THE NEW POSIDIPPUS

THE NEW
POSIDIPPUS

A Hellenistic Poetry Book

EDITED BY

KATHRYN GUTZWILLER

OXFORD
UNIVERSITY PRESS

OXFORD

UNIVERSITY PRESS

Great Clarendon Street, Oxford OX2 6DP

Oxford University Press is a department of the University of Oxford.
It furthers the University's objective of excellence in research, scholarship,
and education by publishing worldwide in

Oxford New York

Auckland Cape Town Dar es Salaam Hong Kong Karachi
Kuala Lumpur Madrid Melbourne Mexico City Nairobi
New Delhi Shanghai Taipei Toronto

With offices in

Argentina Austria Brazil Chile Czech Republic France Greece
Guatemala Hungary Italy Japan Poland Portugal
Singapore South Korea Switzerland Thailand Turkey Ukraine Vietnam

Oxford is a registered trade mark of Oxford University Press
in the UK and certain other countries

Published in the United States
by Oxford University Press Inc., New York

British Library Cataloguing in Publication Data

Data available

Library of Congress Cataloging in Publication Data

Posidippus, of Pella, b. ca. 310 B.C.
[Poems. Selections. English]
The new Posidippus : a Hellenistic poetry book / [edited by] Kathryn Gutzwiller. p. cm.
"This volume stems from a conference on the 'The New Posidippus: A
Hellenistic Poetry Book' held at Cincinnati on 7/9 November 2002"–Acknowledgements.
Includes new translations and essays about the papyrus.
Includes bibliographical references and index.
ISBN 0-19-926781-2 (alk. paper)
1. Posidippus, of Pella, b. ca. 310 B.C.–Translations into English.
2. Posidippus, of Pella, b. ca. 310 B.C.–Manuscripts. 3. Greek poetry, Hellenistic–
Translations into English. 4. Manuscripts, Greek
(Papyri) I. Gutzwiller, Kathryn J. II. Title.

PA4399.P15A25 2005
888'.0102–dc22

2004030578

ISBN 0-19-926781-2 ISBN 978-0-19-926781-1

1 3 5 7 9 10 8 6 4 2

Typeset by Regent Typesetting, London
Printed in Great Britain on acid-free paper by
Biddles Ltd, King's Lynn, Norfolk

Acknowledgements

This volume stems from a conference on the 'The New Posidippus: A Hellenistic Poetry Book' held at Cincinnati on 7–9 November 2002; the comments by Colin Austin originated in a dinner address, while the other essays are revised versions of conference papers. The editor expresses deepest appreciation to the Louise Taft Semple Fund for generously supporting that conference and for assistance with the publication. Many individuals contributed to the success of the Cincinnati event and to the resulting volume: those who presided over sessions—Michael Haslam, Peter van Minnen, Richard Hunter, Nancy Andrews, Holt Parker, Graham Zanker, Ewen Bowie, Benjamin Acosta-Hughes, and Mary Depew—as well as those in the audience who participated in the lively sense of discovery permeating the discussions; my colleagues and students at Cincinnati who enthusiastically supported the project and read the new papyrus with me in weekly sessions; our wonderful librarians Jean Wellington, Michael Braunlin, and Jacquie Riley, who helped with tracking down each new piece of bibliography; Barbara Burrell, who provided special editorial skills and knowledge; my assistants who made the conference possible, Brian Sowers who provided help with many tasks and Valentina Popescu who offered unflagging editorial and bibliographical service and at Oxford University Press, my editors Hilary O'Shea, Lavinia Porter, and especially Leofranc Holford-Strevens, who provided unflagging good humour as well as many useful suggestions. I owe a debt of gratitude to them all.

We acknowledge permission to reproduce an extract from P. Bing, 'Posidippus and the Admiral: Kallikrates of Samos in the Milan Epigrams', *GRBS* 43 (2002/3), 243–66 and selected language from Dirk Obbink, 'Posidippus in Papyri Then and Now' and '"Tropoi": (Posidippus AB 102–103)', in B. Acosta-Hughes, E. Kosmetatou, and M. Baumbach (eds.), *Labored in Papyrus Leaves: Perspectives on an Epigram Collection Attributed to Posidippus* (Cambridge, MA: Harvard University Press, 2004), 16–28 and 292–301. We also acknowledge the following permissions to reproduce illustrations: the

Acknowledgements

Institut de Papyrologie de la Sorbonne for a photograph of P. Sorb. inv. 2272c; LED for several photographs of P. Mil. Vogl. VIII 309; Ny Carlsberg Glyptotek, Copenhagen, for a photograph of Demosthenes, inv. 2782; Archäologisches Institut der Universität, Göttingen, for a photograph of Fittschen's reconstruction of the portrait of Posidippus; Museum für Abgüsse klassischer Bildwerke, Munich, for a photograph of a statuette of Epicurus; National Museum, Athens, for a photograph of the 'Philosopher' from Anticythera.

KATHRYN GUTZWILLER

Cincinnati
December 2004

Contents

Contents

List of Illustrations

Figures

Plates

Abbreviations

AB	Colin Austin and Guido Bastianini (eds.), *Posidippi Pellaei quae supersunt omnia* (Milan: LED, 2002)
AP	*Anthologia Palatina*
APl	*Anthologia Planudea* (= *AP* 16)
BG	Guido Bastianini and Claudio Gallazzi with Colin Austin (eds.), *Posidippo di Pella: Epigrammi (P. Mil. Vogl. VIII 309)* (Papiri dell'Università degli Studi di Milano, VIII; Milan: LED, 2001)
CEG	P. A. Hansen, *Carmina epigraphica Graeca*, 2 vols. (Berlin and New York: Walter de Gruyter, 1983–9)
Dittenberger, *Syll.*³	Wilhelm Dittenberger (ed.), *Sylloge inscriptionum Graecarum*, 3rd edn. (Leipzig, 1915–24, repr. Hildesheim, 1982)
FGE	D. L. Page, *Further Greek Epigrams* (Cambridge: Cambridge University Press, 1981)
GESA	Joachim Ebert, *Griechische Epigramme auf Sieger an gymnischen und hippischen Agonen* (Berlin: Akademie-Verlag, 1972)
GP	A. S. F. Gow and D. L. Page (eds.), *The Greek Anthology: Hellenistic Epigrams*, 2 vols. (Cambridge: Cambridge University Press, 1965)
GP, *Garland*	A. S. F. Gow and D. L. Page (eds.), *The Greek Anthology: The Garland of Philip*, 2 vols. (Cambridge: Cambridge University Press, 1968)
GVI	Werner Peek (ed.), *Griechische Vers-Inschriften I: Grab-Epigramme* (Berlin: Akademie-Verlag, 1955)
IAG	Luigi Moretti, *Iscrizioni agonistiche greche* (Rome: Signorelli, 1953)
K–G	Raphael Kühner and Bernhard Gerth, *Ausführliche Grammatik der griechischen Sprache*, 3rd edn. (Hanover, 1898)
LdÄ	*Lexikon der Ägyptologie*, ed. Wolfgang Helck, Eberhard Otto, and Wolfhard Westendorf, 7 vols. + 3 index vols. (Wiesbaden, 1975–86)
LfrgE	*Lexikon des frühgriechischen Epos* (Göttingen, 1955–)
*OCD*³	*The Oxford Classical Dictionary*, 3rd edn., ed. Simon Hornblower and Antony Spawforth (Oxford, 1996)

Abbreviations

OGIS	*Orientis Graecae inscriptiones selectae*, ed. Wilhelm Dittenberger (Leipzig, 1903–5)
Pack²	R. A. Pack, *The Greek and Latin Literary Texts from Greco-Roman Egypt*, 2nd edn. (Ann Arbor: University of Michigan Press, 1965)
Pf.	Rudolf Pfeiffer, *Callimachus*, 2 vols. (Oxford: Clarendon Press, 1949–53; repr. New York: Arno Press, 1979)
PCG	Rudolf Kassel and Colin Austin (eds.), *Poetae comici Graeci*, 8 vols. (Berlin: Walter de Gruyter, 1983–2001)
Powell	J. U. Powell (ed.), *Collectanea Alexandrina: reliquiae minores poetarum Graecorum aetatis Ptolemaicae, 323–146 A.C.* (Oxford: Clarendon Press, 1925; repr. Chicago: Ares Publishers, 1981)
SH	Hugh Lloyd-Jones and Peter Parsons (eds.), *Supplementum Hellenisticum* (Berlin: Walter de Gruyter, 1983)

Contributors

COLIN AUSTIN, a Fellow of the British Academy, is Professor of Greek in the University of Cambridge and a Senior Fellow of Trinity Hall. His early publications include the *Erectheus* of Euripides (1967), the *Aspis* and *Samia* of Menander (1969), and a corpus of all the then-known comic papyri (1973). More recently, he has edited eight volumes of *Poetae comici Graeci* (with Rudolf Kassel, 1983–2001), a complete Posidippus (with Guido Bastianini, 2002), and a major edition of Aristophanes' *Thesmophoriazusae* (with S. D. Olson, 2004). He is now concentrating on the Menander papyri.

ALESSANDRO BARCHIESI teaches Latin literature at the University of Siena at Arezzo and at Stanford University. He is the author of numerous articles; his books include *The Poet and the Prince* (1994, English trans. 1997) and *Speaking Volumes* (2001). He delivered the 2001 Gray Lectures at Cambridge University and the Jerome Lectures at the University of Michigan in the fall of 2002.

PETER BING teaches classics at Emory University. With interests in theatre, modern German literature, and translation, his research has focused on Hellenistic poetry. He is the author of *The Well-Read Muse. Present and Past in Callimachus and the Hellenistic Poets* (1988) and *Games of Venus: An Anthology of Greek and Roman Erotic Verse from Sappho to Ovid*, co-authored with Rip Cohen (1991), as well as numerous articles on the new Posidippus collection.

MARCO FANTUZZI is a member of the staff of the Graduate School of Greek and Latin Philology of the University of Florence and Professor of Ancient Greek Literature at the University of Macerata. Mainly a scholar of Hellenistic poetry, he has published a number of papers and some books in the field: *Bionis Smyrnaei 'Adonidis Epitaphium'* (1985); *Ricerche su Apollonio Rodio* (1988); and *Muse e modelli: la poesia ellenistica da Alessandro Magno ad Augusto*, with Richard Hunter (2002). He has also published a study of the Greek hexameter, *Struttura e storia dell'esametro greco*, with Roberto Pretagostini (1995–6).

KATHRYN GUTZWILLER is Professor of Classics at the University of Cincinnati. Her research interests include Hellenistic poetry and

Latin elegy, women in antiquity, and literary theory, about which she has produced various articles. Her longer studies include *Studies in the Hellenistic Epyllion* (1981); *Theocritus' Pastoral Analogies: The Formation of a Genre* (1991); and *Poetic Garlands: Hellenistic Epigrams in Context* (1998), for which she received the Goodwin Award of Merit in 2001. She is currently writing a general study of Hellenistic literature for Blackwell Publishers and a commentary on the epigrams of Meleager for Oxford University Press.

WILLIAM A. JOHNSON is an Associate Professor of Classics at the University of Cincinnati. His research has focused on the phenomenon of reading in antiquity, and his numerous articles include the winner of the 2000 Gildersleeve Prize, 'Toward a Sociology of Reading in Classical Antiquity' (*AJP* 121). His book entitled *Bookrolls and Scribes in Oxyrhynchus* was published in 2004 by the University of Toronto Press. He serves on the Board of Directors of the Packard Humanities Institute, the Board of Directors of the American Society of Papyrologists, and various committees of the American Philological Association.

NITA KREVANS teaches in the Department of Classical and Near Eastern Studies at the University of Minnesota. Her research interests include the ancient book as artefactual object and Hellenistic poetry. Her most recent publications include a study of Callimachean prose and (with Alexander Sens) a chapter on Hellenistic literature in the forthcoming *Cambridge Companion to the Hellenistic World*.

ANN KUTTNER has taught at the University of Toronto and, since 1992, at the University of Pennsylvania in the Department of History of Art and in the Graduate Groups in Ancient History, in Art and Archaeology of the Mediterranean World, and Classical Studies. Her research interests in Hellenistic, Roman, and Late Antique art tend to political arts and patronage, landscape architecture, sculpture, and painting—and, in recent years, the relations between visual and verbal language. Her books include *Dynasty and Empire in the Age of Augustus: The Case of the Boscoreale Cups* (1995) and, edited with Alina Payne, *Text and Image in the Renaissance* (2000). Her current project, for the University of California Press, explores the formation and exchange of cultural canons between Hellenistic Pergamon and Republican and early Imperial Rome.

FRANK NISETICH is Professor Emeritus of Classics at the University of Massachusetts, Boston and Visiting Professor of Classics at Boston University. His main publications are *Pindar's Victory Songs* (1980), *Pindar and Homer* (1989), *Euripides: Orestes* (1995), and *The Poems of Callimachus* (2001). His articles deal with Pindar and Euripides, as well as the influence of Pindar on modern poetry. Original poems have appeared in *Partisan Review* and other magazines. *River Moves Till Morning* is currently under editorial consideration.

DIRK OBBINK teaches papyrology and Greek literature at the University of Oxford where he is a Fellow and Tutor in Classics at Christ Church and at the University of Michigan where he is Ludwig Koenen Professor of Papyrology. He is well known for developing an original method for reconstructing the carbonized scrolls from Herculaneum and serves as coeditor of the Oxyrhynchus Papyri and of the Philodemus Translation Project. He is also a recent recipient of a MacArthur Fellowship. Among his many books and articles is a text and commentary of Philodemus' *On Piety*, Part 1 (1996).

ALEXANDER SENS, Professor of Classics at Georgetown University, is well known for his studies of allusion in Hellenistic poetry and as the author of a number of commentaries: *Theocritus: Dioscuri (Idyll 22)* (1997); *Matro of Pitane and the Tradition of Epic Parody in the Fourth Century BCE* with S. D. Olson (1999); and *Archestratos of Gela: Greek Culture and Cuisine in the Fourth Century BCE* with S. D. Olson (2000). He is currently writing a commentary on the epigrams and fragments of Asclepiades of Samos for Oxford University Press.

DAVID SIDER, Professor of Classics at New York University, writes on Greek poetry and philosophy, and is the author of *The Fragments of Anaxagoras* (1981; second edition forthcoming), *The Epigrams of Philodemos* (1997), and (as coeditor with Deborah Boedeker) *The New Simonides* (2001).

SUSAN STEPHENS, a Professor of Classics at Stanford University, works on the social and political context of Greek literature from the Hellenistic through the Late Antique periods. Recent books include *Ancient Greek Novels: The Fragments* with Jack Winkler (1995) and *Seeing Double: Intercultural Poetics in Ptolemaic Alexandria* (2003). The latter contextualizes Alexandrian poetry in terms of the Egyptian as well as the Greek aspects of Ptolemaic kingship.

ANDREW STEWART is Chancellor's Research Professor of Ancient Mediterranean Art and Archaeology at the University of California at Berkeley. His books include *Skopas of Paros* (1977); *Attika: Studies in Athenian Sculpture of the Hellenistic Age* (1979); *Greek Sculpture: An Exploration* (1990); *Faces of Power: Alexander's Image and Hellenistic Politics* (1993); and *Art, Desire, and the Body in Ancient*

Greece (1997). His *Attalos, Athens, and the Akropolis: The Pergamene 'Little Barbarians' and their Roman and Renaissance Legacy*, a study of the so-called Lesser Attalid Dedication on the Athenian Acropolis and its impact, was published in 2004. In addition, he has led the UC Berkeley excavation team at the Canaanite, Phoenician, Israelite, Persian, Greek, and Roman seaport at Tel Dor in Israel since 1986.

DOROTHY J. THOMPSON teaches ancient history at Cambridge, where she is a Fellow of Girton College and Isaac Newton Trust Lecturer in the Faculty of Classics. Her research is mainly on Egypt in the period following its conquest by Alexander of Macedon, on which she has written several books, including *Memphis under the Ptolemies*, and articles. She is a Fellow of the British Academy and President of the International Association of Papyrologists.

1

Introduction

In the second century BC, in the Fayum region of Egypt, an embalmer chose to reuse as mummy cartonnage a discarded papyrus bookroll. Recovered after more than two millennia and published in 2001, this papyrus (P. Mil. Vogl. VIII 309) contains a collection of about 112 Hellenistic epigrams in approximately 606 verses, apparently all by Posidippus of Pella.[1] Although both the beginning and end of the roll are missing, it nevertheless preserves a significant section of an epigram book, copied in the late third century BC. Divided into categories by headings, the epigrams celebrate early Ptolemaic monarchs and their courtiers, praise equestrian victors, famous Greek sculptors, and intricately carved gemstones, describe the use of omens for everyday life and for war, record cures of diseases, and commemorate many ordinary individuals through the old inscriptional forms of dedication and epitaph. In terms of amount of new poetry and its importance for understanding a literary era, the Milan papyrus constitutes the most significant find in decades, comparable to the papyrological recoveries of Bacchylides, Menander, and Sappho. In addition, this epigram collection is our earliest example of a Greek poetry book surviving in any substantial portion in artefactual form. Since Posidippus belonged to the first generation of poets who organized their short poems in aesthetically arranged collections, the new text offers invaluable information about the development of poetry

---

[1] The *editio princeps* is G. Bastianini and C. Gallazzi with C. Austin (eds.), *Posidippo di Pella: Epigrammi (P. Mil. Vogl. VIII 309)* (Papiri dell'Università degli Studi di Milano, 8; Milan: LED, 2001), hereafter BG; this deluxe edition, accompanied by photographic images both printed and on CD-ROM, includes a full introduction, Italian translation, and commentary. The *editio minor*, edited by C. Austin and G. Bastianini, *Posidippi Pellaei quae supersunt omnia* (Milan: LED, 2002), hereafter AB, which offers both English and Italian translations, will be cited throughout. The Austin–Bastianini edition also contains other poetry by Posidippus, including poems of uncertain attribution, and the reader is cautioned that the material from the Milan papyrus constitutes only the first 112 entries.

Preliminary texts of some of the poems, superseded by BG, were published in Bastianini and Gallazzi, 'Il poeta ritrovato: scoperti gli epigrammi di Posidippo in un pettorale di mummia', in *Ca' de Sass*, 121 (March 1993), 28–39 and in *Posidippo: Epigrammi* (Milan: Edizioni Il Polifilo, 1993).

books, which arose in the crucible of the third-century royal courts and later migrated to Rome.

Only two of the epigrams found on the papyrus were previously known (AB 15 = GP 20, AB 65 = GP 18), and both were ascribed to Posidippus. The papyrus retains no direct statement of authorship because the first sheet and the end of the roll are lost. But the editors assume that all the poems are by the Macedonian epigrammatist because the papyrus contains no indication of change of authorship.[2] The most consistent opponent of this view has been Hugh Lloyd-Jones, who argues that the epigrams vary in quality and so seem to represent a collection by multiple hands.[3] It is remarkable, however, that consistency of poetic style, similarity in structuring the epigrams, metrical practice, and meaningful arrangement within some sections of the papyrus all point to the likelihood of a single author.[4] Although absolute proof cannot be obtained, the assumption that the collec-

[2] BG, pp. 22–4. Papyrological evidence supports this reasoning. In P. Köln V 204 (2nd c. BC) the heading Μνασάλκου precedes six epigrams, one of which is ascribed to Mnasalces in the *AP*; all are presumably by the same author. P. Oxy. 3324, containing four epigrams by Meleager, has no author's name between the poems. But other papyri containing sequences of epigrams by different authors bear evidence of attribution preceding each epigram (P. Tebt. 1. 3, P. Oxy. 662, *BKT* 5. 1. 75). See A. Cameron, *The Greek Anthology* (Oxford, 1993), 3, 11–12, 27–8; K. Gutzwiller, *Poetic Garlands* (Berkeley, 1998), 31–5.

[3] Lloyd-Jones has expressed the view that the Milan papyrus contains an anthology, probably the *Soros* known to Aristarchus, in his oral comments after a special panel on the new papyrus at the APA in January 2002, in 'All by Posidippus?', and in his review of BG. S. Schröder, 'Skeptische Überlegungen zum Mailänder Epigrammpapyrus', though rejecting Lloyd-Jones's theory concerning the *Soros*, follows his general view in attempting to demonstrate poor poetic quality for some of the epigrams; he concludes that few if any are worthy of Posidippan authorship. In a more reasoned manner, P. J. Parsons, 'Callimachus and Hellenistic Epigram', 117–18, also maintains the possibility of a mixed anthology; see too F. Ferrari, 'Posidippus, the Milan Papyrus, and some Hellenistic Anthologies', who argues that the cryptic marginal του placed beside eight epigrams on the papyrus indicates poems by other authors that have been added to an edition of Posidippan epigrams originally arranged by the poet himself for the Ptolemaic court. Questions of quality are of course subjective and must be decided by individual readers; for my part, I find the arguments for low poetic quality, especially those of Schröder, to be characterized by special pleading. Since Meleager likely chose for his anthology only the best epigrams, whether the most famous or those he liked personally, it is to be expected that a complete poetry book of the third century would show more variance in quality, subject-matter, and style. Although Posidippus was clearly a poet of importance in the third century, he likely wrote thousands of epigrams, and his aesthetic standards may have differed considerably from those of Callimachus, which came to dominate the Hellenistic tradition in which Meleager worked; see Sider, 'Posidippus Old and New', 33–41. For my views on the importance of reading the epigrams in collected form, see Ch. 15.

[4] Poetic style and epigram structure are rather subjective criteria, but see evidence for repeating vocabulary in Gutzwiller, 'A New Hellenistic Poetry Book', 86 with n. 12. For the similarity between metrical practice in the papyrus and in the 'old' Posidippus, see M. Fantuzzi, 'La tecnica versificatoria del P. Mil. Vogl. VIII 309'. For complex arrangement within sections, see Gutzwiller, 'Posidippus on Statuary'; M. Baumbach and K. Trampedach, '"Winged Words"'; and Fantuzzi, 'Structure of the *Hippika*'.

tion includes only poetry by Posidippus is by far the most reasonable
conclusion, and the majority of scholars working on the papyrus have
accepted the original attribution of the editors.[5]

Documents found with the bookroll bear dates from 188/7 to 178/7
BC. It seems probable that the literary text, whether damaged or dis-
carded for another reason, had a longer useful life, and the style of
the writing is compatible with a date in the second half of the third
century. At the latest, then, this artefact was produced within a few
decades of the lifetime of Posidippus, who received public recogni-
tion as early as the 270s and seems to have continued working into the
decade of the 240s. We cannot rule out the possibility that he lived to
see, or oversee, its creation.

It remains a more open question, however, whether the Milan
papyrus reflects a compilation supervised by the author or an inde-
pendent editor is responsible for its organization and design. The
literary innovations of the third century included the development
of author-edited poetry books, apparently through the influence of
the scholarly editions of earlier Greek poetry that were produced
primarily in Alexandria under the sponsorship of the first Ptolemies.
Callimachus' *Aitia* and *Iambi* and Herodas' *Mimiambi* are now
recognized as sophisticated examples of organization in support
of aesthetic meaning, and I have argued from more circumstantial
evidence that the epigrams of the early Hellenistic epigrammatists,
later anthologized by Meleager of Gadara in his *Garland* (*c.*100 BC),
must have originally existed in epigram books where broad meaning
was conveyed by thematic arrangement. The central question now
at issue for scholars in the volume, as well as elsewhere, is whether
the Milan papyrus preserves part of a such authorially sanctioned
epigram book or constitutes a different type of compilation, made
to suit the idiosyncratic interests of an editor or as representative of
some intermediate stage before the poetic possibilities of aesthetic
arrangement were fully understood and utilized.

Posidippus was a prominent epigrammatist of the third century BC,
a contemporary of the Alexandrian triad of Callimachus, Theocritus,
and Apollonius. Before the discovery of the papyrus, he was best
known as the author of over twenty epigrams preserved in manu-
script sources, several on erotic topics (a category of epigram missing
from the papyrus).[6] Six of these epigrams bear a joint attribution to

---

[5] See e.g. the conclusions of B. Acosta-Hughes, E. Kosmetatou, and M. Baumbach,
'Introduction', 4–5.

[6] The standard commentaries for the 'old' Posidippus are GP and E. Fernández-Galiano,
Posidipo (Madrid, 1987). See too M. Albrecht, 'The Epigrams of Posidippus of Pella' (MA
thesis, Dublin, 1996).

Asclepiades of Samos,[7] an innovative and influential epigrammatist of the early third century, and Posidippus seems to have written a number of epigrams on subjects addressed by Asclepiades, providing early examples of epigram variation. His prominence as a literary figure is shown by epigraphical evidence, two decrees awarding him the honour of serving as a city's foreign representative or proxenos, one from Delphi (276/5 or 273/2 BC) in which the name of Asclepiades occurs close by, and one from Thermon (263/2 BC) which names him as a native of Pella, the capital of Macedon, and speaks of him as a professional composer of epigrams, an ἐπιγραμματοποιός.[8] Another poem, an elegy composed by Posidippus as an old man and commonly called the 'Seal' or cφραγίc, has been found on a wax tablet of the first century BC (AB 118 = *SH* 705). In this poem Posidippus hopes for posthumous recognition in Pella, even a statue of himself holding a bookroll, and claims fame throughout the Aegean islands and mainland Asia. We were aware from other epigrams (AB 115–16, 119 = GP 11–13) that Posidippus belonged to the circle of poets who celebrated the Ptolemies, but the new papyrus makes clear the ideological and political connection between all these geographical points. The early Ptolemaic rulers of Egypt promoted themselves as the direct heirs of the Argead dynasty in Macedon and claimed the right to govern the Aegean basin and Asia Minor: Posidippus was a natural choice to celebrate the scope and heterogeneity of this empire.[9]

One of the most intriguing aspects of the papyrus is its arrangement in titled sections. The epigrams are organized into nine sections with headings centred in the column, and remnants of a tenth section are visible before the papyrus breaks off. These nine are as follows:

Section title	Epigrams	Verses
[λιθι]κά ('stones')	21	126
οἰωνοσκοπικά ('omens')	15	80
ἀναθεματικά ('dedications')	6	38
[ἐπιτύμβια] ('epitaphs')	20	116
ἀνδριαντοποιικά ('statues')	9	50
ἱππικά ('horse-racing')	18	98
ναυαγικά ('shipwrecks')	6	26
ἰαματικά ('cures')	7	32
τρόποι ('characters'?)	8	32

[7] Asclep. 34–9 GP.
[8] *Fouilles de Delphes* III 3, no. 192 (= T 2 AB); *IG* ix²/i. 17. 24 (= T 3 AB). On what is known of the life of Posidippus, see GP i. 481–4, Fernández-Galiano, *Posidipo*, 9–15, and Gutzwiller, *Poetic Garlands*, 151–2.   [9] See J. Bingen, 'Posidippe: le poète et les princes', 56–8.

The sections on dedications and epitaphs, both traditional inscriptional types, correspond to categories of organization that were used by Meleager in his great anthology of Hellenistic epigrams and then later by Cephalas of Constantinople in the epigram compendium that became the basis for our *Greek Anthology*. But in both cases these broad categories shaped book-length sections, rather than short sequences. Nothing in the literary or papyrological record had prepared scholars for the topics of the other sections on the papyrus, but reassessment of what we already knew about Posidippus and other epigrammatists is gradually revealing connections between these categories and various aspects of Hellenistic poetry, particularly the use of prose or scientific sources. By adding so significantly to our knowledge, the papyrus also brings awareness of how little is actually known about the scope of epigrammatic production and collection in the early Hellenistic age.

In almost every case, other epigrams on the topics of the Posidippus collection can be found. The λιθικά section is foreshadowed by Asclepiades' epigram (*AP* 9. 752 = GP 44) on an engraved amethyst ring belonging to Cleopatra, the sister of Alexander the Great, and other epigrams on engraved gemstones are preserved in the *Greek Anthology*.[10] Epigrams on equestrian victories are abundantly represented in the inscriptional record,[11] and Callimachus celebrated the racing victories of Berenice II prominently in his *Aitia*. Epigrams on famous statues also have early parallels and are preserved in good numbers in later Greek epigram, though they seem to be grouped in the Byzantine anthologies with other types of poems under the label 'epideictic'. Records of cures by Asclepius are commemorated in inscriptions and, though rarely found, in the literary archive,[12] while satirical epigrams targeting doctors, including one attributed to Posidippus' contemporary Hedylus (*AP* 11. 123; see too 11. 61, 112–22, 124–6), are likely parodic of a recognized type of laudatory epigram. Likewise, later epigrams satirizing prophets (*AP* 11. 159–64) may be related to Posidippus' section on omens, where specific diviners are praised. The epitaphic section of Meleager's *Garland* grouped together poems on shipwrecked persons and organized other epitaphs by gender, age, and social status, much as the epitaphs (mostly on women) are grouped in the Posidippus collection.[13] Even

[10] e.g. *AP* 9. 746–8, 750–1; on the Asclepiades epigram, see Gutzwiller, 'Cleopatra's Ring'.
[11] Collected in Ebert, *Griechische Epigramme auf Sieger* (Berlin, 1972).
[12] e.g. Aeschines *AP* 6. 330, Callim. *AP* 6. 147 = 24 GP. See BG, p. 222; G. Zanetto, 'Posidippo e i miracoli di Asclepio'; P. Bing, 'Posidippus' *Iamatika*'.
[13] Gutzwiller, *Poetic Garlands*, 307–15.

though certain evidence is now lacking, it seems likely that labelling sections with headings, as in the Milan papyrus, was not unusual in Hellenistic epigram collections.[14] A small sylloge of epigrams ascribed to Theocritus, descending to us in the bucolic manuscripts, easily divides into three separate sections (bucolic, mixed sepulchral and dedicatory, and poems in various metres, mostly on poets), and these sections may once have had headings similar to those in the new papyrus.[15] What the Posidippus collection reveals, conclusively, is the wide variety of subject-matter that third-century epigrammatists incorporated into their poetry, and we should no longer assume that the broad categories known from the Cephalan recension of the tenth century were the only standard. The popularity of the genre, in its Hellenistic literary manifestation, was surely related to its flexibility in commemorating a wide range of human activities.

The chronological limits of the epigrams on the Milan papyrus extend from 284 BC, the date of an equestrian victory by Berenice I (the wife of Ptolemy I Soter), to either 247 BC, if the second victorious βαϲίλιϲϲα of this name is Berenice II, the wife of Ptolemy III Euergetes, as Bastianini and Gallazzi think,[16] or to the 250s, if she is the still unmarried daughter of Ptolemy II Philadelphus, as Dorothy Thompson argues in this volume. This span of time—the 'Golden Age' of Hellenistic literature—fits neatly with what we know or have surmised about Posidippus. Since his professional life was apparently directed primarily to the production of epigrams, and for a period of perhaps four decades, it is only reasonable to assume that he gathered the fruits of his poetic activity into more than one collection. We in fact have evidence that such was the case. A papyrus written about 250 BC (P.Petrie II 49a = *SH* 961) bears the title ϲύμμεικτα ἐπιγράμματα, 'Miscellaneous Epigrams', followed on the next line by the name Posidippus in the genitive case.[17] The introductory epigram or elegy

[14] Neither should we assume that it was the only, or even most common, mode of organization in the early Hellenistic period. The Vienna Papyrus (P. Vindob. G 40611), of the third century, contains a list of about 240 epigram incipits, one of which recurs in Asclepiades *AP* 12. 46 = GP 15; the incipits come from four books, apparently without division by section. See H. Harrauer, 'Epigrammincipit' and Parsons, 'Callimachus and the Hellenistic Epigram', 118–20.

[15] See G. Tarditi, 'Per una lettura degli epigrammatisti greci', 45–52; Gutzwiller, *Poetic Garlands*, 41–5; and L. Rossi, *The Epigrams Ascribed to Theocritus* (Leuven, 2001), 367–75. For a possible section label on a papyrus, see Bastianini, 'Il rotolo degli epigrammi di Posidippo', 115.

[16] BG, pp. 17, 208, 215.

[17] Lloyd-Jones and Parsons, *SH*, pp. 464–5 argue that the retraction of the genitive Ποϲειδίππου on the line after the title indicates that Posidippus was only one of several epigrammatists gathered on the papyrus—a dubious conclusion at best. But Bastianini, 'Il papiro di

consists of twenty-four lines celebrating, seemingly, the marriage of Arsinoe II (less likely Arsinoe I) to Ptolemy Philadelphus, and so dating no later that 274 BC. Although the other epigrams are not preserved on the papyrus, the fragmentary opening poem indicates a fairly early collection, composed under the patronage of the second generation of the Ptolemies. Two other collections are attested by a Homeric scholium (Σ A, *Il.* 11. 101 = AB 144). There we are told that the great Alexandrian scholar Aristarchus of the second century BC found a certain contested Homeric word among Posidippus' epigrams in the *Soros*, but not in his *Epigrammata*, where he had apparently expunged it. The *Soros*, or 'Heap', has been the subject of much, often fanciful speculation on the part of scholars, but what this scholium tells us securely is that it contained epigrams by Posidippus appearing also in his *Epigrammata* and that it was the earlier of the two compilations.[18] While there is no evidence at all that the *Soros* was an anthology of epigrams by various poets, as some scholars have suggested,[19] the other collection mentioned is almost certainly a comprehensive compilation of Posidippus' entire epigram production, as it stood at some point in time. Aristarchus' comment further indicates that Posidippus had editorial control over his *Epigrammata*, which surely ran to multiple bookrolls. Bastianini and Gallazzi argue that the Milan papyrus cannot be a segment of the *Epigrammata*, because certain known epigrams which should fit in the categories found there are missing.[20] But the categorization by generic class is so flexible that, for instance, the epigram on Lysippus' *Kairos* (AB 142 = GP 19), missing from the statue section, might have been accommodated under some lost heading. It seems to me at least a possibility that our papyrus does preserve part of, or is an abridged version of, the *Epigrammata*. In conclusion, then, whether or not the Milan papyrus represents a sylloge originally produced during Posidippus' own life, it does substantiate the multiplicity of Posidippus epigram

Posidippo un anno dopo', 4, after a careful examination of the papyrus in photographic form, has concluded that the title above and the author's name were written by different hands. Thus the idea that 'of Posidippus' was meant to begin a list of epigrammatists falls, and we are left with an early example of epigram collection bearing the name of Posidippus as author.

[18] See now G. Nagy, 'Homeric Echoes in Posidippus'.

[19] First and most famously, R. Reitzenstein, *Epigramm und Skolion* (Giessen, 1893), 96–102, who believed the *Soros* was a joint collection of epigrams by Asclepiades, Posidippus, and Hedylus. The modification of this thesis—that Hedylus constructed an anthology of epigrams by himself and his two friends—offered by Cameron, *Greek Anthology*, 374–6 seems to me equally fanciful. In truth, the *only* epigrammatist whose poems are known to have been included in this *Soros* was Posidippus.

[20] BG, p. 27 and Bastianini, 'Rotolo degli epigrammi', 116–17.

collections made in the third century, of which there were, *at a minimum*, three, and very likely more.

The essays in this volume, originating in a conference held at the University of Cincinnati in November of 2002, assess the new papyrus from a variety of perspectives: papyrology and the study of the ancient book, Hellenistic and Roman literature, visual culture, and Hellenistic history. The range of perspectives brought to bear reflects the complex nature of this collection of Posidippan epigrams, as a series of snapshots of early Hellenistic culture viewed through a Ptolemaic lens. The great advantage of the new literary genre of epigram, especially in collection, was its ability to focus on a large number of individuals and particulars, to span from the past to the present, from great to small, from one place to another. The collection as constituted takes full advantage of these generic possibilities to represent the historical, geographical, and cultural extent of the Ptolemaic world. Here we see the Ptolemies themselves set against the Persian kings they purport to have replaced and the Argeads they revere, usurping the roles of deities after death and assuming the place of great victors while alive; we see the gemstones owned by the elite of their culture and the eastern mountains that produce the stones, as well as the masterpieces of Greek sculpture that shape the artistic standards of the post-Alexandrian world; we see many non-royal individuals, a few of them influential Ptolemaic functionaries who build monuments or make dedications but mostly unknown persons who have their private sorrows and joys commemorated in epigrammatic form. The contributors who here address the issues raised by this rich set of new poems build on the excellent editing work of Bastianini, Gallazzi, and Austin and the many contributions made since by other scholars, particularly with regard to textual problems. The goal of this volume is to address some of the larger problems concerning the papyrus and to begin the process of assessing the importance of the collection for understanding the development of epigram, Hellenistic poetry more generally, and the heritage of the book culture that third-century poets brought into being and passed on to the Romans.

After this Introduction, the reader will find Frank Nisetich's translation of Posidippus' entire corpus, the poems old and new as well as references to other works of prose and poetry. His fine poetic translations of the epigrams, done up in an English version of the elegiac couplet, neatly catch the tone of Posidippus' plain but sophisticated style. Serving as a complement to the scholarly essays, Nisetich's interpretive renderings make their own contribution to our under-

standing of Posidippus' epigrammatic art.[21] The Greek text trans-
lated is that of the complete works of Posidippus as edited by Guido
Bastianini and Colin Austin (the *editio minor*), with select changes
based on new readings and conjectures, as indicated in the notes.

Happily, Colin Austin has contributed a personal memoir of his
participation in the editing of the papyrus. He explains how he came
to collaborate with Bastianini and Gallazzi in producing the com-
mentary for their edition (2001) and then to edit with Bastianini the
complete corpus of Posidippus in a more accessible edition (2002).
The details of how the Posidippus collection came to the attention
of professional papyrologists, of two other papyri awaiting publi-
cation that will also be of great value to scholars of the Hellenistic
world, and of Austin's own fascination with the new Posidippus epi-
grams even in the throes of a life-threatening illness provide a unique
glimpse into the difficulties and joys of the individuals who bring
such materials to the scholarly world.

There follows a set of essays that address papyrological and editor-
ial questions. William Johnson studies the papyrus in relation to other
bookrolls of the Ptolemaic period. He shows that in some respects—
in its short height, small margins, and very small intercolumn—the
papyrus is similar to other bookrolls of the period, while it differs
in other respects: the tiny script, the titles of the sections, the sticho-
metry based on sections, and the marginal sigla. He disagrees with the
editors' assumption that the first column of the papyrus is intact with
only the protokollon, the sheet that may have borne title and author's
name, missing. Johnson argues instead that at least one column, and
likely more, has been lost at the beginning of the papyrus. His gen-
eral approach is to tease out the various cultural circumstances of
the bookroll's production and consumption as a text, including the
purpose for which it was designed and the conditions under which
it was read. Viewing this papyrus as designed more for utilitarian
than aesthetic purposes, he argues that markings in the margins offer
evidence that one reader had gone through the text with an eye to
selecting out certain epigrams.

Nita Krevans considers the activity of the editor in selecting the
epigrams and placing them in labelled sections. Arguing that the titles
are designed to place a heavier emphasis on the sections than the indi-
vidual poems, she considers contemporary comparanda for the type
of headings found in the papyrus. She argues that the titles, which
she calls 'utilitarian', suggest the reference librarian rather than the

---

[21] Unless otherwise noted, the contributors to this volume have provided their own trans-
lations.

9

creative artist who arranges to showcase his compositions. The closest parallels, she concludes, are in scientific collections, such as the 'wonder-books' describing natural rarities created by Callimachus and other Hellenistic authors. She also argues that the ordering within sections may be indebted to the ordering principles employed in such prose texts, so that like topics are placed together and odd or misfitting poems grouped at the end. As Krevans clearly shows, the organizational principles for the Posidippus papyrus are quite different from the complex interweaving of poetic types and topics that are found in Callimachus' *Aitia*, likely the most dazzling and certainly the most influential of Hellenistic poetry books. She concludes that the editor's purpose in following the model of prose treatises had to do with the intended use of this collection, rather than an aesthetic that differed from the Callimachean.

Addressing the concerns of those who would deny unitary authorship on the basis of poetic quality, Dirk Obbink discusses a category of Hellenistic epigram that he calls 'subliterary'. This term describes 'occasional' poems, such as epigrams composed for specific historical circumstances, like victory celebration or funerals, or παίγνια, playful poetic exercises, poems that are not later accepted into the canon of the fully 'literary'. Obbink points out that, although the new Posidippan epigrams were collected and preserved in a professionally produced bookroll, they seem never to have entered the category of canonical poetry, and it may be that their author did not intend them to do so. This view would explain why so few of these epigrams have reached us through the medium of Meleager's *Garland* or in other ancient sources. He illustrates the liminal category of the subliterary by discussing inscribed examples of epigrams similar to those on the Milan roll and other epigrams by Posidippus discovered in private copies, made from professional rolls in the second century BC. He ends by advancing the thesis that the epigram collection on the Milan papyrus may offer an example of the intermediate stage between inscribed occasional verse and authorially sanctioned poetry books with overarching themes and aesthetic arrangements.

Several essays focus on individual sections or on the interaction between thematically related sections. In contrast to Johnson's suggestions about the beginning, Peter Bing reads the first section on stones as introductory to the collection as a whole—'an eye-catching start'. Just as in the sixth *Olympian* Pindar compared epinician song to a portal raised on golden columns, so Posidippus begins with the λιθικά in order to suggest the relationship between the gleam of brilliantly coloured, intricately carved gemstones and the sparkling craftsmanship of his epigrams. Moving beyond the common artistry of stones and poems, Bing explores how the section on stones, which begins with an isolated reference to an Indian river and ends with a prayer to Poseidon not to harm Ptolemaic lands, maps out a political landscape reflecting Ptolemaic aspirations. The evoked landscape of Indian waters and Arabian mountains marks the vast territory won by Alexander and claimed or coveted by the Ptolemies. While providing new readings of epigrams on such diverse subjects as magnets, symposium equipment, and 'Arion's lyre' dedicated to Arsinoe II, Bing shows how the implications for Ptolemaic cultural aspirations introduced in the λιθικά re-emerged in more explicit form throughout various sections of the collection.

Reading the first section from a more art-historical perspective, Ann Kuttner presents the λιθικά as a Ptolemaic gem cabinet, or δακτυλιοθήκη, arranged into planned clusters of related stones/poems. She works back from the late Republican appropriation of Greek regal cultures (including gem cabinets taken from Mithridates) to assemble the evidence that the Ptolemies too had collected valued stones, from defeated Persian monarchs and from their own fabulous mines and territories. Posidippus' catalogue, arranged by cultural types, resembles inscribed temple inventories or the narrated lists of precious objects carried through the streets of Alexandria in Ptolemaic spectacles, she argues. Importantly, she uses the registries of surviving Hellenistic objects—gems set as jewellery, sympotic ware, women's toiletry items—to provide original interpretations of the λίθοι celebrated in these epigrams. From a wide range of prose sources, such as Pliny the Elder and Josephus, she shows how Posidippus reflects, through the organization of his poetic gem cabinet, the cultural uses and symbolic value of these objects in Ptolemaic Alexandria.

David Sider focuses on the surprising and puzzling section on omens, entitled οἰωνοσκοπικά. He offers a detailed reading of the first four poems on weather signs in comparison with the other literature on the subject. By citing parallels with a variety of sources, he argues that Posidippus was most likely 'versifying a text now unknown to us which collected and related signs, perhaps under the rubric of bird signs'. The epigrammatist is thus doing with epigram what Aratus did with hexameter when he turned Eudoxus' prose treatise into epic verse. Sider then considers the relationship of the οἰωνοσκοπικά section to didactic poetry and argues that Posidippus may have invented a category of epigram that the ancients would have considered didactic.

Kathryn Gutzwiller

The section concerning bronze statues, called ἀνδριαντοποιικά, is one of the most fascinating and inventive in the collection. Two essays are devoted to it, one from a historian of Greek sculpture and one from the perspective of Hellenistic poetics. Andrew Stewart takes up the important question of what can be learned about Hellenistic standards of artistic realism and illusion, or 'truth in sculpture', from Posidippus' ecphrastic poems on statuary. He considers the sequence of nine epigrams to constitute a 'tightly structured ensemble' that 'presupposes a single intelligence at work'. Importantly, Stewart shows that Posidippus promotes Lysippus, the favourite sculptor of Alexander, as the true standard of how to represent in stone the appearance of the natural world. In doing so, he illustrates numerous similarities between Posidippus' comments on statues and later remnants of early Hellenistic art criticism, perhaps deriving from a treatise by Xenocrates. As Bing (and others) find the gemstones of the λιθικά to stand in some way for gemlike epigrams, so for Stewart Posidippus asserts a 'sculptural truth' that is 'metonymic for poetic truth'.

Alexander Sens explores more fully the possibility that the statue section makes complex comment on the nature of literary as well as artistic production. Beginning with an analysis of the opening epigram in the section, which calls upon sculptors to 'imitate' statuary works, apparently those of Lysippus, Sens argues that the epigram 'invites readers to suppose that the works . . . described in the ensuing poems . . . may be imagined as a . . . literary hall of statues that could serve as appropriate models for prospective artists'. He then focuses on the second poem in the section, on a statue of the Hellenistic scholar-poet Philitas, as a crucial point in the collection where the literary and the artistic intertwine, as poet represents artist representing poet. Showing important similarities to a programmatic passage in Theocritus' *Idyll* 7 about truth and fiction, Sens argues that Posidippus' epigram sets Philitas' literary activity in parallel with the artistic activity of his sculptor Hecataeus. He then extends this identification of artisan and subject to the other poems in the section and concludes by drawing out the implications of his analysis for questions of authorship and editorial practice.

Susan Stephens focuses on Posidippus' epigrams concerning Queen Arsinoe II to take up the broader issue of his relationship to Callimachus. In a revisionary discussion, she draws attention to the scholium to Callimachus' *Aitia* that places Posidippus, as well as the earlier epigrammatist Asclepiades, among the Telchines, Callimachus' literary detractors. The comment has puzzled because the Telchines criticize Callimachus for writing in the slight style and eschewing long, continuous poems on grand topics, an odd criticism to come from two masters of the new epigrammatic style. Stephens, suggesting that the scholiast has likely misunderstood the nature of the disagreement, contrasts Posidippus' Macedonian focus with Callimachus' Egyptian focus as alternative perspectives on Ptolemaic image-making. In a fascinating reading of the first dedicatory epigram, she argues that Posidippus casts the warlike Arsinoe, whom she argues to be an emblem of Ptolemaic imperial power, in the mould of those fourth-century Macedonian queens who took to the battlefield. Callimachus' poetry on the deified Arsinoe, on the other hand, makes more of the Egyptianizing elements in her new cults. She concludes that the 'quarrel' between these two Ptolemaic court poets was likely just a playful 'duel with epigrams over how to publicize the throne'.

Focusing on the ἱππικά section, Marco Fantuzzi tackles the important topic of Posidippus as court poet. He argues that the homage paid to the equestrian victories of kings and queens 'contributed not only to the ideology of Ptolemaic dynastic power in general but also to the specific ideology of the queens'. He suggestively connects the comparison between Berenice I's Olympic victory and the earlier one by the Spartan Cynisca with the construction of the Ptolemaic monarchy on the model of Spartan kingship, by arguing that Cynisca's heroic honours provided a precedent for the eventual deification of the Egyptian queens. While this section praising equestrian triumphs has a clear parallel in Pindar's epinician poetry, Fantuzzi argues that Pindar's purpose in composing for the occasion of celebration is replaced in Posidippus by a lasting aptitude for victory that afforded the queens the type of heroic honours they could not earn in war.

Surveying Posidippus' entire poetic oeuvre, Dorothy Thompson considers, from a more historical perspective, whether the intended audience was Macedonian, like the poet himself and, through ancestry, the Ptolemies, or whether a wider Hellenic audience was presupposed. She also considers whether we may identify any elements that point to a more local, Egyptian, set of interests. A featured topic is, again, the queens, who are shown to be following the model of earlier Macedonian queens in promoting their independent status and power. She makes a strong case for rejecting the editors' identification of the younger victorious queen as Berenice II, in favour of the unmarried princess of the same name who was the daughter of Ptolemy Philadelphus. She also examines the various loyal servants who appear in the poetry of Posidippus and the way in which the city of Alexandria plays a prominent role. But the Egyptian elements are balanced, she concludes, by multiple references to the Ptolemaic empire and neighbouring lands, so that it is best to view Posidippus not just as an Alexandrian or a Macedonian poet, but a Hellenistic one.

In my own essay I advance the argument that the Milan papyrus constitutes a proper poetry book, 'carefully crafted to suggest meanings that cannot be conveyed in the brevity of a solitary epigram'. The core evidence presented here is a demonstration of thematic coherence, both within sections and across sections. I argue that troubling inconsistencies in categorization within sections are not evidence for posthumous, or non-authorial editing; the basis of organization is theme rather than uniformity of generic type, and this constitutes evidence of an intended literariness promulgated through poetic design. Each section, as far as the condition of the papyrus permits us to observe, begins and ends with a linguistic marker of the section's theme. Three major sections—the ἐπιτύμβια, λιθικά, and οἰωνο-σκοπικά—are examined in detail. I argue that the emphasis on women in the ἐπιτύμβια relates to the theme of connection to family and community, that the section on stones can be read as a miniaturization of cosmological poetry, and that the section on omens, beginning and closing with birds sacred to Apollo, thematizes signification itself and the issue of purposeful design in the universe. A final segment traces the interaction of two dominant themes—the Ptolemies as divinized/heroic monarchs and the artistic aesthetic they promote—across the various sections of the collection and argues that the papyrus, even in its partial state of preservation, offers evidence for authorial organization of the sections into larger units of meaning.

In a coda to this set of essays narrowly focused on Posidippus, Alessandro Barchiesi discusses, more generally and theoretically, the effects of Greek books on Roman poetry books. His essay is premised on a useful distinction between 'perfect' poetry books, which are the more symmetrically and architecturally arranged ones, and 'imperfect' books, organized, perhaps just as self-consciously, from a different aesthetic standard. He makes a strong argument that Meleager's *Garland*, like Callimachus' *Aitia,* was a highly influential model for the perfect poetry book, signalled as such in programmatic passages in Catullus, Propertius, and Vergil. He illustrates how Hellenistic techniques of framing books and sections, as found in Callimachus, Posidippus, and Meleager, are reinterpreted in Martial, Pliny the Younger, and Catullus. The essay concludes with an argument for a 'fuzzy' model for the evolution of poetry books, one that takes account of their original existence as artefacts, which were marked by readers, selectively perused, and recopied, before acquiring a different existence in anthologies or private arrangements. The result is a call for a new approach to poetry books, one that blurs the distinction between self-conscious artistic design and the real world of production and use. Barchiesi thus shows how one of the great benefits of the new Posidippus papyrus is its physicality, making us aware of how the artefactual nature of texts affects their use and so should be woven into their interpretation.

The purpose of this volume is not to present a thesis about the Milan papyrus (although some of the essays do that) but to explore broader topics and issues. As a result, it is inevitable, and proper, that the scholars should present a variety of points of view, reflecting much of the range of discussion that this remarkable discovery has elicited. Even so, a core of themes recurs throughout the essays. In addition to traditional categories based on inscriptional types, such as epitaphs, dedications, equestrian victories, and records of cures, the papyrus contains epigrammatic categories for which there were prose didactic sources, such as books of weather signs, treatises on stones, histories of art, and wonder books. Is this an indication that new types of epigrams by Posidippus were categorized by an editor in the manner of prose collections, or evidence of the Hellenistic aesthetic preference for poeticizing non-traditional sources, here in the form of an epigram sequence? While the collection offers a panorama of humanity, it seems weighted toward women, including royal women. Does this reflect the audience for whom Posidippus composed his epitaphs, dedications, and celebratory epigrams over the course of his career, or does it reflect a collection arranged to appeal to the interest of a principal patron, even Queen Berenice herself? Two sections concern artistic objects admired and collected by the elite of early Hellenistic society. Does the gathering of Posidippus' epigrams on precious stone jewellery and famous statues reflect merely his commissions and occasions for which he wrote, or are these sections emblematic, intended to convey the poet's aesthetic preferences in poetry as well as art? The first three generations of the Ptolemies, their Macedonian ancestors, and their court officials appear repeatedly throughout the collection, although Egypt itself is, curiously, mentioned only uncertainly, almost under erasure. Yet we know that Posidippus worked in other parts of the Hellenic world—in mainland Greece, the Aegean Islands, and Asia Minor. Does the Ptolemaic focus reflect, then, some Egyptian portion of his career from which the epigrams on this papyrus were gathered, or does it have to do with an intended audience of Ptolemaic patrons?

While the contributors to our volume would likely provide different answers to these questions, their analyses constitute a significant step in understanding what is at stake in calling the new Milan papyrus a 'Hellenistic poetry book'.

2

The Poems of Posidippus

TRANSLATED BY FRANK NISETICH

This is a translation of *Posidippi Pellaei quae supersunt omnia*, edited by C. Austin and G. Bastianini (Milan, 2002). Arabic numbers at the top of each poem follow that edition. Roman numerals in parentheses at the bottom of each of the poems in the Milan Papyrus designate the column of the papyrus, followed by the lines. Words in square brackets render editorial supplements and conjectures. Asterisks designate poems of doubtful or dual ascription. Notes follow the translation.

THE MILAN PAPYRUS

I. [STON]ES

1

Indian Hydaspes . . .   (I 1)
    . . .

. . .
    . . . delicate . . .
                                         (I 2–5)

2

. . . lies a drinking horn . . .
    by [the hand of] Cronius [. . .] going [. . .
. . . the b[oy . . .] to pour the wine . . .
    . . . hollowed from below [. . .] Ind[ian].
                                         (I 6–9)

3

This blazing [ruby], on which [the engraver has carved]
    a drinking cup, captures the melting glance and sends it
on to [flowers] traced [in gold], with triple tendrils. [Receive it],
    lady, [with joy] at the banquet, [fond as you are] of nov[elties].
                                         (I 10–13)

4

Seeing the blue-green [stone . . .]
  . . .] of Darius, the engraver . . .
. . .] rivalling the moon . . .
  . . .] by the lamp, all n[ight . . .
Mandene draped the gift, the Persian gem
  mounted in gold, from her en[tic]ing arm.
(I 14–19)

5

Timanthes carved it—this sparkling lapis lazuli
  rayed in gold, this semi-precious Persian stone—
for Demylus, and for a tender kiss the dark-haired
  Coan Nicaea [owns it] now, a [lovely] gift.
(I 20–3)

6

Heros [is greatly taken] with this stone, [admired]
  by all—an image of Iris carved [by Cronius]
in glittering b[eryllion]; and now it's set,
  [beautifully], into Niconoe's golden [necklace],
a gift freely given, to lie upon her [virgin] breast
  [and never pale], a shimmering cube of light.
(I 24–9)

7

Rolling the yellowy [ru]bble down Arabian m[ountains]
  to the sea, the storm-swollen r[iver] swiftly [swept]
this gem, like honey in complexion, which the hand of Cronius
  engraved and bound in gold. Now [it makes sweet]
Niconoe's inlaid necklace [shine], its honeyed sparkle
  smiling in the whiteness of her breast.
(I 30–5)

8

No woman's throat, no woman's finger ever wore
  this cornelian, but it was fastened to a golden chain,
a gleaming gem with Darius on it, and under him
  his chariot is carved, a span in length, illumined
from below. No Indian rubies would stand the test
  of brightness against it, so uniform its radiance.

It measures [three] spans around; and the marvel is that no
   discoloration [from within] beclouds its broad expanse.
                              (I 36–II 2)

9

[You chose] the lyre for your seal, Polycrates, the lyre
   of the singer [who pl]ayed [at your] feet.
[. . .] rays; and your hand [to]ok
   [. . .] possession.
                              (II 3–6)

10

         . . . cylinder
            . . . of a torrent
            . . . the craftsman's
            . . . through them
            . . . Nabataean   5
   . . . king of Arabian cavalrymen
                              (II 7–16)

11

No glint of silver on every side, nor is it [stone] that's mounted
   here, but Persian shell from the shores of the sea—
call it mother-of-pearl: and cupped in the hollow of it
   Aglaia is depicted, [with the gleam of topaz].
And there's a film of wax over the surface, keeping   5
   [the light] on the image rising, [now, to our gaze].
                              (II 17–22)

12

[It is of the] sea, yes, and shell, but mounted
   skilfully with [gilded] stone, it is deemed semi-precious
[. . . . .] of emerald
   [. . .] welded [. . .]—from the hollow
in its golden be[zel] he set it, to bear   5
   . . . small, [a new] engraving [on display].
                              (II 23–8)

13

This is a tr[icky] stone: smear it with oil, and all around
    it swims in [radianc]e, a marvel of [decei]t;
but when it's dry, all of a sudden the Persian [. . .
    . . .] lightens, reaching for the beautiful sun.
                         (II 29–32)

14

Pegasus etched upon misty jasper—the artist's
    hand and mind, working together, have caught it
superbly: Bellerophon has fallen to Cilicia's
    Aleian Plain, his colt has pranced off into the deep
blue sky—and so he carved him, on this ethereal stone,   5
    free of the reins, shuddering, still, at the bit.
                         (II 33–8)

15 (GP 20)

It wasn't a river with murmuring banks but a bearded
    serpent's head that once kept this stone, thickly
streaked in white. And the eye of a Lynceus etched
    a chariot into it—a mere fleck on a nail:
you wouldn't see the chariot, except in the imprint,   5
    or feel a crease on the surface. And here's
the marvel of the thing: how its sculptor
    did not blur his eyesight on the job!
                     (II 39–III 7)

16

Radiant rock crystal: an Arabian torrent washes it
    endlessly down to the beach, torn from the mountains
in massive gobs: that's why, fools as we are, we men
    do not put it to the touchstone smudged with gold.
If it were *rare* from its source, its transparency   5
    would be as priceless as the beautiful sun.
                    (III 8–13)

17

Ponder the nature of this stone, torn from the roots
   of Mysian Olympus, wondrous for its double power:
now, with ease, it draws the iron pitted against it,
   like a magnet; now it thrusts in the opposite
direction, away from itself. And the marvel is how   5
   the one stone acts like two, pushing and pulling.
                 (III 14–19)

18

Come on, all nine of you, back on the couch
   [together]! For I'm [. . .] three [. . . . . .]
with the boy who pours the wine [. . . . . .]
   No problem: [I'll] hold four gallons.
[Lo]ok: I'm five [feet] across here, where [the colander's]   5
   at[tached], three spans here, [much] thicker [there],
[and] where I'm square, over a gre[ater] extent [. . .]
   six [cubits . . .] here, and here, from [. . .]
                 (III 20–7)

19–20

Think [not] how many waves [rolled this] massive
   [rock] far from the raging sea:
Poseidon [easily broke] it off, then tossed it
   mightily, lobbing it on one hard [wave]
toward [the cities], a stone fifty feet across and   5
   scarier than the door-bar to Polyphemus' cave!
Polyphemus, Galatea's diving suitor, the goatherd
   crossed in love, could not have lifted it
nor did it roll down here, a boulder from a cliff: *this* prodigy
   is from the trident, and the Capherean main.   10
Restrain, Poseidon, your huge hand, send from the sea
   no towering wave to crash upon the naked shore:
four and twenty cubits of stone wafted from the deep,
   how easily will you mow down an entire island—
as, long ago, with a single surge, an enormous tidal wave   15
   smote lofty Helice and swept it, cliffs and all,
into the dunes, and would have risen against Eleusis too
   had not Demeter put her lips to your hand!
But now, Lord of Geraestus, together with his islands
   keep Ptolemy's lands and shores unshaken.   20
                 (III 28–IV 6)

II. OMENS

21   (IV 7)

At a ship's launching, let a hawk appear in all
    its power, while the shearwater is *not* washing its wings.
A bird diving into the deep bodes ill, but if it soar
    into the sky [. . . . .] all the way.
So from that oak in Ionia darted a swift-winged hawk   5
    at the launching, Timon, of your sacred ship.
(IV 8–13)

22

Let the wagtail show to the farmer's delight—
    a catcher of flies and a good sign for crops.
But what *we* want, making for Egypt over the open sea,
    is a Thracian crane gliding ahead of the forestays—
a favourable sign to the pilot as [it restrains] the billows,   5
    serenely sailing in the plains of heaven.
(IV 14–19)

23

Catching sight of a shearwater as it dives in the morning
    under the waves, consider it, fisherman, a good sign.
[Let down] a line full of hooks and cast both drag[net]
    and traps: you will not go home empty-handed.
(IV 20–3)

24

[Arise, fisherman,] when you've seen the black Theban [bird]:
    trusting in the shearwater, [you] won't [. . . . .]
. . .
    the harsh [. . .] Archytas [. . . . .]
For the [. . .] bird darts to the headland beaten   5
    by waves—sign of a good catch, ignored by others.
(IV 24–9)

25

An old man is good to meet, before you take to the road
    or set sail, and if you're looking to marry
let a priest in his garlands, or one whose pride
    in children now grown is assured, be [your sign].

But father and brothers—what bad luck, O bride,   5
   to run into *them*! Meet your in-laws instead.
(IV 30–5)

26

For acquiring a servant, the grey heron is your best
   bird of omen—Asterie the prophetess calls on it.
From it Hieron took his cue, hiring one man
   for his fields, another—just as luckily—for his house.
(IV 36–9)

27

Your best bird of omen for the birth of children
   is the vulture: it does not wait on a god's testimony
or for a proud eagle to perch beside it. But when it shows
   on the left, the most telling sign of all,
a vulture ushering your child to the light will make him   5
   a mighty orator in council, dashing, too, in war.
(IV 40–V 5)

28

If a man on his way to deadly battle meets
   an old man crying at the crossroads,
that man will not return again. He should postpone
   going at that time, till another war.
Timoleon of Phocis, scorning this very sign,   5
   came back from the war to his own dirge.
(V 6–11)

29

A hostile sign, catching sight of larks and finches
   in one place: they are bad when they appear together.
Euelthon saw them so, and evil thieves did him in
   on the road in Aeolian Sidene.
(V 12–15)

30

A statue has sweated: what toil for a man of the city,
   what a blizzard of spears is coming against him!
Beseech the sweating god, though, and he will drive away
   the fire, turn it upon the enemy's house and harvest.
(V 16–19)

23

31

An eagle swooping from the [clouds] and lightning
    striking at the same time meant victory
in war for Argead kings, but Athena before her temple
    moved her foot from its lead clamp
for Alexander alone, a sign when he conceived   5
    fire to destroy innumerable armies of Persians.
                    (V 20–5)

32

Antimachus was hastening to meet the Illyrian [enemy];
    a servant bringing him his arms and his belt
slipped near the stone door of the inner court of the house
    and fell. Antimachus was dismayed
at the omen of his servant, who presently returned   5
    from the enemy, bringing the bulky hero—a handful of ash.
                    (V 26–31)

33

Aristoxeinus the Arcadian had a dream too big
    for himself, and reached (fool that he was) for greatness.
He seemed to sleep, married to Athena, all night long
    in her golden boudoir, in Olympian Zeus' palace.
Up in the morning, he rushed to the front lines,   5
    Athena's heart, as he thought, beating in his breast.
But black Ares put him to bed—the pseudo-bridegroom
    who strove with gods and went to Hades.
                    (V 32–9)

34

From this hill with a view all around it
    Damon of Telmessus, noble in his ancestry,
prophesies from augury. Come, this is the place
    for consultation of the oracles and omens of Zeus!
                    (VI 1–4)

35

Here lies Strymon of Thrace, hero and prophet,
    under his crow, that 'Steward of Omens Supreme',
as Alexander styled it, who conquered the Persians
    three times, listening, each time, to this man's crow.
                    (VI 5–8)

III. DEDICATIONS

36   (VI 9)

Arsinoe, yours be this tissue of linen from Naucratis
  here hung up (may the breeze play through its folds!):
in my dream, beloved, your eager struggles over, you seemed
  to reach for it, as if to wipe the fragrant sweat
from your limbs—I see you still, Philadelphus, the sharp   5
  spear in your hand, the hollow shield on your arm.
Here, then, it is: to you from maiden Hegeso, of Macedonian
  lineage, this delicate strip of white cloth.
                              (VI 10–17)

37

Arsinoe, a dolphin of Arion has brought you
  this lyre, that [a poet's] hand once made to speak.
Up from the wave he lifted it, poised, un[hurt], on his tail
  but when, un[hoped-for saviour], he skimmed away
across the sea—yet another act of kindness done—[. . .   5
  the nightin[gales] burst into songs [. . .] afresh!
Re[ceive] too, [O Phil]adelphos, as an offering, this [strain]
  of Arion—a gift [from L]ysus, your temple guard.
                              (VI 18–25)

38

Epicratis [set] me up here to Arsinoe [when she drank]
  from the bowl for the first time [the water] of freedom
and said 'C[ome], and hail! [goddess of] freedom—
  and take this gift of Epicratis [. . .].'
                              (VI 26–9)

39

Whether you're to brave the sea or grapple your ship
  to shore, shout 'Hail!' to Arsinoe of Good Sailing,
calling our lady goddess from her temple—the son of Boiscus,
  admiral at the time, Samian Callicrates, put her here,
sailor, especially for you. And not only for you—often   5
  have others, in need of good sailing, looked to her.
On your way in, then, or out, forth on the godly sea
  you'll find she gives ear to your prayers.
                              (VI 30–7)

40

Cast your offering to Leto down my mouth—yes, make
  your deposit, nor be afraid if, wolf that I am, I yawned.
I'm a treasury, that Ly[cus] dedicated—[the pries]tess
  will tell you [. . .]
                                               (VI 38–VII 2)

41

An eagle's [talons] letting go, the tortoise
  . . . [on] the head
of And[romenes . . .] Half dead,
  . . .
vio[lent]—the tortoise's   5
  sh[ell Andromenes, sa]fe, [dedicated here].
                                               (VII 3–8)

IV. [EPITAPHS]

42   (VII 9)

The [servant of] Hecate [. . . . .]
  lies [. . . . .]
still safe, a[nd her glory re]doubled in her t[wo so]ns:
  both are of genuine blood, a noble race.
                                               (VII 10–13)

43

Nicostrate has gone to the place of the blest, the sacred
  rites of the mystai, the pure fire of Triptolemus.
Again . . . [. . .] of Rhadamanthys, [. . .]
  Aeacus [. . .] to the home and gates of [Hades],
having seen [her house full] of children—always the gentlest   5
  way to approach the harbour of [grim] old age.
                                               (VII 14–19)

44

Pella and the Euiades [cried], ah! three times
    in grief, [when Fate] brought Nico, [the youngest]
of twelve children, [love]ly in virginity, handmaiden
    of Dionysus, down from the Bas[saric] mountains.
(VII 20–3)

45

C[orinna] of Marathus has [here] taken her hands
    in old age from the [difficult] loom,
eighty [years] old, but still able to weave
    with shrill shuttle the de[licate] warp.
Wish her joy of her devotion! [Her toils over now], five times
    she saw,   5
    in a life without weariness, the harvest of a daughter.
(VII 24–9)

46

A poor old woman, I grew old in charge of babies,
    Batis, hireling of Phocian Athenodice.
I taught them how to tend to wool and twist the thread
    for delicate headbands, the plaiting of nets for their hair.
Now as they come to the threshold of their bridal chambers   5
    they've buried me in old age, holding my staff of office.
(VII 30–5)

47

This tomb holds Onasagoratis, who lived to see her children
    and her children's children, four times twenty in number,
generation linked to generation. The hands and hearts of eighty
    were there, then, to support her when she reached the end—
whom now, at the age of a hundred, the Paphians have laid,   5
    Onasas' blessed nursling, in this dust [left by the fire].
(VII 36–VIII 2)

48

For Bithynis the wise, this is enough, O Themis:
    a slave's grave; nearby, masters who were good.
And I am blest, who did [not] toil to be free,
    to have a tomb better than liberty.
(VIII 3–6)

49

[With sharp cries] to the wail of the flute, [her mother]
    Philaenion here put to rest sad Hegedice,
ei[ghteen] years [old], drenched in tears. And down
    from the unrelenting looms the shrill shuttles
[clattered] [. . .] for the girl's golden lips   5
    are stilled, [. . .] in this dark chamber.
                        (VIII 7–12)

50

A dark cloud went through the city, when Eetion
    groaned, putting his girl under this gravestone
and calling 'Hedea, my child!' The wedding god knocked
    not at her bedroom door, but at her tomb
and [all] the city felt it. Let the [tears] and cries   5
    of those who have lost her be enough.
                       (VIII 13–18)

51

'[Go on, on] with your tears, your arms raised to [the gods]'—
    that's what you'll say, Caryae, on the spur
of the moment, at the tomb of the child, Telephie. But when
    with flowering [branches] from the grove in spring, you go
to the contest, sing of the [budding] girl who ran like the wind   5
    and add to your tears lyrics divine, worthy of Sa[ppho].
                       (VIII 19–24)

52

Timon built this [sun]dial, to measure the hours.
    Look, he [lies th]ere now beneath the plain.
This girl, whom he left behind, [tends to him], wayfarer,
    as long—well, how long *is* a maiden to read the hours?
But go, yourself, to old age: the girl beside the tomb—   5
    for a heap of years—will measure the beautiful sun.
                       (VIII 25–30)

53

Maiden Calliope, here you lie, lamented by your friends—
    lamented too, the party that night, a pain to remember
now, when—your mother's pride, the loveliness of heavenly
    Aphrodite—down from the high roof you fell.
                       (VIII 31–4)

54

You are stained with tears, Earth: her brothers have burned
    and buried Myrtis, ten years old and unhappy,
the blood of Cyrene. But alive then, and unaware, Nicanor
    was travelling the world, crossing other boundaries . . .
       [2 verses missing]

(VIII 35–8)

55

All Nicomache's joys, whispers answering whispers
    to the music of the morning shuttle, as in Sappho—
Fate took away before her time: the city of the Argives
    burst into lamentation for the unlucky girl, a bud
raised in the arms of Hera. Ah, cold stayed the beds   5
    of the lovers who came courting her then!

(IX 1–6)

56

For five labours Eleutho took up her bow,
    standing, noble woman, by your bed;
from the sixth you died, and your baby
    died, quenched on its seventh day,
reaching, still, for the swollen breast, and those   5
    who buried each wept for both, the same tears.
Five of your children, then, the gods will mind;
    one, Asian woman, you'll keep in your lap.

(IX 7–14)

57

Once, when Philonis was having her baby, as fierce as *this*
    a [serpent] uncoiled its spire above her head,
a dark hood of scales, already on its way, fire [darting
    from its eyes], to [the hair] loosed over her shoulders
when, [the horror of it!], it lunged [to snatch] the baby   5
    [and the mother, just delivered,] collapsed in fear.
These prodigies were the death of you, woman, but your son
    [survived] then and in time got a grey [head].

(IX 15–22)

29

58

When Protis, [trained as a lyrist from her mo]ther's lap,
    went to her bridal bed, there was an end of her going
to maiden [feasts], [playing in] Boeotian style, but for [fiv]e
    decades of loving years she lived with her husband
[quietly], and having seen her children [flourish], men   5
    [among men], she set sail happily for the Isle of the [Blest].
                (IX 23–8)

59

Menestrate, who grew old in happiness [. . .],
    you saw an entire eighth [decade] of years,
and two generations of children [reared] the grave site
    [you deserve]. The gods having done their part by you,
[be as generous,] dear old woman: share in shining   5
    old age with those who [pass] your sacred tomb.
                (IX 29–34)

60

[Just now], down [the path] from pyre to Hades
    descended Mnesistratus, praying this prayer:
'Weep not for me, children! I welcome the dust—
    pile it now, at the end, over your [cold] father
as custom prescribes. Not heavy with age but light on my feet   5
    I quit the air [at sixty, on my way] to the blest.'
                (IX 35–40)

61

Slow down as you pass this tomb, and greet Aristippus,
    an old man who aged well, and now lies here.
Look, too, at his tearless stone—a stone that he feels
    as a light weight upon him under the earth. For he had
what an old man cherishes most: children who buried him   5
    and children of his daughters, whom he'd lived to see.
                (X 1–6)

V. THE MAKING OF STATUES

62   (X 7)

Imitate these works, O creators of living shapes,
   and, yes, hurry past old-fashioned rules of statuary!
For if ancient works [of the sculptor's] hand—either Hagelaides,
   that absolute antique, older than Polyclitus,
or the stiff figures [of Deinomenes]—had entered the field,   5
   what would be the point, lining up here the new
creations of Lysippus as our touchstone? But if it must be so
   and [a contest] comes about, [he set the limit] for *modern* artists!
                 (X 8–15)

63

This bronze, resembling Philitas in every detail, down
   to the tips of his toes, painstaking Hecataeus fashioned,
his eye on [the measure] of humanity, its dimensions
   and textures, nothing of the heroic thrown in;
with all the resources of art, adhering to the strict   5
   canon of truth, he captured the old man
deep in thought, on the brink of speech—with so much character
   in his rendering, he's [alive], though made of bronze!
'[Thanks to Ptol]emy who is both god and king at once, and for
   the Muses' sake, here [I stand], the man of Cos.'   10
                (X 16–25)

64

[. . .] warmly the bronze Idomeneus
   of Cresilas! Perfection here's so easily seen
Idomeneus finds a voice: 'Run, noble Meriones!
   [. . . . . .] you've been standing still too long.'
              (X 26–9)

65 (GP 18)

Lysippus of Sicyon, sculptor, you've a bold hand
   and plenty of technique: the bronze you've shaped
to Alexander's form has fire in its eyes. Why blame the Persians?
   Are not cattle forgiven, when they flee a lion?
              (X 30–3)

66

[. . . . . .] the little ox [seemed] ready to plough
    [. . .] and extremely valuable. . .
[when he] touched [it], he found, amazed, a thing of skill
    [. . .] but it was Myron's doing.

                        (X 34–7)

67

[. . . . .] of the chariot, observe up close
    how much effort went into Theodorus' work—
you'll see the bands securing the yoke, the reins, the bridle ring
    and the axle and the driver's eyes and finger-tips;
and there, plain to see, [the pole, thin as a hair], and on it   5
    you might see a fly al[ight, the size of the chariot].

                        (X 38–XI 5)

68

The Rhodians wanted to make [enormous] Helius
    twice the size, but Chares of Lindos drew the line—
no artist would make a colossus even larger
    than his. And if the venerable Myron mastered
the four-cubit limit, Chares was first [to rival] the earth   5
    [in size] with a bronze image tastefully done.

                        (XI 6–11)

69

I wear a shirt of bronze [. . . . .] of me
    Tydeus [. . . . .]
But if you touch [. . . . .] Myron
    has made a cl[oak . . . .] that fits me well.

                        (XI 12–15)

70

And the [works] of Polyclitus [. . . . .] of all
    as in the flesh and [. . . . .]
all upon Alex[ander . . . .] from the hands
    of Lysippus [. . . . .].

                        (XI 16–19)

VI. EQUESTRIAN POEMS

71   (XI 20)

This racehorse, Aethon, mine, [came in first]
   as did I, at the same Pythiad, [in the sprint]:
that's twice Hippostratus was proclaimed the winner—
   with my horse and by myself, O mistress Thessaly.
(XI 21–4)

72

Admire the mettle of this colt, how he pants
   from end to end, flanks strained to the limit
as when he ran at Nemea. To Molycus he brought the crown
   of celery, winning by a last thrust of his head.
(XI 25–8)

73

Right from the starting line at Olympia, I ran like this,
   [needing no] spurs [and no encouraging]—pleasant
was the weight I [carried] at full speed, [and] with a branch
   [. . .] they crowned Trygaeus, [the son of . . .].
(XI 29–32)

74

When at Delphi, contending in the chariot race, this filly
   nimbly pulled alongside a Thracian team
and won by a nod, the drivers raised a great outcry,
   O Phoebus, before the regional umpires
who suddenly dropped their staves to the ground and left   5
   the charioteers to claim the crown by lot.
But she, who ran in the traces on the right, lowered her head
   and, on her own sweet whim, picked up a judge's staff,
brave girl among stallions! The crowds with one
   universal shout drowning all protest   10
proclaimed the great crown hers. Amid the roar, then,
   Callicrates of Samos took the laurel garland
and dedicated to the Sibling Gods this tableau depicting
   [the contest] as it was, [chariot and] driver wrought in bronze.
(XI 33–XII 7)

75

[Winning with the chariot] we four mares
 took from Zeus the Charioteer,
O Pisatans, one Olympic garland after another
 [for Dius, son of Lysimachus,] the Lacedaemonian.
 (XII 8–11)

76

He's at full stride, on the tips of his hooves: so for Etearchus
 he takes the prize, this [glorious] Arabian horse.
Having won the Ptolemaea and the Isthmia, and twice at Nemea,
 he couldn't [overlook] the crown they give at Delphi.
 (XII 12–15)

77

In the chariot [. . .] three times I won at Olympia—
 Eu[. . .] with not a little expense
[. . .] for the upkeep [. . .]
 if it's enough for glory, I miss nothing.
 (XII 16–19)

78

Speak, poets all, of my renown, [if ever you enjoy]
 saying what's known: my glory's [not of yesterday].
My grandfather [Ptolemy won] in the chariot,
 driving his steeds over the courses at Pisa,
and Berenice, mother of my father, and my father,   5
 again in the chariot, triumphed, king after king,
Ptolemy after Ptolemy; and Arsinoe won all three
 harness victories at a single [competition].
[. . .] sacred line [. . .] of women
 [. . .] maiden [. . .]   10
Olympia witnessed [all these exploits] of a single house,
 the children and *their* children winning in the chariot.
Sing then, O women of Macedon, of the garland taken by royal
 Berenice in the chariot drawn by full-grown horses!
 (XII 20–33)

79

The royal maiden, yes it is she! Berenice in her chariot
    winning at once every single harness garland
in your contests, O Nemean Zeus! Many a driver was left
    in the dust [. . .] by her speeding chariot
when her horses, racing under the rein, came [like fire-]   5
    brands, first to greet the Argive umpires.
                          (XII 34–9)

80

. . .
  crowns
[. . .] O Nemean Zeus
    [. . .] this for a girl on her own.
                          (XIII 1–4)

81

. . . Dorian leaves of celery
  [honour] a single head
. . .
    [. . .] twice in the chariot drawn by full-grown horses.
                          (XIII 5–8)

82

[Poseidon looked on a great triumph]—Berenice's
  horse win[ning] [. . .] in the races.
And the sacred spring [of Peirene] near Acrocorinth, together
  with her father Ptolemy, marvelled at the Macedonian girl
[decked in garlands]. For so many times, royal, in your own right,
  you had your house proclaimed victorious at Isthmus.   6
                        (XIII 9–14)

83

This Thessalian steed, three times winner at Olympia in the race
  for single horses, [is dedicated here], sacred to the Scopadae:
I, the first and only. Come, put me to the test! I say I won three
    times
    [. . .] upon the banks of Alpheus. The Iamidae are my witnesses!
                      (XIII 15–18)

84

You were [the first] to bathe [this] swift horse in the Alpheus—
  you, Thessalian Phylopidas, victor at Olympia!
[And if your] great house went on to win later crowns,
  [everyone agrees that] first delights come closer to divinity.
(XIII 19–22)

85

I, Amyntas, brought you [this] horse, distinguished
  for his speed, from my own herd [to take
the prize], O Zeus of Pisa, nor did I fall short of my country
  Thessaly's renown in horses from of old.
(XIII 23–6)

86

. . . ran . . . bold . . . for at Nemea in the race for single riders
  this horse was four times victorious, and twice
at Pytho as well he ran the sprint, Messenian Aethon
  and each time got the crown for me, Eubotas.
(XIII 27–30)

87

We were the ones—still [mares] at the time—who gained
  Macedonian Berenice the Olympic garland
so famed throughout the world that we have stripped
  Cynisca of her glory days in Sparta!
(XIII 31–4)

88

We are the first and only trio of kings to win
  the chariot race at Olympia, my parents and I.
I, named after Ptolemy and born the son of Berenice,
  of Eordaean descent, am one, my parents the other two:
and of my father's glory I boast not, but that my mother,   5
  a woman, won in her chariot—*that* is great!
(XIII 35–XIV 1)

VII. SHIPWRECKS

89   (XIV 2)

This empty tomb calls in mourning for beloved Lysicles
    and blames the gods for what he suffered, the first
voice of the Academy, but by now the shores
    and sounding seas [have claimed him for their own].
                                        (XIV 3–6)

90

[Boreas] pummelled Archeanax into the Aegean Sea
    as he swam for scaly Scyros, eyeing
the land from here, from there, but one-fourth
    of a mile of sea is more than a dozen plains.
                                        (XIV 7–10)

91

Think about it four times over, and if you've ever sailed
    be in no hurry to navigate the Euxine
now you've seen this empty tomb of Dorus, whom
    some beach somewhere detains, far from Parium.
                                        (XIV 11–14)

92

As the ship went down, every sailor in the crew
    perished with it, [. . .] swam free:
for a god [. . . ..] him
    swimming [. . . ..]
                                        (XIV 15–18)

93

Wherever you hold Pythermus the good, who died
    under the chill of Capricorn, cover him lightly,
black Earth. But if it's you, Father of the Sea, who keep him
    hidden, put him out now, intact, on the bare sand
in full view of Cyme, giving, as you should, the dead man,   5
    O Master of the Sea, back to his native land.
                                        (XIV 19–24)

94

I died at sea. Quickly (he was in a hurry himself,
   a traveller in a foreign land) Leophantus
bewailed and buried me. But I am too small
   to thank Leophantus in a large way.
                                    (XIV 25–8)

VIII. CURES

95   (XIV 29)

As this bronze image of thinly breathing bones
   barely gathers the life into its eyes,
so were those he saved from disease, the man who found
   the cure for the dread bite of the Libyan asp—
Medeus, son of Lampon of Olynthus, whose father   5
   taught him all the panacea of the Asclepiads:
to you, Pythian Apollo, as a token of his art, he has dedicated
   this shrivelled frame, the remnant of a man.
                                    (XIV 30–37)

96

Over the byways, a cane in each hand, dragging
   his feet, Antichares came to you, Asclepius,
and sacrificed, and stood up on both his feet—
   his many years abed behind him now.
                                    (XIV 38–XV 2)

97

This silver libation bowl is yours, Asclepius,
   in thanks for the recovery of Coan Soses
whose six-year ailment you came and wiped away
   in a single night, and left, taking his epilepsy too!
                                    (XV 3–6)

98

For six years Archytas had nursed in his thigh
   the deadly bronze [. . .] a festering gash,
when, O Paean, [at sight] of you, as in a dream, [he shed]
   his pain [and escaped], cured of a long agony.
                                    (XV 7–10)

99

Asclas of Crete, deaf, able to hear neither the sound
   of the shore nor the roar of the wind, prayed
to Asclepius and left for home, fated now to hear
   what people were saying behind their brick walls.
                                        (XV 11–14)

100

When Zeno, blind for five and twenty summers,
   ought to have gone peacefully to his rest, at the age
of eighty he was suddenly cured, and [glimpsed] the sun
   but twice before he looked grim Death in the eye.
                                        (XV 15–18)

101

The best man asks, Asclepius, for wealth in moderation—
   and great is your power to give it, when you wish;
and he asks for health: remedies both. Indeed they seem
   to be the lofty citadel of character.
                                        (XV 19–22)

IX. TURNS (CHARACTERS?)

102   (XV 23)

What brings you people here? Why not let me sleep?
   Why ask who I am, who's my father, where I'm from?
Pass by my tomb! I'm Menoetius, son of Philarchus,
   from Crete (a foreigner here, I don't talk much).
                                        (XV 24–7)

103

Not even asking, for the sake of custom, where I'm from
   or [who] I am or who my parents were, you walk by:
[notice] me, though, [resting] in peace: I'm the son
   of Alcaeus, Co[an] Soses—[the same, once,] as you.
                                        (XV 28–31)

104

Have the kindness to stop—it's a modest, not a big
    [request] that I make of you: to know [. . . . .] of Eretria.
And if you come a step closer, learn, too, my friend, that I
    went to school with Menedemus—a wise man, Father [Zeus,
      for sure].

(XV 32–5)

105

Say hello to him—he lies beneath the tombstone,
    an old man, lacking but five of a h[undred] years,
from Adramyttion—like this: 'Adramyttian son of Timanthes,
    happy Battus . . .'.

(XV 36–XVI 1)

106

Say [. . . . .]
    greetings, Hegesa[. . . . .]
whose . . . this [. . . . .]
    letters [. . . . .]

(XVI 2–5)

107

I lie upon a fo[reign [. . . . .]
    nor [. . . . .]
stranger, to [. . . . .]
    welcome, d[ear . . . .]

(XVI 6–9)

108

It's good, when [. . . . .] to see
    [. . .] other [. . . . .]
of the dead [man . . . .]
    be safe, best of men [. . . . .]

(XVI 10–13)

109

How [. . . . .]
    Silence [. . . . .]
[. . . . .]
    cold [. . . . .]

(XVI 14–17)

X. (TITLE LOST)

110 (XVI 18)

In spring [. . .] the west wind [. . . . .]
  [. . . . .]
[. . . . .]
  to hesitate [. . . . .]
                               (XVI 19–22)

111

All is str[etched . . . .]
  [. . . . .]
[. . . . .]
  [. . . . .]
                               (XVI 23–6)

112

[. . . . .].
  [. . . . .].
                               (XVI 27–8)

POEMS FROM OTHER PAPYRI

*113 (*SH* 978)

A Shrine of the Nymphs, built in honour of Arsinoe

. . . . . .
  the feast [. . . . .] ablaze [. . .]
silent [. . . . .] and Ptol[. . .]
  welcome gladly, O ki[ngs], the homage [of this man]
who has also reared [a work] of stone, a spacious addition
  to your house—opening a way for the shining water   5
into a semi-circular basin, its wall of Parian marble
  adorned with fluted columns, a frieze in Ionian style
along the edge, and granite flecked in red from Syene
  gleams along the base: here the columns stand.
And stone of Hymettus, glistening wet, cups   10
  the spring's draft as it gushes from the cave.

He had your image, nymphs, carved in rich white marble,
  buffed and polished, and there, in the middle, he put
Arsinoe, honoured as a nymph all through the year. Come, then,
  spirits of the water, grace this fountain with your presence!   15

*114 (SH 961)

Wedding Poem (?) for Arsinoe

. . . . . .
[. . . . .]
  [. . . . .] of Arsinoe, restrain [. . . . .]
[. . . . .] is here from Ol[ympus. . .]
  [. . . . .] gifts of the gods [. . .]
[. . . . .] dew from a go[lden] bowl   5
  [. . . . .] brought, of nine years
[. . . . .] Hera bathed, a maiden
  [. . . . .] entering the bridal chamber on Olympus
[. . . . .] you will disobey my [. . . . .]
  [. . . . .] I said, instructed by the Muses.   10
[. . . . .] from the spring [. . .] you will bring leaves and
    flo[wers]
  [. . . . .] a drink will not quench your thirst
[. . . . .] of Arsinoe [. . .] the river took a turn [. . . . .]
  . . . .]of the porticoes, an ample swell brings
[. . . . .] in the herd, the bridal chamber seen even from
    there   [.   15
  . . . .] rain from heaven [. . . . .]
[. . . . .] the fountain [. . .] sacred [. . .] of the gods
  [. . . . .] pure waters, where the dear girl bathed
[. . . . .] with deep-girdled Dione's child
  [. . . . .] rejecting the bride as her daughter-in-law 20
[. . . . .] without a spindle [. . . . .]
  [. . . . . .] of the nymphs, the sacred sun [. . . . .]
[. . . . .] husband [. . .]
  [. . . . .] gave [. . . . .].

115 (GP 11)

The Greeks' saviour god—O mighty Proteus—shines from Pharos
  thanks to Sostratus of Cnidos, son of Dexiphanes.
For Egypt has no cliffs or mountains as the islands do
  but a breakwater, level with the ground, welcomes her ships.
And so this tower cutting through the breadth and depth   5
  of heaven beacons to the farthest distances

by day, and all night long the sailor borne on the waves
    will see the great flame blazing from its top—nor miss
his aim: though he run to the Bull's Horn, he'll find
    Zeus the Saviour, sailing, Proteus, by this beam.   10

116 (GP 12)

Between the Pharian headland and the mouth of Canopus
    among the waves shining all around me, I have my place—
this windy spur of Libya rich in lambs, reaching
    far toward the breath of Italian Zephyrus:
here Callicrates has raised me up and named me   5
    Queen Cypris Arsinoe's temple.
But come, chaste daughters of the Greeks,
    to her who will be called Aphrodite Zephyritis,
and come, too, men who toil in the sea: the admiral made
    this temple's haven safe from *every* wave.   10

117 (GP 24)

[. . . . .] dear Muses, here is a piece of writing
    [. . .] by the skill of its words
    [. . .] the man—and he's like a brother to me—
    [. . . . .] of connoisseurs.

118 (*SH* 705)

The Seal of Posidippus

If, O Muses of my city, you have heard with ears attuned
    Phoebus playing on his golden lyre, a lovely sound
along the folds of snowy Parnasus or the slopes of Olympus
    as you begin the rites of Bacchus every other year,
take up with Posidippus now the theme of grim old age,   5
    writing in your golden tablets, line by line.
Leave your peaks on Helicon, and come, daughters
    of Castalia, to the walls of Piplean Thebes!
And if ever, god of Cynthus, far-shooting son of Leto,
    you loved Posidippus, [. . .] a shaft [. . . . .]   10
. . .
    an oracle, to the snow-white house of the Parian—
proclaim and cry aloud from your sanctuary, O Lord,
    a like immortal directive in my behalf,
that the Macedonians—those on [the islands] and those   15
    along the coast of Asia, end to end—may honour me.

I hail from Pella. There, in the busy market place,
   let there be a statue of me, a book in both [hands], reading.
To the nightingale of Paros, his due of lamentation [. . .]
   in streams, vain tears pouring from your eyes,   20
and groans—but through my friendly lips [. . .]
   [. . . . .]
. . .

   and not a tear for me, from anyone: but may I make
my way along the mystical path to Rhadamanthys   25
   through old age—missed by the people, missed by them all—
on my own feet, without a cane, my speech still masterful,
   my children heirs to my home and wealth.

POEMS QUOTED BY ATHENAEUS

119 (GP 13)

While on the sea and when on land, keep in your prayers
   this shrine of Arsinoe Aphrodite Philadelphus
whom admiral Callicrates first consecrated here
   to rule over the headland of Zephyrium.
She'll grant good sailing or make the sea, for those   5
   who call upon her in the storm, smooth as oil.
                           (Ath. 7. 318 D)

120 (GP 14)
. . .
and to win a bet once I ate a Maeonian ox—
   Thasos my fatherland, you see, couldn't feed
Theogenes; whatever I ate, still I asked for more—
   and so I stand in bronze, holding my hand out.
                        (Ath. 10. 412 D)

121 (GP 16)

Here in this broken ditch lies Phyromachus, the all-
   devouring glutton, the crow at the party,
wrapped in the rags of his Pellenian cloak. Still, anoint
   his tombstone, man of Attica, and garland it
if ever he partied with you, tagging along, appearing   5
   with bleary eyes, blackened brows, and toothless mouth,
running from meal to meal with only his flask: that's how he looks
   now that he's come, those battles over, to the comic stage.
                        (Ath. 10. 414 D)

122 (GP 17)

Doricha, dust long ago were your bones, and the band
   binding your curls, and the robe, steeped
in perfume, that you shared with Charaxus once,
   body to body, drinking deep into the night.
But the radiant lines of Sappho's song   5
   remain, and will remain to tell of you.
Blest is your name here, in Naucratis' keeping
   as long as ships sail from the Nile to the open sea.
                           (Ath. 13. 596 c)

POEMS FROM THE GREEK ANTHOLOGY

123 (GP 1)

Rain, Cecropian pitcher! Rain with the dewy drops
   of Bacchus—fill all our cups for an opening toast!
And let's not hear from Zeno, wisdom's swan, or the Muse
   of Cleanthes: *Eros the bittersweet* be on our minds today!
                          (*AP* 5. 134)

124 (GP 10)

Four drinkers invited, a girl included for each:
   that makes eight. One Chian jug won't do.
Off to Aristius, boy! Tell him his first delivery
   was off by half, two gallons missing
for sure, and more, if you ask me. But run—   5
   the party starts at eleven a.m.
                          (*AP* 5. 183)

125 (GP 2)

Don't think you deceive me, Philaenis, with persuasive tears.
   I'm not taken in. You love 'absolutely no one more' than me—
for as long as you lie at my side. But if another held you
   in his arms, you'd say he's the one you 'love more'.
                          (*AP* 5. 186)

*126 (GP Asclep. 34)

The Loves themselves, leaving the golden boudoir of Aphrodite,
  looked with favour on the delicate Eirenion,
a sacred flower from head to foot, a statue
  of pure white marble, brimming with maidenly graces:
and many an arrow they aimed at the young men, their hands   5
  making the purple bowstrings twang.

(*AP* 5. 194)

*127 (GP Asclep. 35)

The purple whip and shimmering reins that deck
  the horse-ennobled portico are gifts of Plangon
who beat Philaenis, fierce contender, racing bareback, steed
  against steed, the colts of evening just starting to whinny!
Beloved Cypris, grant her the glory she deserves   5
  in victory, a touch of your beauty that lasts for ever!

(*AP* 5. 202)

*128 (GP Asclep. 36)

It was off your shore, Paphian Cytherea, that Cleandrus saw
  Nico swimming in the savage waves
and took fire, drawing up into his heart
  dry coals of love from the glistening girl!
Down went his ship right where he stood, while she   5
  still tasting the sea stepped softly to land.
Now both burn together in longing—for not in vain
  were the prayers that he prayed from that shore.

(*AP* 5. 209)

129 (GP 3)

Why after me again, tears and revels, into another pit of Cypris'
  coals even before I've pulled my feet from the fire?
Desire never leaves me alone, always some new longing—
  prolonging the pain—comes my way from Aphrodite!

(*AP* 5. 211)

130 (GP 4)

If Pythias is busy now, I'm off; but if she's sleeping
  alone in there, by Zeus, let her invite me in for a bit!
Tell her, for a sign, I've made my way through droves
  of thieves, drunk, the boldness of love guiding my steps.

(*AP* 5. 213)

*131 (GP 21)

Three-year-old Archianax, playing around the well,
  followed the lure of his own silent image.
His mother tore her son, drenched, out of the water,
  looking to see if there was life left in him.
The child hadn't defiled the waters. It is in   5
  his mother's lap that he sinks, and goes to sleep.
                      (*AP* 7. 170)

132 (GP 15)

Sailors, why are you burying me close to the sea? Far from *there*
  is the place for the miserable grave of a shipwreck.
I shudder at the roar of the wave that was my death! But never mind
  and fare you well, who felt pity for Nicetes.
                      (*AP* 7. 267)

*133 (GP 22)

What's the best path to take in life? In the market place,
  wrangling and ruthless dealing; in the home,
worries; out in the fields, toils enough; on the sea,
  terror; abroad, if you have anything, dread;
if you don't, anxiety. Are you married? Life's   5
  not without cares. You won't marry? It's too lonely.
Children are pain; a childless life, disability. The young
  are foolish; grey hairs, at the other end, feeble.
It all boils down, then, to a choice of two: never
  to be born or, once born, to die on the spot.   10
                      (*AP* 9. 359)

*134 (GP Asclep. 37)

There's no feeling for women in my heart, but men
  have set it ablaze, buried in coals unquenchable!
This is the hotter fire: as the male is stronger than the female,
  so is desire for him sharper than desire for her.
                      (*AP* 12. 17)

135 (GP 5)

Go ahead and shoot, Loves: let fly all at once,
  at one target (here I am!). It's stupid not to shoot,
for if you lay me low, archers famed among the gods
  will you be, and lords of the bulging quiver!
                      (*AP* 12. 45)

*136 (GP Asclep. 38)

If you donned a pair of golden wings and slung
    a quiver full of arrows over your silvery shoulders
and took your stand next to gleaming Eros, by Hermes
    Aphrodite herself wouldn't know her son!
                         (*AP* 12. 77)

137 (GP 6)

Desire has strapped the Muses' cicada to a bed of thorns
    and set fire to its ribs, hoping to silence it:
but the soul that has toiled long among books reaps yet
    other harvests, heaping blame on its troublesome fate.
                         (*AP* 12. 98)

138 (GP 7)

I am well armed and will resist you and not give in
    though I am mortal. No more attacks, then, Eros!
If you catch me drunk, lead me away, betrayed. While I'm sober
    I have Reason—he'll stand at my side, against you.
                        (*AP* 12. 120)

139 (GP 8)

Goddess who visit Cyprus and Cythera and Miletus
    and the lovely plain of Syria echoing with hooves,
come now with favour to Callistion—*she*
    never drove a lover from her porch!
                       (*AP* 12. 131)

140 (GP 9)

Pour two for Nanno and Lyde, and one each for Mimnermus,
    love's celebrant, and Antimachus, its master.
Dip a fifth ladle for me and a sixth, saying, Heliodorus,
    'Here's for whoever happens to be in love.'
A seventh goes to Hesiod, say, and an eighth to Homer,   5
    the ninth to the Muses, the tenth to Mnemosyne.
I'll take my drink, Aphrodite, from a brimming cup. For the rest,
    O Loves, a sober drunkenness is not at all disagreeable!
                       (*AP* 12. 168)

*141 (GP Asclep. 39)

This is a statue of Aphrodite. Oh? Be sure it isn't of Berenice!
Which of the two it resembles more, I can't say.

(AP 16. 68)

142 (GP 19)

Who's the sculptor, and from where? *From Sicyon.* The name,
    please!
  Lysippus. And you—who are you? *All-conquering Time.*
Why are you standing on tiptoe? *Always in a hurry.* And why the
    wings
  sprouting on either side of your heels? *I fly with the wind.*
And the razor in your right hand? *So men may know*   5
  no edge is sharper than mine.
Why is your hair in your face? *A handle for the one who meets me,*
  by Zeus! And the reason you're bald behind?
Once I've passed you, running by on winged feet, you won't
  latch onto me from behind, for all your desire.   10
Why did the artist fashion you? *For your sake,*
  stranger: and he put me in the portico, a lesson to all.

(AP 16. 275)

OTHER FRAGMENTS

FROM THE *EPIGRAMS*

143

(Aglais, *SH* 702)

Athenaeus 10. 415 A: *And a woman, Aglais, daughter of Megacles, gave the signal on the trumpet for the procession in the first great parade conducted in Alexandria, wearing a wig and a plume on her head, as Posidippus reveals in his* Epigrams. *And she used to eat, herself, twelve pounds of meat and four days' worth of bread, and would drink a jug of wine.*

FROM THE *HEAP*

144

('Berisos', *SH* 701)

Scholion A to *Il.* 11. 101, iii. 144. 13 Erbse: βῆ ῥ᾽ Ἴϲον: 'he went [to kill] Isos'. *Zenodotus read the phrase without the rho:* βῆ Ἴϲον. *Aristarchus says that the (poem with) 'Berisos' is not now included in the* Epigrams *of Posidippus, but that he did find it in the so-called* Heap. *He also says it is likely that Posidippus, under criticism, deleted it.*
Scholion T, Erbse, iii. 144. 17: βῆ ῥ᾽ Ἴϲον: *Posidippus (read)* Βήριϲον *as one (word).*

FROM THE *ASOPIA*

145

(The Peleae, *SH* 698)

nor do the Peleae set cold at evening
(Quoted, with ascription to Posidippus in his *Asopia*, by Athenaeus 11. 491 C.)

FROM THE *AETHIOPIA*

146

(Doricha, *SH* 699)

Athenaeus 13. 596 C: . . . *and Posidippus composed this epigram (= 122) on Doricha, whom he mentioned indeed many times also in his* Aethiopia.

FROM *ON CNIDUS*

147

(The Aphrodite of Praxiteles, *SH* 706)

Clement of Alexandria, *Protrepticus* (*Exhortation to the Greeks*): *As Posidippus in his* On Cnidus *clearly shows, Praxiteles, when fashioning the statue of Aphrodite of Cnidus, made it resemble his lover Cratine (53. 5) . . . Aphrodite on Cnidus was a stone and was beautiful; another man fell in love with her, and had intercourse with the stone. Posidippus tells the tale . . . in his* On Cnidus (57. 3).

FROM UNCERTAIN SOURCES

148

(Pandarus buried, *SH* 700)

nor did Lycaonian Zelie welcome you back
but Hector and the sons of Lycaon who fight hand to hand
set this tomb up for you by the mouth of the Simois.

(Quoted by Eustathius on the *Iliad*, p. 354. 9, with the comment *Posidippus says that Pandarus was buried beside the Simois.*)

149

(*baris*, *SH* 707)

Stephanus of Byzantium, 159. 8: βάρις means 'house' as in Posidippus
. . .

150

(Heracles left behind, *SH* 703)

Scholion to Apollonius of Rhodes 1. 1289 (p. 116, 12 W): *Hesiod in the* Marriage of Ceyx (fr. 263 M.–W.) *says that he* (i.e. Heracles) *was left behind when he had disembarked in search of water in Magnesia, near the place called Aphetae from his release. But Antimachus in his* Lyde (fr. 58 Wyss = fr. 69 Matthews) *says that he was put out by the heroes* (i.e. the Argonauts) *because he weighed the ship down. The latter is the version followed by Posidippus the epigrammatist and Pherecydes*
. . .

NOTES

The following notes are of two kinds, those that concern the Greek text, and those that are meant to help the non-specialist.

I have as a rule rendered the editorial supplements bracketed in the Greek text. In a few places, I have left them out or rendered others that seemed more plausible.

The translation stays closer to the literal than it might have under other circumstances. Solicited to appear with the essays that follow, it should not very often, I felt, depart so far from the text considered in those essays as to become a puzzle to their readers. But I also had in mind readers who would want to experience something of the poetry of Posidippus, and for them a strictly literal rendering would not do. The result, I hope, strikes a balance between these sometimes conflicting interests.

I wish to thank Kathryn Gutzwiller for inviting me to translate Posidippus and Sir Hugh Lloyd-Jones for many helpful comments. Readers of this translation are very much in his debt.

9

1 *for your seal, Polycrates*: the famous ring of Polycrates, made by Theodorus (see 67). Polycrates, tyrant of Samos, who lived in the sixth century BC, was a great patron of art and poetry. Ibycus and Anacreon visited his court.

11

4 *Aglaia*: one of the three Graces. The name means 'Radiance' or 'Splendour'.

15

This is the first of the two poems in the papyrus that were previously known and ascribed to Posidippus. The other is 65.
3 *Lynceus*: an Argonaut, famed for his powerful eyesight.
5 *in the imprint*: the stone described is a seal.

18

4 *I'll hold four gallons*: evidently a mixing bowl is speaking, though this is hard to fit with the ensuing details.

19–20

BG present 19 and 20 as two separate epigrams, giving their reasons on p. 133. Austin (AB, p. 42) takes them together as a single epigram, followed by W. Lapini, with fuller arguments, in 'Note posidippee', 42–4. Combination results in fewer problems, and so it is adopted here.
7 *Galatea's diving suitor*: Galatea was a Nereid, living in the sea. Theocritus (11. 54–6) depicts Polyphemus wishing he had gills, so he could dive into the sea after her.
9 *nor did it roll down here, a boulder from a cliff*: adopting Lapini's emendation of Ἀνταίου to ἀκταίου ('Note', 44).
15 When the two poems are taken separately, 20 begins here.
an enormous tidal wave: Lapini's interpretation of the phrase ('Note', 42–3).
16 *Helice*: an Achaean city, submerged by a tidal wave caused by an earthquake in 373/2 BC.

16–17 *and swept it . . . and would have risen*: following Austin in AB, but keeping the third person of the papyrus in l. 16 (ἤγαγεν) and changing from second to third person in l. 17 (ἤρθη), with Lapini, 'Note', 43.

17 *Eleusis*: probably the one in Egypt, near Alexandria.

21

1–2 *in all | its power*: the appearance of the hawk would seem to have its full authority as a favourable sign only if it is not qualified or cancelled by another.

2 *while the shearwater is* not *washing its wings*: according to a number of ancient sources, cited by D. Sider, Ch. 9, a shearwater cleaning its wings indicates windy or stormy weather. For the interpretation of this difficult clause (genitive absolute), see Sider.

22

5 *restrains*: adopting Sider's ἴςχει ('Addenda et corrigenda').

23

1 *in the morning*: following Sider's interpretation.

24

1 *the black Theban bird*: the sea eagle. As Sider points out, the sea eagle goes where the fish are.

6 *ignored by others*: reading οὐχ ἑτέροιςι κριτόν with Sider ('Addenda et corrigenda').

25

5 *what bad luck*: renders the emendation of αἰςχρῶς to ἐχθρῶς by Lapini, 'Note', 45.

27

3–4 *But when it shows | on the left*: adopting Lapini's change of ἀλλὰ τελείη to ἀλλ' ὅτε λαιῆι in 'Posidippo, Epigr. 27'.

31

3 *Argead kings*: the Macedonian royal line, named for the Argead clan, the dominant branch of the Temenid family which traced its ancestry back to Heracles through Temenus, legendary king and hero of Argos.

5 *for Alexander alone*: reading οἴωι instead of οἷον (the papyrus): H. Lloyd-Jones, 'Posidippus fr. 31'.

34

2 *Telmessus*: city on the western coast of Lycia, known for its mantic practitioners.

36

1 *Arsinoe*: Arsinoe II Philadelphus, sister-wife of Ptolemy II Philadelphus, deified after her death in 268 BC and worshipped as 'Arsinoe Aphrodite' (116. 6, 119. 2) in her temple at Zephyrium (see on 39. 4). The two following poems also feature dedications to her. The poet calls her by her personal name first, by her official epithet later (l. 5).
2 *here*: evidently, in her temple.
5 *Philadelphus*: 'beloved of her brother', also 'loving her brother'. When paired with Ptolemy II, the epithet has the complementary meaning 'beloved of his sister', 'loving his sister'. The two were worshipped together as Theoi Adelphoi or 'Sibling Gods' (see on 39. 4).

37

1 *a dolphin of Arion*: i.e. a dolphin like the one that rescued the singer Arion from the sea. Similarly, '*this strain | of Arion*' in the last two lines means something like 'this poem, worthy of Arion'.
7 *Philadelphus*: see on 36. 5.

38

4 *this gift*: perhaps the bowl in l. 2.

39

2 *Arsinoe of Good Sailing*: Arsinoe II Philadelphus, now deified. See on 36.
4 *Samian Callicrates*: admiral and powerful courtier of Ptolemy II and Arsinoe II, the Philadelphoi. He erected statues to them at Olympia and is the first recorded official priest of their cult as the 'Sibling Gods' (74. 13).
  put her here: i.e. built her temple at Zephyrium (on the sea, midway between Alexandria and Canopus: 116. 1). The temple is the same as that mentioned in 116 and 119.

40

3 *Lycus*: the dedicator's name means 'Wolf'.

42

1   *The servant of Hecate*: may designate the deceased as an initiate in religious mysteries. Hecate, according to some ancient sources a daughter of Zeus and Demeter, hence the sister of Persephone, was an important goddess at Eleusis in Attica (see next note).

43

1–2   *the sacred | rites of the mystai, the pure fire of Triptolemus*: the deceased had evidently undergone initiation at Eleusis. Triptolemus was an Eleusinian prince, to whom the goddess Demeter taught her mysteries.
3   *Again*: initiation into the Mysteries gave one a glimpse of the after-life. In this sense, Nicostrate in dying sees the underworld 'again'.
3–4   *Rhadamanthys . . . Aeacus*: judges in the underworld. The Eleusinian Mysteries prepared the initiate for the afterlife.

44

1   *Euiades*: Nico's companions in the worship of Dionysus.
    three times: it was traditional to call upon the dead three times.
4   *Bassaric*: Dionysian, sacred to Dionysus, or haunted by him.

45

5–6   *five times . . . the harvest of a daughter*: i.e. she lived to see the grandchild of her great-grand-daughter, a possibility if each of the girls in the succession beginning with her daughter married at the average age of 15. Inscriptions testify to similar feats of longevity.

46

4   *delicate*: reading παιπαλέαις with Livrea, 'Critica testuale ed esegesi', 62–3.

48

1   *Themis*: goddess of Justice.

51

2   *Caryae*: a town in northern Laconia, where Artemis was worshipped by maiden choruses.

52

3   *This girl*: reading αὔτη with E. Bowie, as accepted by C. Austin and G. Bastianini, 'Addenda et corrigenda'. Statues of girls were frequently placed on the bases of sundials.

5–6 *the girl . . . will measure*: punctuation and reading—μετρεῖ (indicative) instead of μέτρει (imperative)—follow Gutzwiller, as in Austin and Bastianini, ibid., and Ch. 15, p. 283.

54

3 *Nicanor*: evidently, the dead girl's father.

56

1 *Eleutho*: Eileithyia, goddess who delivers women from the pangs of childbirth.

6 *the same tears*: the meaning seems to be that those who mourned the mother continued mourning for the child.

62

1 *these works*: evidently, the works praised in the ensuing epigrams (63–70).

2 *statuary*: 'colossi' in the Greek. E. Kosmetatou and N. Papalexandrou, 'Size Matters' define 'colossus' as 'any lifelike statue' (55), and argue that the connotation of gigantic size is a later accretion. See, however, M. W. Dickie, 'What was a *Kolossos?*'

3 *of the sculptor's*: reading πλάϲτα with Gutzwiller, 'Posidippus on Statuary', 45 n. 10. Others suspect that *the name* of a sculptor occurred here. Austin in AB suggests Canachus of Sicyon, who worked in bronze and flourished *c.*490 BC. But see A. Stewart, below, Ch. 10.

Hagelaides or *Hageladas*: sculptor, sixth century BC. The man himself here stands for his works.

4 *Polyclitus*: of Argos, famous sculptor, worked in bronze, active 460–410 BC.

5 *the stiff figures*: on 'hardness' or 'rigidity' as a term of ancient art criticism, see Stewart, Ch. 10.

Deinomenes: 'Didymides' in the papyrus is unidentifiable and probably corrupt. BG, p. 186 suggest Deinomenes, a pupil of Polyclitus. Gutzwiller ('Statuary', 45 n. 10) suggests Daedalides, 'a son of Daidalus', and lists several sculptors who might have been so designated; descent from Daedalus, connoting extreme antiquity, would suit the context well. See also Stewart, Ch. 10.

had entered the field: adopting Austin's change in AB from aorist infinitive to aorist indicative.

7 *Lysippus*: of Sicyon, Alexander the Great's favourite sculptor, authorized as his official portraitist, worked in bronze. Posidippus refers to him also in 65. 1, 70. 4, 142. 2.

8 *he set the limit*: adopting Austin's reading in AB, but with a differ-

ent interpretation. The imperfect verb suggests not the fulfilment of an unreal condition but a *fait accompli*: 'If there should be a contest, he has won already.'

63

1   *Philitas*: a famous poet, born *c*.340 BC on the island of Cos, tutor of Ptolemy II Philadelphos.
2   *Hecataeus*: evidently, a sculptor who worked in bronze, possibly the same person described by Pliny (*NH* 34. 85) as a silver engraver.
9–10   With the change of a single letter in the restored text (from -ται to -μαι), the statue, in the first person, quotes its own inscription: R. Scodel, 'A Note on Posidippus 63 AB'.
9   *Ptolemy*: Ptolemy II Philadelphus (see on l. 1), the dedicator of the statue.

64

1   *Idomeneus*: of Crete, Homeric hero, who appears in the *Iliad*, accompanied by Meriones (l. 3).
2   *Cresilas*: famous Cretan sculptor, fifth century BC.

65

See on 15.

66

4   *Myron*: of Eleutherae, sculptor, worked in bronze, active 470–440 BC. His *Cow* is the subject of numerous epigrams in the Greek Anthology (*AP* 9. 713–42).

67

2   *Theodorus*: Samian engraver, sculptor, and architect, mid-sixth century BC. See on 9.

68

2   *Chares of Lindus*: disciple of Lysippus, creator of the Colossus of Rhodes (*c*.300 BC), one of the Seven Wonders of the World, a bronze statue of Helius that stood 105 feet high. For the meaning of the word 'colossus', see on 62. 2.

74

12   *Callicrates of Samos*: see on 39. 4. He appears again in 116 and 119.
13   *the Sibling Gods*: official title of Ptolemy II Philadelphus and his sister-wife Arsinoe II Philadelphos. See on 36. 1, 5.

77

1   *In the chariot*: literally 'In the mature chariot', i.e. 'in a chariot drawn by full-grown horses'. Why this detail is mentioned is uncertain here. See on 78. 14.

2   *with not a little expense*: in epinician poetry, the victor is often praised for his willingness to incur expense in pursuit of glory.

78

A sequence of five poems celebrating victories gained by a certain 'Berenice' begins here and ends with 82. BG, p. 205 identify her as Berenice II, daughter of Magas of Cyrene and, after her marriage to Ptolemy III, Queen of Egypt; if this is correct, the victories involved would fall between 249 and 247 BC. Dorothy J. Thompson in this volume more plausibly identifies her as Berenice, the daughter of Ptolemy II and Arsinoe I, who left Egypt in 252 BC to become the bride of the Seleucid king Antiochus II of Syria. In that case, the victories would be earlier than 252 BC.

3   *My grandfather Ptolemy*: Ptolemy I Soter.

5   *Berenice, mother of my father*: Berenice I, mother of Ptolemy II Philadelphus. See 87.

7   *Arsinoe*: Arsinoe II Philadelphus.

10   *maiden*: she is so characterized again in 79. 1. The epithet almost always describes a young girl, just shy of marriageable age (see 80. 4 and 82. 4).

13   *women of Macedon*: the poem celebrating a girl's achievements is fittingly addressed to the women of her circle. The early Ptolemies stressed their connection with Macedon, home of Alexander the Great.

13–14   *royal | Berenice*: the Greek here (as at 79. 1 and 82. 5) could designate either a queen or a princess. The former would suit Berenice II, the latter Berenice, young daughter of Ptolemy II (see 82. 4).

14   *in the chariot drawn by full-grown horses*: as opposed to a chariot drawn by fillies or colts. Here and at 81. 4 there may be an implicit compliment: the young girl (l. 10, above) enters a team of mature steeds.

79

1   *The royal maiden*: see previous note.

3   *in your contests, O Nemean Zeus!* If Berenice II were the person praised here, the occasion of this epigram would be identical with the one celebrated by Callimachus at the opening of *Aitia* 3.

80

4 *a girl*: she is so characterized again in 82. 4.
on her own: evidently she entered her own horses, on her own initiative. So too at 82. 5.

82

4 *her father Ptolemy*: Ptolemy II Philadelphus. See next note.
5 *royal, in your own right*: her independence is emphasized. Her father, the king, is present, but only as spectator, witness to his young daughter's triumph.

83

2 *Scopadae*: a powerful Thessalian clan, famed for their patronage of the great fifth-century poet Simonides, who wrote victory odes and dirges for them.
4 *Iamidae*: hereditary priests of Zeus' oracular altar at Olympia.

87

2 *Berenice*: apparently Berenice I (*c*.317–277 BC). See A. Cameron, *Callimachus and his Critics* (Princeton, 1995), 243–4.
4 *Cynisca*: daughter of King Archidamus of Sparta, first woman to win the chariot race at Olympia (396, 392 BC).

88

3 *I*: Ptolemy II Philadelphus.
Ptolemy: his father, Ptolemy I Soter.
Berenice: his mother, Berenice I
4 *Eordaean*: from Eordaea, in western Macedon, ancestral home of Ptolemy I.
5 *and of my father's glory I boast not*: reading κοὐ and restoring ἐμοῦ with Austin and Bastianini, 'Addenda et corrigenda'.

98

3 *at sight of you*: reading ϲ' εὐθὺϲ ἰδών, τότ' with Lapini, 'Note', 51.

103

4 *once*: rendering the alternative supplement in BG, p. 230.

*113

The authorship of this poem is not known for certain. AB, interpreting l. 3 as a reference to Ptolemy III and Berenice II, assign it to

Posidippus. The editors of *SH*, preferring a reference to Ptolemy IV, consider it too late for Posidippus.

3   *O Kings*: see previous note.

    this man: the dedicator of the shrine, unidentified.

6   *Parian marble*: the text has *lychnites*, rendered 'lamp-stone' in AB. According to D. L. Page, *Greek Literary Papyri*, i (Cambridge, MA, and London, 1942), 451, Parian marble was called *lychnites* (from *lychnos*, 'lamp') because it 'was quarried underground by lamplight'.

9   *here the columns stand*: evidently on the wall, forming a miniature colonnade.

14   *Arsinoe*: Arsinoe II Philadelphus.

*114

On the ascription of this poem to Posidippus, see Gutzwiller, Introduction, pp. 6–7 with n. 17. It is not certain, but seems probable, that the poem, like Callimachus 392 Pf., celebrates the nuptials of Arsinoe II Philadelphus. Unfortunately, of the Callimachean epithalamium only one hexameter survives intact; of the Posidippan, these 24 elegiac couplets, all of them illegible at line-beginning and not a few at line-end as well.

7–8   The marriage of Hera to her brother Zeus is called to mind by Theocritus (17. 131–4) in connection with the marriage of Arsinoe to her brother Ptolemy.

19   *deep-girdled Dione's child*: Aphrodite.

115

1   *The Greeks' saviour god*: the statue of Zeus the Saviour, situated on top of the famous lighthouse of Pharos, in the harbour of Alexandria.

    Proteus: a sea god, son of Poseidon. Menelaus encountered him on Pharos on his way home from the Trojan War (*Od.* 4. 454–9).

2   *Sostratus*: statesman, friend and envoy of Ptolemy II Philadelphus, responsible, as P. Bing has shown ('Between Literature and the Monuments', 21–9), for placing the statue of Zeus the Saviour atop the lighthouse.

9   *the Bull's Horn*: evidently, the main entry into the harbour.

10   *Zeus the Saviour*: the statue mentioned in l. 1.

116

1   *the Pharian headland*: a periphrasis for Alexandria, in whose harbour Pharos was located.

5   *Callicrates*: of Samos, son of Boiscus. See on 39. 4.
8   *Aphrodite Zephyritis*: Arsinoe as 'Aphrodite of Zephyrium', as in Callimachus, *Ep.* 5 Pf. (= GP 14). See on 36.1.

117

The ascription of this poem to Posidippus derives from the heading in the papyrus, in which only the last four letters of the poet's name are legible. It may, then, belong to someone else.

118

The title of the poem is taken from Lloyd-Jones, 'The Seal of Poseidippus', where the poem's ascription to our Posidippus and its character as a 'seal' or 'signature poem of a collection' (95 = 190) are both established.

1   *with ears attuned*: according to Lloyd-Jones ('Seal', 81–2 = 169), καθαροῖc οὔαcιν, literally 'pure ears', means 'clean ears', i.e. ears that are not stopped with wax, ears that belong, then, to people who are 'quick in the uptake'. I take it a step further, interpreting it to mean sensitive to finer sounds, namely the nuances and subtleties of well-crafted poems.

5   *Posidippus*: the poet names himself (as again in l. 10), putting a 'seal' or 'signature' to the collection in which this poem originally appeared.

8   *the walls of Piplean Thebes*: evidently, Thebes in Boeotia. Posidippus appears to be writing the poem there. As Lloyd-Jones observes ('Seal', 87 = 176) a Theban connection can be inferred from 145, *Asopia*, having to do with Asopus, the famous Boeotian river, father of Theba, eponymous nymph of Thebes. Piplea was in Pieria, a district of Thessaly, north of Mt. Olympus. Here, according to the oldest sources, the Muses were born. Hesiod in the opening line of his *Works and Days* summons them from Pieria, but in the *Theogony* he makes the Boeotian mountain Helicon in the vicinity of Thebes their haunt. The phrase 'Piplean Thebes' suggests that, thanks perhaps to Hesiod, the Muses are now as much at home in Thebes as they are in their birthplace.

12   *the Parian*: Archilochus, the famous poet, born on Paros, where there was a temple in his honour, built in response to a Delphic oracle. Posidippus in ll. 13–16 asks Apollo to decree a similar honour for himself, presumably at his birthplace, in Pella (l. 17).

18   *a book in both hands*: reading ἀμφοῖν. If the statue is to depict Posidippus perusing a book while standing, both his hands must be

employed. But there is no clear indication of his position, no mention of 'hands', and the word here rendered 'both' is uncertain.

The photograph on the cover of AB shows the statue of a seated figure, an unopened roll of papyrus on his lap, in his right hand, his left raised across his chest. The statue, in the Vatican museum, has the name Ποσείδιππος inscribed on its plinth. According to M. W. Dickie, 'Which Posidippus?', the statue depicts our Posidippus; others (including A. Stewart, below, Ch. 10) think it depicts the contemporary and fellow Macedonian comic poet of the same name.

19 *his due of lamentation*: Archilochus died in battle, presumably not yet in old age.

21 *but through my friendly lips*: Posidippus may be contrasting the more congenial character of his own Muse with that of Archilochus, known for his unfriendly poems—fierce attacks on various enemies. But what, exactly, Posidippus imagines passing through his lips at this point cannot be determined.

24 *and not a tear for me*: as for Archilochus (see on l. 19).

119

2 *this shrine*: see on 39. 4.

120

1 *and to win a bet once*: Athenaeus starts his quotation of the poem at some distance from its opening.

3 *Theogenes*: of Thasos, renowned athlete.

121

8 *to the comic stage*: the Greek has 'beneath Lenaean Calliope', i.e. 'under the sway of the Lenaean Muse'. Comedies were the main attraction at the Athenian festival called the Lenaea.

122

1 *Doricha*: courtesan who detained Sappho's brother Charaxus in Egypt.

124

6 *at eleven a.m.*: in Greek, 'within the fifth hour'. Rather early for a drinking party.

*126

'Asclep.' to the left of the epigram number in this and subsequent headings indicates that the poem is ascribed also to Asclepiades and will be found so numbered among the epigrams of Asclepiades in GP, where epigrams with dual ascription are as a rule printed only once. Asclepiades is not necessarily preferred to Posidippus as the author of the epigram in question.

*127

6   *a touch of your beauty that lasts for ever*: reading cὴν ἐπιθεῖca with Lapini, 'Note', 51–2.

129

4   *prolonging the pain*: reading μηκύνων with Lloyd-Jones (*per litteras*) instead of μὴ κρίνων.

*131

This epigram appears again later in *AP* 7, after no. 481, where it is ascribed to Callimachus, and in *APl*, where it is ascribed to Posidippus.

5   *The child hadn't defiled the waters*: by dying in them. Death pollutes a temple or sacred site.

It is: the present tense suggests a picture (a grave-relief, perhaps), the preceding lines describing what happened before the moment depicted in it.

sinks, and goes to sleep: literally, 'has the deep sleep'. Elsewhere, as GP observe, 'deep' is not among the adjectives applied to 'sleep' when the meaning is 'death'. The poet seems to have wanted us to think of the child, unconscious when pulled from the well, breathing his last in his mother's arms.

*133

There is an alternative ascription of this epigram where it appears in *AP*, to Plato the comic poet.

*134

This epigram is labelled 'anonymous' in *AP* 12. 17, but ascribed to 'Asclepiades or Posidippus' in the epigram sylloge known as the Appendix Barberino-Vaticana (44).

137

3–4   *reaps yet | other harvests*: reading ἄλλα θερίζει with AB and following Gutzwiller, *Poetic Garlands*, 160–1.

140

1   *Nanno and Lyde*: two women, also the titles of two books cele-brating them: *Nanno* by Mimnermus, *Lyde* by Antimachus.

*141

There being no other example of a distich by Posidippus, the poem probably belongs to Asclepiades.
1   *Berenice*: identity uncertain; possibly Berenice I.

142

2   *Lysippus*: see on 62. 6.

144

Zenodotus: of Ephesus, pupil of Philitas, whom he succeeded as tutor of the children of Ptolemy I Soter. Born *c.*325 BC, he came to Alexandria early and was appointed first head of the Alexandrian Library. He initiated the scientific study of the text of Homer, edit-ing both the *Iliad* and the *Odyssey*, as well as other ancient works.
    Aristarchus: of Samothrace, head of the Alexandrian Library from *c.*153 BC. He was renowned as editor and commentator, dealing with Homer and many other ancient poets.

145

The *Asopia*: see on 118. 8.
1   *the Peleae*: the constellation more commonly known as the Pleiades.

148

Pandarus: fought on the Trojan side against the Greeks. Homer calls him the son of Lycaon and leader of the contingent of fighters from 'Zeleia' (*Il.* 2. 826–7). It is he who breaks the truce between the armies by wounding Menelaus in the thigh with an arrow (*Il.* 4. 85–219). He is killed by Diomedes at *Il.* 5. 290–6.
1   *Zelie*: Homeric Zeleia (see previous note), home of Pandarus, some 70 miles east-north-east of Troy.
2   *the sons of Lycaon*: evidently, the men who followed Pandarus to Troy.
3   *set this tomb up for you*: seems to indicate that the lines are quoted from a fictional epitaph or an epitaph composed to adorn an actual monument identified fancifully as the tomb of Pandarus in the Troad.

PART ONE

PAPYRUS ROLLS, READERS, AND EDITORS

3

Back from the Dead with Posidippus

COLIN AUSTIN

In papyrology a primeval urge, akin to love or madness, drives me on relentlessly: Posidippus is my seventh direct encounter on this mystic journey back in time. It all started in Paris during the swinging sixties. Seeing me captivated by the newly discovered *Sikyonios* of Menander, Jean Scherer, the then Director of the Institut de Papyrologie at the Sorbonne, came up to me and said: 'Nous avons aussi un texte tragique, Monsieur Austin. Je vous le donne: il est à vous.' The *Erectheus* sealed my fate as a devotee of Greek papyri.[1] Two years later I was in Geneva: Martin Bodmer himself had heard of my Paris escapade and summoned me for a week to help out with the *Aspis* and *Samia*.[2] My room was above the library and he gave me the key. Being alone in the building, I could easily have absconded with all fifty-two pages of the original codex; instead, I worked at them non-stop, day and night. Those were heady days, a truly golden era, when the *Misoumenos* and other surprises were also resurfacing in London, thanks to Eric Turner. Years later, in Cambridge, with the connivance of Klaus Maresch, Maryline Parca, and the late Bill Willis of Duke University, I caroused to my heart's content with the latest novelties on the horizon: a raving young man in a Cologne comedy, ecstatic about a girl whose face he has never seen,[3] Odysseus attempting to enter Troy in disguise after addressing a cosmic prayer to Athena,[4] and finally the *Silouros*, an exotic fish from the Nile, whose gills are said to be as attractive as 'the beautiful hip of a white-thighed maid'.[5] More recently Peter Parsons fed my insatiable desires with dainty new morsels from Oxyrhynchus, notably the spicy *Hymnis*, another Menandrean hetaira, this time from Miletus.[6] Posidippus

---

[1] 'De nouveaux fragments'.
[2] R. Kasser with C. Austin, *Ménandre: La Samienne* and *Ménandre: Le Bouclier* (both Cologny-Geneva, 1969).
[3] *PCG* viii, fr. 1147 = Men. *fab. incert.* 8 Arnott.
[4] M. G. Parca, *Ptocheia* (Atlanta, GA, 1991).   [5] *PCG* viii, fr. 1146, ll. 29–30.
[6] 'From Cratinus to Menander', 44–7. See also P. Oxy. 4302 = *PCG* viii, fr. 1152 (the *Aischron* play).

was next: I met him rather late in the day, but the shock was all the more electric.[7]

Ten years ago an antiques-dealer came up with three priceless pieces, of the third, second, and first centuries BC. Posidippus was the oldest, 1½ metres in length, with over 600 lines of verse or 112 epigrams, two of which were already known under the poet's name. The second roll, I am told, has several columns of a historical narrative of the Ptolemaic period, while the third is clearly the star of the show, 2½ metres long, a fine illustrated edition of the geographer Artemidorus of Ephesus, who was active around 100 BC. This unique document contains the earliest known map of the Iberian peninsula, with rivers running across Spain, all dotted with complex drawings of buildings and towers. For some unknown reason the map itself was never completed and at a later stage in antiquity the unused parts of the papyrus were filled in with sketches of animals as well as portraits and drawings of the human body.

The first two rolls, Posidippus and the historical text, were bought by Cariplo, a wealthy Italian bank, for the University of Milan, while the Artemidorus was acquired by an anonymous collector. A provisional description of its content was published in 1998 in volume 44 of *Archiv für Papyrusforschung* by Claudio Gallazzi and the German papyrologist Bärbel Kramer of the University of Trier; and there is a brief summary in English by Kramer herself in the international journal for the study of cartography *Imago Mundi*, 53 (2001), 115–20, with a picture of the map. On p. 204 of *AFP* there is a splendid portrait of a grumpy-looking Zeus. The Artemidorus papyrus was originally so tattered and crumpled that it cannot have been used as a pectoral like the Posidippus, but rather, it seems, as very rough stuffing for a sacred animal, an ibis or crocodile.

The Posidippus discovery was announced in the Cariplo magazine *Ca' de Sass* for 1993, but as the papyrus required careful restoration and often microscopic deciphering the full publication could not appear immediately. I first met Guido Bastianini a few years later when I gave a lecture on Menander in Florence. In the library he allowed me a lightning glimpse of his transcript. All I could take in at the time was that Polyphemus was αἰπολικὸς δύσερως, 'a goatherd madly in love'. Back home I sent Bastianini a card saying I felt a bit like his Cyclops. He knew what I meant and nobly put in the post the relevant epigram. In due course he slowly supplied me with the others, one or two at a time, taking great care not to drown me

---

[7] See now the *editio minor* (AB).

with too much at once. Our little game had been going on for quite a while when early in 2000 I received an urgent message: the Milan authorities had decided that the papyrus must be published before the Vienna Congress in July 2001. The problem was that more than half the commentary had yet to be written. I told Bastianini not to worry: as a *quid pro quo* for his generosity I would write the rest 'illico presto' while he and Gallazzi concentrated on other things.

We were making excellent progress—I writing in French, Bastianini turning it all into Italian—when I was suddenly struck down with unstable angina. Three times I was rushed to hospital for emergency heart treatment. A particularly dramatic moment occurred during my second stay in Papworth, the specialized clinic. I had just been operated on early in the morning and was recovering in the ward, when my wife came with the mail and a large envelope from Italy. She told me to be patient and open it later but I could not wait: I tore the wrapping and out fell the funeral epigrams of those who had met an untimely death. Within half an hour I had collapsed again and was being wheeled back to theatre. Above my eyes, too close for comfort, a strange light was hovering in a sinister way: like Meleager, I felt my life was ebbing away. It took the doctors over two hours to repair and reconnect my damaged arteries. Half a dozen stents were needed to ensure my survival. The *editio princeps* duly came out a few days before the Vienna deadline. Thanks are therefore due to Persephone for resurrecting the dead and to Posidippus for keeping the scholarly world enthralled.

4

The Posidippus Papyrus: Bookroll and Reader

WILLIAM JOHNSON

The Posidippus papyrus is of intense interest in a number of specific respects: for the sudden access to the poetic character of an author whose name was well known to us, but whose work was almost entirely lost; for the poetry itself, which ranges in quality but has many interesting pieces; for illuminating the exact content of an early epigram collection; and, lastly, but perhaps most importantly, for what it may tell us about the way that a poetry book was used and put together at this, the time of the beginnings of such poetic collections.

I wish here to pursue that final set of questions: how an ancient poetry book was put together, and how it was used. I will concentrate on what the Milan papyrus tells us as an artefact. That is, what conclusions can we draw from the ways in which this bookroll was constructed and copied, and what we can say about its history *as an object* prior to its discard and reuse as cartonnage in the early second century BC? I organize my discussion around two questions: (1) What seemed usual or unusual about this bookroll when the Ptolemaic reader picked it up in his or her hand? (2) What can the papyrus tell us about its use by readers over time, and was there anything exceptional about that use?

The huge majority of extant papyri are from the Roman era. The corollary is that there are relatively few literary papyri from the Ptolemaic period, and, as it happens, most of these are in poor, fragmentary condition.[1] Even expert papyrologists are, consequently, far less acquainted with what is typical of a Ptolemaic bookroll such as the Milan papyrus, and it will be useful to summarize what about the artefactual details of the papyrus is routine, and what is not.

In the most general terms the look and feel of this bookroll are unexceptional. By 'look and feel', I refer in particular to the way in

---

[1] The Leuven Database of Ancient Books (http://ldab.arts.kuleuven.ac.be/) lists about 300 bookroll fragments surviving in the period from iv BC to the crossover to i BC (i.e. including papyri dated ii/i BC); 2,100 bookrolls from AD ii–iii, including crossovers (i.e. papyri dated i/ii AD, iii/iv AD).

which the rather wide columns are tightly spaced so as to flow almost one into the next—that is, in technical terms, the intercolumn is very narrow, as narrow in fact as logistics allow (Pl. 1). These columns are flanked at top and bottom by, again, quite narrow white space; the upper margin in particular is very narrow. The overall effect is of an extended and somewhat oversized rectangular block of nearly continuous writing that dominates the run of the bookroll. That look, which would be unusual in a well-written Roman-era bookroll, is in fact easy to parallel among Ptolemaic verse texts. I think it fair to say, in fact, that this is one characteristic look for verse texts of the third and second centuries BC. The rather typical example in Pl. 2 (P. Sorb. inv. 2272+72, a well-known late third-century-BC cartonnage from el-Ghorab containing Menander's *Sikyonios*) is slightly shorter in the column (with a height of about 13–14 cm rather than 16 cm), but otherwise noticeably similar in look, particularly in the tendency for longer verse lines almost to intersect with the next column. The height of the column of the Milan papyrus (*c.*16 cm), and the height of the roll itself (*c.*20 cm), are reasonably typical for a Ptolemaic verse text of this type. The column width, though somewhat narrow in comparison with other Ptolemaic verse texts (on which more below), is not far out of the expected range.[2]

The fact that the overall look and feel are typical of the era does not, however, mean that in matters of detail the bookroll is entirely run-of-the-mill. The section headings are unusual in several respects, most remarkably in their mere presence.[3] In formal terms, the most striking feature is simply the script itself, which is unusually tiny, especially for a Ptolemaic book hand. Pl. 2, in which the Menander text and the Posidippus text are set side by side at the same scale, conveys an idea of how tiny the script is. The small script accounts directly for the somewhat more narrow than usual column width, and the large number of lines contained within what is, in physical dimensions, a normal height of column. For this column height, one expects roughly twenty-five lines; the Milan papyrus, by con-

---

[2] A. Blanchard, 'Les papyrus littéraires grecs extraits de cartonnages'; W. A. Johnson, *Bookrolls and Scribes in Oxyrhynchus* (Toronto, 2004), §3.3 (column height), §3.6 (roll height), §3.2.4 (column widths).

[3] The subject headings are 'more specific than the very general divisions familiar from *AP* and first attested for Agathias' *Cycle*': Parsons, 'Callimachus and the Hellenistic Epigram', 121–2. The only close parallel is P. Strassb. WG 2340 (iii BC) = Pack² 1749, which contains a heading, πολεμικά, above very fragmentary elegiacs (cited in Bastianini, 'Il rotolo degli epigrammi di Posidippo', 115); cf. K. Gutzwiller, Introduction n. 15. Of different type are explanatory titles for individual epigrams, found in P. Oxy. LIV 3725, LXVI 4501–2 (i AD, ascribed by Parsons to the same hand), and *SH* 985 (iii BC); and similarly for titles transmitted in the manuscripts of Theocritus.

trast, has forty lines in the column. The overall effect, as we see, are columns considerably less squat in appearance than in the usual Ptolemaic bookroll, an effect which is entirely the consequence of the size of script.

The copy was made by someone trained in the craft, not necessarily a professional scribe but at least someone who knew how to produce a book-like product. The script, though not entirely regular and with a tendency to lapse into a faster mode of writing, is assured and easy, the lines reasonably even and regularly spaced. The column height remains stable within a variation of very few millimetres over the run of sixteen columns. The width from column to column is likewise consistent within tight limits, obviously the product of routine measurement. The measurements from column to column are within 2 mm of 9.5 cm with the exceptions of cols. II, IX, and X; in each of these columns the first line itself exceeds 9.5 cm, necessitating a slightly wider column of 10.1–10.2 cm (Pl. 3). This is what I mean by intercolumns that are as narrow as logistically possible. The tendency towards strict parameters for the physical measurement of column height and the width from column to column is characteristic in all periods for scribal production of bookrolls (as opposed to less formal productions).[4]

Still, this was not a very fine bookroll production. The hand is workaday. The tiny script gives the column a cramped look, as though the scribe were trying to accommodate as many lines as possible within the space. The margins, especially the top margin, are about as small as margins can be, even in the context of a Ptolemaic roll (Pl. 1). Moreover, the papyrus itself is of middling, not high quality, which is unusual for a bookroll. It is rare to have a bookroll in a well-trained hand that is not written on what by the Elder Pliny's time would be called an *optima charta*. The width of the sheets in this roll (19.4–19.7 cm) qualifies the papyrus for two grades below the *optima* (what Pliny later called the 'Fannian'). In my own survey of papyrus sheet sizes in literary bookrolls, only two (one Ptolemaic) use papyrus of this low a grade;[5] Alain Blanchard has reported a couple of additional Ptolemaic examples in this lower category;[6] but clearly the mediocre quality is unusual for a bookroll. Because of physical damage over time, it is very difficult to judge the surface quality of ancient papyrus, especially ancient papyrus from cartonnage. Even

---

[4] Johnson, *Bookrolls*, §2.4.

[5] Ibid. §3.1.1. On the question of the size of papyrus sheets as indicator of papyrus quality, see Plin. *NH* 13.74–8 and Johnson, 'Pliny the Elder and Standardized Roll Heights'.

[6] Blanchard, *Papyrus littéraires grecs*, 21.

so, the glue joins (κολλήϲειϲ) seem noticeably ragged in places (Pl. 4*a*). Col. XIV preserves an interesting example of a κόλληϲιϲ where the top layer is bent over, creating an awkward surface; and yet the papyrus was written upon without smoothing or repair (Pl. 4*b*). This sort of irregularity is to be expected to some extent in hand manufacture, but there seems good cause to conclude that the papyrus surface itself was not meticulously prepared, and not of the quality usual for a bookroll production. The workaday hand and cramped appearance seem to accord with this observation.

When we try to imagine what impression the manuscript gave to a Ptolemaic owner as he or she picked it up, it would be, then, that the bookroll was not the work of an amateur, but rather utilitarian: certainly far from a showpiece designed to impress elite friends with the quality of the book-as-object. Ancient books were normally custom manufacture, meaning that the product resulted from a negotiation between buyer and scribe as to the quality of paper used, the beauty of the writing employed (that is, how rapid or slow the writing, which in turn determined the rate of payment per line).[7] This bookroll summons to our imagination a roll of an unimpressive kind, created with a view perhaps to content rather than to display. The very fact that the bookroll seems to have been created with utilitarian purpose makes striking the (otherwise banal) observation that it appears to have been not at all heavily used. Or at least we do not find evidence of the sort of lectional marks so common on bookrolls used in the usual utilitarian reading contexts: that is, in the schoolroom, or in reading circles where the text was used as entertainment, or in circles where 'scholars'—serious readers—seem to have been studying a text. We find no marks indicating word grouping or division, no apostrophes to mark elision, no dots to mark breath pauses, no signs of διόρθωϲιϲ or of variants, or of correction to even the most obvious scribal errors, aside from a few corrections made by the original scribe in the process of the original copying and a very small number of later corrections and additions, mostly in reaction to damage to the roll. Indeed one of the most conspicuous features of this roll is the number of uncorrected errors, which range from the most trivial (and thus perhaps unimportant since easy enough for a reader or lector to correct on the fly) to errors serious enough to intrude materially upon the sense of certain epigrams.[8]

---

[7] *Edictum Diocletiani de pretiis rerum venalium*, col. vii, ll. 39–41; cf. E. G. Turner and P. J. Parsons, *Greek Manuscripts of the Ancient World* (London, 1987), 1–4.

[8] Many small corrections are made *in scribendo* by the scribe, but there is no evidence of systematic διόρθωϲιϲ; the very few corrections by a reader are limited to cols. IV and V, except

The roll did, however, grow old, whether in the first owner's hands or in another's; and it is in its latter years that the life story of this bookroll becomes particularly intriguing. At some point in its life, the roll was damaged. We can see moisture damage and overtracing quite clearly at a couple of places (Pl. 5, highlighted area).[9] The editors imagine a spill of water, but moisture damage from long storage without adequate exercise and airing of the roll is at least as likely. Whatever the cause, it is clear that the beginning of the roll deteriorated to the point that the front edge had to be refashioned. I will linger for a moment on this front, repaired edge, since it has, I think, much to tell us not only about the later history of the roll's life, but also about its use.

The editors conclude from three related pieces of evidence that the protokollon was a later addition, not part of the original manufacture—that is, that the current protokollon is the result of a repair.[10] First, the left sheet of the manufactured roll is only 11.3 cm wide in a roll in which the other sheets are consistently 19.5 cm (Pl. 1).[11] Secondly, no blank space between the protokollon and the left edge of the manufactured roll is found; the writing begins directly to the right of the protokollon, contrary to custom. It looks, in short, as if the blank space that normally precedes the first column of writing (the agraphon) was cut away. Thirdly, the protokollon is affixed in an unusual fashion. In Greek bookrolls, joins were made so that the left sheet overlaps the right sheet. The rule seems to be as true of the protokollon as of any other sheet in a bookroll. In this case, however, the protokollon is attached so that the sheet at the right overlaps the protokollon. This arrangement is necessary, since the protokollon otherwise would have obscured the first letters of the column (the overlap is usually about 2 cm wide). The editors conclude that this protokollon cannot belong to the original manufacture. Their conclusion is not in every respect unassailable, but the physical details do seem to fit best a scenario in which the torn original roll was cut at the very left of 'col. I', and a new protokollon affixed to repair the front edge of the bookroll.[12]

---

a single correction, by a different reader, in col. XI: BG, p. 15. On instances of reaction to damage, see just below.

[9] So col. XI, ll. 12–15; the correction at col. V, l. 1 has a similar appearance. See BG, p. 13.

[10] Ibid.

[11] Variation, even cheating, is normal for the specified size of a sheet (κόλλημα) in manufactured rolls, but one does not expect or find such wide variation in the very first κόλλημα: Johnson, *Bookrolls*, §3.1.1.

[12] Damage at the front of the roll, which received the most wear and tear, was common; cf. e.g. P. Oxy. 223 for damage and repair similar to the Milan papyrus.

The apparent fact that the protokollon is a repair job may fit in with another detail, one not remarked by the editors. The first line of the first column appears to be in a different ink. The difference in ink is particularly apparent in the infrared image (Pl. 6, right), but also apparent in the colour image (left). I say 'appears to be' and 'apparent' both because a variation in ink flow was natural to ancient writing and because of the problems of variation of appearance in ancient papyri, especially papyri surviving from cartonnage. Still, the ink does appear noticeably distinct, and though I am not so rash as to affirm a difference of hand on the basis of so few letters, it is perhaps worth remark that the letters seem in part differently formed (Pl. 7a).[13] What is tantalizing about the apparent difference in ink is the placement of the line itself, which appears to be not in fact at the expected top of the column, but above the top of the column. I want, in short, to raise the possibility that the first line is a later addition. As observed earlier, the papyrus has a narrow, but quite consistent top margin (of 1.2–1.4 cm) that, despite repeated breaks, survives all along the top of the sixteen surviving columns of the roll (Pl. 1). The same line of margin appears to be in place above the first column, but such that l. 2, and not l. 3, is located at the expected extent (1.4 cm from the top edge: Pl. 8). I am acutely aware of the dangers of such an argument—my own book provides the best available documentation for the capricious breakage of margins in ancient papyri[14]—but the coincidence of apparent difference in ink, script, and extent of margin for the top line of col. I is a conjunction at least worth bringing to notice.[15] Though by no means certain, the real possibility exists that the first line of poetry as we have it was inserted later to fill out that first poem, presumably as part of the repair that occasioned the cutting and refashioning of the front edge of the roll.

One final detail concerning the top of the first column. In the top margin, the editors read a dotted kappa and dotted alpha. These traces are the basis for their supposition that the heading to this section appeared above the first column (restored as [λιθι]κά).[16] In

---

[13] e.g. oval back-leaning omicron extending over the full bilinear height of the script; hastae of iota and mu straight and squared off at the ends, in contrast to the bent hasta with rounded, globular ends characteristic of the main scribal hand. [14] Johnson, *Bookrolls*, §3.5.

[15] Overlaying the adjacent column ('col. II') at its least distorted point gives the viewer a strong impression that the top line of col. I is a later addition. (This is not, however, fully consistent among all the columns, since the column height varies over the course of the roll by a few millimetres.)

[16] BG, p. 13 give the section heading as one of the primary reasons for believing the first column to be the original col. I. At 13 n. 23, they list examples for titles in the top margin of the first column, but these are very few and mostly not unambiguous (for details, see Bastianini's article there cited).

William Johnson

Pl. 9, I highlight the area where the editors describe these letters to be. I have not seen the papyrus in person, and I think the editors, Bastianini and Gallazzi, have been remarkably and laudably careful; but the section heading has to be judged an uncertain reading by any standard. Stray ink is an endemic problem in papyri recovered from cartonnage.

I have dwelt on the first column because the details of that column dovetail in ways that are suggestive for our view of the contents and use of this bookroll. Before trying to put the pieces together, however, we need to examine a final exceptional feature, the stichometry. The stichometry was added after the text, but whether at the time of the original copying or later is uncertain. The editors resist the conclusion that the stichometric letters could be written by someone other than the original scribe, even while conceding that some of the letters are differently formed.[17] In fact, it is difficult to judge (Pl. 7*b*). Now the addition of stichometry was normally a part of the activity of the bookroll's manufacture. In the Milan papyrus, there is no evidence of a systematic corrector (διορθώτης); so one expects the stichometry to have been the original scribe's reckoning of the line totals, as a help towards securing the accuracy of the line counts and as a measure for payment. But the stichometry in the Milan papyrus is quite unusual, indeed unique (so far as I know), in another, obvious respect. The totals are *running totals* for each section of poetry, and not therefore suited for the usual purposes of controlling or measuring the scribe's overall work in copying the book.[18] Moreover, if, as suggested, the first line of the first column is a later insertion and not part of the original column now labelled 'col. I', then the stichometry would be not only not original to the roll, but added after the repair. This follows from the fact that the count for 'col. I', written at the bottom, reads mu, that is, 40, but the lines only add up to forty if we count the (apparently) inserted line at the top; and similarly for the running total given at the end of the first section on gemstones.[19]

---

[17] BG, p. 15.

[18] The use of running totals does occur when individual works (such as short speeches) or books of epic (Homer) are included together in a single large bookroll. But that is quite different from the case here. See BG, p. 16 and n. 28 for some Homeric examples; generally on stichometry K. Ohly, *Stichometrische Untersuchungen* (Leipzig, 1928); D. Obbink, *Philodemus, On Piety, Part 1* (Oxford, 1996), 62–73, esp. 62 n. 1. S. Stephens and D. Obbink, 'The Manuscript', 15 suggest that the running totals may be added as a control to the creation of an epigram collection created from an incipit list.

[19] One can easily imagine a scenario in which this hand was in fact the original scribe. If the owner had a relationship with a scribe trained to write a bookhand, whether a 'professional' scribe, his or her own slave, or the slave of one of his or her friends, it would be natural to reuse that same person for the process of manufacture of a new epigram roll.

Now if we put these various features together—the protokollon added later, with the left part of the manufactured roll cut away; the initial line very possibly added later; the stichometry also possibly a later addition; the problem that the section heading at the top of the first column may itself be a later addition, or even a phantasm—we can imagine a manuscript with a history rather different from that supposed by the editors.

The original bookroll may, I suggest, have extended not just to the right of the fragmentary bookroll that we possess but also to the left. That is, there is no compelling reason to think that 'col. I' was the original first column of the roll, and thus no reason to think that the original bookroll even began with the section on gemstones.[20] The owner seems to have negotiated with the scribe for an economical copy, but the reader or readers of the bookroll neither corrected the text, even in the most obvious or egregious instances, nor made any of the usual lectional markings, like punctuation or word groupings, in this sometimes difficult poetry. Over the course of its life, the roll suffered moisture damage. Some blotted lines were crudely overtraced to correct for that; and the damage to the front of the roll (which may also have been water damage, but of course we do not know) occasioned the cutting-off of some papyrus at the front, apparently including at least one and perhaps many columns of writing.[21] Someone took the trouble to count the number of lines in each section of the poetry and add running totals; perhaps after the repair.[22] Someone, possibly the same someone, set a mark—$\tau o\hat{v}(\tau o)$—alongside a very few of the epigrams, presumably for the purpose of either reading or copying out certain selected epigrams. We do not know when this person sat down to make these notes of selection. But it is certainly striking that the unusual counting activity occurs in the same roll as the equally unusual activity (among papyrus witnesses, that is) of selecting out certain epigrams.

Indeed what seems most significant about the users' activities, or at least the traces we have of those activities, is the absence of marks for

---

[20] The line added to the top of our 'col. I' would have been taken from the bottom of the previous column before the cut and repair was made. (Ancient manuscripts do not accommodate to the modern habit of ending a column with the pentameter.)

[21] H. C. Gotoff points out to me that at least two columns would be probable at the left. The c.8 cm cut away from the left of the first κόλλημα is too narrow to have held a complete column (of 9.5 cm) by itself. We need therefore to assume, probably, at least one additional κόλλημα (of 19.5 cm), thus 27.5 cm (19.5 + 8) of available space, enough to accommodate two columns of 9.5 cm with 8.5 cm of space for the agraphon at the left. Whether one κόλλημα or several preceded what is now 'col. I' is of course anyone's guess.

[22] If the original scribe, then working with the owner a second time. See above, n. 19.

reading in combination with these exceptional indications of count-
ing and selecting. In the study of ancient bookrolls we commonly see,
especially in non-calligraphic productions, those marks of punctua-
tion, correction, and even marginalia that reveal the use of a book
by a lector or reader, often with implications of the book's use by
readers, including groups of readers, for reading entertainment, or
for more serious study.[23] The very fact that in this particular bookroll
the lack of lectional marks combines with the presence of marks of
counting and selecting seems to speak to how the bookroll was used.
Readers' interaction with this epigram book seems to have differed
in a fundamental way from their use of, and activities surrounding,
other types of poetry books. This artefact shows, rather, marks sug-
gesting that the *selection and editing* activity was an *essential* aspect of
the readers' approach to the text.[24]

Other early examples of epigram are by now well documented and
reasonably well known.[25] Most are too fragmentary to draw firm con-
clusions about the nature of the collection. But the few examples we
have display a notable interest in balance, arrangement, and indeed in
the numbers. The still-unpublished incipit list in Vienna (P. Vindob.
G 40611), dating to the third century BC, contains a list of the open-
ing lines of epigrams, together with line counts, divided by books.[26]
Kathryn Gutzwiller has pointed out that the first book documented
by the Vienna incipit list, with 83 epigrams and 344 lines, averages
just a hair over four lines per epigram, while the second book (33
epigrams, 264 lines) averages eight. Her conclusion is that this differ-
ence in average line length 'suggests that the length of individual
poems was one criterion for organization'.[27] Berol. 9812, also a third-
century-BC papyrus, gives fragments of three four-line poems, all
dedicatory.[28] P. Köln V 204, a second-century-BC papyrus, contains
six epigrams by Mnasalces, all four-line poems, and all inscriptional

---

[23] K. McNamee. 'Greek Literary Papyri Revised by Two or More Hands'; Johnson,
'Toward a Sociology of Reading in Classical Antiquity'; id., 'Scholars' Texts and Reading
Communities in Hellenic Egypt'.

[24] See Gutzwiller, *Poetic Garlands*, 14 and *passim*.

[25] Good, accessible account ibid., 20–36; cf. Cameron, *Greek Anthology*, 1–18, esp. 7 ff.;
Parsons, 'Callimachus and Hellenistic Epigram', esp. 115–22.

[26] See Parsons, 'Callimachus and Hellenistic Epigram', 118–20; Gutzwiller, *Poetic Garlands*,
24 and n. 34; Cameron, *Greek Anthology*, 9–10. Cf. also P. Oxy. 3724, a similar incipit list from
the 1st c. AD with markings that look like someone working on the arrangement and what was
to be included. These two incipit lists can be, and have been, interpreted as catalogues of an
existing poetry book rather than as witnesses to the work surrounding the creation of a new
poetry book.

[27] Gutzwiller, *Poetic Garlands*, 24.

[28] In one sense or another. See discussion at Gutzwiller, *Poetic Garlands*, 30 for the question
of the unity of type.

in type. Again, following Gutzwiller,[29] the consistency of length of poem and 'ostensibly inscriptional' type creates a 'formal coherency' within which the arranger can then create ποικιλία through variety of theme and through associative and dissociative juxtaposition. A formal unity, that is, is combined with clever linkage and thematic diversity. With these witnesses as background, it is worth remarking that the epigram-selecting activity we find in the Milan papyrus marks only quatrains—perhaps, then, a mark of formal unity as a criterion for the selection.[30] Be that as it may, it is clear that the Milan papyrus bears witness to reader interest in counting, in the numbers, that seems more likely to be a facet of the editing process—of selecting and re-collecting poems—than of scribal control.

Selecting, collecting, organizing the 'gems' seems, then, fundamental to the idea of the epigram collection from its earliest witnesses. At a minimum the artefactual details of the Milan papyrus suggest that the next generation, as it were, of interaction with this bookroll was focused on the activity of selecting and re-collecting for the next bookroll, that is, on the editorial work of *creating a fresh collection*. Though the basis of evidence is not wide, there does seem to be reason to suppose that the Milan papyrus falls into a *type* of early reader interaction with epigram collections, in which the focus is not only on the authorial production but also on the editor's arrangement, very like the attitude of a viewer presented with artistic photographs collected in a scrapbook or photo essay—in which, that is, the viewer's awareness is of both photographer and designer.

Finally, it is important to distinguish this situation from the Roman poetry collections we know, which also show a strong interest in arrangement, balance, and to limited extent also in the numbers.[31] Catullus perhaps aside, the Roman poetry books that come down to us are almost all authorial collections, and the ancient reader

---

[29] Gutzwiller, *Poetic Garlands*, 31.

[30] The quatrain is, however, the most common size for epigram.

[31] The extent of Roman interest in such matters has been muddied by understandable scholarly reaction to various efforts to box the Augustan poets within the confines of a radical numerology or schema: e.g. G. Duckworth on Vergil (*Structural Patterns and Proportions in the Aeneid*, Ann Arbor, 1962), H. Dettmer on Horace (*Horace: A Study in Structure*, Hildesheim, 1983), O. L. Richmond on 'stanza-schemes' in Propertius (*Sexti Properti quae supersunt omnia* (Cambridge, 1928), esp. 27 ff.), O. Skutsch on the *Monobiblos* ('The Structure of the Propertian *Monobiblos*', in which, despite some valid pairings of poems, the insistence on a consistent overall scheme is faulty). The work of, for example, M. Santirocco on Horace has helped to clarify the principle that interest in balance and arrangement does not require a strict or mechanical overall scheme; and that interest in ποικιλία does not imply a thoroughgoing lack of deliberate, formal structural design. For theoretical discussion and references to earlier work, see Santirocco, *Unity and Design in Horace's Odes* (Chapel Hill, 1986), 3–13.

will have presumably supposed in the reading that the author was in control of the original sequence and linkage among poems. I raise here the possibility that the Ptolemaic reader may not have had this disposition. If that selecting activity was at all essential and common in the reader's interaction with the text (a hypothesis which, again, stands on slim if very intriguing evidence), then the *reader's attitude* towards that peculiar pairing of unity and diversity characteristic of epigram collections will be marked by the relationship of reader to editor, of a reader's willingness to delight in the newness brought to poetry by the crafting of fresh arrangements and newly created relationships between poems.[32] It may well be, that is, that the Ptolemaic reader would no more assume the *author's* hand in the selection and arrangement of an epigram poetry book than he or she would assume the author's hand in the punctuation of a text of Homer or Simonides or, for that matter, Callimachus or Herodas.

---

[32] This sort of reader interaction with the text can be seen as part and parcel of the delight in imitation of the original context, that conveyance of the occasional that seems to inform the gentlemanly hobby of epigram-collecting; just as one might store in one's head the right selection of poetry for a symposium (cf. Parsons, 'Callimachus and Hellenistic Epigram', 104), so one could put together an elegant compilation into a poetry book to demonstrate one's cultural taste and credentials.

The Editor's Toolbox: Strategies for Selection and Presentation in the Milan Epigram Papyrus

NITA KREVANS

This study focuses on editorial strategies in the new Posidippus papyrus, and it will be useful before describing those strategies to clarify the term 'editor'. The editor may be distinguished from both the author and the scribe by the tasks he performs, although such a distinction is not always easy to make. After all, the editor of a poetic anthology might be *the* poet (Callimachus in the *Aitia*), *a* poet (Meleager in the *Garland*), or an anonymous copyist. Nevertheless, simplistically, one can say that the author or authors create the work or works (orally or in writing). The scribe produces the individual copy. The editor's sphere lies somewhere in between: for an anthology like the Milan collection, for example, editorial responsibilities might include selecting poems, organizing those poems (sequencing, subdivisions, etc.) and creating extra-textual material such as dividers, titles, prologues, epilogues, etc. In other words, the editor might overlap with the author or clash with decisions on these matters already made by the author (giving the work a different title, for example). In addition, the editor may develop guidelines for displaying both authorial text (poem) and editorial text (titles, commentary, division markers) on the page. Here he might overlap with the scribe (he might even *be* the scribe, as in the case of the autograph manuscript of Planudes),[1] but he might also find his decisions ignored by the scribe.

As I have argued elsewhere,[2] the editor of an artistically designed poetic collection must balance two conflicting imperatives: the need to maintain the integrity of each individual poem, and the need for the collection to function as a coherent and artistic whole. In the case of the Milan papyrus, which may or may not be designed to be read as a unit, there is the further question of utility versus aesthetics. Is

---

[1] See Cameron, *Greek Anthology*, 16, 75–7.
[2] N. Krevans, 'The Poet as Editor' (Princeton, 1984).

the editor a symphony conductor—or a reference librarian? A survey of various features of this epigram collection which reveal this editor at work will suggest that while there is some evidence for the symphony conductor, there is also considerable evidence for the reference librarian. In particular, parts of this collection show a close relationship with prose encyclopaedias in the selection, arrangement, and labelling of the poems (for a table of the sections with numbers of poems and line counts, see the Introduction, p. 4).

FORMATTING

As William Johnson observes,[3] the papyrus , while containing some errors, is conventional in its format. It follows normal practice for the presentation of anthologized items in other examples from the Hellenistic period.[4] There is little or no use of vertical spacing; little or no use of enlarged letters in headings.[5] Separation of items relies on the paragraphos discreetly inserted at the left margin and on centred headings. Often in anthologies these headings show us a change in the author; sometimes the word *ΑΛΛΟ* is used to indicate that the next item is by the same author as the previous one.[6] (Thus, given the absence of any author-headings in this papyrus, and the faithful observance of editorial norms in every other respect, it is very unlikely that this is a multi-author anthology.) The result of these formatting conventions is that the poems appear visually as a unified block on the page, *except* when a centred heading interrupts the block. The editor of the Milan papyrus, if he envisioned a competent scribe executing his decisions, would know that his sections would be starkly and dramatically marked off from each other by the centred subtitles, whereas individual poems within sections would be bound together in the neat rectangle of the column.

---

[3] Johnson, above, Ch. 4.

[4] Compare e.g. P. Heid. 187, trimeter anthology, iii BC; P. Hib. 7, Euripidean anthology, iii BC; P. Berol. 9772, drama anthology, ii BC. Further discussion in Turner and Parsons, *Greek Manuscripts of the Ancient World*, 8 and pl. 45.

[5] Possible slight enlargement of the headings here at BG VI. 9, XIV. 2, XIV. 29?

[6] Author heading: e.g. P. Berol. 9772, drama anthology, ii BC; *ΑΛΛΟ* e.g. P. Heid. 187, anthology in trimeters. In P. Louvre 7172 = P. Didot, ii BC this heading separates two epigrams of Posidippus (although this papyrus has some other features which are quite odd, including the centring of part of the incipit to serve as a title; see Turner and Parsons, *Greek Manuscripts*, pl. 45).

SECTIONS AND THEIR TITLES

Since the sections are delineated so emphatically in visual terms, it seems appropriate to begin an investigation of editorial strategy with the divisions they create. What definitions has the editor imposed on the epigrams in this manner? What do the sections tell us about the editor's tastes and preferences?[7]

A comparison with the books of the *Greek Anthology* is instructive. Two sections match the thematically organized books of the *Anthology*: ἀναθεματικά (= *AP* 6) and *ἐπιτύμβια (= *AP* 7). In the second case, however, the heading is restored, and although the epigrams themselves correspond well to the contents of book 7, some caution might be warranted on the exact word used for the title.

Other headings are not only unparalleled in the *Anthology* but seem bizarre to readers whose notion of epigram categories has been shaped by Meleager and Cephalas. Stone-poems? Poems on bird-augury? Even headings like ἱππικά and ἰαματικά look odd—not so much because epigrams on these topics are rare (although, relatively speaking, they are), but because the headings are so specific. When ἀναθεματικά is already available as a category in this very collection, why separate seven healing poems, most of which are votive in tone? Similarly, many (if not all) of the ἱππικά are votive, associated with statues of the victorious horses. ἀνδριαντοποιικά is very precise and limiting in comparison to the later ἐπιδεικτικά of the *Anthology*, which could also include the gem-poems. Turning to funerary topics, it should be noted that both the ναυαγικά and the τρόποι would be filed under ἐπιτύμβια in the *Anthology*.[8] In other words, the editor has chosen to set off small groups of poems under extremely specific headings even in cases where the papyrus itself offers an appropriate larger category for those poems.

Another surprise, perhaps the biggest surprise, is the headings which are *not* here. Where are the amatory and sympotic epigrams? The papyrus is incomplete, of course, and at the very end some tantalizing words in the tenth section (whose title is missing) suggest that *AP* 5 and 12 might have had some precursors here as well: Zephyrus? spring? 'everything is stretched'? (AB 110, 111).

If we compare Posidippus in the *Greek Anthology* with what actually survives in the Milan papyrus, however, we find completely different proportions in the subject-matter of the epigrams.

[7] Some aspects of this topic also in BG, pp. 24–7, a discussion of the roll as 'edition'.
[8] Noted also by Obbink, '*Τρόποι*'.

Admittedly, this is a somewhat imprecise task, since a number of epigrams are plausibly attributed to both Posidippus and another poet (commonly Asclepiades).[9] Excluding the Planudean material (book 16), and following Austin and Bastianini for the resolution of some attribution problems there are eighteen epigrams by Posidippus in the *Anthology*. Of these *fifteen* are in the amatory books, 5 and 12. Two are in 7 (funerary), one in 9 (epideictic). The contrast between the editorial preferences of the Milan editor and the Anthology editor (or, more accurately, chain of editors leading up to the Greek Anthology, with Meleager figuring prominently)[10] could not be more dramatic.

It happens that there are some poems in the Milan papyrus which could be considered amatory/sympotic. They have been classified, however, in a manner which emphasizes the non-amatory features of each poem. I refer to a number of poems in the λιθικά. This is by far the oddest of the sections devised by our editor. Even the bird-augury section has at least a remote parallel in book 14 of the *Anthology*, προβλήματα ἀριθμητικά, αἰνίγματα, χρηϲμοί ('Puzzles, Riddles, and Oracles').[11]

This unusual section has been created, in part, by taking amatory poems about beautiful jewels given as gifts to the beloved and shifting the emphasis from 'girl' to 'jewel'.[12] Frankly, in the case of most of these poems, the emphasis *is* on the jewel. Still, there is a poem in the *Anthology* which compares a boy named Heracleitus to a magnet (*AP* 12. 152 = GP anon. 29, Hellenistic in date). It is not in book 9 (the 'epideictic' book), which does contain some non-amatory poems about carved gems and rare stones. Rather, the Heracleitus poem is where it belongs, in book 12, with the other amatory poems about boys. Another *Anthology* epigram lovingly describes a gold-mounted amethyst on Nico's breast, a stone which she employs as a love-charm (*AP* 5. 205 = GP anon. 35, Hellenistic in date); again, it is in book 5—that is, it is classed as amatory.

Here in the Milan papyrus the editor has taken a different path. Consider the first seven poems of the λιθικά section (and thus,

---

[9] See GP i, p. xxx, ii. 115–18; Gutzwiller, *Poetic Garlands*, 120–2. More generally, on the question of pre-Milan vs. post-Milan Posidippus see Sider, 'Posidippus Old and New'.

[10] Cameron, *Greek Anthology*, 24–33, on Meleager's book divisions; on Meleager as editor more generally see Gutzwiller, 'The Poetics of Editing in Meleager's *Garland*'.

[11] The 'oracles', however, are not really epigrams like those in the Milan papyrus but famous verse prophecies, mostly from Delphi, harvested from sources such as Herodotus. On these see Cameron, *Greek Anthology*, 211–15.

[12] As noted in G. O. Hutchinson, 'The New Posidippus and Latin Poetry'.

perhaps, the opening poems of our book).[13] Poem 1 is extremely fragmentary, but contains the feminine adjective λεπτή and what looks like a proper name beginning with Ζην-. The stones in poems 2 and 3 are incised with images of drinking vessels (compare poems in the *Anthology* about amethysts with pictures of Dionysus; the amethyst, as its name indicates, was thought to protect against inebriation);[14] poems 4–7 name three girls who are wearing dazzling stones; the epigrams linger over the play between two different types of beauty and desirability: jewel and girl.

In some sense, then, these are all poems which evoke the themes of wine, women and song we associate with Hellenistic epigram.[15] Yet those themes are muted—perhaps nearly smothered—by the aggressive titling and organization of the section, which requires the reader to look for stones and ignore girls and wine. The classification scheme of the Milan papyrus editor, so different from the choices made in the later epigram tradition, has a radical effect on the reader's view of these poems.

It is clear from this brief comparison that Posidippus in the *Anthology* looks very different from Posidippus in the Milan book, in part because of different principles of selection, but also because of different principles of classification and labelling. There are, however, three additional poems preserved in the Planudean corpus (*AP* 16). As soon as these poems are included, the contrast between the later anthologists and the Milan papyrus editor softens slightly. *AP* 16. 119, in fact, is our poem 65, on Lysippus' statue of Alexander. *AP* 16. 68 (AB 141, also attributed to Asclepiades) is on a statue of Aphrodite (used to generate a compliment to Berenice); *AP* 16. 275 (AB 142) is a dialogue with a statue of Kairos. These last two could both easily join their fellow Planudean piece in the ἀνδριαντο-ποιικά section of the papyrus; all three come from the fourth book of Planudes' anthology, on monuments and statues.

Poems of Posidippus preserved outside the *Anthology* and its appended Planudean collection (either on papyrus or by authors such as Athenaeus) offer an even better match to the Milan material. Echoing the emphasis on Ptolemaic achievements in some sections of our papyrus, we find two epigrams on Arsinoe's temple, one on the

---

[13] See further discussion of this question below.

[14] *AP* 9. 748, 752 (possibly by Asclepiades) and *AP* 5. 205. Or perhaps these epigrams describe drinking vessels ornamented with gems (A. Kuttner, below, Ch. 8).

[15] Even if, as A. Kuttner and K. Gutzwiller suggest (below, Chs. 8, 15), the first three poems are for royal women, the association with sympotic poetry would still be present in AB 2 and 3.

Pharos, one on a Nymphaeum, and an epithalamium for Arsinoe.[16] An epitaph for a parasite (Ath. 10. 414 D = AB 121) would fit nicely in the τρόποι.[17] A tomb-poem for Doricha, mistress of Sappho's brother, could join the numerous other epigrams for women in *ἐπιτύμβια (Ath. 13. 596 C = AB 122). The statue of an athlete who ate a bull (Ath. 10. 412 D = AB 120) resembles Myron's calf in the sculpting section. And the snakestone poem from the λιθικά (AB 15) is also preserved in Tzetzes' *Chiliades*, only the second of these one hundred-plus epigrams to have survived outside the Milan papyrus.

In concluding this brief survey of how the Milan editor compares to later excerpters and arrangers, it should be noted that there is evidence for yet another editor in the papyrus itself. του- abbreviations in the margins in eight places (AB 40, 69, 70, 72, 73, 77, 86, 112) are, as Bastianini and Gallazzi point out in the *editio princeps*,[18] very likely the word τοῦτο meaning, 'copy this one'.[19] This second editor has very different taste from the editor who compiled the Milan papyrus. In the ἀναθεματικά, for example, he picks out the wolf-shaped box dedicated to Leto, leaving all the Arsinoe poems untouched;[20] similarly, he manages to select four ἱππικά epigrams, not one of which is connected with Berenice or the Ptolemies.

The headings themselves, unlike the sections they define, are formed in a very conventional manner. Except for τρόποι and the restored *ἐπιτύμβια they are similar to most of the book-titles used in the Anthology: neuter plural adjectives formed using the suffix -κά. ἀναθεματικά, as mentioned earlier, is the title of AP book 6. Other parallel forms: book 9 ἐπιδεικτικά; book 10 προτρεπτικά; book 11 συμποτικὰ καὶ σκωπτικά. This style of title is found in both Greek and Latin from the fourth century all the way into the Middle Ages. It is used for both prose treatises (works with titles like *Chronica, Exegetica, Prognostica*), and poetic works—*Argonautica* and *Bucolica* are two famous examples. The subject-matter as described by the adjective

[16] P. Louvre 7172 = P. Didot = AB 116; Ath. 7. 318 D = AB 119; P. Louvre 1712 = P. Didot = AB 115; P. Cair. 65445 = *SH* 978 = AB 113, attribution disputed; P. Petrie II 49 = *SH* 961 = AB 114.

[17] The meaning of this heading is uncertain; 'Characters' has been suggested; another possibility is 'Twists', since the legible poems all seem to have some Martial-like bite to them.

[18] BG, p. 16.

[19] Cf. the two incipit-papyri with lists of epigrams, clearly used to select poems to copy: P. Oxy. 3724; P. Vindob. G 40611. On the latter see Harrauer, 'Epigrammincipit'; further discussion now in Parsons, 'Callimachus and Hellenistic Epigram', esp. 118–20. On these lists see also Gutzwiller, *Poetic Garlands*, 23–4; detailed discussion of P. Oxy. 3724 with re-edition and commentary in D. Sider, *The Epigrams of Philodemos* (New York, 1997), 203–25.

[20] Even the four-line poem 38, whose omission I note here given William Johnson's observation (Ch. 4) that all the selected poems are quatrains.

usually marks poetic examples clearly. Interestingly, though, certain titles of this form are used across the prose/poetry boundary: *Georgica, Theriaca, Halieutica,* and *Cynegetica* all exist in both prose *and* verse. The reason for this (as Schmalzriedt and Henriksson found in their exhaustive studies of titulature) is that neuter plural titles in -κά are strongly associated in poetry with didactic, a genre with obvious links to prose treatises.[21]

In some sense the comparison is disingenuous. These section headings are just that, headings. They are not book-titles. The title of this collection, which was likely at the now-lost end of the roll, remains a mystery—although in my opinion it is more likely to have been something like cύμμεικτα ἐπιγράμματα Ποςειδίππου (the label on the Petrie papyrus) than cωρός ('Heap', the metaphorical title of a work cited by Aristarchus with reference to Posidippus at Σ A on *Il.* 11. 101).[22] Nevertheless, it is not inappropriate to consider the associations these headings would have. And even if it is not right to treat them as full titles, it may prove instructive to recall the intertextual debate between Pliny and Aulus Gellius on the subject of metaphorical versus descriptive titles.

Pliny spends a good deal of energy in the preface to his *Natural History* (*NH* praef. 24–6) defending his choice of a 'plain' title and skewering the allusive Greek titles many Roman authors preferred.[23] Following the preface is book 1 of the *Natural History*, which is nothing but a detailed table of contents of the remaining thirty-six books. The entry for each book has not only a list of topics covered, but also a list of authors used as sources, and that list is further subdivided into Latin sources and Greek sources. In other words, Pliny is the model for the 'reference librarian' editor. He wants clear, accurate titles and well-organized, indexed material. Title and organization both emphasize utility: Pliny's reader must be able to find specific items easily.

Gellius replies to Pliny in the preface to his *Attic Nights* (*NA* praef. 4–10), ostensibly deprecating his own choice of title.[24] In fact, Gellius' long list of titles (both Greek and Latin, both plain and ornamental) demonstrate the elegance of his own choice. Gellius is the

---

[21] E. Schmalzriedt, Περὶ φύcεωc (Munich, 1970), 105, showing that e.g. φυcικά alternates with the title περὶ φύcεωc; K.-E. Henriksson, *Griechische Büchertitel* (Helsinki, 1956).

[22] On this work see Gutzwiller, *Poetic Garlands*, 155–6, 169–70; Cameron, *Greek Anthology*, 369–76, GP ii. 116–17.

[23] He does not cite cωρός, but two of his victims, λειμών and cχεδίον—'meadow' and 'impromptu'—are very similar.

[24] On this preface see further L. A. Holford-Strevens, *Aulus Gellius* (Oxford, 2003), 28.

model for the 'symphony conductor' editor. Although Gellius provides the *Attic Nights* with a list of topics covered in each book, he does not give details, nor does he furnish any bibliographic notes. In fact, rather than revealing the careful organization of the work, the lists emphasize the lack of thematic unity within each book. Gellius' work is meant for browsing, for enjoying adjacent anecdotes which jostle each other as though by chance when in fact Gellius has placed every one of them carefully. He therefore needs a metaphorical title, to unite his varied and deliberately disordered collection. cωρός is not as artistic as *Attic Nights*, but it would have worked.

The assertively utilitarian headings of the Milan papyrus, then, indicate the reference librarian. They serve the same function as Pliny's table of contents: they divide the work and make it easy for the reader to find a specific poem. Their form agrees with that mission, but it is no coincidence that these headings recall both didactic poetry and prose treatises. The content of the more unusual sections of the Milan collection has strong links to prose writing, a link these epigrams share with contemporary didactic poets such as Nicander.

STONES AND BIRD-SIGNS

The first two sections of the Milan papyrus in some ways dominate the book.[25] For one thing, together they make up a third of its length. For another, they are the most unusual sections in terms of their subject matter. They are not only unusual as categories of epigram, but unlike some of the other 'odd' sections (ἰαματικά, ἱππικά) they cannot easily be seen as a specialized subset of a recognizable epigram type (votive, funerary, etc.).

This is not to say that these epigrams are completely unparalleled in the corpus. I have already mentioned two 'stone' epigrams which appear in the amatory books of the *Anthology* and a few 'drinking' epigrams about engraved amethysts; in addition there are single epigrams here and there which echo the themes of these first two sections. A sweating statue appears in *AP* 9. 534, there is one animal oracle (D. L. *AP* 7. 744, a steer which licks a man's cloak, predicting his death) and one humourous bird-oracle (Nicarchus 11. *AP*

---

[25] A repair at the beginning of the papyrus raises the possibility that other sections preceded the λιθικά; see Johnson, above, Ch. 4, but also the arguments of the original editors (BG, p. 13) and the discussion by Stephens and Obbink, 'The Manuscript', 13–14. For the present, in spite of these uncertainties, it seems appropriate to treat the λιθικά as the opening section, especially since even in Johnson's reconstruction at least one editor (the scribe making the repairs) judged that these poems could serve as the beginning of the roll.

186, the night-raven as an omen of death is conquered by the song of Demophilus). Stone poems are more common, although still rare.[26]

The closest parallels to the overall content of these two sections, however, is in prose, and a Hellenistic author closely linked to Posidippus in other respects happens to have written two treatises which include material related to the themes found in these epigrams. That author is Callimachus, and the treatises are (respectively) *Collection of Marvels throughout the World, by Location* (frr. 407–11 Pf.) and *On Birds* (frr. 414–28 Pf.).

The first of these two works is particularly interesting. The excerpts from Callimachus' wonder-book are the first surviving examples of the genre of paradoxography. Some argue that he founded the genre; others believe he found it already partially developed in fourth-century sources.[27] In either case, his treatise is recognized as giving the genre its defining shape and character, and the form remained popular throughout antiquity.[28]

The wonder-book and the study of birds are not his only non-poetic works. Callimachus was a prolific prose author. Titles (and in many cases citations) survive from seventeen different works, and although some may be duplicates (e.g. *Local Month-Names* might be a sub-section of *Local Nomenclature*), his range and output is impressive. The most famous work is the Πίνακες (frr. 429–53 Pf.), whose full title in English is *Registers of all those Pre-Eminent in Literature and of their Writings in 120 Books*. This was long taken (erroneously) as a catalogue of the Alexandrian library; numerous fragments survive, and it has been extensively studied by historians of bibliography.[29] Most of the other prose works are lexicographical (glosses, compilations of local terms) or aetiological (foundation stories, barbarian customs, a treatise on nymphs, another on athletic contests). The treatises on marvels and birds are the only ones oriented more towards nature than culture.

The citations from the treatise on birds are primarily from either Athenaeus or the scholia to Aristophanes' *Birds*, and these two

---

[26] Jasper carved with cows: 9. 746, 747, 750; Indian beryl carved by Tryphon: 9. 544; veining on a piece of acoetonus: 11. 695. On 9. 752, an amethyst ring, see Gutzwiller, 'Cleopatra's Ring'.

[27] R. Pfeiffer, *History of Classical Scholarship* (Oxford, 1968), 134–5; P. M. Fraser, *Ptolemaic Alexandria* (Oxford, 1972), i. 454; more generally on the development of the genre K. Ziegler, 'Paradoxographoi'.

[28] Texts of the paradoxographers in A. Giannini, *Paradoxographorum Graecorum reliquiae* (Milan, 1966).

[29] F. Schmidt, *Die Pinakes des Kallimachos* (Berlin, 1922); R. Blum, *Kallimachos*, trans. H. H. Wellisch (Madison, 1991).

authorities not surprisingly focus on rare bird-names. But the treatise also included material on bird-omens: the last fragment (fr. 428 Pf.) reports that the corncrake (κρέξ) is a bird unlucky for weddings. Compare AB 25, which describes three omens (in this case based on meeting particular types of people rather than birds),[30] two of which are omens connected with weddings.

There were presumably more passages like this one in the *On Birds*, but we also find bird-omens in the *Collection of Marvels*. We hear from Callimachus of birds guarding the island of Diomedes who recognize the nationality of visitors: they are hostile to barbarians but welcome Greeks (fr. 407, §172). The Eneti consult jackdaws to discover whether enemies will invade across various parts of their border (fr. 407, §173). The city of Krannon always has two crows (fr. 408).

In this second treatise we also find some material on stones. There are rivers which turn anything dropped into them into stone (fr. 407, §161) and several examples of stones which catch fire (fr. 407, §§166, 168,[31] 170). If more of the treatise survived there would probably be further parallels, but the extended excerpt from Callimachus' work preserved in Antigonus of Carystus (*Mir.* 129–73) is largely about water-marvels—rivers which catch fire, springs which bleach hair, rivers which cure disease, springs in which nothing floats, etc.[32]

The connections with Posidippus appear even more clearly in later wonder-books derived from Callimachus, like the pseudo-Aristotelian *Mirabiles Auscultationes*.[33] In the Palatine wonder-book, if someone afflicted with jaundice sees a yellow bird called the ἴκτερος, he will be cured (*PP* 3); the Celts use an oracle of a pair of crows to decide guilt and innocence in trials (*PP* 10). In the *Mirabiles Auscultationes* we hear of stones shaped like cylinders which are placed in the temple of Cybele as offerings; the Palatine wonder-book tells of bizarre

[30] πρέcβυc, the first 'omen' here and the subject of poem 28, is possibly a pun: this word is also the name of a kind of wren. See D. Petrain, 'Πρέcβυc'.

[31] Cited from Theophrastus' *On Stones*. The paradoxographers from the beginning report their sources, see Ziegler, 'Paradoxagraphoi', 1141.

[32] Antigonus organized his own wonder-book by type of marvel rather than by location, and he seems to have been primarily selecting aquatic marvels when he copied these selections from his predecessor (ibid.).

[33] There is some justification in considering these (potentially) as contemporary sources for Hellenistic epigram in spite of their later date, because the paradoxographers copy from their predecessors faithfully and frequently. The Callimachean report about the birds of Diomedes, for example, turns up in the *Mirabiles Auscultationes* (*MA* 79) and in Pliny's *Natural History* (*HN* 10. 127). The crows of Krannon reappear in Antigonus of Carystus (Antig. Car. 15, with two further variants) as well as at *MA* 126 and in a variant at *MA* 137, where they guard the temple of Zeus in Pedasus.

polygonal stones found in Spain which 'give birth' to baby stones (*MA* 162, *PP* 12. 1; compare AB 10 and 19) We also hear of stones which change colour (*MA* 174, compare AB 13, 16, and perhaps 8). The second-century-BC paradoxographer Apollonius tells us that magnets draw by day but are inert at night and that adamant does not grow hot when placed in the fire (Apollon. *Mir.* 23, compare AB 16, 17).

Emphasis on artistry in carving of stones is not inconsistent with wonder-books either. Incised gems are treated by Pliny in the *Natural History* and several surviving 'marvels' in the paradoxographers involve feats of craftsmanship (e.g. *MA* 96, on a tapestry; 155, on security measures Pheidias built into his statue of Athena.)

The wonder-books thus contained material very similar to the prodigies and rare stones celebrated in the opening sections of the Posidippus papyrus.[34] But the connection goes further than that. The importance of paradoxography for the Milan epigrams lies, I think, in a fundamental difference between Callimachus *qua* paradoxographer and his scientific sources.[35] Wonder-books present examples of phenomena which appear to break the laws of nature. Although they present these items in a rational, objective manner, scrupulously citing sources like Eudoxus as witnesses to the incredible facts they are reporting, they do not explain the violations of natural law in scientific terms.[36] Their aim is not the satisfied 'aha!' of understanding but the round-eyed 'oh!' of wonder.

Consider the phenomenon of the statue as prodigy, the subject of poem 30. Theophrastus treats sweating statues like the one in our poem in his treatises on plants, and explains them logically as the result of fluid in the wood emerging under the influence of moist, southerly air (*Hist. Plant.* 5. 9. 8; *Caus. Pl.* 5. 4. 4). By contrast, the pseudo-Aristotelian *MA* reports on a statue of a golden bull at the temple of Artemis Orthia which utters sounds when hunters enter the shrine. No explanation is given (*MA* 175).

The connection between the wonder-books and many of the Milan

---

[34] In considering the stone and omen sections together, I leave aside many other potential programmatic implications involved in opening the collection with the stone poems. P. Bing, below, Ch. 7, comments on the geographical range of the poems; Hutchinson, 'The New Posidippus and Latin Poetry', is one of many to note the analogy between the 'small-scale artistry' of the gems and Posidippus' own epigrams.

[35] These sources are named in the citations and include Aristotle, Theophrastus, Eudoxus, Timaeus, Theopompus, and Lycus.

[36] When explanations are offered, they are typically aetiological. For example, the birds of Diomedes who can distinguish Greeks from foreigners are said to be the transformed companions of the hero (Call. fr. 407, §172).

epigrams, then, does not lie merely in the coincidence of reports about oddly shaped stones or magnets or vatic birds. They share an aesthetic of surprise, a fascination with the incredible. So big! So small! Cured instantly! Changes appearance! Poem 17, describing the action of the double-action magnet stone, tells us (ll. 5–6):

> . . . ὅ καὶ τέρας ἐξ ἑνὸc αὐτοῦ,
> πῶc δύο μιμεῖται χερμάδαc

'It's quite a prodigy, how on its own | it can imitate two [different] stones.'[37]

ὅ καὶ τέρας, 'it's quite a prodigy!' is a metrical paraphrase of the conventional formulae of the wonder-book inviting us to say 'oh!': θαυμαcτόν, θαυμάcια, τερατωδέcτερον, ἴδιον.[38] Further examples of wonder-formulae appear both in the magnet poem and other stone poems. In AB 13, a stone which changes appearance when wet is called θαῦμ' ἀπάτηc (13. 2) The snakestone is a great wonder, θαῦμα . . . μέγα (15. 7). The magnet is not only a prodigy, but a marvel, θαυμάcιον (17. 2). And if the restored text is correct, the gigantic stone cast ashore by Poseidon is described as a 'monster-work' (τειρατο-εργόν, 19. 10).[39] Now *this*, the formulae advertise, is truly amazing, truly prodigious, truly singular.

The λιθικά and οἰωνοcκοπικά sections, then, provide a very distinctive opening to the Milan epigram papyrus. Their strong links to prose treatises, especially wonder-books, establish a didactic tone which colours the whole collection.[40] Adaptation of prose material is common in Hellenistic poetry, as Aratus and Nicander demonstrate. Nevertheless, the connection with Callimachean prose in particular is significant. Not only have scholars already noted links to the poetry of Callimachus in both the previously published works of Posidippus and the Milan text, but Callimachus himself clearly uses his own prose treatises as source material for his verse.[41]

---

[37] Translation adapted from that in AB.

[38] Antig. Car. 7. 1, 8. 1, 20. 1, Apollon. *Mir.* 23, Ps.-Arist. *MA* 40, 61, 92, etc.

[39] Restored from the papyrus text τερραγοεργον; see BG ad loc.

[40] See Obbink, 'Posidippus on Papyri Then and Now', who argues (17) that the omen-poems have 'subliterary' overtones. Note too that Bing, 'Posidippus' *Iamatika*' believes the cure-poems to be based not on inscribed verse epigrams in shrines of Asclepius but rather on elaborate prose inscriptions at Epidaurus recording 'wonder-cures'.

[41] On Callimachus and Posidippus, see L. Lehnus, 'Posidippean and Callimachean Queries' with further references. As Lehnus points out, the links raise intriguing questions when juxtaposed with the assertion in the Scholia Florentina (on fr. 1. 1 Pf.) that Posidippus is one of the Telchines. In a recent essay (Krevans, 'Callimachus and the Pedestrian Muse') I argue that Callimachus' own poetry shows consistent and detailed correspondences with the material in his prose treatises. Posidippus and Callimachus must be distinguished, however, from the

ORGANIZATION WITHIN SECTIONS

Finally, there remains the important question of how the editor arranges poems within sections.[42] It must be conceded at the outset that answers to this question are somewhat speculative, given the lacunae in several key locations. I emphasize also that I survey here only the broad outlines of the editor's choices, ignoring subtleties such as verbal echoes or linked allusions to earlier poets.[43] Even on this surface level, evidence for the 'symphony conductor' can be found, notably in the section on sculpture, which will be discussed in more detail below. For the most part, however, organization within sections is at least compatible with the preferences of the reference librarian.

Two basic principles govern the sequencing of poems within sections in this collection, both variants of the command 'keep like with like'. The first principle is to keep poems on similar topics adjacent to each other. The λιθικά section contains fifteen consecutive poems about incised stones; within that sequence are four poems in a row (AB 4–7) naming girls who wear the stones. The following section begins with four adjacent poems about birds as weather-omens for seafarers (21–4);[44] it also contains four poems about war omens (30–3) and closes with a pair of poems about prophets (34–5). The votive section opens with four poems about offerings to Arsinoe. The funerary poems may begin with three poems about initiates (42–4);[45] more secure sequences include four poems about old women (45–8) and seven about young women (49–55). Two poems about childbearing are adjacent (56, 57), as are the only two poems about men (60, 61), which close the section.[46] The ἱππικά contain a sequence of five poems about Berenice (78–82)[47] and close with a pair of poems about Ptolemaic equestrian victories (87, 88). The cure-poems begin

verse paradoxographers such as Archelaus. The former include paradoxography among many other learned references in various types of verse; the latter write narrowly defined didactic versions of the prose treatises. On the verse paradoxographers see Fraser, *Ptolemaic Alexandria*, i. 778–80.

[42] On this topic see the preliminary survey by Gutzwiller, 'A New Hellenistic Poetry Book'.

[43] But see K. Gutzwiller, below, Ch. 15.

[44] See D. Sider, below, Ch. 9.

[45] BG ad loc.

[46] AB 52 mentions a dead man, but the focus is on his daughter, who guards the sundial which marks his grave.

[47] The question of which Berenice (Berenice Syra, as suggested by D. J. Thompson, Ch. 14, or Berenice II, as proposed in BG and AB) has important implications for the dating of Posidippus' poetic activity. If Berenice II is meant, the victories in AB 78 and 79 would extend his lifetime into the 240s, amply justifying his claim in AB 118.

with four adjacent epigrams which are either explicitly or implicitly votive (95–8; the crutches in 96 and the piece of shrapnel in 98 would have been dedicated at the shrine as thank-offerings). Within that sequence are two adjacent poems containing six-year illnesses (97, 98). Finally, even in the fragmentary τρόποι the first three poems all concern requests for information from tombstones.

This first principle is not incompatible with an artistic arrangement.[48] It is Meleager's preferred method of arranging poems in the *Garland*,[49] although in that case the variety of authors offers a pleasing tension against the repetition of subject-matter and creates the illusion of a literary conversation. Nevertheless, consistent grouping of like with like is a feature of prose reference works and facilitates location of specific items within the work. Callimachus the prose-editor groups his marvels by location; his imitator Antigonus groups them by subject (animals, birds, humans, etc.). By contrast, when Callimachus the poet-editor arranges items in the *Aitia* he is careful to juxtapose contrasting poems as well as similar ones.[50]

The second principle this editor seems to follow is: keep items which best match the section titles at the head of the section; place items whose connection is less clear at the end of the section.[51] The λιθικά open with a sequence of fifteen poems about artistically worked stones, most of which are named precious or semi-precious gems.[52] From that point on there is much less uniformity. The rock-crystal (AB 16) and the double magnet (17) at least still refer to stones, but the last three poems start to look like miscellaneous tag-ons: a giant stone object (drinking vessel or table, 18),[53] huge round boulders tossed ashore by storms (19), and a prayer to Poseidon which does not even mention stones, unless you count the word κρημνός (banks, cliffs; 20. 2). οἰωνοσκοπικά has a general meaning of augury, but the literal meaning of bird-omen is acknowledged when the section opens with four poems about bird-omens (21–4).[54] The last two poems do not treat omens *per se*, but praise two bird-diviners, Damon and Strymon. In

[48] See e.g. the studies of Fantuzzi and of Baumbach and Trampedach on the equestrian and omen sections respectively: Fantuzzi, 'The Structure of the *Hippika*'; Baumbach and Trampedach, '"Winged Words"'. On the latter topic see also Petrain, 'Πρέςβυς'.

[49] K. Gutzwiller, 'The Poetics of Editing'; ead., *Poetic Garlands*, 277–322 with Tables II–VI.   [50] Krevans, 'The Poet as Editor', ch. 4.

[51] Noted also by Hunter, 'Notes on the *Lithika* of Posidippus', who speculates on the aesthetic effects of this choice.

[52] The restoration of the word βαναύςου in 10 is the only evidence for the working of the stone in this very fragmentary poem; AB 13 is also uncertain but the restoration there of the incised lion is more certain.   [53] Drinking vessel: BG; table: Bing, below, Ch. 7.

[54] If one accepts the pun πρέςβυς (old man) and πρέςβυς (name of the wren) as a link with birds, then the first 9 poems are linked to the title more strongly than 30–5.

the ἰαματικά, the first five poems (95–9) acknowledge specific cures (as the title leads us to expect); the sixth poem describes a cure which is voided by the sudden death of the patient (100); the seventh is a meditation on wisdom addressed to Asclepius (101). As a corollary to this second principle, it is noteworthy that even if items match the title the editor places them at the end of the section if they do not match the other poems in the section. Thus, all the poems in the ἀναθεματικά section are dedicatory, but the two offerings which are not to Arsinoe are at the end (40, 41),[55] just as the two funerary poems about deceased men are the last two poems in the funerary section (60, 61).

Again, this second principle is not necessarily inconsistent with artistic effect. The prayers which conclude λιθικά and ἰαματικά are effective conclusions to those sections, as are the two poems praising famous bird-seers at the end of οἰωνοσκοπικά. Nevertheless, the practice of reserving miscellaneous items for the end of works or sections of works is one found more often in prose treatises than in poetry collections. For example, in Pliny's *Natural History*, the book on stones (36) opens with marble and famous works in marble, proceeds through some three dozen other types of stone and the drugs derived from them, then treats building materials related to stone, mosaics, sand, glass, and finally, as though not sure where else to put them, two anomalous sections on ash and 'wonders of the hearth'. The following book, on gemstones (37) begins with the origin of gems. Then come sections on 'famous' stones: gems belonging to famous figures, famous engravers and their work (note the similarity to the λιθικά here), other expensive non-gem stones (rock crystal, murrine vases). Next come, in alphabetical series by type of stone, over sixty chapters treating dozens of specific precious and semi-precious stones. The last four topics, however, are the shapes of stones, the testing of gems, local variants of stone-types, and comparison of prices.

Before concluding this survey of poem sequencing it should be noted that there is one section which does not follow either of the two guidelines proposed above. The ἀνδριαντοποιικά appear to have a clear ring-composition frame established by the similarity of the opening and closing poems (62, 70), which both contain allusions to Lysippus as well as programmatic statements about sculpture involving a comparison of Lysippus and Polyclitus. Other possible pairs—two poems on Myron (66, 69), two on Alexander-statues (65,

[55] AB 41 is so fragmentary that one cannot exclude any particular deity as the recipient; still, the presence of Leto in 40 after four epigrams to Arsinoe strongly suggests that it is unlikely to return to the deified queen.

70), two on legendary heroes (64, 69)—are in this section separated rather than set next to each other. A triptych of poems about realism so great it deceives the viewer (64, 65, 66) again features Lysippus in its centre. More detailed studies of this section have shown not only many additional links between the poems, but, just as significant, numerous contrasting juxtapositions—*variatio*.[56] The contrast between this section and the determined grouping by theme in the other sections is striking.

With this one exception, then, the ordering of the poems within sections is consistent and predictable. Poems on similar subjects are adjacent to each other; miscellaneous items are appended at the end of sections. While such a scheme is not necessarily incompatible with the type of carefully woven elegance found in many author-designed collections, it does evoke the utilitarian features of prose treatises.

CONCLUSIONS

The editor of this papyrus seems especially interested in highlighting connections between the poems in this collection and contemporary prose works, particularly the 'wonder-books' describing natural rarities inaugurated by Callimachus and popular throughout the Hellenistic period. The wording of the headings, the prominence of the 'wonder' topics (λιθικά, οἰωνοσκοπικά) at the head of the collection, the selection of epigrams, and the impression (even if partly false) of utilitarian sequencing within the sections all tend to create an epigram book with strong didactic colouring. A secondary emphasis on the Ptolemies, notably the queens, is not inconsistent with this didactic strain, but the flavour of this collection would be very different if the votive and equestrian sections (currently third and sixth) had instead been first and second. One section of the papyrus, however, displays a markedly different editorial aesthetic. The sculpture poems, with their symmetrical framing and thematic *variatio*, resemble other author-designed collections such as Callimachus' *Aitia*. This section was perhaps copied in its entirety from an exemplar organized in quite a different fashion—perhaps even one designed by Posidippus himself. Whatever its origins, the sculpture section ends by serving as a dramatic foil to the remainder of the book, a display piece which reveals the paths this editor chose not to take.

---

[56] Lysippus as model for sculptors is followed by Philitas as model for poets (AB 62, 63; these programmatic poems are closely linked but also set off against one another); the miniature workmanship of Theodorus is paired with the colossus of Rhodes (AB 67, 68). See A. Sens, below, Ch. 11; Gutzwiller, 'Posidippus on Statuary'.

6

New Old Posidippus and Old New Posidippus:
From Occasion to Edition in the Epigrams

DIRK OBBINK

THE CENTURY OF PAPYROLOGY AND THE NEW POSIDIPPUS

Theodor Mommsen is supposed to have said that the twentieth century would be the 'Century of Papyrology'. If he indeed said it (and Peter van Minnen has pointed out that nobody knows exactly where he did so[1]) he probably had in mind that papyrology, then in its infancy, together with new papyrus finds and the growing number of published papyri, would one day fill out the documentary record, as epigraphy and the study of inscriptions had begun to do in the nineteenth century.

But Mommsen cannot have foreseen the way in which the twentieth century would become the century of the 'New Text' on papyrus, varying our diet of Greek and Latin literature on an almost constant basis and filling the pages of the *ZPE*. The 'New Text' on papyrus created the cult of the ephemeral and the scandalous, Sappho and the novel, for example, as it raised the fragment to the status of a whole, and fuelled the project, begun in the Renaissance, of collecting between two covers the remains of those authors who, by the close of antiquity, had failed to get themselves sufficiently firmly transferred from the papyrus roll to the vellum codex. This was a project begun already in antiquity in the editions of ancient scholars who, working in centres of learning like Alexandria and Pergamum in conjunction with book producers and collectors, began the process of sifting through and amalgamating the available texts of Archaic, Classical, and contemporary Hellenistic literature of note. But had the epigrams of Posidippus been collected systematically from their monumentally inscribed versions on statues or dedications in sanctuaries, they would have looked radically different (at best geographically organized) than they do situated in the groupings which host them in the Greek Anthology or the Milan roll.

---

[1] P. van Minnen, 'The Century of Papyrology (1892–1992)'.

The 'New Texts' may also be said to have raised more problems than they have solved, as is so often the case with new evidence: problems of authorship, circumstances of preservation, and literary merit. The processes of selection and canonization to which Classical and Hellenistic poetry was subject in later antiquity have elided or at any rate obscured the original occasions for which much literature was composed: both the reasons for which the texts which survived were preserved and the literary merit accorded to them by their original composers, commissioners, and audiences or readers. The tastes which govern selection and preservation were rarely identical with those that governed the original composition and reception. Those processes themselves beg many questions. The 'New Texts' of the 'Century of Papyrology' have made any easy answer to these questions impossible. The majority of the epigrams of the Milan roll are new poems, augmenting the corpus of those previously known from the *Greek Anthology* and earlier papyrus finds. But what and how strong are the arguments for unitary authorship of these poems? How did they come to be collected in a single edition? Why do so few of them figure in the later roster of known Greek epigrams, while many other poems penned by Posidippus on the same topics covered by the Milan roll and known to later antiquity, are not found there? In what follows I try to adduce some answers (or partial answers) to these questions by means of a new approach.

THE MILAN EPIGRAMS AS SUBLITERARY COMPOSITIONS

Another question that the new papyrus of Posidippus seems not yet to answer, or at least not unequivocally, is the degree to which the poems contained in the roll, and the type of poetry there exampled, are occasional. It is the relevance of this category for conceptualizing the poems of the Milan roll that I wish to consider here, especially for the comparisons they afford with the epigrams of Posidippus previously known—both in the later anthologies and on papyrus—and with other poems of an occasional nature preserved on papyri and by inscriptions. By 'occasional' I mean not only the aspect of having seemingly been composed for a particular, historical occasion (together with questions of address and performance or enactment that this raises), but also the aspect of having seemingly been composed in first instance as something other than (or at least in addition to) a work of literature in the canonical sense. This latter sphere, sometimes termed 'subliterary', is a broad category on which not much formal work has been done. The category of subliterary text and in particular subliterary epigram deserve to be examined more closely. There are a growing body of studies[2] and no shortage of examples,[3] not all of which have received the editorial attention they deserve. If you blanch at the term 'subliterary' and its implications of deficiency in literary merit or subordination in a hierarchy, you can revert to the phrase 'Near-Literary' coined by Eric Turner,[4] connoting aspiration to canonical or at least literary status, and one may compare the term *Gebrauchspoesie* used by some literary critics.[5]

The definition of subliterary is difficult, but the examples which follow show what is meant. If poetry performed on a particular occasion is included, then Pindar and indeed classical tragedy become subliterary. In the early Hellenistic period, at least, literary works were not necessarily composed to belong to different canons, because canons are, in many cases, an after-effect; nor indeed had Pindar and the tragedians thought in those terms. The subliterary, instead, may be defined as verses composed only for an ephemeral existence and in fact not received into the canon. The subliterary could move into the literary as part of the historical record or as *belles-lettres*, based on how it was received and appreciated. Therefore: subliterary is not a category based on quality (although quality may affect its reception), but based on use and reception, that is to say, the degree to which it is perceived as literary. In the Milan roll we see, in part, the means by which such a transition could take place.[6]

By occasional poetry I refer not only simply to poems composed for a particular occasion (inscriptional dedication, for example), but also to those seemingly composed with no particular purpose other than

---

[2] R. Cribiore, *Writing, Teachers, and Students in Graeco-Roman Egypt* (Atlanta, 1996); ead., *Gymnastics of the Mind* (Princeton, 2001); M. van Rossum-Steenbeek, *Greek Readers' Digests* (Leiden, 1997); T. Morgan, *Literate Education in the Hellenistic and Roman World* (Cambridge, 1998). Catalogue of literary passages attested in school texts: Cribiore, 'Literary School Exercises'. Specifically with regard to epigrams: J. Wissmann, 'Hellenistic Epigrams as School-Texts'.

[3] D. L. Page, *Greek Literart Papyri*, i (London, 1942); G. Manteuffel, *De opusculis Graecis* (Warsaw, 1930); E. Heitsch, *Die griechischen Dichterfragmente der römischen Kaiserzeit*, 2nd edn., 2 vols. (Göttingen, 1963–4).

[4] E. G. Turner, *Catalogue of Greek and Latin Papyri and Ostraca in the Possession of the University of Aberdeen* (Aberdeen, 1939) ix. *Kleinkunst* carries some of the same connotations of seeming triviality and lack of aspiration towards canonical status, but can also connote finely detailed craftmanship, which is less often associated with 'occasional' or 'subliterary' texts. I suggest that the new epigrams might best be considered under a combination of such categories, in order fully to appreciate both the qualities that exhibited artistic refinement making them memorable as works of art and candidates for transmission, and the elements of occasionality that made them seem topical and fashionable.

[5] H. Lausberg on 'Kleine Gattungen', *Handbuch der literarischen Rhetorik*, 3rd ed. (Stuttgart, 1990) paras. 1157 (p. 553) and 1242 (p. 601).

[6] I am grateful to comments of the anonymous reviewer for clarification in this regard.

the creation of an exemplum, exercise, or παίγνιον (compare Catullus' *nugae*). Both types (along with a corresponding experimentation with genre) have an affinity with one strand of Hellenistic poetry later associated with the Neoterics, and with epigram and elegy and other obscure or subordinate genres of poetry like didactic. This is of course ambiguously evaluative. It is a hallmark of the Neoteric movement that poetry that seemed minor, trivial, or technical (sub-literary?) becomes the most literary of all (if ironically and ambiguously so). It may well be, as some believe, that this paradox was inspired by early third-century Greek Hellenistic poetic theory and practice. If so, the question becomes 'did Posidippus participate in it?'

To some extent what I have to say may be true of epigram as a genre in general, and I will no doubt seem to be beating a dead horse. But I think that at least some of the characteristics of these poems I have in mind have passed notice or been lost in the project of making the case for Posidippus as the sole author of the new epigrams (a case I find broadly convincing), while others continue to be cited by those who impugn Posidippus' authorship in some or all cases or their date or literary merit.[7] But ultimately my characterization of the poems as occasional is not intended as a comment on their merit literary or otherwise, but rather to situate them compositionally in an actual milieu for which they were composed, in which the places, objects, and people described in the poems were seen and experienced. By focusing on the occasions (in some cases trival) of the poems and treating them as literary artefacts, we can revivify the presumed circumstances that made their conventions intelligible to a Hellenistic readership. We must remember that the poems were composed by a real poet for real people, and that behind their jocular and ironic tone lies a world in the constructing and fashioning of which the poet, his patrons, and his readership collaborate. In this way we can see exactly how the previously known poems of Posidippus fertilize the new epigrams of the Milan roll to form a composite interpretative whole.

Within the subsection titled οἰωνοϲκοπικά, 'divination from bird signs' in the Milan roll, there appears an unassuming epigram advertising the divinatory services of one Damon (AB 34):[8]

---

[7] As cited by Gutzwiller, Introduction, n. 3, especially the considerations (some more probative than others) raised by Schröder, 'Skeptische Überlegungen'; see too A. S. Hollis, 'Heroic Honours for Philitas?', 60 n. 24.

[8] Cf. D. Obbink, 'Posidippus on Papyri Then and Now', 16–18, where this epigram is discussed in similar terms. In line 2 ἀγαθῶν is my conjecture for ἀγαθόϲ of the papyrus.

New Old Posidippus, Old New Posidippus

ἐκ τούτου τοῦ πάντα περισκέπτοιο κολωνοῦ
Δάμων Τελμηςςεὺς ἐκ πατέρων ἀγαθῶν
οἰωνοσκοπίας τεκμαίρεται· ἀλλ' ἴτε φήμην
καὶ Διὸς οἰωνοὺς ὧδ' ἀναπευςόμενοι.

From this hill which commands a panoramic view
    Damon of Telmessus of good paternal stock
makes his predictions from bird signs. But do come along
    to consult here the prophetic voice and omens of Zeus.
                     (Translation after Austin in AB)

Was this poem to be read as serving a purely practical purpose, like
the advertisement of Kres from Saqqara given below? Is the pan-
oramic view provided by the vantage point described in the epigram
of Posidippus on Damon designed artfully to complement the far-
sightedness of Zeus' prophecies which it advertises? Both epigrams
are localized by their respective texts by deictic pronouns (τάδε in the
epigram of Kres, and ἐκ τούτου τοῦ κολωνοῦ in AB 34), and individu-
ated by objectively naming a professional practitioner. Both have
an ostensibly practical purpose—and in that sense are occasional—
namely, to monumentalize (if unambitiously so) within the circum-
scribed contexts of their respective advertisers' lives and occupations.
In both we are briefly allowed a private glimpse into the business life
of a private diviner, at once mundane and mysterious, practical and
portentous.

One might suppose that few 'shop-signs' in Graeco-Roman anti-
quity can have been quite as literate as this one. Even fewer will have
been in verse. Those known from Pompeii and Herculaneum, for
example, consist often of painted pictures without words.[9] A good
parallel, however, to Posidippus' epigram comes from a painted
limestone stele from Saqqara, just south of the pyramids at Giza
(now in the Cairo Museum).[10] Its painted inscription, datable by its
letter shapes, advertises the services of a Greek oracle-seller, Kres
(or perhaps: 'a Cretan') who has enterprisingly set up shop outside
the precinct of the nearby Memphite Serapeum, itself an oneirotic
oracular shrine of an institutional type. Apart from depicting a Greek
temple (steps to a raised floor, roof, and columns with Egyptianizing
Caryatids), and altar with approaching bull (perhaps recalling the
Apis bulls, entombed in their huge sarcophagi in the underground
sanctuary nearby), it bears a metrical epigram of anonymous

---

[9] For signs with words see P. Saqqara inv. 1972 GP 3 (c.331–323 BC) in Turner and Parsons,
Greek Manuscripts, 138–9, no. 79, described by Parsons (p. 136) with further examples.
[10] E. Bernand, *Inscriptions métriques de l'Égypte gréco-romaine* (Paris 1969), no. 112 (late iv/
early iii BC) = SB 685.

composition, addressing the passer-by, with a practical purpose—in light of which we might hesitate to call it poetry, but verse and an epigram it remains:

> ἐνύπνια κρίνω τοῦ θεοῦ πρόσταγμα ἔχων
> τυχἀγαθᾶι· Κρής ἐςτιν ὁ κρίνων τάδε.

I interpret dreams at the god's command,
Good luck! It is Kres who interprets these dreams.

In the Milan roll, the epigrams grouped under οἰωνοσκοπικά, the topic of divination itself lends these verse a subliterary cast: the entire section of οἰωνοσκοπικά constitutes virtually a verse manual on divination from bird signs in miniature, though each can be read as an individual epigram and some are paired. A good comparison here is afforded by the collection of horoscopic epigrams in elegiacs by Anubion,[11] which includes some written for famous figures of history or myth (Oedipus, Philip of Macedon) or professions, e.g. the orator. The theme of divination occurs elsewhere in the new Posidippus epigrams. AB 36 describes the dedication of a statue to Arsinoe, upon receipt of a command from her in a dream to do so. AB 33 is a grave epigram which describes the death of the deceased as ironically and tragically determined by acting on an erroneous interpretation of a dream. AB 40 describes a temple thesauros in the shape of a statue through whose mouth money is received by a priestess in return for an oracle-response. The epigrams of the Milan roll that depict individuals (most of them women) as participants in the mysteries might also be cited in this connection (AB 43–4, 46, 58). Book 11 of *AP* contains a section of related poems on astrologers and diviners, many of them skoptic. The fact that ordinary people in antiquity commonly had recourse to some form of divination in decision-making of every sort from whom and when to marry and have children to when to go to battle. In prose Theophrastus' *Character* of the 'superstitious man' epitomizes the everyday element embodied by this subgenre. In poetry Theocritus' *Idyll* 2 with its epigrammatic refrain nicely parallels Posidippus' section on divination from bird signs in its attempt to depict the concerns, moods, and melodramatic language of a middle-class woman in love. AB 34 on Damon instantiates what can only be an epigrammatic subgenre that I would characterize as subliterary and occasional in its content if not in its composition, per-

---

[11] P. Oxy. LXVI 4503–7 with Callimachean metrical preferences: e.g. 4504 ii 16–18 (horoscope of Oedipus); 4505 fr. 2. 9–10 (of a good orator μ]ύθων τε ῥητῆρα ταχὺν πρη[ςτῆρα φέροντα; cf. Posidippus, AB 27. 5–6 φήνη παῖδ' ἀγαγοῦςα καὶ ἐν θώκοις ἀγορητήν | ἡδυεπῆ θήςει, 'a vulture as a child's omen will make him a sweet-speaking orator').

haps with literary aspirations, in so far, that is, as it seems to aspire to conformity to a type, but admits of significant variation: i.e. not a copy or metaphrastic version but another example of its class.[12]

THE MILAN SUBTITLES AND HELLENISTIC THEORY OF GENRE

This generic sense of belonging to a type or subgroup, with specifiable criteria for inclusion or exclusion, is implied already by the subtitles that so strikingly turn out to be separating the sections of the Milan roll.[13] Under these headings, unique for their period,[14] the epigrams of each type are grouped by their affinities for a type of technical, occasional, or subliterary type of writing. This is conveyed in particular by the neuters plural, which connote prose and historical narrative, whereas titles of poetic works show an overwhelming (though not of course exclusive) preference for feminine. One might of course object that the exception to the preference for the feminine in titles of poetry is that of ἐπιγράμματα, which is neuter plural, and that the neuters plural of the Milan roll modify this. But even in this case, they suggest the miscellaneous, piecemeal nature of the collection of epigrams. The titles thus serve to establish expectations for the poems which follow, suggesting that they ought to be read in terms of and as commenting on one another, read according to a generically constructed set of rules for the use of the sophisticated reader, in a way that is made possible only by the chaining of the epigrams into an anthology, and only in these particular groupings.

It is not necessary for my purpose to prove that any of Posidippus' epigrams were actually set up for display in the manner of the epigram of Kres at Saqqara (though a number of them seem in fact to have been), or even composed expressly for such a purpose. The deictic function of the pronoun is sufficient to establish at least the fiction of its display or purpose and so its occasionality. In fact, deictic

---

[12] On subliterary epigram as a type see Wissmann, 'Hellenistic Epigrams as School-Texts'.

[13] On the placement of titles in general see D. Albino, 'La divisione in capitoli nelle opere degli antichi'; W. E. H. Cockle, *Euripides: Hypsipyle* (Rome, 1987) 219–22; J.-C. Fredouille et al. (eds.), *Titres et articulations du texte dans les œuvres antiques* (Paris, 1997); M. Hengel, *Die Evangelienüberschriften* (Heidelberg, 1984); W. Luppe, 'Rückseitentitel auf Papyrusrollen'; E. Nachmanson, *Der griechische Buchtitel* (Göteborg, 1941); R. P. Oliver, 'The First Medicean MS of Tacitus'; Schmalzriedt, Περὶ φύσεως. On titles and *agrapha* at the beginnings of rolls see Bastianini, 'Tipologie dei rotoli e problemi di ricostruzione', 25-7. In Roman books: B.-J. Schröder, *Titel und Text: Zur Entwicklung lateinischer Gedichtüberschriften* (Berlin, 1999).

[14] I know of no contemporary parallel for centred subheadings of this type. Such examples as are witnessed from the period mark absence rather than presence of a type of text different than that of the main body, e.g. μαρτυρία in oratory or χορός/-οῦ in drama.

pronouns directing the reader's attention to the poem as mounted on an object or to the physicality of that object appear in a majority of the poems contained in the Milan roll (and those poems of Posidippus known from other sources). In another large subset of the poems the device of having the object or monument or person associated with it speak similarly situates the poem and grounds its existence in physical presence, real or illusory. The poems tend either to localize themselves, or concern objects which prima facie suggest place. And while many (perhaps as many as half) of the new epigrams could have been plausibly inscribed in some medium or context (and it is hard to think how some, e.g. AB 61, could have been destined for any other use), even in the one instance (see below) where this appears certainly to have been the case, transmission of the poem can be seen to have occurred by scribal means: i.e. through copying from a manuscript rather than from the monumentally inscribed version.

P. M. Fraser adduces the interesting argument that the 'publication of epigrams in roll form explains how such pieces written by poets in one part of the Greek world were imitated in other parts, for it is not likely that isolated short poems would have travelled in the same way that complete rolls did',[15] while inscriptions on stone, of course, do not move at all. This would have been a decisive development: collections of epigrams are not present in the fourth century, but exist by the time of Posidippus. Thus the epigram became divorced from its lapidary context, which in turn facilitated the enlargement of and alteration of the genre's scope. We must envisage a time when poems written for the book and poems written for stone were not fundamentally different, in order to see how even actually inscribed epigrams came to circulate through written copies.

ANOTHER SUBLITERARY ANTHOLOGY OF POSIDIPPUS' EPIGRAMS

A similar relation between poem and monument may be observed in some of the poems of Posidippus known on papyrus before the Milan roll came to light. There is at least one case of an epigram independently attested in connection with its inscription on a monument. It derives from the same location at Saqqara, where in the Memphite Serapeum a large archive of papers comprising a temple archive (one them bearing a pair of epigrams by Posidippus) were recovered by archaeologists in the late nineteenth century.

[15] *Ptolemaic Alexandria*, i. 608.

New Old Posidippus, Old New Posidippus

The papyrus is P. Louvre 7172 ('P. Firmin–Didot'), containing AB 115–16 = GP 11, 12 = Page, *GLP* 104a–b.[16] Written before 161 BC, on an opisthographic papyrus roll, it consists of poems written by the orphaned sons of a Macedonian mercenary in the Memphite Serapeum.[17] The roll includes excerpts from comedy and tragedy as well. The name Ποceιδίππου and the title ἐπιγράμματα, together with the beginning of the first epigram inset as an incipit-title, are given as a heading[18] to the texts of two otherwise unknown epigrams—one (AB 115 = GP 11) on the dedication of the lighthouse by Sostratus of Cnidus, and another (AB 116 = GP 12) on the shrine of Arsinoe-Aphrodite at Cape Zephyrium by Callicrates of Samos:

Ποceιδίππου ἐπιγράμματα
Ἑλλήνων Cωτῆρα, Φάρου cκοπόν,
ὦ ἄνα Πρωτεῦ, | Cώcτρατοc ἔcτηcεν Δεξιφάνουc Κνίδιοc·
οὐ γὰρ ἐν Αἰγύπτωι cκοπαὶ οὔρεοc οἷ᾽ ἐπὶ νήcων,
ἀλλὰ χαμαὶ χηλὴ ναύλοχοc ἐκτέταται.
τοῦ χάριν εὐθεῖάν τε καὶ ὄρθιον αἰθέρα τέμνειν   5
πύργοc ὅδ᾽ ἀπλάτων φαίνετ᾽ ἀπὸ cταδίων
ἤματι, παννύχιοc δὲ θοῶc ἐν κύματι ναύτηc
ὄψεται ἐκ κορυφῆc πῦρ μέγα καιόμενον,
καί κεν ἐπ᾽ αὐτὸ δράμοι Ταύρου Κέραc, οὐδ᾽ ἂν ἁμάρτοι
Cωτῆροc, Πρωτεῦ, Ζηνὸc ὁ τῆιδε πλέων.   10
— ἄλλο
μέccον ἐγὼ Φαρίηc ἀκτῆc cτόματόc τε Κανώπου
ἐν περιφαινομένωι κύματι χῶρον ἔχω,
τήνδε πολυρρήνου Λιβύηc ἀνεμώδεα χηλήν,
τὴν ἀνατεινομένην εἰc Ἰταλὸν Ζέφυρον,
ἔνθα με Καλλικράτηc ἱδρύcατο καὶ βαcιλίccηc   5
ἱερὸν Ἀρcινόηc Κύπριδοc ὠνόμαcεν.
ἀλλ᾽ ἐπὶ τὴν Ζεφυρῖτιν ἀκουcομένην Ἀφροδίτην,
Ἑλλήνων ἁγναί, βαίνετε, θυγατέρεc,
οἵ θ᾽ ἁλὸc ἐργάται ἄνδρεc· ὁ γὰρ ναύαρχοc ἔτευξεν
τοῦθ᾽ ἱερὸν παντὸc κύματοc εὐλίμενον.   10

[16] I discuss this pair of epigrams as a kind of mini-anthology of epigrams on papyrus in 'Posidippus Then and Now', 19–27. Here I simply note the occasional nature of the poems themselves, and their transmission as subliterary texts, not in book form.

[17] For the Egyptian context: D. J. Thompson, 'Ptolemaios and "The Lighthouse"'; ead., *Memphis under the Ptolemies* (Princeton, 1988), 261. The title and author, together with the text of the epigrams, contain numerous copying errors and orthographical idiosyncrasies characteristic of the level of competence of the writer and consistent with Ptolemaic copying practice. The new edition by AB (followed here) corrects simple orthographical errors, but wisely eliminates the emendations (most of them unnecessary) by early editors which appear in the editions of Page (*GLP*) and GP and returns to a text closer to that given by the copyist. For example, in AB 115. 5 previous editors have consistently emended τέμνειν to the participle τέμνων, whereas AB retain the infinitive of the papyrus.

[18] I give the text as laid out on the papyrus. See further the discussion below.

(i) As a saviour of the Greeks, this watchman of Pharos, O lord Proteus,
    was set up by Sostratus, son of Dexiphanes, from Cnidos.
For in Egypt there are no look-out posts on a mountain, as in the
    islands,
but low lies the breakwater where ships take harbour.
Therefore this tower, in a straight and upright line,
    appears to cleave the sky from countless furlongs away,
during the day, but throughout the night quickly a sailor on the waves
    will see a great fire blazing from its summit.
And he may even run to the Bull's Horn, and not miss
    Zeus the Saviour, O Proteus, whoever sails this way.

(ii) Midway between the shore of Pharos and the mouth of Canopus,
    in the waves visible all around I have my place,
this wind-swept breakwater of Libya rich in sheep,
    facing the Italian Zephyr.
Here Callicrates set me up and called me the shrine
    of Queen Arsinoe-Aphrodite.
So then, to her who shall be named Zephyritis-Aphrodite,
    come, ye pure daughters of the Greeks,
and ye too, toilers on the sea. For the captain built
    this shrine to be a safe harbour from all the waves.

                                  (Transl. Austin)

The first epigram (115) addresses Proteus, tutelary Greek divinity
of Pharos Island in the harbour at Alexandria, and tells of a dedica-
tion there by Sostratus of Cnidus, one of the King's wealthy φίλοι.
The second epigram (116) describes the construction and dedica-
tion of a temple of Aphrodite (soon to be identified with Arsinoe) by
the Ptolemaic admiral Callicrates of Samos at Cape Zephyrium and
invites young Greek women to choral performances at her festival
there.[19]

The pair of epigrams AB 115–16 form a piece with the new epi-
grams by Posidippus in the Milan roll. Egypt attracts celebrities
from the entire Greek world (Cnidus, Samos). Greeks are mentioned
twice: prominently in AB 115. 1 and again in 116. 8 nearer the end
of the poem, thus forming a ring. Thus I argue that the epigrams are
paired, both here on the papyrus in a manner of a mini-anthology,
and in composition, as evidenced by the framing references to
(i) Greekness and Sostratus at the beginning of AB 115 and (ii) to
Greekness and Callicrates at the end of 116. However, in this case

---

[19] On Callicrates, Posidippus, and their Ptolemaic connections see P. Bing, 'Posidippus and
the Admiral'.

the physical separation of the two monuments precludes that they were ever actually paired in an inscribed monumental context, for the two monuments in question were dozens of miles apart. Rather, they must have originally been paired in a book.

The epigrams were probably inscribed (and known in antiquity as inscribed) in monumental contexts. Peter Bing argues that Sostratus dedicated not the monument itself, but the statue of Zeus Soter that stood astride the top of the tower.[20] The epigram, he suggests, may have been inscribed on the tower, rather than right beneath the statue of Zeus, where it would have been hard to see.

We can be confident that Ptolemaeus, one of the two brothers resident in the Memphite Serapeum who copied the roll as part of his tuition, did not know the epigram from the inscription on the monument. Rather, he copied it, along with the epigram on Callicrates' dedication on the temple of Arsinoe-Aphrodite at Cape Zephyrium from a Hellenistic poetry book where he found them paired. This is clear from the graphic features which it exhibits. Among these may be counted the scribal errors, which are those of a beginner or a bilingual writer copying from a book: dittographies and hyperiotacisms abound, along with numerous errors of a visual sort caused by the slip of the eye from one sequence to a subsequent identical sequence of letters, as well as seeming phonetic errors caused by misremembering what a copyist has read.[21]

Ptolemaeus is copying from a professionally produced book: he manages to replicate the significant features of the form of the Hellenistic poetry book.[22] We are thus entitled to bring the epigrams of Posidippus on papyri previously known before the discovery of the Milan roll into conjunction with the new epigrams of Posidippus from that book. The pair of epigrams informally copied by Ptolemaeus can be seen to derive from a professionally produced collection like the Milan roll. As such, it comprises a subset, and

---

[20] P. Bing, 'Between Literature and the Monuments'.

[21] This is only partly due to the limited competence of young Ptolemaeus as he is learning to write: papyri of the Ptolemaic date appear to be far more tolerant than their Roman-period counterparts of the sort of errors that a trained reader might have been expected to correct, and this is true of the errors of the Milan roll of epigrams of Posidippus as well.

[22] For example, the pentameters in his versions of AB 115–16 begin at the same point as the hexameters, as was standard in copying of elegiacs in ancient manuscripts. They are inset (unusually) in P. Lit. Lond. 62 = *SH* 982; Cornelius Gallus eleg. fr. (i BC anthol. of Latin elegiac quatrains ed. Anderson–Parsons–Nisbet, 'Elegiacs by Gallus', qq.v. p. 130 for the normal practice); P. CtYBR inv. 4000 (iv AD anthol. of Greek epigrams), and P. Lips. 1445 verso (iii AD anthol. of Greek epigrams ed. W. Luppe, 'Ein Leipziger Epigramm-Papyrus')—all presumably exceptions which prove a more general rule: see also S. Barbantani, 'Un epigramma encomiastico', 259–60 and tav. II.

can be seen in itself as a kind of mini-anthology of Posidippus. The two epigrams of Ptolemaeus' collection appear neither in the Milan roll (where we might have expected them among the other poems given under the heading ἀναθεματικά), nor in *AP* or related later anthologies, though the existence of at least one of them is noted by a periegetical writer, and the second has a close parallel with *AB* 119 (recorded not in the Milan roll, nor in the *AP*, but by Athenaeus 7. 318 D) which purports to be inscribed on the same monument, and possibly with AB 110 in the Milan roll where Ζεφ[υρ- in l. 1 seems to refer to Aphrodite Zephyritis (likewise AB 36 and 39 are dedications to Arsinoe as identified with this goddess, while the latter is sited specifically at the monument in question).[23] They were copied by standard scribal techniques from a collection that either was more exhaustive of the poet's oeuvre than either of these, or at any rate contained additional material—and the lack of overlap between the three can hardly be said to point to the existence of a single authoritative edition on which all three are drawing. This, together with the circumstances of copying, might point in a subliterary direction or at least lead to doubts about authorial composition of any one of these collections. The epigrams were copied as a pair, as indicated by the connecting subtitle ἄλλο—thus constituting a mini-Posidippus anthology incorporated in a larger personal anthology. They came equipped in their source with titles (the latest book-technology of the day), including the use of the incipit as a title, as employed in Callimachus' *Pinakes*.[24] Thus they show signs of derivation not from monument or memory but from state-of-the-art book-production. At the same time their selection for this particular anthology, as in the case of many poems in the Milan roll, seems to have been guided by geographical and political considerations.

The conclusion necessitated then is that monumentality is not a necessary condition for occasionality in these poems, but only a sufficient condition. It is highly unlikely that many (if any) of the epigrams of Posidippus owe their survival (as opposed to their composition) to their inscription on stone or any other medium than papyrus.

---

[23] On this constellation of poems see Bing, 'Posidippus and the Admiral'.

[24] On Callimachus' Pinakes see Blum, *Kallimachos*; F. Schmidt, *Die Pinakes des Kallimachos* (Berlin, 1922); O. Regenbogen, "Πίναξ", 1412–26; R. Pfeiffer, *History of Classical Scholarship* i (Oxford 1968), 127–34 and addenda pp. 287–8.

POSIDIPPUS OLD AND NEW

It is instructive to consider the poems of the Milan roll which do appear in the later tradition. These I call the New Old Posidippus: new in that they recently came to light in the Milan roll; old in so far as they are transmitted through more standard channels. They form the main basis for authorship of the rest of the epigrams in the Milan roll. These are AB 15 (= GP 20), on an engraved gem, also quoted by Tzetzes (*Chil.* VII 653–60, who knows at 661 ἕτερα μυρία by Posidippus), and AB 65 (= GP 18), praising the realism of a statue of Alexander by the Sicyonian sculptor Lysippus; this also appears in the later Planudean appendix:[25]

Λύσιππε,, πλάστα Cικυώ,νιε, θαρc,αλέα χείρ,
   δάϊε τεχνί,τα, πῦρ τοι ὁ χα,λκὸc ὁρ,ῆι,
ὃν κατ' Ἀλεξά,νδρου μορφᾶc ἔθευ· οὔ τί γε μεμπτοί
   Πέρcαι· cυγγνώ,μα βουcὶ λέοντα φυγεῖν.

1 θαρcαλέη Planudes *AP* 16. 119 (cf. Theocr. 24. 117 θαρcαλέωc τιc ἔμεινεν ἀεθλεύοντ' ἐν ἀγῶνι) : δαιδαλέη Himerius *Or.* 48. 14 (cf. Lucr. 4. 551 *verborum daedala lingua*)   3 εθευουτιγε pap.: χέεc οὐκέτι Planudes

Lysippus, sculptor of Sicyon, bold hand,
   cunning craftsman, fire is in the glance of the bronze
which you made in the form of Alexander. In no way can one blame
   the Persians: cattle may be forgiven for flying before a lion.

(Trans. Austin)

Poems (especially in elegiacs) in praise of Lysippus are numerous: in fact, AB 62 is another, while AB 142 (= GP 19) is another, recounting a dialogue between a passer-by and a statue of Kairos, 'Time', by Lysippus. This poem is not in the Milan roll, but appears in the Planudean appendix which gives AB 65. Even Propertius 3. 9. 9 has a verse in praise of this sculptor.

The other previously known epigrams of Posidippus (other than those copied by the brothers in the Memphite Serapeum) might be thought to have some guarantee of their date and Posidippan authorship from their pedigree, that is from being found within portions of the *Greek Anthology* deriving more or less directly from Meleager's *Garland*. The two poems in the Milan roll known to the later tradi-

---

[25] Note that his poem also appears in a papyrus collection (P. Freib. 4 = *SH* 973) following another epigram on a statue by Theodorides. On epigram collections on papyri in general see Parsons, 'Callimachus and the Hellenistic Epigram'; Stephens and Obbink, 'The Manuscript'.

tion (and reported to have been authored by Posidippus) fall outside these sections of the *AP* and therefore lack this pedigree (a criterion in any case questionable since several of the epigrams known before the Milan roll and ascribed to Posidippus in the *AP* have alternative attributions there). This does not necessarily call into question their authorship or date (as Page for example thought). But Planudes was apparently using Cephalas' anthology or a copy thereof, rather than Meleager himself.[26] Therefore Planudes cannot simply be counted upon to have taken the epigram on Lysippus, together with its ascription to Posidippus, from Meleager's *Garland*. (The plausible source for Tzetzes' quotation of AB 15 is anything but clear.) A third-century date for both of these poems is now secured by the date of the Milan roll in which they appear.

But what is clear is that the poems of the Milan roll do not represent an authoritative and exhaustive edition of the epigrams of Posidippus. The lack of overlap with the other epigrams ascribed by the later tradition to Posidippus (as many as thirty-eight if one includes those with disputed—i.e. double—ascriptions to Asclepiades), the failure of the Milan roll to include e.g. AB 142 on Lysippus shows that we have a subset: a selection (perhaps a new instalment) or an early edition of poems composed, or at any rate collected, before the poems known to the later tradition.

Second, the fact that the Milan roll includes two epigrams on Lysippus (AB 65, 70) but omits AB 142 and, more importantly, fails to pair it with AB 62 (which it does include) shows a certain lack of design, a failure to take advantage of an opportunity to link the two poems successively, with no apparent motive or gain in connection between poems elsewhere. We are at least entitled to ask whether we have here a poetry book or a book of poems. A collection without such elements of design[27] would have affinities with many subliterary collections. But we might also see these otherwise unexampled poems as frozen in time, as the poetry book evolves from an inchoate state as a subliterary collection to the design exhibited by the artfully chained sequences of the later garlands and the careful editing manifest in Latin poetry books.

One scenario for this process of selection can be glimpsed from the second-century-BC grammarian Apollodorus of Athens, when

---

[26] So Cameron, *Greek Anthology*, e.g. 342–3.

[27] For an argument for structure in the ἀνδριαντοποιικά section see Gutzwiller, 'Posidippus on Statuary'. In Latin poetry books: cf. G. O. Hutchinson, 'The Catullan Corpus, Greek Epigram, and the Poetry of Objects'.

he excerpted a lost (and otherwise unknown) local Coan epic, the
Meropis:

περιεπέϲομεν δὲ ποιήμαϲιν, ἐφ' ὧν ἦν ἐπιγραφὴ Μεροπίϲ, οὐ δηλοῦϲα τὸν ποήϲῳ
(l. -ϲα)[ντα], 'I came across a poem with the title *Meropis* and no indication
of the author . . .'.

Here a noted second-century-BC polymath grammarian, compiler,
and anthologizer is seen in action—as chancing upon an anonymous
work not known to him (possibly in the royal library of Alexandria
or Pergamum, but possibly in the course of his own book-collecting),
and which would not before or after be mentioned in literary his-
tory independent of this citation.[28] He takes the time and trouble, in
the course of an expansive study of the etymological significances of
divine epithets, to give an epitomized version of the poem in mini-
ature, recording it (as he says) 'because of the peculiarity of its narra-
tive'. Apollodorus in the twenty-two books of his Περὶ θεῶν selected,
copied out, grouped, and arranged literally thousands of such excerpts
from many works of literature obscure and famous, canonical and
subliterary alike into his collection as materials for his study and
theme and no doubt because many of these texts were inaccessible to
his readers. Might not the compiler of the Milan roll have worked in
a similar way and, in part, out of similar motives?

EPIGRAM, OCCASION, AND EDITION

We can now be more specific about the subliterary or occasional
aspects of the epigrams of Posidippus. One has already been men-
tioned: namely the deictic pronouns and other self-references (e.g.
speaking statues) by which many of the poems are objectified. More
than half of the poems of Posidippus are complete enough to identify
one or more such devices in each. In a purely occasional, subliterary
text such pronouns would refer to the material or place of the object
on which the epigram was inscribed (or intended to be inscribed).
In later Hellenistic epigram, of course, the presence of such devices
does not of course guarantee occasionality of the historical and monu-
mental sort; a number of epigrams, identified by historical anachron-
ism or other impossibility, are manifest fictions. But it does show the

---

[28] Apollodorus Atheniensis Περὶ θεῶν (P. Köln III 126 ii 9-11 = *SH* 903A = *PEG* i. 131–
5). On Apollodorus as a Hellenistic collector see Parsons, 'Identities in Diversity', 167 and
A. Henrichs, 'Response to Part Two'. The anonymous epic *Meropis* (cf. *SH* 903A) is otherwise
mentioned only in a citation in Philodemus' *De pietate* which derives from Apollodorus' Περὶ
θεῶν: see Henrichs, 'Zur Meropis'.

work of a poet who, consistent with his genre, habitually insinuates an impression of occasionality.

In addition the poems of Posidippus can be seen to exhibit an air (rarely mentioned) of insouciant irony or humour or sarcasm, often associated with skoptic and obscene epigram, well exemplified by the new epigrams of Nicarchus published by Peter Parsons in *The Oxyrhynchus Papyri*, vol. LXVI.[29] In Posidippus, AB 15, for example, the irony resides in how the epigram, which expresses wonder at the straining of the engraver's eyes, would have been inscribed on such a tiny object:[30]

οὐ ποταμὸς κελάδων ἐπὶ χείλεςιν, ἀλλὰ δράκοντος
  εἶχέ ποτ' εὐπώγων τόνδε λίθον κεφαλή
πυκνὰ φαληριόωντα· τὸ δὲ γλυφὲν ἅρμα κατ' αὐτ,ο,ῦ
  τοῦθ' ὑπὸ Λυγκείου βλέμματος ἐγλύφετο
ψεύδεϊ χειρὸς ὅμοιον· ἀποπλαςθὲν γὰρ ὁρᾶται   5
  ἅρμα, κατὰ πλάτεος δ' οὐκ ἂν ἴδοις προβόλους·
ἧι καὶ θαῦμα πέλει μόχθου μέγα, πῶς ὁ λιθουργός
  τὰς, ἀτενιζούσας οὐκ ἐμόγηςε κόρας.

It was not a river resounding on its banks, but the head
   of a bearded snake that once held this gem,
thickly streaked with white. And the chariot on it
   was engraved by the sharp eye of Lynceus,
like the mark on a nail: the chariot is seen incised
   but on the surface you could not notice any protrusions.
And that's why the work causes such a great marvel: how did the pupils
   of the engraver's eyes not suffer as he gazed so intently.

(Transl. Austin)

A more blatant example is AB 102, in which the laconic deceased complains of being bothered with questions by a passer-by.[31] This epigram is artfully paired with its following one, in which the occupant of a tomb complains that you—who after all will one day be dead like him—didn't trouble to ask him who he was. Such detailed character drawing, redolent of high art but also of the exemplum or παίγνιον, earned these poems a special place in the Milan roll with a new and unattested subheading, τρόποι, thus inventing a new subgenre.[32]

---

[29] Nos. 4501–2. See also G. Nisbet, *Greek Epigram in the Roman Empire* (Oxford, 2003); id., 'Is There a Book in this Text?'.

[30] For the ecphrastic technique cf. Susan T. Stevens, 'Image and Insight: Ecphrastic Epigrams in the *Latin Anthology*'.

[31] For the motif see M. Baumbach, '"Wanderer, kommst du nach Sparta...". Zur Rezeption eines Simonides-Epigramms', *Poetica* 32 (2000) 1-22.   [32] See D. Obbink, '"*Tropoi*"'.

New Old Posidippus, Old New Posidippus

τί πρὸς ἔμ' ὧδ' ἔcτητε; τί μ οὐκ ἥacaτ' ἰαύειν,
εἰρόμενοι τίc ἐγὼ καὶ πόθεν ἢ ποδαπόc;
cτείχετέ μου παρὰ cῆμα· Μενοίτιόc εἰμι Φιλάρχω
Κρήc, ὀλιγορρήμων ὡc ἂν ἐπὶ ξενίηc.

Why have you stopped here, next to me? Why haven't you let me sleep,
asking who I am, where I come from, or to what country I belong?
Go past my tomb. I am Menoetius, the son of Phylarchus,
from Crete, a man of few words as you'd expect in a foreign land.

(Trans. Austin)

(ii) AB 103

οὐδ' ἐπερωτήcαc με νόμου χάριν οὔτε πόθεν γῆc
εἰμὶ παραcτείχειc οὔτε [τίc ο]ὔτε τίνων·
ἀλλὰ cύ μ' ἡcυχί[ωc ἴδε κείμεν]ον, εἰμὶ δ' ἐγὼ παῖc
Ἀλκαίου Cωcῆc Κῷ[ιοc, ὁμόc, φίλ]ε, cοῦ.

In breach of custom, you didn't even ask me from where I come,
and you walk by: not even who I am, or from what family.
Come on then, take a good look at me lying here in peace: I am the son
of Alcaeus, Soses of Cos, the same sort, friend, as you.

The epigrams record the speech of two dead men, each speaking from
the tomb on the same theme, each suggesting a different attitude of
the passer-by toward them and their burial. The first is unfriendly
and unwelcoming; Menoetius of Crete is portrayed through his
speech as a misanthrope or δύcκολοc; the second is similarly critical of
the passer-by for ignoring him, and instead demands attention and
sympathy. The second directly inverts some of the same topics used
in the first ('why are you asking who I am, from where I come from,
or what country I belong' in AB 102 becomes 'why didn't you ask me
from where I come . . . not even who I am, or from what family' in
AB 103, both in the second line of their respective poems)—so that
the second is a more or less symmetrically balanced, perfect reversal
of the first, an inverted variation on exactly the same theme. τρόποι,
we may conclude, are generic 'turns' or stereotyped 'adaptations' of
characterizable ways of speaking. Callimachus, famously, in *AP* 9.
507 = *Epigr.* 27. 1 Pf. = GP 56. 1 uses the term τρόποc to refer to
Hesiod's and Aratus' 'mode' or 'genre' of composition:

Ἡcιόδου τό τ' ἄειcμα καὶ ὁ τρόποc· οὐ τὸν ἀοιδῶν
ἔcχατον, ἀλλ' ὀκνέω μὴ τὸ μελιχρότατον
τῶν ἐπέων ὁ Cολεὺc ἀπεμάξατο· χαίρετε λεπταί
ῥήcιεc, Ἀρήτου cύμβολον ἀγρυπνίηc.

1 τό τ' Blomfield: τόδ' *AP*, *V. Arati* I 66 (Martin)   ἀοιδῶν Scaliger: ἀοιδόν *AP*, *V. Arati*
4 cύμβολον ἀγρυπνίηc Ruhnken whence Pfeiffer: cύντονος ἀγρυπνίη *AP*: cύγγονος ἀγρυπνίηc *V.*
Arati I 69 (Martin), Theon (= *V. Arati* III 35–6 Martin) whence cύγγονοι ἀγρυπνίηc Scaliger

113

It's Hesiod's music and it's Hesiod's genre:
Not the ultimate one that poets [or poems?] can have,
But I swear it: Aratus of Soli has certainly taken as a model
the best of his verses. We praise these terse, subtle tokens of long
effort at night.[33]

Referring to the genre and style of Aratus' poetry (rather than its contents), Callimachus makes Hesiod rather than Homer Aratus' model in order to align him with Alexandrian poetic fashion: small in scope, recherché in subject, refined in treatment.[34] Like the epigrams of Posidippus, they display genuine yet lightly worn learning. Callimachus' tribute to a contemporary here through these complimentary verses is nicely paralleled by a poem of Posidippus preserved on a Tebtunis papyrus long known (AB 117):

,] Μοῦcαι φίλαι, ἐcτὶ τὸ γράμμα
τ]ῶν ἐπέων cοφίηι
]ν ἄνδρα—καὶ ἔcτι [μ]οι ὥcπερ ἀδελφός
]ν κάλ' ἐπιcταμεν[.]ν.

Though woefully fragmentary, its affinity with the Callimachean poem (as well as e.g. Catullus 95) shines through like a beacon. Its missing parts are easily fathomed: the distichs praise the poetry of a friend (Austin suggests e.g. τοῦτ' Ἀcκληπιάδου,] in l. 1; in line 3 ἀνθ' ὧν, followed by Barigazzi's τόνδε, which is needed *metri gratia*). cοφίηι in 2 singles out the excellence of the poetry (ἐπέων). Mention of the Muses is not infrequent in Posidippus (also 63. 10, 114. 10, 118. 1, 137. 1, 140. 6).

Finally, I must mention one respect in which these poems are not subliterary or occasional—and that is in having a fixed paradosis. Many subliterary texts on papyrus, Lives of Aesop or dramatic hypotheses, for example, are characterized by having no fixed text: they tell the same story sometimes with identical phrasing in part, but no two of them are, or ever were, the same, but they have an

---

[33] Translation after S. Lombardo and D. Rayor, *Callimachus: Hymns, Epigrams, Select Fragments* (Baltimore, 1988) 60.

[34] A quotation of Callim. *Epigr.* 27 Pf. in a new Oxyrhynchus papyrus, P.Oxy. LXVIII 4648, on Aratus' use of Hesiod confirms the previously conjectural reading ἀοιδῶν in l. 1, although it does not preserve the beginning of the line. On Aratus' debt to Hesiod see R. Hunter, 'Written in the Stars', esp. 2–4; C. Fakas, *Der hellenistische Hesiod* (Wiesbaden, 2001); M. Fantuzzi and R. Hunter, *Muse e modelli* (Rome and Bari, 2002), ch. V. 6 '"Fenomeni" di Arato e la tradizione didascalica' pp. 302–22, 329–32. Cf. H. Reinsch-Werner, *Callimachus Hesiodicus* (Berlin, 1976); B. Meissner, *Die technologische Fachliteratur der Antike* (Berlin, 1999). Cameron's discussion of Callim. *Epigr.* 27 Pf. in *Callimachus and his Critics*, 374–6 queries whether ἔcχατον can mean 'ultimate' in a good sense, or whether there is any reference to scale of poems in the epigram.

ever-shifting textual basis. The poems of the Milan roll, however, do exhibit a concern for fixity in so far as the stichometric counts at the end of each section can only have functioned as a control in checking that the correct number of lines in each section had or would be copied, thus guarding against omission.[35] In addition, the text of the Milan roll itself demonstrates the existence of an already fixed paradosis: not only did a corrector (the second according to the original editors) add a variant in AB 73. 2 (BG XI 30, also again in the upper margin), but also he (or another corrector) filled in an entire line that the original scribe had left unwritten, AB 24. 4 (BG IV 27), presumably because his exemplar was deficient at this point. Both interferences with the text imply the collation from another, contemporaneously existing text available for comparison and not subject to an excessive degree of textual lability.

To conclude, the poems of the Milan roll show an affinity with occasional poetry not in terms of scribal production like the epigrams by Posidippus in P. Firmin–Didot (AB 115–16) discussed above (the roll is a professionally produced book), but in the content of some of its poems and in the selection and certain aspects of arrangement of its poems as measured against the later reception and transmission. These are poems which have become frozen on papyrus at an early stage of transmission (only two will surface in the later tradition), before the rigorous process of selection and arrangement to which the epigrams of Callimachus, Theocritus, Asclepiades, Meleager, Philodemus, Nicarchus, and others in the *Greek Anthology* were subjected. The implications of this 'cybernetics' of subliterary preservation and transmission helps account for the discrepancy perceived by some between the literary quality (or lack of it) and their ascription to a single epigrammatist of the stature (such as the stature of an epigrammatist was) of a Posidippus. The Greek poetry book can be seen *in statu nascendi*, at the transition from the composition of individual or at most paired poems to their gathering into collections by readers and editors.

---

[35] See Stephens and Obbink, 'The Manuscript'; cf. stichometric totals included in the entries of Callimachus' *Pinakes*—with the section-titles another facet in which the Milan roll exhibits the latest, state-of-the-art book-technology of the day.

PART TWO

A BOOK IN SECTIONS

7

The Politics and Poetics of Geography in the Milan Posidippus Section One: On Stones (AB 1–20)

PETER BING

At the start of his Sixth Olympian Ode, Pindar—comparing the construction of his song to that of a conspicuous palace whose portal is raised on golden columns—memorably states that 'when a work of poetry is begun we must make the entrance far-shining (l. 4 τηλαυγές)'. The new Posidippus papyrus was arranged in at least nine sections, each headed by a title. Of these nine, the first and longest with its 126 verses, was evidently on 'Stones'. Its fragmentary title may with some plausibility be restored as [λιθι]κά in light of the consistent subject-matter of its 21 epigrams.[1] That it was the first section of the roll seems likely. For although stichometric annotations appear in the margins at the end of each section to record its length, only in that on 'Stones' is there a further stichometric note at the bottom of the first column, strongly suggesting that it held a special place as the first of the roll.[2]

Further, as an opening to a poetic work, the section on Stones provides precisely that splendid introduction Pindar recommended. Indeed, that special brilliance embodied in Pindar's τηλαυγές insistently recurs in the terms Posidippus uses to describe the luminosity of his gemstones: αὐγή AB 8. 6, αὐγάζω 3. 1, διαυγές 16. 5, but also nouns like ϲέλας 6. 6 and φάη 7. 6, the verbs ϲτίλβω 11. 1, μαρμαίρω

[1] Diodorus Siculus cites Λιθικά as the title of a work by Orpheus (7. 1. 1), perhaps the same mentioned by the *Suda* (s.v. Orpheus) as being on eighty gemstones and their engraving. And indeed, such a work is extant: the Orphic Λιθικά, cf. R. Halleux and J. Schamp, *Les Lapidaires grecs* (Paris, 1985), and generally D. Plantzos, *Hellenistic Engraved Gems* (Oxford, 1999), 10.

[2] Cf. generally BG, p. 13. To be sure, the start of the papyrus was repaired with a new protokollon, leaving the chance that there were segments preceding what is now the first column (ϲελίϲ) of writing. Nonetheless it is likelier that the section on 'Stones' formed the original opening. Damage such as that repaired by the new protokollon is characteristic of the outermost, i.e. the opening part of the scroll, where the papyrus is most exposed to mishap, cf. E. G. Turner, *Greek Papyri* (Oxford, 1980), 5. W. A. Johnson is more sceptical that this formed the beginning of the roll, cf. this volume, Ch. 4.

6. 3, and ϲυλλάμπω 7. 6, adjectives such as πολιόϲ 16. 1, but above all terms evoking celestial phenomena such as ἀϲτερόειϲ 5. 1, ἀντιϲέληνοϲ 4. 3, ἥέλιοϲ 16. 6, ἠερόειϲ 14. 1, αἰθέριοϲ 14. 6, and ἀϲτράπτω 13. 4.

An eye-catching start. But to what end? In what follows I argue that the λιθικά draw our attention right from the first to fundamental themes which figure prominently elsewhere in the scroll, illuminating important aspects of both politics and poetics, and frequently tying them together. In particular, I hope to show how the stones exemplify in their geographical distribution and social construction both the territorial and cultural/artistic aims of the Ptolemies and of their poet, Posidippus.

To begin with poetics, many of the poems of this section linger on the artist's exquisite workmanship, and it is tempting to read them programmatically: as art contemplating art, they invite a self-reflexive interpretation likewise apt for the beginning of a work.[3] David Schur suggests that such an interpretation may extend even to the title, for inasmuch as epigram is by its origin and history inescapably linked with stone, the possibility that this opening section was called λιθικά—'things having to do with stones'—suggests a high degree of generic self-awareness.[4] Indeed, in this sense λιθικά could be taken as a title for the overall collection.

In any case, the concern with artistry seems to reflect a number of standard 'Alexandrian' preoccupations: it is linked here, for instance, to *diminutive* works in a *minor* artistic genre, *Kleinkunst* as the Germans call it. Though I shrink to mention it, the term λεπτή—'slender, delicate, refined'—appears in the very first poem (AB 1. 4). This, of course, was a crucial watchword of Hellenistic poetics, notably in the programmatic opening poem of Callimachus' *Aitia* with its 'slender' Muse (fr. 1. 24 Pf., cf. *AP* 9. 507 = *Epigr.* 27 Pf. = GP 56) and in Aratus' celebrated acrostic at *Phaenomena* 783–7; thereafter also in Augustan poetry.[5] A section leading off with gems provides an ideal platform to highlight this refined aesthetic, for again and again Posidippus calls attention to the delicacy of the engraver's art. Delicacy of this sort is, moreover, a result of τέχνη and μόχθοϲ. In one of the two previously known epigrams, the speaker claims that the engraved chariot on a snakestone must have been carved with

[3] One thinks, for instance, of Theocritus 1 or the prologue to Callimachus' *Aitia*.

[4] Cf. D. Schur, 'A Garland of Stones', 120.

[5] For the term and its impact in Roman poetry, cf. e.g. N. Hopkinson, *A Hellenistic Anthology* (Cambridge, 1988), 90, 98–101. We will see that Posidippus uses metapoetic water imagery in ways similar to Callimachus (below, at n. 17). Further, the similarities between the 'seal-poem' on his old age (*SH* 705 = AB 118) and the prologue to Callimachus' *Aitia* have long been noted.

the superhuman vision of a Lynceus (τοῦθ᾽ ὑπὸ Λυγκείου βλέμματος ἐγλύφετο AB 15. 4 = *AP* 16. 119. 4 = GP 20. 4), finding it a marvel that such 'toil' (μόχθος) did not hurt (cognate ἐμόγησε) the artist's eyes (Ἦ καὶ θαῦμα πέλει μόχθου μέγα, πῶς ὁ λιθουργός | τὰς ἀτενιζούσας οὐκ ἐμόγησε κόρας 15. 7–8).[6] Yet other epigrams in the section suggest that tiny works like these—though marginal—are prized by connoisseurs, particularly royalty: A sadly fragmentary poem (AB 9) evokes the famous seal-ring of Polycrates, which in Herodotus (3. 41) was the Samian tyrant's most treasured possession. The epigram introduces a significant innovation vis-à-vis Herodotus in that it has Polycrates take as his emblem on the seal 'the lyre of a singer-man, strumming his song at your feet' (ἀνδρὸς ἀοιδοῦ | τοῦ φο]ρμίζ[οντος coῖc] παρὰ π[occ]ὶ λύρην AB 9. 1–2). This most likely refers to Anacreon, whom Herodotus describes as present in Polycrates' banqueting hall (3. 121). Thus Posidippus brings us back to the contemplation of poetry. Indeed, inasmuch as this tiny seal (cφρηγ[ῖδα 9. 1) is embodied in the comparably brief compass of his epigram, he suggests that the one art form can stand for the other. In so doing, he indirectly presents us with a sphragis of his own, bearing the stamp and conveying to us the impression of an important poetic forerunner.

But more than possibly delineating programmatic parameters, the section on Stones explores and maps out a political landscape reflecting certain aspirations of sovereignty which set the tone for the whole work (i.e. it outlines the 'world' we are dealing with).[7] In this regard, we do well to recall the long section in Theocritus' *Idyll* 17. 86–92, the *Encomium to Ptolemy*, which recounts the lands Ptolemy Philadelphus counted as his own in addition to Egypt:

καὶ μὴν Φοινίκας ἀποτέμνεται Ἀρραβίας τε   86
καὶ Cυρίας Λιβύας τε κελαινῶν τ᾽ Αἰθιοπήων·
Παμφύλοιcί τε πᾶcι καὶ αἰχμηταῖς Κιλίκεccι
cαμαίνει, Λυκίοις τε φιλοπτολέμοιcί τε Καρcί
καὶ νάcοιc Κυκλάδεccιν, ἐπεί οἱ νᾶες ἄρicται   90
πόντον ἐπιπλώοντι, θάλαccα δὲ πᾶcα καὶ αἶα
καὶ ποταμοὶ κελάδοντες ἀνάccονται Πτολεμαίωι.

And he cuts off for himself part of Phoenicia and of Arabia
and of Syria and Libya and of the black Ethiopians.
And he holds sway over all the Pamphylians and Cilician spearmen,
and over the Lycians and war-loving Carians

---

[6] For the emphasis on τέχνη in Hellenistic poetics, cf. Callimachus *Aitia* 1.17–18. For 'toil' as part of the poet's self-image, cf. the παίγνιον of Philitas (fr, 10, p. 92 Powell = fr. 12 Sbardella, with commentary). Posidippus (*AP* 12. 98 = GP 6 = AB 137) describes his ψυχή as ἐν βύβλοις πεπονημένη (l. 3).

[7] Susan Stephens thinks in similar terms in 'For You, Arsinoe', 170–1.

and over the Cycladic isles, for his ships are the best
that sail the sea, *indeed all the sea and all the earth,
and the thundering rivers are ruled by Ptolemy.*

As Gow comments (on l. 92) 'the hyperbole in Theocritus is remark-
able'. But Callimachus is no less hyperbolic when he speaks in his
fourth hymn (ll. 166–70) of that same sovereign, 'beneath whose
crown shall come—not unwilling to be ruled by a Macedonian—both
continents and the lands that are set in the sea, as far as where the ends
of the earth are and the source from whence the swift horses of Helios
carry him' (ὧι ὑπὸ μίτρην | ἵξεται οὐκ ἀέκουca Μακηδόνι κοιρανέεcθαι |
ἀμφοτέρη μεcόγεια καὶ αἳ πελάγεccι κάθηνται, | μέχρις ὅπου περάτη τε καὶ
ὁππόθεν ὠκέες ἵπποι | Ἠέλιον φορέουcιν).[8]

The first words of the first poem in Posidippus' section on Stones
are Ἰνδὸc Ὑδάcπηc, the 'Indian river Hydaspes' (AB 1. 1)—the source,
it appears, of the gem that formed the subject of the poem. This river
was essentially the furthest limit of Alexander's conquests in the East.
The section ends with a poem about a massive boulder in Euboea, in
the traditional Greek motherland, and closes with a prayer on behalf
of Ptolemy: 'But now, Geraestian lord (Poseidon), along with the
islands of Ptolemy preserve his land unshaken and also his shores'
(νῦν δέ, Γεραίcτι' ἄναξ, νήcων μέτα τὴν Πτολεμαίου | γαῖαν ἀκινήτην
⟨ἴ⟩cχε καὶ αἰγιαλούc 20. 5–6). This closing prayer, suitably open-ended
in its definition of Ptolemaic boundaries, retrospectively colours our
understanding of the geographic parameters within which the sec-
tion unfolds, setting it all in a Ptolemaic perspective:[9] the range of

---

[8] Cf. R. Hunter, *Theocritus: Encomium of Ptolemy Philadelphus* (Berkeley, 2003) on ll. 86–92
on both these passages as reflecting conventions of the 'oriental rhetoric of kingship' (168) and,
in particular, of Alexander as a model.

[9] Lest we miss how the reader retroactively acquires a Ptolemaic orientation, the first two
poems of the following section—the οἰωνοcκοπικά—reinforce the shift by turning our atten-
tion toward Egypt. The section is launched with an epigram about launching a ship (AB 21),
beginning and ending with the words νηΐ καθελκομένηι (for similarly artful equivalence between
beginnings and ends of a journey and of a poem cf. D. Wray, 'Apollonius' Masterplot', 241–
5). It is followed by one in which the speaker presents himself as a traveller heading toward
Egypt: 'For us who are about to seek out the Egyptian sea, may the Thracian crane be our
guide along the forestays' (ἡμῖν δ' Αἰγύπτου πέλαγος μέλλουcι διώκειν | Θρῆιccα κατὰ προτόνων
ἡγεμονέοι γέρανος AB 22. 3–4). διώκειν suggests that the speaker is far from Egypt and that
the Αἰγύπτου πέλαγος is his goal (cf. LSJ s.v. διώκω I 2). In all likelihood his journey is from
Europe (Macedonia?) to Egypt since, as R. Kannicht observes on Eur. *Hel.* 1478–94, the crane
is known above all as an intercontinental traveller, and it is only his migratory flight in autumn
from north to south that appears in literature: 'der notorische Kranichzug [ist] immer nur
der des Herbstes, weil eben nur der Herbstzug beobachtet werden kann; denn nur im Herbst
lassen sich die Kraniche sozusagen Zeit, fallen hier und da in die Länder, die auf ihrer Route
liegen, ein, rasten, und fliegen cτολάδες weiter. Deshalb ist in den literarischen Zeugnissen fast
ausnahmslos der herbstliche Nord-Süd-Zug gemeint. . . . Der Rückflug im Frühjahr bleibt
dagegen in der Regel unbemerkt, weil die Kraniche dann ohne Verzug und in sehr großer

lands available to the Ptolemies as a source of wealth corresponds to no less than the empire won by Alexander. In addition to India, which was famously rich in gems[10] (cf. also 2. 4, 8. 5), the stones in these epigrams derive notably from Persia (4.5, 5. 2, 11. 2, 13. 3), Arabia (7. 1, 16. 1), Lydia (8. 1), Mysia (17. 1), Samos (9. 1), and the depths of the sea (11. 1, 12. 1). As Theocritus says in *Idyll* 17, 'In wealth Ptolemy could outweigh all other kings, so much comes each day to his sumptuous house *from everywhere* (Ὄλβωι μὲν πάντας κε καταβρίθοι βασιλῆας· | τόccον ἐπ' ἦμαρ ἔκαcτον ἐc ἀφνεὸν ἔρχεται οἶκον | πάντοθε 17. 95–7).[11]

The evocation of Alexander's empire in the geographic distribution of stones in the λιθικά finds confirmation in a little-noted passage from Theophrastus' *Characters*. There, in describing the *alazon*, 'the idle boaster', Theophrastus tells how this character is apt to claim that he was on close terms with Alexander the Great himself on his Eastern campaigns (23. 1–3):

ὁ δὲ ἀλαζὼν τοιοῦτός τιc, οἷοc . . . καὶ cυνοδοιπόρου δὲ ἀπολαῦcαι ἐν τῆι ὁδῶι δεινὸc λέγων, ὡc μετ' Ἀλεξάνδρου ἐcτρατεύcατο, καὶ ὡc αὐτῶι εἶχε, καὶ ὅcα λιθο-κόλλητα ποτήρια ἐκόμιcε· καὶ περὶ τῶν τεχνιτῶν τῶν ἐν τῆι Ἀcίαι, ὅτι βελτίουc εἰcὶ τῶν ἐν τῆι Εὐρώπηι, ἀμφιcβητῆcαι· καὶ ταῦτα ψοφῆcαι, οὐδαμοῦ ἐκ τῆc πόλεωc ἀποδεδημηκώc.

The *alazon* is the sort who . . . on a journey is apt to put one over on a travel companion by relating how he campaigned with Alexander, and how Alexander felt about him, and how many gem-studded goblets he brought back as booty, and arguing that the craftsmen in Asia are better than those in Europe (he says all this even though he's never been out of town). (After J. Rusten, *Theophrastus: Characters*)

Wonderful how Theophrastus here slyly suggests that the journey and companionship of the road prompt the *alazon* to 'recall' his imagined journeys and friendship with Alexander—only to divulge in the end that the present journey is strictly parochial: The boaster has never in his life strayed beyond the narrow limits of the *polis*! What is most interesting in this passage for our purposes, however,

Höhe direkt ihre nördlichen Brutgegenden anfliegen' (p. 388). For the transitional function of the first two poems of the οἰωνοcκοπικά, cf. further D. Petrain, 'Homer, Theocritus and the Milan Posidippus', 381; Stephens, Ch. 12.

[10] Plantzos, *Hellenistic Engraved Gems*, 106.

[11] M.-D. Nenna describes Ptolemaic interest in gems from the Arabian desert as follows: 'Une des premières décisions des Ptolémées fut de réorganiser l'exploitation des carrières du désert arabique. Cette industrie minière, fondée sur la recherche des émeraudes, topazes ou de pierres semi-précieuses . . . était soigneusement surveillée par les collecteurs et les convoyeurs de pierreries appointés par le souverain': 'Gemmes et pierres dans le mobilier alexandrin', 156.

is what this provincial *alazon* associates with those campaigns: 'gem-studded goblets' and superb craftsmen. The passage is revealing in a number of ways. First of all it suggests that the topic of rare gems and their artistic use was easily linked in the public mind with Alexander. Secondly it shows how the Macedonian's conquests were viewed as having made accessible the great mineral wealth of the East (that is what Alexander's 'comrades in arms' would have brought back from their campaigns as booty: ὅϲα . . . ἐκόμιϲε, *LSJ* s.v. κομίζω II 2). Finally it reveals that people from all strata of society—not just the ruling classes—were aware of these precious objects, knew of their exotic provenance, and had some appreciation for the artistry involved in turning them into jewels: travelling-companions might idly chat about them to pass the time on a journey, and debate the relative merits of Asian and European craftsmen. That broad awareness, together with the association of gemstones with Alexander, would make λιθικά a politically charged topic and an appealing vehicle for promoting Ptolemaic aspirations.

Those aspirations were not restricted to the Ptolemies, however; they could extend as well to those in their employ: it is striking that the territorial aims of the Ptolemies on view in these poems match those of Posidippus himself. For the poet sets similar parameters to his own fame in his 'Seal-poem', the elegy in which he considers his legacy from the perspective of old age (*SH* 705 = AB 118). There, he asks Apollo to give an oracle 'so that the Macedonians may do me honour, both those on the islands and the dwellers near the coast of all Asia' (ll. 14–15 ὄφρα με τιμήϲω[ϲι] Μακηδόνεϲ οἵ τ᾽ ἐπὶ ν[ήϲων | οἵ τ᾽ Ἀϲίηϲ πάϲηϲ γ⟨ε⟩ίτονεϲ ἠιόνοϲ). In particular, the phrase 'all Asia' (Ἀϲίηϲ πάϲηϲ) invites readers to think of this continent in the most expansive terms, as for example in Herodotus (4. 36–41, cf. 2. 16) where Asia extends from the Hellespont all the way to India.[12] In this way, the lines attest to the radical expansion of Macedonian power in the aftermath of Alexander's conquests, notwithstanding its humble beginnings,[13] for here again we are dealing with territory that

---

[12] This rather than the more limited sense noted by Dodds for Ἀϲίαν τε πᾶϲαν at Eur. *Ba.* 17, where it is used 'in the restricted sense of western Asia Minor, as the context shows'. Posidippus' reference to 'the dwellers near the coast of all Asia' accords with the idea in Herodotus that Asia is largely defined and bounded by its coasts (4. 44).

[13] This contrast is stressed by Polybius (1. 2. 2): 'The Macedonians ruled Europe from the regions along the Adriatic sea to the Danube river, which seems an altogether small part of the above-mentioned land. Later, by overthrowing the Persian dynasty, they added sovereignty over Asia' (Μακεδόνεϲ τῆϲ μὲν Εὐρώπηϲ ἦρξαν ἀπὸ τῶν κατὰ τὸν Ἀδρίαν τόπων ἕωϲ ἐπὶ τὸν Ἴϲτρον ποταμόν, ὃ βραχὺ παντελῶϲ ἂν φανείη μέροϲ τῆϲ προειρημένηϲ χώραϲ· μετὰ δὲ ταῦτα προϲέλαβον τὴν τῆϲ Ἀϲίαϲ ἀρχήν, καταλύϲαντεϲ τὴν τῶν Περϲῶν δυναϲτείαν).

may be considered coextensive with Alexander's dominions. Now the Ptolemies were eager to present themselves as 'Macedonians', as the Milan papyrus repeatedly demonstrates (AB 78. 32–3, 82. 3, 87. 2, 88. 4, with Paus. 6. 3. 1, 10. 7. 3, and Callimachus *H.* 4. 166–70, cited above),[14] and so was Posidippus, one of the principal poets who served them: 'My family is from Pella,' he declares in the very next line (Πελλαῖον γένος ἁμόν *SH* 705. 17 = AB 118. 17), thus identifying himself with his public and also justifying his expectation of honour from them. We may thus see Posidippus' hopes for recognition from the Macedonians as being bounded only by the limits of Ptolemaic territorial ambition. Here, then, political and poetic aspiration coincide, and the geographic breadth of opportunity available to the poet expands with that of his patrons.[15]

Within these geographic parameters the details of the journey from physical source to cultural application are a persistent theme of the λιθικά—i.e. the passage from earth, sea, or shore, to the artisan who shapes the natural object and through his representational skills makes it signify; how, further, it may be bound in a frame as a jewel, and finally take its place in a social setting, on a person's finger, neck, breast or furniture. To illustrate let me cite just one poem, AB 7 (with the admittedly uncertain, but plausible supplements of Bastianini and Gallazzi):

ἐξ Ἀράβων τὰ ξάνθ' ὁ[ρέων κατέρ]υτα κυλίων,
  εἰς ἅλα χειμάρρους ὡκ' [ἐφόρει ποταμός
τὸν μέλιτι χροιὴν λίθ[ον εἴκελον, ὃ]ν Κρονίο[υ] χείρ
  ἔγλυψε· χρυσῶι σφι⟨γ⟩κτ[ὸς ὅδε γλυκερ]ῆι
Νικονόηι κάθεμα τρη[τὸν φλέγει, ὡ]ς ἐπὶ μαστῶι
  συ⟨λ⟩λάμπει λευκῶι χρωτὶ μελιχρὰ φάη.

Rolling the yellow debris from the Arabian mountains,
  the storm-swollen river carries swiftly to the sea
this honey-coloured stone, which the hand of Cronius
  carved. Bound fast with gold for sweet
Niconoe it blazes as a necklace chain, so that on her breast
  its honeyed radiance gleams together with her fair skin.

The poem starts with a detailed echo of a Homeric simile at *Il.* 13. 137–43 in which Hector, in his assault on the Achaean ships, is likened

[14] Cf. M. Fantuzzi, below, pp. 250–2.

[15] It is worth considering, as Kathryn Gutzwiller suggests to me in conversation (and see below, Ch. 15), whether this poem may have been placed as the closing piece in the missing final part of the Milan papyrus. Certainly there it would have stood in appropriate balance to the geopoetic concerns of the opening section in the λιθικά. For the relationship of Posidippus' seal to the biographical literature of the time, cf. P. Bing, 'The *Bios* and Poets' Lives'.

Peter Bing

to a great stone pried lose from its rock by a winter storm, and carried
irresistibly down into the plain, but then coming powerless to a halt:

>   . . . ὀλοοίτροχος ὡς ἀπὸ πέτρης,
> ὅν τε κατὰ στεφάνης ποταμὸς χειμάρροος ὤσηι
> ῥήξας ἀσπέτωι ὄμβρωι ἀναιδέος ἔχματα πέτρης·
> ὕψι δ᾽ ἀναθρώισκων πέτεται, κτυπέει δέ θ᾽ ὑπ᾽ αὐτοῦ   140
> ὕλη· ὃ δ᾽ ἀσφαλέως θέει ἔμπεδον, εἷος ἵκηται
> ἰσόπεδον, τότε δ᾽ οὔ τι κυλίνδεται ἐσσύμενός περ·
> ὡς Ἕκτωρ εἷος μὲν ἀπείλει μέχρι θαλάσσης . . .

>   . . . like a great rolling stone from a rock face
> that a river swollen with winter rain has wrenched from its socket
> and with immense washing broken the hold of the unwilling rock face;
> the springing boulder flies on, and the forest thunders beneath it;
> and the stone runs unwavering on a strong course, till it reaches
> the flat land, then rolls no longer for all its onrush;
> so Hector for a while threatened as far as the sea . . .

Posidippus varies the source of stone from the *Iliad*'s rocky height
(l. 138 στεφάνης) to Arabian mountains; for Homer's κυλίνδεται (l. 142)
he substitutes the more modern form κυλίων (7. 1); he apparently
reverses the Homeric ποταμὸς χειμάρροος (l. 138) with χειμάρρους . . .
ποταμός (7. 2); and he transposes Homer's mention of the sea as stopping
point (l. 143 μέχρι θαλάσσης) from the framing narrative about Hector
into his account of the stone (7. 2 εἰς ἅλα). If we follow the reconstruc-
tion of the editors, the yellow debris reveals a honey-coloured stone,
which the skilful hand of an artist like Cronius—mentioned by Pliny
as being second in fame after Alexander's personal gem-engraver,
Pyrgoteles (*NH* 37. 8)—transforms into a jewel. Shaped thus, and
translated to another kind of hill (ἐπὶ μαστῶι 7. 5),[16] it can match the
radiance of human beauty in the lovely Niconoe. While discarding
the overt *form* of the Homeric simile, the poet recalls its *function* by
subtly comparing and equating (cυ⟨λ⟩λάμπει 7. 6) the stone's honeyed
colour (τὸν μέλιτι χροιὴν λίθ[ον εἴκελον 7. 3, μελιχρὰ φάη 7. 6) to the
fairness of the woman's skin (λευκῶι χρωτὶ 7. 6), and perhaps also to
her sweetness, if we accept the thrust of the supplement γλυκερ]ῆι (7.
4). But unlike Hector, whose onslaught—like the boulder's—finally
grinds to an impotent halt, Niconoe's power is undimmed, for the
meaning of her name implies that the possessor of such a beautiful
gem has been and will be 'triumphant in her plans', whatever those
may be. In that light, the costly journey from exotic source, through
the artist's transforming hand and into the possession of a Greek

---

[16] For this double meaning of μαστός, cf. Pi. *P.* 4. 8, Callim. *H.* 4. 48 with Mineur's note.

owner, proves worthwhile indeed—a potent figure for the exploitation and mastery of the earth in an implicitly Ptolemaic context.

At the same time, from a poetological standpoint, the Homeric simile of the massive stone thundering down the mountain is an apt image of the epic hero. The development of that simile, then, by Posidippus—which focuses on the fine gem extracted from what's swept down by the torrent and how it is artfully cut into a jewel—may stand as an allegory of the Hellenistic poet's reception and transformation of Homeric raw material to new ends.[17] Such a poetological subtext will hardly surprise in a section dealing so insistently with 'sources'.

Without a doubt, it is in the λιθικά that the politics and poetics of geography (as I call it in my title) intersect most prominently. Yet this section represents only a particularly rich lode in a vein that ramifies throughout the scroll. One could, for instance, productively mine poems of the ἀνδριαντοποιικά or of the ἱππικά for the convergence of geopolitics and geopoetics. One exemplary instance, however, AB 37, from a different section—that on dedications, the ἀναθεματικά—will suffice to suggest the ongoing importance of this theme, and sensitize us to be on the lookout for its possible presence elsewhere. Let us set aside our gemstones for a moment, then, to explore it; we will return to them shortly. As in the poem on the seal-ring of Polycrates, this one concerns a lyre, and as in many of the λιθικά it charts an object's route from exotic source into a new Ptolemaic context:[18]

> Ἀρσινόη, coὶ τή[v]δε λύρην ὑπὸ χειρ[ὸc ἀοιδο]ῦ
> φθεγξαμ[ένην] δελφὶc ἤγαγ' Ἀριόνιο[c
> ου__ελου[__]αc ἐκ κύματοc ἀλλ' οτ[
> κεῖνοc ἀν[__]c λευκὰ περᾶι πελά[γη
> πολλαπο[__]__τητι καὶ αἰόλα τῆι__[5
> φωνῆι π[__]ακον κανον ἀηδου[
> ἄνθεμα δ', [ὦ Φιλ]άδελφε, τὸν ἤλαcεν [__Ἀρ]ίων,
> τόνδε δέ[χου,]υcου μ⟨ε⟩ίλια ναοπόλο[υ.

3 οὐρῆι BG : ἔλ' οὐ [βλάψ]αc ex. gr. Austin : cώc]αc, κέλc]αc, ἐρύc]αc vel sim. BG   ἄλλοτ[ε δ' οὔτω Lapini : ἄλλοτ[ε δ' ἄλληι Bettarini 4 ἀν[ωίcτω]c ex. gr. Austin : ἀν[ἠρ cὤο]c Lapini : ἀν[ίδρυτο]c Bettarini   5 πο[εῖ φιλ]ότητι καὶ αἰόλα ex. gr. Austin : τε[ηι θε]ότητι Luppe : πο[ῶν φιλ]ότητι Bettarini   6 π[ῆμ' ἔλ]ακον κα(ι)νὸν ἀηδου[ίδεc ex. gr. Austin : π[ῆγμ' ἔλ]ακον Bettarini : π[λοῦν ἔλ]ακον Bing   7 [οἶμον Ἀρ]ίων Austin : [εἰκόν'__]ίων Luppe

---

[17] In its programmatic *Bildersprache* it resembles Callimachus' *Hymn to Apollo* (ll. 108–112) with its opposed images of the 'masses of waste and refuse that the great stream of the Assyrian river sweeps along', and 'the trickling drops from the pure and unpolluted spring'. For Posidippus, however, the debris-carrying torrent is itself the ultimate source of the gem. For another Iliadic simile about surging water (11. 492–7) and its impact as a stylistic metaphor in Hellenistic and Roman poetry, as well as in rhetoric, cf. the illuminating discussion of

[*See p. 128 for n. 17 cont. and n. 18*]

Arsinoe, Arion's dolphin brought you this lyre
    which once resounded at the touch [of a singer]
. . . from the wave. But when.[
    that one . . . crossed the foaming sea
many things . . . and various with [
    his voice . . .
But this offering, O Philadelphus, which Arion played
    please accept it, a dedication of . . . your temple custodian.

This poem records the dedication to Arsinoe Philadelphus by her temple-keeper (ναοπόλος) of a lyre brought ashore by 'Arion's dolphin' (δελφὶς . . . Ἀριόνιο[ς).[19] It seems plausible to infer from the text that this sea-borne offering was made in—perhaps even found near—the temple of Arsinoe-Aphrodite Zephyritis, the celebrated foundation of the Ptolemaic admiral, Callicrates of Samos, which (as Posidippus put it in the epigram from the Didot papyrus, GP 12 = AB 116. 2–3) occupied 'the windy headland among the encircling waves' (ll. 2–3 ἐν περιφαινομένωι κύματι χῶρον ἔχω | . . . ἀνεμώδεα χηλήν).[20] If this is correct, then the poem represents a striking example of how an object, the lyre, may be made to embody the cultural/historical herit-

Hunter, 'Reflecting on Writing and Culture', 219–23. Concerning Homeric allusion elsewhere in the Milan papyrus, cf. Petrain, 'Homer, Theocritus and the Milan Posidippus', and Hunter, 'Notes on the *Lithika* of Posidippus'.

[18] I repeat here my discussion of this poem in 'Posidippus and the Admiral', 260–5.

[19] Contrary to my discussion cited in n. 18, I now hesitantly follow BG, who suggest that the masculine pronouns of ll. 7 and 8 refer to a synonym of the lyre lost in the lacuna at the end of l. 7—though it must be admitted that no plausible candidate has been found till now. Alternatively, Austin proposes that the pronouns refer to a word such as οἶμον, and that the epigram thus represents itself as a 'song' of Arion. More speculatively, L. Bettarini goes beyond Austin, proposing that the missing word is ὕμνον. This would refer to a separate hymn, perhaps by 'Arion', dedicated with the lyre, and possibly inscribed in the temple as well (cf. his n. 81). That hymn would be comparable to, or even a version of that at *PMG* 939, which Aelian (*NA* 12. 45) says Arion composed to thank Poseidon for his rescue by the dolphin. In the context of Ptolemaic Egypt, the maritime deity now honored is Arsinoe-Aphrodite Zephyritis rather than Poseidon. This latter point is also eloquently argued by M. Fantuzzi, 'Sugli Epp. 37 e 74 Austin-Bastianini', 31–3.

Different reconstructions of the closing lines, and other parts of the poem, have been suggested by Lapini, 'Note posidippee', esp. 39–42 and Luppe, 'Ein Weih-Epigramm Poseidipps auf Arsinoe'. Lapini thinks the object dedicated was a statue of the dolphin-riding poet Arion with his lyre (like that at Cape Taenarum commemorating Arion's landing there, Herodotus 1. 24). Thus he suggests the supplement τὸν ἤλασεν [ἰχθὺν Ἀρ]ίων, with the verb used in the sense of 'forged'. This, however, does not explain why the lyre alone (τή[ν]δε λύρην l. 1) is highlighted with deixis as the dedication at the start of the poem. More plausibly Luppe proposes that the dedication was a sculpture of the lyre, hence [εἰκόν(α), while the end of the lacuna]ίων conceals the artist's name. On this view, however, there remains a worrying disjunction between the lyre itself, 'which Arion's dolphin brought to you, Arsinoe', and its presumed sculptural representation dedicated in the temple: or does Luppe mean that the dolphin brought the *statue* ashore (inscribed with the artist's name)?

[20] The identification of the site is also made by BG in their introduction to VI 18–25, though their characterization of the shrine as the 'tempio di Arsinoe a Canopo' is misleading.

age, and become (quite literally) the vehicle by which that heritage is transmitted to a new place. For the epigram clearly alludes to the legend of Arion as told by Herodotus (1. 24). In that account, upon being threatened with robbery and death by the crew of the ship on which he was sailing, Arion —'the best singer in the world'—leaped into the sea in full citharodic regalia. He was saved, however, through the miraculous intervention of a dolphin—the most musical of creatures—who caught him up and carried him safely ashore at Cape Taenarum. There, a statue of a man riding a dolphin was dedicated in a temple of Poseidon to commemorate the singer's deliverance. Clearly Posidippus' poem evokes not just the story of the rescue, but also the subsequent dedication—both of them made at a coastal shrine on a rugged cape. By describing how this lyre—together with the tradition it evokes—came to Egypt, the poet links the third-century-BC shrine of Arsinoe to one of the great figures of archaic poetry from the seventh century, and with him to the rich tradition of Lesbian lyric including Terpander, Sappho, and Alcaeus.

But a further, less obvious model may be floating just below the surface here as well. For the story of the lyre's wondrous appearance on Egyptian shores may be intended to recall and provide a modern counterpart to a well-known Lesbian tale linked with Methymna, likewise about a wondrous poetic windfall—the story of Orpheus' lyre which, after the legendary singer had been torn apart by the Thracian maenads, floated across the sea together with his severed head until running aground, as Ovid put it, 'on Methymnaean Lesbos' shore' (*et Methymnaeae potiuntur litore Lesbi*, Met. 11. 55).[21] This tale is memorably recounted in an elegy of Phanocles, plausibly of early Hellenistic date (fr. 1 Powell, pp. 106–7):

Τοῦ δ' ἀπὸ μὲν κεφαλὴν χαλκῶι τάμον, αὐτίκα δ' αὐτὴν
  εἰς ἅλα Θρηϊκίηι ῥῖψαν ὁμοῦ χέλυϊ
ἥλωι καρτύνασαι, ἵν' ἐμφορέοιντο θαλάσσηι
  ἄμφω ἅμα, γλαυκοῖς τεγγόμεναι ῥοθίοις.
Τὰς δ' ἱερῆι Λέσβωι πολιὴ ἐπέκελσε θάλασσα·   15
  ἠχὴ δ' ὡς λιγυρῆς πόντον ἐπέσχε λύρης,
νήσους τ' αἰγιαλούς θ' ἁλιμυρέας, ἔνθα λίγειαν
  ἀνέρες Ὀρφείην ἐκτέρισαν κεφαλήν,
ἐν δὲ χέλυν τύμβωι λιγυρὴν θέσαν, ἣ καὶ ἀναύδους
  πέτρας καὶ Φόρκου στυγνὸν ἔπειθεν ὕδωρ.   20
Ἐκ κείνου μολπαί τε καὶ ἱμερτὴ κιθαριστὺς
  νῆσον ἔχει, πασέων δ' ἐστὶν ἀοιδοτάτη.

---

[21] Lucian, *Adv. indoct.* 11 retells it at length, calling it a Λέσβιος μῦθος. Cf. W. Burkert, *Homo Necans* (Berkeley, 1983), 202 with nn. 30 and 33.

They cut off his head with a sword of bronze, and threw it at once
   in the sea along with the Thracian lyre
binding them strongly with a nail, so they would both be carried
   on the sea together, soaked by the billowing surf.
And the foaming sea drove them to sacred Lesbos.
   And when the clear echo of the lyre spread across the sea
and over the islands and sea-beaten shores, thereupon men
   interred the clear-sounding Orphic head
and set in the tomb the bright-ringing lyre, which used to persuade
   even mute stones and the hateful water of Phorkos.
From that time forth, songs and lovely cithara music
   have occupied the island, the most musical of them all.

In effect this tradition about the lyre of Orpheus constitutes an *aition* of the poetry of Lesbos, lending the authority of one of poetry's founding fathers to that island's status as a great repository and source of song. Transmission and preservation of the lyre here function virtually as a charter. Inasmuch as this early Hellenistic text invests the geographic transfer of this instrument with such poetological significance, I think it plausible to take the tale in Posidippus' epigram in a similar way—that is, to see it as emblematic of the Ptolemies' claim to be the true inheritors and guardians of the literary legacy of Hellas, in particular here the great tradition of Lesbian song. The Lesbian lyre has been passed on; today its home is Egypt.[22]

At the same time, our epigram on the dolphin and the lyre may point to important *political* ties in the mid-third century BC between Egypt and Arion's native Methymna on Lesbos. That city came to serve as an important strategic base for Ptolemaic interests in the northern Aegean, and its third-century coinage included the image of the citharodic dolphin-rider as its emblem.[23] The extent of Egypt's influence here is plain in epigraphic sources, which attest, for instance, to a priest of the divinized Ptolemy there between 267 and 260 (*IG* xii Suppl. 115), worship of Arsinoe Philadelphus (*CIG* ii Add. no. 2168, *IG* xii/2. 513), regular celebrations of the Ptolemaia on the model of those in Alexandria (*IG* xii Suppl. 115, cf. also at Eresos *IG* xii/2. 527

[22] In this sense, the poem serves a function comparable to that of the epigram about the seal-ring of Polycrates, with its image of the lyre, for by setting that lyre-bearing gem in the context of his λιθικά, with its pointedly Ptolemaic orientation, Posidippus similarly linked his monarchs with a grand figure of the lyric heritage, in that case Anacreon, as well as with Polycrates as an important Archaic model of artistic patronage.

[23] Cf. W. Wroth, *Catalogue of the Greek Coins in the British Museum*, xvii: *Troas, Aeolis, and Lesbos* (London, 1894), 179 no. 16 (note also the lyre and dolphin on no. 14), 180 no. 27, 181 no. 35. Cf. also H. G. Buchholz, *Methymna* (Mainz, 1975), pl. 12. The lyre alone appears already on Methymnaean coins of the late 5th and 4th cc., but this is an emblem which it shares with the coins of its rival Mytilene.

and Suppl., p. 33) and perhaps a month named Ptolemaion (*IG* xii
Suppl. 115).[24] Hence a poem commemorating Egypt's acquisition of
the lyre through the miraculous agency of 'Arion's' dolphin would
certainly have conveyed a potent political message at just the time
when Methymna had become a vital part of the Ptolemies' maritime
empire.[25] As in the λιθικά, then, we see how a precious object embody-
ing Egypt's geopolitical/poetic ambitions enters the eager, inclusive
embrace of Ptolemaic power.[26]

The flip-side of this ambition—i.e. to make Egypt also a source
disseminating that poetic heritage to the world—is apparent else-
where in Posidippus, namely in his epitaph for Doricha, a hetaira
of Naucratis in Egypt, famous as the mistress of Sappho's brother
Charaxus (Ath. 13. 596 c = GP 17 = AB 122).[27] In commenting on
the enduring power of Sappho's verse, Posidippus here significantly
links it with its written medium: 'The bright resounding papyrus-
columns of Sappho's | dear song abide, and will yet abide' (ll. 5–6

<hr>

[24] See generally P. Brun, 'Les Lagides à Lesbos' and G. Labarre, *Les Cités de Lesbos aux
époques hellénistique et impériale* (Lyon, 1996), 54–6, who doubts Brun's dating of the priest-
hood for the divinized Ptolemy, placing it rather—as originally proposed by C. Habicht,
Gottmenschentum und die griechischen Städte (Munich, 1970), 109 and R. S. Bagnall, *The
Administration of the Ptolemaic Possessions outside Egypt* (Leiden, 1976), 162—in the reign of
Philopator. The month name Ptolemaion is plausibly conjectured in the *IG*, cf. Buchholz,
Methymna, 230; C. Trümpy, *Untersuchungen zu den altgriechischen Monatsnamen und Monats-
folgen* (Heidelberg, 1997), 247.

[25] i.e. most likely in the 260s, since the cult of Arsinoe-Aphrodite Zephyritis was established
either shortly before or after the death of the queen, generally dated to 270 BC. Recent investi-
gations, however, plausibly date it down to 268, cf. E. Grzybek, *Du calendrier macédonien au
calendrier ptolémaïque* (Basel, 1990), 103–12, R. A. Hazzard, 'The Regnal Years of Ptolemy II
Philadelphos'; id., *Imagination of a Monarchy* (Toronto, 2000), 3, etc. See the discussion of
their findings in H. Hauben, 'La chronologie macédonienne et ptolémaïque mise à l'épreuve',
esp. 160 ff. For Callicrates' foundation of the cult of Aphrodite-Arsinoe Zephyritis to mark the
deified queen's special patronage of the Ptolemaic navy cf. L. Robert, 'Sur un décret d'Ilion',
201–2.

[26] In this respect, the poem about the lyre's migration takes its place beside comparable
epigrams concerning objects dedicated at the shrine of Arsinoe-Aphrodite Zephyritis such as
Callim. *Epigr.* 5 Pf. (Κόγχος ἐγώ, Ζεφυρῖτι = GP 14 = Ath. 7. 318 D), which charts the passage
to the land of Egypt of the roving nautilus shell, and its itinerant dedicator—a certain Selenaea
from Aeolian Smyrna (v. 12) who found the shell on the beach at Iulis on Ceos, a way-station
perhaps on her way from Smyrna to Alexandria. It has been observed that the nearby Cean
town of Coresia became an important Ptolemaic port in the mid-3rd c. BC, which (significantly)
was renamed *Arsinoe* following the queen's death, cf. L. Robert, 'Sur un décret des Korésiens'.
It is probably also important that Ceos has literary significance as the birthplace of Simonides
and Bacchylides.

[27] Cf. already Hdt. 2. 135, who calls her by her nickname 'Rhodopis'. Cf. D. L. Page, *Sappho
and Alcaeus* (Oxford, 1955), 49 n. 1. However, J. Lidov, 'Sappho, Herodotus, and the *Hetaira*',
now proposes that Rhodopis and Doricha only came to be identified with one another in the
Hellenistic biographical tradition, for which Posidippus is our earliest source. Doricha also
appears in Sappho's poetry (frr. 7, 15 LP), though not immediately connected with Charaxus
(fr. 5, and generally 202 LP).

Caπφῶιαι δὲ μένουcι φίλης ἔτι καὶ μενέουcιν | ὠιδῆc αἱ λευκαὶ φθεγγόμεναι cελίδεc). The importance of writing as a means of preservation is further stressed in the following couplet, which addresses Doricha: 'Most blessed is your name, which Naucratis will preserve ὧδε | as long as a ship sails out from the Nile across the salt sea' (ll. 7–8 οὔνομα cὸν μακαριcτόν, ὃ Ναύκρατιc ὧδε φυλάξει, | ἔcτ' ἂν ἴηι Νείλου ναῦc ἐφ' ἁλὸc πελάγη). In the sepulchral context we would normally expect ὧδε (l. 7) to be used in its conventional deictic sense 'here'. But Posidippus pointedly thwarts epitaphic expectation. For ὧδε here refers back to the ability of the *papyrus-scroll* to bestow permanence on its subject (ll. 5–6 μένουcι . . . ἔτι καὶ μενέουcιν | αἱ λευκαὶ φθεγγόμεναι cελίδεc), and therefore means that it is 'thus', 'in this way',[28] i.e. 'through the medium of the scroll', that Naucratis will preserve the hetaira's name. It will do so, moreover, 'as long as a ship sails out from the Nile across the salt sea' (l. 8). P. A. Rosenmeyer elucidated the particular point of this conclusion, acutely observing that the ship was probably laden with papyri.[29] Naucratis was indeed ideally located in the Delta to play a significant part in the papyrus trade.[30] Its very name (l. 7 Ναύκρατιc), 'the city whose power is in ships', bespeaks its mercantile strength and age-old standing as a base of maritime trade between Egypt and far-flung points in the Mediterranean.[31] That connotation of the city's name is deftly activated by Posidippus in the final line (l. 8 ἔcτ' ἂν ἴηι Νείλου ναῦc ἐφ' ἁλὸc πελάγη), inasmuch as the ναῦc envisioned there implies that Naucratite ships—with their precious cargo of scrolls—will sail down the Nile and out to sea for ever.[32] Here then Posidippus, famous in the Greek world as a poet of epigrams for monuments,[33] shows himself equally aware of the memorializing power of papyrus. In particular, he is mindful of Egypt's special role not just in collecting and preserving, but in disseminating the precious poetic heritage of Greece.

Precious objects could be of various sorts, however, even amongst the λιθικά. Returning now to our stones, we find there Ptolemaic interests of another, though related, kind reflected in the epigram that

---

[28] Cf. GP on ὧδε (on 17. 7), who note that *thus* 'seems more likely' than *here*.

[29] P. A. Rosenmeyer, 'Her Master's Voice: Sappho's Dialogue with Homer', 132.

[30] Thus E. Marion Smith, *Naukratis* (Vienna, 1926), 35.

[31] See most recently A. Möller, *Naukratis* (Oxford, 2000); U. Höckmann and D. Kreikenbom (eds.), *Naukratis* (Möhnesee 2001).

[32] The verses may be viewed as an update—from the perspective of book-conscious Hellenistic Egypt—of what is implied already about the easy dissemination of written verse in an image such as Pindar's at *N.* 5. 2–3: ἀλλ' ἐπὶ πάcαc ὁλκάδοc ἔν τ' ἀκάτωι, γλυκεῖ' ἀοιδά, cτεῖχ' ἀπ' Αἰγίναc διαγγέλοιc', 'on every merchant ship, on every boat, sweet song, go forth from Aegina proclaiming the news'.

[33] Cf. the honours bestowed on him as ἐπιγραμματοποιόc at Thermon.

follows the initial sixteen-poem series —the 'gemstone sequence', as Gutzwiller has called it.[34] This epigram has to do with a stone whose natural properties, rather than any artful craftsmanship applied to it secondarily, make it a marvel worthy of contemplation (AB 17):[35]

σκέψαι ὁ Μύσιος οἷον ἀνερρίζωσεν Ὄλυμπος
τόνδε λίθον διπλῆι θαυμάσιον δυνάμει·
τῆιδε μὲν ἕλκει ῥεῖα τὸν ἀντήεντα σίδηρον
μάγνης οἷα λίθος, τῆιδε δ' ἄπωθεν ἐλᾶι,
πλευρῆι ἐναντιοεργός· ὃ καὶ τέρας ἐξ ἑνὸς αὐτοῦ,   5
πῶς δύο μιμ⟨ε⟩ῖται χερμάδας εἰς προβολάς.

3 ἀντήεντα BG: ἀντήοντα pap.   5 ἐναντιοεργός BG: ἐναντιοεργές pap.

Look upon this stone, such a one as Mysian Mt. Olympus grew,
    wondrous for its double power.
With one side it easily pulls the iron set before it,
    like a magnet-stone, with the other it drives it far away
with opposing effect. Even that is the marvel, how from one itself
    it imitates two stones with regard to movements.

This poem suggests that the Ptolemies were not simply interested in claiming the wealth of the world, but also in gathering together its wonders (note l. 2 θαυμάσιον, l. 5 τέρας). But what is the nature of this marvel? Bastianini and Gallazzi were puzzled by the idea that one stone imitates two: 'It would not be clear', they say, 'what the two χερμάδες are, which are imitated by the stone described: one could be the μάγνης λίθος, which attracts iron; the other, however, which repels it, is not described in any way. Above all, finally, the phrase would add nothing of substance to what was previously said, while the connective ὃ καὶ τέρας necessarily implies that the topic is something new.'[36] Without minimizing the difficulty of the final couplet, I think that the commentators fail to account here for the longstanding ignorance in ancient sources about magnetic polarity, i.e. the fact that every magnet has two poles and that when two magnetized objects of the same pole meet, they repel, while opposite poles attract. Surprisingly, the earliest known text—prior to the discovery of our epigram—to describe a stone that can simultaneously attract and repel

[34] 'A New Hellenistic Poetry Book', 88.
[35] On this poem, cf. Luppe, 'Weitere Überlegungen'.
[36] On III 19: 'non si capirebbe quali siano le due χερμάδες imitate dalla pietra descritta: una potrebbe essere il μάγνης λίθος che attira il ferro, l'altra però, che lo respinge, non sarebbe indicata in nessun modo; sopratutto, infine, la frase non aggiungerebbe nulla, in sostanza, rispetto a ciò che è detto prima, mentre il nesso ὃ καὶ τέρας implica necessariamente che si dica qualcosa di nuovo.'

comes from the fifth century AD.[37] In rare instances, authors note that magnets can occasionally repel but, as A. Radl remarks in his study *Der Magnetstein in der Antike*, that is 'an exception'. Such a faculty 'is more usually attributed then to "another stone" altogether'.[38]

Thus the standard view in ancient sources is that magnets attract. That is why our epigram compares its subject to a magnet when seeking to illustrate that ability alone: 'With one side it easily pulls the iron set before it | like a magnet-stone' (ll. 3–4 τῇδε μὲν ἕλκει ῥεῖα τὸν ἀντήεντα cίδηρον | μάγνηc οἷα λίθοc). Those that repel, by contrast, are normally considered different stones—here the *second* of the δύο . . . χερμάδαc which our stone imitates. This epigram is thus by far the earliest evidence for a single stone that incorporates both powers. Inasmuch as this flies squarely in the face of prevailing wisdom, it would indeed be perceived as a 'marvel' (l. 5 τέραc) that this stone from Mysian Olympos, being only one, 'imitates two stones with regard to movements'.[39] The unexpectedness and novelty of the phenomenon justifies our taking the relative phrase ὃ καὶ τέραc as retrospective, looking *back* to the preceding description of the stone's paradoxical doubleness, and amplifying it ('even this is a marvel'), rather than introducing some new wonder.[40]

The poem reflects the Hellenistic interest in paradoxography, which was given a decisive impetus and new scope through the conquests of Alexander the Great. One may see how the influx of carved gems into the Ptolemaic realm, as described in the λιθικά, is paralleled by the collecting of wonders initiated by Callimachus in his

[37] Cf. Marcellus Empiricus (*De medicamentis liber* 1. 63); thereafter Johannes Philoponus' commentary on Aristotle's *Physics* 403. 24, cf. A. Radl, *Der Magnetstein in der Antike* (Stuttgart, 1988), 7, who, discounting the testimony of Marcellus, concludes: 'Lediglich einmal [sc. in Philoponus] wird als ganz besondere Kuriosität bemerkt, daß ein und derselbe "Stein" sowohl anzieht als auch abstößt'; cf. also H. Rommel, *RE* xiv/1. 477: 'Neben der Anziehung beobachtete man auch die Abstoßung . . . ohne daß man sich aber über die Polarität ganz klar wurde.'

[38] 'Über eine abstoßende Wirkung wird ebenfalls berichtet; aber nur als Ausnahme, die dann eher einem "anderen Stein" zugeschrieben wird' (p. 7). Cf. Lucretius 6. 1042–3: *fit quoque ut a lapide hoc ferri natura recedat | interdum*. Similarly Plutarch, *de Iside et Osiride* 62, 376 B, citing Manetho (*FGrHist* III C, no. 609 F 21), speaks of a stone that *at different times* (πολλάκιc μέν . . . πολλάκιc δέ) attracts and repels. Pliny (*NH* 20. 2) sees the stone that repels as a different stone.

[39] The phrase ἐξ ἑνὸc αὐτοῦ recalls philosophical discussions concerning τὸ ἓν αὐτό, cf. Plato, *Parm.* 137 B 3 and esp. Arist. *Met.* 1001ᵇ5, which pointedly asks 'from whence is there to be another one besides the one itself?' (ἐκ τίνοc γὰρ παρὰ τὸ ἓν ἔcται αὐτὸ ἄλλο ἕν:). That seems precisely what is miraculous about the one stone that embodies the function of two.

[40] i.e. if we took ὃ καὶ τέραc with the editors as meaning 'and this, too, is a wonder'. Granted that that is its sense at AB 8. 7, we need not assume that the phrase will always be used in the same way.

Θαυμάτων τῶν εἰc ἅπαcαν τὴν γῆν κατὰ τόπουc cυναγωγή.[41] Or again in verse-paradoxography of the same period there are the poems of the Egyptian Archelaus (*SH* 125–9) who, according to Antigonus of Carystus, 'explained paradoxes in epigrams to Ptolemy'.[42] In other words, what flows into the Ptolemies' domain is not merely *material* wealth (ὄλβοc)—as the passage in Theocritus 17. 95–7 quoted before might suggest—but comprises as well the wealth of cultural/scientific information, including strange fact and fancy, that accompanied territorial expansion (or its ambitions).[43]

The Ptolemaic interests as surveyed in the section on stones are not simply geographic but cut across time. We have already mentioned the epigram concerning the ring of Polycrates. There are other antique gems described in this section as well, particularly associated with Persian royalty (AB 4, 8) through which Posidippus suggests the Ptolemaic appropriation—following the ever-present model of Alexander—of the artistic inheritance of that empire as well. Perhaps we may find traces of the Persian legacy—again via Alexander—in yet another poem where it has not previously been suspected: I mean in the poorly preserved AB 18 which, with its opening invitation to recline (l. 1 ἀνακλίνθητε), its apparent references to a young wine steward (l. 3 οἰνο]χόωι cὺν παιδί), as well as to an amphora (l. 4 ἀ]μφορέα), seems to point to a sympotic context.

δεῦτ' ἐπ' ἔμ', ἐννέα φῶτεc, ἀνακλίνθητε δ[ ]ειc·
    ] ω γὰρ ἐγὼ τρεῖc [ ] λιθε[
οἰνο]χόωι cὺν παιδὶ μ[ ] ἀποδ [
ρηι]δίωc ἔκχουν δεξ[ ] ἀ]μφορέα·
ἠνί]δε· τῆι μὲν πέντ' ἀ[νδρῶν] πάχοc, ἧι δεδ[5
τῆ]ι δὲ τριcπίθαμοc τ[ ] πιότ[ε]ροc
    ] τετραγλώχιc πλε[ ] ἐ]πὶ μῆκοc ε [
τῆι] μὲν ἐφ' ἕξ προcθε [ ]εcι, τῆι δ' ἀφ[

1 δ' [ἀολλ]εῖc Austin   3 μ[έθηc] ἀποδώτ[ορα τερπνῆc Austin   4 δέξ[ομαι Austin
5 πέντ' ἀ[νδρῶν Fantuzzi : πεντά[πεδοc Austin   δέδ[εθ' ἁρμόc Austin   6 τ[ῆι πολὺ]
πιότ[ε]ροc Austin   7 πλε[ῖον δ' Austin

---

[41] Callimachus is seen as the first fully fledged exponent of the genre paradoxography, exerting important influence on his contemporary Antigonus of Carystus, who wrote Ἱcτοριῶν παραδόξων cυναγωγή. Cf. F. Susemihl, *Geschichte der griechischen Literatur in der Alexanderzeit*, i (Leipzig, 1891), 463 ff.

[42] The reference is either to Ptolemy II Philadelphus or III Euergetes (*Mir.* 19. 3–4 = *PGR*, p. 42 Giannini); cf. Fraser, *Ptol. Alex.* i. 778–80. Cf. also the verse and prose paradoxes of Callimachus' student Philostephanus of Cyrene.

[43] Our poem is of course only an explicit example of a scholarly/paradoxographical interest that pervades the whole section, as has been shown by Martyn Smith in his examination of Posidippus' use of technical treatises in 'Exceptional Stones'. For paradoxography in the Milan papyrus generally, cf. N. Krevans, above, Ch. 5.

> Come to me, you nine men, and lie down [together?]
>   . . . for I . . . three . . . of stone
> with a young wine-pourer . . .
>   easily . . . will hold a six-chous amphora
> Look! Here the width is that of five [men] where [the
>   joint is held together (?);
>   here it is of three spans; [here it is much] fatter (?)
> with four corners, [but greater (?)] in length
>   on the one hand six, on the other . . .

Bastianini and Gallazzi on III 23 propose that the subject of this poem, and its speaker, may be a large and costly stone krater, 'which declares . . . its own capacity', to wit more than a six-chous amphora, which it holds easily—that is, more than twenty litres. 'If', say the editors, 'we are truly dealing with a stone krater then we might be able to understand why the epigram would be included in this section' (on III 22–3, cf. also introduction to III 20–7).

But something is not right with this picture. A six-chous amphora is not particularly large. The standard capacity of a storage amphora is *twelve* choes (= 1 μετρητής, cf. *OCD*[3] s.v. 'measures'). A container somewhat more than half that size, even if this were a deliberate under-statement, does not mesh with the description of an object whose width alone suffices to hold five men (l. 5 πέντ' ἀ[νδρῶν] πάχος),[44] and which appears to have four corners (l. 7 τετραγλώχις).

I think it more likely that we are dealing with one of two possibilities: (i) a *kline*, or couch,[45] possibly big and sturdy enough to hold the nine men (not the usual one or two to a couch), who are invited in the opening line to 'come to me . . . and lie down'. In this connection, M. Fantuzzi notes that we should reject the editors' supplement, πεντά[πεδος] πάχος (l. 5), as it ignores the central caesura—an exceedingly rare occurrence in the history of epigram, and one which we should certainly not create through conjecture.[46] He suggests instead πέντ' ἀ[νδρῶν] πάχος, 'a width of five men', a characterization which—in addition to observing the caesura—aptly describes a couch large enough along its length and breadth to carry nine men. (ii) The sec-

---

[44] Much less 'five feet thick' (πεντά[πεδος] πάχος), the supplement proposed by BG, on which see below.

[45] In a similar direction cf. Luppe, 'Ein gastlicher Stein', who suggests that because the epigram belongs to the λιθικά the speaker must be a boulder with three bench-like outcroppings capable of holding three men each. However, this suggestion with its bold supplements lacks plausibility inasmuch as it is supported by not a shred of archaeological evidence—are there examples of sympotic furniture built thus into a natural outdoor setting?—or by any suggestion as to where such a structure might have been.

[46] The same goes for Luppe's proposal (ibid.), πεντα[χερὲς] πάχος.

ond possibility is a massive table perhaps set up in the conventional manner in front of the couch where the men are reclining.[47] Couch or table, I agree with the editors that λιθε[at the end of line 2 suggests that stone or gems figured in the construction.

Now where would such a grand couch or table be found? In a setting, I suggest, that evokes a heroic context. A cue that prompts us in this direction may lie in the appeal to 'nine men', ἐννέα φῶτες. This is, first of all, a Homeric combination.[48] More importantly, it recalls a passage from the *Iliad* (7. 161) where, in response to Nestor's scolding challenge, nine great heroes spring up to volunteer to fight Hector: οἱ δ' ἐννέα πάντες ἀνέσταν. Significantly, this line is quoted verbatim in a sympotic context in Hippolochus of Macedon's description of the sumptuous wedding feast of Caranus the Macedonian (Ath. 4. 129–30). There, after one of the feasters empties at a single draught a cκύφος χοαῖος, a capacious six-pint cup of barely diluted Thasian wine (πληρώcαc οἴνου Θαcίου ὀλίγον τι ἐπιρράναc ὕδατοc ἐξέπιεν), the host responds by offering to give the cup as a Homeric-style γέρας to all who can match this feat. 'At these words', continues the narrator, citing Homer, '*all nine sprang up* and seized a cup, each striving to outstrip the others' (ἐφ' οἷc λεχθεῖcιν "οἱ δ' ἐννέα πάντες ἀνέσταν" ἁρπάζοντες κάλλος ἄλλον φθάνοντες). In other words, the convivial *agon* is made parallel to the heroic *agon*. I suspect that, in view of the Macedonian authorship and subject of this description, the Homeric phrase may have had some currency in Macedonian circles, including that of the Ptolemies. With its nine men, our epigram similarly evokes the Homeric model, and thereby lends a touch of epic grandeur to its imagined symposium. At the same time, of course, it humorously undercuts that grandeur by inverting the Iliadic ἀνέσταν ('all nine stood up') with ἀνακλίνθητε (l. 1 'nine men, lie down').

Larger-than-life opulence may be evoked in another way as well. Despite its tattered condition, the epigram strikes us at once by its profusion of numbers and measurements (l. 1 ἐννέα φῶτες, l. 2 τρεῖς, l. 4 ἔκχουν, l. 5 πέντ' ἀ[νδρῶν], l. 6 τριcπίθαμος, l. 7 τετραγλώχις, l. 8 ἕξ). This feature immediately calls to mind the periegetic prose of the Hellenistic period, in particular those elaborate accounts of gigantic royal tents, ships, and processions—gaudy narrative show-pieces

---

[47] In that case, we might consider whether τρεῖc in line 2 might refer to the standard three-legged sympotic table, and whether πόδαc might be part of a plausible supplement in the gap following τρεῖc.

[48] It appears just once in Homer, *Il*. 16. 785, of Patroclus' final murderous assault, τρὶc δ' ἐννέα φῶταc ἔπεφνεν.

obsessed with quantity and size,⁴⁹ and meant to convey an impression of endless wealth and power.

Oswyn Murray has emphasized the importance in the development of the Hellenistic royal symposium of the Persian model, combined with Macedonian customs of royal feasting. He stresses 'the central importance of *tryphê* and feasting in the life of the [Persian] king', recognized as early as Herodotus, and notes how 'Alexander's banquets were certainly compared to those of the Persian king' in this regard.⁵⁰ Alexander's lavish feasting-pavilion (Ath. 12. 538 B–539 A) was in turn the clear model for the great banquet tent of Ptolemy Philadelphus described by Callixenus of Rhodes (Ath. 5. 196 A–197 C). That tent, with its 130 gold couches (Ath. 5. 197 A), each with a pair of three-legged gold tables set before it, seems deliberately to echo—and outdo—Alexander's furnishings, which included only a hundred couches of silver—the sole couch of gold belonged to Alexander himself. Most significantly for our epigram, in Ptolemy's tent there was a couch (κλίνη), 'in full sight of the sympotic assembly', that could hold a great pile of goblets, cups, and utensils—all of gold, and studded with jewels (ἃ δὴ πάντα χρυσᾶ τε ἦν καὶ διάλιθα, θαυμαστὰ ταῖc τέχναιc), and weighing ten thousand silver talents (5. 197 C). The text does not say of what material this *kline* was made, but to bear such a load—fully 300 tons (!)—it seems a fair bet that it must have been of stone.⁵¹ If the object described in our epigram is a *kline*, it was doubtless more modest than this one. But I think that in exploring the context of royal symposia—'Hellenistic . . . *gigantosymposia*', as Bergquist has called them⁵²—we are looking in the right place.

A comparable royal context would be suitable if we consider the object in our poem a table, for we have a detailed source describing Ptolemy Philadelphus' special interest in the manufacture, and exquisite craftsmanship, of a gem-encrusted table made of gold. I am referring to the sumptuous table said to have been given by the king

---

⁴⁹ A verse counterpart might be the description of the statue of Olympian Zeus in Callimachus' *Iambus* 6.

⁵⁰ 'Hellenistic Royal Symposia', 18–19 and 19 respectively. It is worth noting—especially in light of Posidippus' interest in the ring of Polycrates, mentioned above—that there may also be a Greek model for the display of de luxe furniture at work here as well. A tantalizingly brief notice in Herodotus (3. 123) tells us that Polycrates' secretary, Maeandrius, following his master's death, dedicated in the Heraion of Samos all the furniture from the tyrant's banquet hall—'a sight worth seeing': τὸν κόcμον τὸν ἐκ τοῦ ἀνδρεῶνοc τοῦ Πολυκράτεοc ἐόντα ἀξιοθέητον ἀνέθηκε πάντα ἐc τὸ Ἥραιον.

⁵¹ Cf. Cleopatra's βαcιλικόν cυμπόcιον for Antony, ἐν ᾧ πάντα χρύcεα καὶ λιθοκόλλητα περιττῶc ἐξειργαcμένα ταῖc τέχναιc (Ath. 4. 147 F). In this case, the use of stone inlay appears to have extended to the furniture.

⁵² 'Sympotic Space', 53.

to the high priest of Jerusalem, Eleazar, and minutely described in an extended ecphrasis in the *Letter of Aristeas* (51–72). To be sure, its dimensions were smaller than what our epigram describes: δύω πήχεων τὸ μῆκος, τὸ δὲ ὕψος πήχεος καὶ ἡμίσους (57), i.e. roughly 3 feet long by 2 feet high: Ptolemy had hoped to make it colossal in size (προεθυμεῖτο μὲν οὖν ὁ βασιλεὺς ὑπέροπλόν τι ποιῆσαι τοῖς μέτροις τὸ κατασκεύασμα 52), but naturally he bowed to biblical authority in this regard. What the table lacked in size, however, it more than made up for in its art and precious materials. These are lovingly set out in the elaborate ecphrasis mentioned above, that—as in our epigram—repeatedly stresses the dimensions of each detail. I propose, then, that we may have here in verse a counterpart to the sensational prose descriptions—the Hellenistic answer to the tabloids of today—of spectacular objects on display at royal symposia, quite possibly Ptolemaic symposia.

To conclude, it is worth noting that the Ptolemaic orientation revealed in this section on stones recurs with far greater emphasis in those on dedications (ἀναθεματικά), on victories in equestrian contests (ἱππικά) where numerous epigrams celebrate the institutions and achievements of the first three generations of Ptolemaic kings and queens, and on cures (ἰαματικά), which seems to take its cue from the interests of a high Ptolemaic official.[53] Posidippus was evidently active in quite disparate parts of the Greek world, and served a variety of masters. We know from an inscription in Thermon that in 263/2 he received proxeny from the Aetolian league in his function as writer of epigrams (ἐπιγραμματοποιός, *IG* ix²/1. 17 A = AB T 3), and he appears to come up in a proxeny list from the 270s at Delphi as well (*Fouilles de Delphes* iii/3, no. 192 = AB T 2). Further he seems to have maintained close ties to his native Pella in Macedonia (cf. his poetic sphragis, *SH* 705 = AB 118). The remarkable emphasis on Ptolemaic themes in the Milan papyrus, then—to the exclusion of almost any other regional power's political interests—strongly suggests that the epigrams in this collection were selected with a Ptolemaic audience in mind.[54] An apparent exception like AB 83, commemorating a victory of one of the Thessalian Scopadae in a horse race at Olympia, in fact just adds lustre to the Ptolemaic victories so prominently described by evoking the precedent of Simonidean epinician (cf. similarly

[53] Cf. my articles 'Medeios of Olynthos' and 'Posidippus' *Iamatika*'.
[54] This squares with the Ptolemaic emphasis found in the previously known epigrams of Posidippus, where such notables as the *nauarch*, Callicrates of Samos, or Sostratus of Cnidos, the dedicator of the statue of Zeus Soter atop the Pharos, are prominent, cf. Bing, 'Between Literature and the Monuments'.

Theocr. 16. 34–47). Bearing in mind the striking number of epigrams that focus on women—the first seven poems of the λιθι]κά,[55] almost all those from the section on epitaphs, the prominence of Ptolemaic queens among the ἀναθεματικά and ἱππικά[56]—we may even contemplate a collection shaped to the interests of a Ptolemaic queen, or to one in her service.

[55] 'Nel sottogruppo concernente le pietre incise (I 2–III 7), prima troviamo riuniti insieme tutti gli epigrammi che hanno per tema gemme intagliate offerte in dono a donne (I 2–35)': BG, p. 25.

[56] Note especially how the last two poems of the ἱππικά insistently situate the achievement of these queens in a female context and according to feminine criteria, AB 87. 3–4 τὸ Κυνίσκας | ἐν Σπά[ρ]ται χρόνιον κῦδος ἀφειλόμεθα (sc. the horses of Berenice), 88. 5–6 ἀλλ᾽ ὅτι μάτηρ | εἷλε γυνὰ νίκαν ἅρματ⟨ι⟩, τοῦτο μέγα. For the prominence of women in the poems of the Milan papyrus generally, cf. H. Bernsdorff, 'Anmerkungen zum neuen Poseidipp', 38–41, and Hutchinson, 'The New Posidippus and Latin Poetry', esp. 2.

8

Cabinet Fit for a Queen: The Λιθικά as Posidippus' Gem Museum

ANN KUTTNER

ΔΑΚΤΥΛΙΟΘΗΚΗ

How might the λιθικά, the gem-poems that are the first section pre-
served in our new scroll of Posidippus' poetry, most excite an art
historian? Beyond the fascination of any single object among them,
they are, with the section on masterpiece statues (ἀνδριαντοποιικά),
unparalleled responses by a cultured Hellenistic eye to Hellenistic
visual culture and its sociology. Each poem addresses a different stone,
λίθος, in its setting. The series is like a collection of luxurious and
marvellous artefacts. Consequently these columns of coloured words
give the oldest extant text about the most splendid of Hellenistic elite
displays: the gem and jewellery collection, δακτυλιοθήκη ('ring display
space'), and the cabinets, stands, shelves, cases, cupstands—*abacus*,
armarium, πλινθίον, τράπεζα, κυλικεῖον—of luxury drinking ware and
furnishings (cυμποτικά, καταcκεύαcμα). Extant gem-collecting texts
mostly document the formation and appropriation of Greek regal
collections, by rivals and then by Romans, starting with the first
courts of Alexander's successors and their spoils from the Persian
kings' massive treasures. The λιθικά too discuss both the ornaments
of the symposium, and gems which come from acts of conquest.[1]

The materiality of the collection is therefore this essay's premiss

I thank Kathryn Gutzwiller for attentive editorship and the chance to learn from supportive
colleagues at the original conference. This constricted essay plays off pendants in the volume,
Bing's especially. I am indebted to colleagues who commented on a related presentation at the
University of Pennsylvania, especially Julie Davis, Zirka Filipcek, Ralph Rosen, and graduate
students too numerous to name. Alina Payne gave rigorous art-historical perusal; I remain as
always in debt to her *amicitia* and critical dispassion, as to that of Brian Rose and Alessandro
Barchiesi. Barbara Burrell was an inestimable critical editor. Flaws are my fault.

[1] Pliny's review of *dactyliothecae* is *HN* 37. 11–14. For an exemplary royal collector, who
had Ptolemaic treasures too, see App. *Mith.*, esp. 23, 115–17, for Mithridates' practices. For
texts, H.-P. Bühler, *Antike Gefäße aus Edelsteinen* (Mainz, 1973), 1–26. On the value to the
Ptolemaic treasury of gemware spoils see J. Manning, 'Twilight of the Gods', 866.

and armature. It explores how the poems reciprocally contribute to that implied context, and are informed by it; for the gemmed artefacts, singly and in assemblage, can illuminate their poet's authorial project for raising the status of miniature poetry (epigram), and also some of the dynamics of Hellenistic readership. The gem in Posidippus is not just a sign of luxury (τρυφή), but a metaphor for the poem as material artefact, and vice versa: fragile papyrus recreates perdurable stone.

The λιθικά are amassed of stones made into, or decorating, artefacts familiar to its original readers, as vessels and jewellery in traditional or newly fashionable forms. Current editors consider AB 1–15 to be pictorial signets, sorted as gifts to women (AB 1–7), or not (AB 8–15). Given that numbing banality, the boulder poems at the end (AB 16, 19, 20) seem either messy afterthoughts, or clumsy means towards an amusing pattern of scale shifts between poems and clusters. However, the range of artefacts is in fact more varied than just a ring-stone set, and most gems in the book are not carved with an intaglio design. Instead, they are the lustrous plain jewels beloved for Hellenistic jewellery and vessels; carved figuration here is but one possible quality of the gem. Etched pictures did not necessarily add value. Though metal settings for stones could be dense with miniature sculpture, Hellenistic diadems, earrings, necklaces, and many luxurious rings contained unfigured gems.[2] The epigrams are mostly about pure pleasure, blank stones which are 'only' colours and light, not passed off as usefully durable signet hardstones. 'Many hold it almost criminal to violate some gems with seal designs, so much do they value their variety, colours, substance, aesthetic effect . . . so that many hold that any one gem suffices to give a total, extraordinary meditation on Nature' (Pliny, *HN* 37. 1).

The λιθικά seem to contain planned clusters, as well as poems that could be singletons, absorbed from earlier *ad hoc* work about real or fictive pieces. Lucidly curated by the standards of Hellenistic visual programmes and material collections, the sequence merits that

[2] Intaglios, because pictorial, alas dominate gem scholarship: Plantzos, *Hellenistic Engraved Gems*; S. Michel, 'Steinschneidekunst'. Studies of 'Greek gold' correct any impression that intaglios prevailed: see W. Rudolph, *A Golden Legacy*, 106–218 for Hellenistic items, plus core bibliography; D. Williams and J. Ogden, *Greek Gold* (New York, 1994); E. M. De Juliis et al. (eds.), *Gli ori di Taranto in età ellenistica* (Milan, 1984); S. Walker and P. Higgs (eds.), *Cleopatra regina d'Egitto* (Milan, 2000), 39–42, 52, 82–4, 86. Invaluable on gems' settings if not on gems: M. Pfrommer, *Metalwork from the Hellenized East* (Malibu, 1993); id., *Untersuchungen zur Chronologie früh- und hochhellenistischen Goldschmucks* (Tübingen, 1990); id., *Greek Gold from Hellenistic Egypt* (Los Angeles, 2001) with S. I. Rotroff's review. For colour, see websites of the Boston Museum of Fine Arts, the Metropolitan Museum of Art, the J. Paul Getty Museum, the British Museum, the Louvre, and the Hermitage.

respect for nuanced internal design given to multi-authored antholo-gies.[3] AB (1?) 2–3, gemmed vessels, set a royal couple's symposium. AB 4–7, elements of a woman's now-standard parure (bracelet, ring, necklaces), hint at dynastic success and fertility, conceptualize and name the gem museum (δακτυλιοθήκη), and gloss the cultural absorp-tion of the East. AB 8–10, men's jewels, historical rulers' gemstones, contain both positive and monitory portents; they showcase AB 9, the epigram which perhaps most clearly exposes the author's self-reflective metapoetic programme. AB 11–12, seashells for perfum-ing, women's fashionable Aphrodisian boudoir implements, have cultic and courtly overtones. AB 13–15 is a recondite intaglio (ring) bestiary; AB 16–17, rock masses like scientific specimens; and finally, AB 18–20, rocks that are gods' and monsters' weapons, and therefore artefacts too.

This internal ordering by generic clusters delineates a cultural anthropology, of how we exploit something–probably stones, λίθοι (as the title is not fully preserved). The λιθικά play on new gem encyclopaedias[4] that were also instrumentalist, cataloguing medical, technological, and magical uses.[5] Certain physical properties of gems may produce pleasure, but value and meaning are culturally deter-mined, as the poem on a lovely yet unesteemed quartzite mass, AB 16, stresses. Coloured stones engage sight; held in the hand and worn on the body, they also engage touch. The λιθικά frequently evoke how such ornaments can suggest, even substitute for, live flesh and physi-cal contact with it; they also appeal to the manner in which character-istics of the described gem can seem to be a sort of costume that decks the person seen using the gem with particular associations.[6]

Decoration as ordered accumulation has special valency; meanings are generated by the reasons why objects moved between collections and collectors. Thus Posidippus (AB 4, 5, 8, 9) colours in Theocritus'

---

[3] On which see Gutzwiller, *Poetic Garlands*, 35–6. Hutchinson, 'The New Posidippus and Latin Poetry', 8 sticks up for order and self-referentiality.

[4] See Theophrastus' Περὶ λίθων, ed. Eichholz (cf. K. Gutzwiller, below, Ch. 15); it is worth gleaning Pliny, *HN* 37 for the Alexandrians, e.g. Sotacus' work, Satyrus' treatise in poetic form (*HN* 37. 31), to compare with Posidippus.

[5] Mystic λιθικά are attributed to Orpheus by the 1st-c. D.S. 7. 1. 1; Plantzos, *Hellenistic Engraved Gems*, 10, 110; S. Michel, *Bunte Steine — dunkle Bilder* (Munich, 2001). See AB 9 (Polycrates' gem magic), nn. 37, 46 (fertility gems). The Egyptian and Near Eastern back-ground is crucial. Note that amuletic gems exhibit potent inscriptions and were manipulated with written paper.

[6] Overlooked in 'Classical' gender and sexuality studies, which tend to ignore that jewellery was male too. Typically, N. B. Kampen (ed.), *Sexuality in Ancient Art* (Cambridge, 1996), has adornment studies for second-millennium-BC Egypt and the Near East. See J. Westenholz, 'Metaphorical Language in the Poetry of Love in the Ancient Near East' (Paris, 1992), 383–4 on gem metaphors, erotic and cultic, that prefigure Posidippan strategies.

salute to Ptolemy I and II in *Idyll* 17, for virtuously passing on their treasures to temples, cities, vassals, courtiers—and poets. Both of Posidippus' sections on art reflect how Macedonian dynasties from the fourth century onwards fostered collecting as a means of status display, self-fashioning, ideological persuasion, and intellectual self-assertion.[7] Ordinary readers could own items named in the λιθικά, such as cups, rings, and bracelets. But historical and masterpiece gems imply extreme wealth. Individual epigrams emphasize acquisition as such (Achaemenid treasures, AB 4, 8;[8] *cυμποτικά*, AB 18), and clusters evoke particular fashions for collecting. The beasts of AB 13–15 miniaturize new royal zoos and hunting parks, as if one hand could hold the Ptolemies' collections; as in Ptolemaic parades, weird animals come after drinking wares.[9] The mock-solemn poems on specimens like AB 16–17 and the tiny half-globe AB 5 mirror the Museum's Aristotelian study collections, where work on optics prompted Posidippus' observations on luminosity and refraction (e.g. AB 8, 13, 15).[10]

From what fits human hands to what fits only a god's, the reader, scroll on lap, palms the whole paper tray of precious things. That implicates the reader in the aesthetics and ethics of τρυφή:[11] an ideological agenda in which power, by sharing pleasure, seduces as well as compels obedience. The cult of collecting—'collectionism'— endorsed acquisition, so long as it had a worthy cultural agenda: the more stuff, the more lessons.[12] Macedonian courts introduced a kind

---

[7] With care, post-antique evidence is indispensable to envision Hellenistic practices undocumentable otherwise. Useful orientation: J. Elsner and R. Cardinal (eds.), *The Cultures of Collecting* (Cambridge, MA, 1994). Hellenistic and Republican collecting, brief references: A. Kuttner, 'Republican Rome Looks at Pergamon'; B. Bergmann, 'Greek Masterpieces and Roman Recreative Fictions' (paintings), and E. Gazda, 'Roman Sculpture and the Ethos of Emulation' (sculpture). Good to think with for Hellenistic luxury art and the jewel, and the construction of literature about it, is P. Fumerton, *Cultural Aesthetics* (Chicago, 1991); for courtly cultures, see N. Z. Davis, most recently *The Gift in Sixteenth Century France* (Madison, WI, 2000), and for courts and merchant aristocracies in eras of geographic expansion, L. Jardine, *Worldly Goods* (London, 1996).

[8] E. Schmidt, *Persepolis II* (Chicago, 1958).

[9] The Parade's animals and colossal images (Ath. 5. 200 E–202 D): E. E. Rice, *The Grand Procession of Ptolemy Philadelphus* (New York, 1983); D. J. Thompson, 'Philadelphus' Procession', 369, 371, with n. 23 on Theoc. *Idyll* 2. 68. Sculptural fantasizing at Memphis: Kuttner, 'Hellenistic Images of Spectacle from Alexander to Augustus', esp. 105 and fig. 4. For Egyptian/Ptolemaic hunts and zoos, though not for art: J. Lindsay, *Leisure and Pleasure in Roman Egypt* (London, 1965), 192–213; Near Eastern representation: B. Lion, 'La Circulation des animaux exotiques au Proche-Orient', including (365) glyptics.

[10] *HN* 37. 136–7 praises *iris*' refractive qualities (see AB 6), describing experiments of hanging prisms in rooms for coloured light-shows on walls.

[11] Thompson, 'Philadelphus' Procession'; H. von Hesberg, 'The King on Stage', 68–9 (parade), 72–3 (pavilion).

[12] Cf. A. Erskine, 'Culture and Power in Ptolemaic Egypt'.

of potlatch morality to symposia, where the rich now displayed status by giving away expensive furnishings to guests. Lovers exchanged jewels, kings distributed costly artefacts, on the understanding that they contributed to others' amassing. All λιθικά bijoux were potential objects of distribution, whether or not actual donation was narrated; poems about such objects were also (pretending to be) valuable gifts.

The naming of artists establishes 'gallery-effect'. Macedonian courts now elevated gem carvers from mere artisans, βάναυcοι (AB 10), to artists of record; Posidippus invites the reader to endorse an analogous elevation of inscription composers to epigrammatic poets (epigram-makers). Alexander had firmly set the court fashion, to assemble a salon of active makers, their works highlighted by collections of 'old masterpieces'. Here and in the ἀνδριαντοποιικά, new artists honour ancient paradigms by innovating as the ancients had, not by slavish replication. Contemporary and recent artists (Cronius, AB 2, 7; Timanthes, AB 5; Heros, AB 6)[13] join renowned Archaic masters (Theodorus, AB 9). In AB 6–7, Niconoe, like a great hetaira, seemingly receives jewels directly from the artists, like Phryne taking statue gifts from her lover Praxiteles, a favourite art-historical paradigm; collecting artists with stones, she wittily impersonates regal patronage.[14] AB 19 mythopoetically endorses all artists, for Poseidon's hand, carving rocks with a trident, consummates the series of artists' hands gouging gems with little chisels; this geography, divinely engraved, elegantly links microcosm and macrocosm, epigrammatic with epic creation.

Martial's *Apophoreta* epigrams align many cup types (including gemmed and gemware), a *dactyliotheca* (11. 59), and more jewellery, cataloguing a rich man's house and self;[15] the λιθικά attest the Hellenistic generic ancestor for such Roman works. Posidippus' lists deliberately resembled royal spectacle inventories, as narrated by Callixenus in the second century (Posidippus saw the original spectacles). His assemblage also evoked prose itineraries through treasuries, in colloquy with Herodotus and with the contemporary art historians with whose works the λιθικά and ἀνδριαντοποιικά closely engage.[16] Like Callimachus (*Iambi* 6 and 13), Posidippus mocks (AB

[13] According to syntax and grouping, Heros made it, not Cronius as restored; the ἀνδριαντοποιικά never repeat artists for adjacent artefacts.
[14] Contemporary hetairai expecting gems, Plantzos, *Hellenistic Engraved Gems*, 108. Posidippus discussed Praxiteles' mistresses (AB 147).
[15] On Martial, A. Barchiesi, below, Ch. 16.
[16] On this rapport, G. Zanker, 'New Light'; Stewart (below, Ch. 10) is the first art historian to do that project.

18) number-obsessed, factoid-blinded antiquarians. Arrangement and vocabulary teasingly miniaturize a genre exemplified by the Delian temples' inventories, full of assorted gemmed cups, seals, jewellery, rulers' dedications, lesser men's and women's personal votives, ancient tokens. (Posidippus likely knew them, if he led a royal θεωρία to Delos, depositing a votive phiale, cf. *IG* xi/2. 226 B 5.)[17] In Egypt, Naucratis' ancient shrines and Alexandria's new temples must have been similarly packed. For a reader, the tidy columns of pseudo-inscriptions (ἐπιγράμματα) on the papyrus could easily seem a humorous miniature of stone temple walls where engraved columns of text listed the god's treasures and their donors.

The λιθικά, though, do not inventory any one museum, and they leave specified votive scenarios to the ἀναθεματικά. Palatial treasures hint at Ptolemaic collections, rescued from the oblivion that overtook the Atreidae's undocumented gold (Theocritus, *Idyll* 17. 118–20, a mandate to compose object poetry). Objects of any upper-class reader's experience join perhaps fictive stones (and artists); and the poems suggest a range of viewing situations (a bedroom on a side street, or deep within a palace). This paper can give only a short, selective look at a few art-historical *realia* that are significant to the λιθικά's programmatic aim, hoping to induce readers to return to the poems on their own.

As shown by Hutchinson, AB 1's 'Hydaspes' had lasting fame in Roman poetry.[18] If the last line names Zeus,[19] it matches the closing poems AB 19–20, his brother Poseidon's pseudo-hymns: between sky and sea lies an Aegean, Egyptian, and Asian cosmos of κόσμος, decoration. From l. 1, the watery eastern frontier Ἰνδὸς Ὑδάσπης, readers arrive vertiginously at here and now, Ptolemaic Alexandria; that repeats the triumphant journeys back from India of Zeus' sons ancient and modern, Dionysus and Alexander. Alexander allied with the defeated Porus after the battle of the Hydaspes river, and Ptolemy

---

[17] Dated to 279 BC: R. Hamilton, *Treasure Map* (Ann Arbor, 2000); id., review of D. Harris, *The Treasures of the Parthenon and Erechtheion* (Oxford, 1995); B. Dignas, '"Inventories" or "Offering Lists"?'; ead., *Economy of the Sacred in Hellenistic and Roman Asia Minor* (Oxford, 2002); M.-F. Baslez, 'Le sanctuaire de Délos dans le dernier tiers du ivᵉ siècle', for historic Hellenistic donors.

[18] Hutchinson, 'The New Posidippus and Latin Poetry', 11, citing Vergil, Horace, Statius, Seneca.

[19] I thank Kathryn Gutzwiller for direction to R. Hunter's reading, 'Notes on the *Lithika* of Posidippus', 95.

II made close relations with the Indian emperor Aśoka; so the stone embodies war become amity, angry water a friend. Subsequent books suggest an appearance by Alexander in the λιθικά; if so, it was here, making AB 1 the first ruler-stone.

AB 2–3, and perhaps AB 1, show in use the costly, novel διάλιθος and λιθοκόλλητος Greek drinking wares popularized by Alexander and his successors, in imitation of Persian practice. Cronius (*HN* 37. 8) anchors this banquet-gear in Alexander's age at the earliest. Such cυμποτικά (formal drinking equipment) of precious metal studded with gems, or vessels cut from gemstones, crowd the early spectacle texts: ten thousand talents' worth just for Ptolemy's Pavilion (Ath. 5. 197 C). The phiale of AB 3 nests gemstone in spiralling live-springing (φυή) tendrils, miming a fruit, and a drop of that wine evoked by the 'fluid glance'.[20] The real ornament, and the language about it, are paralleled in known royal commissions of this poet's era, the foliage studded with jewelled fruit on the table which Ptolemy II gave the Temple in Jerusalem, in an astounding hoard of gemmed gifts (including thirty phialai; Josephus, *AJ* 12. 40–84, esp. 82). This is λιθοκόλλητος ware, like extant Hellenistic silver bowls sheathed in fantastic three-dimensional acanthus foliage, blossoms, and fruits, sometimes nesting garnets in a central boss.[21] There seems to be red in every epigram cluster: vessel inlays were always garnet, strengthening the restoration ἄνθραξ, the prized Indian garnet. If l. 3 contained 'new', καινός, a patroness relishes new gemmed metalwork gifts (and poems); καινουργία, originality, was a salient and desirable attribute of Ptolemy's gifts (ibid. 12. 70, 77).

The κέρας (drinking horn) of AB 2 is a rhyton.[22] At opening, 'it lies' (κεῖτ[α]ι) empty, on a table, or in a servant's or drinker's hand. The closing direction βυccόθεν, 'from below', evokes a now-filled, upright rhyton, wine spurting from bottom spouthole to mouth; such horns typically ended in figure sculpture, an animal protome. Precious metal rhyta of this originally Achaemenid type immediately

[20] *Contra* BG and AB, the text does not demand that the cup be engraved into stone. Their list of gem parallels is too small, and such intaglio motifs are extremely rare in the enormous corpus, almost exclusively Roman of the 1st c. onwards. BG admit that the stone is set in sculptured gold vegetation, but there are no such Hellenistic (or earlier) settings for ring stones.
[21] Pfrommer, *Metalwork*, 21–2, 26–7 on tendril styles, Macedonian or South Italian in origin, figs. 16, 27, 39.
[22] The basic animal-horn shape represents a hero's cup in Theophrastus' *On Drunkenness*. Throne displays in the Parade carried golden and gilt κέρατα, Ath. 5. 202 B; Ptolemy II assigned cornuacopiae to Arsinoe II's images (Ath. 11. 497 B–E) and put doubled ones on the reverse of coins in her memory: O. Mørkholm, *Early Hellenistic Coinage* (Cambridge, 1991), 102–3, figs. 294–5.

became popular in the Successor courts;[23] in Egypt, workshops of the Persian period simply kept producing. It may even be gemware,[24] to make Cronius famous; compare the garnet chunks big enough to be the feet of Ptolemy II's table for Jerusalem (J. *AJ* 12. 74). The material could be onyx (sardonyx, agate), like extant Ptolemaic gemstone κέρατα used that patterned brown-white Indian stone (l. 2) for animal-head rhyta.[25] Perhaps the poem once specified a particular iconographic motif, for in Alexandria in this period Hedylus (GP 4) praised a colossal rhyton wine-fountain shaped like Bes, the Ptolemaic Egyptianizing dwarf god, for ritual feasts to Arsinoe-Aphrodite at Cape Zephyrium;[26] Theocles described the actors' guild ritually draining a rhyton[27] shaped as Arsinoe II's double cornucopia, before 'our dearest king'.[28]

Posidippus pairs a banqueting man's rhyton with a similar phiale poem which addresses a πότνια: this epic salute for princesses and goddesses evokes Arsinoe II beside her brother-husband Ptolemy.[29] The

[23] Seleucus I dedicated three stag-rhyta among begemmed banquet fittings to Didymaean Apollo in 288/7: Dignas, *Economy*, 40–1 and n. 24, '"Inventories" or "Offering Lists"?', 242–3; briefly, Plantzos, *Hellenistic Engraved Gems*, 105. Early Ptolemaic hoards' metal animal rhyta, and the Ptolemaic Tomb of Petosiris' images of Achaemenid-style vessel production: A. Kozloff, 'Is There an Alexandrian Style?', fig. 7. See Pfrommer, *Metalwork* 47–9, n. 383, cat. 74, and nn. 511–39 (Egyptian faience, n. 511, winged lion); D. Arnold et al., *Ancient Art from the Shumei Family Collection* (New York, 1996), cat. 15, 16, 27.

[24] 'Amethyst' should not be restored with Austin, 'Paralipomena Posidippea', 22: it is invalid to restore gem names in a lacuna with no other cues. As *HN* 37 shows, too many exist, and Posidippus uses periphrasis too (e.g. AB 7, 'honey stone'). Metal rhyta had tiny gems as animal eyes, but they were unlikely to make Cronius famous. For the many 4th- and 3rd-c. authors mentioning rhyta, Ath. 11. 496 F–497 E. I introduced the interpretation that AB 2–3 portray vessels at the 2002 conference; E. Kosmetatou, 'Posidippus, *Epigr.* 8 AB and Early Ptolemaic Cameos' makes AB 2 a horn, but keeps 3 as an intaglio picturing a cup.

[25] One has a calf's head: found along ancient caravan routes near Koptos in Egypt, with eight agate drinking vessels: Bühler, *Antike Gefäße aus Edelsteinen*, cat. 8, in 1–9; Walker and Higgs, *Cleopatra regina d'Egitto* 38, cat. I. 6. The other has a horned ibex head. It is from a 9th-c. Chinese context (heirloom, Silk Road): Pfrommer, *Metalwork*, n. 480; Nenna, 'Gemmes et pierres dans le mobilier alexandrin', 157, cat. 94; Carlo Gasparri (ed.), *Le gemme Farnese* (Naples, 1994), 75, fig. 102. See *HN* 36. 59, Arabian 'onyx' drinking ware including a nine-gallon mixing bowl, and 37. 91, citing the Alexandrian poet Satyrus' appreciation of onyx's colouring.

[26] By Ctesibius. Thompson, 'Philadelphus' Procession', 376 links him to the Parade's liquid-pouring automata; his documented automata (transcribed in the 3rd–2nd c. treatise by Hero of Alexandria; see Fraser, *Ptolemaic Alexandria*, i. 427) include several giant cups.

[27] Compare Ptolemy II's images of his rhyton-bearing pourer, the lovely girl Cleino, that were placed around Alexandria (Plb. 14. 11. 2; Ath. 10. 425 E–F, 13. 576 F).

[28] Ath. 11. 497 C, from Theocles' Ἰθύφαλλοι, 'Ithyphallic Songs', i.e. for the royal cult of Dionysus, patron of actors. See 11. 497 A–B: in a wonderful comedic scene from Epinicos' Ὑποβαλλόμεναι, characters drained enormous ones (Bellerophon on Pegasus, [Egyptian] elephant) in timed contests: cf. AB 18.

[29] The very first poem of the ἀναθεματικά, AB 36, calls Arsinoe πότνια in a similar position in its book; AB 38 dedicates another phiale to Arsinoe, from a woman who drank the 'water of freedom' that Arsinoe symbolically dispensed (emended recently: Lapini, 'Note posidippee', 45).

pair of drinkers make AB 2–3 suggest Ariadne with Dionysus, that icon of Hellenistic royal self-fashioning. The paradisal, Dionysiac, sexual iconicity of woman taking laden vine is plain (Pl. 10). Male and female are humorously sexualized things, phallic horn and receptive open bowl. Rereading AB 2–3 as banquet vessels gives the book structure, illuminating the programme for the last cluster AB 18–20, whose colossal objects have puzzled. The position of AB 18 echoes that of AB 2–3, framing the inmost edge of outmost cluster. AB 18, an overgrown version of Posidippus' drinking-ware party epigrams (AB 123–4, 140), comically celebrates the urge for giant things in collections,[30] like the Parade's fabulously enormous vessels and tables. AB 2, 3, and 18 tease out 19's sympotic motif: the Cyclops' shot at the departing Odysseus recalls how the bad host/guest ate his visitors until, getting him blind drunk, they blinded him; awaking with history's worst hangover, he vainly assaulted an escaping hero saved by wine.[31] The colossal artefacts and protagonists stack up within poems, evoking monstrous banquets that echo the earlier divine ones. With its Theocritean Polyphemus displaying a goatherd's longing for Galatea (cf. *Id.* 6. 7), AB 19 also parodies AB 2–3's banquet/marriage. Finally, in AB 20, loving brother/sister rulers are mirrored by Demeter kissing her brother Poseidon's hand, ironically to avert not invite a gift of stone.

MARINE GODDESSES

AB 11–12 are redolent with meaning. From the fourth century on, real shells and their gem and metal imitations held perfume and cosmetics from the East and were used to scoop aromatics and unguents onto Greek women; depictions of using them made women into bathing goddesses attended by Eros.[32] Aphrodite was envisioned riding the ocean on, or even in, a shell.[33] The Persian ὄστρακον of AB 11

[30] According to Luppe, 'Ein gastlicher Stein', the λιθικά need a talking object, so the now-missing rock speaks AB 18; it *is* the described furniture, a U-shaped carved boulder. I reject this reading. There are no parallels, excavated or described, in the Graeco-Roman corpus of banquet sites, especially not in the Hellenistic age; and Graeco-Roman literature lacks talking furniture—chairs, couches, tables. Cf. Bing, Ch. 7, pp. 135–9

[31] Hutchinson, 'The New Posidippus and Latin Poetry', 3, suggests a tale where Cyclops throws at Galatea's lover; even so, one should never rule out the Homeric association.

[32] A. Kuttner, *Dynasty and Empire in the Age of Augustus* (Berkeley, 1995): dishes, 208, 303–4 nn. 25–6; perfuming and bathing shell-dish scenarios in Hellenistic, Etruscan, and Roman images and jewellery, 26–8, 223–5 nn. 48–61. Second-c. Delos inventories' 'phiale with shell boss/ornament' κογχωτή, ID 1444 Aa 6, 11; note χρυσοκογχύλιον (gold, or gilded real shell), in pseudo-Democritus (ii. 44 l. 19 ed. Berthelot).

[33] Naval cult of the goddess born of the *concha*, Plautus' 3rd-c. *Rudens* 702–5, the setting

contains in its mother-of-pearl interior one of the Charites, Aglaia or 'Gleam'—the shell endows its users with beauty as the gems of AB 6 may have bestowed χάρις on Niconoe. The pictured sea-nymph emphasizes the shell's marine origins. Readers familiar with art would likely imagine her with bared torso, erotically suggestive of the vision of a woman using the shell to bathe; Hellenistic epigrams (anon. *AP* 9. 325, sleeping Eros), also describe shells adorned with carvings.[34] Emerald, again Eastern, suggesting the new Ptolemaic mines at the Red Sea, is set like a drop of seawater in the gold-framed shell of AB 12. (Shell containers do gain metal ornament like silver handles and feet[35] by the third century.) If AB 11–12 are pendants, they recall ancient Egyptian jewellery;[36] if dishes, a vessel pair like AB 2–3. The place names evoke coastlines of what Greeks called the 'Red Sea' (which ancient geographers stretched from Egypt and Arabia across the Persian Gulf to India); this befits the link between shell dishes and aromatics, for costly perfumes like Arabian myrrh came along the same routes to support the royally controlled perfume industry.

AB 11 can be clarified by one third-century silver bivalve shell (Pl. 11);[37] on its lid, gold stripes mimic a shell's striations planed flat to expose an inner colour (as specified for the carving of the poem). On either side of the lid, relief tondos show a bejewelled nymph riding on a garnet-eyed sea-beast. A carving of Aglaia could have occupied a similar area inside the top shell of AB 11. But how were wax and γλύμμα associated? A seal carved on the flat bottom of a vessel,[38] or more likely, a shell sealed up, perhaps to contain perfume. Women would dream of holding these exotic new 'Indian' versions of a now-standard possession, male readers of seeing (and smelling) naked women at toilette—a favoured Hellenistic image in the visual arts.[39]

before Venus' shrine (related to the Cape Zephyrion Arsinoe/Aphrodite shrine?): E. Leach, 'Plautus' Rudens'; Gutzwiller, *Poetic Garlands*, 69. *Rudens* obviously has an Alexandrian source (woman named Ptolemocratia!).

[34] A post-Hellenistic shell poem specifies an Aphrodite, *AP* 9. 681: Kuttner, *Dynasty and Empire*, 304 n. 26, and for technique in the poem, cf. 224 n. 55, palmettes 'carved' in bronze patera shell-hinges.

[35] Women's excavated graves at Taranto set the chronology. See De Juliis, *Ori* 372 no. 7, 355–6 cat. 318. Several graves contained many shells, like 490 nos. 37–9; 498, nos. 30–4. S. Italian and Sicilian luxury arts had close links to Macedon, Pergamon, and Alexandria.

[36] e.g. a 3rd–2nd-c. golden cowrie chain (Pfrommer, *Greek Gold from Hellenistic Egypt*, 7, fig. 36) replicates Egyptian women's common good luck and fertility jewellery, cf. Rudolph, *A Golden Legacy*, 232 cat. 64.A.; 181–2, cat. 40.B: earrings with golden shell pendants.

[37] De Juliis, *Ori* 58–62, cat. 8, Taranto MN 22. 429–30, from the Tomba degli Ori at Canosa, 16 cm long, 4 cm thick.

[38] Ptolemaic agate dish, Bühler, *Antike Gefäße aus Edelsteinen*, cat. 12. Aristophanes' *Wasps*, 583–5 uses 'shell' (κόγχη) for a guard fixed over seals of wills.

[39] Related is Callimachus, GP 14, votive nautilos for Arsinoe-Aphrodite, with commentary,

Pale curved bodies begemmed, their nacreous, suggestively exposed interiors (for moist things, and to moisten), are metonymic for users' damp jewelled flesh; spreading (warm, white) impressed wax develops that sensuality.

HISTORIC COLLECTIONS AND IMPERIAL SEX

Like the shells, the parure of AB 4–7 is trendy: it combines novel formats like gemmed necklaces, recent booty from Persia, and stones from new Ptolemaic mines or eastern trade routes. It is left uncertain whether the stone of AB 5 was cut for Nicaea or sent from her lover's collection. ἀϲτερόεντα, 'bestarred', signifies that prized lapis lazuli flecked with gold pyrites; by word and image the little round blue bezel (ἡμίλιθοϲ)[40] naturally 'pictures' contemporary astronomers' globes in miniature. Niconoe's pendants in AB 6–7 charmingly replicate attested collecting of gem hangers for necklaces. Despite AB, the ἶριϲ of AB 6 is the prismatic rock-crystal from an island in the Red Sea off Berenice (*HN* 37. 136–7). One could translate 'beryl holding' ἶριϲ': Hellenistic jewellers routinely hung gold-set gems from each other, for earring and necklace pendants.[41]

First of the historic gems which imply royal cabinets, AB 4 signals long-term treasuring of objects of famous provenance; to store important knowledge makes a hoard a museum. I would argue that this poem's l. 2 evokes, though it cannot name, the gem-jewellery museum, δακτυλιοθήκη, at the start of the four jewellery poems. The word Δαρείου suggests Persia's overflowing palace treasuries, started

GP, p. 169; Gutzwiller, *Poetic Garlands*, 193–4, its fertility symbolism. Callimachus' *Lock of Berenice* prescribes cultic toilettes for divinized queens using 'onyches', attested gemware versions of traditional Egyptian unguent flasks in new Indo-Arabian stone (Arabian onyx we would call agate, *HN* 36. 60, 62); on this Egyptianizing ceremony, see L. Koenen, 'The Ptolemaic King as a Religious Figure', 108–10. Callimachus' serio-comic *Hymn* 5, *The Bath of Pallas*, says (13–17): 'do *not* bring the unfeminine Athena alabasters [perfume flasks], myrrh, specially confected unguents'.

[40] Stone: J. Spier, *Ancient Gems and Finger Rings* (Malibu, 1992), 6. It cannot mean 'star-like', as opaque blue stones do not resemble stars. Cf. *HN* 37. 100–1, *sandastros* or *pandastros*, 'starry all over', with sparkles mimicking the constellations Pleiades and Hyades in number and arrangement(!), like the natural forms (Apollo and the Muses) that appeared in Pyrrhus of Epirus' royal agate (*HN* 37. 5). The translation (Austin in AB) 'semi-precious' is not an ancient category; lapis was in any case one of the most precious ancient gems. 'Half-stone' is more likely the much-favoured cabochon-cut gem, like a halved sphere.

[41] M. Gronewald, 'Bemerkungen zum neuen Posidippus', 1 well proposes taking εἰϲ χρυϲέην (AB 8. 2) as 'set into a gold bit of necklace'; but not a focal gem embedded into a chain, which has no parallels; instead, a separate element, as was common. See Rudolph, *A Golden Legacy*, 162–9 no. 35, ten gemmed and/or figured pendants of the late 3rd–1st c.; at 166–7 the two parallels. Gutzwiller, 'Nikonoe's Rainbow' also argues (as in Ch. 15 below) that ἶριϲ is the stone and suggests new supplements for the poem.

by Cyrus, inherited by his successors. There are two possible sources for the jewel if it is in Egypt: dowry of a noble Persian bride (typically, vast amounts of drinking ware and of jewellery), or booty taken from Persian royal treasures by Ptolemy I. His hetaira Thais had her pick from Persepolis' regal γᾶζα; all his subsequent women must have received gifts from it.[42] The colour has suggested a bracelet of chalcedony (Pl. 12); such Persian-style bracelets were solid gem, here ornamented with gold, i.e. metal finials or encircling wire.[43] Mandene sliding off her jewels (disrobing) removes a husband's gift. 'Lamplight' illumines a bedroom, as in other Alexandrian erotic epigrams; the hard ornament's sliding touch on a soft 'desirable' wrist tropes a man's hand.[44] The love-act must be that engendering Cyrus, ideal ruler and nation-maker, the hero of Herodotus (see AB 9) and of Xenophon's *Cyropaedia*, exemplary for the Ptolemies as for Alexander. Imperial femininity looks back to AB 3, and ahead to AB 8's vicious feminizing of Darius III, Cyrus' last, unworthy successor. In the third century, Mandene must have evoked the noble and royal Persian consorts of Alexander and his ἑταῖροι (including Ptolemy I's half-royal bride, Artacama: Arr. 7. 4. 4–6) and their mass wedding at Susa. If the scroll is panegyric, Posidippus here offers an amulet for Ptolemaic queens' fertility and their sons' glory.[45]

KINGS' GEMS: TIME STONES AND TROPHIES

AB 8–10 is another series of body ornaments, this time male rulers' pectoral, ring, and bracelet or necklace. As throughout, that juxtaposes the sexes, shifting private to public, love to war. These stones seal meditations on empire, and on Greeks' relationships with eastern foreigners. AB 8–10 continue AB 4's fascination with pedigree of ornaments worn by historical personages. The stones are fetishized,

---

[42] Strabo 14. 1. 39 refers to the raiding of King Lysimachus' γᾶζα (adopted Persian word for treasure house).

[43] Persian tastes in pale, especially blue/grey, chalcedonies: J. Boardman, *Greek Gems and Finger Rings* (New York, 1970), 304. Gem-in-metal bracelets are not in the Achaemenid repertoire. Cf. De Juliis, *Ori* 246–7, cat. 170–1, paired 'twisted' chalcedony circles, from an early Hellenistic Tarentine grave. Other Persian-style bracelets were solid 'twisted' crystal; extant are broken circles, like that with Persianizing golden animal-head finials and gold wire in the grooves, Williams and Ogden, *Gold*, 77 no. 32, 330–300 BC, from ?Thessaloniki.

[44] In Greek art, males grasping female wrists make tacit sexual claims, initiatory of (marital) copulation.

[45] Queen Timaris (otherwise unknown) said in a 'not inelegant' epigram (*HN* 37. 178) that her gem dedicated to Aphrodite, a *paneros* ('all-love'), aided her fertility. Philip II dreamt of sealing Olympias' womb with a lion intaglio, marking her child with 'lion's nature' (Plu. *Alex.* 2). Note: Xenophon's *Cyropaedia* adapted for the tomb poem AB 60: Hutchinson, 'The New Posidippus and Latin Poetry', 5.

implying the desire to touch the famous dead through what once touched them, to impersonate them by inserting one's body into their costumes.[46] Historicized jewels exemplify how meaningfulness is an artefact too. These old and alien historic stones imply that meanings are transportable through time and across cultures, but must metamorphose in the process. That is especially true for gems of regal pride before great falls (AB 8–9).[47] The monitory coloration arises from new Stoic apprehensions of the inexorable succession of empires, and the dominance of $Τύχη$ (Fortune), to which Posidippus (following $λιθικά$ with $οἰωνοσκοπικά$) was as sensitive as Polybius.

AB 8's enormous sard (carnelian) on its gold chain is much discussed. Here it is identified for the first time as a Persian man's necklace, a real trophy taken by Ptolemy I in Alexander's conquest of Darius III, which signifies because of its function and history, not just because of its image of Darius. It is not a contemporary commission on a display hanger, which would be unparalleled in extant Greek art. 'Hung from no woman's neck' is a clear periphrasis for a man's necklace pectoral, with a hanger on each side. Long gems were indeed suspended laterally, as implied for AB 10, in the Iranian cultural zone, and texts note gems large enough for a horse's pectoral.[48] Spoliation of extraordinary Persian necklaces really occurred (Pl. 13). The pendant of a late Achaemenid enamelled and jewelled torque showed the royal chariot in battle (Pl. 14), analogous to our sard;[49] on the back a Greek, in best proprietorial spirit, has inscribed its weight. Alexander attached a begemmed eastern neckpiece to his battle helmet (Plu. *Alex.* 32). The qualities described convey that the necklace had been a great treasure for its Persian (royal?) wearer; for a Greek man it was functional solely as an heirloom.

The sard's image may have been either intaglio-cut, as there were large Graeco-Persian intaglio gems treasured as 'pictures', or in flattened low relief, resembling Pharaonic stone jewellery. It was not

[46] See Kuttner, 'Spectacle'. Compare Callimachus' vision of Ptolemy donning the Persian kings' headdress, $μίτρα$, to rule their empire, *Hymn* 4. 166. On collecting as fetishizing, John Forrester, '"Mille e tre"'; S. Stewart, *On Longing* (Durham, NC, 1993).

[47] Regal hubris punished by falling is literally denoted by AB 14, the Pegasus gem; the horse soared free, as it is described, after it threw the now old and arrogant king Bellerophon.

[48] Pfrommer, *Metalwork*, 44–5, and nn. 496–7; *HN* 37. 76–9, similar Indian settings for large, elongated beryl crystals, to show off their translucence (especially when they have no white clouded core); §113, greeny-gold chrysoprase (which comes large enough to make small vessels) commonly cut in 'cylinders'; §194, large-scale, 'eastern kings' military production of horses' chest pendants and forehead plaques in polished *cochlides*; Mesopotamian large, flat agate beads, Neolithic to at least 400, Rudolph, *A Golden Legacy*, 45–7 cat. 2.0.1–6, 53–4 cat. 9.

[49] *Treasures of Ancient Bactria* (Shigaraki, 2002), cat. 33, pp. 48, 207–10; Arnold, *Ancient Art from the Shumei Family Collection*, cat. 19.

a cameo, bicolour stone cut so that raised images are on differently coloured ground;[50] Posidippus specifies a clear, monocolour luminous slab with no 'cloud'.[51] Did the style look 'Persian'? Likely not. Achaemenid luxury art was produced by both Hellenic and Egyptian ateliers, in fusion styles familiar to early Alexandrian readers; Graeco-Persian gem prisms and seals especially show pictorially complex hunts and combats with (defeated) Greeks, including chariot scenes.[52]

The gold chain of AB 8 becomes a halter, enslaving the sard and its subject/owner. The bejewelled king is the Greeks' stereotype of effeminate, weak Eastern monarch. The chariot on gem evokes Darius' begemmed war-chariot, Alexander's booty and perhaps a Ptolemaic possession.[53] Persia's empire crumbled at the battle of Issus, when Alexander approached so near Darius' chariot that the panicked king fled, launching his huge army's final rout by Macedon's smaller force (cf. AB 31, 65). As many note, AB 8 evokes the fourth-century Macedonian masterpiece copied in Pompeii's second-century Alexander Mosaic.[54] Thus, formerly a pleasure to Persian owners, the gem's marvel of scale now mocks their former empire with the wonder of its overthrow, and a once-positive Persian portrait is transformed to one about its subject's denigration. Literally, its measure changes: Greek 'handspans' vividly convey grasping the enemy body, effeminized as lovely, καλός.

AB 9, Polycrates' famous emerald, suggests a real royal δακτυλιο-θήκη—but if not, the poet offers readers the chance to imagine, anyway, 'owning the Mona Lisa'. No scholar has yet restored the fragmented text with the name of the ring's famous artist, Theodorus

---

[50] See e.g. M. Henig, *The Content Family Collection of Ancient Cameos* (Leeds, 1990), pp. ix–xvi, 3. Kosmetatou, 'Posidippus, *Epigr.* 8 AB and Early Ptolemaic Cameos', concedes that evidence is strong against any sizeable cameos by Greeks in the 3rd c. Those she adduces are tiny monocolour sculpted bezels with an isolated head (cf. Walker and Higgs, *Cleopatra regina d'Egitto*, 82–3).

[51] Pliny's translation of the Greek technical term for this type of flaw in clear gems is *umbra*: *HN* 37. 68–9.

[52] Spier, *Ancient Gems and Finger Rings*, 56–7, cross-referencing Boardman's authoritative *Greek Gems and Finger Rings*, ch. 6; note especially 321 fig. 309 (now lost), a two-register cylinder inscribed in Aramaic. J. Boardman, *Persia and the West* (London, 2000), 166–74: multi-sided pear-shaped hangers and prisms ('tabloids') are common; a figure per side made up a group. For Persian war-chariots on fretwork plaques, see *Treasures of Ancient Bactria*, 253, cat. 210: perhaps itself nailed to a chariot rim.

[53] Curtius 3. 3.

[54] By 300 its core compositions were quoted from Apulia to Sidon. Most recently, P. Moreno, *Apelles: The Alexander Mosaic*, trans. D. Stanton (Milan, 2001). Kosmetatou, 'Posidippus, *Epigr.* 8 AB and Early Ptolemaic Cameos', 38–9, reads Darius' picture as a fair (καλός) and therefore heroic king under siege. However, technically he was never besieged; ancient sources which call him good-looking also stress his fear of Alexander.

(Hdt. 1. 51, 3. 41): one would have expected the poet to name him, as he did other famous makers of jewellery. The stone was likely blank, like most ancient emerald jewellery.[55] The first line's cφρηγίc need not mean intaglio-carved seal; temple inventories almost always say cφραγίc for single gems, though archaeology shows that many precious gems were plain. A ring can be a badge in its own right, proving identity and authenticity. The poem's lyre is not an intaglio image; rather, the lyre sounds at the poetry-loving tyrant's feet—a vignette of the gem-owner as in other λιθικά. The Samian throne vision collapses time, suggesting our author, and the Ptolemies' poetry contests; he pointedly honours as highly as the tyrant another poet (name absent), whose works have lasted like the ring.

Herodotus (3. 41–3) tells the story: Pharaoh Amasis advised Polycrates to sacrifice a treasure to avert bad fortune. After Polycrates threw this cherished ring into the sea (gem magic)[56] it returned, in a fish served to him at banquet. Amasis withdrew his friendship, to protect Egypt, understanding from the portent that Cyrus (see AB 4) would defeat Polycrates. This story was widely proverbial, not just antiquarian. The marine themes work with other λιθικά (AB 11–12, 19–20); prophecy, and empire, herald the next section on bird-omens. Is the poem's moment before Amasis' warning, while Polycrates is happy, or after the ring ominously returns? This darkened counterpart to the ruler vignettes AB 2–3 matches the closing, apotropaic citations of ancient catastrophes, AB 19–20.

Artist, ruler, owner, stone all engage Greece in Egypt, and also Persian imperialism as in AB 8. Amasis oversaw Theodorus' visits to Egypt, where he learned enough to become Hellas' first monumental architect and sculptor, and to write the first Greek texts on art, his own canons. Posidippus' song brings the ring Amasis saw home to the land of emeralds. The little 'mirror of princes' admonishes Ptolemy: be like Polycrates a master of the seas, good patron to Greek art and literature; but do not be a tyrant. Instead be a god-fearing,

---

[55] I contradict current readings. *Contra* Kosmetatou, 'Posidippus, *Epigr*. 8 AB and Early Ptolemaic Cameos', 36, *HN* 37. 8 references blank emerald as the standard descriptor. Hdt. 3. 41 is trustworthy, by closeness in time and normal accuracy: an emerald, cut by Theodorus, son of Telecles (whom Plantzos, *Hellenistic Engraved Gems*, 105 mistranslated as artist). Strabo 14. 1. 16: 'cut stone', which need not mean intaglio; Paus. 8. 14. 8 also says emerald. Livia reset, and Pliny saw, a sardonyx as the gem of Polycrates but his *HN* 37. 4 shows tactful doubt of the attribution. Though *smaragdi* were carved in Alexander's time (*HN* 37. 8), true emeralds were almost impossible to carve. Cf. *HN* 37. 62–4: for their unique ability to satisfy the eye and extraordinary lucent quality, 'humanity has ordained that emeralds are to be left unengraved, in their natural state'.

[56] V. Rosenberger, 'Der Ring des Polykrates im Lichte der Zauberpapyri'.

wise, lucky Egyptian king who looks after Greeks and their artists. The poem champions the Ptolemies' overlapped Egyptian/Greek ideology; Posidippus begins to emerge its champion as strongly as Callimachus or Theocritus.[57] None could miss Posidippus' polemic for little poems like his own in AB 9 and 67, which choose to celebrate Theodorus' tiny things, not his colossal temple, images, and vessels.[58]

Finally, the Nabataean 'cylinder' of AB 10, in stark contrast to its Persian pendant AB 8, evokes kings' collaboration in war and peace. Line 1 immediately presents a Near Eastern form, made by an anonymous artist for his king.[59] Seal cylinders were strung at the wrist, plain ones around the neck; Greeks from the fifth century onward hung imitations, plain or pictorial,[60] on chains, probably as necklaces for women. The appeal of the alien bracelet or necklace is like that of the Persian bracelet of AB 4: convergent taste is a metaphor for socio-cultural rapprochement. AB 10 implies a real, contemporary, regal alliance, and thus a real gem; no Greek knew of Nabataea until the late fourth century, when it defeated the Antigonids' attempt to seize Petra's royal treasures.[61] This gem signals Nabataea's assistance to Egypt in its third-century south-eastern and Syrian wars (note the epinician ending), and its ward over caravan routes from Arabia and the East. Its warrior king dispelled brigands who would have stolen Niconoe's stones (AB 6–7) en route.

[57] R. S. Bagnall, 'Archaeological Work on Hellenistic and Roman Egypt, 1995–2000' reviews the new evidence for Egyptianizing monuments in Alexandria's palace quarter. On this programme and its literary agents, D. Selden, 'Alibis'; J. Reed, 'Arsinoe's Adonis and the Poetics of Ptolemaic Imperialism'; seminal are Koenen, 'The Ptolemaic King as a Religious Figure' and id., 'Die Adaptation ägyptischer Königsideologie am Ptolemäerhof'. Now see Susan Stephens's formidable book, *Seeing Double* (Berkeley, 2003). I hope to expand on this character of Posidippus' stone poems in a future essay on AB 113, an Egyptianizing nymphaeum.

[58] J. J. Pollitt, *The Ancient View of Greek Art* (New Haven, 1974), 12–14, 35, 121, 123, 408, 431–2; A. Stewart, *One Hundred Greek Sculptors* (Perseus Web Project 1996), s.v. Theodoros. His art works: (i) a giant silver bowl holding 600 nine-gallon measures, dedicated by Croesus at Delphi (Hdt. 1. 51. 2–3); (ii) the self-portrait at the Samian Heraion holding a quadriga and file (*HN* 34. 83) was gone by Pausanias' day (10. 38. 6–7), but the chariot ended at the sanctuary of Fortuna at Praeneste; was it already separate and collectible in Posidippus' age, when the poet wrote about it without mentioning the accompanying self-portrait? (iii) possibly Bathyllus as poet, for the Samian Heraion (Apul. *Flor.* 15).

[59] Austin and Bastianini worry that 10 is too long, perhaps two separate poems; but the Near Eastern artefact in l. 1 binds to the last line's Near Eastern people.

[60] e.g. De Juliis, *Ori*, 310, 312, 315; Plantzos, *Hellenistic Engraved Gems*, 15–16; Rudolph, *A Golden Legacy*, 153 cat. 31.F; Spier, *Ancient Gems and Finger Rings*, 108; on the stylistic range for Greeks, Eastern and Persian to Hellenized: Boardman, *Greek Gems and Finger Rings*, 207, 210, 236, 309, and 293 pl. 595 (colour pl. 203. 3).

[61] In 312 BC: D.S. 19. 94–7, 100; G. W. Bowersock, *Roman Arabia* (Cambridge, MA, 1983), 13–17, 20–1, 46, 64, 70. Nabataean pirates at some point attacked Egyptian Red Sea stations, then were pacified; AB 10 seems to mark a collaborative stage before or after.

CHIMAERA

The cluster AB 13–15 resembles a hunter's παράδεκος and contains 'scientific' observations on optics (AB 13, 15). Fact or clever fiction (is Lynceus real . . .?), it nests a visual joke:[62] Pegasus (AB 14) separates bits of that monster which he helped dismember, lion, and serpent (AB 13, 15). Unlike fixed riddling appositions in (epigrams on) tomb reliefs,[63] this invites you to imagine rearranging your gems/pictures for new contingent meanings. Pegasus' blue jasper sky is another, well-recognized game, pairing colour with iconography as do other, contemporary Macedonian poets.[64]

The gem-beasts again evoke the East, where fierce and wonderful animals were 'mined'.[65] On the Red Sea coast, Ptolemy II founded Ptolemais 'of the Beasts' (Θηρῶν), for hunting the war-elephants vital to third-century land wars, and capturing interesting specimens for game-parks and menageries. Parodying Sotacus' stories about seeing in a king's possession (Ptolemy II) what (Eastern) hunters in chariots dug from the heads of 'dragons', AB 15 humorously depicts its own means of production.[66] It also miniaturizes Ptolemy II's thirty-cubit python, whose capture and transportation were recounted by Posidippus' contemporary, Agatharchides of Cnidus (D.S. 3. 36. 3–37). The king kept that Ethiopian beast in his zoo for 'the greatest, most astounding spectacle (θέαμα) for all strangers visiting the palace';[67] Posidippus and his Alexandrian audience must have visited after its presentation.

As readers knew, AB 14's Pegasus drinks with the Muses at Helicon

---

[62] Similarly playful is AB 35. 3 on Alexander's tomb for his seer Strymon, buried under a crow's image. Alexander 'sealed this image upon him' whom he called his (talking oracular) crow; ϲημήνατο (impressed a seal's design) puns upon both ϲῆμα, monument, and ϲημαίνω, signify. Cf. D. Sider, below, Ch. 9; K. Gutzwiller, below, Ch. 15.

[63] Compare triad structure on a three-jasper man's gold ring: Demetrius II and Cleopatra Thea between a wolf and a Ptolemaic eagle: L. Berg and K. Alexander, 'Ancient Gold Work and Jewelry from Chicago Collections', no. 114. On stela compositions, e.g. S. Goldhill, 'The Naïve and Knowing Eye', 199–200.

[64] Collecting matched image/colour poetic gems, Gutzwiller, 'Cleopatra's Ring'; ead., *Poetic Garlands*, 122; Plantzos, *Hellenistic Engraved Gems*, 111. Real patrons looked for the same match, like the 4th-c. gem-collecting musician Ismenias of Thebes who bought an emerald carved with the sea-nymph Amymone (*HN* 37. 6). We need more scholarship on how often images thus match colour on extant actual intaglios.

[65] Such emphases in the Grand Parade (e.g. Ath. 5. 200 E–201 C): Thompson, 'Philadelphus' Procession', 372; Werner Huss, *Ägypten in hellenistischer Zeit* (Munich, 2001), 292.

[66] *HN* 37. 158; Gutzwiller, 'Cleopatra's Ring', 387.

[67] D.S. 3. 36. 2–4 sums up Ptolemy II's animal collecting and the kings' passion for hunting. Carved stone impossible to carve (Pliny, *HN* 37. 158) surely mocks buyers gulled by the pseudo-science of a Sotacus (cf. n. 4).

and/or at Peirene, whose waters (AB 82) smiled on Berenice II and her own swift horse; Posidippus prayed to Muses of both sites (AB 118). At their pool, Athena, goddess of intellect and craft, granted Bellerophon a magical bridle (here shaken off) to tame Pegasus. 'With his hand, and with his mind ($\nu o \hat{v} c$), the hand-artist cut this': intellection's talisman for the carver-penman, who can control Pegasus. Nous, and aither, activate Platonic metaphors about the superior [poetic] soul whose winged steeds attain the heavens.

PHILOSOPHER'S STONES

AB 16 and 17 are unworked masses of stone, as if scientific specimens preserved in Alexandria's Museum. They are also natural portents on which to philosophize about art and aesthetics, eros and authorship. AB 16 describes a quartzite lump, providing either raw material for Ptolemaic royal portraits in the new translucent stones, or ore-matrix to be ground up to extract the last lines' gold. Either way, the poem savages vulgar collectors who depend on others' criteria of worth. The magnet, AB 17, echoes observations of Epicurean science,[68] and Heraclitus' twinned forces, eros and repulsion. The magnetic *symplegma* looks like ($\mu\iota\mu\epsilon\hat{\iota}\tau\alpha\iota$) one rock with two projections (a copulatory silhouette that plays on Hellenistic sex sculpture), welding another stone to itself by attracting its heart (*HN* 34. 147, 36. 126–7). Stoics would see a providential $\theta\alpha\hat{v}\mu\alpha$ (ll. 2 and 5).[69] But intellectuals would especially recall Plato; the *Ion*'s cosmic magnet (533 C–E) makes poets into jewellery,[70] magnetizing bards/iron rings in dangling chains of authorial filiation.[71]

---

[68] Hutchinson, 'The New Posidippus and Latin Poetry', 3 n. 8; cf. Lucr. 6. 1047. Posidippus in touch with Zeno's school, perhaps with Stoic literary circles around king Antigonus Gonatas of Macedon: Gutzwiller, *Poetic Garlands*, 129–30, 151–2. Stoics discussed $\phi\alpha\nu\tau\alpha\sigma\iota\alpha$ in terms of rings and seals, true impressions being stamped on our souls by what is (D.L. 7. 50, *Suda* s.v. $\Phi\alpha\nu\tau\alpha\sigma\iota\alpha$ $\kappa\alpha\iota$ $\phi\alpha\nu\tau\alpha\sigma\mu\alpha$ $\delta\iota\alpha\phi\epsilon\rho\epsilon\iota$), building on prior metaphors (Pl. *Tht.* 191 A–195 B; Arist. *de An.* 424ª17–24).

[69] Manifest e.g. in *HN* 36. 126–7.

[70] Transforming a scientific experiment: cf. *HN* 34. 147.

[71] AB 123, philosophers' banquet; AB 104, tomb for an Eretrian philosopher, schoolmate of Menedemus of Eretria. '[O]ne area of great importance, regrettably marginalized in the scholarly literature, is the relation between Hellenistic philosophy and Hellenistic literature': Goldhill, 'The Naïve and Knowing Eye', 207; at pp. 207–10 he outlines Platonic, Stoic, Aristotelian, Academic, and Epicurean visual and mimetic theory as (Alexandrian) elites would have known them.

THE SOCIOLOGY OF *ΤΡΥΦΗ*

The λιθικά map[72] τρυφή, luxury, as an empire fecund of gems opened up by Ptolemies I–III. That empire's 'Red Sea' touches almost every gem/poem: sardonyx, garnet, crystal, beryl, topaz, emerald, lapis, shell, quartzite.[73] AB 6's b[eryllion] came from India, its iris from an island in the Red Sea, AB 7's 'Arabian' honeystone (chrysoberyl or topaz) from another Red Sea island, Topazos. 'Arabian' 'mountain' rivers washing down rocks are seasonally flooded wadis (AB 7, 10, 16; landscapes, D.S. 3. 12–15). Mining stations there sifted naturally washed gem-bearing scree, then hand-washed precious matter from smashed ores.[74] AB 16 evoked the Arabian gold mines with their quartz beds, in terms so close to Agatharchides' discussion[75] as to confirm what one might guess, the poet's interest, for his geography of gems, in the royal explorer's factual text (see above, on the python). The λιθικά glitter with this providential stream. Gems begot gems: ideally suited to long-distance trade (value for weight), new corals and topazes were bartered directly in India for gems like AB 3's ἄνθραξ.[76]

Ptolemy II founded Berenice in his mother's name on the Red Sea's western shore (*HN* 37. 136); it was the landfall for the mineral-bearing islands, and guarded the emerald-mining zone (AB 6, 9, 12).

---

[72] A. Hardie, 'The Statue(s) of Philitas', 34: 'the section takes readers on a kind of geographical "tour", requiring them in most cases to identify locations for themselves. This is in keeping with the geographical content in the collection as a whole, including its reflections on the extent of the Ptolemaic empire.'

[73] Most discussions footnote Roman or Arabian studies: J. F. Breton, *Arabia Felix from the time of the Queen of Sheba*, trans. A. LaFarge (Notre Dame, 1999). Compare the programmatic effect of the major gem choices in Ptolemy II's Jerusalem dedication: ἄνθραξ, emerald, crystal, [Ethiopian] amber.

[74] Early Ptolemaic mining activity is hard to trace under later occupations; on gem production and extraction techniques, see I. Shaw, J. Bunbury, and R. Jameson, 'Emerald Mining in Roman and Byzantine Egypt', and Shaw's work generally.

[75] Agatharchides of Cnidus, who explored trade routes and colony sites for Ptolemy I and II, was heavily excerpted by Diodorus. See F. Pfister, 'Das Alexander-Archiv und die hellenistisch-römische Wissenschaft', 60 ff. D.S. 3. 12. 1: at the royal gold mines are 'seams and veins of a lustrous stone (μάρμαρος) of extraordinary whiteness, whose own brilliance (λαμπρότης) outshines everything else whose nature is to have brilliancy'.

[76] See the *Periplus Maris Erythraei* 3, 6, 10–11, 39, 48, 49, ed. Lionel Casson (Princeton, 1989). Studies of Ptolemaic economic policy (e.g. Richard Sidebotham, 'Ports of the Red Sea and the Arabia–India Trade', and Fraser, *Ptolemaic Alexandria*) typically state that the Red Sea zone was colonized not so much for trade or mines as for military resources, to get war-elephants. But indigenously generated wealth supported the court, paid the armies, and fed the elephants—mining emeralds and shipping myrrh was like mining money. Opulence was a weapon of statecraft; see e.g. Huss, *Ägypten in hellenistischer Zeit*, 218, 288–9 with more of a nod to trade motivations.

Royal officials[77] explored for these new mines, giving the queens gem boulders that could be transformed into queens: Ptolemy II commissioned a four-cubit topaz Arsinoe II from the boulder of new stone 'he greatly admired' brought to their mother (*HN* 37. 108). The dynasts absorbed an indigenous theocratic ideology that the king brings Egypt its (coloured) stones for jewels, building, and sculpture.[78] The goddess Hathor, now identified with Aphrodite, had looked after gem-prospecting as well as princes; the bureaucracy of exploration had an ancient Pharaonic pedigree, and imports went directly to court and sanctuary workshops, exiting as jewellery for royal largesse and badges of rank and office. Graeco-Egyptian portraits[79] still wear those traditional necklaces; Ptolemies donned them at Egyptian sanctuaries. Among Hellenistic kingdoms, Egypt's gem arts therefore especially suggested gifts to and from rulers: royal monopolies and court-based ateliers were the main suppliers to elite consumers.[80]

How the λιθικά celebrate this geographic expansion constitutes a fascinating socio-historical document. Here τρυφή takes its ideological sense, fecund peace which rewards and symbolizes power, as in the great Parade. The procession was fun to see, and Posidippan opulence is fun to read. But it would be naïve to miss the ideological programme which the poetry shares with the historic spectacle, of military, political, economic, and cultural dominance converging in Ptolemaic Alexandria.[81] Hellenistic Greeks prized gems because Alexander penetrated the foreign lands of their supply and use. But gems could not matter without settings; fourth-century Macedonian taste put new value on portable, precious, things which could hold the new stones set in new synthetic styles.[82] Posidippus of Pella boasted a Macedonian pedigree (AB 118).[83] His λιθικά, occurring at a moment when poet and audience could still admire their own new material culture as a matter of ethnic pride, address both the

[77] *HN* 37. 24 (Pythagoras), 108 (Philo).

[78] Ptolemaic officials' and priests' rings with royal portraits and cartouches continued the ancient association. See W. Huss, *Der makedonische König und die ägyptischen Priester* (Stuttgart, 1994) 39–40; ibid. 55–6, the Pharaonic-mode 'holy gold gemmed image' for Berenice daughter of Ptolemy III (Canopos Decree, *OGIS* 56; cf. Arnold, *Ancient Art from the Shumei Family Collection*, 4–7); ibid. 166, traditionalist late Ptolemaic Edfu inscriptions to Horos and Hathor citing royal gifts of 'all the precious stones of the quarries'; id., *Ägypten in hellenistischer Zeit*, 304 on Pharaonic royal lists of imported gems.   [79] R. R. R. Smith, 'Ptolemaic Portraits'.

[80] Kozloff, 'Is There an Alexandrian Style?', 248–9.

[81] I take as models Manning, 'Twilight of the Gods', 871–4, and M. Mann, *The Sources of Social Power*, i (Cambridge, 1986).   [82] M. Barry, 'Late Classical to Hellenistic'.

[83] Gutzwiller, *Poetic Garlands*, 151–2, biography. Material culture in Egypt and royally encouraged Macedonian self-assertion: M. Pfrommer, 'Roots and Contacts', 177–9; Kozloff, 'Is There an Alexandrian Style?', 248–50; around the 3rd-c. world, R. Billows, *Kings and Colonists* (Leiden, 1995).

poetic and the tangible miniature arts, celebrating modernist aesthetics in ornament and literature simultaneously. The fantastic authorial δακτυλιοθήκη, studded with stones that are self-referential about poetic authorship (AB 9, 14, 16, 17), suggests that gemcraft did embody critical positions for Posidippus. Showcased in AB 1's last line, λεπτή (delicately worked) could hint the miniaturist polish, λεπτότης, endorsed by the poet-critic Philitas, subject and paradigm of ἀνδριαντοποιικά's first statue poem (AB 63).[84] Scholars toss 'authorial sphragis' (self-emblematizing seal) at any Greek literature. But Hellenistic, Macedonian epigrammatists make the first signet poems, and the λιθικά give the first explicit gems of poetry.[85]

GEMMED WORDS

Epigrams about fine vessels and women's metal jewellery, the poetry of the precious, begin in the later fourth century; the Alexandrian poets contributed much. But so far unique is Posidippus' consistent focus on coloured gems, and so on their sources, settings, and histories (material and social). His gems' origins recall strange journeys, apposing civilized and wild; such poems swoop from maplike panoramic views (another Alexandrian novelty) to close-ups on gemmed breasts. To loving bodies, Posidippus matches hard stones aeons old that will outlive poet, lover, reader. Surely, as Hutchinson intimates, he inspired Latin poets of gems, who also fetishized touching jewels that touch women, traversing waters and lands to attain gemmed women. AB 5's Demylus has an erotic empire to conquer, if his girl consents to wear Persian stone! We can see something of the poet's context in stray epigrams by Asclepiades[86] (*AP* 12. 163 = GP 24; ring gift?)[87] and Adaeus (*AP* 9. 544 = GP, *Garland*

---

[84] λεπτότης praised in Ptolemaic gemmed goldwork: J. *AJ* 12. 75. A polemic for this quality opens the book on statues (AB 62. 1–2), as emphasized by G. Zanker, 'New Light'. Philitas' statue as embodiment of its subject's agenda: Hardie, 'The Statue(s) of Philitas', 32.

[85] 'Seal of Posidippus' now labels AB 118, not a stone; L. Lehnus, 'Posidippean and Callimachean Queries', 12. What was painted on the ring in his marble portrait type? For the presence of the ring, K. Fittschen, 'Zur Rekonstruktion griechischer Dichterstatuen, 2. Teil', 241.

[86] His jeweller-Eros sets [new Egyptian] emerald into gold, to model true male lovers' joining. Symposium and bed enter too: 'ivory in ebony' = Eros as cabinet-maker, suggestively veneering trendy couches in luxurious African materials.

[87] The 2nd–1st c. Leiden agate intaglio is large enough to take a uniquely epigrammatic inscription, above and below the figures of an unusual male–male lovemaking scene on a special love-gift, John R. Clarke, *Looking at Lovemaking* (Berkeley, 1998), 38–42, fig. 9: Παρδάλα πεῖ|νε τρύφα περιλά|μβανε θανεῖν σε | δεῖ ὁ γὰρ χρόνος | ὀλίγος | [bed image] Ἀχαιί, | ζήςαις; 'Leopard, drink, live in luxury [τρυφή], embrace! You must die, for time is short. May you live life to the full, O Greek!' (tr. Clarke.) The oval, banded agate glosses the nickname 'Leopard' by resembling that animal's spots.

9),[88] whose eroticized jewels also seduce readers to meditate on serious relationships between facture, authorship, and response. But our poet's consistent interest in artists, 'famous people's' gems, alien cultural excellence, and the poetic possibilities of matching wine and gem, have yet no match; and his distinctive taste for wrapping the precious thing in story, making a little spectacle of its usage, lets him rival the situations of 'ecphrasis' in more colossal literary genres.[89]

To whom are the λιθικά a possible gift? Their historicized jewels, imperialist overtones stress rulership. Their sensualities recall that jewellery is Aphrodite's sphere; seas, shells, and Poseidon evoke her watery birth and dominion. Given Aphrodite's identification with Arsinoe as patroness of marine empire (AB 39, 113, 116), any Aphrodisian ornaments can seem gifts to royal women. AB 4–7 assemble expensive beauties, just as the Ptolemies collected and displayed women, from princesses (AB 4) to performers (AB 143). Women of ambiguously hetaira-like character, AB 5–7, remind how the polygynous Macedonian nobility and their kings granted courtesans and concubines loftier places than did other Greeks, bringing them on campaign, favouring children by them, sometimes wedding them. In art, cult, and poetry, Ptolemaic ideology offered queens to public (eroticized) fantasy. Posidippus, the new Hephaestus, designs his gems both like the artist of AB 5, and like the cτρατηγοί who brought new gems to queens. The whole λιθικά can be seen as a gemmed 'object,' scintillating with coloured patterns,[90] as when Ptolemy's Parade wheeled an enormous gold crown of variegated gems around Berenice's golden shrine (Ath. 5. 202 D), or women strung gem pendants of different shapes and meanings across their breasts.

CODA

In the λιθικά the materiality of ornament emphasizes poetry about it as book, not song,[91] a material artefact, scratched on paper or wax

---

[88] This foreshadows Ovid's Pygmalion and his Galatea: Tryphon, 'Τρυφή-man', 'persuades' stone with his 'soft hands' into showing the swimming Galene who speaks of her shaping.

[89] Paradigmatic for jewellery scenes are e.g. Aphrodite's bedecking, and undressing by her lover, *h.Hom.* 6; *h.Ven.* 5. 84–91, 160–5; Hera bejewelling herself to beguile Zeus *Il.* 14. 159–85, 214–21; Pandora's adorning, and zoomorphic crown, Hes. *Th.* 570–89, *Op.* 72–82.

[90] Listing the λιθικά poems/gems in their varied colours, one finds AB 1–3: ?/?/red; 4–7: white-grey/blue/green/yellow-brown; 8–10: red/green/?white-pale; 11–12: pearly white with ?-stone colour/green; 13–15: red?/blue/white-pale; 16–17: white-pale/?-iron-black. A dangling rainbow, AB 6 (*iris*) refracts all the repeating colour clusters, interlaced by yellow gold.

[91] On craft and script metaphors for Archaic Greek oral poetics, Gregory Nagy, 'The Library of Pergamon as a Classical Model', 211.

as gems are scraped by engravers. The act of reading reminds that experience of poems, too, can be the visual scrutiny of a marked-up object. Owners pricked their names on metal; artists worked names and votive tags and even signature poems into a γραμματικὸν ἔκπωμα or letter-cup;[92] even gold bezels say Χαῖρε (Greetings!).[93] But few jewels could hold the poems about them; bracelets and rings were not dowelled to pedestals, freezing their proximity to text. Rather, this scroll collects epigrams, as if bits of paper dispersed with or as gifts. Yet the poet does not lose what he gives away; owning nothing, he collects all in his paper museum. Unlike the unique jewel, its description is replicable; intaglio poems, like intaglios, existed to disseminate perfect images of themselves upon writing materials.

Hellenistic gem artistry gave Posidippus powerful metaphors. Gemmed ornament nests substances. To choose, embed, juxtapose a word, or an epigram, remade older metaphors of ποίηcιc. As intertext, other poets are gems to inlay, their lines, heirloom allusions—or plunderable δακτυλιοθῆκαι, exploitable mines! Object assemblage, as the gem and statue sections celebrate it, tropes editorship and anthology. Authors essay gems others will treasure, accumulate; editors who make one assemblage also anticipate reconstellation.[94]

Enduring, gems colour their paper descriptions' fragility. Any hand likely to open the λιθικά wore, like the hand which authored it, at least one ornament. As their fingers traced crabbed letters, hands smoothing the papyrus, readers would be led to meditate the physical and visual alignment of solid and written jewellery. Alexandria's new Museum culture battled entropy: books rot, live memories die, 'texts' disappear.[95] Gem poetry is perhaps gem magic. In reproduction, let my words last like Polycrates' unsinkable emerald—a magic that now turns out to have worked.

---

[92] Around Posidippus' time and homeland, rim inscription on the Derveni krater: *The Search for Alexander* (Boston, 1980), cat. 127. Note Ath. 11. 782 B: a relief cup (contemporary work or collectors' forgery?) of Troy: 'The composition (γράμμα) of Parrhasius, the artistry of Mys: I am the work (ἔργον) of lofty Ilion, that the Aiacids took.'

[93] Williams and Ogden, *Greek Gold*, 73, cat. 29; the onset of classical talking rings (e.g. recipient's name in the dative meaning 'For you, X'): Boardman, *Greek Gems and Finger Rings*, 236; inscribed late Hellenistic and Roman cameos and intaglios: Henig, *The Content Family Collection of Ancient Cameos*, 6–9; cf. the late Hellenistic 'Leopard' agate, n. 88, maybe inspired by then-extant intaglio poems.

[94] Reconstellated Posidippan poems, Gutzwiller, *Poetic Garlands*, 24–5.

[95] Alexandrian preserving and editing vs. material and linguistic corruption of textual bodies: Nagy, 'The Library of Pergamon as a Classical Model', 194–201, 210.

9

Posidippus on Weather Signs and the Tradition of Didactic Poetry

DAVID SIDER

Fifteen of the new poems, AB 21–35, are labelled οἰωνοσκοπικά. The first editors analyse their order and arrangement by noting that the first four 'riguardano l'apparire di ucelli che costituiscono un buon auspicio per la navigazione o per la pesca'.[1] This is true as far as it goes, but it is also important to note that the first four are to be distinguished from those that follow, in that 21–4 are of the sort found in the traditional weather literature, which is devoted to listing, but rarely explaining, signs of imminent changes in the weather that would be of interest to, primarily, farmers and sailors. Aratus' Διοσημίαι section and the end of Vergil's *Georgics* 1 are the most famous examples of this kind of text, but they were but versifications of a much larger prose literature devoted to this subject.[2] The remaining oionoskopic epigrams, all but the last two,[3] in the New Posidippus collection also

---

[1] BG, p. 25. For an important study of the οἰωνοσκοπικά, see Baumbach and Trampedach, '"Winged Words"'. My examination here of the first four οἰωνοσκοπικά complements theirs of the ominal epigrams. I hold Posidippus himself responsible for this particular arrangement of the epigrams in this section (as in the collection as a whole), even if, as will be argued below, he found this same distinction between scientific and ominal in a prose source. On the question of the arrangement of all the epigrams on the papyrus, cf. Gutzwiller, 'A New Hellenistic Poetry Book'. On a possible link between the οἰωνοσκοπικά and the preceding section (λιθικά), cf. Petrain, 'Homer, Theocritus, and the Milan Posidippus'.

[2] For weather literature in general, see R. Böker, 'Wetterzeichen'; for a survey of all known prose and verse texts on the subject, see the introduction to D. Sider and W. Brunschön's forthcoming edition of Theophrastus, *De Signis*.

[3] Each of the last two is on a noteworthy bird seer: AB 34 purports to be an inscription set up on the hill where Damon of Telmessus observed birds and interpreted their signs. The last sentence invites the reader to do the same. Perhaps this is intended as an oblique grave marker. Cf. Thphr. *Sign.* 4, which associates astronomers who observed weather signs with their respective mountains: Matricetas on Mt. Lepetymnus, Cleostratus (who wrote in verse, by the way) on Mt. Ida, Phaeinus on Mt. Lycabettus, 'and there were many others who studied astronomy in this way'. AB 35 is a sepulchral epigram for Strymon of Thrace, noting and explaining why an image of a (prophetic) crow marks his grave: ὧι τόδ' Ἀλέξανδρος ϲημήνατο, i.e. in a mild pun (missed by BG and AB, but see Kuttner, Ch. 8 n. 62 and Gutzwiller, Ch. 15, pp. 309–11), Alexander marked Strymon's ϲῆμα (grave; LSJ s.v. 3) with a ϲῆμα (an appropriate image; LSJ s.v. 5) of the particular ϲῆμα (LSJ s.v. 1), the crow, that served as Strymon's bird

contain predictions, but it would be fair, even by ancient standards, to call them omens; that is, not only do they not predict the weather, they are also less scientific and more religious and superstitious.[4] Homer once, in an odd but effective simile, lumps the two sorts of results together when, during the battle over Patroclus' body, he declares a rainbow a sign of either battle or a winter storm that casts a chill over human activity.[5] More normally, though, as in this section of Posidippus, the two kinds of results are kept distinct. Thus, even though an ordinary soldier (τιc), with none of Calchas' predictive skills, interprets a shooting star seen just before a battle so cautiously as to render it useless as prophecy—ἢ ῥ' αὖτιc πόλεμοc . . . | ἔccεται, ἢ φιλότητα . . . τίθηcιν | Ζεύc (*Il.* 4.82–4)—he at least, even if he does not know whether war or peace is indicated, keeps his categories straight. None the less, the need for experts (such as Posidippus' Damon, AB 34) and, later, technical treatises was clear.

AB 21–4, though, as just said, contain 'scientific' signs (of weather, that is, not war vel sim.), which are typically either themselves meteorological in nature or derived from unusual, but not bizarre, animal behaviour. To judge from the treatises in which these signs were listed and discussed, the Greeks regarded them as generally quite distinct from those sent by gods, which can be of various kinds (dreams, oddities like sweating statues, or chance occurrences). That the epigrams in this section show by their very segregation this same distinction is therefore noteworthy in itself. The remaining poems in this section contain such signs as an old man crying at a crossroads,[6] a moving bronze statue, an armed servant falling, a dream; and results pertaining to the buying of slaves, childbirth, and marriage. None of these signs or results ever appears in the usual weather literature.

---

sign. For a somewhat similar pun on this word, cf. Eur. *Hec.* 1273 κυνὸc ταλαίνηc cῆμα, ναυτίλοιc τέκμαρ, where a sign of one sort serves as a sign of a second sort (cῆμα and τέκμαρ can serve as synonyms in omen literature). On these two epigrams see Bernsdorff, 'Anmerkungen zum neuen Poseidipp', 13; S. Schröder, 'Überlegungen zu zwei Epigrammen'.

[4] The precise relationship between 'science' and 'magic, religion, superstition', etc. is, I am well aware, not so polar as this; cf. e.g. G. E. R. Lloyd, *Magic, Reason and Experience* (Cambridge, 1979), 49–58. None the less, the distinction I make in this chapter is the one implicitly followed throughout ancient weather literature. The gods, including Zeus the weather god, may be thought to signal many events of interest to humans, but not in these texts, where no sign is given a divine origin or cause. Concentrating as I shall do on the first four epigrams in the οἰωνοcκοπικά, therefore, I find it easy to divide this section into (i) scientific, (ii) ominal, and (iii) personal. For other divisions, see Baumbach and Trampedach, '"Winged Words"', 128–37, with a review of other organizational schemes; and D. E. Lavigne and D. J. Romano, 'Reading the Signs' (I thank Don Lavigne for allowing to me to see this paper in advance of publication).

[5] τέραc ἔμμεναι ἢ πολέμοιο, | ἢ καὶ χειμῶνοc δυcθαλπέοc, ὅc ῥά τε ἔργων | ἀνθρώπουc ἀνέπαυcεν ἐπὶ χθονί, *Il.* 17. 548–50.   [6] The 'old man' may in fact be a wren; cf. Petrain, 'Πρέcβυc'.

I

In this section, then, I would like, first, to show in detail the relationship between these four poems and the related scientific literature, especially the work which served as source for all Hellenistic and subsequent literature, the Theophrastan *De signis*. (Some pertinent parallels with this text have already been noted by Bastianini and Gallazzi.) This will lead in section II to the subject of the relationship between these four poems of Posidippus and didactic poetry. Because the poems are still so new to us, however, it will be best first to establish the text and meaning on which we plan to base our interpretation.

21

νηὶ καθελκομένηι πάντα πλέον᾽ ἰνὶ φανήτω
ἴρηξ, αἰθυίης οὐ καθαροπτέρυγος·
δύνων εἰς βυθὸν ὄρνιc ἀνάρcιοc, ἀλλὰ πετέcθω
ὕψο [. . .] [. . .] [.] φ᾽ ὅλωc·
οἷοc ἀπὸ δρυὸc ὦρτ᾽ Ἰακῆc ὠκύπτεροc ἴρηξ   5
ἱρῆι, Τίμων, cῆ νηὶ καθελκομένηι.

For a ship setting out to sea let a hawk appear with altogether great force, while the shearwater does not clean its wings. A bird diving into the deep is hostile [i.e. a bad sign]; rather let fly high [the hawk] . . . wholly. Such a swift-winged hawk rose from an Ionic (oak?) tree, Timon, for your ship, sacred, setting out to sea.

1 πλέον᾽ ἰνί] *ΠΛΕΟΝΙΝΙ* is the reading of the papyrus, which I articulate as πλέον(ι) ἰνί and Gronewald, 'Bemerkungen zum neuen Posidippos', 1–2, as πλέον ἰνί (taking what follows as genitive of comparison rather than gen. absolute: 'Wenn ein Schiff zu Wasser gelassen wird, zeige sich unbedingt *öfter kraftvoll* der Falke als die unreine Möwe'). An elided iota in a dative singular noun or adjective is uncommon; see D. B. Monro, *A Grammar of the Homeric Dialect*, §§373, 376 (3), whose suggestion of original length is confirmed by the survival in Mycenaean of Indo-European *-ei*. Homer offers fewer than fifteen examples and Theognis three (265, 1326, 1329). All examples offered by MSS of tragedy, however, have been emended away, even some that make perfect sense (see e.g. Easterling on S. *Tr.* 675; and for tragedy in general, Jebb, *Soph. OC*, pp. 289–90). On this elision in Attic inscriptions, see L. Threatte, *The Grammar of Attic Inscriptions*, i. 424. Among Hellenistic poets, Lycophron has two instances (894, 918), which is a little perverse, since he is remarkably sparing of elision in general. None the less, an elided iota for

Posidippus still seems defensible, especially given the following long iota, which makes what is here written as elision indistinguishable from crasis when the poem is read aloud; cf. $Δἰ = Διἰ$.[7]

2 ἴρηξ] Only two weather signs involving a hawk were known before this poem (not one, as said by BG ad loc.). The first is Thphr. *Sign.* 17 'If a hawk sitting on a tree and flying directly into it hunts for lice, it signals rain'; the second is Dionysius, *de Aucupio* 2. 9 (30. 6–12 Garzya) φίλτατοι δ᾽ εἰcὶν οἱ ἐρωιδιοὶ τοῖc ἀνθρώποιc καὶ προcημαίνουcιν εὐδίαν τε καὶ χειμῶνα, μάλιcτα πρὸc ἐκεῖνο τὸ μέρος, ὅθεν ἂν μέλληι cφοδρότατος ἄνεμος πνεῖν, ἐπὶ τοῖc cτήθεcι τὰc κεφαλὰc κατακλίνοντεc. ναύτηc γοῦν οὐκ ἄν ποτε ἑκὼν ἐρωιδιὸν ἀποκτείνειεν, ἐπειδὴ πιcτεύονται τοῖc ἁλιεῦcιν ἐν τῆι θαλάττηι cημαίνειν <u>ὁπόcα τοῖc θηραταῖc ἐπὶ τῆc γῆc οἱ ἱέρακεc</u>.[8] That is, the flight of hawks, especially their hovering, can be read for the direction and force of the wind, which is exactly what sailors setting out would like to know in advance.[9]

αἰθυίηc οὐ καθαροπτέρυγοc] Shearwaters flapping their wings and/ or diving are a bad sign;[10] cf. Thphr. *Sign.* 28 αἴθυιαι καὶ νῆτται καὶ ἄγριαι καὶ τιθαccαὶ ὕδωρ μὲν cημαίνουcι δυόμεναι, πτερυγίζουcαι δὲ ἄνεμον, Aristotle fr. 270. 21 Gigon (= Aelian, *NA* 7. 7) νῆτται δὲ καὶ αἴθυιαι πτερυγίζουcαι πνεῦμα δηλοῦcιν ἰcχυρόν (= *CCAG* viii/1. 138. 16 = Anon. Laur. 11. 35[11]), Aratus 918–19 πολλάκι δ᾽ ἀγριάδεc νῆccαι ἢ εἰναλίδιναι | αἴθυιαι χερcαῖα τινάccονται πτερύγεccιν, *Suda* αι 155 (2. 167. 5 Adler) αἱ γὰρ αἴθυιαι ὅταν δύνωcι κάκιcτος οἰωνὸc ὑπάρχει τοῖc πλέουcι, Posidippus AB 23, discussed below. Thus, although sailors,

---

[7] BG and AB emend to πλέοc ἰνί ('. . . may a hawk appear *all full of strength*, as the shear-water's wings are not of good omen'), taking the last three words, as I do, as a genitive absolute without οὔcηc, referring to KG ii. 102 (although this is quite rare in poetry). AB also note that Gronewald's version should call for a generic μή rather than οὐ, but poetry is not always so strict; cf. KG ii. 188. Lapini, 'Osservazioni sul nuovo Posidippo' would read πλόον, 'quando la nave è tratta in mare per un intero viaggio, appaia con forza l'ἴρηξ' (39), but his *per*, which seems to represent both purpose and an accusative of extent, is hard to justify.

[8] In its current state, this work is a prose reworking of a lost didactic epic, which no doubt was in turn a versification of an even earlier prose treatise on weather signs; cf. A. Garzya, 'Sull'autore e il titolo del perduto poema "Sull'aucupio" attribuito ad Oppiano', who argues that the lost poem in question was written by Dionysius the Periegete, who was credited with a Διοcημίαι (a term also applied to the last section of Aratus); cf. O. Crusius, 'Dionysios (94)', 923, who seems sympathetic to Rühl's suggestion that this is the same work as the Μετεωρολογούμενα attributed by the *Suda* to Dionysius of Corinth.

[9] Nobody needs advance warning of bad weather and the skill to detect it so much as a sailor, preferably *before* the ship sets out. Cf. Alcaeus 249. 6–9 V. ἐˌκ γᾶc χρὴ προΐδην πλόˌον | αἴ τιc δύναταˌι καὶ πˌαλˌάμαν ἔˌχˌηι, | ἐπεὶ δέ κ᾽ ἐν πˌόηˌτωι γˌένηται | τῶι παρεόντι †τρέχειν† ἀνάˌγκα; Ar. *Av.* 596–7 προερεῖ τιc ἀεὶ τῶν ὀρνίθων μαντευομένωι περὶ τοῦ πλοῦ· | "νυνὶ μὴ πλεῖ, χειμὼν ἔcται." "νυνὶ πλεῖ, κέρδοc ἐπέcται."

[10] On the identification of the αἴθυια (which sometimes seems to be a cormorant), see W. G. Arnott, 'Notes on *gavia* and *mergi* in Latin Authors'.

[11] This last is an anonymous list of weather signs in Cod. Laur. 28. 32, ff. 12ʳ–15ᵛ edited by M. Heeger, *De Theophrasti qui fertur Περὶ cημείων libro* (Diss. Leipzig, 1889), 66–71.

as Pindar says, sometimes have a need for winds,[12] too much can be dangerous, as only Aristotle, Posidippus, and the *Suda* spell out.

It is also a sign of wind when a shearwater cleans its feathers according to (and before this papyrus only according to) Pliny, *NH* 18. 362 *mergi* (= αἴθυιαι) *anatesque pinnas rostro purgantes ventum* [sc. *significant*]. (Missed by D'A. W. Thompson.) In our epigram, therefore, καθαροπτέρυγος has to be understood with the first element verbal and active: 'wing-cleaning', with which compare Opp. *H*. 2. 482 φερέπτυξ, 'bearing wings, i.e., winged', where, however, φερε-, unlike καθαρο-, can *only* be verbal. Moreover, as LSJ note, the form actually found in Oppian, φερεπτύγων, could be a form of φερεπτέρυγος, -ον, but this difference of form does not matter (as Bastianini and Gallazzi note ad loc.). Even if it were an exact parallel, Posidippus' formation would have struck his contemporaries as quite odd, which is sometimes precisely the aim of a Hellenistic poet. The translations in AB are therefore inadequate ('poiché la berta non è propizia di ali', 'as the shearwater's wings are not of good omen'). Closer to the truth is W. Lapini's 'quando la berta non ha le ali pure', which he spells out as 'quando le ali della berta sono incrostate di salsedine, segno che si è tuffata in mare.'[13] As a weather sign, however, this is most impractical. How can an observer be expected to know that the gull's wings are clean? To be consistent with the many weather signs found in the technical and didactic literature (Theophrastus, Aratus, Vergil, and Pliny are but the best-known examples), what is needed is an action, here the act of cleaning feathers with a beak (or, as in Aratus, beating the wings on the ground). With this self-conscious coining of a hapax legomenon, compare AB 62, where Posidippus praises Lysippus for being a καινοτέχνης; but since Posidippus has (in all likelihood) just coined this word, he thus manages to praise himself for being this same kind of artist.

ἰρῆι] why is the ship sacred? In part, I suspect, simply because Posidippus liked the jingle of ἴρηξ ἰρῆι. (May we compare *Dies irae?*) In this case, however, it would also allude to the notion of like-to-like that lies behind some weather signs.[14] For examples, cf. Thphr. *De*

---

[12] For the reference to Pindar's Eleventh *Olympian*, see below, n. 23.

[13] Lapini, 'Note posidippee', 45.

[14] Like-to-like is an important notion among Presocratics and some medical writers. Note how Socrates sums up his scientific predecessors by referring to their fondness for this relationship at *Lysis* 214 B οὐκοῦν καὶ τοῖς τῶν σοφωτάτων συγγράμμασιν ἐντετύχηκας ταῦτα αὐτὰ λέγουσιν, ὅτι τὸ ὅμοιον τῷ ὁμοίῳ ἀνάγκη ἀεὶ φίλον εἶναι· εἰσὶν δέ που οὗτοι οἱ περὶ φύσεώς τε καὶ τοῦ ὅλου διαλεγόμενοι καὶ γράφοντες. Cf. C. W. Müller, *Gleiches zu Gleichem* (Wiesbaden, 1965). The two words are not related etymologically, although Chaintraine, *Dict. Etymol.* s.v. ἱέραξ allows for the possibility that its rough breathing is perhaps due to the influence of ἱερός (if not ἵημι).

signis 15 'Nonaquatic birds bathing themselves are a sign of rain or storm. And a toad washing itself and frogs croaking more than usual signal rain', where the water sought by the birds and frogs portend the water that will fall as rain; 16 'if . . . during fair or foul weather (a raven) imitates the sound of raindrops, it signals rain' (similarly with birds and chickens in 17); 42 'the build up of ash [on an oil lamp] signals snow.' The sign looks or sounds like its result. Posidippus' example is of his own poetic devising, however; no known weather sign works so onomastically. Omens do, though: *nomen est omen*. The δεξιός object/hand/side is the δεξιός sign.[15] One has to wonder, therefore, whether Posidippus has converted a sign of an ordinary sort (and birds are the most common animal sign in the weather literature) into a κληδών, a verbal utterance that more than presages its outcome, it was imagined actually to cause it,[16] although a κληδών should be distinguished from those curses and prayers that depend upon visual but non-verbal similarities; for example, while holding a sere leaf one says 'Let so-and-so be like the dead, as is this leaf'—a type of magic imprecation that is called *similia similibus*.[17] These curses work (or are supposed to) even though the intended victim is well out of hearing; for a κληδών to work, not only must the person hear it, he must understand it.[18] Otherwise it is like the tree falling in the forest. Such sensitivity to the meaning of words is of course precisely what a poet would hope to find in his audience, so that in this case the κληδών and poem become one; the meaning of the latter cannot be fully understood unless the former is too. To return to our initial question: the ship is sacred at the end of the poem (it was not so designated in l. 1) *because* of the appearance of the hawk.[19]

The pertinence of these observations is twofold. First, the parallels from the prose weather treatises firmly establish the empirical/scientific nature of the hawk as a weather sign. It is not, that is, a bird sign of the sort we see often in Homer and elsewhere (such as in all but

This would not of course stop a poet; cf. Lavigne and Romano, 'Reading the Signs', 16, and Gutzwiller Ch. 15, pp. 306–7.

[15] Cf. D. Collins, 'Reading the Birds', 29–30, who discusses *LSAM* 30 A (Ephesus 6th–5th c.), which calls a bird δεξιός which raises its δεξιός wing. See also Baumbach and Trampedach, '"Winged Words"', 142–4.

[16] Cf. Fraenkel on Aes. *Ag.* 1653; J. J. Peradotto, 'Cledonomancy in the *Oresteia*'.

[17] Cf. F. Graf, *Magic in the Ancient World*, tr. F. Philip (Cambridge, MA, 1997), ch. 7, 'Words and Acts'. I draw my example of the leaf from his p. 211. Cf. Pos. 28, where the κλαίων πρέσβυς presages Τιμολέων κεκλαυμένος; cf. Petrain, 'Πρέσβυς', 12 n. 18.

[18] As Peradotto, 'Cledonomancy in the *Oresteia*', 8, puts it, 'it goes without saying that hypersensitivity to the spoken word is implied in cledonomancy.'

[19] Hutchinson, 'The New Posidippus and Latin Poetry', 4, points out how the last line of Catullus 16 also closely echoes the first.

the last two of the remaining epigrams in this section of the papyrus), a sign of divine favour or displeasure. Contrast, for example, Bastianini and Gallazzi's linguistic parallel, *Od.* 20. 101, where Odysseus asks Zeus for a favourable sign (Διὸς τέρας ἄλλο φανήτω), whereupon Zeus immediately produces thunder. Posidippus' sign, on the other hand, is exactly of the sort we see throughout the ancient literature of weather signs from Democritus to the Byzantine work known as the *Geoponica*. This brings us to our second point, however. While the hawk sign is indeed *of the sort* we see in ancient weather literature, this particular sign is not in fact to be found there, although repetition of signs from text to text is a hallmark of weather literatures, where truth and usefulness are considered far more valuable than originality. Indeed, some signs attributed to Democritus are still to be found in the *Geoponica*.[20] It is only thanks to the parallel found in Dionysius, added rather casually only to illustrate Dionysius' main point, that we can account for its meaning.

Similarly, the precise meaning of the oddball formation of the hapax legomenon καθαροπτέρυξ can be discerned only thanks to the one passage in Pliny. Posidippus thus neatly manages to allude to a rarely recorded fact with a unique word. He has, it seems, gone out of his way to to find weather signs beyond those found in the traditional sources. What are these sources? Writers on the subject whose works were available to Posidippus were Democritus, Aristotle, Theophrastus, and Eudoxus; also available was *De signis* (the only such text now extant). What about Aratus, who may well have been an exact contemporary of Posidippus? (310 BC has been put forth on entirely separate grounds as a likely birth year for each poet.) And more than being merely his contemporary, Aratus, as ancient evidence is united in telling us, was commissioned to compose his *Phaenomena* by none other than King Antigonus of Pella, Posidippus' home town.[21] Previously this last fact had been of minimal interest, but it is now tempting to imagine Posidippus present during Aratus' stay in Pella in the years 276 and following, writing these epigrams as a (friendly?) coda in the form of epigrammatic alternatives (on which more below). Aratus, then, would not be Posidippus' source (see further below), but rather a text to be supplemented.

---

[20] The *Geoponica* often specifically credit Democritus with particular observations on the weather: 1. 5. 3, 1. 12. 5, 11, 17, 28, 40. For an argument that Democritus did indeed record weather signs, cf. Sider, 'Demokritos on the Weather'.

[21] *V. Arat.* 1 (8. 3–9 Martin) ὃς παρὰ τῷ βασιλεῖ γενόμενος καὶ εὐδοκιμήσας ἔν τε τῆι ἄλληι πολυμαθείαι καὶ τῆι ποιητικῆι προετράπη ὑπ᾿ αὐτοῦ τὰ Φαινόμενα γράψαι, τοῦ βασιλέως Εὐδόξου ἐπιγραφόμενον βιβλίον Κάτοπτρον δόντος αὐτῶι καὶ ἀξιώσαντος τὰ ἐν αὐτῶι καταλογάδην λεχθέντα περὶ τῶν φαινομένων μέτρωι ἐντεῖναι; sim. §3 (16. 24–8).

22

ὄρνις μὲν β[ο]υκαῖος ἐπήρατος ἀνδρὶ γεωργῶι
φαινέςθω, λήπτης καὶ περὶ φύτλ' ἀγαθό[ς·
ἡμῖν δ' Αἰγύπτου πέλαγος μέλλουςι διώκειν
Θρῆςςα κατὰ προτόνων ἡγεμονέοι γέρανος,
cῆμα κυβερνήτηι καταδέξιον, ἢ τὸ μέγ' [ἴςχει   5
κῦμα, δι' ἠερίων cω[ιζο]μένη πεδίων.

2 λήπτης : ληιςτής Gronewald   5 ἴςχει Sider εἰςι BG ἀθρεῖ Austin ἔχθει Gronewald

To the farmer let appear a welcome wagtail, a catcher of flies and (a) good (sign) for plants.[22] But for us about to follow the sea to Egypt let a crane from Thrace lead, (flying) over the forestays, a favourable sign for the pilot, and it (sc. the crane) holds in check the great wave, keeping itself safe through the plains of air.

The first distich is a brief priamel: 'Some people (farmers) like the wagtail, but we (sailors) like . . .'.[23] It is also hard to pin down. Although the bird in question seems to be a common wagtail (as ably demonstrated by Bastianini and Gallazzi), the mere appearance of so common a bird can hardly have predictive value since it would be seen before all kinds of weather. If only it could be shown to be a cπίνος, a finch, which is credited with the ability to predict rain; e.g. Thphr. *Sign.* 23 'a chaffinch singing . . . in the afternoon signals rain.'[24] And rain, if not in excess, is 'good for plants'. With this last phrase, cf. §25 'it is better for plants and animals if the rain comes first from the north', Aratus 1087 γίνεται οὔτε φυτοῖς χειμὼν φίλος οὔτ' ἀρότοιςιν.

Αἰγύπτου πέλαγος: rather than 'mare d'Egitto' (Bastianini and Gallazzi) or 'Egyptian sea' (Austin in AB), perhaps we should understand the genitive with πέλαγος as that with ὁδός, the road/sea *toward* something; cf., e.g., Eur. *Hipp.* 1197 Ἄργους κἀπιδαυρίας ὁδόν, Parm. B 1. 2–3 ὁδὸν . . . δαίμονος. Note also Opp. *H.* 1. 620–1 on the (northward) flight of the cranes, ἀπ' . . . Αἰγύπτοιο ῥοάων | ὑψιπετὴς γεράνων

---

[22] For this translation, cf. Pl. *Prot.* 313 D χρηςτὸν ἢ πονηρὸν περὶ τὸ cῶμα. Here ἀγαθός means 'a good sign'; cf. 22. 5 cῆμα . . . καταδέξιον, 23. 2 cῆμα ἀγαθόν, and the *Suda* passage cited above, κάκιςτος οἰωνός. This seems more in accord with the qualities looked for in weather signs—so also Lapini, 'Note posidippee', 45—and certainly preferable to the editors' renderings 'buon acchiappatore anche intorno alle piante', 'a good fly-catcher even among the plants', which makes too much of the καί.

[23] Cf. Pi. *O.* 11. 1–2 ἔςτιν ἀνθρώποις ἀνέμων ὅτε πλείςτα | χρῆςις· ἔςτιν δ' οὐρανίων ὑδάτων—easily unpacked to mean that sailors sometimes need wind and farmers sometimes need rain—which serves as a priamel for what follows; cf. E. Bundy, 'The Eleventh Olympian Ode', 4–11; Sider, 'Pindar *Olympian* 11 and Greek Weather Lore'.

[24] More examples in D'A. W. Thompson, *A Glossary of Greek Birds* (Oxford, 1936), s.v.; Hutchinson, 'The New Posidippus and Latin Poetry', 4, adduces Sen. *Oed.* 604–6, Lucan 7. 832–4, and Stat. *Theb.* 12. 515–18.

David Sider

χορὸς ἔρχεται. We can now understand πέλαγος as the direct object of διώκειν, 'pursue, seek after' (LSJ s.v. I 2), which is more natural than assuming ναῦν vel sim. (Bastianini and Gallazzi). 'Seeking the sea to Egypt' because there is no guarantee of a successful voyage, especially at this time of year (see below).

ἴσχει: in defence of my reading, note that Ael. NA 1. 44 takes cranes not merely as a sign of rain, but as the actual cause: τῶν γεράνων αἱ κλαγγαὶ καλοῦςιν ὄμβρους; cf. Theocr. 7. 57 ἀλκύονες στορεσεῦντι τὰ κύματα, Lucr. 5. 1085–6 (some birds change their songs) ubi aquam dicuntur et imbris | poscere et interdum ventos aurasque vocare, Vergil, Aen. 10. 264–6.

γέρανος: Bastianini and Gallazzi could be clearer in explaining the relevance of the crane, or rather cranes, whose twice-yearly migrations in V-formation between northern Europe and Africa were notable features in the sky and the early Greek calendar.[25] Their arrival in the fall was taken by Hesiod as a sign of winter and bad weather (Op. 448–51):

φράζεσθαι δ᾽ εὖτ᾽ ἂν γεράνου φωνὴν ἐπακούσῃς
ὑψόθεν ἐκ νεφέων ἐνιαύσια κεκληγυίης,
ἥτ᾽ ἀρότοιό τε σῆμα φέρει, καὶ χείματος ὥρην
δεικνύει ὀμβρηροῦ.

The winter migration south of the European crane (ardea rus Linn.) occurs throughout October and November,[26] or in Greek, or more specifically Attic, terms τοῦ Μαιμακτηριῶνος (Arist. HA 597ᵃ24), and takes them from northern Europe (over Greece, especially Thrace as many but not all veer towards Turkey to keep the mainland beneath) to Ethiopia and Sudan.[27]

Yet, for all the regularity of the appearance of cranes overhead, their flight must be studied for its shape, size, sound, altitude, direction, and time of appearance, which in various combinations signal storm, winter, or fair weather. Thus storm is imminent when οὐδ᾽ ὑψοῦ γεράνων μακραὶ στίχες αὐτὰ κέλευθα | τείνονται, στροφάδες δὲ παλιμπετὲς ἀπονέονται (Arat. 1031–2). The storm will be severe when γέρανοι ἐκ τοῦ πελάγους ἐς τὴν γῆν πετόμεναι (Arist. fr. 270. 21 Gigon = Ael. NA 7. 70); cf. Ael. NA 3. 14, Hdt. 2. 22. 4 γέρανοι δὲ φεύγουσαι

---

[25] On migrating birds and their use in describing the typical weather at the time of their northward and southward migrations, cf. J. Morton, The Role of the Physical Environment in Ancient Greek Seafaring (Leiden, 2001), 296–301.

[26] Cf. L. Walkinshaw, Cranes of the World (New York, 1973), 24.

[27] Ibid. 45; cf. further Pliny, NH 10. 60; S. Cramp et al., Birds of the Western Palaearctic, ii (Oxford, 1998), 618–26.

τὸν χειμῶνα τὸν ἐν τῆι Cκυθικῆι χώρηι γινόμενον φοιτῶcι ἐc χειμαcίην ἐc τοὺc τόπουc τούτουc, i.e. Egypt; Theognis 1197–9 ὄρνιθοc φωνήν . . . ὀξὺ βοώcηc | ἤκουc᾽, ἥτε βροτοῖc ἄγγελοc ἦλθ᾽ ἀρότου | ὡραίου.²⁸

If the storm ahead is severe they may deviate from their usual straight path or even choose to land; Arist. *HA* 614ᵇ19–21 εἰc ὕψοc πέτονται πρὸc τὸ καθορᾶν τὰ πόρρω, καὶ ἐὰν ἴδωcι νέφη καὶ χειμέρια, καταπτᾶcαι ἡcυχάζουcιν ~ Antig. *Mir.* 40 (note the πρόc: they fly high *in order* to see a long distance). As Homer puts it more simply, γεράνων . . . αἵ . . . χειμῶνα φύγον (*Il.* 3. 3–4; cf. Vergil, *Georgics* 1. 374–5).

The crane in Posidippus therefore tells us that this particular ship is setting out toward the end of the sailing season, when storms are more likely.²⁹ The poetic use of ἡγεμονέοι (4) should not mislead us: it is not that 'il volo della gru verso l'Egitto deve indicare alla nave la rotta da seguire' (BG ad loc.). Heaven help the pilot who needs to wait up to six months for the flight of cranes to guide him to Egypt (and then only at the end or beginning of winter). Rather, the pilot knows that if the high-flying cranes (cf. ὑψιπετῆ . . . γέρανον, Antip. Sid. *AP* 7. 172. 2 = GP 22) deviate it is because they see a storm far in advance of what can be seen at sea level. A straight course is taken as a cῆμα . . . καταδέξιον (5).

23

ἠερίην αἴθυιαν ἰδὼ[ν ὑπ]ὸ̣ κῦμ[α] θαλάc[cηc
δυομένην, ἁλιεῦ, cῆ[μα φ]ύλα[c]c᾽ ἀγαθ[όν·
καὶ πολυάγκιcτρον κ[αθίει] καὶ βάλλε cαγ[ήνην
κ]α̣ὶ κύρτουc· ἄγρηc οὔ[ποτ᾽ ἄ]πε[ι] κενεόc.

Seeing a shearwater diving under a sea wave in the morning, regard it as a good sign, fisherman; and drop your many-hooked line and cast your net and pots. You will never return from fishing empty-handed.

The adjective ἠέριοc is often used of flying birds (LSJ s.v. II 2, and well illustrated by BG ad loc.), but since a diving bird can hardly have been doing anything else in the moment before but flying, this meaning is rather vapid here. I am not as impressed as BG are by the antithesis of ἠέριοc/δυομένην. However, ἠέριοc = 'in the morning' should not be ruled out, first because this is indeed the time of day that sailors would set out (cf. Hes. *Op.* 579–81); and second because the time of day is frequently one of the criteria for establishing the precise meaning of a sign in the texts on weather (none of which are

---

²⁸ Cf. Mynors on Verg. *Georg.* 1. 374–5.

²⁹ Ar. *Av.* 710–11 specifically says it is time for the sailor to sleep when the crane migrates south: ὅταν γέρανοc κρώζουc᾽ εἰc τὴν Λιβύην μεταχωρῆι, | καὶ πηδάλιον τότε ναυκλήρωι φράζει κρεμάcαντι καθεύδειν.

David Sider

here adduced by BG); cf. Thphr. *Sign.* 16 'if a raven *in the morning* producing many different sounds repeats one of these quickly twice over and shakes its wings to make a whirring sound, it signals rain', §18 'a heron uttering his *cry early in the morning* signals rain or wind', §38 'if a flock of cranes flies *in early morning*, it will storm early.' Since, however, for the Greeks themselves the meaning of this adjective was (so to speak) up in the air,[30] it may be that Posidippus, by placing the word first, was playing with his readers' expectations and presenting them with a test of interpretation.

The diving shearwater signals rain (cf. Thphr. *Sign.* 28, quoted above), a good sign for an fisherman. And if, as with the two previous epigrams, there is anything unusual about this weather sign, it is that it is directed to the fisherman. When, before the publication of these new epigrams, I attempted a complete census of all those explicitly identified as audiences for weather literature, I found, in addition to the standard pair of farmers and sailors (see the first epigram above), herdsmen (of goats, sheep, and cattle), millers, physicians (note especially *Airs Waters Places* 1–2), and the rather vague 'luckless man' (ἄνολβος ἀνήρ, Aratus 1073). Nobody in all the weather literature specifies the fisherman. Posidippus may have felt a Hellenistic poetic urge to correct this lack, here and in the next poem.[31]

24

γήθ]εο τὸν Θηβαῖον ἰδών, ἁ[λιεῦ], μέλα[ν ὄρνιν·
αἴ]θυίηι πεισθεὶς ουκα [. . .] . α [
. . . [.] . [.] . . . [.] . [. . . . .] ε ά υτ [
τρηχη . ς Ἀρχυτα[. . .]θεν ἐπα[
εἰς γὰρ κυματοπλῆγ᾿ ἀκ[τὴν ἵ]εθ᾿ οκλρυρο[.]ὄρ[νις   5
ς]ῆμ᾿ εὐαγρείης οὐχ ἐτέ[ροισι] κριτόν.

1 γήθ]εο De Stefani : ὄρς]εο BG AB   6 ἐτέ[ροισι] κριτόν Sider : ἐτέ[ροις᾿ ἄ]κριτον BG
AB: ἐτέ[ρως πα]ριτόν Luppe

[Rise, fisherman,] if you see the black Theban [bird]; if you trust to the shearwater, [you] won't . . . Rough . . . Archytas[32] . . ., for the [   ] bird

[30] Amongst those arguing for a derivation from ἠερι-, 'at dawn', are Chantraine, *Dict. étymol.*, F. Bechtel, *Lexilogus zu Homer* (Halle, 1914), 151, Heubeck on *Od.* 9.52, and Kirk on *Il.* 1. 497; arguing for a derivation from ἀήρ is E. Risch, *Wortbildung der homerischen Sprache*[2] (Berlin, 1974), 113–14. Homeric scholia favoured 'in the morning' (ἑωθιναί, ὀρθριναί), although 'in spring' (ἐαριναί) was also proposed; cf. e.g. Σ A on *Il.* 1. 497, Σ D on *Il.* 3. 7, *LfrgE* s.v.

[31] The fisherman, though, as Ewen Bowie reminded me, does make several appearances in Hellenistic poetry, from New Comedy on (Menander's Ἁλιεῖς). Note in particular [Theocr.] 21 Ἁλιεύς, with its distinctly anti-ominal message: ἴca δ᾿ ἦν ψεύδεσιν ὄψεις (64).

[32] Understood here as a vocative; so too the editors. Lapini, 'Osservazioni sul nuovo Posidippo', 40 doubts whether a second vocative after the 'fisherman' of v. 1 is likely, but, to anticipate my conclusion, alternation, sometimes rapid, of addressee is common in didac-

rushes to the wave-battered headland, a sign of a good catch, not recognized by others.

This epigram's cῆμα is not a weather sign, but is on the same empirical level and contains a similar syntax. Note in particular the ἰδών of this and the preceding poem, which is equivalent to the typical conditional form of a weather sign: if *X* (is observed), then *Y* (will occur), where the protasis may contain a conditional participle. Here the presence of many fish just below the surface draws the sea-eagle, which in turn will draw the observant fisherman.

BG's text of the end of l. 5 alters the text in the immediate neighbourhood of a lacuna: ἰ̂]κ⟨θ⟩' ὁ κρ⟨ιτ⟩ὸ[c] ὄρ[νιc, a violation of Youtie's Law. After ἀκ[τῆν, which the editors fully justify on the basis of Soph. *OC* 1240–1 ἀκτὰ κυματοπλήξ, it is better simply to print the papyrus and wait for a better suggestion; cf. Luppe, 'Ein unbekannter Vogelname'. All the more so, since their jingle of the two forms of κριτός in ll. 5 and 6 seems insufficiently motivated.

Far more interesting for our general purposes, however, is Bastianini and Gallazzi's convincing explanation of the reference in l. 1 to a sea-eagle (ἁλιαίετοc) on the basis of Dionysius *De aucup.* 2. 2 (23. 15–16 Garzya) οἱ ἁλιεῖc δ' αὐτοὺc ὡc εὐκτήν τινα καὶ αἴcιον ὄψιν ἀcπάζονται. Once again, Dionysius the Periegete (assuming he really is the birdcatcher) is our only parallel. It now seems possible to conclude that what Posidippus is doing in these four epigrams is versifying a text now unknown to us which collected weather and related signs, perhaps under the rubric of bird signs. This would have been the same prose source used later by Dionysius (second century AD), not knowing or not caring that some of them had earlier been versified by Posidippus. As I have said, the weather literature is rather conservative in tending to list the same sources over and over. For the epigrammatist, I think, a main point of the poem would have been the very obscurity of the signs; hence my conjecture on l. 6. ('Take that, Aratus!')

Who could this source have been? Perhaps one of those Pliny lists (in Book 1) for the 2,060 facts (by his reckoning) recorded in his Book 18, since one of Posidippus' obscure signs also appears elsewhere only in Pliny, whose insatiable appetite for texts is well known. Among the names he lists, Aristotle, Eudoxus, Theophrastus, and Aratus collected weather signs, but these were the authors Posidippus wanted

tic poetry; cf. Obbink, 'The Addressees of Empedocles', 51–98. Luppe, 'Ein unbekannter Vogelname' would get rid of the vocative by reading ᾁ[λιον], thereby burdening this bird with a third adjective. For De Stefani's reading see his 'Integrazioni e congetture', 166.

to supplement. Perhaps it was a certain Dionysius, who, Pliny says, translated a work written by the Mago the Carthaginian (*qui Magonem transtulit: HN* 1. 8). A Phoenician text would be likely to contain bird/weather signs unknown to the usual Greek tradition. But this, like any other name in Pliny's list, can only be a guess.[33]

II

We have seen that the four poems we have examined are versifications of material found in scientific prose treatises. Were it not for their brevity, this would normally qualify them for consideration as examples of didactic poetry. Epigrams, however, have not been thought of in this way, but perhaps it is time to broaden the definition. The Hellenistic age saw an efflorescence of didactic.[34] If we, for the sake of convenience here, like the ancients, lump just about all archaic didactic poetry under the name of Hesiod,[35] there remain in addition to Hesiod prior to the Hellenistic period only Parmenides, Empedocles,[36] Xenophanes, Cleostratus, Evenus, and Scythinus.[37] Thereafter, however, the genre flourishes.[38] Our only complete works from the Hellenistic period are those by Aratus and Nicander, but testimony and fragments exist (mostly in Powell and *Supplementum Hellenisticum*) for didactic works written by Aglaias, Alexander Aetolus, Alexander of Ephesus, Anubion, Archelaus, Archestratus,

[33] Another intriguing possibility, admitedly tenuous, is 'Archytas', the name that appears in 24.

[34] And recent years have seen a renewal of interest in this form; cf. A. Schiesaro, P. Mitsis, and J. S. Clay (eds.), *Mega nepios* (Pisa, 1994); P. Toohey, *Epic Lessons* (London, 1996); C. Atherton (ed.), *Form and Content in Didactic Poetry* (Bari, 1998); K. Volk, *The Poetics of Latin Didactic* (Oxford, 2002); and C. Fakas, *Der hellenistische Hesiod* (Wiesbaden, 2001). And perhaps we should grandfather in B. Effe, *Dichtung und Lehre* (Munich, 1977). On the Hellenistic revival of didactic, see Toohey, *Epic Lessons*, 49–51. Note, however, that Fraser, *Ptolemaic Alexandria*, i. 623–4, dismisses (his word) didactic poetry as a genre 'favoured in Alexandria'.

[35] An exception may be the *Bougonia*, attributed to Eumelus, a title that looks like a work on (at least) cattle-raising; cf. Boeus' *Ornithogonia*. Cf. Eumelus T 4 and 14 Bernabé. On Eumelus as a catch-all name attached to works of different authors, cf. M. L. West, '"Eumelos": A Corinthian Epic Cycle?'

[36] On these two, see now M. R. Wright, 'Philosopher Poets', with C. Osborne's response, 'Was Verse the Default Form for Presocratic Philosophy?'

[37] On the period between classical and Hellenistic didactic, cf. G. Wöhrle, 'Bemerkungen'.

[38] This is not the place to attempt a definition of the constantly evolving genre of didactic poetry as a whole, but a good working definition of *Hellenistic* didactic is 'a translation into dactyls of a pre-existing technical prose treatise' (as distinct from earlier poets, who composed, even if from age-old lore, their own works). This certainly applies to the first four oionoskopic poems and may well, as Baumbach and Trampedach, '"Winged Words"', argue *passim*, to the ominal ones as well, although the precise sources can only be guessed at. The remaining epigrams of Posidippus are exercises in other genres; only 17 (cκέψαι . . . οἷον . . . τόνδε λίθον) seems to qualify for the didactic label.

Archimedes, Cleanthes,[39] Dorotheus, Eratosthenes,[40] Eudemus, Euthydemus, Hegesianax, Hermippus, Matro, Menecrates, Mnesitheus, Numenius, Pancrates, Philo of Tarsus, Posidonius of Corinth, Satyrus, Sminthes, Timachidas, and Zenothemis.[41] Nor was this idle toil on the part of these poets. There is ample evidence for their poems' being received with great pleasure. Note in particular what one Hellenistic poet who did not himself write didactic poetry says about the performance of a poem, sung by Orpheus to the crew of the Argo, whose contents were the same as any Presocratic treatise (prose or otherwise) on cosmogony and cosmology (Ap. Rh. 1. 496–511):

> Ἤειδεν δ' ὡς γαῖα καὶ οὐρανὸς ἠδὲ θάλασσα,
> τὸ πρὶν ἐπ' ἀλλήλοισι μιῆι συναρηρότα μορφῆι,
> νείκεος ἐξ ὀλοοῖο διέκριθεν ἀμφὶς ἕκαστα·
> ἠδ' ὡς ἔμπεδον αἰὲν ἐν αἰθέρι τέκμαρ ἔχουσιν
> ἄστρα, σεληναίης τε καὶ ἠελίοιο κέλευθοι·   500
> οὔρεά θ' ὡς ἀνέτειλε, καὶ ὡς ποταμοὶ κελάδοντες
> αὐτῆισιν νύμφηισι καὶ ἑρπετὰ πάντ' ἐγένοντο.
> ἤειδεν δ' ὡς πρῶτον Ὀφίων Εὐρυνόμη τε
> Ὠκεανὶς νιφόεντος ἔχον κράτος Οὐλύμποιο·
> ὥς τε βίηι καὶ χερσὶν ὁ μὲν Κρόνωι εἴκαθε τιμῆς,   505
> ἡ δὲ Ῥέηι, ἔπεσον δ' ἐνὶ κύμασιν Ὠκεανοῖο·
> οἱ δὲ τέως μακάρεσσι θεοῖς Τιτῆσιν ἄνασσον,
> ὄφρα Ζεὺς ἔτι κοῦρος, ἔτι φρεσὶ νήπια εἰδώς,
> Δικταῖον ναίεσκεν ὑπὸ σπέος, οἱ δέ μιν οὔπω
> γηγενέες Κύκλωπες ἐκαρτύναντο κεραυνῶι,   510
> βροντῆι τε στεροπῆι τε· τὰ γὰρ Διὶ κῦδος ὀπάζει.

He sang of the past age when earth and sky were knit together in a single mould; how they were sundered after deadly strife; how the stars, the moon, and the travelling sun keep faithfully to their stations in the heavens; how mountains rose, and how, together with their Nymphs, the murmuring streams and all four-legged creatures came to be; how, in the beginning, Ophion and Eurynome, daughter of Ocean, governed the world from snow-clad Olympus; how they were forcibly supplanted, Ophion by Cronos, Eurynome by Rhea; of their fall into the waters of Ocean; and how their successors ruled the happy Titan gods when Zeus in a Dictaean cave was still a child, with childish thoughts, before the earthborn Cyclopes had given him the bolt, the thunder and lightning that form his glorious armament today. (Trans. E. V. Rieu)

---

[39] Not the *Hymn to Zeus*, but the iambic fr. 3 Powell, which begins τἀγαθὸν ἐρωτᾶις μ' οἷόν ἐστ'· ἄκουε δή.

[40] On whose poetry, see now K. Geus, *Eratosthenes von Kyrene* (Munich, 2002), 98–138.

[41] For post-Hellenistic poetry we mention only Anubio (edition forthcoming by D. Obbink), Damocrates (edition forthcoming by Sabine Vogt), and Andromachus. On medical poems, see H. von Staden, 'Gattung und Gedächtnis', esp. 75–8.

His audience was stunned:

> ἔτι προύχοντο κάρηνα,
> πάντες ὁμῶς ὀρθοῖσιν ἐπ' οὔασιν ἠρεμέοντες
> κηληθμῶι· τοῖόν σφιν ἐνέλλιπε θέλκτρον ἀοιδῆς.   515

the heads of all were still bent forward, their ears intent on the enchanting melody. Such was his charm—the music lingered in their hearts.

Similarly pleased are Chromis and Mnasyllos, who force the hung-over Silenus to sing, among other things (Vergil, *Eclogue* 6. 31–40):

> uti magnum per inane coacta
> semina terrarumque animaeque marisque fuissent
> et liquidi simul ignis; ut his exordia primis
> omnia, et ipse tener mundi concreuerit orbis;
> tum durare solum et discludere Nerea ponto   35
> coeperit, et rerum paulatim sumere formas;
> iamque nouom terrae stupeant lucescere solem,
> altius atque cadant submotis nubibus imbres,
> incipiant siluae cum primum surgere, cumque
> rara per ignaros errent animalia montis.   40

how, through the vast void, the seeds of earth and air, and sea, and liquid fire withal were gathered together; how from these elements all nascent things, yes all, and even the young globe of the world grew together; how the earth began to harden, to shut off the Sea god in the deep, and little by little to assume the shapes of things; how next the lands are astonished at the new sun shining, and how rains fall as the clouds are lifted higher, when first woods begin to arise and here and there living creatures move over mountains that know them not. (Trans. Fairclough–Goold)

And in the *Aeneid*, we read that *cithara . . . Iopas | personat aurata* (1. 740–1), Iopas, who

> canit errantem lunam solisque labores;
> unde hominum genus et pecudes; unde imber et ignes;
> Arcturum pluviasque Hyadas geminosque Triones;
> quid tantum Oceano properent se tinguere soles   745
> hiberni, vel quae tardis mora noctibus obstet.

sings of the wandering moon and the sun's toils; whence sprang man and beast, whence rain and fire; of Arcturus, the rainy Hyades and the twin Bears; why wintry suns make such haste to dip themselves in Ocean, or what delay stays the slowly passing nights. (Trans. Fairclough–Goold)

Whereupon *ingeminant plausu Tyrii, Troesque sequuntur*. Can we also consider here Odysseus' catalogue of women and its favourable reception in the court of the Phaeacians? Two shorter passages where the performance of a didactic poem is both described and praised are *h.Merc.* 418–37 (Hermes sings a theogony and is praised by Apollo) and Vergil, *Georgics* 4. 345–7:

> Inter quas curam Clymene narrabat inanem   345
> Vulcani Martisque dolos et dulcia furta,
> aque Chao densos divum numerabat amores . . .

Clymene was telling of Vulcan's baffled care, of the wiles and stolen joys of Mars, and from Chaos on was rehearsing the countless loves of the gods. (Trans. Fairclough–Goold)

The existence of such a ready audience for didactic poetry led poets to stretch the boundaries, some of them verging on parody, such as, I suppose, Euthydemus' poem on dried fish (*SH* 455).[42] It now seems likely that among the experiments in didactic poetry are the four epigrams Posidippus produced on weather signs. They, if any do, deserve the rubric didactic epigrams. Could the two vocatives in our four poems be meant to echo this feature of didactic, from Perses on?[43]

Are there other 'didactic epigrams'? Since Hesiod is the granddaddy of didactic poetry (as in Callimachus' Ἡσιόδου τό τ' ἄεισμα καὶ ὁ τρόπος, *AP* 9. 507. 1, in praise of Aratus[44]), and his lists and catalogues were noteworthy, perhaps we can consider epigrams containing similar lists as qualifying for the term. For example, Antipater of Thessalonica *AP* 9. 26 (= GP, *Garland* 19) lists the nine women poets nourished by Helicon and Pieria, places and a number that surely are

---

[42] Parody, however, can be of any thing or genre; cf. S. D. Olson and A. Sens, *Archestratos* (Oxford, 2000), pp. xxviii–xliii.

[43] On this feature of didactic poetry, cf. Schiesaro et al., *Mega nepios*; Volk, *The Poetics of Latin Didactic*, 37–9. Volk, in fact, is so strict in her definition of didactic poetry that she would exclude Parmenides because he does not address his poem to anyone; but the goddess's address to Parmenides can be seen as a variation which allows the poet (Parmenides) to have the narrator receive the instruction usually directed to the reader; cf. Sider, 'How to Commit Philosophy Obliquely'.

[44] And of himself; the *Aitia*, although, like the epigram, elegiac in metre, clearly play with the idea of didactic; cf. Toohey, *Epic Lessons*, 73–6, who, however, would 'disqualify it from the didactic subgenre' (75); see also Cameron, *Callimachus and his Critics*, ch. 13, 'Hesiodic Elegy', who argues that Hesiod's influence on Callimachus has been greatly exaggerated by modern scholars. In any case, 'Hesiod' is but one element of this most complicated programmatic proem; cf. Acosta-Hughes and Stephens, 'Rereading Callimachus' *Aetia* fragment 1'. This is not the place to examine the question at length, but as one consideration of Callimachus' ability to incorporate natural science into his poetry, cf. Fraser, *Ptolemaic Alexandria*, i. 587–8, who nicely demonstrates how Call. *Ep.* 5 Pf. = GP 14 = Ath. 7. 318 D (spoken by a conch) works Peripatetic science into a dedicatory epigram. It is further interesting to note that B. Kramer, 'Il rotolo di Milano e l'epigramma ellenistica', 40–1, makes this same point about some of Posidippus' epigrams, comparing (*inter alia*) Posidippus' λιθικά with Theophrastus' work on stones. Her remark that 'anche negli οἰωνοσκοπικά assistiamo all'elaborazione artistica di osservazioni naturalistiche' (41) serves as a prelude to my argument, but she speaks more of the general Alexandrian interest in science and less of Posidippus' specific poetic programme.

meant to recall not only the canonical nine lyric poets (see below) but also the nine Muses who inspired Hesiod on Mt. Helicon. Indeed, vv. 9–10 of this poem spell this out and enumerate for those too lazy to count ἐννέα μὲν Μούcαc μέγαc Οὐρανόc, ἐννέα δ' αὐτὰ | Γαῖα τέκεν.

Some other list poems are helpfully recorded by Gow and Page, *Garland of Philip*, ii. 36: Antipater of Thessalonica 9. 58 = GP, *Garland* 91 lists the Seven Wonders of the World, Antipater of Sidon *AP* 7. 81 = GP 34 and an anonymous epigram (*AP* 9. 366) list the seven sages (the latter cleverly including the most famous saying of each), and two anonymous epigrams present the nine lyric poets (*AP* 9. 184, 571).[45] For us, though, even though it was written after Posidippus, Antipater's list of the female canon is the most interesting because it is intriguingly similar to a poem (ignored by Gow and Page in this context) written by none other than Posidippus.[46]

As I try to show elsewhere,[47] Posidippus 140 = *AP* 12. 168 = GP 9, on the surface merely a list of toasts to be made at a symposium, actually is a compilation of the interdependent components of the poet Posidippus, including his literary models, one of whom is Hesiod:

> Ναννοῦc καὶ Λύδηc ἐπίχει δύο, καὶ φιλεράcτου
> Μιμνέρμου, καὶ τοῦ cώφρονοc Ἀντιμάχου·
> cυγκέραcον τὸν πέμπτον ἐμοῦ· τὸν δ' ἕκτον ἑκάcτου,
> Ἡλιόδωρ', εἶπαc, ὅcτιc ἐρῶν ἔτυχεν·
> ἕβδομον Ἡcιόδου, τὸν δ' ὄγδοον εἶπον Ὁμήρου,   5
> τὸν δ' ἔνατον Μουcῶν, Μνημοcύνηc δέκατον.
> μεcτὸν ὑπὲρ χείλουc πίομαι, Κύπρι· τἆλλα δ', Ἔρωτεc,
> νήφοντ' οἰνωθέντ' οὐχὶ λίην ἄχαρι.

Pour in two measures for Nanno and Lyde, and one for the lover's friend Mimnermus and another for prudent Antimachus. For the fifth measure mix in myself. Then, Heliodorus, add the sixth measure with a toast to each person who ever happened to be in love. Say the seventh is Hesiod's, the eighth Homer's, the ninth the Muses', and the tenth Mnemosyne's. I drink a cup slopping over the brim, Cypris. And then, Cupids, to be sober while drunk on wine is not to be too graceless.

At first glance Hesiod may seem like an odd insertion, but even within the poem (which is all that I attempted in my earlier study, 'Posidippus Old and New') it can be justified as an acknowledgement that it was to Hesiod that Posidippus owes the poetic list format currently in progress in 140—an acknowledgement reinforced by the

---

[45] These are merely the early examples; see further S. Barbantani, 'I poeti lirici del canone alessandrino nell'epigrammatistica'.

[46] Also qualifying as didactic epigram are Aglaïs (medical; *SH* 18) and Archelaus Chersonita (*mirabilia*; *SH* 125–9).   [47] 'Posidippus Old and New'.

fact that no. 9 is 'the Muses'. Each item in the list, by the way, is explicitly numbered, a unique feature among list poems.[48]

I now want to suggest an external reason for Hesiod's being listed among Posidippus' literary debts: Posidippus, perhaps only in his own mind (but probably in fact) the inventor of the didactic epigram, included Hesiod along with Homer, Mimnermus, and Antimachus because he was proud of this accomplishment. If he wrote more than these four and the remaining oionoskopic epigrams, which may have come from the same omen book—and if my argument is correct he must have—they, like these, did not make the cut when Meleager came to selecting those epigrams he thought best.

How strange would the idea of a didactic epigram have been to Posidippus' contemporaries? Probably not much. For the first generation of Hellenistic epigrammatists, almost every deviation from the classical topoi of inscribed epitaphs was an experiment. And inscriptional epigrams are limited almost exclusively to sepulchral and dedicatory monuments. The few deviations in Hansen's two volumes of *Carmina Epigraphica Graeca* tend to be verses on pots identifying the object and its owner. Where Hansen leaves off, Hellenistic epigrams begin; and I do not mean only chronologically. At this point, a new spirit of experiment prevails, and, as we see in the New Posidippus and in Meleager's *Garland* in general, all sorts of types or topoi are tried.[49] Probably the easiest to adapt to epigrams were the subjects of classical elegy, since the elegiac metre was common to both; *in primis* love songs and other sympotic subjects, especially as epigrams were performed in similar settings. Soon, though, the evolutionary niches left vacant by the absence of a lively performance culture for epic, skolia, and lyric would be filled by epigrams.[50] The composition of

---

[48] In this context, 'list' means a passage that itemizes names, pretty much one after the other. When the matter between names takes up more space (a few lines, say), the term is 'catalogue'. But this is not always used of a whole poem or major section of a poem that also itemizes things on the same level; e.g. Nicander and Aratus, prime examples of Hellenistic didactic poetry. They are, though, merely following their prose sources, which tend to be empirical (as opposed to theoretical) treatises. Cf. W. D. Smith, 'Analytical and Catalogue Structure in the *Corpus Hippocraticum*', 277–84.

[49] See Baumbach and Trampedach, '"Winged Words"', 151–2.

[50] For epigrams' taking the place of lyric epinicia, consider the new Posidippus epigrams gathered under the rubric ἱππικά (AB 71–88), and cf. S. Barbantani, 'Epinici in distici di età ellenistica'. Posidippus also wrote poetic invitations (AB 124 = GP 10), for which epigrammatic form, see Sider, *Epigrams of Philodemos*, 161, where I argue that any poem hand-delivered by a slave early in the morning which mentions a dinner later that day at such-and-such an hour (along with some comments about the food to be brought or served) would be understood by its recipient (and hence by us) as an invitation. On epigrammatic 'epistles' in general, see P. A. Rosenmeyer, 'Epistolary Epigrams in the *Greek Anthology*'. Posidippus' ἰαματικά are verses based on the prose inscriptions left with votive offerings at shrines to Asclepius.

didactic epigrams would have been thought worth trying—but not, it seems, worth pursuing. Even if, as is quite likely, other didactic epigrams were written that were lost to us because they were not chosen by Meleager, it still seems clear that other topoi better fit the bill of what Hellenistic authors and their audiences came to desire in an epigram.[51]

[51] I thank Frank Nisetich, Leofranc Holford-Strevens, and Kathryn Gutzwiller for their helpful comments.

10

Posidippus and the Truth in Sculpture

ANDREW STEWART

On 23 October 1905, Paul Cézanne wrote a letter to his friend Émile Bernard. In it, he made a striking promise: 'I owe you the truth in painting and I will tell it to you.' And over two millennia earlier the poet Posidippus of Pella declared that in his portrait of Philitas, the sculptor Hecataeus had 'held to the straight canon of truth' (AB 63).[1] What do these two statements mean? What (if anything) might they have in common? What circumstances prompted them? And *cui malo*: whom are they directed against?

But first, some remarks about the context of the *Philitas*, the Milan papyrus' ἀνδριαντοποιικά (AB 62–70).

THE *ΑΝΔΡΙΑΝΤΟΠΟΙΙΚΑ*: SOURCES AND STRATEGIES

This is a tightly structured ensemble. Its nine poems deal exclusively with sculpture in bronze; the words χαλκός, χαλκεία, and χαλκουργεῖν echo through them like a litany. The poet opens and concludes with a hero and his foil. His hero is a 'modern' sculptor and the favourite of the Macedonian court, Lysippus of Sicyon; his foil is an 'old master', Polyclitus of Argos. For the first epigram in the series (AB 62) champions Lysippus' new grace—so self-evident that 'there is no reason at all to invoke it as a touchstone' as opposed to the rigidity of 'oldies' such as the archaic Hageladas and the classical Polyclitus. And the final one (AB 70), although grotesquely mutilated, moves from the 'fleshy' statues of Polyclitus back to Lysippus, apparently contrasting the two once more.[2]

I thank Kathryn Gutzwiller, Christopher Hallett, Donald Mastronarde, Peter Schultz, Alexander Sens, and Graham Zanker for their kind assistance with this chapter. As usual, all remaining mistakes and indiscretions are my own. For fuller discussion of Lysippus' Alexanders, the *Philitas* and its contemporaries, and classical/Hellenistic portrait realism, together with remarks on Posidippus' σκέλετος (AB 95), see the author's companion essay, 'Alexander, Philitas, and the Skeletos'; the two essays are complementary and should be read in tandem.

[1] J. Rewald, *Cézanne. Correspondance* (Paris, 1995), 315; cf. AB 63. 6—though Austin's translation inexplicably omits the word 'straight'.

[2] Gutzwiller, 'Posidippus on Statuary', 42, groups the poems into two sets of four and a

The seven intervening poems develop these themes and add more. AB 63 and 64 celebrate two masterpieces of realism, Hecataeus' *Philitas* (quoted below)[3] and Cresilas' *Idomeneus*. The next pair, AB 65 and 66, returns to Lysippus and presents a different kind of foil to him. AB 65 was already known from the *Anthology*, which explicitly attributes it to Posidippus.[4] It praises the boldness of the Sicyonian's *Alexander*, which precisely captures the fearsome and leonine character of the king, chasing the Persians as a lion chases cattle. AB 66 responds with a neat piece of bathos: Myron's *Cow*—the classic exemplar of the lumbering bovine 'good for the yoke'—which predictably fools the naïve oxherd into believing it to be real.[5]

AB 67 and 68 offer a different kind of antithesis. They juxtapose the archaic sculptor Theodorus' tiny *Chariot* and the *Colossus of Rhodes* by Chares of Lindus—a contemporary virtuoso and pupil of Lysippus. En route, announcing the penultimate poem (AB 69), we are told that Myron had not managed anything even one-tenth as big. (His *tour de force* measured only four cubits against the Colossus' seventy or so).[6] Unfortunately AB 69 itself, on Myron's *Tydeus*, is almost completely destroyed. And finally AB 70, in equally bad shape, returns us to Polyclitus and Lysippus.

This tightly structured ensemble presupposes a single intelligence at work. Who else but Posidippus? Its equally strong aesthetic and critical agenda supports this conclusion. For Posidippus wrote a great

coda, as follows: 'The first set of four consists of two poems praising Lysippus surrounding two poems that feature pre-Lysippan and post-Lysippan sculptors and are linked by the theme of the speaking statue. The second set of four consists of two poems praising Myron surrounding two poems that feature sculptors who predate and postdate Myron and are linked by a contrast between miniaturism and great size. The final epigram, though very poorly preserved, contains references to Lysippus and Polyclitus and, in all likelihood, reiterated in some way the message of the opening poem that the art of Lysippus, rather than that of Polyclitus, represented the *telos* of Greek bronze sculpting.' The two schemes complement each other, demonstrating how tightly structured this section is. Kosmetatou, 'Vision and Visibility', 188–9, deftly characterizes the politico-literary agenda of the ἀνδριαντοποιικά, and on p. 205 recasts their structure in evolutionary terms, 'the framework for an art-historical model that Posidippus drew from one of his contemporary art-historians . . . the rule and trajectory of perfection in sculpture'. As will appear, however, the poet drew on no single source for his musings.

[3] Hecataeus is known only from Pliny, *HN* 33. 156 and 34. 85—if this is the same man. See A. Hardie, 'Philitas and the Plane Tree'; id., 'The Statue(s) of Philitas', for arguments that the *Philitas* stood on Cos. For despite repeated statements to the contrary, there is no evidence that intellectuals were ever honoured thus in Alexandria: on the city's dearth of portraits other than those of the Ptolemies, see A. Stewart, 'The Alexandrian Style: A Mirage?', 240. So l. 9 of the epigram must be understood as it is by AB, p. 87: the portrait was erected *at Ptolemy's behest*.

[4] *AP* 16. 119; also (without an attribution) Himer. *Or.* 48. 14 (p. 203 Colonna).

[5] For the previously known epigrams on Myron's Cow, see Gutzwiller, *Poetic Garlands*, 245–50.

[6] On the Colossus of Rhodes see M. W. Dickie, 'What was a *Kolossos*?', 252 n. 42, listing the different estimates of its size; cf. Kosmetatou and Papalexandrou, 'Size Matters'.

deal about Lysippus[7] and evidently saw himself as an advocate for the truth of his art. Indeed, he was perhaps the first Greek intellectual who actively and consistently promoted an artist in this way. For although Socrates and Aristotle (for example) both judged Phidias and Polyclitus the best in their respective professions, and Aristotle vastly preferred the paintings of Polygnotus to those of Zeuxis, these casual acknowledgements, usually made to illustrate philosophical or literary points, fall far short of Posidippus' sustained, outspoken promotion of Lysippus and his art.[8]

So Posidippus was a pioneer—a dangerous occupation—and was apparently well aware of it. What was his *authority* for this venture? Here it is necessary to look again at his proem, AB 62:[9]

μιμ[ή]cαcθε τάδ᾽ ἔργα, πολυχρονίους δὲ κολοccῶν,
  ὦ ζ[ωι]οπλάcται, ν[αί,] παραθεῖτε νόμους·
εἴ γε μὲν ἀρχαῖαι [Δρυ]όπα χέρεc, ἢ Ἀγελάιδηc
  ὁ πρὸ Πολυκλείτο[υ πά]γχυ παλαιοτέχνηc,
ἢ οἱ Δαιδαλιδῶν cκληρ[οὶ τύ]ποι εἰc πέδον ἦλθον,   5
  Λυcίππου νεαρὴν οὐδ[ε]μία πρόφαcιc
δεῦρο παρεκτεῖναι βαcάνωι χάριν· εἶ[τα] δ᾽ ἐὰν χρῆι,
  καὶ πίπτηι ὦθλος καινοτεχνέων, πέρας ἦν.

3 suppl. Livrea   5 Δαιδαλιδῶν Livrea : Διδυμίδου pap.   ἦλθον Austin : ἐλθεῖν pap.
7 ἐὰν: εαγ pap.   8 ὦθλος BG: οαθλου ex οαλλου corr. pap.

Imitate these works, and the antique laws of colossi,
    statue-makers—yes!—outrun them!
For if the ancient hands of Dryopas, or Hageladas,
    a pre-Polyclitan, wholly primitive practitioner of the art,
or the hard creations of the Daedalidae had entered the field,
    there'd be no reason at all to invoke Lysippus' new grace
as a touchstone. But if need should arise,
    and a contest among moderns occur, he'd overtake them all.

Posidippus surely composed this poem as a programmatic introduction, either to this particular collection or to an earlier, comprehensive book of sculptural epigrams which the Milan papyrus' editor excerpted. In it he establishes his authority in two main ways.

First, he boldly throws down the gauntlet. 'Imitate these works, sculptors, yes! and outrun the antique laws of colossi.' As the papyrus'

[7] Himer. *Or.* 48. 14 (p. 203 Colonna); only the three in the Milan papyrus and one other, *AP* 16. 275 on the *Kairos* (AB 62, 65, 70, and 142), have survived.
[8] Xen. *Mem.* 1. 4. 3; Pl. *Men.* 91 D; *Hp. Ma.* 290 A; Arist. *EN* 6. 7. 1, 1141ᵃ9–12; *Poet.* 6, 1450ᵃ25–8; *Pol.* 8. 5. 7, 1340ᵃ35–40.
[9] Text, incorporating improvements in ll. 3 and 5 made by Livrea, 'Critica testuale', follows Acosta-Hughes and Kosmetatou, 'New Poems Attributed to Posidippus', except that in l. 5 I adopt Austin's ἦλθον.

Andrew Stewart

editors realized, his use of the deictic τάδε, 'these', places him, the sculptors he challenges, and us, his audience, squarely before the very works whose imitation he is advocating. His contemporary Nossis employs a similar device, but does so in a more literal way. She leads her audience through what seems to be an actual collection of votives in a temple of Aphrodite, describing them one by one.[10] Posidippus, though, keeps us in suspense. Although κολοccοί are defined by their immobility (*not* primarily by their size),[11] and thus anything that 'out-runs' them must be mobile by definition, what are these mysterious masterpieces and who made them? He does not—yet—care to say.

Second, he appeals to a piece of art criticism: a sculptural 'hard-ness scale'. For with these novel creations, it is as if the 'hard images' by Hageladas and others, even Polyclitus, had suddenly come to life and walked off their pedestals. Hitherto this criterion was known only from Cicero, Quintilian, and Lucian; now we can be confident that it is authentically pre-Hellenistic.[12] It describes what we call the transition from the archaic style to the classical. By referencing it, Posidippus shows us that he is *knowledgeable in sculpture*. He has consulted its literature—still in its infancy—and is familiar with its discourses. He is an insider, an expert, a true scholar-poet, so we must take his opinions seriously.

But his account of this hardness scale is heterodox and by no means neutral. Not only does it differ completely from the version(s) that circulated in Roman times,[13] but it includes several implicit attacks on received wisdom—statements that establish (or seek to estab-lish) the poet as an independent authority in the field.[14] For as we have seen, even the great Aristotle, Lysippus' own contemporary, judged not him but Polyclitus to be the supreme exponent of Greek ἀνδριαντοποιία—even though he was surely familiar with Lysippus' work from his years with Alexander and the Macedonian court. Others agreed:

---

[10] Posidippus: BG ad loc. Nossis: Gutzwiller, *Poetic Garlands*, 80–4, on *AP* 6. 265, 275, 353–4; 9. 332, 604, 605 (Nossis GP 3–9); ead., 'Posidippus on Statuary', 46.

[11] Against AB ad loc. see esp. D. T. Steiner, 'Eyeless in Argos'; ead., *Images in Mind* (Princeton, 2001), 137; and Kosmetatou and Papalexandrou, 'Size Matters'.

[12] Cic. *Brut.* 70; Quint. 12. 10. 9; Lucian, *Rh. Pr.* 9; see Pollitt, *The Ancient View of Greek Art*, 82–3 and s.vv. cκληρóc, *durus*; A. Rouveret, *Histoire et imaginaire de la peinture ancienne* (Rome, 1989), 424–36, 444–5.

[13] Canachus, Calamis, Myron, Polyclitus (Cicero); Callon, Hegesias, Calamis, Myron, Polyclitus (Quintilian); Hegesias, 'circle of Critius and Nesiotes' (Lucian).

[14] *Contra*, Kosmetatou, 'Vision and Visibility', 205–11, who argues that the entire ἀνδριαντο-ποιικά section derives from a single source, probably Duris of Samos' book on τορευτική listed in Plin. *HN* 1. 34; yet the only surviving citation from it is the anecdote about Eupompus and Lysippus paraphrased in *HN* 34. 61 (quoted below), which tells us nothing of its contents.

186

Polyclitus Sicyonius, Hageladae discipulus, Diadumenum fecit molliter iuvenem, centum talentis nobilitatum, idem et Doryphorum viriliter puerum. fecit et quam Canona artifices vocant liniamenta artis ex eo petentes veluti a lege quadam, solusque hominum artem ipsam fecisse artis opere iudicatur. (Pliny, *HN* 34. 55)

Polyclitus of Sicyon, *a pupil of Hageladas*, made a *Diadumenus*, a supple youth famous for having cost a hundred talents, and a *Doryphorus*, a virile-looking boy. He also made a statue that artists call the 'Canon' and from which they derive the principles of their art *as if from some kind of a law*, and he alone of men is deemed to have rendered art itself in a work of art.

Now Pliny probably took some of this from the sculptor and art critic Xenocrates of Athens, a second-generation member of the Lysippic school. Active early in the third century, he was Posidippus' exact contemporary, a writer on bronze sculpture and on painting, and among Pliny's key sources. Pliny lists him in his bibliography to *HN* 34 next to a certain Antigonus, who was probably the late-third-century polymath Antigonus of Carystus, also a sculptor. Other clues, particularly a long citation of their comparison between the styles of the painters Zeuxis and Parrhasius, suggest that Antigonus edited and republished Xenocrates' book and thereby made it accessible to Roman scholars such as Varro and Pliny himself.[15]

Scholars realized long ago that Pliny probably based much of his account of Greek sculptural evolution at the hands of Phidias, Polyclitus, Myron, Pythagoras of Regium, and Lysippus (in that order!) in *HN* 34. 54–67 upon Xenocrates' and Antigonus' work. For not only do these chapters indeed present a relatively consistent, clear, and integrated development that coincides at several points with their known interests, but the misrepresentation in 34. 55 of

[15] On Xenocrates and Antigonus see Plin. *HN* 1. 34; 34. 83, 84; 35. 67–8; Wilamowitz, *Antigonos von Karystos* (Berlin, 1881), 130–68; B. Schweitzer, 'Xenocrates von Athen'; Pollitt, *The Ancient View of Greek Art*, 73–7; Rouveret, *Histoire et imaginaire de la peinture ancienne*, 436–40; A. Stewart, *Greek Sculpture* (New Haven, 1990), 21, 63, 82, 238, 254–5, 262–4, 289, 291–3, 299, 303; G. Sprigath, 'Der Fall Xenokrates von Athen' (sceptical). Was Xenocrates the author of the hardness scale also (so Pollitt, op. cit. 360–1, contradicting his own comments on p. 83)? In favour is Pliny's description of the Diadoumenos as *mollis*, 'supple': cf. the accounts of the hardness scale in Cic. *Brut.* 70; Quint. 12. 10. 9; Lucian, *Rh. Pr.* 9. Against are: (1) Posidippus' comment that Hageladas was a 'pre-Polyclitan, wholly primitive practitioner of the art', which implicitly contradicts Pliny's 'Xenocratic' biography of Polyclitus; (2) the scale does not otherwise appear in Pliny and uses a tactile criterion that is quite different from the formalistic Xenocratic triad of συμμετρία, ῥυθμός, and ἀκρίβεια (see below); (3) it correctly dates Myron before Polyclitus, but the 'Xenocratic' scheme of *HN* 34. 54–67 incorrectly switches the two; and (4) it culminated with Polyclitus, whereas the 'Xenocratic' scheme culminated with Lysippus (*HN* 34. 65). Probably, then, someone else (a late- 5th- or 4th-c. partisan of Polyclitus?) invented it and a subsequent editor (Antigonus of Carystus? Varro? cf. *HN* 34. 56, 35. 68) inserted it into Xenocrates' work.

Polyclitus' hometown as Sicyon—he was from Argos—seems to clinch the matter. For who but Xenocrates, a partisan of the Sicyonian Lysippus, would want to deracinate the great Argive, blatantly and unhistorically, in order to co-opt him as a direct ancestor to Lysippus and his Sicyonian following?[16]

What does Posidippus *do* with all this information? Again, he treats it sceptically and critically. Not only does he vigorously dispute that Hageladas was Polyclitus' teacher—far from it, he was a 'much earlier practitioner of the art'—but he brusquely turns Polyclitus' own canonical status on its head. *No* long-standing law, he declares—neither Polyclitus' nor anyone else's—now governs the field. So whose law does? His last three lines reveal the truth: Lysippus'. His new grace is so self-evident that 'there is no reason at all to invoke it as a touchstone'. No contest: Easily overtaking both old and new, and implicitly rivalling the acknowledged contemporary master of 'grace', the painter Apelles,[17] Lysippus wins the prize. For as Posidippus hints and others later emphasized, his works were both elegant and supremely *alive*. And Cicero, in an oft-misunderstood passage (since Overbeck's authoritative 1868 collection of testimonia omitted its second half), tells us that when Lysippus acknowledged Polyclitus as his master, he did so with tongue in cheek![18]

Scattered remarks elsewhere in the ἀνδριαντοποιικά reinforce Posidippus' position and his authority to hold it.

First, in epigram 63 on the *Philitas* (quoted below) he remarks that Hecataeus accurately modelled it 'to the tips of its toenails . . . holding fast to the straight (ὀρθόν) canon of truth'. With this remark he takes a double swipe at Polyclitus, whose *Canon* or 'Rule' with its pretensions to absolute correctness (ὀρθότης) in attaining ideal truth must be the target—making its strong Platonic overtones doubly

---

[16] Oddly overlooked by Schweitzer, 'Xenocrates', 6 in his discussion of Xenocrates' pro-Sicyonian bias.

[17] Plin. *HN* 35. 79; Quint. 12. 10. 6; Ael. *VH* 12. 41; etc.; cf. Pollitt, *The Ancient View of Greek Art*, s.vv. χάρις, *elegantia*; for possible echoes of Posidippus' judgment see Call. *Descr.* 6. 2; Himer. *Or.* 31. 5; cf. Plin. *HN* 34. 66, quoted below.

[18] Elegant: Plin. *HN* 34. 66, quoted below; for possible echoes of this judgement, praising the χάρις of his statues, see Call. *Descr.* 6. 2; Himer. *Or.* 31. 5. Alive: *AP* 9. 777 (Philip, GP, *Garland*, 64): ται τέχναι γὰρ ἐμπνέει; Prop. 3. 9. 9: *gloria Lysippo est animosa effingere signa*; cf. AB 65, 142. Lysippus and Polyclitus: Cic. *Brut.* 296 *ut Polycliti Doryphorum sibi aiebat, sic tu suasionem legis Serviliae tibi magistram fuisse. haec germana ironia est.* On Lysippus and his brother Lysistratus, see, in general, P. Moreno, *Testimonianze per la teoria artistica di Lisippo* (Rome, 1973); id., *Lisippo*, i (Bari, 1974); id., *Vita e arte di Lisippo* (Milan, 1987); Stewart, *Greek Sculpture*, 186–91, 289–94; C. Rolley, *La Sculpture grecque*, ii (Paris, 1999), 323–62; for a sceptical view see B. S. Ridgway, *Fourth-Century Styles in Greek Sculpture* (Madison, 1997), 286–320.

ironic.[19] Moreover, the treatise that accompanied Polyclitus' statue declared that 'the work is hardest when the clay is at [or on] the [toe/finger]nail'—when the modelling process reaches the body's extremities. This remark soon became proverbial.[20] Once again, Posidippus takes pains to prove that he knows sculpture and its discourses.

Second, in AB 64, on Cresilas' *Idomeneus*, Posidippus mobilizes his friends in support. 'How accurately it is wrought, we saw well,' he exclaims, validating his personal opinion of the statue by inserting himself as narrator into a fictional group of spectators who allegedly share it. He thus presents himself as merely the spokesman for a collective and therefore authoritative community of voices. This is a well-known ecphrastic strategy of Philostratus, Callistratus, and the Second Sophistic; Xenophon's vivid picture of Socrates and his coterie visiting artists' studios and discussing their work is an obvious precedent (*Memorabilia* 3. 11. 1–3). In the third century, Theocritus 15 and Herodas 4, where women visit shrines and discuss their artworks, dramatize this scenario. But on present evidence very few epigrammatists followed suit. Nossis (*AP* 9. 332 = GP 4) urges us to accompany her to the temple of Aphrodite to see Polyarchis' statue of the goddess; and an epigram attributed to either Asclepiades or Posidippus (*AP* 16. 68 = AB 141 = GP Asclep. 29) advises us to check out another Aphrodite to see if it really portrays Queen Berenice. But that is all.[21]

Our poet, though, presents the judgement of his companions as a *fait accompli*. Outnumbered, outside this privileged community, and not having seen the *Idomeneus* ourselves, we can only follow its lead. Did Posidippus introduce this topos into Greek literature?

Finally, in AB 70, Posidippus describes Polyclitus' statues as σάρκινα, 'fleshy', apparently in contrast to Lysippus' Alexanders. This recalls Pliny's 'Xenocratic' judgement that Lysippus' figures were *graciliora siccioraque*, 'slenderer and leaner' than his predecessors'

---

[19] For ὀρθότης, 'correctness', as an aesthetic criterion see Pl. *Crat.* 430 B–432 D and especially *Lg.* 667 B–670 C, where it is closely correlated with Truth: cf. Pollitt, *The Ancient View of Greek Art*, 45 and esp. S. Halliwell, *The Aesthetics of Mimesis* (Princeton, 2002), 44–8, 65–70, with pp. 63–4 and 138–47 on Plato's critique of the inadequacy of verisimilitude. The phrase 'straight canon of truth' may not be Posidippus' own, since (as an anonymous reader of this essay notes) it is used by his contemporary, Timon of Phlius, apparently to describe the philosophy of his teacher Pyrrho: *SH* 842.

[20] Plu. *Mor.* 86 A, 636 B–C; on the meaning of this statement see C. C. Mattusch, *Greek Bronze Statuary* (Ithaca, NY, 1988), 159–61; A. Stewart, 'Nuggets: Mining the Texts Again', 274–5 ('Two More Citations of Polyclitus' Canon'); and A. d'Angour, 'Ad unguem'.

[21] On Nossis as both dramatic narrator and author-compiler see Gutzwiller, *Poetic Garlands*, 83–4.

(*HN* 34. 65, quoted in full below),[22] and once again suggests that the poet is parading his knowledge of the field and its discourses.

POSIDIPPUS AND LYSIPPUS: TRUTH, BEAUTY, AND GRACE

Lysippus was Posidippus' hero, and as remarked earlier, we know that the poet wrote a great deal about him.[23] So his four extant epigrams on the sculptor (AB 62, 65, 70, and 142) must represent only a fraction of his work on him. Who was this Lysippus and why should Posidippus have cared about him? In *HN* 34. 51 Pliny dates him to the 113th Olympiad (328–325 BC) and a few pages later (*HN* 34. 61–6) has this to say about him, quoting from the early Hellenistic historian Duris of Samos at the beginning, and another source—surely Xenocrates again—towards the end.

(61) Lysippum Sicyonium Duris negat ullius fuisse discipulum, sed primo aerarium fabrum audiendi rationem cepisse pictoris Eupompi responso. eum enim interrogatum, quem sequeretur antecedentium, dixisse monstrata hominum multitudine, naturam ipsam imitandam esse, non artificem. (62) plurima ex omnibus signa fecit, ut diximus, fecundissimae artis, inter quae destringentem se, quem M. Agrippa ante thermas suas dicavit . . . (63) nobilitatur Lysippus et temulenta tibicina et canibus ac venatione, in primis vero quadriga cum sole Rhodiorum. fecit et Alexandrum Magnum multis operibus, a pueritia eius orsus . . . (64) idem fecit Hephaestionem, Alexandri Magni amicum, quem quidam Polyclito adscribunt, cum is centum prope annis ante fuerit; item Alexandri venationem, quae Delphis sacrata est, Athenis Satyrum, turmam Alexandri, in qua amicorum eius imagines summa omnium similitudine expressit; hanc Metellus Macedonia subacta transtulit Romam. fecit et quadrigas multorum generum. (65) statuariae arti plurimum traditur contulisse, capillum exprimendo, capita minora faciendo quam antiqui, corpora graciliora siccioraque, per quae proceritas signorum maior uideretur. non habet Latinum nomen symmetria, quam diligentissime custodiit nova intactaque ratione quadratas ueterum staturas permutando, uulgoque dicebat ab illis factos quales essent homines, a se quales uiderentur esse. propriae huius uidentur esse argutiae operum custoditae in minimis quoque rebus. (66) filios et discipulos reliquit laudatos artifices [D]aippum, Boedan, sed ante omnes Euthycraten, quamquam is constantiam potius imitatus patris quam elegantiam austero maluit genere quam iucundo placere.

(61) Duris says that Lysippus of Sicyon was nobody's pupil. Originally a bronze smith, he joined the profession after hearing a response from the painter Eupompus. When asked which of his predecessors he followed,

---

[22] Cf. Pollitt, *The Ancient View of Greek Art*, s.vv. *gracilis, siccus.*
[23] Himer. *Or.* 48. 14, p. 203 Colonna.

Eupompus pointed to a crowd of people and said that it was Nature herself, not another artist, whom one should imitate.

(62) Lysippus was a most prolific artist, and made more statues than any other sculptor, among them an *Apoxyomenus* or *Man Scraping Himself with a Strigil* which M. Agrippa dedicated in front of his baths, and which the emperor Tiberius was astonishingly fond of . . .

(63) Lysippus is famed for his *Drunken Flute Girl*, his *Hounds and Huntsmen*, and particularly for his *Chariot of the Sun* at Rhodes. He also made many studies of Alexander the Great, beginning with one in his boyhood . . . (64) He also sculpted Hephaestion, Alexander's friend, which some ascribe to Polyclitus, even though he lived a century earlier, and made an *Alexander's Hunt* dedicated at Delphi, a *Satyr* now at Athens, and an *Alexander's Squadron* in which he rendered the portraits of the king's friends with the highest degree of likeness possible in each case; Metellus removed this to Rome after the conquest of Macedonia. He also made chariot groups of various kinds.

(65) Lysippus is said to have contributed much to the art of sculpture, by rendering the hair in more detail, by making the heads of his figures smaller than the old sculptors used to do, and the bodies slenderer and leaner, to give his statues the appearance of greater height. Latin has no word for the *symmetria* that he most scrupulously preserved by a new and untried system that modified the foursquare figures of the ancients; and he used to say publicly that whereas they had made men as they were, he made them as they appeared to be. A distinguishing characteristic of his is seen to be the scrupulous attention to detail maintained in even the smallest particulars.

(66) He left three sons who were his pupils, the celebrated artists Daippus, Boedas, and above all Euthycrates, who, however, imitated his father's toughness rather than his elegance, preferring to find favour through an austere style rather than a pleasing one.

Finally, Pliny tells us that Lysippus' brother, Lysistratus, was the first to use life masks taken from the human face as a basis for portraiture. But significantly, Lysistratus then made sure to touch up the end products where necessary, 'making corrections upon a casting produced by pouring wax into this plaster mould'.[24]

Quintilian briskly agrees with all this:

Ad ueritatem Lysippum et Praxitelen accessisse optime adfirmant: nam Demetrius tamquam nimius in ea reprenditur et fuit similitudinis quam pulchritudinis amantior. (*Inst.* 12. 10. 9)

Critics agree that Lysippus and Praxiteles best attained representational truth. For Demetrius is blamed as too extreme in this respect, and was fonder of likeness than of beauty.

---

[24] *HN* 35. 153.

Where do these remarks get us? First, it is clear that most ancient critics (Posidippus included) indeed presented the history of classical Greek sculpture as a quest for representational truth (ἀλήθεια/ *veritas*). Yet (second) it is equally clear that—received wisdom to the contrary[25]—the quest was by no means straightforward, its goals were by no means clear-cut, and hardline realists were few and did not necessarily reap the highest esteem.

To begin with this second proposition.

In *Poetics* 25, Aristotle tells us that there are three kinds of mimesis, 'of things as they were or are; of things as they are said or seem to be; and of things as they ought to be'—i.e. (in art-historical jargon), realism, phenomenal idealism, and categorical idealism. The passages cited above and the extant sculptural remains demonstrate that all three took truth to nature as their basic premise; that each prevailed at different times; that no simple line of development connects them; and that each foray from a formalized naturalism into hardboiled realism provoked a backlash of some kind.

For naturalism and realism are not identical. Although Greek artists committed themselves to truth to nature from the very start, they almost never aimed at realism *per se*. Instead, they sought what Roland Barthes once famously called in another context a 'reality *effect*'.[26] Since art's basic aim was to please gods or men or both, they sought Beauty (κάλλος/τὸ καλόν) above all, and for the most part—like John Keats two millennia later—unproblematically equated it with Truth (ἀλήθεια)—or rather, surreptitiously redefined Truth as what seemed to be the 'most beautiful' (τὸ κάλλιστον) at the time.[27]

This is the so-called 'Greek ideal'. Tacitly defined as the general and typical, as the highest common factor in human or animal, it required the invention of visually satisfying, all-purpose conventions (ῥυθμοί, cχήματα) for key features such as muscles, lips, eyes, hair, clothing, and so on, and for the endless variety of postures available to the human body. This commitment to universals, to what J. J. Pollitt has perceptively called 'the representation of the specific in the

---

[25] e.g. R. R. R. Smith, 'Theory and Criticism'.

[26] R. Barthes, *The Rustle of Language*, trans. R. Howard (New York, 1986), 141–8.

[27] See Pollitt, *The Ancient View of Greek Art*, s.v. ἀλήθεια/*veritas*, τὸ κάλλος, ῥυθμός, cχῆμα, *numerosus/numerus* and *pulchritudo* (there is no entry for κόcμοc) with e.g. Schweitzer, 'Xenocrates'; C. Karouzos, "Τί τὸ κάλλιcτον;"; C. H. H. Hallett, 'The Origins of the Classical Style in Sculpture'; Stewart, *Greek Sculpture*, 78–85; Steiner, *Images in Mind*; Sprigath, 'Der Fall Xenokrates von Athen', 413–16; R. T. Neer, *Style and Politics in Athenian Vasepainting* (Cambridge, 2002), 10–13; all citing numerous texts in support. *Contra*, Plato, who was well aware of the mimetic tension between truth to appearances and truth to a (supposed) inner reality: cf. e.g. *Soph.* 325 D–E; *Crat.* 432 A–D; *Rep.* 596–602, with Halliwell, *The Aesthetics of Mimesis*, 44–50, 136–8.

light of the generic', tempers Greek naturalism with a certain degree of formality, with an appropriate dosage of κόϲμοϲ, or Order.[28]

But how much Order sufficed in the particular case? For as E. H. Gombrich has remarked, 'the more a painting or a statue mirrors natural appearances, the fewer principles of order and symmetry it will automatically exhibit. Conversely, the more ordered a configuration, the less it will be likely to reproduce nature.' So, on the one hand, as Plato declared, 'Measure and proportion (ϲυμμετρία) are everywhere equated with beauty and virtue.' But on the other, the drive to satisfy the demands of natural Truth led not merely to greater naturalism, but to its corollary, greater *illusionism* and thus greater power for the artist over the hapless spectator—philosophers included.[29]

By the late fifth century, intellectuals like Gorgias had understood this uncomfortable fact, and by the early fourth, Plato—aghast at the thought of conceding such power to mere artisans (βάναυϲοι)—was vigorously attacking it. Whereas Gorgias was fascinated by illusionistic deception (ἀπάτη) in the arts, Plato's immediate reaction was to condemn it as a 'lie' (ψεῦδοϲ). He particularly targets contemporary painting for its obsession with ϲκιαγραφία (perhaps best translated as 'chiaroscuro'), but makes several jabs at sculpture too. For by unscrupulously deceiving the eye, ϲκιαγραφία and other exercises in illusion (φανταϲτική) are nothing less than a kind of 'sorcery' that exploits our 'weakness' and results in our 'enslavement'. Yet contrary to general belief, except for a highly rhetorical passage in the *Republic*, Plato never attacks or wants to ban the visual arts *per se*. For the most part he assails only those artistic developments that (he felt) gave the ignorant and unscrupulous βάναυϲοϲ power over the unsuspecting public's hearts and minds, usurping what should be the proper role of the philosopher.[30]

There is no evidence that anyone outside philosophical circles took much notice of these debates. The inherently unequal contest between Nature and Order continued inexorably to favour the former, as artists slowly learned how to integrate the two and began

[28] J. J. Pollitt, *Art and Experience in Classical Greece* (London, 1972), 6.
[29] E. H. Gombrich, *Norm and Form*, i (London and New York, 1966), 94 (quoted by Hallett, 'The Origins of the Classical Style in Sculpture', 80 n. 53); Pl. *Phlb.* 64 E. On naturalism, illusionism, and power, cf. Halliwell, *The Aesthetics of Mimesis*, 123–4 and W. J. T. Mitchell, *Picture Theory* (Chicago, 1994), 323–38, 329–44.
[30] On Gorgias and Plato see Pollitt, *The Ancient View of Greek Art*, 41–52, with 247–54 on ϲκιαγραφία (esp. *Phaedo* 69 B and *Rep.* 10, 602 D); Rouveret, *Histoire et imaginaire de la peinture ancienne*; Steiner, *Images in Mind*; Halliwell, *The Aesthetics of Mimesis*, esp. pp. 57–58, 134–42 on the rhetorical and satirical character of *Rep.* 10. 595–607.

to ease the latter tactfully but firmly into the background—usually taking care, however, not to abandon it altogether. For Pliny (see above) takes pains to stress that although Lysippus introduced several major mimetic innovations, and tempered his robust manner with an appropriate measure of elegance and grace (*elegantia*; Posidippus' χάρις), he scrupulously preserved at least one key principle of Order: cυμμετρία or proportionality. Indeed, he even reinforced it by boldly devising a 'new and hitherto untried system' that regulated the flux of appearance more firmly—if less obviously—than ever before.

Hardboiled realism—the direct, uncompromising transcription of individually specific traits, even personal quirks—was potentially disruptive to this aesthetic of formalized naturalism. So its most blatant advocates like the early-fourth-century sculptor Demetrius of Alopece—interestingly omitted from Posidippus' catalogue of realists—always remained on the fringes of the art, at least in the eyes of the critics (see Quintilian, quoted above), even though he apparently achieved considerable commercial success.[31]

Of course, naturalism and realism are by no means absolutes and are easily inflated in the mind of the beholder—and then, when something more compelling appears, just as speedily deflated.[32] So did Posidippus' own poetic agenda (see Alexander Sens, below, Ch. 11) cause him to exaggerate and somewhat distort Lysippus' sculptural one? Perhaps not. For in the extant poems he never praises Lysippus as a realist *tout court*, and everything he says about him can be reconciled with the judgements of Pliny, Quintilian, and Plutarch. Indeed, Plutarch stresses that Alexander much preferred Lysippus over the realists (*Moralia* 335 A–B):

Διὸ καὶ μόνον Ἀλέξανδρος ἐκέλευε Λύσιππον εἰκόνας αὐτοῦ δημιουργεῖν. μόνος γὰρ οὗτος, ὡς ἔοικε, κατεμήνευε τῶι χαλκῶι τὸ ἦθος αὐτοῦ καὶ cυνεξέφαινε τῆι μορφῆι τὴν ἀρετήν· οἱ δ' ἄλλοι τὴν ἀποστροφὴν τοῦ τραχήλου καὶ τῶν ὀμμάτων τὴν διάχυcιν καὶ ὑγρότητα μιμεῖcθαι θέλοντες οὐ διεφύλαττον αὐτοῦ τὸ ἀρρενωπὸν καὶ λεοντῶδες.

Alexander ordered that only Lysippus should make his portraits. For he alone, it seemed, brought out his real character in the bronze and caught his essential genius (*arete*). For the others, in their eagerness to represent his crooked neck and melting, limpid eyes, were unable to preserve his virile and leonine demeanour.

---

[31] On Demetrius' realism see also Lucian, *Philops.* 18, though a number of inscribed bases from the Acropolis show that despite the criticisms, he was well supplied with portrait and other commissions (see Stewart, *Greek Sculpture*, 274–5).

[32] For this insight see especially Hallett, 'Origins of the Classical Style', 77–8.

Unlike Lysippus, then, these individuals failed to capture the essence
of the king's character—exactly the achievement that Posidippus
praises in his epigram on Lysippus' Alexanders (AB 65).

So to work chronologically using the artists singled out by these
authors, and accepting their judgements about them at face value, we
arrive at the following schematic chart:

TABLE 1: *Mimesis and the Masters*
(after Aristotle, Posidippus, Pliny, Quintilian, and Plutarch)

Name	Floruit	Realism ('were or are')	Phenomenal idealism ('said or seem to be')	Categorical idealism ('ought to be')
[Dry]opas	?			×
D[aedalidae]	?			×
Theodorus	550	×		
Hageladas	500			×
Myron	460	×		
Phidias	450			×
Polyclitus	440			×
Cresilas	420	×		
Demetrius	400	×		
Praxiteles	360		×	
Lysippus	330		×	
Lysistratus	330	× ⟶	×	
Hecataeus	270	×		

To summarize, Posidippus saw Theodorus' *Chariot* and Myron's
Cow and *Idomeneus* as true masterpieces of *realism* for their time—
and thus as trail-blazers for Lysippus and his art.[33] By contrast, the
'hard' statues of Hageladas *et al.* and Polyclitus' *Canon*, respectively,
were paradigms of *categorical idealism*. Next, Demetrius of Alopece
produced *overrealistic* portraits, to critical disdain. Then, in reaction,
Praxiteles and Lysippus mastered the art of *phenomenal idealism*,
and Lysistratus developed the key technical means—life casting—
to ground this more temperate approach in reality. And finally (if
Posidippus is to be believed), Hecataeus developed the *canonical*

---

[33] For the suggestion that Posidippus saw Myron as Lysippus' artistic ancestor, see
Gutzwiller, 'Posidippus on Statuary', 54, 58–60. This is another implicitly anti-Xenocratic
judgement, since Plin. *HN* 34. 58 censures Myron for his relatively crude rendering of the hair
and pubes, 'no more accurate than that of rude antiquity', despite his command of movement
and proportion.

realism of his *Philitas*—the 'straight canon of truth' in sculpture (AB 63):[34]

τόνδε Φιλίται χ[αλ]κὸν [ἴ]ϲον κατὰ πάνθ' Ἑκ[α]ταῖοϲ
ἀ]κ[ρ]ιβὴϲ ἄκρουϲ [ἔπλ]αϲεν εἰϲ ὄνυχαϲ,
καὶ με]γέθει κα[ὶ ϲα]ρκὶ τὸν ἀνθρωπιϲτὶ διώξαϲ
γνώμο]ν', ἀφ' ἡρώων δ' οὐδὲν ἔμειξ' ἰδέηϲ,
ἀλλὰ τὸν ἀκρομέριμνον ὅλ[ηι κ]ατεμάξατο τέχνηι   5
πρ]έϲβυν, ἀληθείηϲ ὀρθὸν [ἔχων] κανόνα·
αὐδήϲ]οντι δ' ἔοικεν, ὅϲωι ποικίλλεται ἤθει,
ἔμψυχ]οϲ, καίπερ χάλκεοϲ ἐὼν ὁ γέρων·
ἐκ Πτολε]μαίου δ' ὧδε θεοῦ θ' ἅμα καὶ βαϲιλῆοϲ
ἄγκειμ]αι Μουϲέ{ι}ων εἵνεκα Κῶιοϲ ἀνήρ.   10

1 πάνθ' : παντα pap.   4 ἔμειξ' : εμειξε pap.   10 ἄγκειμ]αι Scodel : ἄγκειτ]αι BG

This bronze, just like Philitas in every way, Hecataeus
  moulded accurately down to the toenails.
Following a human standard in scale and feature,
  he blended it with none of the form of the heroes,
but modelled the old perfectionist with all his skill,
  holding fast to the straight canon of truth.
He seems about to speak, so characterful is he—
  the old man's alive, though he's made of bronze:
'Here, thanks to Ptolemy, god and king as well,
  for the Muses' sake I stand, a man of Cos.'

The poet cleverly repeats the root *akr-* to make his point. Hecataeus has modelled Philitas ἀ]κ[ρ]ιβὴϲ ἄκρουϲ . . . εἰϲ ὄνυχαϲ, precisely duplicating the old scholar-poet's own anxious perfectionism (ἀκρομέριμνον). The power relation of artist over spectator that is inherent in illusionistic art—an art of deception (ἀπάτη)—is now decisively inverted.[35] Because Hecataeus has patiently modelled his *Philitas* 'accurately down to the toenails', following 'a human standard in scale and feature' and 'holding fast to the straight canon of Truth', we all now have direct access to the 'real' Philitas, the 'man of Cos' whose outer and inner self leap vividly alive before our eyes, and who now even addresses us directly. Thanks to Hecataeus' trenchant honesty, we have regained power over reality. In truth, poet, audience, sculptor, image, and subject all match perfectly.

---

[34] Text taken from Acosta-Hughes and Kosmetatou, 'New Poems Attributed to Posidippus', who in l. 10 follow R. Scodel, 'A Note on Posidippus AB 63'.
[35] Cf. Mitchell, *Picture Theory*, 325.

POSIDIPPUS, PHILITAS, AND THE TRUTH IN SCULPTURE

So what is this Straight Canon of Truth? In order to frame an answer to this question, it is necessary to examine the other testimonia on Philitas' portrait and to consult some other early Hellenistic portraits that help to elucidate Posidippus' description of it.[36]

The longest text is by Philitas' pupil and friend, Hermesianax (fr. 7. 75–8 Powell):

> οἶcθα δὲ καὶ τὸν ἀοιδὸν ὃν Εὐρυπύλου πολιῆται
> Κῶιοι χάλκειον θῆκαν ὑπὸ πλατάνωι
> Βιττίδα μολπάζοντα θοήν, περὶ πάντα Φιλίταν
> ῥήματα καὶ πᾶσαν ⟨τ⟩ρυόμενον λαλίην.

> You know the singer, that the Coan citizens of Eurypylus
> set up under a plane tree, the bronze one,
> singing of his nimble Bittis—Philitas,
> worn out on all words and all dialect.

Philitas himself apparently discussed it too (Philitas fr. 14 Powell):

> θρήcαcθαι πλατάνωι γραίηι ὕπο . . .

> . . . to be seated under an old plane tree.

The context of his four-word comment is unknown, but it might have been a sphragis-type poem like the one by Posidippus mentioned earlier, in which he was fishing for heroic honours and a portrait statue at Pella. Finally, Propertius (3. 1. 1–2) contributes the crucial fact that Philitas was heroized:

> Callimachi Manes et Coi sacra Philitae
> in uestrum, quaeso, me sinite ire nemus.

> Shade of Callimachus and sacred rites of Coan Philitas
> suffer me, I pray, to come into your grove.

As to Hecataeus, Pliny mentions a silversmith by this name (*HN* 33. 156, 34. 85) but hints that he lived much later; a *Pandora* search has turned up nothing more.

The portrait comparanda are the *Demosthenes* (Fig. 1), the *Epicurus* (Fig. 2), and our epigrammatist's namesake, Posidippus the Athenian

---

[36] Recently, the *Philitas* bibliography has mushroomed: see especially Hollis, 'Heroic Honours for Philitas?'; Hardie, 'Philitas and the Plane Tree'; id., 'The Statue(s) of Philitas'; F. Angiò, 'Filita di Cos in bronzo'; Bernsdorff, 'Anmerkungen zum neuen Posidipp', 23–5; A. Sens, 'The New Posidippus', and below, Ch. 11; Gutzwiller, 'Posidippus on Statuary', 46–50. On the poet himself see most recently Bing, 'The Unruly Tongue', with the commentaries by L. Sbardella, *Filita* (Rome, 2000), and K. Spanoudakis, *Philitas of Cos* (Leiden, 2002).

Fig. 1. Demosthenes. Roman marble copy after a bronze original by Polyeuctus, 280/79 BC. Copenhagen, Ny Carlsberg Glyptotek, inv. 2782. Photo: Museum

FIG. 2. Epicurus. Plaster cast of a Roman marble statuette in the Palazzo dei Conservatori. Original c.270 BC. Munich, Museum für Abgüsse klassischer Bildwerke. Photo: Museum

FIG. 3. Reconstruction by Klaus Fittschen and E. Funk of the portrait of the Athenian comic poet Posidippus. Original *c*.250 BC. Composite plaster cast of an inscribed Roman marble copy in the Vatican of the entire statue and a Roman marble copy in Geneva of the head. Göttingen: Archäologisches Institut der Univerität. Photo: Stephan Eckhart

FIG. 4. Bronze 'Philosopher' from a wreck off Anticythera, c.250–200 BC. Athens, National Museum Br. 13400. Photo: DAI Athens

comic poet (Fig. 3). All are known only in copy. Alongside them, I illustrate the sole original of any use, the bronze *Philosopher* from the Anticythera wreck (Fig. 4).[37] Brilliantly naturalistic—even realistic—to a fault, they help us to understand Hecataeus' aims in making his *Philitas*.

The *Demosthenes*, commissioned by the Athenians in 280 from a certain Polyeuctus, has Philitas' anxious, focused intensity and meagre body, sharing the latter trait with the *Epicurus*. For in addition to being an obsessive perfectionist, Philitas was also extraordinarily thin. Some alleged that he was literally emaciated by his studies, others that he wore weighted shoes so the wind would not blow him away! This tradition has been dismissed as a mere literary topos, but Alan Cameron has shown that it must be authentic and must derive from Attic New Comedy.[38] Never strong, Philitas perhaps suffered—like Epicurus—from a wasting disease that contemporaries jokingly attributed to the consuming passion of his pedantry. Hecataeus, determined to adhere inflexibly to the 'straight canon of truth' in portraiture, clearly confronted all this head on.

The portrait of the Athenian comic poet Posidippus is a composite, brilliantly reconstructed by Klaus Fittschen. For the head of the inscribed, full-length marble copy in Rome was completely recut in Roman times.[39] The restorer left untouched only a few locks on the nape of the neck, but these were enough for Fittschen to recognize the head type in another series of copies and to reunite it in plaster cast with the body. As to its identification as the Athenian comedian and not our Macedonian epigrammatist, not only is there no evidence that the latter's coveted portrait at Pella was ever set up, but an Athenian location for any intellectual reproduced in Roman copy is far more likely than a literary backwater apparently ignored by the copyists. A backhanded remark by Pausanias furnishes a suitable context for the comedian's statue: 'In their theatre, the Athenians have portrait statues of poets, both tragic and comic, but they are mostly nonentities. With the exception of Menander no comic poet

[37] On these portraits see most conveniently G. M. A. Richter, *The Portraits of the Greeks* (London, 1967), 2, 38, fig. XL (Anticythera head), 194–200, figs. 1149–1225 (Epicurus), 215–23, figs. 1397–1512 (Demosthenes), 238–9, figs. 1647–50 (Posidippus); Fittschen, 'Zur Rekonstruktion griechischer Dichterstatuen, 2. Teil'; with comments in P. Zanker, *The Mask of Socrates* (Berkeley and Los Angeles, 1994), 77–145; also B. Andreae, *Schönheit des Realismus* (Mainz, 1998), 52–4, 66–74.

[38] Ael. *VH* 9.14; Ath. 12. 552 B; Cameron, *Callimachus and his Critics*, 488–93; and cf. now Bernsdorff, 'Anmerkungen zum neuen Posidipp', 23.

[39] Illustrated without comment on the front cover of AB, with caption on p. 1; cf. Dickie, 'Which Posidippus?'

represented here won a reputation, but tragedy has two illustrious representatives, Euripides and Sophocles.'[40]

Despite its well-fed appearance, the Athenian *Posidippus* has the same sober, unheroic demeanour as the *Philitas* apparently had, and emphasizes, too, that writing is hard work. It is also enthroned, as Philitas must have been, since despite the latter's unheroic appearance and purely human demeanour, he was officially heroized and the recipient of cult (Propertius, quoted above). The relevance of the intense, haggard Anticythera *Philosopher* to all this goes without saying.

The *Philitas*, then, was no aberration. Far from it. It must have been a paragon of its time and style—a brilliant exercise in descriptive realism. But what of Posidippus' own stance? How did he understand the Straight Canon of Truth in Sculpture? This is less straightforward, and deeply imbricated with his own view of art and the poetic enterprise (see Sens, Ch. 11). For the purposes of this essay, it may be approached from two complementary directions, via the keywords 'straight' (ὀρθόν) and 'truth' (ἀλήθεια). The first describes Hecataeus' method and the second its outcome.

Four modalities of artistic 'straightness' (ὀρθότηc) come to mind, prompted by the entries in Liddell and Scott's *Greek–English Lexicon*:

First, Hecataeus' method is *straightforward*. He correctly understands both sculptural technique in general and the demands of this particular commission. Doing justice to the old perfectionist entails a directly mimetic approach, an accurate 'human standard' with no admixture of the heroic or divine, that presents him simply as a 'Coan man'.

Second, Hecataeus' canon is *objectively straight*. He uses a rule that is straight and accurate, sizing up his subject exactly with yardstick, hand, and eye. Using all his skill-at-hand (τέχνη), he has produced an objectively measured guide to the reality or Truth of Philitas.

Third, Hecataeus' canon radiates *moral rectitude*. Eschewing all illusion (φανταcτική), deception (ἀπάτη), and fiction (ψεῦδοc), he cleaves to an upright moral vision that exactly matches his exacting subject and the dignity of his own commission—a portrait commanded by a god-king and dedicated to the divine truth-tellers, the Muses.

And fourth, his work appeals to us *straightforwardly and directly*.

---

[40] Paus. 1. 21. 1; AB 118 = *SH* 705, ll. 17–18—though *pace* Austin's translation, 'standing ... in the crowded market-place', the Greek has only κείμενοc, 'placed'.

He makes no twists and turns; we need no particular expertise to follow his 'human standard', no mental gymnastics to filter out inappropriate heroics. The real Philitas is straightforwardly present to our eyes, as if alive and about to speak.

What results—for Posidippus—is nothing less than Truth itself. This returns us, finally, to Cézanne's promise. Jacques Derrida has offered four separate readings of it—four separate modalities of artistic Truth—all of which are relevant to Posidippus' agenda and are underpinned by the four modalities of ὀρθότης explored above.[41] They begin where the other four leave off. Translating painting into sculpture and keeping Figs. 1–4 and the Philitas epigram in mind, the following paragraphs paraphrase and gloss Derrida's analysis.

First, there is the truth that pertains to *the thing itself*: to the portrait image. The anxious old perfectionist really seems to be singing; his character sparkles out (ποικίλλεται); indeed, he's so characterful that he looks alive (ἔμψυχοc) even though he's bronze. The portrait transcends the limitations of its own medium; it *obliterates* it with its truthfulness. It's the real Philitas, the real McCoy.

Second, there is the truth that pertains to adequate *representation*. For after all the portrait is bronze and is seemingly alive even though it is bronze. With consummate technique Hecataeus has modelled it accurately down to its toenails. The sculptor's perfectionism mirrors his subject's. In size and feature, it is the truth faithfully represented in its portrait, trait for trait and with no false heroics. This image is anxious old Philitas' double—Philitas in the flesh—but precisely other by virtue of its *being* a likeness—of its being *bronze and accurate* (ἀκριβής, ὀρθόc).[42] So it is still the truth of truth, but this time the value of adequation has *pushed aside* that of unveiling.

Third, there is the truth that pertains to *sculpture*: in Philitas' case, the truth *in bronze*. For truth could be presented quite otherwise, according to other media. Here it is done *in bronze sculpture*, and not in painting, poetry, theatre, or whatever. In emphasizing this, Posidippus opens our eyes to what is proper to an *art form*: the truth 'in sculpture' just as in Cézanne's case it would be 'in painting'. In our first two modalities, 'sculpture' figured the presentation or representation of a *model*, which happened to be the truth. But none of this three-dimensional accuracy (ἀκρίβεια, ὀρθότης) of character, flesh,

---

[41] J. Derrida, *The Truth in Painting*, trans. G. Bennington and I. McLeod (Chicago, 1987), 5–7.

[42] On the portrait double see Plato, *Crat.* 432 B–C; see most recently Steiner, *Images in Mind*, 69–70; Halliwell, *The Aesthetics of Mimesis*, 46–7. Heroics would be appropriate for Alexander (AB 65) and *a fortiori* for Ptolemy (AB 63. 9), but definitely not here.

age, height, and so on could be represented in painting, still less in poetry. Indeed, some of it could not be represented adequately even in marble (cf. Figs. 1–4). And although Greek painting climaxed in these very years—'it flourished primarily from around Philip's time down to Alexander's successors'[43]—even so, Posidippus did not *write* about painting. He wrote about sculpture, specifically about *bronze sculpture*. The material regulates the possibility of play, of divergences, of the equivocal—a whole economy of the trait. And here, Hecataeus emerges as a truly straight man. There is no room for hucksters and conmen in his economy.

And finally, we *will see* this truth and other artists *will acknowledge* it. From the first line of epigram 62, Posidippus constantly asserts his own authority, telling us exactly what we will see and citing his reading and his friends to back up his statements. He is a 'Master of Truth' in the classic poetical manner: his remarks, also dedicated *de facto* to the Muses, are sworn testimony.[44] He opens our eyes to the truth *on the subject of* sculpture; he writes that which is *true on* the art that is called sculptural. If sculpture has the highest truth-value of all the representational media, then he is the one who writes the truth about it: he writes truth on truth. He is 'knowledgeable in sculpture'; he knows the truth about the truth, he owes it to us, and he will tell it to us. And this sculptural truth is metonymic for poetic truth, Alexandrian-style.[45]

---

[43] Quint. 12. 10. 6. Apelles epitomizes the truth in painting for Posidippus' contemporary Herodas: *Mimiambi* 4.72–8; he was also the acknowledged master of grace, χάρις, in this medium: Plin. *HN* 35. 79; Quint. 12. 10. 6; Ael. *VH* 12. 41; etc.

[44] Cf. M. Detienne, *The Masters of Truth in Archaic Greece*, trans. J. Lloyd (New York and Cambridge, MA, 1996), with Stewart, *Greek Sculpture*, 53–5; Neer, *Style and Politics*, 10–13.

[45] Sens, below, Ch. 11.

11

The Art of Poetry and the Poetry of Art: The Unity and Poetics of Posidippus' Statue-Poems

ALEXANDER SENS

In Theocritus' fifteenth idyll, Praxinoa and Gorgo, Syracusan women residing in Egypt, travel to the royal palace at Alexandria in order to celebrate Arsinoe's festival of Adonis. As they enter the palace Gorgo invites her companion to consider the refinement of the tapestries that hang there (78–9), and Praxinoa elaborates on their realism (80–3). 'What workers', she observes, 'must have made them, and what artists drew the accurate lines. How truly the figures stand and how truly they whirl, alive, not woven. Man is a clever thing!' (*coφόν τι χρῆμ' ἄνθρωποc*). Shortly thereafter, a female singer performs a hymn to Adonis, in response to which Gorgo offers a similar reaction: 'The woman is a most clever thing' (145; *τὸ χρῆμα coφώτατον ἁ θήλεια*). As Richard Hunter has observed, the parallelism between the women's reactions to the tapestries and the song suggests the analogy not only between these two artefacts but also between them and the poem in which they are contained.[1] However one assesses the competence of Praxinoa and Gorgo as critics of art and poetry,[2] their reactions to what they see and hear in Arsinoe's palace represent a comment on Theocritus' own project as well.[3] A similar connection between ecphrasis and poetic programme is forged in Theocritus' first idyll, where the goatherd's description of scenes engraved on the elaborate cup he promises to Thyrsis in exchange for a song both suggests the equivalence of poetry and artefact and calls attention to the artifice involved in the poet's treatment of similar 'naturalistic' themes.[4]

I am grateful to Marco Fantuzzi, Nita Krevans, and Enrico Magnelli for comments on a written draft of this chapter, as well as to the participants in the Cincinnati conference for their remarks on the preliminary oral presentation.

[1] R. Hunter, *Theocritus and the Archaeology of Greek Poetry* (Cambridge, 1996), 116–23.

[2] Cf. J. Burton, *Theocritus' Urban Mimes* (Berkeley, 1995), 93–122.

[3] Hunter, *Theocritus and the Archaeology of Greek Poetry*, 119.

[4] Cf. K. Gutzwiller, *Theocritus' Pastoral Analogies: The Formation of a Genre* (Madison, 1991), 90–4; R. Hunter, *Theocritus: A Selection* (Cambridge, 1999), 76–7.

Posidippus, too, exploits the parallels between visual and literary craft. Among the notable features of the new papyrus is its interest in works of art ranging from carved stones to statues, and critics have pointed out that the poems in the section on stones (λιθικά), inasmuch as they emphasize the refinement of small, highly wrought objects in a 'minor' artistic genre, may be read as programmatic comments on the author's own small and elegant poetry.[5] A number of the poems on statues that make up the ἀνδριαντοποιικά, a section characterized by careful and symmetrical organization,[6] similarly play on the relationship between the aesthetic qualities of the art objects they praise and the literary characteristics of the poems themselves by creating an elaborate nexus of connections that link the artist, the narrator, and the sculpted object.

Perhaps more than any other section of the papyrus, the epigrams grouped under the generic label ἀνδριαντοποιικά invite a programmatic reading, since the opening of the first poem (AB 62) is explicitly cast as a set of instructions for artists:[7]

μιμ[ή]cαcθε τάδ' ἔργα, πολυχρονίους δὲ κολοccῶν,
  ὦ ζ[ωι]οπλάcται, ν[αί], παραθεῖτε νόμους·
εἴ γε μὲν ἀρχαῖαι [ ] πα χέρες, ἢ Ἀγελαίδης
  ὁ πρὸ Πολυκ⟨λ⟩είτο[υ πά]γχυ παλαιοτέχνης,
ἢ οἱ †Διδυμιδουτ cκληρ[οὶ τύ]ποι εἰc πέδον ἦλθον,   5
  Λυcίππου νεάρ' ἦν οὐδ[ε]μία πρόφαcιc
δεῦρο παρεκτεῖναι βαcάνου χάριν· εἶ[τα] δ' ἐὰν χρῆι
  καὶ πίπτηι ὦθλοc καινοτεχνέων πέραc ἦν·

5 ἦλθον Austin: ελθειν pap   7 ἐὰν: εαγ pap.   8 ὦθλοc BG: οαθλου ex οαλλου corr.
pap.   πέραc BG: πετεc pap.   ἦν Austin: ηι pap.

Imitate these works, and run past—yes, do—
the long-standing rules for statues,[8] sculptors.
Even if the ancient hands of (?) or Hagelaides
the craftsman of the very old style before Polyclitus
or the rigid sculptures of Didymides (?) had come into the field,
there would be no reason to lay out here the novelties of Lysippus
for examination. Then if it were necessary
and the contest of craftsmen of the new style fell, he would be
  the best (?).

---

[5] P. Bing, above, Ch. 7; Schur, 'A Garland of Stones'; Hutchinson, 'The New Posidippus and Latin Poetry', 2–3.
[6] For the careful arrangement and thematic unity of the ἀνδριαντοποιικά, cf. Gutzwiller, 'Posidippus on Statuary'; ead., 'A New Hellenistic Poetry Book'; A. Stewart, above, Ch. 10.
[7] The text and sense of the final verses are uncertain; I print the text of the *editio minor*.
[8] For the sense and possible significance of κολοccῶν here, cf. below, n. 44.

In urging sculptors to 'run past the long-standing rules for statues', the epigram sets up an opposition between the older, monumental-izing style of representation and the new style embodied in the works the speaker urges artists to imitate. As the first editors note, the open-ing phrase, with its deictic τάδε, suggests that the speaker is standing before a series of sculptures, and in the internal logic of the poem, the works he asks sculptors to imitate appear to be the 'novel' statues of Lysippus, who as Andrew Stewart has demonstrated at length is here as elsewhere treated as a master of the modern, realistic sculp-tural style.[9] At the same time, the phrase's placement at the head of the section invites readers to suppose that the works mentioned in the opening clause are also those described in the ensuing poems, so that the section may be imagined as a sort of literary hall of statues that could serve as appropriate models for prospective artists—as, in other words, a typically Hellenistic project of assembling, ordering, and classifying the cultural heritage of the past. Read this way, the section may perhaps be understood as doing for the plastic arts what a work like Alexander Aetolus' *Muses*,[10] apparently a gallery of poetic masterpieces, does for literature. In any case, however we under-stand the phrase, the speaker's demand that sculptors imitate certain sorts of statues but not others fundamentally casts the artist's activity as an engagement with artistic models. Mimesis, as represented by the speaker of the opening poem, is, in other words, not merely the imitation of life as it is, but also life as it is represented in art. To the extent that artists are to be successful in creating the appearance of lifelikeness, they do so through the imitation of other sculptures.[11]

The opposition between the monumentalizing practices of the past and the modern style that artists are urged to adopt runs through many of the epigrams in the ἀνδριαντοποιικά and finds analogues in passages like the *Aitia* prologue, in which Alexandrian poets oppose their own allegedly innovative works to those that seek merely to emulate the standards of a former day, especially those of Homeric

---

[9] Cf. BG, p. 185; Gutzwiller, 'Posidippus on Statuary', For Lysippus, cf. Moreno, *Testimonianze per la teoria artistica di Lisippo*; id., *Vita e arte di Lisippo*; id., *Lisippo: l'arte e la fortuna*; A. Stewart, *Greek Sculpture: An Exploration* (New Haven, 1990), i. 186–91, and above, Ch. 10.

[10] For this work and its likely contents, cf. E. Magnelli, *Alexandri Aetoli Testimonia et Fragmenta* (Florence, 1999), 21–3. About Callimachus' *Grapheion* almost nothing can be known (cf. Pfeiffer on fr. 380), but it is not impossible that it engaged in a similar strategy.

[11] For 'imitation' mediated by artistic models, cf. D. Konstan, 'The Dynamics of Imitation: Callimachus' First Iambic'; Hunter, *Theocritus and the Archaeology of Greek Poetry*, 116–23. Duris ap. Plin. *HN* 34. 61 is said to have reported that Lysippus himself was inspired to take up sculpture by the painter Eupompus, who asserted that nature itself was to be imitated (*naturam ipsam imitandam esse, non artificem*).

PLATES

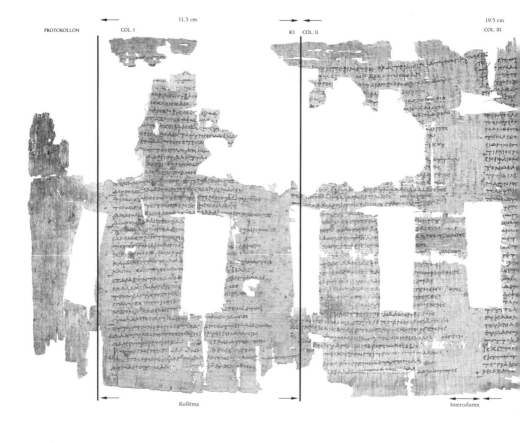

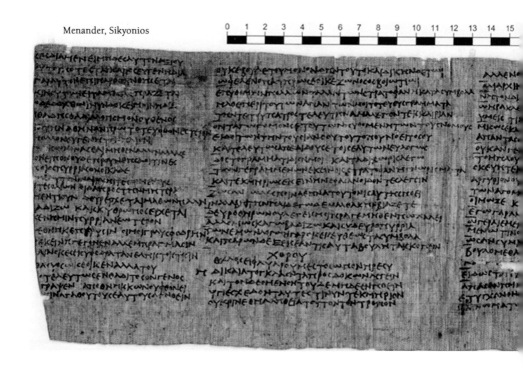

Menander, Sikyonios

PL. 1. P. Mil. Vogl. VIII
309, cols. I–VI. Labels
mark the protokollon
(a first sheet added to the
left of the manufactured
roll), the κολλήματα (the
sheets of the manufac-
tured roll), the column
of writing, and the inter-
column (blank space
between columns)

PL. 2. Left: P. Sorb. inv.
2272+72 (iii BC, el-
Ghorab). Right: P. Mil.
Vogl. VIII 309, cols.
V–VI. Set alongside at
the same scale

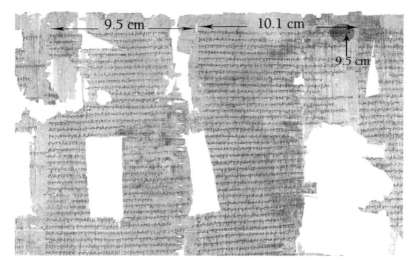

PL. 3. P. Mil. Vogl. VIII 309, cols. VIII–IX. Column to column measurement is consistently 9.5 cm except in instances like col. IX, where the initial line oversteps the 9.5 cm limit (see highlighted area)

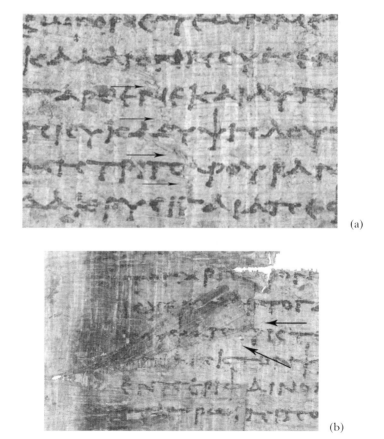

(a)

(b)

PL. 4. (a) Col. VIII. (b) Col. XIV. Rough edges at the point of κόλληϲιϲ (glue join between papyrus sheets)

Pl. 5. Col. V. Moisture damage and rewriting. Infrared

COL. I

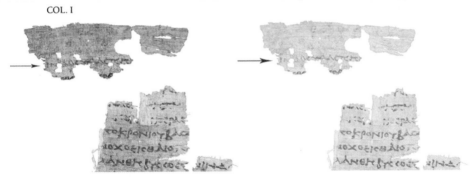

Pl. 6. First line of 'Col. I'

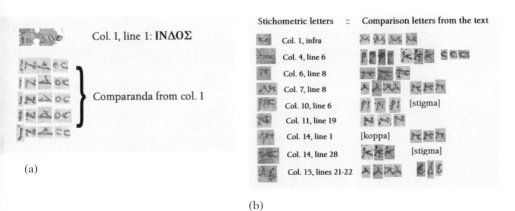

(a)

(b)

Pl. 7. (a) First letters of Col. I, l. 1 compared with letters drawn from elsewhere in column; (b) Stichometric letters compared with letters drawn from elsewhere in text

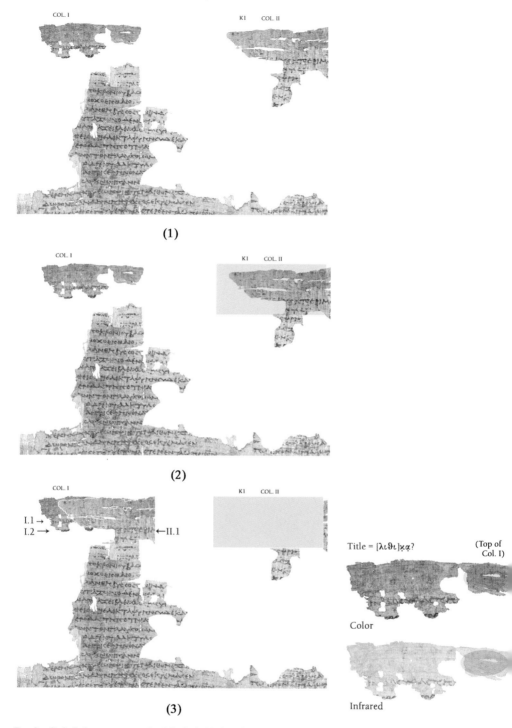

COL. I   K1   COL. II

(1)

COL. I   K1   COL. II

(2)

COL. I   K1   COL. II

I.1 →
I.2 →   ←II.1

(3)

Pl. 8. Col. I, l. 1 compared with Col. II, l. 1 for distance from top of margin (three stages)

Title = [λιθι]χα?   (Top of Col. I)

Color

Infrared

Pl. 9. Col. I. Highlight of the remains of the supposed section heading in the top margin

PL. 10. Silver drinking bowl with acanthus-style relief decoration, gilding, and garnet inlays; found in 1811 at Città Castellana; Naples, Museo Archeologico Nazionale, inv. 25284. Cf. AB 3

(a)

(b)

(c)

PL. 11. Shell box, silver with gilding and garnet inlays. Late 3rd–early 2nd c. BC. 4 × 16 cm. From Canosa, the Hellenistic Tomba degli Ori; Taranto, Museo Nazionale Archeologico, inv. 22429–30: (a) upper valve, outer face, nymph on sea-panther; (b) upper valve, inner face, nymph on κῆτος; (c) lower valve with inscribed hinge. Cf. AB 11

PL. 12. Chalcedony
bracelet, diam. 8.5–9 cm.
4th–3rd c. BC. From a
Hellenistic South Italian
tomb at Salandra (exca-
vated in 1910); Taranto,
Museo Nazionale
Archeologico, inv. 6445.
De Juliis et al., *Gli ori di
Taranto in età ellenistica*,
cat. 170. Cf. AB 4

PL. 13. Carnelian
scaraboid, 24 × 18 mm,
from Mesopotamia.
London, British Museum,
inv. 1911.4-15.1. Mounted
Persian attacks with his
lance a running biga.
(Other, flat face has a
hound.) Boardman, *Greek
Gems and Finger Rings*, no.
864; G. M. A. Richter,
*Engraved Gems of the
Greeks and Etruscans*
(London, 1968), 130, no.
502. Cf. AB 8

PL. 14. Torque (pectoral) in gold, enamel, and gems,
from an Egyptian workshop for an Achaemenid
patron, 4th c. BC? Main pendant: Persian battle scene.
On the torque, mounted warriors. *Treasures of Ancient
Bactria* (Shigaraki, 2002), cat. 43, pp. 207–10

epic. These connections, to which we shall return, raise the possibility of understanding τάδ' ἔργα in an additional sense, as a reference not merely to the plastic works described in the opening epigram and the others in the section, but also to the poems in which those works are described. On such a reading, the epigrams of the ἀνδριαντοποιικά stand as analogues to the works they describe, and embody a similar set of aesthetic principles. As such, they are to serve as models for poets in the same way that the sculptures they laud should serve as models for the plastic arts.

Support for such a reading is to be found in the next poem (AB 63), which more directly suggests the similarity and comparability of the plastic and literary arts. The epigram praises a bronze statue of the poet Philitas of Cos:[12]

τόνδε Φιλίται χ[αλ]κὸν [ἴ]ϲον κατὰ πάν⟨θ⟩'{α} Ἑκ[α]ταῖοϲ
ἀ]κ[ρ]ιβὴϲ ἄκρουϲ [ἔπλ]αϲεν εἰϲ ὄνυχαϲ,
καὶ με]γέθει κα[ὶ ϲα]ρκὶ τὸν ἀνθρωπιϲτὶ διώξαϲ
γνώμο]ν', ἀφ' ἡρώων δ' οὐδὲν ἔμειξ' ἰδέηϲ,
ἀλλὰ τὸν ἀκρομέριμνον ὅλ[ηι κ]ατεμάξατο τέχνηι   5
πρ]έϲβυν, ἀληθείηϲ ὀρθὸν [ἔχων] κανόνα·
αὐδήϲ]οντι δ' ἔοικεν, ὅϲωι ποικίλλεται ἤθει,
ἔμψυχ]οϲ, καίπερ χάλκεοϲ ἐὼν ὁ γέρων·
ἐκ Πτολε]μαίου δ' ὧδε θεοῦ θ' ἅμα καὶ βασιλ⟨ῆ⟩οϲ
ἄγκειτ]αι Μουϲέ{ι}ων εἵνεκα Κῶιοϲ ἀνήρ.   10

1 πάνθ' : παντα pap.   4 ἔμειξ' : ἔμειξε pap.

Hecataeus accurately made this bronze equal to Philitas
in every respect down to the tips of nails.
In size and body he followed closely the one discerning (?)
      in a human way,
and he mixed in nothing from the form of heroes.
But he copied with all his skill the exactingly careful
old man, holding the straight yardstick of truth.
Although made of bronze, the old man seems like one about
      to speak,
with so much character is he decorated,
alive (?). So by the order of Ptolemy, god as well as king,
the Coan man has been dedicated for the sake of the Muses.

Posidippus' praise of Hecataeus' realism, in emphasizing the sculptor's care and precision, sets up a clear parallelism between the

---

[12] An inchoate version of the following discussion, based on a paper delivered orally at the American Philological Association's January 2002 annual meeting, was posted as 'The New Posidippus, Asclepiades, and Hecataeus' Philitas-Statue', at www.apaclassics.org in February 2002.

sculptor and his subject, who displays similar qualities. Hecataeus is
ἀκριβής, 'exact', 'precise', 'accurate'; Philitas is ἀκρομέριμνος, a hapax
legomenon meaning 'taking the greatest care'. Indeed, the charac-
terization of Philitas as ἀκρομέριμνος at the head of the fifth verse is
juxtaposed to the account of Hecataeus' skilful accomplishment, ὅληι
κατεμάξατο τέχνηι, in the second half of the line. This opposition is
perhaps already anticipated in the first pentameter, where ἀκριβής
is juxtaposed to ἄκρους in the phrase ἄκρους εἰς ὄνυχας. The parallel-
isms in the opening couplets cannot be accidental, and it seems clear
that what Posidippus has done is to attribute to the sculptor the very
exactitude for which Philitas himself was otherwise well known, and
at which the anonymous author of a fictitious funerary epigram pokes
fun, adesp. *FGE* 134 ap. Ath. 9. 401 E ξεῖνε, Φιλίτας εἰμί· λόγων ὁ
ψευδόμενός με | ὤλεσε καὶ νυκτῶν φροντίδες ἑσπέριοι 'Stranger, I am
Philitas. The lying word and nights' evening cares destroyed me.'

Against this background, the terms in which the artist's careful real-
ism are described are significant—especially the claim that Hecataeus
added 'nothing from the form of heroes' (ἀφ' ἡρώων δ' οὐδὲν ἔμειξ'
ἰδέης) but used the 'straight yardstick of truth' (ἀληθείης ὀρθὸν [ἔχων]
κανόνα)[13] in representing Philitas' true form. Given the analogy that
the epigram sets up between sculptor and poet, Hecataeus' refusal
to inflate the size and appearance of his Philitas statue by imposing
on it distorting elements from the heroic tradition may represent a
comment on Philitas' own verse, and by extension on aesthetics and
the use of the heroic in both poetry and visual arts in particular.[14] In
this regard, the epigram seems to evoke what might be considered
a fundamental feature of refined Hellenistic poetry, namely an aver-
sion—such as that inscribed in the proem to Callimachus' *Aitia*—to
the production of literary art that merely adopts the style and content
of early heroic poetry in an unsophisticated and unnuanced way.

Indeed, the opposition that the epigram sets up between truth-
fulness and heroic monumentality finds an interesting parallel in
a famous passage of Theocritus' seventh idyll. In that poem, the
narrator, Simichidas, encounters the goatherd Lycidas in a scene
that owes a great deal to literary representations of divine epiphanies.
Simichidas remarks, with what seems to be false modesty,[15] that he is

---

[13] The phrase recurs at Timo Phliasius *SH* 842. 2, where the narrator asserts of the nature of
his assertions 'the divine and the good' are true. For the relationship of the epigram's language
to ancient discussions of ἀλήθεια in art, cf. Gutzwiller, 'Posidippus on Statuary'.

[14] Spanoudakis, *Philitas of Cos*, 43 recognizes in the parallelism a programmatic com-
ment on Philitas' own poetry; cf. Kramer, 'Il rotolo di Milano e l'epigramma ellenistico', 42;
Bernsdorff, 'Anmerkungen zum neuen Poseidipp', 19–26.

[15] Cf. C. Segal, 'Simichidas' Modesty'.

not yet a match for Philitas or Asclepiades; his interlocutor Lycidas laughs sweetly and gives Simichidas his staff, expressing admiration for his honesty and disdain for those who attempt great things of which they are not capable (Theoc. 7. 39–48):

> "οὐ γάρ πω κατ᾽ ἐμὸν νόον οὔτε τὸν ἐcθλόν
> Cικελίδαν νίκημι τὸν ἐκ Cάμω οὔτε Φιλίταν   40
> ἀείδων, βάτραχοc δὲ ποτ᾽ ἀκρίδαc ὥc τιc ἐρίcδω."
> ὣc ἐφάμαν ἐπίταδεc· ὁ δ᾽ αἰπόλοc ἁδὺ γελάccαc,
> "τάν τοι", ἔφα, "κορύναν δωρύττομαι, οὕνεκεν ἐccί
> πᾶν ἐπ᾽ ἀλαθείαι πεπλαcμένον ἐκ Διὸc ἔρνοc.
> ὥc μοι καὶ τέκτων μέγ᾽ ἀπέχθεται ὅcτιc ἐρευνῆι   45
> ἶcον ὄρευc κορυφᾶι τελέcαι δόμον Ὠρομέδοντοc,
> καὶ Μοιcᾶν ὄρνιχεc ὅcοι ποτὶ Χῖον ἀοιδόν
> ἀντία κοκκύζοντεc ἐτώcια μοχθίζοντι."

'Not yet in my opinion am I able to beat in my singing
good Sicelidas of Samos or Philitas
but like a frog I compete against crickets.'
So I spoke, intentionally. And the goatherd, laughing sweetly,
said, 'I give you this staff, for you are
a shoot of Zeus all fashioned for the truth.
Hateful to me is the builder who seeks
to make a house equal to the peak of Mt. Oromedon,
and as many of the cocks of the Muses who, crowing
against the Chian bard, toil in vain.'

Scholars have noted that the gift of the staff situates the episode in the tradition of poetic inspirations dating back to Hesiod's *Theogony*, in which the Muses comment on their ability to tell both lies and the truth (Hes. *Th*. 22–34).[16] The passage contrasts the positive 'truthfulness' of Simichidas to the negative qualities exhibited by those who would seek to build a monumental house or to rival Homer.[17] It thus sets up a dichotomy between heroic grandeur and truthfulness analogous to that which the epigram sets up between Hecataeus'— and by implication Philitas'—'truthfulness', on the one hand, and the idealization of the heroic tradition, on the other.[18] As critics have recognized, the idyll as a whole may owe a deep debt to Philitas' poetry,[19]

---

[16] For a recent discussion see Hunter, *Theocritus: A Selection*, 149–50; A. S. F. Gow, *Theocritus*² (Cambridge, 1952), ii. 142 recognizes the Hesiod background to the gift of the staff. For the specific Hesiodic background to Theocritus' ἐπ᾽ ἀλαθείαι πεπλαcμένον cf. G. Serrao, *Problemi di poesia alessandrina I* (Rome, 1971), 36–55; Hunter, op. cit. 164.

[17] Cf. Serrao, op. cit. 43–55, esp. 45–6.

[18] M. Puelma, 'Die Dichterbegegnung in Theokrits "Thalysien"' takes ἐπ᾽ ἀλαθείαι πεπλαc-μένον as a reference to 'true art' and to 'Callimachean' poetics in particular.

[19] Cf. E. L. Bowie, 'Theocritus' Seventh Idyll, Philetas, and Longus'; Hunter, *Theocritus:*

and Lycidas' words come in response to Simichidas' self-deprecatory
claim the he does not yet rival Philitas. Read against this background,
Lycidas' pointedly ironic[20] description of Simichidas as ἐπ᾽ ἀλαθείαι
πεπλαcμένον bears an interesting resemblance to Posidippus' claim
that Hecataeus has sculpted (ἔπλαcε) his statue of Philitas accord-
ing to the yardstick of truth.[21] One passage may look to the other,
but it is also possible that both allude to a passage of Philitas (who
in that case would also have been influenced by the Hesiodic refer-
ence to truthfulness).[22] If so, one might even speculate that, given the
thematic and verbal connections between the passages of Posidippus
and Theocritus, Philitas associated falseness with crudely 'heroic'
poetry in some sense.[23]

The scanty remains of Philitas' own poetry do not allow any clear
insight into what features of it Posidippus might have in mind pre-
cisely. But if the description of Hecataeus' sculpture does constitute
an analogical comment on Philitas' own art, or perhaps even a refer-
ence to a specific, programmatic passage of that poet, the point might
be that, like Hecataeus, Philitas in some sense refused to 'mix in the
form of heroes'. Since Philitas, himself a Homeric critic, manifestly
did draw on and adapt epic language and themes, the point cannot
be that he did not borrow from the heroic tradition at all, but it is not
impossible that he shared with many of his successors an interest in
representing even the grandest of figures from the heroic tradition as
if they were more ordinary people,[24] which is to say that he may have
engaged in the sort of 'reduction' of the heroic to the quotidian that
can be seen clearly in, *inter alia*, the depiction of Jason by Apollonius

A Selection, 149. Spanoudakis, *Philitas of Cos*, 223–73 argues for extensive connections
between the idyll and Philitas' *Demeter*, and suggests that the encounter between Lycidas and
Simichidas has its background in an encounter between Chalcon and Demeter in that work.

[20] Cf. Segal, 'Simichidas' Modesty', 131–3 = 170–2.

[21] Cf. also Angiò, 'Filita di Cos in bronzo', 21.

[22] In the humorous epitaph for Philitas (adesp. *FGE* 134; cited above, p. 210), λόγων ὁ ψευδό-
μενοc is said to have been responsible for Philitas' death, though that phrase seems to refer to
the so-called Liar's Paradox rather than to his poetry; cf. Cameron, *Callimachus and his Critics*,
490–1.

[23] An intriguing parallel to Posidippus' treatment of Philitas in this epigram may be offered
by Callimachus' treatment of Xenomedes, who, he claims, was (like Philitas) an old man
concerned with the truth (fr. 75. 76 πρέcβυc ἐτητυμίηι μεμελημένοc). Callimachus inverts the
Hesiod scene (in which the Muses are the source of truth in poetry) by making the prose writer
Xenomedes provide the truth to the poet's Calliope (fr. 75. 77). For the possible programmatic
significance of old age in Hellenistic poetics, cf. also Call. fr. 1 and Posidipp. AB 118 = *SH*
705.

[24] So Spanoudakis, *Philitas of Cos*, 43. For Philitas' poetic fragments, cf. also Sbardella,
Filita.

or of Amphitryon and his family or the Dioscuri in Theocritus' 'epi-
cizing' idylls.[25]

Whatever the realities of Philitas' own verse, the reduction of the
heroic to the quotidian that one sees in other Hellenistic poetry finds
a parallel in the interest that Posidippus' Hecataeus shows in the aged
and physically ordinary Philitas rather than in the idealized 'form of
heroes'. But in a more complex way, the reduction of the grand to the
ordinary may also be seen in the poem's apparent engagement with
another early third-century epigram.

Asclepiades or Archelaus *AP* 16. 120 (= Asclepiades GP 43),
praises a statue of Alexander by Lysippus:

τόλμαν Ἀλεξάνδρου καὶ ὅλαν ἀπεμάξατο μορφὰν
  Λύσιππος· τίν᾽ ὁδὶ χαλκὸς ἔχει δύναμιν.
αὐδασοῦντι δ᾽ ἔοικεν ὁ χάλκεος ἐς Δία λεύσσων·
  "γᾶν ἐπ᾽ ἐμοὶ τίθεμαι, Ζεῦ, σὺ δ᾽ Ὄλυμπον ἔχε."

The boldness of Alexander and his whole form were imitated
by Lysippus. What power this bronze has!
The brazen man, as he looks, resembles someone about to say,
'I subject the land to myself; Zeus, you keep Olympus!'

The authorship of this poem is controversial, since it is ascribed by
its lemma alternatively to Asclepiades or to a poet called Archelaus.
No other poems are attributed to Archelaus in the *Greek Anthology*,
but a poet of this name is known to have written elegiac poems
detailing the generation of various creatures from the dead bodies
of other species (*SH* 125–9). Given how little of Archelaus' work is
known, stylistic arguments for and against Asclepiadean authorship
are unpersuasive, as are arguments from the epigram's placement
in the *Anthology*. On the one hand, the epigram directly follows a
thematically related poem by Posidippus, and since Meleager regu-
larly juxtaposed epigrams by Asclepiades and Posidippus, its con-
junction with one ascribed to Posidippus might be thought to speak
for Asclepiadean authorship. On the other hand, the frequency with
which epigrams by the two poets are juxtaposed could also explain
why some supposed the poem to be by Asclepiades, and indeed the
attribution to Archelaus may seem less likely to be conjectural.[26]

To the issue of authorship, the Philitas-statue poem has something

---

[25] Cf. e.g. A. E.–A. Horstmann, *Ironie und Humor bei Theokrit* (Meisenheim am Glan, 1976);
B. Effe, 'Die Destruktion der Tradition'; K. Gutzwiller, *Studies in the Hellenistic Epyllion*
(Meisenheim am Glan, 1981).
[26] Cf. GP ii. 147; I. G. Galli Calderini, 'Su alcuni epigrammi dell'*Antologia Palatina* cor-
redati di lemmi alternativi', 277–80.

to contribute. Whether or not the editors are correct to supplement
αὐδήϲοντι in the fourth hexameter of that epigram, it is clear that one
poem was written with the other in mind. The phrase ὅληι κατεμάξατο
τέχνηι is clearly related to ὅλαν ἀπεμάξατο μορφάν, as]οντι ἔοικεν is to
αὐδαϲοῦντι ἔοικεν;[27] χάλκεοϲ appears in close conjunction with these
related phrases in both epigrams. The epigrams of Posidippus in the
Greek Anthology share numerous points of contact with the poetry of
Asclepiades,[28] and the verbal connections between the Philitas- and
Alexander-statue poems are most naturally explained as yet another
example, despite the surprising fact that the poems preserved on the
papyrus do not otherwise seem to have connections to the extant
corpus of Asclepiades.

The relative chronology of the two passages cannot be known with
certainty. If, however, Posidippus is the borrower, the reuse of a
description of Lysippus' Alexander statue in the context of a poem
praising a realistic image of the physically humble Philitas constitutes
a subtle game. It is true that the Lysippan Alexander of Asclepiades'
poem is imagined to acknowledge that he is to be king only on earth,
and to relegate Olympus to Zeus, but Alexander's manifest arrogance
clearly pushes the outer limits of that distinction.[29] That Posidippus
should have used a poetic description of such a statue as a model
for his account of Hecataeus' statue of Philitas is striking, and the
allusion underscores the differences between text and intertext. It is
well known that Alexander, whose line was thought to have traced
from Heracles, represented himself and was flattered by his con-
temporaries as a new Achilles and a successor to epic heroes.[30] By
reapplying Asclepiades' description of him to a notably more humble

[27] The witnesses to the text of the Asclepiadean poem offer various forms of the participle.
Pl and Tzet. *Chil.* 8. 200. 426–7 have αὐδάϲοντι, but the archetype of Plu. *Mor.* 331 A and 335
B, where the MSS have αὐδαϲοῦντι, αὐδᾶϲ οὖν τί, αὐδᾶν οὖν τί, αὐδάϲοντι, and αὐδήϲοντι, seems
likely to have been αὐδαϲοῦντι. This contracted Doric future seems less likely to have been the
product of corruption and should perhaps be preferred as *lectio difficilior* (the assertion of GP
ii. 147 that the form would be surprising in an epigram of Hellenistic date depends on circular
assumptions). Cf. N. Hopkinson, *Callimachus: Hymn to Demeter* (Cambridge, 1984) 80, on
Call. *h.* 6. 3.

[28] For the connections between these two poets, cf. e.g. Cameron, *The Greek Anthology from
Meleager to Planudes*, 369–76; Gutzwiller, *Poetic Garlands*, 120–1.

[29] I am thus not persuaded by A. Stewart, *Faces of Power* (Berkeley, 1993), 23 that the poem
participates in any significant way in a debate about the proper way of representing Alexander
in art. The poem takes its point of departure from the idea that character can be shown in art,
and makes the nature of Alexander's τόλμα its central problem: the first word of the epigram is
only explained by the final verse and a half.

[30] Cf. e.g. Arr. *An.* 7. 14. 4.

man, Posidippus cuts the haughty Alexander of Lysippus' statue and Asclepiades' poem down to size. Posidippus' epigram, in other words, does precisely what Hellenistic poets—and indeed perhaps Philitas himself—do so often, namely to take material used more grandly in an antecedent and to reapply it to less 'heroic' figures.[31]

Read against this background, the final couplet of the poem becomes especially interesting. According to Posidippus, the statue of Philitas was dedicated 'from (ἐκ) Ptolemy, god and king', which must be to say that it was set up through an order of Ptolemy.[32] Whatever the historical reality, the poem's rather pointed insistence that Ptolemy is both god and king sets the monarch in sharp opposition to the man honoured by the statue. In contrast to Philitas, who is treated on conspicuously human scale (cf. ἀνθρωπιστί), Ptolemy, the man responsible for the dedication, has surpassed the limits of ordinary humanity. He is both βασιλεύς and θεός—in other words, he resembles at some level the sort of heroic figures said *not* to have been a model for the Philitas statue. One reading of the final couplet might therefore be that Posidippus, in his own description of Ptolemy, has done something very much like what he praises Hecataeus for not doing, thereby turning on its head the apparently straightforward literary programme of what precedes.[33] Another explanation, however, now seems to me far more compelling, namely that the poem's implicit admiration of Hecataeus' truthful realism suggests that the poet is himself telling the truth about what may have seemed to some Alexandrians a controversial claim about Ptolemy's divine status. The final verse, on this interpretation, does not reject the aesthetic programme implicitly endorsed elsewhere in the epigram, but instead

---

[31] In this regard, it may be worth noting that whereas Asclepiades imputes to the Alexander statue a specific speech, Posidippus, if the final verse is correctly supplemented, restricts himself to observing that the statue of Philitas appears to be going to speak. In so doing, he deprives of words a man whose greatest concern was verbal precision, but at the same time eliminates the hybris of Alexander's speech. Scodel, 'A Note on Posidippus 63' notes that ἄγκειμ]αι could be printed in the last verse and the final couplet treated as direct speech placed in the mouth of Philitas. If this were correct, however, the nature of the statue's words would differ from that of speeches attributed to other statues in other early Hellenistic epigrams, since it would advert directly to the circumstances of the statue's dedication; more often, speech in the mouth of sculptures is designed to suggest the 'realism' of the statue.

[32] Hermes. fr. 7. 75–8, p. 100 Powell reports that the Coans themselves erected a statue in honour of the poet, but that object need not have been identical with the statue by Hecataeus that is praised in this poem. For discussion of the Coan statue, cf. Hollis, 'Heroic Honours for Philitas?'; Hardie, 'Philitas and the Plane Tree'; id. 'The Statue(s) of Philitas'; Sbardella, *Filita*, 38; Spanoudakis, *Philitas of Cos*, 34–7; Angiò, 'Filita di Cos in bronzo'. For statues of poets, cf. Rossi, *The Epigrams Ascribed to Theocritus*, 92–8.

[33] This suggestion, initially advanced in Sens, 'The New Posidippus', is adopted by Bernsdorff, 'Anmerkungen zum neuen Poseidipp', 26.

depends on its acceptance in order to make an encomiastic point:[34] to call Ptolemy a god is, the poem implies, no less truthful than to depict Philitas as a man.

The rejection of the heroic mode of representation in the Philitas-statue poem plays out in interesting ways in the next epigram (AB 64). This poem describes a statue of an overtly epic subject, the Homeric hero Idomeneus:

αἴ]νεέ γ'{ε} Ἰδομεν⟨ῆ⟩α θέλων χάλκειον ἐκεῖν[ον
Κ̣ρής̣ιλ⟨α⟩· ὡς ἄκρως ἠργάσατ' εἴδομεν εὖ·
γ]α̣ρύ[ει] Ἰδομενεύς· "ἀλ[λ'] ὦ 'γαθὲ Μηριόνα, θεῖ
.......] πλασται δὰν [ἀδό]νητος ἐών."

Willingly praise that bronze Idomeneus
by Cresilas. How precisely he made it, we saw well.
Idomeneus cries: 'Come, good Meriones, run!
. . . having been long immobile'.

The contrast between the heroic theme of this epigram and the explicitly unheroic statue of Philitas is surely a mark of careful arrangement,[35] and invites an exploration of the relationship between the two poems.

As in the case of the Philitas-statue poem, the point of the epigram is that Cresilas' statue is realistic. Like other early ecphrastic epigrams,[36] the poem depends on the longstanding convention that a work of art would seem entirely lifelike if only it could talk,[37] and the words imputed to the statue in the second couplet thus serve as a mark of the statue's mimetic power, as a means to suggest that it has surpassed even the limitation imposed by bronze's natural muteness. In this connection the dialect and style of Idomeneus' words are particularly interesting.[38]

---

[34] For the encomiastic strategies employed elsewhere in the papyrus, cf. M. Fantuzzi, below, Ch. 13.

[35] Cf. Gutzwiller, 'A Hellenistic Poetry Book'.

[36] I use 'ecphrasis' as a broad and general term without implying that these poems contain detailed descriptions of the works they praise. G. Zanker, 'New Light' argues that 'ecphrastic' is a misleading term for the poems of the ἀνδριαντοποιικά, and suggests 'andriantopoeic' instead.

[37] e.g. A. fr. 78a. 6–7 εἴδωλον εἶναι τοῦτ' ἐμῆι μορφῆι πλέον | τὸ Δαιδάλου μ[ί]μημα· φωνῆς δεῖ μόνον; Erinna, *AP* 6. 352. 3–4 = 3 GP ταύταν γοῦν ἐτύμως τὰν παρθένον ὅςτις ἔγραψεν | αἰ καὐδὰν ποτέθηκ' ἧς κ' Ἀγαθαρχὶς ὅλα. For the appearance of speech as a mark of realism, cf. Hp. *Ep.* 3. 804 δοκέει λαλεῖν τὸ ἄγαλμα; Herod. 4. 32–4 πρὸ τῶν ποδῶν γοῦν εἴ τι μὴ λίθος, τοὔργον, | ἐρεῖς, λαλήσει. μᾶ, χρόνωι κοτ' ὤνθρωποι | κἠς τοὺς λίθους ἔξουςι τὴν ζοὴν θεῖναι with W. Headlam and A. D. Knox, *Herodas: The Mimes and Fragments* (Cambridge, 1922) 186; Sens, 'An Ecphrastic Pair', 251–2.

[38] What follows abbreviates an argument laid out in detail in Sens, 'Doricisms in the New and Old Posidippus', 75–6.

The language spoken on the island of Crete, birth-place of the sculptor Cresilas and literary home of Idomeneus, ranks among the Doric dialects that Ahrens termed 'Doris severior',[39] in which the secondary long [e:] produced by contraction or compensatory lengthening was represented by η rather than ει, and secondary long [o:] represented by ω rather than ου. At least by the end of the fourth century, Cretan had also come to show the influence of other dialects, particularly the Attic *koine*. Such local linguistic specifics are of no concern to the Homeric tradition. All Homeric heroes, including the Cretan king Idomeneus, speak the same artificial literary dialect.[40] In Posidippus' epigram, however, both the narrator and the embedded speaker, the Cretan king Idomeneus, speak a language that, albeit stylized, resembles to some extent that actually spoken on Crete. Indeed, the form ἠργάcατο in the second verse may be understood as a severe Doricism,[41] and since the only other severe Doricisms in the papyrus appear in an epigram in which another Cretan is the speaker, it is possible that Posidippus is self-consciously evoking the colouring of Cretan speech. Since this form occurs with other Doricisms like γαρύει in the narrative, the effect is to suggest that the speaker of the epigram comes from the same linguistic community as do both the artist whom he honours and the Homeric hero whom Cresilas depicts so vividly. The association that is thus created forms part of a larger pattern in the ἀνδριαντοποιικά, in which, as we shall see in more detail, the speaker, the artist, and the artist's subject are regularly assimilated to one another.

That the words ascribed to Idomeneus also seem to have a Doric colouring (cf. δάν) is important to the project of the epigram as a whole. In attributing to him words appropriate to his supposed place of origin, the narrator of the epigram departs from—and caps—the practice of early epic: the Cretan hero is imagined to speak not the language of epic, but a version of the language of his supposed homeland. Idomeneus thus speaks in the manner not of a Homeric hero,

---

[39] H.L. Ahrens, *De Graecae linguae dialectis* (Göttingen, 1839–43), ii. 153–72, 201–7, 403–22.

[40] Readers since antiquity have noted other sorts of stylistic markers in the language of individual Homeric speakers, most notably Achilles; cf. R. Martin, *The Language of Heroes* (Ithaca, NY, 1989), 146–205.

[41] The matter is considerably complicated by the fact that manuscript and inscriptional evidence suggests that the augmented form of the verb was commonly if not regularly spelled this way in Attic as well; cf. D. J. Mastronarde, *Euripides: Phoenissae* (Leipzig, 1988), p. xxiii. None the less, this is the only example in the papyrus of η as the product of the contraction of ε + ε, and the fact that the only other 'strong' Doricism in the papyrus appears in another poem involving a Cretan strongly suggests that the form should be understood as a Doricism here.

but of an ordinary person—a status also reflected in his use of the col-
loquial and un-Homeric form of address ὦ 'γαθὲ Μηριόνα. The poem
may thus be read as an embodiment of the aesthetic principles dis-
cussed in the preceding poem: both the poet and the sculptor whose
work he depicts treat an epic subject, but the language with which
the statue is described and the words that Cresilas' Idomeneus is
represented as speaking reveal the extent to which both artists have
diverged from the traditional, heroic mode of representation.

The final line of Idomeneus' speech is too poorly preserved for us
to know precisely what he says to his companion Meriones, but what
does survive is tantalizing in at least two ways. First, whether πλαϲται
at the head of what survives is to be understood adjectivally (i.e.
πλαϲτᾶι) or nominally (i.e. πλάϲται),[42] the form is surely appropriate
in a sculptural context, and may even involve an explicit and direct
reference to sculpture. If so, the speech attributed to Idomeneus in
order to show the realism of the statue simultaneously calls atten-
tion to its artificiality: the hero, freed from the limitations previously
imposed on sculpture, comments on his (and Meriones') previously
static 'existence'.

Second, the words spoken by Idomeneus share several verbal and
thematic points of contact with the programmatic opening lines of
the ἀνδριαντοποιικά as whole. At the beginning of the first poem in the
grouping, sculptors (ζ[ωιο]πλάϲται, if the supplement is correct) are
urged to 'run past' (παραθεῖτε) the long-standing rules (πολυχρονίουϲ
. . . νόμουϲ) for making colossi. The imperative παραθεῖτε is perhaps
suggestive of an athletic contest, but is somewhat strangely used with
νόμουϲ, as though a more positive variation of παραβαίνετε. In any case,
παραθεῖτε finds an analogue in the Idomeneus poem, where the statue
of the Cretan hero is imagined to urge his companion Meriones—
presumably a statue grouped with that of Idomeneus—to run, θεῖ,
the only other imperative of the simplex θέω or of one of its com-
pounds in the papyrus.

This point of contact is reinforced by other connections between
the passages. As we have noted, the damaged state of the pentameter
makes it impossible to know the sense of πλαϲται at the head of what
survives. Whatever that word means in its context, however, it is
striking that these syllables occupy the identical metrical position in
the first pentameter of the opening poem, where the editors supple-
ment ζ[ωιο]πλάϲται. The result is that in each passage the second-

---

[42] Cf. BG, pp. 190–1; for the text, cf. also F. Angiò, 'La statua in bronzo di Idomeneo, opera
di Cresila'.

person plural imperative of the simplex or a compound of θέω is accompanied, in the same metrical *sedes* of the pentameter, by πλάςται as a single word or as a component of a compound.

In addition to the verbal similarities, there seems also to be a thematic connection between the two passages. Although the precise point of the final pentameter remains obscure, Idomeneus—if it is in fact he who continues to speak—seems to be urging his *therapon* to take advantage of his mobility after long having been static in prior sculptural representations. If the editors' δὰν [ἀδό]νητος ἐών is correct—and it must be said that despite the editors' puzzlement there is nothing dialectally problematic about ἀδόνητος, which is the regular Doric form[43]—the phrase as a whole finds a parallel in πολυχρονίους . . . νόμους, which suggests both 'ancient' and 'long-standing' practices, in the Idomeneus-statue poem: the customary ways of making colossi,[44] after all, were what guaranteed the immobility of earlier statues. Thus Idomeneus' words set up an opposition between the long-standing practices of earlier sculptors and the new artistic style, and in this regard his command to Meriones recapitulates the voice of the narrator of the opening poem, who advises sculptors to set aside the long-prevailing rules of sculpture and take up the practices embodied in the works of artists like Lysippus.

These links between Idomeneus' command to Meriones and the narrator's advice to sculptors add another strand to the nexus of associations in the ἀνδριαντοποιικά. As we have seen, dialect and place of origin link speaker, sculptor, and subject, much as the preceding epigram establishes a connection—already implicit in the opening poem—between the artist Hecataeus and his subject Philitas. Both the opening epigram and the Philitas-statue poem further suggest a parallelism between poets and artists. To this pattern, the link between the narrating voice of the opening poem and the embedded voice of Idomeneus in the third conforms nicely. In the Idomeneus-statue poem, the words spoken by the Cretan hero closely mirror the words spoken by the 'poet', if one may so designate the speaker of the opening poem. This makes good sense, since the identification of

[43] *Pace* BG, p. 191, ἀδόνατος would be hyper-Doric.

[44] The widely accepted view advanced by Wilamowitz, 'Heilige Gesetze', 169 that κολοςςός came to imply enormous size only late in the Hellenistic period, via its association with the Rhodian statue of the Sun, has been challenged by Dickie, 'What was a *Kolossos*?' If the word did connote large size already in the 3rd c., the opposition that the poem sets up between the old rules for creating enormous sculptures and the new practices embodied in Lysippus' work would find parallels in the contrast that Hellenistic poets draw between 'big' works and their own more refined compositions, of which the miniaturization of epigram is a striking instantiation. For a different view, see E. Kosmetatou and N. Papalexandrou, 'Size Matters'.

Alexander Sens

sculptor and poet, on the one hand, and that of sculptor and subject, on the other, implies an identification of poet and subject-matter as well.

The next epigram, an ecphrasis of a statue of Alexander by Lysippus (AB 65),[45] continues the complex association of the artist and his subject:

Λύcιππε,, πλάcτα Cικυώ,νιε, θαρc,αλέα χείρ,
δάϊε τεχνί,τα, πῦρ τοι ὁ χα,λκὸc ὁρ,ῆι
ὃν κατ᾽ Ἀλεξά]νδρου μορφᾶc ἔθευ. οὔ τί γε μεμπτοὶ
Πέρcαι· cυγγνώ,μα βουcὶ λέοντα φυγεῖν.

1 θαρcαλέη Pl : δαιδαλέη Himerius Or. 48 (14). 14 (1)   3 χέεc. οὐκέτι Pl

> Lysippus, Sicyonian sculptor, bold hand,
> clever/fierce craftsman, that bronze, you know, has a look of
>   fire in its eyes
> which you put over the form of Alexander. One cannot blame
> the Persians at all: it is forgivable for cattle to flee a lion.

Here again the basic point is that the statue is wholly realistic: Lysippus has captured the ferocious look in Alexander's eyes so successfully that viewers can understand the terror experienced by the king's real-life Persian enemies. In this context, the epithets applied to the sculptor, especially the adjective δάιοc in the second verse, can serve as a key for understanding the project of the epigram as a whole. Critics take the adjective as a cognate of *δάω meaning 'clever' or the like ('cunning' Austin, 'provetto' Bastianini). The word in that sense is extremely rare, attested only in adverbial form in a possibly corrupt fragment of Epicurus,[46] but it well suits the context. At the same time, the word's more common sense, 'destructive, hostile', may also be operative. In Homer, the adjective δήιον is most often used as an epithet of fire, and the epic phrase δήιον πῦρ comes to be adopted by other high-style poetry as well.[47] This Homeric usage lends special point to the word as it appears in the context of Posidippus' poem. In the second verse, after addressing Lysippus as δάιε τεχνίτα, the narrator of the epigram remarks that the bronze statue he has produced has in its eyes a look of fire, the very substance with which the epithet used to describe the sculptor is traditionally most associated. Thus while at a surface level δάιοc in the epigram has the rare

---

[45] The epigram was previously known from *AP* 16. 119 = GP 18, where it is ascribed to Posidippus; it is thus of crucial importance for the authorship of the poems contained on the papyrus. Cf. BG, pp. 22–4.

[46] Fr. 183 δαίωc codd.: δαιμονίωc Usener.

[47] Cf. *Il.* 2. 415; 6. 331; 8. 181; 9. 347, 674; 11. 667; 16. 127, 301; 18. 13; A. *Th.* 222; E. *Hel.* 197; *Tro.* 1300–1; *Ion* 214–15.

meaning 'clever', it also suggests a link between the sculptor and his product, both of which have qualities that could warrant their being called δάϊος. Lysippus, in other words, not only captures the fire of Alexander's gaze but also *has* a conventional attribute of fire.

This use of δάϊος in the second verse provides a useful entrance point for looking at the narrator's description of the sculptor at the end of the preceding hexameter. The papyrus, which preserves only the end of the adjective modifying χείρ, confirms the Doric colouring[48] of the entire epigram but provides no indication of whether Posidippus wrote δαιδαλέα (δαιδαλέη Himerius) or θαρcαλέα (θαρcαλέη Pl).[49] The regularity with which δαίδαλος, δαιδάλεος, and their cognates are used of artistic production may suggest that Himerius' text is a trivialization,[50] and modern editors have preferred the alternative. A more important consideration is that the description of Lysippus as 'bold' conforms to a larger pattern in the poem. As we noted, the argument is that the realism of Lysippus' representation explains the Persians' cowardly response to Alexander. In this context, the boldness of the sculptor in the first line stands in direct opposition to the flight of the Persians in the final verse. In the most obvious sense, Lysippus' bold-ness lies in his innovative approach. At the same time, 'boldness', in both its positive and negative senses, was one of Alexander's most striking and obvious characteristics, as is evident from Asclepiades *AP* 16. 120 (discussed above, pp. 213–15), in which Lysippus is said to have captured the king's τόλμα as well as his form. In the context of the epigram, then, Lysippus stands, in pointed oppósition to the Persians, as a fitting counterpart to his subject-matter. Understood in this light, the sculptor's daring lies not merely in his novel approach, but even more basically in his ability to produce an image that would naturally put others to flight.

Thus the first four epigrams of the ἀνδριαντοποιικά reveal a web of verbal and thematic connections that associate the poet and the sculptor, the sculptor and his subject-matter, and even the speaker who views the work of art and the individual who is represented in it. These identifications suggest the self-referential character not only of the epigrams in the section, but of art and poetry in general. The artists whose work the poet describes effect an innovative style that departs from the static 'heroic' mode of representation used by their predecessors; the identifications we have seen imply that the same

---

[48] Cf. Sens, 'Doricisms', 69–70.

[49] Cf. D. L. Page, *Epigrammata Graeca* (1975), 120: 'fort. 1 θαρcαλέα, 4 cυγγνώμα'.

[50] Cf. GP ii. 498; P. Schott, *Posidippi epigrammata* (Berlin, 1905), 85, who suggests that Himerius' version may be due to the influence of 'Plato' *AP* 9. 826. 1 = *FGE* 22(a). 1 δαιδαλέη χείρ; cf. Leon. *AP* 6. 204. 1 = GP 7. 1 δαιδαλόχειρ.

is true for the epigrams themselves. Indeed, the Idomeneus-statue poem, which describes a work of art depicting epic subject-matter in a new way, embodies the same aesthetic principle by representing direct speech of a Homeric hero in a novel, 'realistic' manner. In the Alexander-statue poem, the point of the final line depends not only on Alexander's famously leonine appearance but also on the frequency with which lions appear in similes describing Homeric warriors. At the same time, the novel realism of Lysippus' representation of the king finds an analogue in the way in which the epigram renews the traditional language of epic by separating the adjective δάϊος from its traditional Homeric referent, fire—here present in the ferocious gaze vividly depicted by Lysippus—and reapplying it, in a new sense, to the creator of the art object. The novel take on the heroic tradition that is praised in the sculptures and inscribed in the epigrams themselves thus closely resembles what might be called the larger project of the works of Hellenistic poets like Apollonius, Callimachus, and Theocritus. To the extent that it is possible to tell, in other words, there is nothing in the epigrams to explain why, if the Florentine scholia to the opening of Callimachus' *Aitia* are accurate,[51] Posidippus would have ranked among the Telchines against whom Callimachus defends himself, or to suggest that he would have found fault with Callimachus' views about the appropriate relationship of contemporary poetry to the early epic tradition.[52] Indeed, the brevity and precision required of epigram in general make the form a perfect vehicle for those who, like Callimachus' intended audience, prefer the chirping of cicadas to the braying of asses (cf. Call. fr. 1. 29–30). Inasmuch as they enact in a written context the break with heroic tradition for which, in the plastic arts, the work of Hecataeus, Cresilas, and Lysippus is lauded, Posidippus' statue-poems seem perfectly to instantiate the aesthetic principles enshrined in the *Aetia* prologue.

With this as background, let us turn to one further epigram from the section, a poem describing a chariot wrought by the sculptor Theodorus of Samos (AB 67):[53]

[51] For scepticism about the identification of the Telchines in the scholia, cf. M. Lefkowitz, *The Lives of the Greek Poets* (London, 1981), 123–5, 138, and see S. A. Stephens, below, Ch. 12 n. 4.

[52] Posidippus and Asclepiades, who is also named as one of the Telchines, disagreed with Callimachus about the quality of Antimachus' *Lyde*; for this dispute and for the men identified as Callimachus' Telchines by the Florentine scholia to *Ait.* fr. 1, cf. Cameron, *Callimachus and his Critics*, 185–232; Lehnus, 'Posidippean and Callimachean Queries'. Krevans, 'Fighting Against Antimachus' argues that Callimachus disapproved of Antimachus' metrical practices.

[53] The poorly preserved state of the intervening epigram (AB 66), on Myron's statue of a

].·.[..]. ἄντυγος ἐ⟨γ⟩γύθεν ἄθρει
τῆς Θεοδωρείης χειρὸς ὅσος κάματος·
ὄψει γὰρ ζυγόδεϲμα καὶ ἡνία καὶ τροχὸν ἵππων
ἄξονά θ᾽ [ἡνιό]χου τ᾽ ὄμμα καὶ ἄκρα χερῶν·
ὄψει δ᾽ εὖ [c.12   ] . . . εος, ἀλλ᾽ ἐπὶ τῷιδε   5
ἑζομέν[ην ἂν ἴϲην ἅρματι] μυῖαν ἴδοις.

4 θ᾽] τε pap.   6 suppl. AB

. . . of the chariot, observe from close up
how great is the toil of Theodorus' hand.
For you will see the yoke-band, the reins, the ring on the
    bit of the horses,
the axle, as well as the driver's eye and the tips of his hands.
And you would see well . . . and sitting on this a fly the size of
    the chariot (?).

The basic point of the epigram appears to be that Theodorus has pro-
duced a work of wondrous detail but miniature size, since, to judge
from a corrupt and problematic passage of the elder Pliny,[54] the final
verse seems to indicate that the chariot was covered entirely by a fly.
What Pliny makes clear but is not explicit in what survives of the epi-
gram is that Theodorus' depiction of the chariot formed part of the
artist's depiction of himself in the act of crafting the work: in his right
hand, he holds a file, in his left the chariot and team. Although the
self-reflexivity of the original sculpture may never have been made
explicit in the poem, it is natural to suppose that Posidippus expected
his audience to recognize that it was a self-portrait. In this regard,
Theodorus' statue is a fitting subject for Posidippus' ἀνδριαντοποιικά,
which seem to contain a self-reflection on the principles of literary
and artistic production and in which the activities of the poet, the
sculptor, and the embedded subject-matter are regularly identified
with one another.

Beyond this, the speaker's admiration for Theodorus' accomplish-
ment depends on the juxtaposition of the small size of the product

cow, makes assessment of it difficult, but its concluding words, ἀλ]λὰ Μύρων ἐπόει, may involve
a play on a common form of artist's signature. If so, the point might be that the sculpture
seemed to be a cow until the viewer looked more closely, at which point he saw the signature
Μύρων ἐπόει. Thus the epigram would conflate the viewer's revised assessment ('Myron made
it [and it's not a real animal]') with the words actually inscribed on the statue.

[54] *NH* 34. 83 *Theodorus, qui labyrinthum fecit Sami, ipse se ex aere fudit . . . dextra limam tenet,
laeva tribus digitis quadrigulam tenuit . . . tantae parvitatis ut miraculo fictam* (*pictam* codd., corr.
Sillig) *eam currumque et aurigam integeret alis simul facta musca* ('Theodorus, who made the
labyrinth at Samos, cast himself in bronze . . . In his right hand he holds a file, and with three
fingers in his left hand he held a little chariot-team . . . of such small size that a fly made at the
same time covered the miraculously moulded team and the chariot and the charioteer with its
wings').

and the enormity of the labour that went into it. That the terms of the contrast are equally applicable to the sort of poetry admired by Posidippus' learned contemporaries is made clear by the opening of Callimachus' *Aitia*, as well as by works like Asclepiades *AP* 7. 11 (= GP 28), an epigram in honour of Erinna,[55] the small quantity of whose labour, cut short as it was by untimely death, stands in contrast to its great quality:

ὁ γλυκὺς Ἠρίννας οὗτος πόνος, οὐχὶ πολὺς μέν
    ὡς ἂν παρθενικῆς ἐννεακαιδεκέτευς
ἀλλ᾽ ἑτέρων πολλῶν δυνατώτερος· εἰ δ᾽ Ἀίδας μοι
    μὴ ταχὺς ἦλθε, τίς ἂν ταλίκον ἔσχ᾽ ὄνομα;

This is the sweet labour of Erinna, not large in size,
seeing that she was a nineteen-year-old maiden,
but more powerful than many others. Had Hades not come for me
early, who would have had so great a name?

As this Asclepiadean epigram and numerous other examples make clear, Greek words for toil like πόνος may denote either the act or the product of labour. At the surface level, the κάματος mentioned by Posidippus is a reference to Theodorus' painstaking craftsmanship, but κάματος also sometimes denotes the 'product of toil'.[56] In the Theodorus poem, both uses may be operative, and if so, the phrase ὅσος κάματος, understood in the sense 'how great the product of labour', constitutes a joke, since the work in question turns out to be minute.[57] Second, if, as seems at least possible, the chariot depicted by Theodorus was intended to be in motion, the word κάματος would capture not only the toil of the artist but that of his subject as well, since κάματος was an appropriate term for the exertion of horses.[58] The result of this is that the poem does what we have seen in other epigrams in the section, namely to suggest a parallelism between the activity of the sculptor and that of the figure he represents.

The fragmentary state of most of the other epigrams in the section makes a detailed literary discussion of them difficult, and it is thus not clear to what extent the later poems in the section show the same thematic association of author, sculptor, and, subject-matter that can be seen in the earlier epigrams. The relatively well-preserved epigram on Chares of Lindus' intercession to limit the still unprecedented

---

[55] On this poem, cf. Sens, 'Asclepiades, Erinna, and the Poetics of Labor'.

[56] e.g. H. *Od.* 14. 417; Hes. *Th.* 599.

[57] χειρός may involve a similar play, since the work is both a product of Theodorus' hand (for χείρ to refer to the skill of a craftsman, cf. Herodas 4. 72 with Headlam–Knox 206) and, according to Pliny, held in the hand of the sculpted figure of the artist.

[58] A. fr. 192. 6; Σ⸀ᵀ *Il.* 4. 27; Ael. *NA* 3. 2; Opp. *Hal.* 5. 183; Pollux 1. 206.

enormity of the Rhodian Sun statue (AB 68) treats a theme—the restriction of excessive size—of obvious importance in Hellenistic poetics and shows some of the same dialectal play as does the epigram on Cresilas' *Idomeneus*,[59] but does not otherwise seem to engage in the sort of identifications to be found elsewhere. It thus may well be that the thematic and verbal links that run through the first poems did not extend throughout the entire section. Whatever the case, the sophisticated thematic organization of at least the first few epigrams none the less seems to me to go well beyond the grouping of like subject-matter with like subject-matter.[60] I would not wish to insist that this thematic unity must be the product of authorial rather than merely editorial arrangement, but the programmatic and unified character of the opening epigrams of the ἀνδριαντοποιικά does seem to me to suggest that at least this section reflects the work of the poet rather than that of even the cleverest compiler.

[59] Cf. Sens, 'Doricisms in the New and Old Posidippus', 76–9.
[60] Cf. Krevans, above, Ch. 5.

PART THREE

POSIDIPPUS IN A PTOLEMAIC CONTEXT

12

Battle of the Books

SUSAN STEPHENS

At the opening of his long elegiac poem, the *Aitia*, Callimachus labels his critics 'Telchines', a term that links them with antiquated ways and malevolent behaviour.[1] According to the Florentine scholia, Posidippus, along with his fellow epigrammatist Asclepiades, was one of these Telchines.[2] The scholiast thought the source of animosity to be the etiolated nature of Callimachus' poetry (τὸ κάτιςχνον τῶν ποιημάτων) and a problem of length (μῆκος). Since Posidippus and Asclepiades were themselves writers of short poems, the nature of their objections to Callimachus is not immediately obvious. In an effort to find an issue, modern scholars, on the basis of their respective epigrams, have taken the 'quarrel' to be the result of differing valuations of Antimachus' poem, the *Lyde*.[3] Callimachus stigmatized it as 'fat' and not 'acute' (παχὺ γράμμα καὶ οὐ τορόν, fr. 398 Pf.), while Posidippus and his fellow epigrammatist, Asclepiades, found it praiseworthy (*AP* 9. 63, 12. 168 = *AB* 140). The insufficiency of this argument has led to some vacillation on the truth-value of the scholium, and to question the idea of a poetic 'quarrel' at all.[4] Now, however, the publication of the Milan epigrams allows us to consider the matter from a somewhat different perspective. This roll, which has been plausibly attributed to Posidippus by the original editors, though there are still doubters,[5] not only gives us a large sample of poetry against which we may read Callimachus, it also provides several points of direct comparison.

In the second epigram of the second section (entitled οἰωνοσκοπικά)

---

[1] See G. Crane, 'Tithonus and the Prologue to Callimachus' *Aetia*'; Magnelli, 'Quelle bestie dei Telchini'. [2] Lines 3–9 on fr. 1 Pf.

[3] See R. Pfeiffer, *Callimachus*, i (Oxford, 1949), 3 n.7; Cameron, *Callimachus and his Critics*, 303–7 on Callimachus and Asclepiades on the *Lyde*.

[4] Lefkowitz, *The Lives of the Greek Poets*, 123–5, 138 regards the quarrel as a construct of ancient biographical writing, while Cameron, *Callimachus and his Critics*, 230–2 is inclined to give it more substance.

[5] For a balanced assessment, see Parsons, 'Callimachus and the Hellenistic Epigram', 117–18. For reasons that will emerge I think the identification with Posidippus to be correct.

of the new Milan roll we encounter the following statement (AB 22. 3–6):

> ἡμῖν δ' Αἰγύπτου πέλαγος μέλλουσι διώκειν
> Θρῆισσα κατὰ προτόνων ἡγεμονέοι γέρανος,
> cῆμα κυβερνήτηι καταδέξιον, ἢ τὸ μέγ' [ἀθρεῖ   5
> κῦμα, δι' ἠερίων cω[ιζο]μένη πεδίων.

But as we are about to sail over the Egyptian sea, may the Thracian crane, along the forestays, guide us on our way, a favourable sign for the pilot, as [it observes] the great wave, safely gliding through the high expanses of air.

The phenomenon of the cranes' seasonal migration from Thrace to Egypt in the spring marked the beginning of safe sailing, an event that is noted in a Homeric simile in *Il.* 3. 3–6 as well. For the Milan epigrammatist, Thracian cranes augur a favourable voyage, and the direction of their journey—towards Egypt—parallels the movement discernible in the opening of the roll. In the *Aitia* prologue, however, where Callimachus lays out his poetic agenda, the cranes are dispatched from Egypt back to Thrace:

> . . . .]ον ἐπὶ Θρήϊκας ἀπ' Αἰγύπτοιο [πέτοιτο
> αἵματ]ι Πυγμαίων ἡδομένη [γ]έρα[νος

. . . let the] crane, delighting in the blood of Pygmies, [fly] from Egypt to Thrace. (fr. 1.13–14 Pf.)

Elsewhere we have argued that Callimachus used the simile of the small and non-heroic Pygmies and cranes, which Homer likens to the Trojan and Greek armies, to co-opt the father of large poetry to his own poetics.[6] In Homer, as in the Milan roll, the cranes move from Thrace to Egypt. Callimachus certainly must have been aware of their importance for navigation—his own nautilus shell takes the same route as it drifts towards Egypt (*Epigr.* 5 Pf. = GP 14 = Ath. 7. 7. 318 D). Why then does Callimachus dismiss the cranes? In part because in Homer, if not in Callimachus (his text is broken), cranes are raucous birds, and within the *Aitia* prologue elegant and attenuated sounds signal the new aesthetic. Also, via Homer's simile, the cranes are associated with warfare. This may be all there is to it. Still, the migration of Thracian cranes is a rare motif in Greek poetry, and the likelihood of these two contemporary poets' independently chancing upon it is not high, especially since the twin poles of the migration—Thrace and Egypt—have personal associations for the poets themselves. If Callimachus' rejection of the Thracian cranes

---

[6] Acosta-Hughes and Stephens, 'Rereading Callimachus' *Aetia* Fragment 1', 247–8, 250. Homer refers to their κλαγγή (*Il.* 3. 3).

is in some sense directed at the Pellaean poet, what—whether real or simulated—might be the bone of contention?[7]

It is unlikely to have been a dispute about the quality of the *Lyde*, or if we extend the logic, to a disagreement over suitable poetic length. Admittedly it might have centred on various ideas about arranging epigrams into longer units. Posidippus seems to have organized at least four rolls of epigrams[8] and is bound to have had an opinion on the subject, and Callimachus has a sizeable number of epigrams that may well have been collected into an anthology by the poet himself.[9] There are, however, more easily accessible differences. From even a casual reading of the two poets it is clear that they wrote poetry about the Ptolemies in markedly different ways. Each operates within an idiosyncratic poetic geography, and each constructs and incorporates his encomiastic subjects into a poetic framework in ways that not only differ; they often seem to be antithetical.

EGYPT VERSUS MACEDON

Let us begin with geography: Callimachus was a Cyrenaean by birth, whose pride in his connection with the former ruling house of the Battiadae is commemorated in two familiar epigrams.[10] In his poetry he makes no claims to have lived anywhere but Cyrene and Alexandria. In contrast, Posidippus styles himself a Macedonian. He was from Pella, and in his elegy on his old age, a papyrus fragment discovered before the Milan roll (AB 118), he imagines that his statue, 'unrolling a book', has been erected in the Pellaean town square (ll. 17–18). Surely he belonged to the wave of Macedonians who travelled to Egypt to the court of the early Ptolemies.[11] The

---

[7] Another epigram that may have an anti-Posidippan tinge is *AP* 7. 524 = 13 Pf. = GP 31. This poem plays on a conventional theme, that tales of the underworld and afterlife are no more than fictions. The last two lines read: οὗτος ἐμὸς λόγος ὕμμιν ἀληθινός· εἰ δὲ τὸν ἡδύν | βούλει, Πελλαίου βοῦς μέγας εἰν Ἀΐδηι. The reference in the last line to the 'Pellaean' is usually taken to refer to a coin type, as in the opening of the first *Iambus*, ll. 1–2, and to mean something like 'things are cheap in Hades'. But this may be a double entendre: 'If you want good news, you can get a large ox in exchange for a Pellaean (= Posidippus).'

[8] K. Gutzwiller, *Poetic Garlands*, 150–70.

[9] There are other scenarios, but Gutzwiller, *Poetic Garlands*, 19, 38–40, 183–5 makes a compelling case. See also Parsons, 'Callimachus and the Hellenistic Epigram', 100–5.

[10] *AP* 7. 415, 520 = 35, 21 Pf. = GP 30, 33. It may not be wholly accidental that Posidippus in AB 105 has chosen the name of Battus. This was famously the name of the Cyrenaean royal house, but Posidippus' Battus is from Adramyttion in the Troad. Since Battus means 'Stutterer' the joke of the epigram would seem to be the stuttering effect achieved by the repetitions of consonants in l. 3: Ἀδραμυτην[ὸς ἀνήρ, Τιμάνθεος Ἀδραμυτηνὲ | Βάττε, μάκαρ[.

[11] It is tempting to understand the 'well-laden ship' of AB 21, the opening epigram of the οἰωνοσκοπικά, as conveying Posidippus' own poetry along the course marked out by cranes in the next epigram.

two poets seem to have been near contemporaries[12] and many of their poetic subjects overlap, but the difference in countries of origin has ramifications for their normative geographies. Callimachus' focus is the southern Mediterranean and he often locates or contextualizes his court poetry in terms of North Africa and Egypt, while Posidippus continually emphasizes Macedon and Northern Greece. We have already seen the one welcoming, the other banishing the Thracian cranes. In one other place in his poetry, 'Thrace' serves as the antithesis of Callimachus' own poetic values. In a fragment now plausibly assigned to the opening of *Aitia* book 2,[13] his poetic persona attends a banquet given by an Athenian newly arrived in Egypt,[14] who is celebrating the Attic feast of the Aiora. Seated next to a man from Icos, Callimachus remarks on their similar dislike of deep drinking (fr. 178. 11–12 Pf.):

καὶ γὰρ ὁ Θρηϊκίην μὲν ἀπέστυγε χανδὸν ἄμυστιν
οἰνοποτεῖν, ὀλίγωι δ' ἥδετο κιссυβίωι.

For he disliked greedy drinking of unmixed Thracian wine, and preferred a small cup.

This passage is unlikely to have been directed at Posidippus. Rather, here Callimachus capitalizes on the Macedonian and Thracian reputation for excessive and often blustering behaviour,[15] as a foil for his own aesthetics. The strong military profile of Thrace and its dynastic associations with Alexander, who necessarily evokes a context of war and conquest, may also be in play here, since these are subjects Callimachus consistently avoided in his poetry.[16] But Posidippus demonstrates that an inclination towards military themes is not necessarily dependent on length or genre. Alexander is commemorated in four of the new epigrams (AB 31, 35, 65, and 70), in three as conqueror of the Persians. The specific nexus of Thrace and Alexander is visible in the final epigram of the οἰωνοσκοπικά, the section that begins with the omen of the Thracian cranes. In this last poem, the Thracian prophet, Strymon, is singled out for his hermeneutic skills. He was an expert reader of bird signs who thrice provided Alexander with favourable omens in his battles against the Persians (AB 35).

The victory poems show a similar geographical divergence.

---

[12] Fraser, *Ptolemaic Alexandria*, i. 557–8; Cameron, *Callimachus and his Critics*, 183–4, 231, 242–4.   [13] J. E. G. Zetzel, 'On the Opening of Callimachus, *Aetia* II'.
[14] Presumably the symposium was set in Alexandria, but it is worth emphasizing that Callimachus names the location as 'Egypt' (fr. 178. 6 Pf.).   [15] See e.g. Ath. 10. 442 E–F.
[16] An explicitly political reason to reject Thrace, if we want one, could be found in the fact that Arsinoe II's marriage to Lysimachus of Thrace was a particularly violent affair that culminated in the death of her sons, before she returned to Egypt to marry her brother Ptolemy.

Consider the opening of Callimachus' epinician for Berenice II's chariot victory at the Nemean games (*SH* 254. 1–6):

> Ζηνί τε καὶ Νεμέηι τι χαρίσιον ἔδνον ὀφείλω,
> νύμφα, κα[ϲιγνή]των ἱερὸν αἷμα θεῶν,
> ἡμ[ε]τερο [. . . .] εων ἐπινίκιον ἵππω[ν.
> ἁρμοῖ γὰρ Δαναοῦ γῆϲ ἀπὸ βουγενέος
> εἰϲ Ἑλένη[ϲ νηϲίδ]α καὶ εἰϲ Παλληνέα μάντ[ιν,   5
> ποιμένα [φωκάων], χρύϲεον ἦλθεν ἔποϲ.

To Zeus and Nemea I owe a debt of gratitude, bride, holy blood of the sibling gods, . . . our epinician for your horses. For lately a golden report came from the land of cowborn Danaus to Helen's isle and the Pallenaean prophet, shepherd of [seals].

Callimachus begins his poem by moving away from Nemea. We are conscious of the event not as it happens but as it is reported in Egypt, and victory as report is reinforced by the long embedded μῦθος of Heracles and Molorchus. This is partly the result of Callimachus' habit of imitating Pindaric epinician, in which the victor is often celebrated in his home community. But in these opening lines Callimachus goes further: he describes both Greece and Egypt via Greek myths of Egyptian–Greek consanguinity (Danaus and his progenetrix Io) or interaction (Helen and Proteus).[17] The reference to Proteus as 'the Pallenaean prophet', for example, reinforces a contrast of Egypt and Thrace. The Egyptian Proteus was once married to Torone of Thracian Pallene, but in despair at its lawlessness he returned to Egypt via an undersea passage opened for him by his father Poseidon.[18] The allusion to Helen is similar. Her double mythology gives her close ties to Egypt. The tale of divine intervention that kept her in Egypt, dispatching only her phantasm to Troy, preserved her reputation[19] and allowed her to be adapted as a fit model for Ptolemaic queens.[20] Callimachus also identifies the queen as 'holy blood of the sibling gods', a reference to the Egyptian practice of brother–sister marriage adopted by the Ptolemies. It is gratuitous, however; Berenice, the poem's subject, was not the daughter of Ptolemy II and Arsinoe II, but of Magas of Cyrene. She was her husband's cousin, not his sister, though Ptolemaic ideology blurred the distinction.

In contrast Posidippus in the section entitled ἱππικά turns the reader of the epigram into a spectator of the victorious moment, often with a

[17] Stephens, 'Egyptian Callimachus', 246–7, 268–9.
[18] The story is told in Lycophron, ll. 115–26.
[19] The story is most familiar from Hdt. 2. 112–20 and Euripides' *Helen*.
[20] Callimachus associates Arsinoe with Helen in the *Apotheosis* (fr. 228 Pf.) on which see below.

unique or memorable feature, such as the Macedonian child winning in the presence of her father (AB 82. 3–5). This is not simply a result of disparity in length—Callimachus' epinicians are much longer than any of Posidippus'—and the different aesthetics that a poem of no more than four to fourteen lines requires. Rather it results from the way in which each poet geographically centres his poems. For Posidippus, a Ptolemy victorious in the isolympic sites constituted the core of praise, the *raison d'être* of the epigram. His poems are constructed to provide the mimesis of these events as they happen. Callimachus stresses the reaction at home, both in the opening of the *Victory of Berenice* and again in the *Victory of Sosibius*.[21] Further, Posidippus insists on the Macedonian heritage of the queens three times (AB 78, 82, 87). Elsewhere he links the Ptolemies with Alexander and employs eponyms like 'Eordaean' (AB 88. 4) or 'Argead' (AB 31. 3), a habit that strengthens the family's Macedonian connection, and may even perpetuate an idea that the Ptolemies are legitimate heirs to the throne of Macedon. At no point in Posidippus' victory poems are we made aware of the Egyptian location of the Ptolemaic kingdom, and within the more than 100 surviving poems of the new collection, the name 'Egypt' occurs only in the epigram on Thracian cranes. Even the poems on the Cape Zephyrium temple mute the temple's location. In AB 39, for example, no location is given at all, and Callicrates is identified as ναυαρχῶν Cάμιος. Two epigrams not in the Milan roll (AB 116 and 119) exhibit similar behaviour: 119 mentions only the Zephyrian promontory, while 116 locates the temple in 'sheep-rich Libya', between the Pharos (the only Alexandrian monument Posidippus ever mentions) and Canopus.

The reverse is true for Callimachus. Only once does he make explicit reference to Macedon in his poetry, and this is the more striking because so much more of his poetry survives than of Posidippus'. In the *Hymn to Delos* Apollo prophesies from the womb, instructing his mother to avoid Cos because it is destined to be the birthplace of Ptolemy II (165–8):

> ἀλλά οἱ ἐκ Μοιρέων τις ὀφειλόμενος θεὸς ἄλλος
> ἐcτί, Cαωτήρων ὕπατον γένος· ὧι ὑπὸ μίτραν
> ἵξεται οὐκ ἀέκουcα Μακηδόνι κοιρανέεcθαι
> ἀμφοτέρη μεcόγεια . . .

But another god is owed her [Cos] from the Fates, of the lofty race of the Saviours, under whose crown shall come—not unwilling to be ruled by a Macedonian—the Two Lands . . .

[21] Fr. 384 Pf. See especially ll. 24–34 and the speech of the Nile.

Callimachus inserts the 'Macedonian' into a poem that, as a number of scholars have demonstrated, consistently appropriates pharaonic Egyptian motifs.[22] ἀμφοτέρη μεσόγεια is the Greek equivalent of the term Egyptians used to designate their own country, Upper and Lower Egypt, or 'The Two Lands'.[23] Apollo's instructions from the womb imitate a standard feature of pharaonic ideology, the *post-eventum* prophecy placed in the mouth of the unborn king to announce his future accomplishments. Callimachus' choice of Μακηδόνι cannot be innocent, because as Apollo's prenatal prophecy continues Ptolemy the 'Macedonian' seems to be shedding his Macedonian identity. He is destined to be born on Cos, not in Macedon, and the signal exploit that distinguishes him takes place in Egypt. As the poem works itself out imaginatively, Ptolemy's projected defeat of the Gauls, who have invaded Egypt, functions on the human level to mirror Apollo's defeat of Pytho on the divine level. In doing so Ptolemy replicates pharaonic behavior by destroying enemies of Egypt and restoring order from disorder.[24]

But Posidippus, even when his poem must take place in Egypt, seems to efface it. For example, in an epigram on the Lighthouse known before the Milan roll (AB 115), the Pharos is likened to mountain watchtowers, familiar from the Greek islands. The Pharos is thus defined in terms of geographies more naturally occurring of the islands and indeed the rest of Greece, while the breakwater on which the Pharos is situated is assimilated to the long line of Greek islands that populate the Aegean.[25] In the new collection, the final epigram of the first section, a prayer for the wellbeing of 'Ptolemy's land and shores' (AB 20. 6), is framed in terms of saving Eleusis. Within the poem itself this fact, combined with the naming of Demeter and Poseidon, occasions some confusion. Is this the more famous Eleusis in Attica or, as must be the case, the Alexandrian suburb named for the former, probably because the Eumolpids introduced a form of the Eleusinian mysteries into Egypt under Soter?[26] The movement of objects over the opening section of the roll—from the periphery

---

[22] W. H. Mineur, *Callimachus: Hymn to Delos* (Leiden, 1984), 12–13, 165–6 summarizes the main points. For further detail see the following notes.

[23] P. Bing, *The Well-Read Muse* (Göttingen, 1988), 136; Koenen, 'The Ptolemaic King as a Religious Figure', 82.

[24] Bing, *The Well-Read Muse*, 128–39, Koenen, 'The Ptolemaic King as a Religious Figure', 81–4, and S. A. Stephens, *Seeing Double: Intercultural Poetics in Ptolemaic Alexandria* (Berkeley, 2003), 117–21.

[25] See below where Callimachus calls Mt. Athos an obelisk.

[26] Fraser, *Ptolemaic Alexandria*, i. 200–1 and Satyrus, 'On the Demes of Alexandria', P. Oxy. 2465, fr. 3.4–11. See now Lehnus, 'Posidippean and Callimachean Queries', 11–12.

ever closer to the kingdom of the Ptolemies—surely requires the reference be to Alexandrian Eleusis. For Posidippus, who seems to have been an initiate into the Mysteries elsewhere,[27] Alexandrian Eleusis would have been a natural place for him to identify in Egypt, and one with which he could easily have been familiar. However, by naming Egyptian spaces as if they were part of mainland Greece, he casts the entire Ptolemaic adventure in Egypt as an ever-widening extension of Macedon.

ARSINOE AND MACEDON

Whether we regard this behaviour as deliberate poetic technique or unconscious habit of mind, it is even more striking when we observe how it plays out in the depiction of Ptolemaic queens, and in particular Arsinoe II. The third section of the new roll, entitled ἀναθεματικά, includes four poems dedicated to her. The first reads as follows (AB 36):

> Ἀρσινόη, coὶ τοῦτο διὰ cτολίδων ἀνεμοῦcθαι
> βύccινον ἄγκειται βρέγμ᾽ ἀπὸ Ναυκράτιος,
> ὦι cύ, φίλη, κατ᾽ ὄνειρον ὀμόρξαcθαι γλυκὺν ἱδρῶ
> ἤθελεc, ὀτρηρῶν παυcαμένη καμάτων·
> ὡc ἐφάνηc, Φιλάδελφε, καὶ ἐν χερὶ δούρατοc αἰχμήν,   5
> πότνα, καὶ ἐν πήχει κοῖλον ἔχουcα cάκοc·
> ἡ δὲ coὶ αἰτηθεῖcα τὸ λευχέανον κανόνιcμα
> παρθένοc Ἡγηcὼ θῆκε γένοc Μακέ[τη.

Arsinoe, this linen headpiece from Naucratis is dedicated to you to be caught by the wind in its folds. With it, dear one, you wished in a dream to wipe the sweet sweat when you ceased from busy toils. You appeared thus, Brother-loving one, holding a spear in your hand and with a hollow shield on your arm. And at your request the white strip was dedicated by the girl Hegeso, of Macedonian stock.

The roll as a whole opens with a section in which luxury items as well as mundane objects are inexorably drawn towards New Macedon on the Nile. The section immediately preceding this poem, the οἰωνοcκοπικά, engages the reader in acts of omen interpretation via a series of epigrams focused on sea and land travel (AB 21–4), as we saw with the epigram on the Thracian cranes, and with war (AB 28, 30–3, 35). It ends with a poem on Alexander (AB 35). This first dedication to Arsinoe draws together several earlier strands: it is both a culmination of earlier movement towards Egypt and an omen that

---

[27] A golden *lamella* found at Pella is inscribed: 'to Persephone, Posidippus pious initiate' (AB T1); see also AB 43–4.

permits multiple interpretations as Arsinoe is linked via image and event with Macedon and Alexander.[28] Posidippus stresses that the dedicator is a Macedonian, and the gift from Naucratis. Although originally established under the Saite pharaohs as an entrepôt for foreign traders, Naucratis was the one city in Egypt that Greeks could and did claim as their own.[29] Situated on the Canopic branch of the Nile some 70 miles south of the coastline, the city epitomized Greek commercial enterprise and was emblematic of Greek naval power, as its very name implies ($ναῦc + κράτοc$). The object given to Arsinoe is of linen ($βύccινον$), a material grown and processed in Egypt for international export as well as local consumption. But by being designated as 'linen from Naucratis' the native material is constructed as a Greek commercial product: it joins the procession of goods flowing inevitably towards the Ptolemies.

This first dedication to Arsinoe experiments with images of dynastic power by linking Arsinoe with Alexander, who appears in the final couplet of the immediately preceding epigram. Throughout the first two sections of the roll, Alexander was recalled as conqueror of the Persians,[30] and the Ptolemies were associated with him in victory in AB 31. Arsinoe, who is here depicted with a spear and shield, suits well the Ptolemaic claims for the Macedonian legitimacy of the line as well as the image they laboured to project of themselves as the heirs of Alexander. As part of this legitimating process Arsinoe was included in the ancestor-cult of Alexander, and like Alexander (and the other Ptolemies) was modelled on coins with the ram's horns that marked Alexander as the son of Zeus Ammon.[31] But the association may be even more intimate. Arrian (*An.* 7. 21. 2–5) records the following anecdote about Alexander as he approaches Babylon shortly before his death. When he was navigating the marshes, a strong breeze fell upon him and carried off his hat[32] and $διάδημα$. The diadem—essentially a strip of white cloth tied at the brow, with its ends left to hang down the back[33]—was carried by the breeze to land upon a reed. A sailor retrieved the diadem and tied it upon his own head to free

[28] She is also associated via the images of previous epigrams with Athena. See my discussion in 'For You, Arsinoe...', 167–8.
[29] Fraser, *Ptolemaic Alexandria*, i. 133–4, and see also Hdt. 2.178–9.
[30] See my discussion in 'For You, Arsinoe...', 163–6, 169.
[31] H. Kyrieleis, *Bildnisse der Ptolemäer* (Berlin: 1975), 79 and pl. 70, 1–2.
[32] This was the καυcία, a broad-brimmed hat particularly associated with Macedon; see *AP* 6. 335 and discussion below.
[33] R. R. R. Smith, 'Spear-Won Land at Boscoreale', 116 n. 59 states: 'A combination of literary, numismatic, and sculptural sources makes it clear that the royal diadem . . . was a flat white band of cloth with free-hanging ends behind.'

his hands for swimming. According to Arrian: 'most of those writing about Alexander say that he gave him a talent for his zeal, but ordered his head cut off because the prophets instructed him not to leave anyone who had worn the royal diadem alive' (7. 21. 4). Arrian adds that some historians claimed that it was Seleucus who returned the diadem, and that this presaged the death of Alexander and the transfer of the empire to Seleucus (7. 21. 5).[34] For Arrian as well as other Alexander historians who recorded it, the incident of the diadem carried on the wind was significant both as omen of transition of power and for Alexander's own ability to interpret omens.[35] The story itself forms part of the rich omen literature that surrounded Alexander's demise and the ensuing skirmish among his successors to promote signs of legitimacy. Elizabeth Baynham characterizes the recording and exchange of these omens as follows:

What is apparent from the tradition of the Successors is that they and their attendants were a highly educated and literary group, as much at home with witty repartee, allusion, and riddle as any gentleman at a fashionable Athenian symposium.[36]

One of these Successors, who also wrote a history of Alexander, was Ptolemy I of Egypt, Arsinoe's father.

In fact many signs point to the linen strip as a surrogate diadem: the previous section (οἰωνοϲκοπικά) was not only about omens and proper omen interpretation, its final epigram focused on propitious omens for Alexander. I have already mentioned the transition of power from Alexander to the Ptolemies sketched in AB 31.[37] Although the object that is given to Arsinoe is not called a diadem, it bears a close resemblance. It is marked for the forehead by its name, βρέγμα, and is in shape a white strip, λευχέανον κανόνιϲμα, whose folds are carried by the wind, διὰ ϲτολίδων ἀνεμοῦϲθαι. These are salient characteristics of the object that Alexander wore and that the Ptolemies and their queens continued to wear.[38] Arsinoe often wears it on commemorative coins.[39] The diadem might also appear as a fillet tied around

---

[34] Both Diodorus 17. 116. 5–7 and Appian, *Syr.* 9. 56 record versions of the event.

[35] L. Pearson, *The Lost Histories of Alexander the Great* (London, 1960), 158–9; and see next note.

[36] E. Baynham, 'A Baleful Birth in Babylon', 253. This is part of her discussion of the prodigies associated with Alexander's last days.

[37] The epigram plays off of the iconography of Ptolemaic coinage in which an eagle with the thunderbolt (a Ptolemaic image) is protected by Athena (an image familiar from many coins of Alexander); see Stephens, 'For You Arsinoe . . .', 165, and next note.

[38] J. N. Svoronos, *Die Münzen der Ptolemäer* (Athens, 1908), pls. *A–B*.

[39] Ibid. Also see below on Thmuis mosaics.

the δίκερας, the double cornucopia that Ptolemy II was said to have designed as an emblem in his sister's iconography.[40] There are further signs that we as readers are being encouraged to identify the gift as a symbol of royal power: the gift-giving girl is Macedonian, and she bears a name—Hegeso—that could mark leadership or power. (The verbal form ἡγήςω means 'you led'). The queen herself solicits the object, ostensibly to wipe her 'sweet sweat'. 'Sweet sweat' could refer to no more than the fragrance connected with divinity, but it may also recall Alexander, whose εὐωδία was often noted.[41]

Although much later, a series of Roman wall paintings is instructive for understanding this epigram. The villa at Boscoreale outside Pompeii has a much-discussed set of painted panels that present an allegory of Macedonian power.[42] One of the panels contains two seated women, the left wearing the characteristic Macedonian hat (καυςία) and diadem, holding a spear and Macedonian shield. The second, seated lower and at the right, wears a rather crushed μίτρα. Consensus holds them to be personifications of Macedonia and Asia, with the former claiming the latter as 'spear-won land' (δορίκτητος γῆ).[43] Although the date of the frieze is between 60 and 30 BC, scholars agree that it must derive from a late fourth- or early third-century Macedonian original, probably celebrating the Antigonids. In three facing panels, taken to be a royal wedding combined with an allusion to the couple's future offspring, we find the presence and absence of the diadem—the husband does not wear one, his future son does—to be part of the allegorical play.[44] From these friezes we may infer that the manipulation of symbols of power in art, like the riddling games of the Successors' symposia, were a familiar feature of Posidippus' Macedonian world. To return to Arsinoe: apart from the καυςία, her appearance is the same as the Boscoreale Macedonia—bearing a shield and spear. Macedonian Hegeso receives via a dream Arsinoe's request for diadem-like object made from linen. Is this poem also an allegory? Are we to understand Arsinoe to be claiming Egypt (the linen diadem) as spear-won land, tacitly ceded by Macedon?[45] If this

---

[40] Ath. 11. 597 c cites evidence that Ptolemy II himself ordered the manufacture of the δίκερας, a kind of double rhyton, as an attribute for her statues (φόρημα τῶν Ἀρcινόης εἰκόνων).

[41] See e.g. Plu. *Alex.* 4. 4–5.

[42] See Smith, 'Spear-Won Land at Boscoreale', 108–12 and fig. 4; also B. Virgilio, *Lancia, diadema e porpora* (Pisa, 2003), 76–85 and fig. 16, who reprises much of Smith's argument.

[43] For the term as applied to the claims of the Successors, see Smith, op. cit. 110 n. 43.

[44] Ibid. 113–20 and fig. 11.

[45] It may also be relevant that Arsinoe seems to have worn the diadem briefly as Ceraunus' wife (Justin 24. 3. 3). See E. Carney, *Women and Monarchy in Macedonia* (Norman, OK, 2000), 232–3 and n. 142.

line of argument is correct, the riddling epigram may convey a sub-
tle compliment to the queen, or be disingenuous in its hint at her
desire for imperial power, or it may be packaging the status quo (the
Ptolemies' control over Egypt) as a clever cap to an already familiar
tale (Alexander's diadem) that made the rounds as sympotic enter-
tainment.

In any case Hegeso's dream of Arsinoe resonates particularly well
as a Macedonian image, since Macedon was distinguished by its cul-
ture of war. In Macedon queens too might behave as warriors, espe-
cially if they came from neighbouring Illyrian peoples, with whom
Macedonian royalty regularly married. Queens as warriors are also
found among the Ptolemies. Indeed it is possible to assemble a nearly
continuous line of evidence[46] from Olympias, the wife of Philip II,
to Arsinoe III. Several historians note that after Alexander's death,
when Olympias appeared in front of her army ranged against the
army of Eurydice, the Macedonian soldiers with the latter immedi-
ately defected, so moved were they by the spectacle of Olympias,
their former queen. Although the account in Diodorus 19. 11 is more
balanced, Duris' version, found in Athenaeus, is worth quoting for
the colourful image it projects (Ath. 13. 560 F):

> Duris of Samos says that the first war between two women was that
> of Olympias and Eurydice, in which the former came forth rather like a
> Bacchant with tambourines (βακχικώτερον μετὰ τυμπάνων). Eurydice was
> armed completely in the Macedonian manner (Μακεδονικῶς καθωπλισμένην),
> having been trained in military affairs by Cynna, the Illyrian [her mother].

Cynna (= Cynana) was a daughter of Philip II, and according to
Polyaenus fought by her father's side in an Illyrian campaign, killing
an Illyrian queen (8. 60).[47] Duris' vignette reads like sensational fic-
tion, but it is likely to have captured and/or reflect the popular view
of these queens, if the Vergina tomb finds are any indication. Gilded
weapons and armour were deposited in an antechamber close to the
entombed queen, who has been identified as either Philip II's wife,
Cleopatra, or as the Eurydice of Duris' anecdote.[48] Note that Duris
claims Eurydice wore a distinctive Macedonian battle garb, though
in what aspects is now not clear. So Arsinoe with shield and spear
would have some historical (in addition to an allegorical) precedent.
It is against this kind of background that I suspect we should read

---

[46] The evidence is of varying credibility if we are trying to establish historical facts. Its inter-
est here is for the consistent set of images of these women that seems to have circulated within
ancient literature.   [47] See Carney, 'The Career of Adea-Eurydike'.
[48] O. Palagia, 'Hephaestion's Pyre', 190–1; Carney, 'The Career of Adea-Eurydike', 500–1.
See also Carney's discussion of royal tombs in *Women and Monarchy in Macedonia*, 234–44.

Posidippus' epigram. His portrait of the armed queen asserts the Macedonian (and queenly) blood of Arsinoe at the same time that she (via the poem's position) is associated with Alexander and a symbol of his power, the diadem.

Given the variety of representations of Arsinoe in Alexandria and elsewhere, it is possible that Posidippus' epigram refers to a real image of the queen, though this cannot be proven. It might also serve to indicate her power. There has been considerable debate over the character of Arsinoe and the degree to which she did or did not shape her brother's political policy. The only concrete evidence for Arsinoe's participation in the normally male affairs of state comes from two inscriptions. The first is *SIG*³ 434/5, which reads in the relevant part: 'King Ptolemy in accordance with the policy of his ancestors and his sister is visibly concerned for the common freedom of Greece.' The second is the Canopus decree, which asserts that she was present with her husband to inspect the repairs of the dikes and to oversee the return of the gods (sc. statues of the native Egyptian gods) from Persia.[49] Whatever her political influence—and the evidence, however meagre, is more than for other contemporary queens—Posidippus' epigram provides in some sense the missing link between the earlier representations of the warrior queens of Macedon and the military activities attributed to later queens of the Ptolemaic dynasty.

Hyginus, in his discussion of Berenice's catasterized lock in the *Astronomica,* tells us that she participated in battle along with her 'father', Ptolemy II.[50] Hyginus' text is instructive—note the relationship between the events themselves and Callimachus' poetic evocation of them (*Astr.* 2. 24. 11–18 Bunte):

This Berenice, as some like Callimachus have said, bred horses and had been accustomed to send them to Olympia. Others add this further: that Ptolemy the father of Berenice, terrified by the number of the enemy, sought safety in flight, but his daughter, as she was often accustomed, mounted a horse, held the remaining force of the army, killed many of the enemy, and then put the rest to flight. For this reason Callimachus called her *magnanimam.*[51]

Hyginus apparently elicits his historical 'facts' from poetry or com-

[49] *OGIS* i. 56. J. K. Winnicki, 'Carrying Off and Bringing Home the Statues of the Gods', discusses the symbolic and practical aspects of this claim.

[50] She was in fact the daughter of his half-brother Magas and subsequently married to Ptolemy III.

[51] The Greek text of the *Lock of Berenice* is missing at the point in question, but Catullus' lines are: *a ⟨te⟩ ego certe | cognoram a parva virgine magnanimam.* Scholars have conjectured that *magnanimam* is translating an epithet like μεγάθυμον or μεγαλόψυχον.

mentaries on poems—he depends on the *Victory of Berenice* for the first part of his statement and the *Lock* for the conclusion. But he has found some other source for the intriguing middle section alleging Berenice to have taken an active part in her father's battles. Another elegiac fragment of Callimachus (388 Pf.) has been put forward as the source because it names Magas, Berenice II's father, and includes the word πολύπαλτος, the root of which, παλτός, is always connected to weapons.[52] Whether poetic narrative or commentary, Hyginus does seem to have some relatively contemporary source for his claims about Berenice,[53] and though undoubtedly exaggerated, they dove-tail with subsequent claims made for Arsinoe III, her daughter. Historical sources—Polybius 5. 83. 3 and 3 Maccabees 1. 4—state that Arsinoe III addressed the troops before the battle of Raphia in 217 BC. Posidippus' epigram does not require us to impute similar paramilitary activities to Arsinoe II, but it does contribute to a representational continuum for Macedonian and Ptolemaic queens, and in Egypt is likely to have been promoted as part of imperial ideology.

In this context it is worth a brief consideration of the Thmuis mosaics.[54] These are two floor inserts assigned to the end of the third century BC, but thought to be copies of earlier originals or templates. They feature a woman wearing a corslet with shield and spear, crowned by a ship. One of them is signed by Sophilus, the other is usually thought to be a less skilful imitation. The mosiacs have generally been taken to represent a personified Alexandria, but recently Wiktor Daszewski has put forward the appealing thesis that these are images of Berenice II as mistress of the Mediterranean.[55] Ann Kuttner refines his argument, proposing that they are two different women—one Berenice II, the other Arsinoe II.[56] It is unnecessary for my argument to establish that the mosaics were portraits of former queens. What is significant is that the complex representation of the figure(s) has features in common with the Arsinoe of the epigram. Like the Boscoreale Macedonia, the female of the Thmuis mosaics carries a shield and spear. Daszewski reminds us that shields are common devices on coinage of the early Ptolemies,[57] while personified females

[52] See Pfeiffer, *Callimachus*, i. 321 (notes on fr. 388, where a better text of Hyginus is printed) and Fraser, *Ptolemaic Alexandria*, ii. 1021–2, n. 101.
[53] See N. Marinone, *Berenice da Callimaco a Catullo* (Bologna, 1997), 22 n. 28, for a discussion of Hyginus' source.
[54] I am indebted to Ann Kuttner for bringing these mosaics to my attention and for her help with bibliography.
[55] W. A. Daszewski, *Corpus of Mosaics from Egypt*, i (Mainz, 1985), 146–58.
[56] Kuttner, 'Hellenistic Images of Spectacle', 111–13.
[57] Daszewski, *Corpus of Mosaics from Egypt*, 149–50.

holding spears may well allude to 'spear-won lands'. Other features of the mosaic image include a fillet tied around a standard, which Daszewski identifies as the diadem.[58] Whether or not the mosaics are officially sanctioned portraits of a former Ptolemaic queen, like Posidippus' epigram, they encapsulate what came to be enduring elements of Ptolemiac iconographic repertory—power represented as women, often divinized, accoutred with symbols like shield and diadem. Posidippus' epigram belongs at the beginning of the trend, and may well indicate that the iconographic repertory was originally Macedonian. Callimachus, in contrast, seems uninterested in portraying the queens in these specific ways. If we can extrapolate from Hyginus, Callimachus acknowledged the queens' real or imagined military exploits only tangentially, conveying whole narratives in one word.

ARSINOE THE GODDESS

We have seen how Callimachus and Posidippus construct the identities of their subjects as 'Macedonian' or 'Egyptian'. We have also seen the way in which queens may be imagined as warriors. In this final section I want to turn to the mythological encodings of Arsinoe II as a goddess. Here too the poets differ, not only in the selection of model by means of which they choose to articulate the experiments in Ptolemaic self-fashioning, but also in the degree to which they present the queen as divine. These are not entirely bookish experiments: both poets focus on known cult temples of Arsinoe in their poems. Whether the poems were written to commemorate real dedications or events that took place at these shrines cannot now be ascertained, though it is prima facie likely. It is fair to say that both Callimachus and Posidippus in their poems recreate a sense of living cult practice.

Let us first consider the epithalamia for the marriage of Arsinoe II and her full brother, Ptolemy II, an unusual poetic challenge, to which both Callimachus and Posidippus responded. Only the first line of Callimachus' poem survives: Ἀρσινόης, ὦ ξεῖνε, γάμον καταβάλλομ᾽ ἀείδειν (fr. 392 Pf.). We know nothing of its content, but even in the first line we can see the temporal displacement—the poem will not be a direct mimesis of the event itself, but a recollection for a guest or outsider. The choice of καταβάλλομαι further constructs a context: it is a Pindaric allusion to the habit of competitive performance—

[58] Daszewski, *Corpus of Mosaics from Egypt*, 149.

καταβολαί were the initial poems in the sacred contests, according to the scholiast on Pindar, *N*. 2. 1a, and from this comes to mean simply 'beginnings'. With Callimachus we can be sure that the original sense retained some force. In fact we have two other poems on the marriage, one most likely to be by Posidippus (AB 114)[59] and another anonymous piece in a papyrus belonging to the University of Chicago,[60] so that Callimachus' positioning of his poem as competitive may not be far from the mark. Posidippus' epithalamium is also fragmentary but we can see better how he treated his subject. Like Callimachus he speaks in the first person, but locates himself as having learned from the Muses (*Μου*]*cέων εἶπα διδασκόμενοc* l. 10). His poem proceeds not unlike Theocritus' *Idyll* 17. 131–4 in comparing the bride to Hera. Posidippus draws an analogy between the marriage rites of Hera on Olympus and those of Arsinoe via allusion to the bowl with which she performed her nuptial ablutions (ll. 7–8). There is a comparison also with Aphrodite—*cὺ*]*ν παιδὶ βαθυζώνοιο Διώνηc* (l. 19). This is consistent with a number of other of Posidippus' poems in which he links Arsinoe and Aphrodite. Aphrodite is the mythological exemplum of choice in the anonymous Chicago papyrus as well—col. III. 5 refers to *Ἀφρογένεια*, and in col. II. 14 Arsinoe is hailed as *κρατοῦca cὺ πόντον*.

Although we have no details of his treatment of the marriage in his epithalamium, elsewhere in his poetry Callimachus seems never to employ the usual analogy of Hera and Zeus for Arsinoe and Philadelphus. His compliments to Arsinoe fall along the reliable lines of poetic patronage. She is the tenth Muse according to the scholiast,[61] and although he does so inferentially, he never identifies Arsinoe directly with Aphrodite. In his poem on Arsinoe's death and apotheosis (fr. 228 Pf.), written in archebouleans, she is not co-templed with an Olympian divinity. Callimachus begins that poem with a panorama of Egypt in mourning, the smoke from the funeral pyre visible over the Thracian sea (ll. 39–44). We see the death through the eyes of Arsinoe's sister, Philotera, who is already dead

[59] It is preserved on a Ptolemaic papyrus (P. Petrie II 49a = P. Lit. Lond. 60), on the back of which is written *cύμμεικτα ἐπιγράμματ*[α] *Ποcειδίππου*.

[60] Chic. Lit. Pap., no. II; printed in Powell, 82–9. The surviving text is an epithalamium for Arsinoe in hexameters. Col. III mentions Aphrodite, but it is not attached to the first two columns. Since there are poems to other gods in subsequent columns it is not entirely clear if cols. I–III belong to a continuous poem, though given what can be inferred of the content, this is very likely. See Fraser, *Ptolemaic Alexandria*, i. 667–8, ii. 935–6, nn. 399–402; see also Sylvia Barbantani's study of P. Chicago, 'Osservazioni sull'Inno ad Afrodite-Arsinoe dell'antologia P. Goodspeed 101'.

[61] See the discussion in Cameron, *Callimachus and his Critics*, 141–2.

and deified, in conversation with Charis. To Charis she expresses her concerns that 'my Libya is being harmed' (l. 51). Charis explains that the land of Egypt is clad in black to mourn Arsinoe (ll. 67–75). From the scholium we know that Callimachus went on to tell of Arsinoe taken up by the Dioscuri, from which it seems likely that she was associated with Helen, a divinized 'human' figure from heroic past. He also described the altar and temenos that were established for Arsinoe in Alexandria near the Emporium. This was the Arsinoeion, an elaborate shrine that Ptolemy II had built for his sister. Apparently he even had an obelisk conveyed to this precinct, though it was still unfinished at the time of his death.[62] Pliny claims that the cult statue was made of topaz (37. 108). He also informs us that the roof was magnetic in order that a statue of Arsinoe could be suspended above it (34. 148). The sheer lavishness of the monument as Pliny describes it must have made it an arresting feature of the city's landscape. Coupled with it was the institution of the Arsinoeia, the festival held in Arsinoe's memory. Satyrus' *On the Demes of Alexandria*, now surviving as a papyrus fragment, includes what appear to be guidelines given to the residents of Alexandria as they prepared to celebrate this event.[63]

No other poets mention Arsinoe's mortuary temple. But we do have, by current count, three epigrams written by Posidippus— one from the new roll (AB 39) and two earlier discoveries (AB 116, 119)—on Arsinoe's temple located at Cape Zephyrium. In each of these he praises Callicrates' dedication and specifically identifies Arsinoe with Aphrodite. In Posidippus' epigrams Arsinoe becomes or is promoted as a marine goddess, and her sphere of influence is said to have encompassed not only seafarers but 'daughters of the Greeks' as well. The temple is mentioned twice in Callimachus, but it is doubtful that we would be able to identify it very accurately, if we did not have Posidippus' epigrams. In part this is a reflection of poetic style. Callimachus' approach is to highlight the insignificant or mundane while consigning manifestations of the royal house to the background—in the Selenaea epigram (GP 14 = 5 Pf.), for example, we are focused on the speaking conch shell and its aleatory route to the shores of Egypt.[64] The girl who makes the dedication and the

---

[62] Plin. *HN* 36. 67–9. See Fraser, *Ptolemaic Alexandria*, ii. 72–3 n. 168.

[63] P. Oxy. 2465, fr. 2, col. I. 1–9. L. Robert, 'Sur un décret d'Ilion', 198 would connect this celebration with the shrine of Aphrodite-Arsinoe at Zephyrium because he regarded the instruction to place sand on the altar as a marker of the sea deity. Fraser, *Ptolemaic Alexandra*, ii. 379 n. 318 demurs, pointing out that the ubiquity of sand in Egypt deprives it of any symbolic value.

[64] Gutzwiller, 'The Nautilus, the Halcyon, and Selenaia', 198; Selden, 'Alibis', 309–13.

Susan Stephens

dedicatory shell converge in Iulus in Ceos (a town recently renamed
for Arsinoe) and their journeys end in Egypt, though we know much
more about the conch than the girl. The temple where the dedica-
tion is made is identified only by the triple vocatives—Ζεφυρῖτι (l. 1),
Κύπρι (l. 2), and Ἀρσινόη (l. 8)—distributed throughout the poem. The
vast political apparatus that underlies and enables the journey is only
vestigially present. We find a similar treatment in the *Lock of Berenice*
(fr. 110 Pf.). There Arsinoe II, Berenice's 'mother', is first intro-
duced in connection with Mt. Athos, which is described as her 'obe-
lisk' (l. 45),[65] then Zephyrus is introduced via his brother, 'Ethiopian
Memnon'. (Again note the explicit Egyptianizing of Callimachus'
detail.) The lock is 'placed in the lap of Cypris. Zephyritis herself
chose [the lock], she who is resident on the Canopic shore' (ll. 56–8).
Arsinoe and Aphrodite are co-present in these lines, but they are
never specifically equated.

Many scholars, following Louis Robert's defining article on the
subject, take the Cape Zephyrium temple to have been the most
important of the Ptolemaic temples to Arsinoe.[66] But what was the
nature of its fame? Was the temple the central focus of the cult, or
merely the subject for continuous promotion in surviving poetry?
What is the relationship of these dedicatory poems to real events?
Did Posidippus create or merely reflect the importance of the tem-
ple? If we cannot answer these questions, we can be cautious in con-
structing history from poetry. About the Cape Zephyrium temple, we
have no other information beyond the poems and a brief reference in
Strabo, who mistakes its location.[67] Two passages in Athenaeus take
their information from the poems they preserve: the first includes
Callimachus' Selenaea epigram and Posidippus AB 119 (both men-
tioned above), and tells us that 'Posidippus wrote on the Aphrodite
honoured at Zephyrium' (7. 318 D). The second passage (11. 497
D–E) includes an epigram of Hedylus on a rhyton in the shape of
Bes, an Egyptian grotesque, supposedly dedicated at the same tem-
ple.[68] In modern discussions there is a tendency to construct rites
and prerogatives for the temple based solely on the evidence of the
poems, and its promotion by Posidippus acts as a magnet to draw

[65] Koenen, 'The Ptolemaic King as a Religious Figure', 98–9.
[66] L. Robert, 'Sur un décret d'Ilion'.
[67] Stephen of Byzantium (s.v. Ζεφύριον) notes it, but claims Callimachus as his source.
[68] Hedylus' epigram is preserved because of its reference to a rhyton. Given the tenor of
the passage, it is possible that this poem is intended as a parody of other poetic dedications to
Arsinoe. In vocabulary Hedylus is often indebted to Callimachus. See GP 4 and commentary
ad loc.

246

other poems or events into its orbit.[69] Within the dynamics of reading this may be correct, but evidence from documentary sources suggests that Arsinoe worship was not principally concentrated on that temple. Satyrus' *On the Demes*, as noted above, provides us with regulations for celebrating the Arsinoeia within the private spaces of Alexandria.[70] The large number of dedicatory oinochoai with figures of Ptolemaic queens found throughout the Mediterranean testify to the popularity of these women as objects of worship.[71] The oinochoai provide an important counterweight to poetry that associates Arsinoe with Aphrodite, because their iconography is never that of Aphrodite, but of Isis-Demeter or Agathe Tuche.[72]

The Cape Zephyrium temple with its cult figure of Arsinoe-Aphrodite is distinctively different from the mortuary cult of the divinized queen at the Arsinoeion or the co-templing of Arsinoe in shrines of other deities throughout Egypt. The most significant aspect of this temple, if we go by the evidence of Posidippus, is that there was only one cult statue, not two, as we find in other shrines, and that Arsinoe was completely identified with the goddess. He identifies the figure as Cypris-Arsinoe (AB 116 and 119) and Arsinoe Euploia (AB 39), employing a cult title of Aphrodite. In Theocritus, *Id.* 17. 34–50 we learn of Berenice I being taken off by Aphrodite to share in her honours, but no shrine is named.[73] Scholars debate the meaning of this tribute. Does it refer to a separate co-templing of Berenice I and Aphrodite? A co-templing in the Cape Zephyrium temple before the subsequent dedication of the temple as that of Aphrodite-Arsinoe? Or is it a delicate poetic 'premonition' of this supposedly later event? What we can infer from the poems is that the movement to equate the queen or queens with an Olympian goddess was a Greek, not an Egyptian, phenomenon, and was taking place at a very early moment in the dynasty's history. The prerogative seems even to have been extended to Ptolemy II's mistress, Bilistiche, to whom, according to Plutarch,[74] a shrine was dedicated as Bilistiche-Aphrodite. Whether

---

[69] See e.g. Bing's discussion in 'Posidippus and the Admiral', 255–66.

[70] P. Oxy. 2465, fr. 2, col. I. 1–9.

[71] D. B. Thompson, *Ptolemaic Oinochoai* (Oxford, 1973), 51–9.

[72] Ath. 11. 497 B–C cites material to the effect that Ptolemy II himself was responsible for the δίκερας or double cornucopia that became emblematic of Arsinoe II both on the oinochoai and on her coins.

[73] A shrine to Berenice-Aphrodite is known in the chora, but whether it is to the first Berenice or not is unclear. See Gow, *Theocritus*, ii. 334–5, n. 50.

[74] *Erotikos*, 753 E. See Cameron's discussion on Bilistiche, *Callimachus and his Critics*, 241–6. For cults of queens and royal mistresses associated with Aphrodite, see Carney, *Women and Monarchy in Macedonia*, 216–24.

Callicrates himself was the prime mover or whether he was acting for
the throne, the dedication of the Cape Zephyrium temple marked a
new phase in imperial promotion. Louis Robert was undoubtedly
right in seeing this as part of Callicrates' project to expand the sphere
of influence of the Ptolemaic navy throughout the Mediterranean, in
part by using the figure of the queen—now Aphrodite Euploia—as
patron of the maritime empire.[75] Although it is tempting to draw
all evidence for Arsinoe worship into one orbit and to connect it to
the grand schemes of Callicrates, a more likely scenario is that the
Ptolemies via their dependants—whether poet or admiral—experi-
mented with a variety of symbols and formats to promote their new
regime. These apparently took the form of temples of queens and
mistresses identified with Aphrodite, ancestor and mortuary cults,
co-templing with Egyptian gods, elaborate civic festivals, as well as
the creation and promulgation of specific icons like the δίκερας, the
diadem, and the oinochoai, as well as commemorative coinage.

Callimachus and Posidippus fit well into this broader model. The
reason to juxtapose them is not in order to draw conclusions about
poetic quality: to make one out to be a crass propagandist and the
other a slightly subtler practitioner of the flatterer's art. Rather it is
to illustrate the various ways in which Ptolemaic image making was
necessarily an evolving and even competitive process. The 'quarrel'
may not have existed at all—it could have resided rather in the minds
of scholiasts, who were as capable as we are of seeing the divergences
of the two poetic styles. If Callimachus and Posidippus are squaring
off, it will not necessarily have been rancorous or serious; more like-
ly it belonged in the realm of imperial entertainment—a duel with
epigrams over how best to publicize the throne.[76] The newly evolv-
ing monarchy after all provided the poets with a dizzying array of
moments to experiment with the hermeneutics of power.

[75] L. Robert, 'Sur un décret d'Ilion', 201–2.
[76] The epigram on Plangon (AB 127. 4), attributed to Posidippus or Asclepiades, for
example, clearly transplants a line from Callimachus' *Hymn to Athena* (ending ἄρτι φρυασσο-
μένων) into a sexual context. (Callimachus was describing the horses of a dust-covered Athena
delaying her bath until she had attended to them.) Since we now have the sequence in the new
roll of a sweating divinity (AB 30), Athena as the subject of an erotic dream (AB 33), and a
sweating Arsinoe, who appears in a dream (AB 36), we may wish to conclude that not all this
image-making was entirely serious. Cameron, *Callimachus and his Critics*, 241–6 connects the
Plangon epigram to a dedication of Ptolemy II's mistress, Bilistiche; but for another view see
V. Matthews, 'Sex and the Single Racehorse'.

13

Posidippus at Court: The Contribution of the Ἱππικά of P. Mil. Vogl. VIII 309 to the Ideology of Ptolemaic Kingship

MARCO FANTUZZI

As a famous argument put by Alcibiades to the Athenians at Thucydides 6. 16. 1–3 makes clear, the 'impression of power' was a quintessential ingredient of the ideology of the κῦδος that victory in chariot races provided:

Athenians, I have a better right to command than others . . . the Greeks, after expecting to see our city ruined by the war, concluded it to be even greater than it really is, by reason of the magnificence with which I represented it at the Olympic games, when I sent into the lists seven chariots, a number never before entered by any private person, and won the first prize, and was second and fourth, and took care to have everything else in a style worthy of my victory. Custom regards such displays as honour, and they cannot be made without leaving behind an impression of power (νόμωι μὲν γὰρ τιμὴ τὰ τοιαῦτα, ἐκ δὲ τοῦ δρωμένου καὶ δύναμις ἅμα ὑπονοεῖται).

The Olympic games were the most expensive agonistic competitions of ancient Greece, and therefore provided good evidence of the financial power with which political power quite often corresponded (in ancient times no less than today). Indeed it seems likely that Alcibiades chose horse-breeding and equestrian competition deliberately to demonstrate his own power: according to Isocrates 16. 33,

although in natural gifts and in strength of body he was inferior to none, [Alcibiades] disdained the gymnastic contests, for he knew that some of the athletes were of low birth, inhabitants of petty states, and of mean education. Therefore he tried his hand at horse breeding, work of the uppermost crust and not possible for a poor man, and he beat not only his competitors, but all previous winners.

This chapter has profited from suggestions by Hugh Lloyd-Jones, C. Catenacci, N. Luraghi, and A. Sens (who also helped me to improve its English form); finally, the copy-editor of this book, Leofranc Holford-Strevens, saved me from some last slips.

The same applied to Alexander the Great, at least according to the Alexander Romance 1. 18–19: when Alexander decided to participate in the Olympian games, both his father (versions A and B) and one Nicolaus 'king of the Acarnanians' he had met at Pisa (version B) advised him to compete in wrestling or in some other athletic speciality; instead, he opted for the chariot race—and of course won.[1] Indeed, of the forty-five epinician songs of Pindar known to us, fourteen—almost one-third—deal more or less directly with 'monarchic figures',[2] and of these fourteen poems twelve with equestrian victories.

In view of the high esteem in which equestrian chariot victories were held, celebrations of success in this event naturally contributed to the image of politically important people in all cities and periods of Greek history. For fourth- and third-century dynasties and those who celebrated them, the view that equestrian victories created an 'image of power' appears to have been particularly widespread. In the case of the Ptolemies, the ideological importance of success in equestrian events is shown in an official context by the friezes representing horse races which can be found in the Ptolemaion of Limyra (usually dated 290–280 BC); similar decorations were found in the Mausoleion of Mausolus of Halicarnassus and in the Prince-Tomb of Vergina (end of the fourth or beginning of the third century).[3] Furthermore, a certain Attalus (= Attalus I ?) was victorious with the chariot at Olympia (280–272),[4] and the same personal interest in the event can be assumed for Hieron II, the tyrant-king of Syracuse, who dedicated two statues of himself (standing and as a rider) at Olympia, perhaps after an equestrian victory of which no record has survived.[5]

In Egypt in particular, the Ptolemies' keen interest in racing reflects the long-standing interest that the Macedonians had in horses, but it also may have represented the resumption of the traditional pharaonic passion for racing,[6] especially since the Ptolemies represented themselves as the natural successors of the pharaohs, at least to the native

---

[1] The information is of course unreliable, but testifies to the diffusion of the idea that equestrian victories fit a great king.

[2] As noticed by C. Catenacci, 'Il tiranno alle Colonne di Eracle', 27 n. 68.

[3] On all these friezes, cf. K. Tancke, 'Wagenrennen'.

[4] *IAG* 37 = *GESA* 59.

[5] The hypothesis of an equestrian victory is maintained by H. Berve, *König Hieron II.* (Munich, 1959), 81 on the basis of the statement of Polyb. 1. 16. 10, who calls Hieron II φιλοστεφανῶν καὶ φιλοδοξῶν εἰς τοὺς Ἕλληνας, and of some of Hieron's coins, where an image of Nike is displayed. For a sound criticism of Berve's thesis, cf. B. Hintzen-Bohlen, *Herrscherrepräsentation im Hellenismus* (Weimar and Vienna, 1992), 113–14.

[6] Cf. W. Decker, *Sport und Spiel im alten Ägypten* (Munich, 1987), 54–62.

Egyptian audience. The founder of the dynasty, Ptolemy I Soter, competed with the cυνωρίc and won at Delphi in the Pythian games of 310 BC, as Pausanias tells us (10. 7. 8). From Pausanias again (6. 3. 1) we know that in the inscription commemorating his victory, Ptolemy I called himself 'Macedonian', and he did the same when he dedicated a statue of himself in the Altis of Olympia. The emphasis he placed on his Macedonian ethnicity might be thought a reflection of the fact that he had not yet assumed the title of king;[7] or it might show the special bond of affection that this king, born (unlike Ptolemy II) a private citizen in Macedonia, may have felt for his Macedonian origins; this ethnic may also have stood higher in the Ptolemies' favour than it did in the other kingdoms of the Diadochoi.[8] These hypotheses, however, now appear hardly satisfactory: the fact that Ptolemy I officially referred to himself as 'a Macedonian' at Delphi and at Olympia finds an intriguing parallel in the remarkable emphasis that the ἱππικά give to the Macedonian ethnicity of the later Ptolemaic queens Berenice II (or Berenice the Syrian[9]) and Berenice I in the context of celebrating their victories at the Isthmian games and at Olympia,[10] as well as in the final apostrophe of the long epigram summarizing the series of equestrian victories attained by the whole dynasty of the Ptolemies and their queens at Olympia (AB 78. 13–14): ἀείδετε . . . ὦ Μακέτα[ι] 'celebrate, o ye Macedonians', where the Macedonians appear to be addressed as the whole body of the fellow-citizens of Berenice.[11] A more probable explanation of the Ptolemies' emphasis on their Macedonian background is therefore that participation in the pan-Hellenic games was conceived by the Ptolemies as a part of their keen interest in and support for the impulses of Greek poleis to revolt against the predominance of Antigonid power in continental Greece, impulses that led amongst other things to the so-called Chremonidean war (begun in 268/7 or 265/4 and concluded in 263/2 or 262/1 with the siege of Athens). It is against this background, I believe, that the Ptolemies deliberately presented themselves not as

[7] Cf. G. Maddoli, M. Nafissi, and V. Saladino, *Pausania. Guida della Grecia. Libro VI: l'Elide e Olimpia* (Milan, 1999), 185–6.

[8] As suggested by Paus. 10. 7. 8. Cf. C. Bearzot, 'Πτολεμαῖος Μακεδών'.

[9] Bastianini and Gallazzi proposed to identify the Βερενίκη of AB 78. 13, 79. 1 and 82. 1 with Berenice II, the daughter of Magas of Cyrene and wife of Ptolemy III, whose Nemean victory in a chariot race was celebrated by Callimachus (*SH* 254–69). D. J. Thompson, below, Ch. 14 has now persuasively suggested that Posidippus' Berenice should be Berenice the Syrian, daughter of Ptolemy II and Arsinoe I, and sister of Ptolemy III: after the Second Syrian War she was married to Antiochus II and was killed when her husband died in 246.

[10] In AB 82. 3, 87. 2 respectively; see also 'Εορδαία γέννα 'Eordaean stock' in 88. 4, on another Olympian victory.

[11] Cf. Bingen, 'Posidippe: le poète et les princes', 58.

Marco Fantuzzi

'kings of Egypt', but as 'Macedonians' in the context of pan-Hellenic games from which non-Greeks were excluded. With this ethnic designation the Ptolemies may also have strengthened their persistent claim to be the real and legitimate successors of Alexander the Great by continuing the tradition of Alexander I Philhellen, the son of Amyntas, and of Philip II, both of whom had participated and won in the Olympic games: Philip in 356 with the κέλης; Alexander in the stadion, having been admitted to participate in the Olympic games only after he could prove his Argive origins as a *Macedonian* king.[12] Of course this emphasis possibly was also a way for Posidippus—if Posidippus was the author of all the epigrams of P. Mil. Vogl.[13]—to indulge in the national pride he certainly showed in AB 118. 15– 17 (ὄφρα με τιμήcωcι Μακηδόνεc οἵ τ' ἐπὶ ν[ήcων | οἵ τ' Ἀcίηc πάcηc γ⟨ε⟩ίτονεc ἠϊόνοc. | Πελλαῖον γένοc ἁμόν 'so that the Macedonians may honour me, both the islanders (?) and the neighbours of all the Asiatic shore. From Pella is my family'); yet, in my opinion he would hardly have engaged in such ethnic chauvinism in the ἱππικά if his Ptolemaic patrons did not wish to present themselves as Macedonians in order to establish their place in the pan-Hellenic games and, perhaps, to further their interests in continental Greece.[14]

The homage that the ἱππικά paid to the equestrian victories of kings and queens most probably had further and more specific implications, since it was endowed with a deeper meaning and function that contributed not only to the ideology of Ptolemaic dynastic power in

---

[12] To judge from Hdt. 5. 22 Alexander was initially excluded from participation by 'those who manage the contest' (probably the Hellenodikai), since even at the beginning of the 5th c. at least some if not most Greeks appear not to have been immediately ready to recognize the Macedonians as Greeks. Alexander could be admitted only when he 'demonstrated' at least that, as a member of the dynasty of the Macedonian kings, he had Argive origins (such a claim most probably still implied the awareness that the body of his Macedonian subjects was not Greek): cf. the analysis of the ancient sources on the Greekness of Macedonian ethnicity by J. M. Hall, 'Contested Ethnicities'. Of course this kind of objection could hardly be raised by the Hellenodikai in the 4th c. of Philip II, when at least the Macedonian aristocracy was fully Hellenized, and, more importantly, Greece was more and more at the mercy of the Macedonians.

[13] I personally believe Bastianini and Gallazzi's idea (now mainly accepted) that all the epigrams of P. Mil. Vogl. are from the hand of Posidippus. In any case, my analysis of the ἱππικά suggests a substantial unity underlying the ideology of the epinician epigrams for the Ptolemies.

[14] Bingen, 'Posidippe: le poète et les princes', 56–9 would rather explain the emphasis of the ἱππικά on the Macedonian ethnicity of the Ptolemies by saying that in general 'la légitimité du pouvoir se situe à Alexandrie dans la continuité de la succession d'Alexandre le Macédonien'. In fact, the Ptolemies appear to have officially emphasized their Macedonian origins above all in connection with events in continental Greece: see also the list of the members of the royal family honoured in the exedra on the monument in their honour in Apollo's temple at Thermon, all qualified by Μακεδών or Μακέτα: IG ix/1². 56.

252

general, but also to the specific ideology of the figure of the queens.

In AB 87, the first of the final pair of ἱππικά that focus on Berenice I, the poetic voice of Berenice's mares not only may mimic the *persona loquens* of Berenice's lock in the major encomiastic poem at the end of the Callimachean *Aitia*,[15] but explicitly points to another model that highlights the specific κῦδος it bestows on Berenice I: in the second distich the horses are said to provide Berenice I with the victory at Olympia, 'the much celebrated glory, with which she has erased the long-lasting κῦδος of Cynisca'.

A member of the royal dynasty of the Spartan Eurypontids, daughter of Archidamus II, and sister of Agesilaus II and of Agis II, Cynisca won at least twice with the four-horse chariot at Olympia, most probably at the Olympiads of 396 and 392 BC.[16] She was considered to have been the first woman to breed horses and to enter and win a chariot competition in pan-Hellenic games (Paus. 3. 8. 1, 3. 15. 1). Indeed she had recorded the reason for her κῦδος in the epigram inscribed on the round pedestal holding a chariot and a team, as well as Cynisca and the charioteer, by the Megarian sculptor Apelle(a)s, one of the two monuments erected in Olympia to commemorate her enterprise (Paus. 6. 1. 6).[17] The text of Cynisca's epigram (both preserved on the stone, with some gaps—*GESA* 33 = *CEG* 820—and transmitted as an adespoton at *AP* 13. 16) reads:

> Cπάρτας μὲν βασιλῆες ἐμοὶ πατέρες καὶ ἀδελφοί,
> ἅρματι δ᾽ ὠκυπόδων ἵππων νικῶσα Κυνίcκα
> εἰκόνα τάνδ᾽ ἔcταcα. μόναν δ᾽ ἐμέ φαμι γυναικῶν
> Ἑλλάδος ἐκ πάcαc τόνδε λαβεῖν cτέφανον.

My father and brothers were Spartan kings,
I won with a team of fast-footed horses, and I Cynisca
put up this monument: I say I am the only woman
in all Greece to win this crown.

Celebratory inscriptions usually had 'the tendency to add . . . a 'surplus-value' to that of the victory itself',[18] by emphasizing some special feature that gave it extra distinction: the epigram for Cynisca accomplishes this by underlining the exceptional quality of the victory of a woman in an Olympic context (women were not allowed

---

[15] I have developed this idea in 'The Structure of the *Hippika* in P. Mil. Vogl. VIII 309'.

[16] As established by C. Robert, 'Die Ordnung der olympischen Spiele und die Sieger der 75.–83. Olympiade', 195. The most plausible alternative chronology of Cynisca's victories is 380 and 376: cf. *IAG*, p. 43.

[17] The other monument, representing the 'horses of Cynisca', was situated in the temple of Zeus: cf. Paus. 5. 12. 5.

[18] Cf. H. W. Pleket, 'Games, Prizes, Athletes, and Ideology', 79.

even to enter Olympia during the games); however, it also shows a striking boldness—Cynisca is the *only* woman in the whole of Greece to win this crown—instead of making the more prudent claim that she was the only one 'among all those who are living', or that she was the 'first' (πρώτη) to do so. The former claim is found for instance in the inscription of the Lacedaemonian Damonon (νικάhας ταυτᾶ hᾶτ' οὐδὲς πέποκα τὸν νῦν 'after winning victories in this way as no one of our contemporaries has yet done': *IAG* 16, dated 440–435, or shortly after 403), while the latter appears to be the most common expression in the record-boasts by the agonistic winners of the Hellenistic age: for instance *GESA* 64, 68, 69, 71 (?), 72, 73 (of the third and second centuries BC) and *IAG* 45 (200–180 BC).[19]

That Cynisca's epigram makes no attempt to narrow the scope of her achievement to a limited time unavoidably exposed her glory to the risk of being 'surpassed', and the author of the ἱππικά took advantage of the opportunity by representing his Berenice as having eclipsed Cynisca's prior record (and boast). The poet who wrote the ἱππικά, by contrast, appears to have recognized that epinician's inherent generic inclination to exaggerated boasting risked exposing his victors to the same fate as Cynisca. Yet in truth his royal *laudandi* are safe from this danger: he is very careful as far as other Ptolemies are concerned, and stresses only records that are by definition almost unbeatable, since they concern specific, ideal competitions with other kings. This is especially clear in AB 88. 1, where the speaker, Ptolemy II, makes the daring claim πρῶτοι τρεῖς βασιλῆες . . . καὶ μόνοι ἁμές 'we were the first and only three kings'.[20] In another epigram the scope of the competition is even limited to the Ptolemaic family itself: Berenice II (or Berenice the Syrian) is said to be the only member of the family able to crown her house at the Isthmian games, though her house was well accustomed to so many victories:[21]

ἐκήρυξας γὰρ ἐν Ἰςθμῶι | τοςςάκις ἀθλ[οφ]όρον δῶμα μόνη βαςιλίς 'you

[19] It is self-evident that 'while μόνος includes πρῶτος, πρῶτος does not necessarily involve μόνος': M. N. Tod, 'Greek Record-Keeping and Record-Breaking', 111–12.

[20] This phrase may have been already 'technical' in celebratory inscriptions (as we may suspect from the few surviving instances: e.g. *GESA* 45, of the 5th c., and 67, of the 3rd), but as can be easily seen from *IAG* it becomes very common only in the imperial age (above all in the forms μόνος καὶ πρῶτος τῶν ἀνθρώπων or μόνος καὶ πρῶτος ἀπ' αἰώνων).

[21] This seems to me the most reasonable interpretation of 82. 5–6, though Bastianini and Gallazzi prefer to translate: 'tu infatti, regina, da sola, hai fatto proclamare la casata così tante volte vittoriosa', where 'da sola' ('alone' or 'single-handedly') is inexplicable to me. AB, which came to my hands only after the text of the present paper had long been submitted, wavers between the translation of the *editio maior* and the interpretation I favour: the English version, 'for you proclaimed at the Isthmus your house so often victorious—a Queen on your own' assumes the former, whereas the Italian 'tu infatti all'Istmo sei l'unica regina che abbia fatto

were the only queen to proclaim her house victorious at the Isthmus so often' (AB 82. 5–6; the same idea probably underlay 80. 4 τοῦτ' ἐπὶ παιδὶ μόνηι). Much more daringly, the same phrase used in 88. 1 also appears in 83. 3 for the κέλης of a winner declared to be the πρῶτος καὶ μόνος 'first and only' to win three victories at Olympia. In this case, however, we are dealing with a non-royal victor, for whom the risk of being overtaken by another and thus to lose his status as μόνος 'the only one', was far less dangerous than it was for a king: the claim that 'no defeat would be greeted with so much ridicule' as the defeat of a king in an equestrian competition appears in the mouth of the Simonides of Xenophon's *Hieron* (11. 6),[22] a treatise to which we will later return. Furthermore, the author of this epigram clearly recognizes the risk involved in his boast, and by issuing the command ἐλέγχετε 'please check', the speaking statue of the victorious Thessalian horse appears explicitly to challenge all earlier racehorses. Indeed the poet knew well the history of equestrian records: other κέλητες had won crowned games more than twice—Hieron's horse Pherenikos had won at least once at Olympia (476 BC, maybe also 472) and at least once at the Pythian games (478 BC, maybe also 482)[23]—but no single racer appears to have won the Olympic games more than twice; besides, three successive victories at Olympia would have involved an exceptional, though not impossible, span of racing time for a single horse, nine years.[24] At the same time our epigram may also be offering a sly challenge to the literary tradition of epinician poetry, a challenge analogous to that issued by the horse towards the tradition of agonistic exploits. The record boasted

---

proclamare così tante volte le vittorie del suo casato' implies the latter. In fact no Isthmian victory except the one described in our epigram is certainly attested for the Ptolemies, but AB 81. 1 Δωρικὰ φύλλα σελίνων 'Dorian leaves of celery' may also point to an Isthmian victory (the localization cannot be ascertained, since the 'celery' is both used as a reference to Isthmian and Nemean games, and at least AB 80 celebrates a Nemean victory). If AB 81 celebrates the same Berenice, as it seems to me most probably to do—cf. BG, p. 210—she possibly won twice at Corinth, and 81. 4 δίς might point to this fact (together with 80, AB 81. 4 may, however, point as well to a double victory by her at Nemea). In any case our Berenice appears to have felt her primacy in the Isthmian games an important achievement to celebrate, and the emphasis on this primacy, in my opinion, explains the qualification μόνη.

[22] Xenophon was most probably thinking of the misfortune that befell Dionysius I, who had participated in the chariot race at Olympia of 388 BC, but had all his chariots leave the track, or break to pieces during the competition (D.S. 14. 109. 4).

[23] See B. Gentili's note on Pi. *P.* 3.73 f., in edn. (Milan, 1995), 417.

[24] According to Hdt. 6. 103 Miltiades' father, Cimon, won three times at Olympia in the four-horse chariot with the same horses; only the Spartan Euagoras enjoyed the same success. The case of these chariot-horses, however, is rather different from that of the single κέλης, because the quality of endurance needed in a chariot-horse fitted ageing horses better than the speed of the single racer: cf. H. Maehler, *Die Lieder des Bakchylides* (Leiden, 1982), ii. 79 n. 6.

Marco Fantuzzi

by the Thessalian horse is represented as a μνῆμ' ἱερὸν Ϲκοπάδαιϲ its 'sacred memorial to the Scopadae': the epigram does not use for its *laudandus* the usual ethnic 'Thessalian' (AB 74. 2, 84. 2; cf. also 85. 4) but refers to him as contributing new glory to the Scopadae. This is, I suggest, a device by which the author implicitly compares his celebrative skills to the talent of Simonides, since this famous epinician poet is often mentioned at the beginning of the third century as a successful provider of immortal glory to his *laudandi*, above all in connection with his eulogies for the Thessalian dynast Scopas II.[25]

As late as Pausanias' day the epigram for Cynisca was considered an exceptional event in the long and highly conservative story of the Spartan dyarchy. As Pausanias himself correctly acknowledged (3. 8. 2): 'the Spartans seem to me to be of all men the least moved by poetry and the praise of poets; for, with the exception of the epigram upon Cynisca, of uncertain authorship, and the still earlier one upon Pausanias that Simonides wrote on the tripod dedicated at Delphi, there is no poetic composition to commemorate the doings of the royal houses of the Lacedaemonians.' Not only were these two instances isolated episodes, but the Lacedaemonians had radically regretted the latter: the epigram in honour of Pausanias, ascribed to Simonides (*FGE* 17(a)), was immediately deleted from the tripod. Condemned as an act of celebratory self-indulgence, it was replaced with the list of the towns that had shared the anti-Persian alliance of the second Persian war.[26] In the case of Cynisca, however, the Lacedaemonians even heroized her after her death, and built a posthumous heroon for her near the Platanistas, the most important gymnasium of Sparta (cf. Paus. 3. 15. 1). The heroic honours afforded Cynisca were exceptional not only in Sparta, but more generally in fourth-century Greece, since most of the heroized athletic victors known to us either won their events in the first half of the fifth century or are eighth-century victors who appear to have begun receiving cult honours in the fifth.[27]

It is beyond doubt that the chariot victories of the queenly Cynisca—'queenly' not only in reality but also in the emphasis that her epigram places on her origins, as do epigrams honouring Archedice, the daughter of the last Peisistratid tyrant of Athens, Hippias,[28] and

[25] Cf. Theoc. 16. 36 and Callim. fr. 64.14; also Cic. *De orat.* 2. 351–3; Quintil. 11. 2. 11–16.
[26] Cf. Thuc. 1. 132.
[27] Cf. F. Bohringer, 'Cultes d'athlètes en Grèce classique'; L. Kurke, 'The Economy of Kudos'.
[28] *FGE* 'Simon.' 26(a). 3–4 πατρός τε καὶ ἀνδρὸς ἀδελφῶν τ' οὖϲα τυράννων | παίδων τ' 'her father and husband, her brothers and children were tyrants'.

Olympias, the wife of Philip II and mother of Alexander[29]—greatly improved her image. It is not necessary to assume, however, that all Lacedaemonians felt the same way about Cynisca's glory. Her ostentatious pride about her agonistic success, after all, stood in manifest contradiction to the egalitarianism of the Spartans and to their preference for martial bravery and training over agonistic performance, a preference that dates at least from Tyrtaeus. Even Agesilaus is said to have juxtaposed the useful breeding of war horses to the useless breeding of race horses, and to have encouraged the agonistic career of his sister only in order to show through her victory that 'such a stud marks the owner as a person of wealth, but not necessarily of merit', since he believed that 'a victory in the chariot race over private citizens would add not a whit to his renown' (Xenophon, *Ages.* 9. 6–7). The claim, repeated after Xenophon in Plutarch (*Ages.* 20. 1; cf. also *Apophth. Lac.* 212 A–B), well befits the μεγαλοψυχία that can be credited to the king.[30] Therefore we would not put it past him to have suggested to Xenophon what to say about Cynisca, though of course neither can we in principle rule out that the words he is made to utter may also in part represent Xenophon's own (more radical?) reinterpretation of his views. Anyway Xenophon was personally so fond of these ideas that he put them again in the mouth of Simonides in his long didactic speech to Hieron (*Hier.* 11. 5–6):

what about the breeding of chariot horses, commonly considered the noblest and grandest business in the world? By which method do you think you will gain most credit for that, if you outdo all other Greeks in the numbers of teams you breed and send to the festivals, or if the greatest number of breeders and the greatest number of competitors are drawn from your city? . . . Indeed my own opinion is that it is not even seemly for a great despot to compete with private citizens. For your victory would excite envy rather than admiration, on the ground that many estates supply the money that you spend, and no defeat would be greeted with so much ridicule as yours (ἐγὼ μὲν γὰρ οὐδὲ προσήκειν φημὶ ἀνδρὶ τυράννωι πρὸς ἰδιώτας ἀγωνίζεσθαι. νικῶν μὲν γὰρ οὐκ ἂν θαυμάζοιο ἀλλὰ φθονοῖο, ὡς ἀπὸ πολλῶν οἴκων τὰς δαπάνας ποιούμενος, νικώμενος δ' ἂν πάντων μάλιστα καταγελῷο).

Apart from Cynisca's, a single other dedication for equestrian victories is known from Spartan sanctuaries, that of Damonon in the sanctuary of Athena on the Spartan Acropolis.[31] Although for the

---

[29] τῆςδε πατὴρ καὶ ἀνὴρ καὶ παῖς βασιλεῖς, καὶ ἀδελφοί, | καὶ πρόγονοι 'her father and husband and son were kings, and her brothers, and her ancestors' ap. Plut. *Quaest. conv.* 747 F.

[30] Cf. P. Cartledge, *Agesilaos and the Crisis of Sparta* (London, 1987), 149–50.

[31] I rely on the analysis of the testimonies (and of the case of Damonon) by S. Hodkinson, *Property and Wealth in Classical Sparta* (London, 2000), 303–7.

classical period Spartan inscriptions are rather rare all told, the scantiness of the evidence may testify to a broader Spartan view that equestrian victories were less valuable than victories in other athletic contests, since equestrian competition did not normally involve the personal participation of the owner/breeder of the horses.[32] If it did exist, however, such a bias would clearly not be relevant in the case of a woman, who could not personally enter any athletic pan-Hellenic agon, and in any case one king, Damaratus, had in fact participated in and won the four-horse chariot race of Olympia in 504. If Agesilaus had really had such a low opinion of his sister's agonistic victories, he would hardly have allowed Cynisca's athletic achievements to be memorialized as they were—according to Xenophon, he was generally opposed to this kind of self-advertisement[33]—and above all else he would likely have opposed her heroization and the erection of her shrine.[34] In fact the timing of Cynisca's victories in the most pan-Hellenic contest of Greece coincides with the period when Agesilaus was at his most 'pan-Hellenic',[35] and this must be cherished as a clue, however slight, that he exploited Cynisca's victories in order to improve the international prestige of Sparta.

Cynisca's heroic honours must have seemed to every Greek of the third century sure and familiar evidence of the prestige that queenly individuals could win via agonistic successes in chariot races. But Sparta also provided one of only a few instances of monarchy (or rather dyarchy) inside the Greek-speaking world, together with the Battiads of Cyrene and the Macedonian kings. It might therefore seem an alluring model for anyone who felt the need to find unambiguously Greek parallels for the monarchs of the new kingdoms founded after the death of Alexander. That a 'queenlike' Spartan woman was an ideal term of comparison for the new figure of a queen is clear, for reasons having to do with more than gender: Pindar also seems to exploit connections between the Spartan kingship and the absolute dynasts of his age in order to establish as legitimate the authority of the latter. At the beginning of the Tenth Pythian, an ode written for a

---

[32] Of course the Spartan elite was not an exception to the high aristocratic evaluation of success in athletic competitions (cf. Hodkinson, 'An Agonistic Culture?'), and from the 540s to the 360s all Spartan equestrian victors bar two are recorded as having erected some kind of victory monument at the site of the games: cf. Hodkinson, *Property and Wealth*, 307–28.

[33] Cf. *Ages.* 11. 7 'he would not allow a statue of himself to be set up, though many wanted to give him one, but on memorials of his mind he laboured unceasingly, thinking the one to be the sculptor's work, the other his own, the one appropriate to the rich, the other to the good.'

[34] Agesilaus and Cynisca should have been more or less the same age (cf. *GESA*, p. 110), and since Agesilaus was exceptionally long-lived, he more probably outlived her than the reverse.

[35] Cf. Cartledge, *Agesilaos and the Crisis of Sparta*, 150.

certain Hippocleas from Pelinna but commissioned by the Aleuadae, Pindar stresses the analogy between Sparta and Thessaly and between Spartan kings and the Thessalian Aleuadae, since the two royal families of Sparta and the Thessalian dynasts shared a common descent from the sons of Heracles (ll. 1–5):

Ὀλβία Λακεδαίμων,
μάκαιρα Θεccαλία. πατρὸc δ' ἀμφοτέραιc ἐξ ἑνόc
ἀριcτομάχου γένοc Ἡρακλέοc βαcιλεύει.
τί κομπέω παρὰ καιρόν; ἀλλά με Πυθώ
   τε καὶ τὸ Πελινναῖον ἀπύει
Ἀλεύα τε παῖδεc, κτλ.

Fortunate is Lacedaemon,
blessed is Thessaly. Over both rule the descendants
of one father, Heracles, greatest in battle.
Why am I vaunting inappropriately? Rather, Pytho
and Pelinna are calling upon me,
and Aleuas' sons, etc.

The parallelism Pindar draws between the Aleuadae and Spartan kings seems likely to have been intended to gratify the ambition of these dynasts to create a certain image of authority, for though they controlled a great part of Thessaly, *de facto* and *de jure* 'a king of all Thessaly did not exist'.[36]

---

[36] Quotation from N. Robertson, 'The Thessalian Expedition of 480 BC', 106; see now B. Helly, *L'État thessalien*, 69–130. The Aleuadae are also called βαcιλεῖc of Thessaly by Hdt. 7.6.2, and Simon. *PMG* 511 seems similarly to represent Aeatius, celebrated in connection with a victory of his 'sons' with the κέληc, as a βαcιλῆα τελεcφόρον 'king with full authority' of all the people of Thessaly: he may have been the ancestor of the Aleuadae (cf. Gentili, 'Studi su Simonide', 120–1), though we cannot rule out that he was the head of another Thessalian family which claimed descent from Heracles via Thessalus: cf. J. H. Molyneux, *Simonides* (Wauconda, IL, 1992), 130. Pindar often describes Hieron, an especially frequent protagonist of his epinicians, with the epithets ἀρχόc, βαcιλεύc, λαγέταc (τύραννοc), but by using these titles he is merely trying to develop the image of his *laudandus*, ascribing to him an aura of traditional authority he wished for but lacked, since most probably the absolute power gained both by Gelon and by his brother Hieron was not officially institutionalized in any of these terms. In fact, in all the numerous inscribed dedications recorded by both tyrants at Delphi, Olympia, and elsewhere, they always introduced themselves as aristocratic representatives of Syracuse, and nothing else: see now S. E. Harrell, 'King or Private Citizen', though the essence of the problem had been already clearly and carefully presented by N. Luraghi, *Tirannidi arcaiche* (Florence, 1994), 354–68 (which Harrell appears not to know). This maybe happened because they could not show off titles they did not officially have in such a compromisingly public/pan-Hellenic medium as inscriptions; or because they were aware of the widespread anti-tyrannical orientation of the great majority of the Greek poleis in the first half of the fifth century, and refrained from stating their autocratic power in pan-Hellenic seats where the majority of the readers would have shared this hostility to tyrants (the case of *CEG* 397, where the original second hemistich of the first line Γέλαc ἀνέθεκε Fανάcc[ον] was erased, and Π]ολύζαλόc μ' ἀνέθηκ[ε] was superinscribed, may be an especially telling instance).

Marco Fantuzzi

Pindar also made use of the 'guarantee of legitimacy' provided by Sparta in the first Pythian, a poem that celebrates Deinomenes, son of Hieron and regent of the newly founded Aetna, the town whose νόμοι were modelled on the basis of the Spartan constitution: just after calling Deinomenes βαϲιλεύϲ of Aetna at the end of the third epode (ll. 60 and 60a), Pindar, using a succession of thoughts that almost serve to 'gloss' that title, devotes the fourth strophe to an exaltation of the Doric constitution of Hyllus and Aegimius (ll. 62–6) that instituzionalized the dyarchy:

> ἄγ᾽ ἔπειτ᾽ Αἴτναϲ βαϲιλεῖ φίλιον ἐξεύρωμεν ὕμνον·   60
> τῶι πόλιν κείναν θεοδμάτωι ϲὺν ἐλευθερίαι
> Ὑλλίδοϲ ϲτάθ|μαϲ Ἱέρων ἐν νόμοιϲ ἔ-
> κτιϲϲε· θέλοντι δὲ Παμφύλου
> καὶ μὰν Ἡρακλειδᾶν ἔκγονοι
> ὄχθαιϲ ὕπο Ταϋγέτου ναίοντεϲ αἰ-
> εὶ μένειν τεθμοῖϲιν ἐν Αἰγιμιοῦ
> Δωριεῖϲ. ἔϲχον δ᾽ Ἀμύκ|λαϲ ὄλβιοι   65
> Πινδόθεν ὀρνύμενοι, λευκοπώλων
> Τυνδαριδᾶν βαθύδοξοι
> γείτονεϲ, ὧν κλέοϲ ἄνθηϲεν αἰχμᾶϲ.

Come then, let us compose a loving hymn for Aetna's king,
for whom Hieron founded that city with divinely fashioned freedom
under the laws of Hyllus' rule,
    because the descendants of Pamphylus
and indeed of Heracles' sons,
who dwell under the slopes of Taygetus,
are determined to remain for ever in the institutions of Aegimius
as Dorians. Blessed with prosperity, they came down from Pindos
and took Amyclae, to become much acclaimed
    neighbours of the Tyndaridae with white horses,
    and the fame of their spears flourished.

As has been well said, to represent Aetna as a new Sparta allows Pindar to combine the absolute power of the βαϲιλεύϲ (l. 60) with the idea of ἐλευθερία (l. 61), avoiding the paradoxical contrast of the two terms.[37]

Indeed the model chosen by the author of the ἱππικά or by his royal clients could hardly be better. Most obviously, one of the main arguments made by Xenophon (or Agesilaus?)—that 'it is not even seemly for a great despot to compete with private citizens'—may have had some circulation beyond Xenophon and the supporters of an enlightened monarchy. It is also reflected in a saying ascribed

[37] Cf. Luraghi, *Tirannidi arcaiche*, 359.

260

to Alexander, who asserted his readiness to run at Olympia 'pro-
vided that my adversaries are kings' (Plu. *Alex.* 4): according to the
Alexander Romance (versions A and B, §18), Alexander did indeed
compete at Olympia in the chariot race, as we have seen,[38] and in his
case four out of nine competitors were 'kings'. Thus the epigram's
explicit reference to Cynisca and the claim that the κῦδος of that
queen had been eclipsed allowed Berenice I to enter and win not so
much a contest with the 'private citizens' competing at Olympia, but
the diachronic competition that the queenly Cynisca had initiated
with the unwary μόνη of her epigram.[39]

Furthermore, as we observed before, Cynisca was one of the few
Olympic victors who got the official honour of being heroized after
death and having a heroon built for her. Not only was Berenice I also
deified after death (a shrine was built for her, called the Berenikeion[40]),
but the process of her deification probably resembled in some way tra-
ditional heroization like that undergone by Cynisca. Theocritus 15.
106–8 presents Berenice as a mortal whom Aphrodite made immor-
tal (ἀθανάταν ἀπὸ θνατᾶς), thus attributing to her a status (to be born
a mortal and to become immortal) that precisely mirrors the status
of some traditional Greek heroes: Berenice lacked the divine lineage
from Zeus that was ascribed to Soter via Alexander (cf. Theoc. 17.
16–25),[41] or later to both Ptolemy II and Arsinoe as children of divin-
ized parents.[42] She may thus have needed to be deified, through the
direct divine interest of a god (Aphrodite), for her own virtues,[43] as

[38] Above, p. 250.
[39] Cf. Catenacci, 'Il tiranno alle Colonne di Eracle', 16: 'Delfi e Olimpia ... sono splendide
vetrine. Tutti prima o poi vi si recano. Il messaggio di potenza affidato a un magnifico donario
raggiunge così il più alto numero di persone nel modo più impressionante.'
[40] Cf. Callix. *FGrHist* 627 F 2 (34). Another temple existed for her and Ptolemy Soter,
erected by Philadelphus: cf. Theocr. 17. 123 and Lyc. Rheg. *FGrHist* 570 F 16. The date
of Berenice's deification, as well the date of her death, cannot be established with certainty:
cf. Fraser, *Ptolemaic Alexandria*, i. 224.
[41] Cf. S. B. Pomeroy, *Women in Hellenistic Egypt* (New York, 1984), 30: 'the difference
between the deification of Macedonian kings and the deification of the queens is that, for the
kings, they were bound to follow the example of Alexander. There was more to gain by associa-
tion with this great figure than could possibly be acquired by innovation. For the deification
of women there were no binding precedents, though the cult of Berenice could be used on a
much smaller scale.'
[42] 'We must remember that it was the deification of Arsinoe . . . which seems to have marked
a major turning-point in the development of the royal cult, and the deification of her mother
may have been an altogether less grand, "more Greek" affair' (Hunter, *Theocritus and the
Archaeology of Greek Poetry*, 134). Cf. also Fraser, *Ptolemaic Alexandria*, i. 214–19 and L.
Koenen, 'The Ptolemaic King as a Religious Figure', 51–5; G. Weber, *Dichtung und höfische
Gesellschaft* (Stuttgart, 1993), 252–4.
[43] Cf. W. Meincke, *Untersuchungen zu den enkomiastischen Gedichten Theokrits* (Diss. Kiel,
1965), 101–2; F. T. Griffiths, *Theocritus at Court* (Leiden, 1979), 74.

often happened to other humans who became heroes.⁴⁴ We do not know whether Ptolemaic propaganda exploited or anticipated this motif, though the comparison of Berenice I to Cynisca appears to have had the effect of implying or supplying a good reason to divinize Berenice. But we do know that the athletic victories of Berenice II came to be regarded as a part of her heroic status: when Ptolemy IV in 211/10 BC brought the dead Berenice into the Alexander cult to join Arsinoe and his other divine ancestors, the eponymous priestess of Berenice's cult was designated ἀθλοφόρος.⁴⁵

Apart from Cynisca and, perhaps, Berenice, agonistic κῦδος did not provide many other people with immortality, but had been quite often successfully pursued as an ingredient of the image of power. I am not sure whether we have to accept that unlike κλέος the word κῦδος implies the idea of a 'talisman of supremacy', the *mana*, or special power, bestowed by a god that makes a human invincible.⁴⁶ The linguistic evidence aside, in purely cultural terms the view that in a broad sense agonistic glory served as a 'talismanic' symbol of superiority helps explain the fact that the kings of Sparta used to go to battle accompanied by victors who had been crowned in athletic games or that, when these victors entered a city, a portion of the city walls was customarily torn down in order to show that, because of them, the city had no need for walls at all. It is also difficult to deny that the advertisements of the Pythian victory of Arcesilas IV of Cyrene in 462,⁴⁷ were extreme attempts at reinforcing the Battiad dynasty at a time when the aristocracy of Cyrene had already attempted to rebel against the monarchy and would later engage in the successful

---

⁴⁴ As pointedly remarked by Koenen, 'The Ptolemaic King as a Religious Figure', 114, 'Egyptian kingship was based on mythical thinking, which was a thing of the past for educated Greeks . . . the world of myth and mythical thinking had survived in poetry and reappeared in the tales of Hellenistic poets . . . *The hero of old was the thing closest to a divine king on earth*' (the italics are mine).

⁴⁵ As was remarked by Stephens, 'For You, Arsinoe . . .', 170; cf. also Thompson, Ch. 14, p. 274.

⁴⁶ Cf. E. Benveniste, *Indo-European Language and Society*, trans. E. Palmer (London, 1973), 348 and H. Fränkel, *Early Greek Poetry and Philosophy*, trans. M. Hadas and J. Willis (New York, 1973), 80 n. 14 (both cit. by Kurke, 'The Economy of Kudos', 132). Nor should we be sure that Cynisca's heroization reflects 'a final bid for renewed talismanic authority by the Spartan kingship in the face of the encroaching power of the Ephorate', as was cautiously suggested by Kurke, op. cit., 162–3: see above all the criticism of Hodkinson, *Property and Wealth in Classical Sparta*, 309–10. See also Walbank, 'Monarchies and Monarchic Ideas', 88, who draws a parallel between the heroizations granted in Athens to three followers of Demetrius Poliorcetes in 302–1 and the divine cult accorded by the Athenians to the same Poliorcetes (though Walbank correctly specifies that 'nevertheless ruler-cult is not derived from hero-cult': of course court poets could enjoy emphasizing the analogies of historically independent facts). On the renewed interest for heroic cults in the Greek mainland of the 3rd c., cf. Alcock, 'The Heroic Past in a Hellenistic Present'.   ⁴⁷ Celebrated by Pi. *P.* 4 and 5.

putsch that ended in the murder of Arcesilas and the extinction of the Battiads (440 BC). Nor can one deny that several tyrants of the fifth century used their athletic crowns to try to create for themselves the image of special divine protection that could justify their absolute power in the eyes of their citizens.[48] Last but not least, the increasing aristocratic participation in chariot racing in Athens during the fifth century was also a deployment of economic power intended to provide personal charisma as a substitute for the aristocracy's waning cultic power, which had been the institutionalized political charisma of the previous two centuries.[49] The emphasis of AB 87. 3–4 on the traditional word κῦδος will have certainly evoked and depended on these traditional values in order to enhance Berenice's glory.

Hints at a strong interest in Sparta are not new within the ideology of Ptolemaic power,[50] and in the particular case of Berenice I, the mother of Magas, king of Cyrene (the future father of Berenice II), the Spartan connection would also have been felt to involve a hint at the historical filiation Sparta > Thera > Cyrene also advertised by Callimachus at *Hymn* 2. 71–9 (after Pi. *P.* 5. 72–81). The specific precedent of Cynisca, however, provided (or at least could have provided; we do not know whether it was exploited or not by official propaganda) a further clearly identifiable contribution to the making of the public image of the first Ptolemaic queen, an image that is radically new in the theatre of Greek political power. In the ideology of Ptolemaic monarchy, the king was not simply the supreme governmental power, but 'he was, rather, a unique figure . . . ruling by qualities of character rather than position'.[51] Battle and athletic contexts were in Greece the main arenas for the winning of personal κῦδος.[52] There is clear evidence that military victory was perceived as one of the most important proofs and attributes of royalty.[53] But

---

[48] Cf. Catenacci, 'Il tiranno alle Colonne di Eracle'.

[49] As was shown by J .K. Davies, *Wealth and the Power of Wealth in Classical Athens* (Salem, NH, 1981), 97–100.

[50] See e.g. Hunter's reading of Theocr. 18 in *Theocritus and the Archaeology of Greek Poetry*, 149–66.

[51] A. E. Samuel, 'The Ptolemies and the Ideology of Kingship', 192. See also the seminal analysis of the king's qualities according to the Hellenistic idea of kingship in O. Murray, 'Aristeas and Ptolemaic Kingship', 353–9, and H. J. Gehrke, 'Der siegreiche König'.

[52] Cf. Kurke, 'The Economy of Kudos', 132.

[53] Commenting on an eastern expedition of Antiochus III, Polybius remarked (11. 34. 15–16) 'he put his kingdom in a position of safety, overawing all his subjects by his courage and his efforts. It was in fact this expedition which made him appear worthy of the throne . . .' (cit. Walbank, 'Monarchies and Monarchic Ideas', 66). See also the often mentioned definition of βασιλεία in *Suda* (β 147 Adler), which is believed to derive from a Hellenistic source: 'it is neither descent nor legitimacy which gives monarchies to men, but the ability to command an army and to handle affairs competently.'

the arena of war was still most probably off limits for women, though the chances that Ptolemaic queens had for glory would later extend to martial activities as well (at least in the case of Berenice II); AB 36 proves beyond any doubt that as early as Arsinoe's reign the imagery of a queen dressed in arms and engaged in the toils of battle (cf. the ὀτρηροὶ κάματοι of l. 4) could be conceived as the dream fantasy of a girl.[54] The athletic victories of Berenice I will have served as a demonstration of the superiority she needed in the eyes of her subjects. This is even more the case, if we—and Berenice's subjects—are led by our epigram to interpret her victories as a defeat of Cynisca, a queenlike figure and thus one of the few peers to be found in Greek culture for the new image of the first Ptolemaic queen. That the reference to Cynisca formed part of a deliberate strategy of this sort is hard to doubt if we remember that between Cynisca and Berenice I another woman, the Spartan Euryleonis, had won at Olympia[55] and had a statue erected to celebrate her victory (mentioned by Paus. 3. 17. 6). Though *de facto* the κῦδος of Cynisca had already been eclipsed, Euryleonis was not a queenlike figure[56] with whom it was fitting for Berenice I to compete; nor does there appear to have existed any memorial that presented her as a queenlike figure to be surpassed by the new Ptolemaic queen.

'More glory is won by an Olympic victor who comes of a family of Olympic victors; more honourable is that soldier who comes from a fighting stock: there is a keener pleasure in pursuits that have been followed by one's fathers and forefathers.' Though the author from whom I quote this claim, Philostratus (*VS* 611), is later than the age we are considering now, he expressed well a long-lasting aristocratic feeling that characterized most athletic practices, and certainly at least equestrian competitions, the most elite sport of Greece.[57]

Indeed a quite similar statement can also be found in Pindar (*P.* 10.

---

[54] According to Hyg. *Astr.* 2. 24 Berenice II combined equestrian skills and martial valour: 'Ptolemaeum Berenices patrem multitudine hostium perterritum fuga salutem petisse; filiam autem saepe consuetam insiluisse in equum et reliquam copiam exercitus constituisse et complures hostium interfecisse': maybe this is the reason why she was called something equivalent to *magnanima* by Callimachus (cf. Cat. 66. 26: from an original μεγάθυμος?). On the reliability of Hyginus' information, which has been challenged in the past, see Parsons, 'Callimachus: Victoria Berenices', 45 and N. Marinone, *Berenice da Callimaco a Catullo*, 2nd edn. (Bologna, 1997), 22–3 n. 28. As for Arsinoe's possible engagement in foreign politics (and also military campaigns?) see Stephens, 'For You, Arsinoe . . .', 167–8; ead., above, Ch. 12.

[55] Around 386 BC (*IAG* 418).

[56] Cameron, *Callimachus and his Critics*, 244 calls her 'another Spartan princess', but no evidence exists about her social status.

[57] On this point see M. Golden, *Sport and Society in Ancient Greece* (Cambridge, 1998), ch. 5.

22–6): 'blessed and a worthy subject for song in wise men's eyes is that man who conquers by his hands or the excellence of his feet and wins the greatest of prizes with courage and strength, and while still living sees his young son duly win Pythian crowns.' Pindar's odes provide secure and early evidence for the emphasis on the continuity of the 'aptitude for victory' within a family.[58] In *I*. 3. 13–17b Melissus of Thebes, winner with the chariot at a Nemean game shortly after 479 BC, 'brings no disgrace upon the prowess inherited from his kinsmen. Surely you know the ancient fame (δόξαν παλαιάν) of Cleonymus with chariots, and on his mother's side as relatives of the Labdacidae they devoted their wealth to the toils of four-horse chariots.' Again, the main protagonist of the first part of the Fourth Isthmian is the φάμα παλαιὰ εὐκλέων ἔργων, 'the ancient fame for glorious deeds' (ll. 22–3) of the equestrian successes of the family of the Cleonymidae: the ode, which celebrates first an Isthmian chariot victory by the same Melissus and finally his previous victories in the pankration, opens with a mention of Melissus, but mainly speaks throughout the opening section (ll. 1–30) of the original equestrian glory of the family, of the temporary slack period due to the death of four members of the family in war, and only finally of the resurrection of the family glory by Melissus. The same emphasis can be found in the Seventh Pythian ode, in which the predominant aim is to honour the whole Ἀλκμανιδᾶν εὐρυσθενὴς γενεά . . . ἵπποισι 'the mighty race of the Alcmaeonids for their horses' (ll. 2–4), and the poet admits to being led to the celebration of the protagonist, Megacles, by the several victories not only of the man but also of his πρόγονοι 'ancestors'. These victories are then listed all together as common acquisitions of the family (ll. 12–16). Another telling feature of the Seventh Pythian is that the victor to whom the ode is dedicated, Megacles, is only mentioned at l. 17. The postponed naming of the honorand represents a remarkable point of contact with the first of the royal ἱππικά (AB 78), where the winner of the victory being celebrated, Berenice II or Berenice the Syrian, is not mentioned before l. 13, and the real protagonist of the epigram is the continuity of the aptitude for victory of the γένος ἱερόν 'sacred clan' (l. 9): the actual winner is mentioned only after Berenice I and Arsinoe, as well as her grandfather Ptolemy I and her father Ptolemy II.

In any case, there is a substantial difference between the practice of archaic epinician and the target pursued by the royal ἱππικά.

---

[58] For a full list, and a discussion, cf. L. Kurke, *The Traffic in Praise* (Ithaca, NY, 1991), 17–22 and S. B. Pomeroy, *Families in Classical and Hellenistic Greece* (Oxford 1997), 85–95.

Whereas in Pindar the *hic et nunc* of the specific victory celebrated by each poem was always especially relevant, in many epigrams the aptitude for victory of the Ptolemies almost overshadows the specific victory for which the poem was composed. This change of emphasis finds a parallel in Callimachus' epinician for Sosibius (fr. 384 Pf.), in which the Nemean victory that occasioned the poem is almost overshadowed, first by the memory of the Isthmian victory previously gained by Sosibius, and then by the enumeration of all his other victories.[59] The new focus of such poems demonstrates the substantial distance between the function of archaic epinician, commissioned and composed for one performance after the victory (or at any rate no more than a few), and that of the royal ἱππικά as 'advertisements' of a ruling dynasty.

We can track a twofold encomiastic strategy in the ἱππικά. On the one hand, these poems emphasize the continuity of the aptitude for equestrian victory of the members of the Ptolemaic dynasty; on the other, they focus in particular on a series of female victories, which are treated as a 'specialization' of the Ptolemies' aptitude for victory. The two different sections of the royal ἱππικά (AB 78–82 and 87–8) focus either on one aspect or on the other.

The last section mainly focuses on the latter aspect. The victory of Berenice I has a special and exclusive relevance in the penultimate epigram of the ἱππικά, which we considered above: highlighted as a victory for which the queenlike Cynisca provides the sole precedent, the success of Berenice I finds in the Spartan woman an aetiological starting-point for the aptitude to victory of the Ptolemaic queens. In the last epigram (AB 88) the speaker (Ptolemy II) mentions both his own glory and that of his parents. He thus not only implies the continuity of his family's achievement but also stresses the major relevance of his mother's achievement (ll. 5–6: ⟨κ⟩οὐ[60] μέγα πατρὸς ἐμοῦ τίθεμαι κλέος, ἀλλ' ὅτι μάτηρ | εἷλε γυνὰ νίκαν ἅρματι, τοῦτο μέγα 'and I do not claim my father's victory as great, but that my mother won a chariot victory as a woman, *this* is a great thing').

Another exceptional aspect of the victories of the other Ptolemies is shown to be the continuity of the athletic success of both male and female family members. This aspect is featured in the whole first section of the royal ἱππικά. For the image of the reigning dynasty this

[59] Cf. Th. Fuhrer, *Die Auseinandersetzung mit den Chorlyrikern* (Basel, 1992), 203–4.

[60] I accept R. Führer's text in Bernsdorff, 'Anmerkungen zum neuen Poseidipp', 39, which slightly modifies the reading suggested by Gronewald, 'Bemerkungen zum neuen Poseidippos', 5. The 'continuity factor' would be even stronger if we accept the text printed by BG, πρὸς μέγα πατρὸς ἐμὸν τίθεμαι κλέος ('to my father's great glory I add my own').

continuity was probably more than a mere record: rather, it provided much stronger evidence of the talismanic divine favour accorded to them than a few isolated successes by isolated representatives of the dynasty would have done. Furthermore, it thus served as indirect evidence of their substantial identity as members of the same family. As in Theocritus 17, where the kinship between the two Ptolemies is stressed through the identity of their names and martial qualities (cὲ δ', αἰχμητὰ Πτολεμαῖε, | αἰχμηταὶ Πτολεμαίωι ἀρίζηλος Βερενίκα, 'and you, warrior Ptolemy, to warrior Ptolemy renowned Berenice (bore)', ll. 56–7), in the programmatic[61] first poem of the part of the ἱππικά for the Ptolemaic family, AB 78, the main focus is on the continuity of the dynastic aptitude for victory (ll. 11–12: [ἐξ ἑ]νὸς οἴκου | ἅρμασι καὶ παίδων παῖδας ἀεθλοφόρο[υ]ϲ 'and from a single house the children's children winning prizes with their chariots'). This continuity is linguistically reflected both in the repetition of the same words (in addition to παιδ- within l. 12, νικ-, ἅρμα-, βασιλ-) and in the stress placed on the identity of the names and title: see l. 3 ἅρματι μὲν γάρ μοι προπάτω[ρ Πτολεμ]αῖος ἐν[ίκα 'my grandfather Ptolemy won with his chariot' and (textually more certain) ll. 5–7 ἅ]ρ[μ]ατι δ' αὖτ[ιϲ | νίκην εἶλε πατὴρ ἐκ βασιλέω[ϲ] βασ[ι]λεύϲ | πατρὸς ἔχων ὄνομα 'with his chariot my father was victorious, a king son of a king with his father's name'. Indeed the author of the ἱππικά most probably wished to contribute to the motif that accorded the Ptolemaic children a perfect likeness to their parents, a motif that thanks to Theocritus 17 can be shown to be one of the main points of the public image that the Ptolemies adopted for themselves as a dynasty: see ll. 56–7 cited above, and 63–4 ὃ δὲ πατρὶ ἐοικώϲ | παῖϲ ἀγαπητὸς ἔγεντο 'in his father's likeness was he born, the beloved child'.[62]

Some of Posidippus' epigrams for Ptolemaic equestrian victories seem to have been conceived as inscriptions for commemorative statues of the horses and/or chariot (plus, sometimes, driver and victor) or seem to presuppose such a monumental context (see e.g. the deictic reference of AB 74. 14 and 87. 1, which implies that the living horses have become a statue). It is puzzling that, despite this, neither archaeology nor Pausanias offers any evidence for celebratory

[61] By 'programmatic' of course I do not mean that the epigram was composed to be programmatic, but that it was chosen to be the first of the royal ἱππικά, because it included and expressed in an especially clear form the main ideas of its author as an encomiast of the equestrian victories of the Ptolemaic dynasty.

[62] On which R. Hunter correctly comments: 'the Ptolemies are in fact a Hesiodic "limit case", in which the son, who (unusually) bears the same name as the father, is *very* like, perhaps identical with, the father': see *Theocritus: Encomium of Ptolemy Philadelphus* (Berkeley and Los Angeles, 2003), 138.

monuments in honour of victories by the Ptolemies or their leading officials in any of the Panhellenic sanctuaries of mainland Greece. Perhaps Ptolemaic monuments had simply disappeared by the time Pausanias got there. Alternatively, and more probably, Posidippus may have been celebrating the autonomous power of poetry by evoking a purely fictitious monumental tradition: the epigrams would, in normal circumstances, have been parallel to the commissioning of monumental statues by the Ptolemaic victors, but Posidippus may have autonomously constructed a κῦδος for the Ptolemies which did not depend upon the actuality of such commissions.

14

Posidippus, Poet of the Ptolemies

DOROTHY J. THOMPSON

'My family is from Pella' boasts the poet Posidippus; Ptolemy comes from Eordaea.[1] Both were Macedonians. It was, however, in Alexandria that the poet seems to have come to live and work—on the generous payroll, we may assume, of Ptolemy II Philadelphus.[2] What I plan to do in this study is to ask how far the poetry of Posidippus that survives is Macedonian poetry written for a Macedonian audience, though one transposed to a foreign land, how far was it aimed at a wider audience and whether—if at all—it was a more local, Egyptian, readership that the poet had in mind. After somewhat of a digression on the subject of Ptolemaic queens, in the end I shall suggest that although we may identify Egyptian aspects to his oeuvre these were neither significant nor important.[3] The poetry of Posidippus was Hellenistic poetry.

First, the Macedonian side to Posidippus. Here the most obvious and striking feature is how in his poetry the ruling dynasty of Egypt is regularly defined as Macedonian not simply as Greek. Writing later of Cleopatra VII, the last of the Ptolemies, Plutarch in his *Life of Antony* elaborated on her linguistic skills in contrast to those of other Ptolemies; she could converse with Ethiopians, Troglodytes, Hebrews, Arabs, Syrians, Medes, and Parthians. 'Preceding kings', he reported, 'had not tried to master even the Egyptian tongue and

I should like to proffer thanks to Colin Austin, Marco Fantuzzi, and Richard Hunter for particularly constructive comments on earlier versions of this chapter; several other colleagues and participants at the Cincinnati colloquium will recognize their input, for which I am also grateful.

[1] AB 118. 17, Πελλαῖον γένος ἁμόν; 88. 4, Ἐορδαία γέννα, with W. Clarysse, 'Ethnic Diversity and Dialect', 12, on the dialect of AB 88, and Bearzot, 'Πτολεμαῖος Μακεδών', on Ptolemy I (in her view contrasted to II) as a Macedonian.

[2] Theoc. 14. 59, Ptolemy as a generous paymaster; Ath. 11. 493 F–494 B, for scale of σύνταξις payments; cf. 12. 552 C, Panaretus received 12 talents a year from Ptolemy III Euergetes. An Alexandrian residence is accepted by Fraser, *Ptolemaic Alexandria*, i. 558.

[3] Throughout this more general discussion the new poems are integrated, as they must be, into the wider corpus.

some had even ceased to speak Macedonian (μακεδονίζειν)'.[4] With Posidippus, however, we are at the start—in the first hundred years of Ptolemaic rule—and the early Ptolemies were clear about the distinctiveness and superiority of their Macedonian heritage. So too is our poet. In the context of the Ptolemies, the repetition of 'Macedonian' is a striking and repeated feature of his poems. In 78. 14 it is the Macedonians (Macedonian women, I suspect) who are called on to celebrate the equestrian victories of the young Berenice and earlier members of her family.[5] In 82. 3 the same princess is characterized as the 'Macedonian child' when, at the Isthmian games, she once again finds herself victorious with her horses.[6] So too, her grandmother, Berenice I, the mother of Philadelphus who won the Olympic crown with her horses, was—so her horses remind us—a Macedonian.[7] Not only royalty but commoners too; Hegeso, who dedicated a fine linen scarf to Arsinoe Philadelphus is described as of Macedonian stock.[8] And when Posidippus addresses the Muses of Pella in old age, it is the Macedonians who are the first to be named as his readers.[9] Only twice in the full corpus do we find instead a mention of the wider category of Greeks. The great image of Zeus Soter on the Pharos of Alexandria is described as 'saviour of the Greeks'[10] and 'the chaste daughters of the Greeks', together with 'the men who work at sea', are named as worshippers at the shrine of Arsinoe-Aphrodite on Cape Zephyrium.[11] In both cases, a wider world was involved.

Before turning to consider further the non-Macedonian aspect of this poetry, I want briefly to consider some Ptolemaic queens. In the poetry of Posidippus, as elsewhere, the cult of Arsinoe–Aphrodite is given a prominent role. This was Arsinoe II, the second wife of Ptolemy II, Arsinoe Philadelphus who was also his sister.[12] It is to the goddess Philadelphus that various dedications are made: the

---

[4] Plu. *Ant.* 27. 3–4. On Doric as a 'prestige dialect', see Clarysse, 'Ethnic Diversity', 10–13, cf. Sens, 'Doricisms'.

[5] AB 78. 14, ὦ Μακέτα[ι]). For Μακέτα as the standard feminine form of Μακέδων in contemporary documents, see e.g. C. A. La'da, *Foreign Ethnics in Hellenistic Egypt* (Leuven, 2002), 207–9. Both Gell. *NA* 9. 3. 1 and Steph. Byz. s.v. Μακεδονία (cit. BG ad loc.) are much later. For women as addressees, cf. 116. 8.

[6] AB 82. 3–4, Μακέτην . . . παῖδα, cf. l. 6, μόνη βασιλίς.

[7] AB 87. 1–2, Βερενίκας . . . Μακέτας; cf. 88. 3–4, Ptolemy II, the son of a prize-winning mother (and father) is more specifically from Eordaea. On this use of the Macedonian epithet, see Fantuzzi, above, Ch. 13.   [8] AB 36. 8, γένος Μακέ[τη.

[9] AB 118. 15, ὄφρα με τιμήσωσι Μακηδόνες; note the masculine form. On the Macedonian emphasis, cf. Bingen, 'Le poète et les princes', 51, 55–9.

[10] AB 115. 1, Ἑλλήνων σωτῆρα; see Bing, 'Between Literature and the Monuments', 21–9, for this interpretation of what was involved in the dedication of Sostratus son of Dexiphanes.

[11] AB 116. 8, Ἑλλήνων ἁγναί . . . θυγατέρες.

[12] AB 114 may celebrate their marriage.

Naucratite linen scarf already mentioned, a lyre, probably the bowl from which the former slave Epicratis drank on her manumission, and other dedications.[13] Her statue stood at the centre of the fountain described in the poem of the Ptolemaic teachers' handbook (the so-called *Livre d'écolier*),[14] and the temple which Callicrates of Samos put up to her on Cape Zephyrium and where she was worshipped as Aphrodite, Cypris, or Aphrodite Euploia is the subject of several of Posidippus' poems.[15] Posidippus here joins other Alexandrians in fêting this queen and there is no doubt that in Egypt the cults of Arsinoe had a double resonance (both Greek and Egyptian), as also a double form. Arsinoe was first divinized together with her brother-husband during her lifetime when, in 272/1 BC, these Sibling Gods were added to the Alexandrian cult of Alexander as the Theoi Adelphoi. The first known priest in this developing dynastic cult was no other than the same Callicrates, son of Boiscus.[16] Like his wife, Ptolemy II could now be characterized as 'both a god and a king'.[17] Later, following her death, came the Alexandrian cult of Arsinoe Philadelphus, the brother-loving goddess with her own dynastic priestess, a basket-bearer or κανηφόρος.[18] This was the Greek side. The introduction of the cult of the queen to all the temples of Egypt is recorded in the Mendes decree,[19] and it was here, in an Egyptian context, that this queen cult really took off.[20] This was the first of many others and, in the divinization of their queens, the Ptolemies apparently touched a native nerve. It is the Greek side of things, however, to which the poetry of Posidippus refers.

[13] AB 36. 1, 5, linen scarf; 37. 1, 7, lyre; 38. 1, bowl (without epithet Philadelphus); 119. 2, Philadelphus Cypris.

[14] AB 113. 13, cf. O. Guéraud and P. Jouguet, *Un livre d'écolier du IIIe siècle avant J.-C.* (Cairo, 1938); the authorship of this particular poem remains disputed though the emphasis on the different stones built into the fountain is reminiscent of the λιθικά.

[15] AB 39. 2; 116. 6–7; 119. 2.

[16] W. Clarysse and G. Van der Veken, *The Eponymous Priests of Ptolemaic Egypt*, 4; cf. AB 39. 3–4; 74. 12. For Callicrates, see H. Hauben, *Callicrates of Samos* (Leuven, 1970); Bingen, 'La victoire pythique de Callicratès de Samos'; Bing, 'Posidippus and the Admiral'.

[17] AB 63. 9, θεοῦ θ' ἅμα καὶ βασιλῆος.

[18] The first certainly recorded κανηφόρος remains Aristomache daughter of Aristomachos in 267/6, P. Louvre dem. 2424, see Clarysse and Van der Veken, *Eponymous Priests*, 6–7; cf. D. M. Bailey, 'The canephore of Arsinoe Phildelphos', for the office.

[19] K. Sethe, *Hieroglyphische Urkunden der griechisch-römischen Zeit*, ii (Leipzig, 1904), 41. 7–42. 1, 'The king ordered the installation of her statue in all the temples. This pleased their priests, for they were aware of her noble attitude towards the gods and of her excellent deeds to the benefit of all people . . . Her name was proclaimed as: beloved of the ram, the goddess who loves her brother, Arsinoe'; cf. J. Quaegebeur, 'Cleopatra VII and the Cults of the Ptolemaic Queens', 43.

[20] See D. J. Thompson, *Memphis under the Ptolemies* (Princeton, 1988), 126–32; Quaegebeur, 'Cleopatra VII'.

The importance of Macedonian queens has been much discussed in recent years. The independent status that queens enjoyed in Macedon was taken over by Ptolemaic queens; these Macedonian women often played a significant role in court and other matters.[21] The new poems of Posidippus will surely join the dossier, especially his immortal cry of τοῦτο μέγα ('this is the great thing') from her son describing the chariot victory at Olympia of his mother, Berenice I, who won the race as/though (?) a woman.[22] Nevertheless, despite the credit she gained, this was not the first equestrian victory at Olympia won by a female victor. Spartan Cynisca took that crown, as Posidippus recalls elsewhere.[23] Ptolemaic queens played many roles: Arsinoe II was held to have directed her brother's Aegean policy even after her death;[24] queens might enjoy their own cults;[25] some of them owned ships (Nile barges for the transport of grain)[26] or land;[27] and, now we know even better than before, third-century queens had racing stables.

Until recent years a regular summer picture in the British press has been of the Queen, Elizabeth II, together with Queen Elizabeth the Queen Mother, attending the races at Ascot. Successful racing stables are the stuff of queens and kings, today as in the Hellenistic world and, as now, a Ptolemaic princess was prepared to travel to watch her horses win.[28] What is different in the modern world is the acceptable level of public glorification for a monarch's success in the field. No modern poet laureate would boast of royal racing success to the degree that we find in these poems. For Posidippus, in contrast, equestrian success offers an opportunity to praise his immediate patrons and their family members. But who exactly were these? Which races did each of them win, and who were the members of the royal family who owned the winning horses? The following royal victories are recorded in these poems.

---

[21] See Pomeroy, *Women in Hellenistic Egypt* and, especially, Carney, *Women and Monarchy in Macedonia*, with references to her earlier work.

[22] AB 88. 5–6, μάτηρ εἷλε γυνὰ νίκαν ἅρματι, τοῦτο μέγα.

[23] AB 87, Berenice's mares make a virtue of her not being first; Cynisca's fame is now eclipsed. On Cynisca, see M. Fantuzzi, above, Ch. 13.

[24] Dittenberger, *Syll.*[3] 434/5. 16–17.

[25] Quaegebeur, 'Cleopatra VII' with Clarysse and Van der Veken, *Eponymous priests*.

[26] Hauben, 'Le transport fluvial en Égypte ptolémaïque'.

[27] e.g. P. Tebt. III 720 (247–245 BC); *BGU* XIV 2438. 13, 16, 20, 42, 48, 53, 76 (late 2nd c. BC), with J. Rowlandson (ed.), *Women and Society in Greek and Roman Egypt* (Cambridge, 1998), 25–41. Papyrus editions are abbreviated as in J. F. Oates et al., *Checklist of Editions of Greek, Latin, Demotic and Coptic Papyri, Ostraca and Tablets*, 5th edn. (Oakville, CT, 2001).

[28] AB 82. 5, Berenice (described as παῖς) attends the games with her father Ptolemy II, σὺν πατρὶ Π[τολ]ε̣[μ]α̣ίωι.

ROYAL RACING SUCCESSES

Ptolemy I Soter

78. 3–4, with chariot at Olympia (Pisa)

Berenice (I), wife of Ptolemy I and mother of Ptolemy II (and Arsinoe II)

78. 5, with chariot at Olympia (Pisa)

87, Olympic victory (Pisa), in which she has eclipsed Cynisca, celebrated by (statues of) her mares

88. 1–2, 5–6, notable Olympic victory with chariot (B. as wife of Ptolemy I and mother of Ptolemy II, μάτηρ . . . γυνά).

Ptolemy II Philadelphus

78. 6–7, Olympic victory, as for his parents (Ptolemy and Berenice), and for Arsinoe and Berenice

88, celebration of Olympic victory in chariot-race together with that of his father and mother

Arsinoe

78.7–8, triple victory for harnessed horses in one contest at Olympia[29]

Berenice

78.10, 13–14, victory with four-horse chariot at Olympia (B. described as παρθένιος [βαcιλί]c and βαcιλευούcηc)

79, victory (ἀθλοφορεῖ) in all races at Nemea involving horses and chariot (B. as παρθένοc ἡ βαcίλιccα); 80, probably the same victory (B. as παιδὶ μόνηι)

81, possibly B. (not named) wins Doric celery-crown with four-horse chariot for a second time (at Nemea or Isthmus)

82, four-horse chariot victory in Isthmian games (B., accompanied by father Ptolemy, described as [πολυcτέφα]νον Μακέτην . . . παῖδα, μόνη βαcιλίc, and as member of an ἀθλ[οφ]όρον δῶμα)

The winning streak is presented as very much a family affair. AB 78 is the clearest example of this expression. Victorious at Olympia, it is Berenice who speaks:[30]

> My grandfather [Ptole]my [won] with his chariot
> driving his team on the race-courses at Pisa,

---

[29] See BG on XII. 26–7 for details of the three races involved.   [30] Trans. Austin in AB.

> as did Berenice, my father's mother. Then again with his chariot
>   my father was victorious, a king son of a king
>   with his father's name.

She continues with Arsinoe. Finally she returns to her own victory and, if we accept the supplements, she describes herself as 'light of women' and 'virgin' (or is it 'maiden?) queen' ([γυ]ναικῶν . . . [φέγγοϲ] παρθένιοϲ [βαϲιλί]ϲ). Again we note the emphasis on the female side of the Ptolemaic house. This is a house of winners (ἀθλοφόροι) with children's children winning prizes. But who is Berenice?

Understandably, given the existing literary tradition, the *editio princeps* identifies this Berenice with the wife of Ptolemy III Euergetes, daughter of Magas of Cyrene and Apama, whose Lock was dedicated in the temple of Arsinoe (II) Zephyritis before being transported to the heavens. Callimachus, in writing of this miraculous event, calls that queen (Berenice II) the daughter of Arsinoe.[31] Hyginus, who later wrote on astronomy, mentions the Olympic horses of the same queen.[32] Contemporary inscriptions show how Cyrenaean Berenice was fictively adopted into the Ptolemaic royal line as the sister-wife of Ptolemy III.[33] And when, in 211/10 BC under Ptolemy IV, she acquired her own dynastic priestess, this priestess was called her ἀθλοφόροϲ. Berenice, the queen of Ptolemy III, was certainly a prize-winner.[34] The argument for identifying Posidippus' Berenice with the queen of Ptolemy III, already strong, appears to gain further support from P. Lille 82 = *SH* 254, where Berenice, victorious at the Nemean games, is addressed as 'bride, sacred blood-descendant of the Sibling Gods', νύμφα, κα[ϲιγνή]των ἱερὸν αἷμα θεῶν; the scholion included with this text calls the winning chariot that of a queen, βαϲιλίϲϲηϲ ἅρμα.[35] This scholion laboriously makes the point that the queen involved was actually Berenice, daughter of Magas rather than of the Sibling Gods, and in his discussion of this text Peter Parsons first suggested that this victory ode came from the start of *Aitia*,

---

[31] Callimachus fr. 110. 45 Pf., Arsinoe as μητρὸϲ ϲέο, cf. 228. 47 for the Athos connection; it is the adoption of Berenice into her husband's family with the consequent acquisition of two new parents which must lie behind the name Arsinoe used by Justin 26. 3 for Magas' wife Apama.

[32] Hyginus, *Astr.* 2. 24.

[33] *OGIS* i. 56. 7–8 (238 BC), Ptolemy (III), son of Ptolemy (II) and Arsinoe (II), the Sibling Gods, and Queen Berenice (II), his sister and wife, the Benefactor Gods. Since Ptolemy III was actually the son of Arsinoe I, fictive ancestry was not limited to his queen, cf. Σ Theoc. 17. 128 with W. Huss, *Ägypten in hellenistischer Zeit 332–30 v. Chr.* (Munich, 2001), 335.

[34] Clarysse and Van der Veken, *Eponymous Priests*, 16–17.

[35] *SH* 254. 1–2 with AB 78. 9, γένοϲ ἱερόν (BG on XII 28–9), cf. *SH* 255. 23, βαϲιλίϲϲηϲ ἅρμα.

book 3, thus forming a structural link for the second two books of the work with *The Lock* at the end of book 4.[36] Both involved the same queen and that queen was Berenice II, the wife of Ptolemy III. Here, in the poetry of Cyrenean Callimachus, we find commemorated a victorious horseracing Queen Berenice (II), who was fictively adopted more closely into the Ptolemaic royal house than her actual descent might allow. But is this the same victorious Berenice as in the poems of Posidippus?

In tentatively suggesting another, more literal, identification for Posidippus' young victor Berenice as the real daughter of Ptolemy (II) and of his first wife Arsinoe (I), and sister of two brothers (Ptolemy III and Lysimachus), I base this suggestion on details within the relevant poems. First is the emphasis on the youth of Berenice. This young Macedonian horseowner is, as we have seen, twice described as παῖc.[37] Further, at Nemea, she is also termed παρθένοc,[38] a word that always describes a woman who has not married.[39] Finally, there is the detail in 82.5 that her father Ptolemy (II) accompanied his daughter to the races when (as a child, παῖc) she was victorious at the Isthmian games.

What then of παῖc and παρθένοc? Berenice II, the daughter of Magas of Cyrene, married Ptolemy III either when or shortly before he succeeded his father on 28 January 246 BC.[40] Berenice quickly proved a remarkably fertile wife. Shortly after his accession to the throne, the king left for Syria to fight Seleucus II in what is known as the Third Syrian or the Laodicean War. On his return in late 245 or early 244, as we learn from a dedication that they made there to Isis and Harpocrates, the royal couple visited Philae on the southern border of Egypt. Already they had more than one child.[41] Pregnancy had started soon for this queen, who speedily gave birth to many children.[42] But the Berenice who gained victory in those races was

[36] Parsons, 'Callimachus: Victoria Berenices', 49–50.
[37] AB 80. 4 (Nemea), παιδὶ μόνηι; 82. 3–4 (Isthmus), τῆν . . . Μακέτην . . . παῖδα, accompanied by her father.
[38] AB 79. 1 (Nemea), παρθένοc ἡ βαcίλιccα, cf. 78.10 (Olympia), παρθένιοc [βαcιλί]c.
[39] See G. Sissa, *Greek Virginity* (Cambridge, MA, 1990), 76–7, on παρθένοc; the term denotes 'the expectant hiatus between childhood and marriage'; S. Lewis, *The Athenian Woman* (London, 2002), 27–8, 'as yet unmarried'.
[40] For Ptolemy III's succession on 25 Dios = 28 Jan. 246 BC (*OGIS* i. 56. 15–16), see Pap. Lugd.-Bat. XXI 274; for the marriage, A. Laronde, *Cyrène et la Libye hellénistique* (Paris, 1987), 382 (*OGIS* i. 54. 6 records Libya as inherited by Ptolemy III from his father) and G. Hölbl, *A History of the Ptolemaic Empire* (London, 2001), 46.
[41] *I. Philae* 4. 3, τεκνία; for the reading, date, and context (before the adoption of the cult-title Euergetes), see Bingen, '*I. Philae* I 4'; others date this visit to 242, see Clarysse, 'The Ptolemies Visiting the Egyptian Chora', in L. Mooren (ed.), *Politics, Administration and Society in the Hellenistic and Roman World*, 37–8.

just a child, a παῖς; and when her horses won at the Isthmian games, as already mentioned, we possess the telling detail that her 'father' Ptolemy accompanied his young daughter to the races.[43] If it is the same Berenice who is involved here then she must, at least for our poet, have been accepted into her new family some years before her marriage and the death of Ptolemy II.[44] Indeed, as suggested in the *editio princeps*, the equestrian victories of this princess would seem likely to have preceded both these events.[45]

Posidippus' Berenice is a young unmarried victor. She is also described as a 'queen', βαcίλιccα. That in itself should cause no trouble since in Ptolemaic (and later) parlance βαcίλιccα was also used for 'princess'. This can most clearly be found in the case of yet another Berenice, the daughter of Ptolemy III and Berenice II, who died during the course of a priestly synod held at Canopus in 238 BC. Her subsequent mummification and deification is described in detail towards the end of the Canopus decree, a decree of the priests made in honour of her parents, Ptolemy III Euergetes and Berenice II:[46]

And since, while the priests from the whole country, who annually forgathered in his presence, were still in attendance on the king, it happened that the daughter born of the Theoi Euergetai, King Ptolemy and Queen Berenice, called Berenice, who was also immediately recognized as βαcίλιccα (in this context, 'princess'), while a maiden (παρθένοc) was all of a sudden translated to the everlasting firmament . . .

Here we meet a maiden βαcίλιccα from the next generation whose parents are both alive and ruling. That the description of Berenice by Posidippus as βαcιλεύουcα and βαcιλίc might refer to a princess Berenice rather than to a queen need cause us no problems.

Magas, the ruler of Cyrene, had long been hostile to Ptolemy II but shortly before his death the two half-brothers were reconciled. To mark the reconciliation Magas' daughter Berenice was now betrothed to Ptolemy's son, the future Ptolemy III.[47] Magas died sometime

---

[42] C. Bennett, 'The Children of Ptolemy III and the Date of the Exedra of Thermos', 145, 6 children in 6 or 7 years.

[43] AB 82. 4–5. Reference to an earlier joint Cyrenaean/Ptolemaic visit to the races before the two kings' reconciliation seems implausible in the extreme; such a scenario would also involve an anachronistic ascription of the father–daughter relationship.

[44] Unless Posidippus is anachronistic in his reference to a Ptolemaic affiliation, as suggested by Bingen, 'Posidippe: le poète et les princes', 51–2.

[45] BG, pp. 205–6.

[46] *OGIS* i. 56. 46–8; cf. BG on XII. 34. For βαcίλιccα, see now Bennett, 'Children of Ptolemy III', 143.

[47] Paus. 1. 6; Justin 26. 3. 2.

around 250 BC. It is hard to be more precise given the paucity of information that survives.[48] His death was followed by the attempt of his Seleucid wife Apama, daughter of Antiochus I, to replace their daughter's Ptolemaic fiancé with one more favourable to her side of the family. Demetrius the Fair ('Kalos') was summoned to Cyrene from Macedon but murdered some time later when he lived up to his name and was caught in bed with his future mother-in-law. In the typically spicy account of Justin, Berenice was personally involved in his death.[49] So, in the words of Catullus, a young girl (*parva virgo*) had committed a crime that was good (*bonum facinus*).[50] If this same Berenice was the victor hailed by Posidippus we must now imagine that Ptolemy II acted speedily to take the young girl, his future daughter-in-law, into his protection and away from home. On this reconstruction, he will have accompanied her with her racing teams to Greece where, in the spring of 248 at the Isthmian games, her Cyrenaean horses proved their worth.[51] Once safely away in Greece, the young girl—it would appear—had remarkable success with her horses, successfully competing at the Isthmian, Olympic, and Nemean games.

The timetable involved in this scenario is possible, just even plausible, but it is a very, very crowded one. Negotiations with Demetrius in Macedon, his arrival in Cyrene, his affair with the mother of his intended bride, and his subsequent murder must all have taken place in a very short time indeed since, to be present at the Isthmian games in the spring of 248, Ptolemy and Berenice will have had to journey north with her horses before the closure of the seas in October 249.[52] Such a reconstruction would leave Cyrene vulnerable, without a ruler at a critical stage.[53] It would also involve the 60-year-old king of Egypt, who suffered from gout, making quite an adventurous

<hr/>

[48] For this date, based on a (rounded?) 50 years in Ath. 12. 550 B, and the mention of Magas in the rock edict of King Aśoka, see F. Chamoux, 'Le roi Magas', 22; Bagnall, *The Administration of the Ptolemaic Possessions outside Egypt*, 26.

[49] Justin 26. 3. 3–8, where Apama has become Arsinoe. For this episode, see Laronde, *Cyrène*, 380; Huss, *Ägypten*, 333–4.

[50] Catullus 66. 26–7, presumably based on Callimachus.

[51] See BG, p. 206, for a possible timetable.

[52] L. Casson, *Ancient Trade and Society* (Detroit, 1984), 25, seas closed October–April. As implied by the editors (p. 206, with added '?'), a Nemean victory in 249 is even more unlikely. For a late summer date (September) for the Nemean games, see now P. Perlman, 'The Calendrical Position of the Nemean Games', with S. D. Lambert, 'Parerga II'.

[53] This might then be the occasion when the Megalopolitans Ecdemus/Ecdelus and Demophanes were invited in, bringing 'freedom' and 'stability', Plb. 10. 22. 2–3; Plu. *Phil.* 1. 3–4, cf. F. W. Walbank, *A Historical Commentary on Polybius*, ii (Oxford, 1967), 223–4; Laronde, *Cyrène*, 381–2.

journey across the seas somewhat late in his life.[54] More worrying-
ly, and this is where I started, this identification assumes a fictive
adoption made even before the young Berenice was married. We are
left with the question of whether Berenice, the young bride-to-be of
Ptolemy III, really can be the παῖc and παρθένοc of Posidippus.

There is an understandable tendency when possible to identify the
new with the known, and the world of these Hellenistic poets was
certainly one in which poets vied with one another in compositions
on the same theme. Berenice of Posidippus is thus assumed to be
same as the Berenice of Callimachus (and of course Catullus), despite
the difficulties involved. This, then, is where I should like to try to
fly my kite, in making an alternative suggestion. The most straight-
forward identification for our young princess would be to take all the
details of these poems at face value and to assume that horseracing
and victory at pan-Hellenic events formed a regular part of life for
most Ptolemaic princesses and queens, not just for those that we
already know of. After all, before the publication of our new papyrus,
neither Queen Berenice I nor Arsinoe was known to have owned race-
horses.[55] There is another young princess Berenice who might be
the subject of Posidippus' poems, and she was the true daughter of
Ptolemy II. She is, as mentioned above, the young Berenice who left
Egypt in 252 BC when she married Antiochus II of Syria. Berenice,
daughter of Ptolemy II, and Berenice, daughter of Magas, may in
their different times both have been ἀθλοφόροι. Both may have been
celebrated by contemporary poets.

If my suggested identification for Berenice is accepted, we need
to rethink the dating both of Berenice's victories and of Posidippus'
celebratory poems. The only relevant date that we should know for
sure is when Princess Berenice left home. In spring 252 BC, already
termed βαcίλιccα in a contemporary papyrus, the daughter of Arsinoe
I and Ptolemy II was escorted (again?) by her father, this time to the
borders of his kingdom, to be given in marriage to Antiochus II of
Syria, so marking the end of the Second Syrian War.[56] On my inter-
pretation, the equestrian poems would predate 252 when Berenice
became a Seleucid. And she is the youngest in her line to be celebrated

---

[54] Ath. 12 536 E, gout; Str. 17. 1. 5 C 789, more general bodily ἀcθένεια.

[55] See now AB 78. 8.

[56] Jerome, *In Dan.* 11. 6 (termed 'dowry-bringer', *phernophoros*); cf. P.Cairo Zen. II 59242.
4–7 (Nov.–Dec. 253), preparation of galleys; 59251. 1–3 (April 252 BC), Artemidorus (court
doctor) and Apollonius (διοικητής) are back in Alexandria after accompanying the princess
(l. 2, βαcίλιccα) to Sidon. For this princess perhaps commemorated in Berenice Panchrysos, see
J. Desanges, 'Bérénice "comblée d'or"', 1195. See now Criscuolo, 'Agoni e politica', 328–31,
for the same identification made independently.

by our poet.[57] 252 BC, therefore, serves as the only certain date *ante quem* the new poems in the Milan papyrus should be placed.

At Royal Ascot in Berkshire in June others besides royalty can compete though, in the words of the homepage, 'only the privileged have access to the royal enclosure'.[58] Others come to share the excitement of the races and there are other racehorse owners. So it was in Alexandria, though for Alexandrians the races were often further away, across the sea in mainland Greece. Who the 'privileged' might be in a Ptolemaic context is also to be found in Posidippus' equestrian poems. For among the collection of victory odes is one for Callicrates of Samos, the well-known nauarch of the Nesiotic League under Ptolemy II and, like Sostratus son of Dexiphanes from Cnidus who dedicated the statue to Zeus Soter on the Pharos,[59] a loyal member of the royal bureaucracy. We have already met him dedicating the temple on Cape Zephyrium to Arsinoe-Aphrodite and officiating as the first dynastic priest in the cult of the Sibling Gods. Here he competes at the Pythian games in a hotly contested four-horse chariot race.[60] The result of the race is disputed but in the end the victory goes to Callicrates, who loyally dedicates a commemorative bronze statue to the Sibling Gods, the Theoi Adelphoi, whom he serves. He may also have paid for the poem. A fine cameo this makes of what it was to be a Ptolemaic courtier.

There are other loyal servants who appear in these poems—certainly the doctor Medeus of Olynthus[61] and, most probably, Etearchus of poem 76. The name Etearchus is widely found,[62] but not in fact in Egypt. In the *Prosopographia Ptolemaica*, just one certain Etearchus is listed in the index and he is the well-known nomarch who formed part of Ptolemy II's development team in the Fayum, that reclamation area newly named the Arsinoite nome.[63] Etearchus, son of Cleon and brother of Damis and Sostratus, is known to have been a citizen of Alexandria, a member of the Helen deme. Could he be the same as our horseowner?

Two further details are of interest here: the games at which Etearchus competes and his horse. First, the games. The immediate victory for

---

[57] Bingen, 'Posidippe: le poète et les princes', 59, notes the absence of reference to the early euergetic ideology of the reign of Ptolemy III. Berenice/Cypris of AB 141 is most probably Berenice I, cf. Theoc. 15. 106–8.

[58] www.royal-ascot.2001.co.uk.

[59] AB 115. 2. On Sostratus' role as ambassador, see Huss, *Ägypten*, 208–9.

[60] AB 74. 12, with Bing, 'Posidippus and the Admiral'.

[61] AB 95. 5, identified by Bing, 'Medeios of Olynthos'.

[62] So BG on XII 12, based on *LGPN*.

[63] For full references, see Pap.Lugd.-Bat. XXI A, Prosopography, p. 328.

which the ode was written would seem to be a Pythian victory which came at the culmination of a successful racing career. However, as we learn from Posidippus, it was not just Greek games that Etearchus attended with his horses. Winner at the Isthmian games and twice at Nemea, he also entered locally, in the races of the Ptolemaia, the Alexandrian dynastic festival set up by Ptolemy II in honour of his parents, the Saviour Gods, in 279/8 BC. These games were officially described as isolympic or equal to the best of old Greece;[64] in competing here, Etearchus lends support to Ptolemaic claims. Secondly, his horse. The horse of Etearchus victorious at Delphi was an Arab,[65] and in this choice, as in the Ptolemaia, Etearchus shows himself a true Alexandrian, happy to win glory in the local games and enjoying the best of neighbouring lands. Arab horses will have compared well with those from Thessaly, and in the choice of horses these men were connoisseurs.[66]

Here we may leave the royal family and their circle, the ruling family from Macedon, connected—as they claimed—with the Argeads, whose auspicious eagle and thunderbolt became the royal symbol of Ptolemaic coinage,[67] and those courtiers and bureaucrats who came from elsewhere, from the Aegean—from Samos, Cnidus, or other islands—and from the coast of Asia Minor.[68] And, finally, we may turn to consider the role of Posidippus not just as a Macedonian poet and a court poet of the Ptolemaic empire but as a poet whose work in Egypt reflected to some degree the country where he lived.

The city of Alexandria plays a prominent role in the work of this

---

[64] Dittenberger, *Syll.*[3] 390. 21, isolympic; on the date, see D. J. Thompson, 'Philadelphus' Procession', 381–8. See also Posidippus, AB 143 (Ath. 10. 415 A–B), on Aglais, daughter of Megacles, who blew the trumpet for the great procession at the start of this festival.

[65] Arabia (with Arabs) was the term used for the desert (with its inhabitants) east of the Nile (Hdt. 2. 8. 1; 15. 1; Str. 17. 1. 21) but the horses probably came from Arabia proper, cf. AB 10. 9–10.

[66] As visible e.g. among the Zenon papyri: P. Cairo Zen. I 59075. 3, 9 (257 BC), Toubias, the Ammanite chief, sends the king rare animals including horses, cf. V 59802. 2, 18; I 59093. 4 (257 BC), problems in buying a new horse; II 59225. 3, 5, 8 (253 BC), Artemidorus the court doctor tries to acquire a black stallion for breeding; III 59393. 2–6 (mid 3rd cent. BC), problems over price of the 'big horse'; IV 59586. 4 (mid-3rd c. BC), purchase of better horses, perhaps for racing; P. Lond. VII 2053. 1–3 bis (255/246 BC), Zenon's horse-breeding interests; in addition, many accounts of feed. It may be significant that among the literary extracts in the Zenon papyri is an extract from Euripides, *Hippolytus*, where Hippolytus is sent into exile and, following the shoreline with his horses, is overwhelmed by Poseidon, Pap. Lugd.-Bat. XX 15. Of course not all horses were racehorses; most mentioned in the papyri will have belonged to cavalrymen.

[67] Cf. AB 31. 1–3; see too the Alexandrian demotic Argeades and the Arsinoite village Argeas.

[68] Cf. AB 118. 15–16, where the audience of Posidippus in old age is characterized as 'both the [islanders] and the neighbours of all the Asiatic shore'.

poet, not just its festivals but particularly its monuments. It is hard not to conclude that Posidippus once lived here. Poems like that on the Pharos, the shrine of Arsinoe-Zephyritis, and that on the Alexandrian fountain, were used in the teaching of Greek and Greek culture in the many schools of Egypt. In the days before photography or film, it was poems like these that allowed the inhabitants of up-country Egypt to envisage Alexandria, the great new capital city.[69] In the somewhat humorous account in AB 130 of the drunken lover who ventures through thieves there may lurk a reference to the dangers of the Alexandrian streets before the successful clean-up of Ptolemy II.[70] The 'bearded snake' whose eye was once the gemstone carved with a tiny chariot recalls the city's guardian spirit, the Agathos Daimon.[71] Finally, Alexandria was a city of immigrants and we sometimes find echoes of this in the work of Posidippus, an immigrant himself.[72]

So much for Alexandria. In contrast, up-country Egypt does not have a prominent role. Local Aswan granite, Syenitis, is mentioned in the poem on the fountain that featured Arsinoe, if indeed this is by Posidippus.[73] As well as the (pink)-flecked granite of Aswan, in the group of omen poems we meet the black Theban bird,[74] which could be the screeching sea eagle then regularly seen in the south.[75] For an Egyptian reader of these poems, the identification of the vulture of AB 27 as the Egyptian goddess Nechbet would seem inescapable.[76] And the very first omen of all involves the falcon, whom Egyptians recognized as Horus.[77] The best portents carry a range of different meanings; a double cultural reading of these birds might render them more efficacious. What else do we find from Egypt? The fine linen scarf dedicated by Hegeso to Arsinoe derived from Naucratis,[78] and Naucratite Doricha (alias Rhodopis) is the subject of another

[69] See D. J. Thompson, 'Ptolemaios and "The Lighthouse"'; ead., *Memphis under the Ptolemies*, 261; *UPZ* I 78. 28–39, for Ptolemaeus' vision of the city (and perhaps the Pharos in particular) in a dream.
[70] Cf. Theoc. 15. 47–50.
[71] AB 15. 1–3.
[72] AB 102. 3–4, the Cretan Menoetius is (understandably) short of words on foreign soil, ὀλιγορρήμων ὡς ἐπὶ ξενίης, cf. 94. 3, another death away from home, ἐπὶ ξείνης.
[73] AB 113. 8–9, Cυηνὶς cτικτή. Cf. Plin. *HN* 36. 63–4.
[74] AB 24. 1; see BG on IV 24, comparing D.S. 1. 87. 9, for the royal eagle (perhaps Mut's vulture) worshipped by the Thebans.
[75] *Halieëtos vocifer*, see J. Boessneck, *Die Tierwelt des alten Ägypten* (Munich, 1988), 93, with pl. 153b; this identification is very tentative.
[76] On Nechbet, particularly sacred in Kom Ombo, as protector goddess in childbirth, see *LdÄ* iv. 366–7.   [77] AB 21. 2; cf. Gutzwiller, Ch. 15, pp. 306–7.
[78] AB 36. 2. The somewhat surprising martial form of Arsinoe, appearing to Hegeso in a dream, is reminiscent of Athene/Neith, the local Naucratite goddess, cf. *LdÄ* iv. 492–4.

poem.[79] Naucratis, however, was the one Greek city of Egypt which preceded Alexandria. These references are not to Egyptian Egypt. Indeed, such references as we do find here provide barely more than local colour, a mere handful of allusions to the new homeland of the Ptolemies—nothing more.

The Ptolemaic empire and neighbouring lands have a more important role. Etearchus' horse, we noted, was an Arab and the wider range of allusions in Posidippus reflects the wider world over which the early Ptolemies ruled or with which they came into contact.[80] For Greeks this was a new Eastern world, full of wonders, exotic beings, and precious goods, the fruits of empire as displayed in the great procession of Ptolemy II that we know from Athenaeus.[81] When the explorer Philo voyaged down the Red Sea coast he sent back a large topaz for Queen Berenice I.[82] In writing on gems, Posidippus was in some way cataloguing the wealth of the Ptolemaic kingdom and the broader world around; this is a standard imperial enterprise. With the conquest of Alexander, Persia had been conquered for the Greeks.[83] In the post-Alexander world, an Asian woman who perished during her sixth confinement could have her epitaph composed by a poet from Greece.[84] With Alexander, India too had entered the purview of the Greeks. This land made a great impression and remained a point of reference. The great procession at the Ptolemaia included a float that featured Alexander's return from India. Here, there were Indian women dressed as captives on display, Indian hunting dogs, and all-white Indian cattle; the dining room of the ceremonial barge of Ptolemy IV was surrounded by columns made of Indian stone.[85] It is not at all surprising to find in Posidippus reference to the river Hydaspes where Alexander fought with Porus, as recalled on a commemorative issue of coins minted in Babylon.[86] The Indus joined the Macedonian Strymon in the list of rivers that children learnt at school.[87]

---

[79] AB 122; 146, mentioned in his *Aithiopia*; cf. Ath. 13. 596 C.

[80] From the Ptolemaic empire: 45. 1, Marathus (Phoenicia); 46. 2, Phocaea; 47. 5, Paphos; 51. 2, perhaps Caria; 54. 3, Cyrene; see further P. Bing, above, Ch. 7.

[81] Ath. 5. 196 A–203 B.   [82] Plin. *HN* 37. 108.

[83] AB 31. 3–7, Athene provides a good omen for Alexander; 35. 3–4, Alexander's triple victory; 65. 3–4, the power of Alexander's image to put Persians to flight; 4. 2, ring of Darius; 8. 3, image of Darius.   [84] AB 56. 7, 'an Asian woman'.

[85] Ath. 5. 200 D, float with elephants, 201 A, captive women, B, dogs, C, cows, 205 E, Indian stone.

[86] AB 1. 1, Hydaspes; cf. A. Stewart, *Faces of Power*, fig. 68, for this Babylonian five-shekel issue.

[87] Guéraud and Jouguet, *Livre d'écolier*, 9–10 with plate II; the editors suggest this may be the Carian Indus.

Posidippus' view of the world is extensive. It is from Mysian Olympus, Arabia, from Persia or the Persian gulf and from India that those gems and semi-precious stones he writes about in his λιθικά originate.[88] The great crag of the Capherean gulf in south-east Euboea seems somewhat out of place in this group of poems.[89] It takes the last poem of the λιθικά to bring these two worlds together: Poseidon, lord of (Euboean) Geraestus who destroyed the town of Helice, has recently threatened Eleusis, the suburb of Alexandria.[90] Now the god is called upon to protect and keep free from earthquakes 'together with the islands, the land and shores of Ptolemy'.[91]

The audience of Posidippus was limited to Greek-speakers, but the world of the poet, like that of the Ptolemies, was not just Macedon or even Egypt; it was a wider and an even more inclusive world—the land of Egypt, the Greek world of the Aegean, as also Macedon and, now, the new lands of the east. So, in the words of Posidippus, Aphrodite's haunts were some (though not all) of them new—Cyprus, Cythera, Miletus, and the fair plain of Syria.[92] All this makes Posidippus not just a Macedonian poet, not an Egyptian poet, but—I would argue—a true Alexandrian poet whose concern is the wider Hellenistic world.

---

[88] AB 17. 1 (magnetic stone from Mysian Olympus); 14. 3 (Cilician plain); 7. 1 (Arabian mountains), 16. 1–3 (Arabian grey rock-crystal), 10. 9–10 (a Nabataean king of Arab troops, engraved on cylinder); 4. 5 (Persian grey stone), 5. 1–2 (lapis lazuli, a Persian semi-precious stone), cf. 13. 3–4 (image of Persian lion); 11. 2–3 (mother-of-pearl from the Persian gulf); 2. 4 (India?), cf. 1. 1 (Indus), 8. 5 (Indian rubies).

[89] AB 19. 9–10. On this and other λιθικά poems, see Hunter, 'Notes on the *Lithika* of Poseidippos'.

[90] AB 20. 3–4.

[91] Ibid. 5–6.

[92] AB 139.

PART FOUR

A HELLENISTIC BOOK AND ITS LITERARY CONTEXT

15

The Literariness of the Milan Papyrus or 'What Difference a Book?'

KATHRYN GUTZWILLER

The comic goatherd of Theocritus' *Idyll* 3, exasperated by Amaryllis' unwillingness to peek out of her cave and acknowledge his wooing, delivers the following threat: 'You'll make me shred into little pieces (λεπτά) the ivy garland that I'm keeping for you, the one I plaited from rosebuds and sweet-scented celery' (3. 21–3). By dwelling lovingly on the sensual qualities of the flowers and plants of his wreath, the goatherd suggests that its beauty derives from its individual components. But he also suggests, by his threat to dismantle it, that the object is much more valuable as a plaited whole, that its broader meaning lies in the workmanship he brought to bear upon it, as a symbol of his devotion to Amaryllis. The poetic garlands of antiquity of course suffered a similar fate, to be shredded λεπτά, into little pieces. The single epigrams that formed the debris from these collections were mostly lost, sometimes preserved by citation or by removal to a new garland, showing clearly that these poems were valued as separate literary objects, admired for their concise intricacy. But now comes the Milan papyrus, offering an opportunity to understand Hellenistic epigrams, not just as small gemlike objects, but also as components within a poetry book, itself carefully crafted to suggest meanings that cannot be conveyed in the brevity of a solitary epigram.

The advent of literary epigrams, apparently a phenomenon of the third century, seems directly tied to the invention of the poetry book as a literary form. There must have been intermediate stages between elegiac verses contextually embedded on stone and the books of epigrams known to have been admired in antiquity, such as Callimachus' *Epigrammata*.[1] In this intermediate stage we might

I wish to thank J. M. Bremer for reading and commenting on the penultimate version of this chapter. I alone am responsible for any remaining defects.

[1] Substantial evidence exists for a 3rd-c. edition of Callimachus' epigrams; see Gutzwiller,

put editions of verses collected from inscriptional sites or editions of epigrams ascribed, rightly or wrongly, to a poet of the past, such as Simonides,[2] and we might imagine as well a practice of reciting sophisticated poetry, epigrammatic in length and form, at social gatherings for amusement and perhaps critical discussion.[3] The question that arises, then, is whether the Milan papyrus is representative of this intermediate stage, a mechanical gathering of epigrams by one or more poets, or whether it was intended to be read as a literary object composed of multiple individual parts, that is, as a poetry book. The answer is important because it affects fundamentally the privileges we may choose to grant ourselves in reading these poems, whether we should read them in terms of some earlier, original purpose, as inscriptions or symposium chatter and therefore discrete entities in which the historical reality of the subject-matter is of primary import, or whether we are dealing with an aesthetically organized collection that is more than the sum of its parts, where meaning resides as much in the interrelationship of the epigrams as in individual poems.

Missing are the beginning and end of the roll, those places where title and author's name or special introductory or concluding poems might provide clear evidence that this papyrus should properly be called a 'poetry book'. As a result, we must base our assumptions about the purposes for which the collection was made on other clues. The more objective factors remain ambiguous. Although the scribal hand suggests the production of a scriptorium, not a private copy, Johnson shows in this volume that we are dealing with a relatively inexpensive edition perhaps used, at least in part, as a source of epigrams for another edition or for recitation. In addition, Krevans argues that the techniques for organizing the sections were adapted from prose collections of the period. But of course the quality of this copy tells us nothing about the origin of the collection it contains,

---

Poetic Garlands, 183–5 and L. Argentieri, 'Epigramma e libro', 6, who proposes (ibid. 1–2) the terms *sylloge* for the type of collection produced by an editor and *libellus* for a collection organized by the author. Since these terms seem to me too artificial, requiring explanation for the uninitiated, I refer to both types as 'collections' and reserve the term 'poetry book' for those that were apparently author-arranged; I use 'anthology' for multi-authored collections.

[2] Philochorus' *Attic Epigrams* (*Suda* s.v. Φιλόχορος) was apparently a collection from stone made in the early Hellenistic period. For the collection of epigrams attributed to Simonides, see Gutzwiller, *Poetic Garlands*, 49–52 and Argentieri, 'Epigramma e libro', 3–4.

[3] A scholar of the 2nd c. BC quotes an epigram supposedly improvised by Simonides at a symposium (Ath. 3. 125 C–D = *FGE* 'Sim'. 88), which indicates that the practice was well known at the time. For arguments in favour of the symposium as an important site for epigram recitation, see Reitzenstein, *Epigramm und Skolion*, 87–96, Cameron, *Callimachus and his Critics*, 71–103 and Nisbet, *Greek Epigram in the Roman Empire*, 19–21, 33–4.

and poeticization of scholarly practice and prosaic sources is one of the hallmarks of early Hellenistic poetry, traits often associated with the Callimachean revolution and Alexandrian poetics.[4] Nor should we expect uniformity of approach to organization in such diverse Hellenistic poetry books as Callimachus' *Aitia* and *Iambi*, Herodas' *Mimiambi*, and early epigram collections. Third-century poets were working in an era of experimentation, often vying with each other as their innovations evolved and diverged, so that we should not limit the possibilities for reading the Posidippus collection through preconceived ideas of what Greek poetry books were like or how epigrams were received by contemporary readers.

I propose here to explore the more subjective internal evidence of the poetry itself for indications that this epigram collection was intentionally constructed to be read as a literary text. Since the collection as we now have it consists uniformly of the inscriptional (rather than sympotic) type of epigram, characterized by absence of the poet's own voice, much of the literary meaning is generated simply by the arrangement of the poems and the thematic connections between them.[5] The more clearly and extensively the collection promotes recognizable themes, to the greater degree that structural arrangement emphasizes these themes, and the more frequently these thematic messages appear in key epigrams at points of opening, closing, and transition, then the more likely we are dealing with a purposely constructed, or author-edited, poetry book.

The thematic coherence of the collection, I will argue, exists on two levels, within sections and, more broadly, across sections. Organization by section may have been the case in other early epigram books as well, since we commonly find clusters on a single topic among the surviving epigrams of other third-century poets.[6] In what is labelled the *Epigrammata* of Hedylus, for instance, Athenaeus found a sequence of satirical poems on gluttons, from which he quotes

---

[4] For Callimachus' scholarly accomplishments and interest in paradoxography, see Fraser, *Ptolemaic Alexandria*, i. 452–5, with his concluding remark (i. 455): 'There can be no doubt that the abstruse knowledge acquired in the fields indicated by these works was absorbed by him and recreated, illuminated by his imagination, in his poetry, and the part it played in the formation of the whole personality of the poet gives it a particular claim to our attention.'

[5] For some interesting remarks on the contrived variety of Posidippus' arrangement, see D. Del Corno, 'Posidippo e il mestiere di poeta', and for a reading of the collection as a mosaic of interconnected pieces, Stephens, 'Posidippus' Poetry Book'.

[6] There is, however, no certain evidence in other Hellenistic epigram papyri for organization by sections with headings; see Cameron, *Greek Anthology*, 3–12, Gutzwiller, *Poetic Garlands*, 20–36, and Parsons, 'Callimachus and the Hellenistic Epigram', 118–22. But see Bastianini, 'Il rotolo degli epigrammi di Posidippo', 115, who points to the title πολεμικά in P. Strassb. WG 2340, possibly a collection of elegies or epigrams.

samples (8.344 F–45 B = GP 7–9).[7] At the same time, other preserved epigrams by Hedylus—on wine, women, and song—suggest that sympotic topics produced thematic coherence for his collection as a whole.[8] If we make the same kind of distinction for the Posidippus collection between topic and theme(s), then troubling inconsistencies in categorization within sections become less a problem. Why does the long section which the editors labelled ἐπιτύμβια (but which might have been called something else) contain predominantly epitaphs for women? Why do other sections—the οἰωνοσκοπικά, ναυαγικά, and τρόποι—also contain epitaphs? Why is the section labelled ἀναθεματικά so brief, only six poems, when dedications were a very common type of inscribed epigram? And why do epigrams with dedicatory features also appear in other sections, throughout the ἱππικά and in at least one of the so-called λιθικά (AB 4) and in one of the ἰαματικά (AB 95)? Should the οἰωνοσκοπικά, which begins with bird omens and moves to other types of portents, be understood etymologically as 'bird omens' with extraneous material added or as just 'omens' with an emphasis on birds? Why does the ἀνδριαντοποιικά section, which should by title refer only to human statues, also contain an epigram on a sculpted cow and an enormous statue of a god? Richard Hunter has explored the possibility that a play with generic expectations may be at work in some sections, particularly the λιθικά, which moves from engraved gemstones to unusual rocks to large boulders.[9] To some degree, this is likely the case. But I would argue that an important consideration in grouping poems within sections was thematic, that throughout the collection theme trumps generic typologies.

OPENINGS AND CLOSINGS

Dominant themes are overtly signalled in the openings and closings of sections, wherever lacunae do not obscure the transition, and I suspect that this phenomenon appeared throughout. Despite uncertainties at the opening of the papyrus, the preservation of the protokollon shows that, at least in its repaired state, the λιθικά were the

[7] See Fraser, *Ptolemaic Alexandria*, i. 572; Gutzwiller, *Poetic Garlands*, 173–5. An epigram on a glutton is also found among the previously known epigrams of Posidippus (AB 121 = GP 16 = Ath. 10. 414 D), who, like Asclepiades, seems to have been a model for Hedylus.

[8] In *Poetic Garlands*, as here, I have commonly assumed a single epigram collection for a poet for the sake of finding general thematic links between surviving epigrams. But I am of course aware that the reality was more complicated and that epigrammatists may have produced a number of larger or smaller collections.

[9] Hunter, 'Osservazioni sui *Lithika* di Posidippo', 115 = 'Notes on the *Lithika* of Posidippus', 98.

recognized opening section. Richard Hunter has suggested that the Ζην[in AB 1. 4 may refer to Zeus, not to an ordinary girl with a name like Zenophila, as the editors propose.[10] Aratus' *Phaenomena*, Theocritus' *Encomium to Ptolemy* (*Idyll* 17), and Callimachus' *Hymns* all begin with Zeus, and it seems a likely assumption that we have here an epigrammatic counterpart to those openings. If so, then the opening clearly links to the final poem (AB 19–20), an epigram of twenty lines (as it now seems)[11] ending with an prayer to Poseidon to keep Ptolemaic lands 'unshaken' (τὴν Πτολεμαίου γαῖαν ἀκινήτην ἴσχε, AB 20. 5–6; cf. ἴσχε . . . μεγάλην χέρα, AB 19. 11). The οἰωνοσκοπικά open with the hawk (AB 21) and close with a raven (AB 35), the two birds most closely connected to Apollo as god of divination, as I show in greater detail below. So, too, Ἀρσινόη, coί (AB 36. 1; repeated at 37. 1) surely signals that Arsinoe as divinized queen is the focus of the ἀναθεματικά; the penultimate epigram (AB 40), on a treasury to Leto, is related to the Ptolemaic complex of identifications between traditional Greek gods and monarchs (Ptolemy II was identified with Leto's son Apollo), although the almost total loss of the final poem (AB 41) makes it impossible to know with certainty how, or if, the thematic focus was enunciated by the end. The first poem in the so-called ἐπιτύμβια is also extremely fragmentary (AB 42), but the theme of women initiates of the mysteries, appearing in AB 43 and 44, was probably introduced here; as I argue below, it connects to the two final epigrams in the section (AB 60, 61), concerning men who were probably initiates.

The ἀνδριαντοποιικά begin with a request to sculptors to mimic (μιμ[ή]caσθε, AB 62. 1) the new style of Lysippus, as an advance over Polyclitus, and, after a catalogue of famous statues by sculptors who foreshadowed or copied Lysippan style, end with a fragmentary epigram (AB 70) that apparently returns to praise of Alexander's favourite sculptor, again in contrast to Polyclitus.[12] The structure of the section, divided into two sets of four poems plus the final one, seems designed as an epigrammatic history of Greek sculpture, in which Lysippus stands as the pinnacle of developing naturalism and the model for artistic connoisseurs of Posidippus' day.[13] Like-

---

[10] Hunter, 'Osservazioni', 109–10 = 'Notes', 95, who further points out that Κρονίου in AB 2. 2, the engraver mentioned also in AB 7. 3, may suggest the paternity of Zeus.

[11] So Austin in AB and Lapini, 'Note posidippee', 42–4.

[12] The reference to flesh (cάρκινα, AB 70. 2) links back to the second epigram in the section, on the Philitas statue, which reproduces his actual size and the quality of his flesh (caρκί, 63. 3).

[13] Gutzwiller, 'Posidippus on Statuary', first presented at the Hellenic Center conference in April 2002; see too similar conclusions made independently, and from a more art-historical perspective, by Andrew Stewart in this volume.

wise, πότνια Θεccαλία (AB 71. 4) in the first of the ἱππικά acts as a kind of dedication to Thessaly as the mother of racehorses and also foreshadows the thematic focus on the victories of females, especially the Ptolemaic queens, in a traditionally male-dominated field. This theme is clearly marked, for instance, in the fourth epigram where a tracehorse, an 'extraordinary female among males' (δεινὴ θήλεια μετ' ἄρcεcιν, AB 74. 9), claims a disputed victory for her team, as also in the penultimate poem (AB 87) where Berenice's mares, victorious at Olympia, boast that they have taken away the long-standing glory of the Spartan Cynisca, the first woman to gain such a victory. The *theme* of the unique glory of females, especially the Ptolemaic queens, superimposed on the more general *subject* of equestrian victory, appears overtly in the concluding couplet of the section when Ptolemy Philadelphus himself proclaims: 'Not do I set up the glory of my father as great, but *this* is the great thing (τοῦτο μέγα), that my mother, a woman, won victory with a chariot' (AB 88. 5–6).[14]

Enunciation of thematic message occurs also at opening and closing points of the ναυαγικά, a second, seemingly more specialized, epitaphic section concerned with the pathetic separation of mourners from the physical remains of the mourned. The κενὸc τάφοc of the first epigram (AB 89. 1) weeps and blames the gods, thus marking the double pain caused relatives and friends by death and the absence of the body. After a sequence of poems working changes on this theme, the last epigram features the opposite solution to the epigrammatic paradox of loss at sea: the shipwrecked person himself, beginning with an echo of the section title, ναυηγόν με θανόντα (AB 94. 1), speaks of his burial by a kind stranger in a foreign land. The ἰαματικά, which catalogue cures effected on various individuals, begin with a doctor's dedication to Apollo of a statue of an emaciated patient (AB 95), the view 'before' the cure. The section ends with what Cephalas would later call a 'protreptic' epigram, recommending that the virtuous man ask Asclepius only for moderate wealth and health, called from the thematic perspective the 'two cures' (ἄκη δύο, AB 101. 3) of human existence. The τρόποι section, though largely fragmentary, seems to consist of epitaphs in which communication takes place between the deceased and a passer-by. If this is right, then the opening ques-

---

[14] Reading κοὐ μέγα πατρὸc ἐμοῦ. Gronewald, 'Bemerkungen zum neuen Poseidippos', 4–5, first proposed κοὐ, but with BG's ἐμὸν rather than ἐμοῦ as on the papyrus. See Bernsdorff, 'Anmerkungen zum neuen Poseidipp', 39. The ink traces and spacing of the papyrus confirm καιου written in *scriptio plena*, as discovered collaboratively at the Cincinnati conference. One of the first characteristics of the collection noticed by scholars was the dominance of women; see Hutchinson, 'The New Posidippus and Latin Poetry'; P. Bing, above, Ch. 7; and Bernsdorff, op. cit. 38–41.

tion posed by an ill-tempered and laconic deceased—'Why have you stopped here by me? Why do you keep me from sleep with your "who", "from where", and "whose son"?' (AB 102. 1–2)—announces, with irony, the topic of conversation with the dead. The heading, however, suggests that this inscriptional form is here adapted to the theme of various character types, an epigrammatic version of prose collections like Theophrastus' *Characters*. While the character trait spotlighted is lost in most of these epigrams, the deceased in the first explains his bad temper on the basis that he, a Cretan, is a man 'of few words' (ὀλιγορρήμων). As in a related epitaph by Callimachus (*AP* 7. 447 = 11 Pf. = GP 35), there is likely some play here on the brevity of epigrammatic form, so that the section opens with a self-referential allusion to Posidippus' art as epigrammatist.[15]

This evidence that each of the sections, as far as we can tell, opens and closes not just with a reference to its topic but to the thematic treatment of that topic strongly indicates the presence of the author's guidance in designing the collection. I turn now to a more extended discussion of the main themes in three important sections—the ἐπιτύμβια, λιθικά, and οἰωνοσκοπικά —before attempting to tease out the thematic connections that link sections and so create the overall flow of the collection.

ΕΠΙΤΥΜΒΙΑ

The epitaphic section, based on a traditional type of inscription, consists of seventeen epigrams about deceased women and three on deceased men. The marked poems about males occur at points of transition in the section, one at the beginning of the second set of ten epigrams and the other two at the end of the section. These final two epitaphs (AB 60–1) feature men who lived fairly long lives and were survived by children. The other epigram on a male (AB 52) involves a sundial set up by one Timon near his grave and tended by a παρθένος; it occurs in the midst of six epigrams on the deaths of unmarried girls, violating the direct coherence of that sequence. Another odd epigram, which would likely be considered an 'intruder' if found in an epitaphic book of a Byzantine anthology, occurs in the series on women who died in childbirth (AB 57); Philonis, attacked by a snake as she is giving birth, manages to deliver her baby safely but dies her-

---

[15] Cf. Callim. fr. 1. 9, ὀλιγόστιχος, with reference to his poetics, and Philip, *AP* 4. 2. 6 = GP, *Garland* 1. 6, ὀλιγοστιχίην, in the prooemium to his *Garland* (cf. too Parmenon, *AP* 9. 342 = GP, *Garland* 11, on brevity in epigrams). For Callimachus' play on epigrammatic form in *AP* 7. 447, see Gutzwiller, *Poetic Garlands*, 198–200.

self. Since her son lives on to middle age, the poem cannot be an epitaph, and Bastianini and Gallazzi point out that it is 'epideictic' in the later sense of that term.[16] While these topically divergent epigrams could result from an editor's desire to find a place for certain poems in the collection, they fit well enough if theme, rather than generic typology, is recognized as a basic principle for coherence within the section.

The dominant theme of the ἐπιτύμβια is, I submit, the connection of the deceased with family and community. This is of course a common theme in many inscribed epitaphs, but in Posidippus' hands it provides a gendered focus for his section, explaining why so many of the poems concern women, who are more likely to be commemorated for their personal relationships than public or professional ones. In the opening epigram, for example, the lacunose first couplet refers to the deceased woman while the second commemorates the happier circumstance that her lineage is 'safe' through the survival of her 'two sons', legitimate heirs to the nobility of the family (AB 42). Other examples show clearly the connection between the theme of familial or communal bond and female gender: Onasagoratis, dead at age 100 and leaving behind eighty children and grandchildren (AB 47); the unmarried Hedeia mourned by her city and father (AB 50); Eleutho, who leaves behind five children and takes the sixth with her to Hades (AB 56); the slave Bithynis given the gift of burial by her masters (AB 48); the old Batis, who earned her living instructing girls in weaving, now buried by her former students (AB 46). The world represented in the epitaphic section is one in which the young, the old, and those in the midst of life, persons of good family and those who must labour in the homes of others, all receive ceremonial recognition from family or community at the time of their departure from life.

To confirm this, we need only look, by way of contrast, at the ναυαγικά and τρόποι. In the first poem of the shipwreck section (AB 89), no family member or friend gives voice to grief for Lysicles, only his cenotaph, which speaks of the shore or wave that perhaps (a pathetic που) holds him. Likewise, in AB 91 a voice apparently coming from an empty memorial warns against sailing the Euxine by pointing out that a seashore 'far away' perhaps (που) holds the deceased Doros.[17] In another (AB 93) a mourner asks Poseidon to return Pythermus' body to his homeland, and in the last (AB 94) the dead sailor offers thanks to a passer-by who tarried just long enough

[16] BG, p. 179.
[17] Reading που with Austin for the μου of the papyrus; see too Gronewald, 'Bemerkungen zum neuen Poseidippos', 5.

to bury him. The idea that common humanity is sufficient basis for a bond between two strangers, one dead and one living, announces the thematic focus of the τρόποι section, which, as far as we can tell, seems to contain epigrams in which a deceased person speaks from the grave to unknown passers-by. In the first poem (AB 102) Menoetius, a Cretan of few words, requests that strangers do not interfere with his rest and keep moving past his tomb, while the other speakers, at least in those poems that remain relatively intact, are concerned to receive the customary greeting from strangers, owed by the living to the dead. In none of these poems, to the degree they survive for us, is there any mention of mourning on the part of family or community, since this theme had provided the focus of the ἐπιτύμβια.

We return, then, to the seemingly odd poems in the epitaphic section. The epigram about the woman who was attacked by a snake during childbirth now falls into place, since its point is the mother's bond with the child: 'You, lady, died from the monster, *but* (ἀλλ') your son was then safe and in time acquired a grey head' (AB 57). The final two on men of moderate old age survived by children are connected by the rather rare theme of 'no need for tears', an inversion of the conventional epitaphic emphasis on grief;[18] they reflect the poet's view of the blessed life, a Hellenistic version of Solon's story about the Athenian Tellus (Hdt. 1. 30). The 'no tears' motif seems associated with the happy afterlife of the Dionysiac initiate, so that the concluding epitaphs for men link back to the opening ones about female celebrants of the mysteries.[19] The deceased Nicostrate in AB 43 dwells among the 'blessed' (ἐπ' εὐcεβέων, 1), a phrase, often used of initiates,[20] that links forward to the penultimate epitaph (ἐπ' ε]ὐcεβέων, AB 60. 6) for Mnesistratus. We can further assert that Aristippus' tombstone, with its emphasis on familial relationships, appropriately ends the epitaphic section by enunciating a kind of thematic motto: burial by one's children, it proclaims, is 'the dearest possession for an old man' (φιλαίτατον ἀνδρὶ γέροντι κτῆμα, AB 61. 5–6).

The epigram about the sundial (AB 52) deserves lingering attention. Here is my text and translation, differing somewhat from Bastianini and Gallazzi:

> Τίμων, ὃc cκιό[θηρον ἐθή]κατο τοῦθ' ἵνα μετρῆι
> ὥρας, νῦν ἰδ' ἐκ[εῖ κεῖται ὑπ]αὶ πεδίον·

---

[18] See BG, p. 184 and Hutchinson, 'The New Posidippus and Latin Poetry', 5.

[19] For documentation, see Gutzwiller, 'A New Hellenistic Poetry Book', 89; see too Pi. *O.* 2. 66–7, where the afterlife of the blessed is 'tearless'. On the women initiates in the first three poems, see Dignas, 'Posidippus and the Mysteries', 185–6.

[20] See e.g. *GVI*, no. 1916.

αὕτη παῖc θ[εραπεύει, ὁ]δοιπόρε, τὴν ἔλιφ᾽, εἴωc
ἐνδέχετ᾽ ἐλπ[ίδ᾽ ἔχειν π]αρθένον ὡρολογεῖν·
ἀλλὰ cὺ γῆρας ἵκοῦ· κούρη παρὰ cήματι τούτωι   5
cωρὸν ἐτέων μετρεῖ τὸν καλὸν ἠέλιον.[21]

> Timon, who set up this sundial so as to measure time,
>   now, as you see, lies there under the soil.
> This girl tends it, traveller, the one he left behind, for
>   as long as a maiden can be expected to tell time.
> But may you come to old age. A girl beside this monument
>   for a heap of years measures the lovely sun.

Our earliest concrete evidence for Greek sundials comes from the third century BC,[22] and scientific luminaries of the early Hellenistic period, including Berossus the Chaldaean and Aristarchus of Samos, are credited with inventing important new types.[23] Inscriptions commemorating the dedication of a time-telling instrument, either for private use or as a civic benefaction, also begin in the third century.[24] In our epigram that dedicatory form is reworked as an epitaph for Timon, who has been buried near or beneath his sundial. But poetically, the initial couplet sets in parallel Timon's purpose in erecting the sundial, to measure ὧραι, with what the passer-by is asked to observe, that his life is ended, so that the measurement of time and the length of a human life are symbolically associated.[25]

   The second couplet concerns, not, I believe, Timon's daughter in the flesh, as Bastianini and Gallazzi understood it, but an image of a girl placed beneath the instrument. Graeco-Roman sundials, conical

---

[21] The emendation αὕτη in 3 was suggested by Ewen Bowie at the Cincinnati conference; the editors originally took the αcτη of the papyrus as a proper name. The editors also read κούρη in 5 as vocative with cύ and printed the imperative form μέτρει in 6. I suggested the text of 5–6 printed here in my presentation at the Cincinnati conference, and this interpretation, as well as Bowie's αὕτη, has been accepted by Austin and Bastianini, 'Addenda et corrigenda'. Lapini, 'Osservazioni sul nuovo Posidippo', 52 has now also suggested that κούρη is vocative, but in a very different interpretation of the poem which includes an improbable emendation to μετρεῖν. Intriguingly, Gronewald, 'Bemerkungen zu Posidippos', 65 supplements the second line of AB 52 with θεῖον ὁρ]ᾶι πεδίον, which would make reference to the Elysian plain, so that Timon also becomes an initiate.

[22] S. L. Gibbs, *Greek and Roman Sundials* (New Haven, 1976), 7–8. A history of dials can be found in R. Rohr, *Sundials: History, Theory, and Practice*, trans. G. Godin (Toronto, 1970), 3–17; Rohr's description of how ancient sundials worked is especially clear.

[23] Vitr. *De arch*. 9. 8; discussion in Rohr, *Sundials*, 9–10. For Berossus and his association with Cos, see Fraser, *Ptolemaic Alexandria*, i. 505–6 and, for Aristarchus and his likely Alexandrian connections, see ibid. 396–9.

[24] One of the earlier examples is *OGIS* 24, the dedication to a 'King Ptolemy' of a sundial made by Themistagoras of Alexandria; other inscriptions on sundials are quoted by Gibbs, *Greek and Roman Sundials*, esp. 392–4.

[25] Cf. Petron. *Sat*. 26. 9 *Trimalchio, lautissimus homo . . . horologium in triclinio et bucinatorem habet subornatum, ut subinde sciat quam de vita perdiderit.*

or hemispherical in shape like the vault of heaven, were commonly viewed from below and so placed on a column or support that might be decorated with one or more figures. Several sundials supported by figures of young women have been found, and it seems that a dial similar to these was used as a marker for Timon's grave.[26] Cemeteries were common locations for sundials, and particularly interesting, from the second century BC, is the funeral stele of one Theodotus, son of Menephron, which sports two small sundials, each supported by a Sphinx with a Caryatid beneath.[27] Though the nature of the παρθένος as a moulded image is not overtly expressed,[28] the position of the epigram in sequence guides the reader in this interpretation. The preceding poem concerns girls from the Laconian town of Caryae, who would be known to all as Caryatids, like their ancestors who were punished for Medizing by being sculpted as columns to support public buildings (Vitr. 1. 15–16),[29] and in the following poem a deceased maiden is called, metaphorically, a κάλλιστον ἄγαλμα (AB 53. 3), 'most beautiful statue', recalling of course the placement of a κόρη on a girl's grave (cf. Anyte, *AP* 7. 649 = GP 8, where παρθενικά refers to a girl's image on her tomb).

This reading of the Timon epigram is also supported by an important intertext, the inscription supposedly engraved on Midas' tomb, one of the few epigrams known to circulate in literary quotation already before the Hellenistic era:[30]

χαλκῆ παρθένος εἰμί, Μίδα δ' ἐπὶ σήματι κεῖμαι.
ἔστ' ἂν ὕδωρ τε νάηι καὶ δένδρεα μακρὰ τεθήληι,
ἠέλιός τ' ἀνιὼν λάμπηι, λαμπρά τε σελήνη,
καὶ ποταμοί γε ῥέωσιν, ἀνακλύζηι δὲ θάλασσα,
αὐτοῦ τῆιδε μένουσα πολυκλαύτωι ἐπὶ τύμβωι,
ἀγγελέω παριοῦσι, Μίδας ὅτι τῆιδε τέθαπται.

---

[26] An example of a base with female figures from Alsace was published by Rohr, 'Le cadran solaire romain de Bettwiller'; see Gibbs, *Greek and Roman Sundials*, 162, no. 1049. A sundial in the shape of a flower supported by a young woman is known from Aquileia; see L. C. Bracchi, 'Orologi solari di Aquileia', 51, figs. 1–2, Gibbs, 205, no. 2011G; see too Gibbs, 313, no. 3099.

[27] The Theodotus stele was published by N. Firatli, *Les Stèles funéraires de Byzance gréco-romaine*, 54–5 no. 33, Pl. VIII; see too Gibbs, *Greek and Roman Sundials*, 164, no. 1051G with pl. 8. In Petron. *Sat.* 71.11 Trimalchio orders that a clock be placed on his tomb: *horologium in medio, ut quisquis horas inspiciet, velit nolit, nomen meum legat*.

[28] In conversation Ewen Bowie has suggested reading θ[ηρεύει in 3, an intriguing play on cκιόθηρον that would make easier the reader's realization the girl is but a plastic figure.

[29] See Ath. 6. 241 E citing Lynceus of Samos, a writer of the early 3rd c., on the Caryatids as a well-known architectural feature.

[30] Pl. *Phdr.* 264 D; *AP* 7. 153; D.L. 1. 89–90; *Vit. Hom.* pp. 198–9, 235 Allen; Favorinus, fr. 95. 38 Barigazzi. I print the longer form that includes ll. 3–4, as it appears in Diogenes and the Life of Homer. The epigram is attributed to either Homer or Cleobulus of Lindus.

I am a bronze maiden and I am placed on Midas' tomb.
For as long as water flows, tall trees bloom,
the sun rises and shines, the moon is bright,
rivers flow and the sea seethes,
remaining in this spot on his much-lamented tomb,
I will announce to passers-by that here Midas is buried.

Both poems concern maidens who are stationed by a man's tomb, and in both the maiden is responsible for continuing the memory of that man beyond the space of a human life. In the Midas epigram the sun is one of several emblems of eternity, while the Timon epigram focuses on the sun as that fixture of the universe by means of which time is judged. Through these thematic resemblances to the well-known Midas epitaph, as well as a number of similarities in syntax and phrasing,[31] Posidippus expected his reader to understand that the παῖc left behind by Timon was a statue. But the connection between the two epigrams is based on an important difference as well. Midas' epitaph was commonly cited as an example of the folly of trying to preserve memory of oneself through a physical monument. Timon's sundial avoids that illusion: the girl left behind to measure the hours will endure for many years, young as the ὧραι she tends—but yet finitely, only as long as such a maiden might be expected to tell time. The epigram thus plays on the various meanings of ὧραι, which signify the divisions of the day measured by the sundial, the seasons of the year by which the progress of a human life is measured, and *the* season, that of youth and vigour. The final couplet brings the message home to the passer-by who enjoys Timon's gift and reads his reasoned comment on the limits to human life and achievement. If we take κούρη as nominative and μετρεῖ as present tense, the entire poem is then addressed to the passer-by, who, upon reading the inscription, receives a blessing for long life (as in Mel. *AP* 7. 417. 10 = GP 2. 10, εἰc γῆραc καὐτὸc ἵκοιο λάλον),[32] symbolized by the unageing girl on the sundial. In terms of generic typology, this παρθένοc may seem displaced in comparison with the dead maidens who surround her, but thematically she provides a hopeful contrast, continuance replacing loss. Just as Philonis dies but leaves behind an infant son to grow to manhood, so too Timon in perishing leaves behind his symbolic daughter, a κόρη who for many a year will offer the service of time-

---

[31] Both epigrams make reference to a maiden (χαλκῆ παρθένοc, αὕτη παῖc), a temporal limit (ἔcτ', εἴωc), the sun (ἠέλιοc, ἠέλιον), duration over time (τῆιδε μένουcα, cωρὸν ἐτέων), a tomb (πολυκλαύτωι ἐπὶ τύμβωι, παρὰ cήματι τούτωι), passers-by (παριοῦcι, ὁδοιπόρε), and a man's burial site (Μίδαc . . . τῆιδε τέθαπται, Τίμων . . . ἐκ[εῖ κεῖται).

[32] Cf. AB 103. 3, ἀλλὰ cὺ μ' ἡcυχί[ωc ἴδε κείμεν]ον, also addressed to the passer-by.

telling to those who pass her by.[33] This is the central theme of the section, enunciated as well in the opening poem and again in the final words of Aristippus.

ΛΙΘΙΚΑ

Thematically, the λιθικά section is one of the most complex, as it sets up some of the broader themes recurring throughout the collection—precision of craftsmanship, particularly in miniaturism,[34] the replacement of the Persian empire by the even more expansive geography of lands conquered by Alexander, the stability of the Aegean world now ruled by the Ptolemies. Despite the very lacunose beginning, tantalizing clues suggest that the first three epigrams concern the Ptolemies and their iconography. The apparent reference to Zeus in AB 1. 4 may function as covert reference to a Ptolemaic king as his earthly instantiation, as in Callimachus' *Hymn to Zeus*. The two poems after the first, though still quite fragmentary, most likely concern Ptolemaic queens and crafted stone objects associated with them. Apparent references to a horn (κέρας) in AB 2. 1 and to a phiale in AB 3. 1 suggest the cornuacopiae and phialai that played a large role in the worship of the divinized Arsinoe Philadelphus.[35] We now know from one of the dedicatory poems (AB 38) that a phiale used in a manumission ceremony was offered to Arsinoe, and the language of offering apparently occurs in both these phiale poems (δέ[χου, 3. 4; δέξα[ι, 38. 4). Most significantly, πότνια in AB 3. 4 can scarcely refer to an ordinary woman admired by her lover, as the editors prefer, but surely looks forward to πότνα (36. 6) and πό]τνιαν (39. 3) in the dedicatory section, as titles for the divinized Arsinoe.[36] Queens and gems had a natural association in life and in art, and Posidippus seems to have built this sequence of epigrams around a motif taken from Asclepiades' epigram about an engraved amethyst

[33] BG, pp. 173–4 point out the odd coincidence that Timon of Phlius in the *Silloi* called Prodicus a λαβάργυρος ὡρολογητής, which refers to his charging a fee for the type of philosophical instruction that he gave in a work entitled Ὧραι (see Ath. 9. 406 E, Eust. *ad Il.* 24. 262). The present state of our knowledge does not allow us to establish a relationship between that comment and Posidippus' epigram, but it does suggest contemporary interest in exploring the various etymological implications of ὡρολογεῖν.

[34] Hutchinson, 'The New Posidippus and Roman Poetry', 2 suggests a 'metapoetic link between the small-scale artistry and craft of the gems and that of Posidippus' epigrams'. See too Schur, 'A Garland of Stones'; P. Bing, above, Ch. 7; A. Kuttner, above, Ch. 8.

[35] Fraser, *Ptolemaic Alexandria*, i. 240–2 and D. B. Thompson, *Ptolemaic Oinochoai*.

[36] The only other appearance in the papyrus is at AB 71. 4, where 'mistress Thessaly' is personified as if divine. As evidence for πότνια referring to a mortal woman, BG, p. 112 offer only *AP* 5. 270. 2 by Paulus Silentiarius, a very late parallel.

Kathryn Gutzwiller

ring belonging to Alexander's sister Cleopatra (*AP* 9. 752 = GP 44),[37] as he probably built the ἀνδριαντοποιικά section around a poem on Lysippus' *Alexander* (*AP* 16. 120 = GP 43) attributed to Asclepiades (or Archelaus). If the λιθικά, then, constitute the beginning of the roll, the collection did, after all, have an introductory sequence involving the Ptolemies and their iconography.

The fourth poem on a Persian stone bound in gold and apparently set in a bracelet provides a historical precedent for the Ptolemies' association with precious gems (AB 4. 5–6):

> Πέρcην δὲ χρυcῶι cφι⟨γ⟩κτὸν λίθον ἐξ ἀγ[απ]ητ[οῦ
> δῶρον Μανδήνη πήχεος ἐκρέμαcεν.

A Persian stone banded with gold Mandene hung up,
a gift from her lovely arm.

As the Ptolemaic queen, treated as if divine, is receiving the gift of a precious stone engraved with a phiale, here her Persian predecessor seems to offer another stone in dedication,[38] a neat reference to the more exalted status of contemporary monarchs made through the positioning of the poems. Two royal Persian women named Mandene are known, the mother of Cyrus the Great and the daughter of Darius, and the reference to Darius in the fragmentary first couplet strongly suggests that we are dealing with a historical member of the Persian royal family.[39] This technique of insinuating equivalence to famous figures of the past merely by juxtaposition is used a number of times in the collection, both to mark the greatness of the Ptolemies and to associate the epigrammatist with his poetic predecessors who celebrated earlier patrons. But the Mandene epigram links as well, by repetition of vocabulary (Πέρcην, Περcικόν/δῶρον in same position) and theme, to the succeeding poem, about a lapis lazuli stone given by Demylus to Coan Nicaea in exchange for a kiss (AB 5):

[37] On which see Gutzwiller, 'Cleopatra's Ring'.
[38] The verb ἐκρέμαcεν is here the key to the dedicatory form; cf. Hom. *Il.* 7. 83, Pi. *P.* 5. 34–9, Hdt. 1. 66. 4, and, among the many examples from dedicatory epigram, Asclep. *AP* 5. 203 = GP 6 (an erotic epigram with ἐκρέμαcεν in final place), Mel. 5. 191 = GP 73 (same *sedes*), Mnasalces 6. 9 = GP 3, l. 2 (δῶρα παρὰ Προμάχου, Φοῖβε, τάδε κρέμαται), and Leon. 6. 130 = GP 95, ll. 1–2 (δῶρον Ἀθάνᾳ | Πύρρος ἀπὸ θρασέων ἐκρέμαcεν Γαλατᾶν).
[39] For the older Mandene (or Mandane), the daughter of Astyages and wife of Cambyses, see Hdt. 1. 107–8, 111, Xen. *Cyr.* 1. 2–1. 3, D.S. 9.22; Ael. *VH* 12. 42. For the younger one, the sister of Xerxes, see D.S. 11. 57. 1–3. BG, p. 113 argue that Mandene is more likely to be an ordinary person of Iranian descent than one of these queens. Note, however, other evidence for the dedication of precious jewels by royal women: Pliny mentions both Livia's dedication of what was claimed to be Polycrates' ring in the temple of Concord at Rome (*HN* 37. 4) and the dedication of a stone to Venus by Queen Timaris with an accompanying epigram mentioning her success in childbirth (37. 178, a reference I owe to Ann Kuttner).

Τιμάνθης ἔγλυψε τὸν ἀστερόεντα σάπειρον
τόνδε χρυσίτην Περσικὸν ἡμίλιθον
Δημύλωι· ἀνθ' ἁπαλοῦ δὲ φιλήματος ἡ κυανόθριξ
δῶρον Ν[ι]καίη Κῶια ἔδ[εκτ' ἐρατόν.

Timanthes engraved this starry lapis lazuli, this Persian
cabochon-cut stone, shot with gold,
for Demylus. The dark-haired Coan Nicaea received it
as a [lovely] gift in exchange for a tender kiss.[40]

As Martyn Smith has shown, this epigram, one of the most charming in the collection, gives evidence for Posidippus' use of prose sources, since his reference to the 'starry' quality of the dark-blue stone, a metaphorical description glossed by χρυσίτης, 'containing gold', conforms closely to the information found in Theophrastus' *De lapidibus* about lapis lazuli (§23) and the reference to its Persian origin is paralleled by Pliny's discussion (*HN* 37. 119–20), drawn in part from the early Hellenistic Περὶ λίθων of Sotacus.[41] In the epigram, however, the prosaic information about the stone is transformed into poetry primarily because the value of the lapis and the craftsmanship put into it are equated, ironically and meaningfully, with Nicaea's tender kiss. Whether this Nicaea is historical or fictive, courtesan or high-status lady, is not known, nor in the *literary* context of the collection does it fundamentally matter, since she has come to dwell in a world where royal women, non-royal women, and the beautiful gems they own reflect one another as equivalent aesthetic objects.

While crafted stones brilliantly, and metapoetically, introduce the section, what is actually most consistent throughout is an emphasis on the physical origins of the stones—in mountains, rivers, and sea—and on their physical properties—their sparkle, colour, and size.[42] All this, yet again, corresponds quite closely to the treatment of stones found in ancient prose sources. Theophrastus, echoing concepts found in Plato (*Ti.* 59 A–B) and Aristotle (*Mete.* 378^{a}18–^{b}4),

---

[40] For the translation 'cabochon-cut', see Kuttner, Ch. 8 n. 40, who argues against Austin's 'semi-precious'.

[41] M. Smith, 'Elusive Stones', 107–8. On Posidippus' technical source for the *draconitis* or *dracontias* in AB 15, see Gutzwiller, 'Cleopatra's Ring', 387–8. Pliny names Sotacus as one of his 'oldest' (*vetustissimi, HN* 36. 146) sources, and Sotacus wrote on types of stone also mentioned by Posidippus: the fabulous *draconitis* (AB 15), which he observed in the possession of a 'king' (*HN* 37. 158), and magnetic stones (AB 17), of which he described several types (*HN* 36. 128–30, 146–8). For Sotacus and other ancient writers on stones, see Halleux and Schamp (eds.), *Les Lapidaires grecs*, pp. xiii–xxxiv.

[42] Cf. P. Bernardini and L. Bravi, 'Note di lettura al nuovo Posidippo', 148 n. 1 'il vero tratto distintivo di tutti i λιθικά è l'interesse per la provenienza e le qualità del materiale e dell'oggetto'.

begins his *De lapidibus* by stating that 'of all things formed in the earth some are of water and some of earth; metals are of water . . ., and of earth stone including the more unusual types'. He points out that from various processes of formation stones 'derive their smoothness, solidity, luster, transparency, and other such properties' (1. 1–2).[43] What happens in the λιθικά section is that references to the constituent parts of the universe and to the properties of its hardest substances are slyly worked into epigrams which directly deal with the relationship between a stone and the humans who encounter it. The result, I suggest, is a thematizing of nothing less than the physical nature of the universe.

With a bow to the easternmost rim of Alexander's empire, the ruined first poem begins with the Hydaspes River of India, and the paradox of water as the source or formative element for hard substances recurs in several epigrams. A honey-coloured stone (AB 7) was rolled by a swollen river (χειμάρρουϲ . . . ποταμόϲ) from the Arabian mountains (ἐξ Ἀράβων . . . ὀ[ρέων]) to the sea (ἅλα). So too, a chunk of transparent crystal was cast from a mountain to the sea's shore by an Arabian stream (ἐπὶ θῖνα . . . πόντιον . . . ἐξ ὀρέων ὀχετόϲ, AB 16. 1–2), and in a mostly lost epigram yet another raging river (χαρ]άδρηϲ, AB 10. 3) appears, in connection with Nabataean kings. A miraculous repelling and attracting magnet came from the deep roots of Mysian Mt. Olympus (AB 17). But 'no sounding river' (οὐ ποταμ,ὸϲ κελάδων, AB 15. 1) produced the *dracontias*, the hardened eye of a monstrous Indian snake—a negative opening designed to continue a thematic thread in absence.[44] Likewise, two epigrams emphasize that mother-of-pearl, though glistening 'all-silvery',[45] is a generic mismatch for the section, not a stone (οὐ[χὶ λίθο]ϲ, AB 11. 1, Austin's supplement), but a product of the ocean (θαλάϲϲηϲ, AB 11. 1; θα]λάϲϲιοϲ, 12. 1).

While stones have their origin in the earth and its waters, their properties of sparkle and brilliant colour associate them with the heavenly sphere. The blue chalcedony bearing an incised Pegasus is given its technical name, 'skylike' (ἠερόεϲϲαν, AB 14. 1), being an 'airy stone' (αἰθερίωι . . . λίθωι, 14. 6) that provides a background of

---

[43] For discussion of the formation of stones in Theophrastus and his predecessors, see D. E. Eichholz (ed.), *Theophrastus: De lapidibus*, 15–47.

[44] The use of an initial οὐ to mark a theme in its absence is found also in AB 8, where the transition from epigrams on precious stones belonging to women to other types of stones is signalled with the opening οὔτ' αὐχὴν ἐφόρηϲε τὸ ϲάρδιον οὔτε γυναικῶν | δάκτυλοϲ, 'not any neck or finger of a lady wore this carnelian'. See Gutzwiller, 'New Hellenistic Poetry Book', 87.

[45] Reading ϲτίλβουϲ[α π]ανάργυρον (AB 11. 1) with Lloyd-Jones, 'Notes on P. Mil. Vogl. VIII 309', and De Stefani, 'Una nota al "nuovo Posidippo"', 140.

'dark-blue sky' (κυανῆν ἠέρα, 14. 4) for the horse's flight.[46] Nicaea's gold-flecked lapis is 'starry' (ἀcτερόεντα, AB 5. 1), while Mandene's Persian stone shines like the moon (ἀντιcέληνον, AB 4. 3), apparently at lamp-lit parties. A stone with a carved lion is dull when moistened, but, dried out, 'flashes toward the beautiful sun' (ἀcτράπτει πρὸc καλὸν ἠέλιον, AB 13. 4). Likewise, the 'beautiful sun' (καλὸc ἠέλιοc, AB 16. 6) is a suitable standard of comparison for commonplace rock-crystal. Niconoe's sparkling crystal is not, I believe, engraved with an image of Iris, but rather 'draws a coloured rainbow [from the sun]' (ἕλκει δὲ γραπτὴν ἶριν [ἀπ' ἠελίου, AB 6. 2 with my supplement): it is Pliny's *iris* stone (*NH* 37. 136–7), a prism reflecting all the shimmering colours of the rainbow onto the bosom of a girl who wears it on a chain.[47] A carnelian, adorned with Darius on his chariot, is extraordinary for its size, brilliance, and perfection, lacking any 'watery cloud' (ὑδρηλ[ὴ] . . . νεφέλη, AB 8. 8) within: here the term chosen to designate a white vein in a stone continues the subtext of celestial phenomena. Stars, the moon, clouds, the rainbow, the blue sky, and even the sun can, then, be caught, or reflected, in gleaming stones forged in the earth and brought forth by rivers. The final epigram about a boulder that Poseidon has cast from sea onto land (AB 19–20) comes into focus thematically, I argue, if we read this section as presenting us, from an epigrammatic perspective, with the nature of our physical world, which exists not in a steady state but in stages of motion and rest through which natural forces, or equivalent deities, shape our environment.

The λιθικά section can be viewed, I suggest, as the epigrammatic equivalent of cosmologic poetry. In Apollonius' *Argonautica* Orpheus begins his cosmologic song with 'earth, heaven, and the sea' (1. 496), which leads to the 'stars and the paths of the moon and sun' (1. 500) and then the 'mountains' and 'sounding rivers' (ποταμοὶ κελάδοντεc, 1. 501). But the aesthetic of Posidippus' collection does not allow anything so grand as the creation of the world or the age of heroes; rather his epigrammatic poetry is constructed on a human scale and focuses on the world as currently observable. An important parallel to the final poem on Poseidon's hurling of boulders is a passage in Callimachus' *Hymn to Delos*, where the poet introduces the story of Delos as the birth place of Apollo by passing over the origin of the other islands, 'how first the great god smiting the mountains with his three-forked sword made for him by the Telchines, fashioned the islands in the sea, lifted them from beneath as with a lever and rolled

---

[46] Plin. *HN* 37. 115 speaks of a type of *iaspis* from Persia that is *aeri similem, quae ob id vocatur aerizusa*. See Gutzwiller, 'Cleopatra's Ring', 386.

[47] Gutzwiller, 'Nikonoe's Rainbow'.

them into the water' (30–3). Both Callimachus and Posidippus recognize, then, the potential for reporting on the cosmic scale, for defining the current physical world in terms of the past actions of the gods, but both modify such accounts to fit the demands of a new kind of poetry. Writing in the traditional form of narrative hymn, Callimachus yet associates the story of Apollo's birth on Delos with matters of contemporary interest, the birth of Ptolemy Philadelphus on Cos and its Egyptian connections.[48] Composing in the new epigrammatic form where larger themes are suggested through juxtaposition and arrangement of collected poems, Posidippus views the mountains, rivers, sun, and stars only from the perspective of the particular, as the origin of this stone or captured in the gleam of that stone.[49] The poet's source is now some prose treatise recording rational observations of the world, but through the epigrammatic lens this material can still be turned to poetry, a new kind of cosmology for a new kind of culture. The λιθικά section is elegantly rounded off with a prayer to Poseidon to keep Ptolemy's land and shores 'unshaken' (ἀκινήτην)—not the metaphorical prayer for continued good fortune with which Bacchylides closes an epinician for Hiero (ἀκινήτους, 5. 200), but a plea for physical stability in a region prone to earthquakes.

ΟΙΩΝΟΣΚΟΠΙΚΑ

While the λιθικά section focuses on the physical world, with stones acting as a point of linkage for earth, water, and sky, the οἰωνοσκοπικά concern the realm of the unseen as it is signified in the observable world around us. The subject of omens, for which Posidippus again relied on prose sources, was easily adapted to epigram form merely by focusing on a single omen and sometimes adding an example of an individual who did or did not heed the sign. Posidippus, yet again, uses the combination of discrete epigrams in series to offer a panorama of human experience, from ordinary individuals seeking to understand conditions for sailing or fishing or favourable indications for marrying, having children, and finding servants, to those engaged in warfare, both combatants aspiring to individual heroism and the military leaders of the Argead dynasty seeking to conquer the Persian empire. While the *topic* is thus illustrated by a select range of omens, its *thematic importance* is revealed by contemporary philosophical

---

[48] See Bing, *The Well-Read Muse*, 91–143; Stephens, *Seeing Double*, 114–21.

[49] Pliny (*HN* 37. 1) observes that 'many people find a single gem sufficient for a total and perfect contemplation of the universe' (*plerisque ad summam absolutamque naturae rerum contemplationem satis sit una aliqua gemma*).

debate about the reliability of divination. The subject was of crucial importance to various Hellenistic philosophical groups because omens were a traditional proof for the existence of the gods and for their kindly regard for human affairs. While the Epicureans rejected all forms of divination as superstitious fear, the Stoics defended it as reliable, when properly performed, and as evidence of divine purpose permeating the observable world. Following Stoic belief, Aratus in his *Phaenomena* sets forth Zeus as a rational force pervading the cosmos, a form of providence benefiting human beings with signs provided by the constellations and natural phenomena.[50] Posidippus' erotic poetry indicates his own Stoic leanings: in an apparently programmatic epigram he lays aside, temporarily, the strictures of Zeno and Cleanthes in order to sing, under Bacchic influence, of 'bittersweet Eros' (AB 123 = *AP* 5. 134 = GP 1), and in another (AB 138 = *AP* 12. 120 = GP 7) he attempts to employ Stoic reason (λογιςμός) against the assaults of erotic passion.[51] While the specific signs in the οἰωνοςκοπικά are taken from works like Theophrastan *De signis*, Posidippus' examples of individuals who heeded or failed to heed a sign find parallels in philosophical discussions of omens, especially Cicero's *De divinatione*. There Quintus Cicero, citing his brother's translation of Aratus' *Prognostica* (1. 13–15), maintains the central Stoic principle of the interdependence of the gods and divination, before Cicero himself presents the Academic position that nature provides us signs of future events without the intervention of the gods. Since the debate began in the early Hellenistic period, it would be difficult for Posidippus' contemporaries to read his epigrammatic treatment of omens without considering the larger question of the intervention of the gods in the human sphere.

Although the initial group of signs report objectively how natural phenomena indicate coming weather, the first epigram, again, has special importance, introducing the presence of the supernatural through linguistic play and literary allusion (AB 21):

> νηῒ καθελκομένηι πάντᾳ παρὰ θινὶ φανήτω
> ἴρηξ, αἰθυίης οὐ καθαροπτέρυγος·
> δύνων εἰς βυθὸν ὄρνις ἀνάρςιος, ἀλλὰ πετέςθω
> ὑψο..[. ...]..[. ..].[..].φ' ὅλως·
> οἷος ἀπὸ δρυὸς ὦρτ' Ἰακης ὠκύπτερος ἴρηξ
> ἱρῆι, Τίμων, ςῆι νηῒ καθελκομένηι.

πάντᾳ παρὰ θινὶ Luppe (2004) : πάντα πλέος (πλέον pap.) ἰνὶ BG

[50] On Aratus' Stoicism, see Effe, *Dichtung und Lehre*, 40–56; D. Kidd (ed.), *Aratus: Phaenomena* (Cambridge, 1997), 10–12.   [51] See Gutzwiller, *Poetic Garlands*, 157–62.

As a ship is setting sail, let a hawk appear anywhere by the shore
  since the wings of a shearwater lack purity:
A bird that dives into the deep is a bad omen, but let
  [the hawk] fly high . . . . altogether.
Just so a swift-winged hawk rose from the Ionian oak
  when your holy ship, Timon, was setting forth.

If we could identify the historical event that underlies the exem-
plum of a hawk flying from an 'Ionian oak',[52] then we would perhaps
know why Timon's ship is called 'sacred'. But despite that gap in our
knowledge, it is evident that Posidippus draws the reader's attention
to the connection between the hawk and the divine sphere by ety-
mologizing ἴρηξ with ἱρῆι.[53] While many birds were used for augury,
the hawk's special association with prophecy, seers, and Apollo is
evident from as early as Homer.[54] In *Iliad* 13 Poseidon, appearing
to the two Ajaxes disguised as the 'divinely sanctioned bird-seer'
Calchas (θεοπρόπος οἰωνιστής, *Il*. 13. 70), darts away as if 'a swift-
winged hawk rose up in flight' (ὥς τ᾽ ἴρηξ ὠκύπτερος ὦρτο πέτεσθαι,
13. 62), a line that Posidippus echoes in this epigram.[55] In *Il*. 15.
237–8 Apollo himself is compared to a 'hawk, swift slaughterer of
doves, the swiftest of flying creatures' (ἴρηκι ἐοικὼς, ὠκέϊ φασσοφόνωι,
ὅς τ᾽ ὤκιστος πετεηνῶν),[56] and in *Od*. 15. 525–6 a κίρκος, a specific type
of ἴρηξ, appears as a 'good omen' (δεξιὸς ὄρνις), a 'swift messenger of
Apollo'. So too, Aristophanes describes Apollo's relationship with
the hawk as like that of Zeus to the eagle and Athena to the owl (*Av*.
514–16). To begin the οἰωνοσκοπικά with the 'sacred' ἴρηξ, then, is to

---

[52] Analogy with other sections supports the supposition, also in BG, p. 135, that Timon is a
historical figure: both the ναυαγικά and ἰαματικά open with epigrams about prominent persons
of the early Hellenistic period, Lysicles the Academian, mentioned by D.L. 4. 22, and Medeus,
a Ptolemaic official and physician, now identified from the epigraphic record by Bing, 'Medeios
of Olynthos'.

[53] Cf. Serv. on *Aen*. 11. 721 explaining Vergil's use of *sacer ales* to designate the hawk:
Graecum nomen expressit: nam ἱέραξ *dicitur, hoc est sacer;* ἱερεύς *enim graece, latine sacerdos
vocatur. cur autem graece ita dictus sit, ratione non caret, quae nota est sacrorum peritis*. For this
and other etymological plays in the omen section, see Lavigne and Romano, 'Reading the
Signs', an essay that interacts in various ways with my presentation at the Cincinnati confer-
ence. For a survey of etymologizing in Greek poetry, including Hellenistic, see J. J. O'Hara,
True Names (Ann Arbor, 1996), 7–42; for Stoic use of etymology, see A. A. Long, 'Stoic
Readings of Homer', 53–5, 62–5.

[54] J. Pollard, *Birds in Greek Life and Myth* (London, 1977), 144 explains the association on
the basis that 'Apollo as the son of Zeus was represented by a similar, but lesser raptor than
the eagle.' On the ἱέραξ, the generic term for small hawks and falcons, see D'A. W. Thompson,
A Glossary of Greek Birds, 2nd edn. (London, 1936), 65–7 and Pollard, op. cit. 80–1.

[55] As noted by BG, p. 135.

[56] Citing the same etymology found in Posidippus, the T scholiast explains ἱερὸς γὰρ
Ἀπόλλωνος ὁ ἱέραξ.

begin with an emblem of Apollo, god of prophecy, conveyor of Zeus' will to humankind.

Nor should we forget that falcons were sacred animals in Egypt and that the falcon represented Horus, who was not only the divine manifestation of the pharaoh but also identified with Apollo.[57] The iconography of the pharaoh as the Horus falcon and protected by the Horus falcon was adapted by the Ptolemies as early as Soter, and became increasingly common in text and image throughout the third century.[58] As Daniel Selden has effectively shown, Callimachus' close association of Ptolemy Philadelphus with Apollo in his *Hymn* to that god is best explained by an identification of the king and Horus/Apollo that has deep roots in Egyptian religious and political thought.[59] To begin the omen section with the ἵρηξ allowed Posidippus to suggest covertly, to a Greek audience, a divine source for the signs of the natural world and, to an Egyptian or Egyptianizing audience, a close association of this divine source with the Ptolemaic kings. In the complicated new world constructed by the Ptolemaic vision, the ἵρηξ was the perfect symbol of divine presence both for those who followed the new philosophical adaptations of traditional Greek religion and those who saw from the double perspective of the Greek–Egyptian amalgam.

The crucial play on ἵρηξ/ἱρῆι is certainly not the only example of the *figura etymologica* in the omen section; rather an abundance of word plays signals, on the semantic level, that signification itself—meaning indicated through similarity or analogy—is thematized throughout. The arrangement of the section, from bird omens to other kinds of omens, calls the reader's attention to a shift in the meaning of the heading οἰωνοσκοπικά, which refers literally to bird augury and by transference to any interpretation of signs.[60] Although this arrangement may resemble the method found in prose treatises of moving

<hr/>

[57] For the sacredness of hawks/falcons in Egypt, see Hdt. 2. 65, 67; D.S. 1. 87. 7 reports that hawks were sacred in Egypt because seers used them as omens. The symbol for the hawk even came to signify the word θεός (Horapollo 1. 6). The identification of Horus and Apollo is expressly stated in Hdt. 2. 144, 156, and a series of unofficial bronze coins bearing a laureate Apollo on the obverse and a falcon on reverse have been recently discovered buried in a house in Ptolemaic Alexandria; see O. Picard, 'Monnaies de fouille d'Alexandrie', 203–5; id., 'Un monnayage alexandrin énigmatique', pl. 34; Walker and Higgs, *Cleopatra of Egypt*, 108, no. 132.
[58] For inscriptional and iconographical evidence, see Selden, 'Alibis', 387–8 with figs. 4–6; see also Stephens, *Seeing Double*, 55, 159.   [59] Selden, 'Alibis', 384–405.
[60] See Baumbach and Trampedach, '"Winged Words"', 125–6. Ar. *Av.* 719–22 plays up the humourous side of this: 'You think everything that gives prophetic advice is a bird. Any chance word is a bird, you call a sneeze a bird, a coincidence is a bird, any sound is a bird, a servant is a bird, a donkey is a bird. Aren't we [birds] clearly your mantic Apollo?'

from the most specific to less apt examples, editorial arrangement merely on such bases leaves unexplained the way in which the shift in meaning is expressly explored a number of times in the section, or how it relates to other etymological plays in the omen epigrams. Among the first nine poems only two do not concern bird signs, and in both of those (AB 25, 28) the sign is a πρέcβυc. David Petrain has argued that in AB 28 this word refers not to an old man but to a bird called the πρέcβυc, the wren. While the old man seems in fact a better literal interpretation of the omen, which involves meeting a κλαίων πρέcβυc at a crossroads, the ambiguity of the word comes into play, surely, in *both* epigrams, since in AB 25 it is the first word in the poem, creating at least a moment of uncertainty for the reader who has just gone through four epigrams on bird signs in a section entitled οἰωνοcκοπικά.[61] In the four epigrams concerning omens relating to war, AB 30–3, Posidippus twice uses the word οἰωνός in the transferred sense of 'omen' (31. 2, 32. 5), and in the first of these it refers to the two favourable signs for the Argeads, an eagle (for which the word may retain its original meaning) and lightning (for which it cannot).

In addition, the οἰωνοcκοπικά contains a number of 'speaking names', several of them ironical.[62] So a man named Euelthon, 'Good Traveller', was killed on a journey by thieves when he ignored the bad omen of larks and finches seen together (AB 29), and Antimachus, 'Resistant Fighter', unsuccessfully opposed the enemy in war when he ignored the omen of his servant slipping on the threshold (AB 32). Another example of an ironical speaking name may be Aristoxenus, whose name indicates an excellence in matters pertaining to hosts and guests. But he misinterprets a dream about sleeping in the house of Zeus as the bridegroom of Athena and so ends up dying in battle, a bridegroom in the house of Hades (AB 33). A more complex play with names and omens occurs in AB 26, where the 'grey heron' (ἐρωιδιὸc . . . πελλόc), the one that 'the seer Asterie calls to her holy rites' (Ἀ[c]τερίη μάντιc ἐφ' ἱρὰ καλεῖ), is the best bird/omen (ὄρνιc) for acquiring a servant. Most of the bird signs work by similarity or analogy, as, for instance, a diving shearwater signals a sinking

[61] For Petrain, 'Πρέcβυc', the word has the meaning 'wren' in AB 28 but 'old man' in AB 25, even though he notes that AB 25 acts a transition piece between the first four epigrams on birds as weather signs and the next four on bird signs pertaining to domestic affairs. I would argue, rather, that in both epigrams 'old man' is a better literal meaning but that the reader is teased with the ambiguity bird/not bird in both; see too Lavigne and Romano, 'Reading the Signs', 18–19. On the πρέcβυc, see D'A. W. Thompson, *Glossary of Greek Birds*, 150–1.

[62] On 'speaking names' in the οἰωνοcκοπικά, see Baumbach and Trampedach, '"Winged Words"', 130–1.

ship (AB 21). But the heron's connection with choosing a servant is not so self-evident, and can only be found through linguistic awareness. Posidippus speaks of the 'grey' heron, the most common type, but the name of the seer Asterie may remind the reader of another kind of heron called ἀϲτερίαϲ.[63] Aristotle knew an aetiological story according to which 'starry' herons, or bitterns, had metamorphosed from slaves and were consequently very lazy.[64] Here, I assume, the grey heron is the 'best bird/omen' for choosing a servant, the one that the significantly named Asterie calls, because, unlike the 'starry' heron associated with lazy slaves, the more common variety presages a servant of good character. It is significant as well that Hieron, a man whose name announces his obedience to the heron portent produced by Asterie's ἱρά, successfully acquires two such good servants.[65]

As the οἰωνοϲκοπικά opens with the hawk, so it closes with the raven, also sacred to Apollo as the god of prophecy (Ἀπόλλωνοϲ ἱέραξ καὶ κόραξ, Porph. *Abst.* 3. 5).[66] The final epigram is an epitaph for a favourite augur of Alexander, the Thracian Strymon, whose profession is marked by the representation of a raven on his tombstone (AB 35):[67]

> μάντιϲ ὁ τῶι κόρακι Ϲτρυμὼ[ν] ὑπ[ο]κείμεν[ο]ϲ ἥρωϲ
> Θρῆϊξ ὀρνίθων ἀκρότατοϲ ταμίηϲ·
> ὧι τόδ' Ἀλέξανδροϲ ϲημήνατο, τρὶϲ γὰρ ἐνίκα
> Πέρϲαϲ τῶι τούτου χρηϲάμενοϲ κόρακι.

A seer, the hero Strymon who lies beneath the raven,
  a Thracian, is the very best steward of birds,

---

[63] See Arist. *HA* 609ᵇ23–5, 616ᵇ33–617ᵃ1. By postponing πελλόϲ until the beginning of the pentameter, Posidippus is possibly referring to a disputed passage in Homer, *Il.* 10. 274–5 τοῖϲι δὲ δεξιὸν ἧκεν ἐρωιδιὸν ἐγγὺϲ ὁδοῖο | Παλλὰϲ Ἀθηναίη, where the T scholiast comments ἀντὶ δὲ τοῦ Παλλάϲ "πέλλον" γράφειν φηϲὶ δεῖν ὁ Ζώπυροϲ (= *FGrHist* 494).

[64] *HA* 617ᵃ5–7 ὁ δ' ἀϲτερίαϲ ὁ ἐπικαλούμενοϲ ὄκνοϲ μυθολογεῖται μὲν γενέϲθαι ἐκ δούλων τὸ ἀρχαῖον, ἔϲτι δὲ κατὰ τὴν ἐπωνυμίαν τούτων ἀργότατοϲ. Boios related an aetiological myth about the origin of the smaller heron, which metamorphosed from a servant unjustly treated by his masters (Ant. Lib. 7). Ael. *NA* 5. 36 reports that the ἀϲτερίαϲ, a domesticated bird in Egypt, understands the human voice: if someone calls it a slave, it becomes angry, and if someone calls it fearful (ὄκνον), it becomes indignant, as if it had been accused of low birth or laziness.

[65] There seems to be yet another linguistic play in the phrase ἀγαθῶι ϲὺν ποδί in AB 26. 4, since a scholiast to Ar. *Av.* 721 explains that servants who were considered omens ('birds') were called καλλίποδαϲ . . . καὶ καλλοιωνίϲτουϲ. So ἀγαθῶι ϲὺν ποδί is the equivalent of ἀγαθῶι ϲὺν οἰωνῶι.

[66] Ael. *NA* 1. 48 ὁ κόραξ, ὄρνιν αὐτόν φαϲιν ἱερόν, καὶ Ἀπόλλωνοϲ ἀκόλουθον εἶναι λέγουϲι; cf. Bianor, *AP* 9. 272 = GP *Garland* 11, l. 1, Stat. *Silv.* 2. 4. 17. In Callimachus' *Hymn to Apollo* the god assumes the form of a raven to lead his people to Cyrene, propitious for the founder (Λιβύην ἐϲιόντι κόραξ ἡγήϲατο λαῶι | δεξιὸϲ οἰκιϲτῆρι, 66–7). For ravens as birds of augury, see D'A. W. Thompson, *Glossary of Greek Birds*, 92–3 and Pollard, *Birds in Greek Life and Myth*, 127–8.

[67] The epitaphic nature of the poem has been recognized by S. Schröder, 'Überlegungen zu zwei Epigrammen'.

for whom Alexander made this sign. For three times he
defeated the Persians by means of this man's raven.

An epitaph makes an excellent closure device, one used in later poetry
books and, seemingly, already in other third-century epigram collec-
tions.[68] Here there is the additional advantage of closing a series of
epigrams, innovative in type, by reverting to a traditional inscription-
al form. More important, the epitaph provides the section's clearest
statement of the relationship between birds, their interpreters, and
the source of the signs they give. The first couplet, giving the name,
origin, and profession of the deceased, may be read as the engraved
epithet, now embedded in a literary epigram, or it may be construed as
the first half of a poem emanating entirely from the epigrammatist.[69]
The uncertain status of the first couplet sets up the key phrase ὧι τόδ᾽
Ἀλέξανδρος ϲημήνατο, most simply translated 'for whom Alexander
made this sign',[70] where the ϲῆμα is ambiguously the tomb itself, the
raven upon it, and the epitaphic statement of the seer's excellence.
The poet thus makes a final allusion to the complicated thematic role
of signification in the section by this play on ϲημαίνω itself. In addi-
tion, by the act of creating a sign, Alexander becomes, within the
thematics of the section, a godlike figure, belonging to the realm of
the sacred. The verb ϲημαίνω is the proper term to use of the god's
role in sending divinatory signs to humans,[71] and Aratus so uses it
of Zeus, who 'kindly provides humans with favourable signs' (ἤπιος
ἀνθρώποιϲιν | δεξιὰ ϲημαίνει, 5–6) and determined the stars that 'would
make for men signs of the seasons' (ϲημαίνοιεν | ἀνδράϲιν ὡραίων, 12–
13). In the penultimate epigram (AB 34) the augur Damon boasts
of his skill at interpreting the 'birds of Zeus', while in the final one

[68] Propertius closes two of his four books with epitaphic poems: 1. 21–2, 4. 11. Epitaphs that
possibly closed epigram books, or sections within them, include Callim. *AP* 7. 415, 525 = 35,
21 Pf. = GP 30, 29, Leon. 7. 715 = GP 93, and Mel. 5. 215 = GP 54 (an embedded example);
see Gutzwiller, *Poetic Garlands*, 40, 108, 299.

[69] Embedding of an epigram within an epigram appears in other literary epitaphs of the
period, e.g. Theoc. *AP* 7. 262 = GP 23, Callim. 7. 522 = 15 Pf. = GP 40, Heraclitus 7. 465; see
P. Laurens, *L'Abeille dans l'ambre* (Paris, 1989), 105–10.

[70] The editors interpret the verb as referring to the phrase ὀρνίθων ἀκρότατος ταμίης, and
Austin translates 'this is the title Alexander gave him with his seal'. While the middle voice
commonly refers to sealing something (acc.), that is not the construction here; nor does the
image of sealing seem appropriate. The middle with the normal active meaning is found in
Hdt. 9. 118. 2 (as one transmitted reading), Aratus 891 (with a play on ϲῆμα), and Nic. *Alex.*
151. Lapini, 'Osservazioni sul nuovo Posidippo', 46 has proposed reading ϲῆμ᾽ ἤνυτο, 'con-
structed a tomb', which, if accepted, would carry the same variety of meanings as ϲημήνατο. But
the change is, to my mind, unnecessary.

[71] Cf. Heraclitus 22 B 93 DK, of Apollo (ὁ ἄναξ, οὗ μαντεῖόν ἐϲτι τὸ ἐν Δελφοῖς, οὔτε λέγει οὔτε
κρύπτει ἀλλὰ ϲημαίνει), Xen. *Mem.* 1. 1. 3 (τοὺς θεοὺς διὰ τούτων αὐτὰ ϲημαίνειν), Pl. *Ti.* 71Ε–72Α;
for discussion of its meaning with regard to divination, see G. Manetti, *Theories of the Sign in
Classical Antiquity*, trans. C. Richardson (Bloomington, IN, 1993), 16–17.

Zeus' reputed son sets up a bird as a $c\hat{\eta}\mu a$, signifying both Strymon's professional skill *and* Alexander's own victory over the Persians.[72] Through his use of allusion and etymological play, forms of signification here thematized, Posidippus illustrates epigrammatically the Stoic argument that omens prove the existence of the gods, although the divine figures are now largely remade as all-powerful Hellenistic monarchs.

LARGER STRUCTURES: PTOLEMIES AND POETS

Empedocles, Anaxagoras, Democritus, and Epicurus are said to have 'constructed their model of the universe on the gathering of bodies composed of small particles' ($\kappa a\tau\grave{a}$ $cuva\theta\rho oic\mu\grave{o}v$ $\tau\hat{\omega}v$ $\lambda\epsilon\pi\tau o\mu\epsilon\rho\hat{\omega}v$ $c\omega\mu\acute{a}\tau\omega v$ $\kappa oc\mu o\pi o\iota o\hat{v}c\iota$, DK 21 A 44). Having begun with the metaphor of the garland, I now submit that atomistic cosmology is also not a bad metaphor for Posidippus' collection, in which we find a $\kappa\acute{o}c\mu oc$ created through the $\check{a}\theta\rho o\iota c\iota c$, or gathering, of $\lambda\epsilon\pi\tau\acute{a}$, the smallest of poems, complete in themselves and finely worked. I have endeavoured to show that this interweaving of epigrams to form a larger whole was accomplished not just by arrangement and verbal connection, but also by a sophisticated use of thematics to give shape and meaning to the sections. Lastly, I turn to broader thematics, by tracing the movement of thought from section to section, and most particularly the interaction of the Ptolemies as divinized/heroic monarchs with the artistic aesthetic that underlies their new $\kappa\acute{o}c\mu oc$. In doing so, I will argue that the collection, as it now remains for us, consists of two sets of four related sections, followed by a third, mostly lost, set of indeterminate length and theme, and I will speculatively suggest how the collection may have begun and ended. While any set of epigrams by a single author will inevitably contain repetition of theme, the thematic complexity of the collection preserved on the Milan papyrus is strong evidence for aesthetically meaningful organization on the part of the author.

The meagre parallels we have for Hellenistic epigram books offer a significant probability that the new Posidippus collection originally began with a longer introductory poem, anticipating major themes. From another fragmentary papyrus we know that an elegiac poem, apparently concerning the marriage of Arsinoe II to her brother Philadelphus, stood at the head of Posidippus' earlier $c\acute{v}\mu\mu\epsilon\iota\kappa\tau a$

---

[72] Plu. *Alex.* 27. 3–4, 73. 2 preserves stories about ravens providing important omens for Alexander: they led him to the shrine of Zeus Ammon and so saved him from death in the desert, and they sent a dire omen of his death at the walls of Babylon.

Kathryn Gutzwiller

ἐπιγράμματα (AB 114 = SH 961). Meleager is likely responsible for the loss of this and other such poems since he anthologized mainly shorter epigrams and had no interest in court themes; however, he did replicate the introductory form by providing a prooemium of 58 lines for his own *Garland* (*AP* 4. 1). Johnson argues that at least two columns are missing from the beginning of the Milan bookroll, ample room for a title followed by a longer epigram functioning as prooemium. Although at this point I am of course only speculating, the parallel provided by the tattered epigram on the earlier papyrus suggests that Posidippus' focus on the Ptolemies, particularly the queens, was first introduced here. If so, then the opening sequence with its oblique references to the domain of Alexander's eastern conquests and cult practices for Arsinoe (as it seems) would less obtusely introduce the Ptolemaic thematics of the collection. In addition, the twenty-line epigram at the end of the stones section with its prayer to Poseidon to preserve Ptolemaic lands (AB 19–20) may seem less surprising in terms of both length and theme.[73]

The presence of the Olympians in the λιθικά—Zeus (perhaps) in AB 1, Poseidon and Demeter in AB 19–20—supports my reading of the section as an epigrammatic cosmology, a presentation of the universe through individual stones and the human or divine beings who have contact with them. In the οἰωνοσκοπικά, concerned with human ability to discern larger meaning and design through natural and accidental signs, these divine figures vanish, or remain merely in image or symbol (note Athena as statue in AB 31). Poseidon links the λιθικά with the omens section only in the sense that the 'long-winged hawk' of the first epigram recalls through Homeric allusion Poseidon disguised as the seer Calchas (*Il.* 13. 62). By the end of the section, however, Alexander, a mortal become god, functions as the maker of signification, by setting up a seer's tomb with a bird emblem. Reading the final epigram so provides transition to the dedicatory section, where the traditional divine recipients of offerings are replaced by Arsinoe, whose first act is to provide the maiden Hegeso a dream vision—a sign—of her desires. Arsinoe with spear and shield in AB 36 also provides a continuation of the military theme, connected to the Argeads and Alexander, that dominates the later part of the οἰωνοσκοπικά, while the maiden's gift of a linen garment accomplishes a feminization of the theme. This short section of

---

[73] The sisterly kiss of Demeter that saves (Egyptian) Eleusis from the violence directed at the Greek mainland (AB 20. 3–4) likely evokes some protective cult activity on the part of a Ptolemaic queen; note that in AB 116 = GP 12 the shrine of Arsinoe Euploia at Zephyrium acts as a 'good harbour from every wave'.

dedications has the function of introducing a new kind of deity for the Ptolemaic world, a deity who not so long ago was still a human being, who shows herself labouring on behalf of mortals (ὀτρηρῶν . . . καμάτων, AB 36. 4), and who acts as a kindly helper to those who pray for aid, like the sailor who finds Arsinoe Euploia 'ready to listen' (τὴν ἐπακουϲομένην, AB 39. 8; cf. Ζεφυρῖτιν ἀκουϲομένην, AB 116. 7 = GP 12. 7). The association of the goddess-queen with her devoted worshippers leads smoothly to the ἐπιτύμβια, where the reader comes fully into the realm of humanity, with emphasis on the joys and sorrows of family and communal life. The gods now mentioned, notably in the opening two epigrams, are kindly deities of the underworld—Hecate (probably), Triptolemus, Rhadamanthys, and Aeacus (AB 42–3)—those gods who effect continued happiness after death for initiates. The final two epitaphs for men, appropriately placed as transition to a section entitled ἀνδριαντοποιικά, round off the movement of the first four sections by presenting a vision of εὐδαιμονία, the longed-for goal of life in the Hellenistic world, both now and for eternity, possible in this Ptolemaic κόϲμοϲ that Posidippus has presented in its physical, divine, and human dimensions.

The metapoetics of the λιθικά, as the first of four interrelated sections, links forward to the metapoetic opening of the ἀνδριαντοποιικά section, which marks an important point of transition to another set of four sections. In the first epigram on statues the poet himself, stepping outside the bounds of normal practice for inscriptional form, articulates a call to 'imitate these works' (μιμ[ή]ϲαϲθε τάδ᾽ ἔργα, AB 62. 1). While reference to the sculptural 'works' in the coming section shows that this epigram was composed with book placement in mind, reference to the critical concept of mimesis, which spans and links the visual and verbal arts, invites a broader reading. The art-historical account that may be pieced together from the epigrams in the ἀνδριαντοποιικά—a development from the 'rigid' (ϲκληρ[οί, l. 5) statues of archaic sculptors to the more energized art of Myron to the culmination of naturalism in the 'new art' of Lysippus—reappears in Cicero (*Brut.* 70) and Quintilian (*Inst.* 12. 10. 7–9), where statuary provides a parallel for the development of rhetorical style.[74] Since the analogy of literary styles to the arts was a feature of Hellenistic canonization, the ἀνδριαντοποιικά with its emphasis on naturalism would easily suggest to Posidippus' readers a parallel development of poetry

---

[74] See Gutzwiller, 'Posidippus on Statuary', 59–60 and Stewart, above, Ch. 10. Certainly by the Augustan era the terminology originally applied to statuary, ϲκληρόϲ and *durus* versus μαλακόϲ and *mollis*, had been adapted to poetic style.

Kathryn Gutzwiller

toward a new aesthetic of the small-scale and realistic.⁷⁵ Throughout
the collection, a number of references to earlier poets defines the
place of Posidippus and his Ptolemaic patrons in a literary history
that parallels, and is explicated by, gem production and sculpture. In
the λιθικά (AB 9) the famous gemstone of Polycrates, who supported
the personal poetry of Anacreon and Ibycus, offers the reader a fascin-
ating *mise en abîme* in which the poet represents a gemstone repre-
senting a lyre with its player.⁷⁶ In addition, the epigram links directly
to the ἀνδριαντοποιικά (AB 37) section, since Theodorus of Samos,
who appears there as the early master of precision and miniatur-
ism in sculpture (AB 67), was the artist who cut Polycrates' stone
(Hdt. 1. 51, 3. 41). In the ἀναθεματικά a lyre, rescued from the sea by
'Arion's dolphin' and brought to Egypt, is dedicated to Arsinoe II,
a gesture suggesting that the queen has inherited the role of artistic
patron from her mainland predecessors.⁷⁷ An anachronistic epigram
in the ἱππικά (AB 83) celebrates the Scopadae, the Thessalian dyn-
asty praised by Simonides (cf. Theoc. *Id.* 16. 36–47, Callim. fr. 64.
14), who, like Anacreon, offered a model for Posidippus' art, since
epigrams attributed to both poets were published in collected form
in the early Hellenistic period. As a contemporary equivalent of these
famous patrons, the younger Berenice calls upon 'all poets' (AB 78.
1) to tell of her κλέος as a victor carrying on the tradition of Ptolemaic
victories.⁷⁸

The key epigram, in which all the elements defining the aesthetic

⁷⁵ A paraphrase of an earlier literary critic in Philodemus' *On Poems* reveals conclusively
that parallelism between poetry and the arts—not just sculpture and painting but gem carv-
ing as well—was a topos in Hellenistic literary theory (*Tract. tert.* col. XVI. 3–21 Sbordone,
with revised text in M. L. Nardelli, 'P. Herc. 1676', 166 n. 17): 'Just as a gem engraver
(δακτυλιογλύφος) has his particular skill not in producing similarity [to a model], since he shares
that with a sculptor and a painter, but in cuttings made in metal and stone, and yet the value
of his art lies not in cutting but in production of similarity [to a model], so likewise a poet has a
particular skill in the art of composition (σύνθεσις) but hunts for value through thought (διάνοια)
and language (λέξις), the elements that are common to others.' I thank Marco Fantuzzi for
showing me in advance of publication his discussion of this passage in Fantuzzi and Hunter,
Tradition and Innovation.
⁷⁶ In best ecphrastic fashion, the reader is asked to imagine an impossible intaglio. How can
a σφρηγίς described as ἀνδρὸς ἀοιδοῦ τοῦ φορμίζοντος σοῖς παρὰ ποσσὶ λύρην be visualized without
violating the limits of possibility for small-scale engraving? The problem of realistic possibility
disappears if we take the construction as a genitive absolute with λύρην as cognate accusative (so
apparently Kuttner, Ch. 8, p. 155), but this is literarily less interesting.
⁷⁷ Cf. Bing, 'Posidippus and the Admiral', 263, who argues that Posidippus' epigram can be
read as 'emblematic of the Ptolemies' claim to be the true inheritors and guardians of the liter-
ary legacy of Hellas'; see too Bing, Ch. 7, pp. 128–9.
⁷⁸ When at the epigram's end the queen asks a choir of 'Macedonian women' (as seems most
likely) to sing her praises (AB 78. 13–14), she evokes as well earlier poetry by or about women,
just as girls in Caryae sing 'Sappho songs' in lamentation for a departed comrade (AB 51;
cf. AB 55).

314

preferences of the Ptolemies and their artists coalesce, is the one about the statue of Philitas (AB 63), significantly placed just after the transitional poem in which the poet calls for a new form of mimesis. As Alexander Sens has shown so well, Philitas' literary excellence as a precise and intricate thinker (ἀκρομέριμνον, AB 63. 5) is mirrored in Hecataeus' similarly precise (ἀ]κ[ρ]ιβὴς ἄκρους, l. 2), intricate (ποικίλλεται, l. 7), and realistic (ἔμψυχ]ος, l. 8) bronze image of him. If the final couplet is to be read as the comment of the statue itself,[79] then the verbal and the visual reach a final synthesis, as Philitas, represented realistically as one about to speak, does in fact speak, to identify Ptolemy, 'both god and king', as the one responsible for the dedication of a 'Coan man' (meaningful final phrase; cf. ἀνὴρ Cάμιο[c in AB 74. 12 of Callicrates dedicating to the Theoi Adelphoi) for the sake of the Muses. Here most clearly, the art history of the ἀνδριαντοποιικά parallels and explicates the poetic history that informs Posidippus' epigram collection: as Hecataeus continues the principles of Lysippan naturalism into the contemporary world of the Ptolemies, so Posidippus, ventriloquizing the bronze Philitas, positions himself as the heir to the aesthetic principles of this master poet.

The metapoetics of the ἀνδριαντοποιικά marks a new beginning in the flow of the collection, as it introduces a set of four sections focusing on different human occupations or realms of achievement (cf. again τάδ' ἔργα, AB 62. 1)—sculpture, racing, sailing, and medicine—all, again, part of the Ptolemaic κόσμος. Throughout the statues section the emphasis on Lysippus as the culmination of the progression toward sculptural naturalism presupposes his famous position as the favourite sculptor of Alexander (Plu. *Alex*. 2. 2), and so associates the aesthetic preferences of the Ptolemies with those of their Macedonian predecessor. The Ptolemaic connection appears most strongly in the ἱππικά section, where the dynasty's claim to *unique* glory is based on cumulative familial achievement that includes rare victories by queens.[80] To my mind, this section is best divided into three sets of six epigrams.[81] The first six (AB 71–6), written as if to

---

[79] Scodel, 'A Note on Posidippus 63 AB' argues that ἄγκειμ]αι, not ἄγκειτ]αι, should be read in the last line, and is followed by A. Stewart, above Ch. 10; but for objections, see A. Sens, above, Ch. 11.

[80] See Fantuzzi in this volume for the significance of the recurring word μόνος. Note that μουνοκέλης in the opening epigram (AB 71. 1), though it refers to single-horse racing, anticipates verbally the theme of the uniqueness of Ptolemaic achievement and so echoes the closing poem, πρῶτο[ι] . . . καὶ μόνοι, AB 88. 1.

[81] My division, for which I make no 'truth claim', differs from those both of BG, pp. 26, 197 and of Fantuzzi, 'Structure', 213, although all three of us find a break after AB 82 (the principal

be inscribed on images of victorious horses,[82] follow naturally on the statues section. Here the dedication of a 'vivid picture' of Callicrates' team and chariot to the Theoi Adelphoi (AB 74) introduces the Ptolemies as heirs to the victors of the past.[83] The second set of six (AB 77–82), in which the victors speak, centres on the younger Berenice, whose voice is heard in the longest of these (AB 78), while the last six (AB 83–8), returning to the inscriptional mode, represent a brief history of prominence in racing from the Thessalians to the Spartans to the Ptolemies and end with two epigrams celebrating the elder Berenice, distinguished by her place in the history of *women* victors. The remaining two sections, while making no direct mention of the Ptolemies, may nonetheless involve their dynastic cult interests in other arenas of human activity. In ναυαγικά we have a cenotaphic record of what can happen at sea to those, the reader may assume, who fail to elicit the help of Arsinoe Euploia, to whom sailors are advised to give ritual greeting in the ἀναθεματικά (AB 39). Curing the sick was also a Ptolemaic cult preoccupation, as witnessed by the connection of Demetrius of Phalerum, functioning as adviser to Ptolemy Soter, with Sarapis as healing god.[84] The ἰαματικά section opens with a dedication by the Ptolemaic courtier Medeus (AB 95), who boasts about curing the bite of the asp, a particularly Egyptian danger. The concluding prayer to Asclepius for moderate wealth and good health (AB 101), seeming to emanate from the poet's own voice, thus links back to the opening of the ἀνδριαντοποιικά and signals a move away from specific realms of activity to a more general treatment of human moral behaviour.

textual clue). BG propose division into two sections, one devoted to the younger Berenice and one to Berenice I (AB 71–82, 83–8), while Fantuzzi, assuming that a distinction between non-royal and royal victors is the main criterion, divides into four groups (AB 71–7, 78–82, 83–6, and 87–8). Although I agree with much of what Fantuzzi says about the arrangement of the section, he does not take account of the connecting link between the first group of six and the statues section (but see his discussion of epigrams on monuments, esp. 'Anacreon', *AP* 6. 135 = *FGE* 6) and overlooks the sense of history that unites AB 83–8. For parallels between the ἱππικά and horse monuments, see Papalexandrou, 'Reading as Seeing', 250–5.

[82] The first, AB 71, is spoken by the victor, but the opening phrase οὗτος ὁ μουνοκέλης shows with its deixis that the epigram is to be visualized as accompanying an image of the horse. Other deictic references follow: θηεῖσθε (72. 1), οὕτω (73. 1), εἰκὼ ἐναργέα, ὧδ' (74. 13–14), οὗ]τος (76. 2); AB 75, which lacks a deictic word in its extant portion, presupposes an image of the four-horse team that speaks.

[83] Callicrates was the first eponymous priest of the cult of Alexander and the Theoi Adelphoi (P. Hibeh II 199 ii 12); on Callicrates' activities in support of the Ptolemies, see Bing, 'Posidippus and the Admiral', especially 246–52 on this epigram.

[84] Demetrius composed paeans for Sarapis because that god cured him of blindness (D.L. 5. 76) and wrote five books recording dreams, particularly those producing cures by Sarapis (Artem. 2. 44). For the worship of Sarapis as healer, see Fraser, *Ptolemaic Alexandria*, i. 256–7, 375.

Partially on that basis, I conjecture that a new series of related sections began with the τρόποι, which seem to present different personality types through the form of epitaphic conversation. The parallel suggested above between the 'brief-speaking' Cretan (AB 102) and the epigrammatic poet strengthens the likelihood that here too the reader was to recognize a point of transition, with reference to the arts, within the thematic flow of the collection. Although the fragmentary remains of the ninth and tenth sections give little evidence of the Ptolemies, the opening words of the tenth referring to 'spring' and 'Zephyr' may possibly link back, once again, to the cult of Arsinoe at Zephyrium.[85]

I ask the reader's indulgence for one final piece of speculation, namely, that the 'Seal' poem may have concluded this collection of epigrams (or possibly a larger collection from which it was selected).[86] The two poems on men that immediately precede the transitional break at the end of the ἐπιτύμβια provide a clear parallel to this poem of twenty-eight lines on Posidippus' old age. The rare motif of 'no need for tears' linking these two epitaphs (μὴ κλαύσητέ με, AB 60. 3; τὸν ἀδάκρυτον . . . λίθον, 61. 3), plausibly connected with initiates, appears also near the end of the 'Seal', where Posidippus contrasts his own afterlife as an initiate in the Dionysiac mysteries with the ritual lamentation conducted on Paros for Archilochus (AB 118. 19–21, 24–6):

> ἀλλ' ἐπὶ μὲν Παρίηι δὸc ἀηδόνι λυγρὸν ἐφ [
> νῆμα κατὰ γληνέων δάκρυα κειṉὰ χέω[ν
> καὶ cτενάχων, δι' ἐμὸν δὲ φίλον cτόμα [
>
> . . . . . .
>
> μηδέ τιc οὖν χεύαι δάκρυον· αὐτὰρ ἐγὼ
> γήραϊ μυcτικὸν οἶμον ἐπὶ Ῥαδάμανθυν ἱκοίμην
> δήμωι καὶ λαῶι παντὶ ποθεινὸc ἐών.

> Give sad lament for the Parian nightingale . . .,
> Vainly casting streams of tears from your eyes
> and groaning, but through my own mouth . . .
>
> . . . . . .
>
> So may no one shed a tear. Rather in old age
> may I travel the mystic path to Rhadamanthys,
> adored by the city and all its people.

---

[85] For speculation about this section and poetry on sailing in spring, see Bernsdorff, 'Anmerkungen zum neuen Poseidippos', 32–7.

[86] Lloyd-Jones, 'The Seal of Posidippus', who demonstrated the nature of the piece as a *sphragis*, thought of an introductory position. But A. Barigazzi, 'Il testamento di Posidippo di Pella', 201–2 has pointed out that a concluding position is more likely. For my earlier guess that the 'Seal' concluded Posidippus' *Epigrammata*, see Gutzwiller, *Poetic Garlands*, 154–5.

Rhadamanthys also provides an echo of the second epigram in the
ἐπιτύμβια (AB 43), which, it seems, was part of an opening sequence
on women initiates, one of whom is from Pella (AB 44). Since a gold
lamella from a fourth-century Macedonian grave, bearing the inscrip-
tion Περcεφόνηι Πocείδιππoc μύcτηc εὐcεβήc (AB T 1), was buried with
an initiate who was most likely an ancestor of our poet,[87] the 'Seal'
clearly reflects the historical reality of Posidippus' own religious
experience and his Macedonian heritage. But the key positioning of
the epitaphs on women initiates and on the two fortunate men, at the
end of the thematic flow connecting the first four sections, strongly
suggests that a meaningful link was established within the collection
in its original complete form.

The beginning of the ἀνδριαντοποιικά also foreshadows this longer
poem. In the 'Seal' Posidippus asks Apollo, following the precedent
of his oracle establishing the heroic shrine for Archilochus on Paros,
to issue a proclamation concerning himself so that the Macedonians
will honour him. Specifically, he asks that a statue of himself unrolling
a book be set up in the crowded market place of Pella (AB 118. 17–18),
a request that reprises the major aesthetic themes of the Milan col-
lection. Eschewing the heroic honours provided Archilochus, the old
Posidippus fashions for himself honours that mimic those of the eld-
erly Philitas, whose realistic statue was made in human scale without
any of the form given heroes (AB 63. 3–4). The image of Posidippus
unrolling his book in the midst of multifarious humanity resonates
beautifully at the end of the collection where the arts and poetry
repeatedly analogize, one to illuminate the other, and where the ulti-
mate subject is the multiplicity of life in the Macedonian/Ptolemaic
world. After asking the reader repeatedly to visualize an art object in
order to understand his own poetic principles, Posidippus may, at
the end of his collection, ask that he himself, the poet/editor, be visu-
alized holding what can be imagined as the very epigram collection
perused by the reader. Positioned there, a distinguished older man,
beloved by all the people, still steady on his feet (ἀcκίπων ἐν ποccί, 118.
27; cf. 96), a correct speaker in the public forum (ὀρθοεπήc, 118. 27),
a family man leaving a decent inheritance to his children (δῶμα καὶ
ὄλβον, 118. 28; cf. 101), he encapsulates the vision of εὐδαιμονία and
of artistic merit that appears in his collection. He here realizes the
request that he makes at the end of the ἰαματικά for 'moderate wealth'
and 'health', constituting the 'high citadel' of human life, so that the
transitional point after the second set of four sections also links to

[87] See Dickie, 'The Dionysiac Mysteries in Pella', and Rossi, 'Il testamento di Posidippo'.

318

the 'Seal'. In addition, the linguistic quality of ὀρθοέπεια, 'straight speaking,' that marks this elderly Posidippus clearly recalls the artistic canon enunciated in the Philitas poem (ἀληθείης ὀρθὸν . . . κανόνα, 63. 6). Dionysius of Halicarnassus (*Dem.* 26) points out that in style Plato was considered the κανὼν ὀρθοεπείας, even though he sometimes lapsed from Attic clarity toward prolixity.[88] As Hecataeus' realism rather than Polyclitus' classical mimesis now represents the 'straight canon of truth' in sculpture, so Posidippus' epigrammatic simplicity rather than Plato's philosophical prolixity becomes the new 'canon of straight speaking' in the verbal arts. If this argument about the 'Seal' is right, in the end, then, the poet himself comes to embody both the good life and the artistic qualities that he projects in his epigram book.

[88] Plato (*Phdr.* 267 c) uses ὀρθοέπεια to refer to Protagoras' writings on language and grammar, and his own *Cratylus*, concerned with the naturally as well as conventionally correct use of words, bore this term as its title. Posidippus may use the term to refer not only to his simple style, appropriate to his genre, but also to speech that reflects Stoic 'right reason' (ὀρθὸς λόγος), the principle that underlies order in the universe (D.L. 7. 88).

16

The Search for the Perfect Book:
A PS to the New Posidippus

A ROMAN CONTEXT FOR HELLENISTIC BOOKS

My topic for this Roman PS is emphatically not allusions to
Posidippus in Roman poetry: this has been throroughly explored by
Gregory Hutchinson.[1] I used to have something to say on what for
a Latinist is one of the most striking aspects of the new papyrus,
the presence of strategies of textual order that implicate geography
and politics; but that has all been anticipated in the present volume
and in various conferences during the *annus mirabilis* of Posidippus'
career, 2002. So I am talking about a more indirect contact between
the new papyrus and the study of Roman literature: about the way
new research on Hellenistic poetry books can help Latinists to revive
but also revise one of their professional obsessions, the search for the
perfect book.[2]

The Search for the Perfect Book has been the masterplot of
research on Roman poetry in the 1970s and 1980s. Vergil's *Bucolics*,
Propertius, and Horace have emerged as the origins of the poetry book
in the Western canon. Today, when we revisit some of the bibliog-
raphy, the whole approach sounds intolerably idealizing and even
fetishistic. The perfect book, to me at least, sounds like the equivalent
of avant-garde painting in the art market of, let us say, New York,
soon after World War II. That geometric perfection is reminiscent of
Mondrian and his rise: those readers want from Propertius and Horace

For discussions on various aspects of this chapter I am grateful to Brian Breed, Joy Connolly,
Traianos Gagos, Stephen Heyworth, Gregory Hutchinson, Nita Krevans, Ann Kuttner, Ilaria
Marchesi, Jay Reed, Luigi Enrico Rossi, Susan Stephens, Sarah Stroup, and the editor.

  [1] Hutchinson, 'The New Posidippus and Latin Poetry'.
  [2] Ironically for a study of the poetics of books, most of the input for my own approach comes
from oral transmission: an unforgettable paper by the late Don Fowler, supported by a 14-page
handout, to be followed in due course by publication of his posthumous essay on the book;
information from Nita Krevans about her important study of the poetics of Augustan books
(preceded by her Princeton dissertation of 1984: *non vidi*).

the ancient counterpart to abstract art, concentration on structure as a statement of avant-garde.[3] From our present perspective, one main flaw had been the tendency to centre everything on the creative intention of the author and his control of the structure. We will come back precisely to this problem later. But there have been also at least two significant breakthroughs in this search: one is the recuperation of the ancient book as a material object, with its specific features and constraints (particularly in the pioneering approach of J. Van Sickle) and the other is the rediscovery of anti-structural forces, for example in the work of Horace, in a complex situation when the author is aware of the conditioning pressure and of the semiotic richness of the book format, but is also anxious to recreate a sense of performative autonomy for every single lyric poem he publishes (important ideas especially in the approaches of Matthew Santirocco, Michèle Lowrie, and Nita Krevans).[4]

That said, I need a preliminary caveat. For the literary scholar, it is crucial to keep listening to the sceptical voices of papyrologists. Whenever we idealize and essentialize the Book, we need their ironic reaction—'the book, yes, the Book . . .'—ironic, because they immediately see how much abstraction and generalization it takes whenever we try to move from the individual to the species. In today's Classics, dialogue between empiricism and theory has become even more vital. One goes to a conference on Death in Antiquity, where most of the papers are about aesthetic recreations of death in poetry, and there goes the specialist, a respected French historian who writes about torture, executions, proscriptions, and morgues in ancient Rome. 'You had it all wrong'—he says bluntly—'this is not what Death is all about.' Then he shrugs, takes a deep breath and says: 'La Mort, c'est les morts . . .' and goes on to discuss the visibility of corpses in Roman cities, and post-mortem regulations for executed criminals. Similarly, the enthusiastic scholar working on cultural poetics of archaic Greece will always need the cautious voice of the social historian (again, with some ironic inflexion): 'oh yes, the polis, the Polis . . .'. But of course papyrology can offer more than simply antagonism and anti-essentialism: scholars of textual culture are now bridging the gap between semiotics (even cognitive studies)

---

[3] In fact the favourite text of the 'perfect book' approach has been the *Bucolics*, for a long time a favourite area for the New Critics; on links between the New Critics and Abstract Expressionism, see the refreshing paper by J. Connolly, 'Picture Arcadia', esp. 99–104.

[4] See respectively J. Van Sickle, 'The Book-Roll and Some Conventions of the Poetry Book'; Santirocco, *Unity and Design in Horace's Odes*; M. Lowrie, *Horace's Narrative Odes* (Oxford, 1997).

and material culture, and their work is therefore an ideal contact zone with literary interpretation. They are the people who can best explain the value of individual books as acts of communication and expressions of taste and social interaction.[5]

In this evolving context, the focus of my discussion will be the effects of Greek books on Roman poetry books. Let me begin by recapitulating some of the final results of Gutzwiller's research on epigram books from Callimachus to Meleager.[6] Meleager's *Stephanos* was not solely important as a compendium, it was an epoch-making aesthetic object. It had elegiac texts, that is, longer than epigrams, as beginning and end; it had grouping of poems by theme and function. One immediate distinction is needed. The division in formalized categories had ample precedent, as now demonstrated by the new Posidippus. The effect on Roman poets of the first century BC or AD is not great if we think simply about tidy distribution into functional blocks. More original—and here is the new emphasis in Gutzwiller's conclusion—was the structuring in short multi-authorial sequences, often connected by relationships of model and imitation-cum-variation. The impulse here could have been the sequence of epigrams on Myron's *Cow* gathered by Antipater of Sidon. This is interesting because it shows a link between the idea of an artistic book and issues of imitation and reproduction, visual and textual. The *Cow* itself was both a model and a copy: its idea was that of lifelike reproduction, and it became the object of many acts of reproduction. Roman poets cannot have been indifferent to this example, to judge from the situation of Apollo Palatinus in 28 BC. After a long tradition of visual and textual reproduction, four Myron-like lifelike cows *in situ* were admired by Propertius (2. 31. 8 *quattuor artifices, vivida signa, boves*: note the compressed irony of *artifices* and *vivida*), who implicitly continues the tradition of writing about the *Cow*(s), with the added twist that he is a Roman: he lives in Replicaland.[7]

More generally, the diffusion of Meleager as a model in Roman poetry between the times of Caesar and Octavian is striking. It is not just the amount of traceable intertextuality: it is more about the strategic and ambitious positioning of allusions. The alluding texts are Catullus 1, Propertius 1. 1. 1–2, and (probably) Vergil, *Buc.* 1. 1–2 and Horace, *Ode* 1. 38:[8] the programmatic incipits of three of

---

[5] W. Johnson, above, Ch. 4 is representative of this evolution.

[6] *Poetic Garlands*, 321–2 See also ead., 'The Poetics of Editing in Meleager's Garland'.

[7] For a new attention to the semiotic status of the so-called 'Roman copies' see E. Gazda (ed.), *The Ancient Art of Emulation* (Ann Arbor, 2002).

[8] For the first two poems see the standard commentaries; for the Vergilian text, Gutzwiller,

the most ambitious 'perfect books' written in Latin (and the explicit of a fourth) are linked by a shared interest in Meleager. The logical implication is that this reference to a model was important not just as a bow to an individual poet—Catullus, Vergil, Propertius, and Horace had many other options if they wanted to flag a specific Greek model through allusion, and the models are taken from different points of the *Garland*—and not even solely as a generic pointer to epigram as a kind of poetry (significant to the agenda of Catullus and Propertius, not so for Horace and Vergil), but as an icon of the beautiful book, the well-wrought collection.[9] They invoke Meleager at points of inauguration and closure because this particular poet knew how to shape a collection, complete with beginnings, endings, and planned variety of poems.

The other link with Rome—this too helps to explain the popularity of Meleager—is that when Roman poets take to composing books where some of the poems have the status of translations—Catullus mixes his own texts with his own Sapphic and Callimachean versions—Greek poets have already started making books where epigram sequences include past masters and modern variations. Catullan translations can be seen as a response to this strategy, not only as a response to the local tradition of 'Vortit Barbare'. The so-called pre-Neoterics on the other hand would have been perfectly able to draw the lesson too, for there was never a single breakthrough of Greek book culture in Rome, not Meleager, not Parthenius, there was always a *guttatim* process. People like Porcius Licinus and Lutatius Catulus wrote epigrams and short pieces, they were exposed to Callimachus, Bion, Antipater. The problem is that, quite simply, we do not have a clue about collections and books in the generations before Catullus. By the second quarter of the first century BC, anyway, the well-planned book is already the icon of chic communication. Guglielmo Cavallo points out that the elegiac graffiti by Tiburtinus in Pompeii are not average graffiti, but the layout invites comparison with that of a well-planned *liber*.[10] In the age of Cicero and Catullus,[11] the *libellus* is an object of affection and *amicitia*, privileged and fetishized, a cult object in exchange and trade; people are fond of talking about their book-

---

'Vergil and the Date of the Theocritean Epigram Book', 95–7; on Horace, *Ode* 1. 38 and his minimalist wreath, see below.

  [9] For a similar approach to the allusion in Catullus 1 see N. Holzberg, *Catull* (Munich, 2002), 12. I return below to the Catullan poetics of the book.

  [10] Guglielmo Cavallo ap. A. M. Morelli, *L'epigramma latino prima di Catullo* (Cassino, 2000), 341–2.

  [11] Here I am indebted to conversations with Sarah Stroup about her work on these topics, in particular her forthcoming book *A Society of Patrons*.

rolls, display them, mention them in letters and go to bed and travel around with books. Texts seem to be promoted and used as 'objects of affection', and subjects of violence, they can represent and stand in for social relations, they become personified, sometimes like family members, or acquire a certain erotic physicality. This is why the search for the perfect book, for all its modern shortcomings, should not be simply brushed aside: it was part of Roman culture and it was fed by a continuous import of improved books. We cannot prove a direct link with the boom of artistic arrangements in Roman poetry, but we should not dismiss this either as a Neoteric eccentricity.

Now if we look at the Posidippus papyrus as an anticipation of the search for the perfect book, it is not just the separate headings and blocks of poems that attract our attention. More prominent is the distribution of poems within the various categories, and especially the positional privilege awarded to poems about the Ptolemies and Alexander. This strategy has some obvious aspects, but it also includes more subtle effects of positioning. I do not dwell on the details because so many observations have been made by other contributors to this volume. What interests me now is that, starting from this very early example, it should be possible to revisit later evidence on epigram books and look not for dependence on Posidippus and on this particular exemplar as an individual model but for some continuous tradition involving many authors, and if possible readers, producers, and buyers.

The question of whether to believe that an epigram book has artistic arrangement is not exclusive to the age of Posidippus, Asclepiades, and their likes, and it is helpful to have a look at Roman collections that are uncontroversially authorial yet for a long time have not been credited with much of a significant patterning. Martial could be an interesting witness.

THE SELF-CONSCIOUS BOOK AND THE AUTHOR'S AUTHORITY

The simple device of framing a collection of short pieces in praise of a ruler is found e.g. in Martial's so-called book 13, the *Xenia*—incidentally, this slender book in Latin is a part of a tradition of poems on objects that receives some indirect light from Posidippus' gem collection. The book has three programmatic poems and then the first regular piece, i.e. the first distich on objects (13. 4), is:

Tus
Serus ut aetheriae Germanicus imperet aulae
Utque diu terris, da pia tura Iovi.

Frankincense. Give pious incense to Jupiter, and wish that Germanicus may become a ruler of the celestial Court as late as possible, and as long as possible on earth.

while the final epigram (13. 127) is:

Coronae roseae

Dat festinatas, Caesar, tibi bruma coronas:
Quondam veris erat, nunc tua facta rosa est.

Rose garlands. Winter offers you hasty garlands, Caesar: the rose used to belong to the springtime, now it is yours.

Frankincense and roses, sacrifice and wreathing, clearly complement each other, as do the two official titles Germanicus and Caesar. In particular, a poem about garlands at the end of an epigram collection[12] cannot be a coincidence: Meleager begins and ends[13] his anthology with a reference to στέφανοι. Horace, *Ode* 1. 38—in a poem indebted to Meleager, as I think Nita Krevans was the first to argue[14]—had focused on a simple wreath of myrtle (it had been the plant of Callimachus in the complicated garland of Meleager's proem, *AP* 4. 1. 21–2), and refused all the other flowers, especially the costly, exotic and artificial late roses. Martial reinstates the roses, emphatically early ones, as a homage to the emperor, as a seasonal marker, and as part of a sympotic isotopy that runs through the entire book: *unguentum* is the topic of the previous poem (126), fully complementary to roses in the evocation of a banquet. But there is also a neat twist of ironic modesty. *Festinatas*, the adjective that marks the flowers as anti-Horatian winter roses, is also a buzzword in Martial for the allegedly simple and hasty poetics of his epigram books: *festinatis . . . libellis* (Mart. 2. 91. 3)—except that of course the allusions to Meleager and Horace guarantee that this poet can make a pretty garland even in hasty nonchalance.

The problem is that, in order to believe this kind of argument, we have to rely so much on images of the controlling and designing artist—and that involves a continuous process of re-evaluation: was poet X good enough?—but what would help us even more is evidence about how people would read and produce and market book-rolls, and desire a perfect book.

---

[12] Compare the observations on book structure in T. J. Leary, *Martial Book XIII: The Xenia* (London, 2001), 10–11 and 194–5, after the influential paper by D. P. Fowler, 'Martial and the Book', 223–4.

[13] The classic analysis of Meleager GP 129 is Bing, *The Well-Read Muse*, 34.

[14] In her dissertation of 1984 (*non vidi*).

Alessandro Barchiesi

As an author, Martial is important in this whole tradition.[15] His insistence on the spontaneous and improvised character of his book collections implies, by contrast, readers who care about quality. He recapitulates and intensifies the traditional oscillation of epigram collections about 'here' and 'not here', the idea that the epigram has a place in a book but this cannot be the whole story, it also belongs elsewhere, that is to gravestones, objects, gifts, occasions, symposia, private messages, inscriptions: the epigram can be fastened and unique, or mobile and ephemeral. The book offers itself as the ideal compromise: it is permanent and mobile, repeatable and authentic, but the compromise can be easily destroyed. Therefore epigram books like to play on the fragility and stability of their format. The climax of this tradition is his proem to Martial's so-called book 14, the *Apophoreta*, where we encounter the following performative description of the book (14. 1. 5):

> divitis alternas et pauperis accipe sortes

Please accept the alternating lots of the rich and poor.

The epigrams are strikingly called *sortes*. They are *alternae* because the book structure will be based on alternation of cheap and expensive gifts—and also of course because they are in elegiacs, since *alternus* is Ovidian jargon for elegiac couplets (cf. Ov. *fast.* 2. 121; *trist.* 3. 1. 11; 3. 1. 56; 3. 7. 10; (?) *her.* 15. 5). Regarding the *sortes*, it must be significant that there was a tradition of gift lotteries at the Saturnalia: but then the orderly formal principle of alternation 'appears somewhat at odds with the concept of a lottery',[16] to quote a somewhat understated comment. The irony is that the book has a neat sequential order of gifts, very appropriate to the divisions in Roman social cosmology, yet as soon as they—the Saturnalian readers—perform the book, the book will dissolve into a myriad of little cards and the order will be reshuffled in performance. Value will change too: some poems will be validated as cheap, some as expensive. The performative function of the book of *Apophoreta* can be seen through the action of Petronius' *Cena Trimalchionis* (56. 7): *cum pittacia in scypho circumferri coeperunt, puerque super hoc positus officium apophoreta*

---

[15] My chapter has not enough space for references to the many recent and stimulating publications on Martial, but I need to mention at least two forthcoming papers which offer important insights on poetic memory and epigrammatic concentration on 'stuff' (S. Hinds, 'Martial's Ovid', forthcoming) and on the dynamics of text and material object in books 13 and 14 (S. Stroup, 'Invaluable Collections'); also important are L. Roman , 'The Representation of Literary Materiality in Martial's Epigrams', M. Citroni, 'Marziale e la letteratura per i Saturnali', and Fowler, 'Martial and the Book'.

[16] T. J. Leary, *Martial Book XIV. The Apophoreta* (London, 1996), 53.

recitavit. Of course if they do this, people will not only destroy Martial's construction but also its implied social hierarchy, yet this is after all what the Saturnalia are about, controlled suspension of privilege, a temporary licence for chaos.

Therefore the reader should savour the precarious beauty of the order, which is both there and not there: the question that the book is posing is the most basic question that can be offered to a customer of a text entitled 'Take Away', *Apophoreta*: 'is it for here, or to go?', the answer being double-edged: 'for here', the book you are reading, 'to go', the individual gift or poem you are entitled to.

The *Apophoreta* is deeply Saturnalian literature, as should be clear from the incipit:

APOPHORETA
Synthesibus dum gaudet eques dominusque senator
Dumque decent nostrum pillea sumpta Iovem . . .

While the equestrian and the master senator enjoy their *syntheses*, and while *pillea* look good on our Jupiter . . . (14. 1. 1–2)

Domitian is Jupiter in the age of Saturn, or rather, in this mini-age of Saturn which is the Saturnalia: free to be a *libertus*, while Saturnus is a detainee in the perennial age of Jupiter. While he wears the cap of a *libertus*, senators and equites will suspend social distinctions by donning the *synthesis,* the casual dinner dress that they would never wear in public for the rest of the year. How nice, then, that cύνθεcιc is also the Greek for any 'combination, collection, series of matching items'. People of all orders, apparently, enjoy a good collection. As a piece of clothing, *synthesis* is also important because it is the Saturnalian alternative to *toga*, which is, we should not forget, the second word of the matching collection of easy pieces,[17] the *Xenia*:

XENIA
Ne toga cordylis et paenula desit olivis
Aut inopem metuat sordida blatta famem,
Perdite Niliacas, Musae, mea damna, papyros . . .

So that there may be no shortage of togas for tunas and hooded cloaks for olives, and the foul book-worm may not fear debilitating hunger, waste, O Muses, the Nilotic papyrus (the loss is mine) . . . (13. 1. 1–3)

On the one hand, if the beginning boldly covets the same kind of triumphant autonomy allotted to e.g. *Arma virumque*, then *Ne toga*

---

[17] The polarity is clearly laid out at Mart. 14. 142: '*Synthesis*. Dum toga per quinas gaudet requiescere luces | hos poteris cultus sumere iure tuo' (*Synthesis*. While the toga enjoys five days of rest, you are fully entitled to this outfit).

will become a self-contained tag—almost like the book of 'no toga', a prescription for casual dress, as well as a programme for loose, laid-back poetic entertainment. If one extends the tag to *ne toga cordylis*, what we have is of course one of the funniest poetic incipits ever ('No toga for tuna'), but also the typical metaliterary joke on bad poems as wrappings. There is a clear self-reflexive underpinning: the story of poetry-as-wastepaper begins in Latin with Catullus 95. 8 where the *Annales* of Volusius *laxas scombris saepe dabunt tunicas*, and there is a sense of increased waste when *toga* replaces *tunica*: Catullus is for Martial the classic that awaits a successor. But it is interesting to note a much more subtle effect. Martial often displays dependence on Catullus and makes much more oblique declarations about his fundamental but often antagonistic link to the major Augustan poets. Horace had answered the Catullan model at the end of his Letter to Augustus (*Epist.* 2. 1. 269–70):

> deferar in vicum vendentem tus et odores
> et piper et quidquid chartis amicitur ineptis.

I will be transported to the block where they sell incense and fragrances, and pepper, and whatever is wrapped in silly pages.

The choice of perfumes and aromas instead of fish possibly includes a Horatian dig at Catullus: the poem that Catullus was praising above Volusius' stinking fish-wrappers had as a title the most sought-after of *odores*, the *myrrha* (Cinna's *Zmyrna*): so the substitution of perfume-wrappings for fish-wrappings is not innocent, but implies criticism of the Neoteric canon. Martial's first two items in the collection, the first two material poems, are respectively (13. 4) *Tus* and (13. 5) *Piper*, with a recall of the Horatian option for poetry as a present-wrapper.

Similarly rich in intertextuality is the end of the book of *Apophoreta* (14. 223):

Adipata

> Surgite: iam vendit pueris ientacula pistor
> Cristataeque sonant undique lucis aves.

Deep-fried pastry. Arise. Already the baker is selling the boys their breakfast cookies and the crested birds of daybreak are sounding forth on every side.

On a thematic level, the dawn and the idea of 'back to school' are both effective closural devices: end of night-time entertainment, end of winter holidays. But the use of *surgite* reminds us of other strategies of ending: similar invitations can conclude a play (*exsurgite* is the final word of Plautus' *Epidicus*), a book of poetry (Verg. *Buc.* 10. 75 *surgamus*, perhaps alluding to transition to a grander work) and

328

even a three-book sequence of dialogues (Cic. *De orat.* 1. 265. 7 *cum exsurgeret, simul adridens*, end of first book; 2. 367. 11 *quoniam est id temporis, surgendum censeo et requiescendum*, end of second book; *De orat* 3. 230. 7 *'Sed iam surgamus' inquit*, end of third).[18] The choice of *adipata* as the final item, could have a paradoxical kind of implication: another occurrence of this rare word in extant Latin is a Ciceronian metaphor for cheap and heavy, greasy Asianism:

> itaque Caria et Phrygia et Mysia, quod minime politae minimeque elegantes sunt, adsciverunt aptum suis auribus opimum quoddam et tanquam *adipatae dictionis genus* quod eorum vicini non ita lato interiecto mari Rhodii numquam probaverunt, Graeci autem multo minus, Athenienses vero funditus repudiaverunt. (Cic. *Orat.* 25)

Thus Caria and Mysia, since they completely lack elegance and taste, have adopted that fattened kind of style, so appropriate to their ears, that deep-fried style, if I may say so, that was never quite popular with their neighbours of Rhodes, across a short sea channel, and even less with the Greeks, and was totally banished by the Athenians.

But Martial's 'small breakfast cookies for schoolchildren' are, by contrast, an example of the lean cuisine of Atticism, as far as possible from bombastic heaviness.

The general strategy of *Xenia* and *Apophoreta* resembles but also partly inverts the relationship between the λιθικά and material culture explained by Ann Kuttner:[19] Martial's book is the source of an anti-collection of slips of paper, of soon to be distributed gift-labels; instead of being, more obviously, the result of the act of collecting, it is the total of a forthcoming fragmentation—and will survive it. Because of the repeatable and plural nature of texts the users can have their cakes and also eat them, or more exactly the poet/reader can have the cake while the dinner-guest takes it away.

Whether we decide to accept this kind of reading effect or not, the importance of book arrangement is in the eye of the beholder, i.e. depends on our assessment of the author's quality and poetics. Martial scholars have started only recently to accept that Martial's well-known commitment to the imagery and *Realien* language of book-production and book-trade can be related to a deep interest in the effects of book format on the meaning of poems. The same

---

[18] See also Citroni, 'Marziale e la letteratura per i Saturnali', with Fowler, 'Martial and the Book', 223–4

[19] Above, Ch. 8, on the dialectics between the 'slip of papyrus' as a *prière d'insérer* for the costly present, the poem as a substitute for the precious gift, the book as the literary surrogate of gem-collecting.

question is now facing scholarship on the new Posidippus, again with implications about the literary competence and canonic standing of the author.

In Roman imperial culture, the question also invests prose. If we move from Martial to Pliny the Younger, like Martial surely a 'next big thing' in Roman studies, we find again that the status of the author in Roman society, and in modern scholarship, is crucial to the evaluation of the book format, and goes in hand with the problem of whether to believe in declarations of simplicity, improvisation, and spontaneity. The clearest possible statement is the prooemial letter to the powerful 'friend' Septicius Clarus. This is clearly a letter that is designed to be an introduction to the whole collection, yet it says very explicitly that this is not going to be a 'perfect book', and that at the moment of composing 1. 1 the author has not even achieved complete control over his material, since some letters are still out there waiting for the act of collecting, and some have yet to be composed: the genre of 'letters' and the act of collecting and publishing is being enhanced, as befits a preface, yet the arrangement of the letters is and will be a random one, although with some unspecified attempt at selection (*si quas paulo curatius scripsissem*). We may well wonder how far the existence of 1. 1 will condition the composition of future letters, but there is certainly no mention of rewriting the ones which are already 'at hand'. In the meantime, we learn that this author is open to the influence of a powerful friend:

C. PLINIVS SEPTICIO ⟨CLARO⟩ SVO S.

Frequenter hortatus es ut epistulas, si quas paulo curatius scripsissem, colligerem publicaremque. Collegi non seruato temporis ordine (neque enim historiam componebam), sed ut quaeque in manus uenerat. Superest ut nec te consilii nec me paeniteat obsequii. Ita enim fiet, ut eas quae adhuc neglectae iacent requiram et si quas addidero non supprimam. Vale.

Pliny to his friend Septicius Clarus. You frequently advised me to collect and publish my letters, the ones which were written in a less casual way. So I did collect them, without attention to their chronology—obviously I was not composing a history—but in the order of their coming to my hand. The next step is that you do not regret having made your suggestion, and I don't regret your influence. So I will start searching the ones which have hitherto been put away and forgotten, and I shall not destroy the ones I keep adding. Be well.

The final letter of the nine-book collection looks definitely less innocent. It begins by stating that the addressee likes the letter(s) a lot (*scribis pergratas tibi fuisse litteras meas*)—not of course the entire collection, only Pliny's correspondence with him, but how can we not broaden the reference to the entire opus, considering that we are reading the end of Pliny's collected letters?[20] The power situation seems to have shifted since the time of letter 1. 1. The new addressee is evidently less visible than Pliny, and not only enjoys the letters, but wants them to be an image of the author, a person whose status has been steadily growing both in the time elapsed from 1. 1 and through the readerly reception of the *Epistles*, the act of unfolding the whole collection (9. 40. 1–3):

C. PLINIVS FVSCO SVO S.

Scribis *pergratas tibi fuisse litteras meas*, quibus cognouisti quemadmodum in Tuscis *otium aestatis* exigerem; requiris quid ex hoc in *Laurentino hieme* permutem. Nihil, nisi quod *meridianus* somnus eximitur multumque de *nocte* uel ante uel post *diem* sumitur, et, si agendi necessitas instat, quae frequens *hieme*, non iam comoedo uel lyristae post cenam locus, *sed illa, quae dictaui, identidem retractantur*, ac simul memoriae frequenti *emendatione* proficitur. Habes *aestate hieme* consuetudinem; addas huc licet *uer et autumnum,* quae inter *hiemem aestatemque* media, ut nihil de *die* perdunt, de *nocte* paruolum adquirunt. Vale.

Pliny to his friend Fuscus. You write you deeply enjoyed my letter(s), since you had a chance to know how I spend my summer holidays in the Tuscan villa; your question is how far is my winter here in Laurentum different. There is no difference, except that I give up my noon siesta, and that I extend my day during early morning, and evening, thus shortening the night, and, if there is necessity to work, as is frequently the case in the winter, there is no room for a comedian or a lyre-player after dinner, but there is a frequent reworking of what I have been dictating, and a continuous process of improvement through memory. You have the entire routine of winter and summer then: you may add spring and autumn, the intermediate seasons, during which none of the day is wasted, and so very little is stolen from the night. Be well.

The difference from 1. 1 is not only that now the addressee is Pliny's inferior, wants to know about Pliny the author, and enjoys the letter(s) (*pergratas*). There are also formal differences. The sequence of temporal markers is an elegant stylization of the very idea of closure: seasons and times of day complete each other (note the striking redundance of *aestatis . . . hieme . . . meridianus . . . nocte . . . diem . . . aestate . . . hieme . . . uer . . . autumnum . . . hiemem aestatemque . . . die . . . nocte*) just as the collection saturates a mosaic of the lifetime of Pliny. The author emerges from this final letter as a master of

---

[20] Pliny's letters are *epistulae*, but *litterae* need not mean a single letter, cf. Cic. *Phil.* 12. 1, Plin. *HN* 15. 133.

time: his control over his rhythm of work and leisure corrects the asymmetry created by the natural alternation of long winter nights and long summer days. And just when the style becomes more openly self-conscious, the profound difference is that precisely here we encounter a reference to the stages of creative rewriting—*dictatio*, *retractatio*, *memoria*, and *emendatio*, the whole process of textual composition by an illustrious prose writer in Roman culture. To be sure, Pliny is ostensibly speaking only about his oratory, not about letters, but as far as this letter belongs to its place in the book, the implication must be that letter-writing too is not a casual, occasional production when such an important author is the writer. Hence an invitation to revisit the entire nine-book opus as a true collection, planned, rewritten and improved, by a self-conscious author and a perfectionist. As a confirmation, all we need is a glance at the paratext of both letters: if this is a real book, even the addressees must become a part of its meaning, so how casual is it that the modest prooemial letter is addressing the patronizing *Clarus*, Mr VIP, while the addressee of the self-conscious final letter is the devoted fan *Fuscus*, Mr Almost Famous?

When it comes to Hellenistic poetry, the very names Alexandrian and Hellenistic appear to guarantee the search for those bookish effects: but Pliny the Younger has been for a long time allotted to prosopography and social history, so nobody has been looking for them.[21] Yet he had many reasons to be interested in the 'perfect book': the epistolary tradition itself, of course, but also familiarity with epigram/elegy authors, in Greek and Latin. Besides reading and listening, he had been one of those poets occasionally. He knew from inside out a genre in which improvisation must be wedded to planning, and occasion to publication.

The related question is of course how far do Roman authors care for the book form, not for the form of their books, but for the fact that Hellenic models come in books, already arranged in book format? Later I will try to relate this question to my 'fuzzy' model of tradition, but I do not wish to deny out of hand the importance of authorial innovation and one-on-one dynamics. We have already mentioned a couple of aspects of Catullan book-poetics: the allusion to Meleager in poem 1 implies recognition of the cτέφανοc as a model for artistic book-arrangement, the alternation of imitation and

---

[21] The approach to Plinian prose is changing very quickly: see e.g. I. Marchesi, 'A Complex Prose' (diss. Rutgers, 2002); J. Bodel, *The Publication of Pliny's Letters* (Ann Arbor, forthcoming).

translation can be viewed as a response to the potted literary histories in epigram collections. Now we can focus on a more crucial issue. Is there a way for us to connect speculations about the book format of Catullus' oeuvre with his reception of specific Greek models? I choose the sequence of poems 65–116 for a double reason: (i) it has a good chance of being an authorial collection,[22] and (ii) it shows promising traces of close engagement with one Greek model, one model that features in modern research as the *ne plus ultra* of a pre-Roman poetics of the book: the poetic work of Callimachus. The two issues are in fact related: 65–116 is a likely candidate for a Catullan book because it is a sequential *summa* of his output in elegiacs, and Callimachus is famous in Hellenistic–Roman culture essentially as the number one of elegy/epigram (the two genres are overlapping in this respect).

CATULLUS, THE BOOK, AND THE STRUCTURE OF CALLIMACHUS' *AITIA*

Let us start from a minimalist question: what did the incipit of the elegiac masterpiece by Callimachus, the *Aitia*, look like? this is what we can glean from papyrus evidence (Callimachus, *Aitia* 1. 1 Massimilla = Pf.):

......ι μοι Τελχῖνες ἐπιτρύζουϲιν ἀοιδῆι

The Telchines squeak away at me, at my poem

Alan Cameron has recently pointed out[23] that Lobel's πολλάκι must be right: it fits a well-known initial formula of Attic speeches,[24] and this 'much quoted proem' could have influenced the popularity of πολλάκι as an epigrammatic beginning. If we choose πολλάκι over e.g. πάντοθι we also have a refined effect, typical of elegiac composition, whereby a word in the hexameter is capped by a similar word in a following, but not contiguous, pentameter, πολλαῖϲ in 1. 4.[25]

More recently, F. Pontani has secured πολλάκι as the correct reading through a surprising route, a textual discussion of Σ Hom. *Od.* 2. 50.[26] For the first time in ages we are in a position to look at the entire

---

first line of Callimachus *Aitia* and know how it sounded to ancient readers. Admittedly, not an ambitious note: more than a clarion call, a mysterious hum (πολλάκι . . . ἐπιτρύζουςι). But even one very common word could make a difference if it is the incipit of such a famous work.

One text for which the complete version of *Aitia* 1. 1 could make a difference—albeit a shade of meaning, not more than that—is Catullus 116, the last text in our transmitted *Liber*, a poem that, as was shown in a famous paper by Colin Macleod,[27] is a programmatic text for Catullus as well as an important step in the Roman appropriation of Callimachus:

> *Saepe* tibi studioso animo venante requirens
>   carmina uti possem mittere Battiadae,
> qui te lenirem nobis, neu conarere
>   tela infesta meum mittere in usque caput,
> hunc video mihi nunc frustra sumptum esse laborem,
>   Gelli, nec nostras hic valuisse preces.
> contra nos tela ista tua evitamus amictu:
>   at fixus nostris tu dabi' supplicium.[28]

Often for you with passionate thought I've been searching for words, in order to send you poems of the Battiad, that I might win you over, and that you might not try to throw destructive shafts against my head. But now I see this has been for me a useless toil, Gellius, and that herein my prayers have not availed. Those shafts of yours launched against me, I shall evade, and find protection: but you shall be pierced by mine, and pay the penalty.

The dynamics of the poem are deeply involved with the work of Callimachus and its different genres: note e.g. the metaliterary summary by John Ferguson:[29] 'I've long thought to dedicate a translation of Callimachus to you . . . It'll be *Ibis*.' It has always been clear that the unspecified *carmina . . . Battiadae* in l. 2 stand in some kind of relationship to the *carmina Battiadae* of 65. 15–16 (and thus, mediately, to the *Coma*): *mitto haec expressa tibi carmina Battiadae*, 'I send you translated these verses of the Battiad', although, in view of the absence of *expressa*, we are not explicitly told that there will be a Latin version of the original this time.[30] The crucial link seems to be the idea of 'sending' a poem: in 65. 15 *mittere* helps to construct the poem as a cover-letter for the *Coma*, and supports the Callimachean

---

[27] 'Catullus 116'.

[28] I offer a tentative text: the many textual problems do not directly affect my point about *saepe* and the general thrust of the poem from *doctrina* to iambic invective.

[29] *Catullus* (Lawrence, KS, 1985), 346.

[30] Some interpreters have gone too far in claiming a perfect symmetry with the situation of poems 65 and 66. Contrast e.g. the approach of Holzberg, *Catull*, 209.

allusion to the rolling apple of Acontius at the end (65. 19 *missum
. . . malum*); in 116, *mittere* initially invites a link with 65, but by the
end of the poem it has been redefined as the proper word for iambic
aggression, *iambos* from 'hurling', and so the metaphor of *venante*
shifts from intellectual research to the shooting of a moving target.[31]
We are not told whether the *carmina Battiadae* are a Greek original
or a Roman version in 116, but in both cases we might expect some
amount of bilingual allusion and illusion.

In his more than virtual Latin version of Callimachus, the *Coma*,
Catullus had been very careful to offer not a reproduction but a sem-
blance of the actual beginning: *Omnia . . .* (66. 1) responds (inten-
tionally, in terms of superficial form and not in terms of grammar) to
Πάντα . . . (*Aitia* fr. 110. 1 Pf.). Now he recreates for 116 the begin-
ning of the *Aitia*, *saepe + pronominal dative = πολλάκι + pronominal
dative*, and sustains for a moment the pointed impression that he is
going to offer Gellius the most learned work of ancient poetry, then
switches to invective. (This interest in the *Aitia* as a whole dovetails
with the pre-existing arguments[32] about 65 being a poem concerned
with the entire Callimachean collection and not just with the individ-
ual elegy that follows, the *Coma*, and that indeed the *Coma* is being
translated as a part of the *Aitia*.) One can certainly caution that one
common lexical item is not much to build on, but I must say that,
in addition to *carmina . . . Battiadae*, many other clues in this poem
have always made me think about the *Aitia*: they form the entire rest
of l. 1—*studioso*,[33] *animo*,[34] *venante*,[35] and *requirens*,[36] to which one
should add *laborem* in l. 5. This whole language is in tune with what
we know about the reception of the *Aitia* in antiquity: research, the
poet's memory-cum-imagination, hunting for antiquarian rarities,
aetiology, and toil. Since *tu dabi' supplicium* has been recognized as

[31] This subtle effect justifies the blunt repetition of *mittere* at ll. 2 and 4.

[32] Hunter, 'Callimachean Echoes in Catullus 65'.

[33] The poem has an ambiguous relationship to the work of Ennius (see below), the poet who
had pioneered Callimacheanism in Latin literature through his claim to be a *dicti studiosus*
(*Annales* 209 Sk.: I thank Jay Reed for help on this point), i.e. a φιλόλογος.

[34] For the importance of θυμός as a keyword of the *Aitia* see fr. 2. 3 Massimilla with n. (= 1a.
20 Pf.), frr. 35, 89. 21 Massimilla = 31b, 178.21 Pf.; fr. 75, 10 Pf.; Bing, 'A Note on the New
"Musenanruf" in Callimachus' *Aetia*'.

[35] For a link between the Callimachean tradition and 'hunting' for learning note the polemi-
cal use of θηρήτορες in Philip, *AP* 11. 321. 5 = GP, *Garland* 10 'Grammarians, you children of
Stygian Momus, you book-worms feeding on thorns, demon foes of books, cubs of Zenodotus,
soldiers of Callimachus from whom, though you hold him out as a shield, you do not refrain
your tongue, *hunters* of melancholy conjunctions who take delight in μιν and cφιν . . . '. The
poem maliciously casts Callimachean philologists as Telchines.

[36] On pointed usage of *quaeris*, *quaeritis* signalling aetiological genre and Callimachean influ-
ence see A. Barchiesi, 'Discordant Muses', 1.

an allusion to the revenge of Romulus in Ennius' *Annales* (95 Sk. *dabi' sanguine poenas*), involving both fighting spirit and the abrasive roughness of archaic style, it is tempting to view the dynamics of the poem as a regressive movement from Callimachus to Ennius.

If poem 116 was the end of an elegiac collection by Catullus, as many people tend to think, we now have one more instance of the neoteric practice of reversing beginnings and endings:[37] the final poem invokes the *Aitia* prologue, the initial poems—for such is the force of 65 and 66—had been quoting respectively book 3 (Cydippe) and 4 (the Coma) of the *Aitia*. More exactly, 116 could be seen as a violent, warped recapitulation of the entire Callimachean *Aitia*: from the incipit to the final promise of a future iambic oeuvre; or as a progressive abjuration of Callimachus until the scandalous Ennianism *dabi'* expresses the choice of old-fashioned violence over new-wave refinement.[38]

In sum, the architectural effects created by a reading of the book of Catullan elegiacs, poems 65–116, are inseparable from Catullus' interest in the structure of the *Aitia* as a model of the well-planned book. There is, however, something subversive about this interest. Beginning, middle, and end are capriciously mixed up. Even more if we accept the ingenious hypothesis[39] that it is actually at the *beginning* of the sordid poem 67 that Catullus is ironically offering the solemn *closure* of the *Coma Berenices*, a closure missing from the end of 66:

> O dulci iucunda viro, iucunda parenti,
> > salve, teque bona Iuppiter auctet ope,
> ianua

Greetings, door, dear to the beloved husband, dear to the father, and may Jupiter benefit you with kind assistance (67. 1–3).

If there was a continuous tradition of Greek books of poetry framed by poems for rulers—such as the *Aitia*, such as parts of the Posidippus collection—the idea of beginning a Roman book of elegiacs with the sequence 65–7 can only be described as a satiric transformation: the convention becomes outlandish[40] when the Ptolemies are being transferred to Rome.

---

[37] Zetzel, 'Catullus, Ennius, and the Poetics of Allusion', 251–66.

[38] Yet there is a more sarcastic implication for Gellius: the present that was flashed before his eyes then replaced by an invective may have been a civilized alternative but it was, after all, the Reply to the Telchines.

[39] T. P. Wiseman, *Catullan Questions* (Leicester, 1969), 22; Hunter in M. Fantuzzi and R. Hunter, *Muse e modelli* (Rome and Bari, 2001), 549.

[40] Shocking aspects in the transfer include court poetry, ruler cult, sexualization and feminization of power images, and the routinized scandal of 'incest marriage': the last-named issue

TOWARDS A FUZZIER MODEL

Again we have relied on our own image of the controlling author: the difficulty this time was not, as with Martial or Pliny, the weak canonic standing of the author—if anything, modern expectations and presumptions about Catullus would rather create the contrary bias—but the state of our evidence. But are we allowed to look for this kind of effect only if we can take for granted the activity of the original author? The emphasis on single personalities as true inventors of the Poetry book (Callimachus *Aitia* and *Iambi*, Vergil's *Bucolics*) may have distracted our attention from other areas. Epigram books, for example, are interesting because we never know how far and for how long arrangements became canonic, and some of the existing types are clearly the joint work of editors and compilers, of customers and scribes. In my discussion of Catullus, I have concentrated on Callimachean elegy because there we have indications of authentic book-planning. But as far as epigram collections are concerned, we can surmise that Catullus had familiarity with many different kinds of *libellus*, not all of them authorial, some of them occasional; we should even doubt whether his own sequence 1–60 or 1–64 is the result of authorial planning. I quote one significant comment:

The papyri suggest that collections of epigrams were easily modified. In principle, authors, later editors, and readers could omit from or add to an existing collection, or compile their own selection from one (a process which could leave signs of the original planning while not leaving anything like the original book). The informality of many of the papyri of epigram need not make them the less revealing of readers' attitudes and activities. Though there is an important distinction between the very common personal versions and generally circulated texts, it seems doubtful that generally circulated editions of single epigrammatists were always of complete works; the concept of modification, and particular modifications, might matter widely. The do-it-yourself element was not remote from Catullus' Rome.[41]

Hutchinson is clearly trying to come to terms with a couple of recent pieces of evidence in Greek,[42] such as the Oxyrhynchus papyrus (LIV 3724) of the late first century AD, containing a list of seventy-five incipits written in a documentary hand, which should

is of course a paradoxical link between the triumph of Ptolemaic marriage in the Coma poem (66) and the obscure, provincial nexus of marriage, adultery, and incest that forms the topic of poem 67.

[41] Hutchinson, 'The Catullan Corpus', 206–7.

[42] Parsons, 'Callimachus and the Hellenistic Epigram'; see also Sider, *The Epigrams of Philodemos*.

indicate that it was a privately made copy. Twenty-seven of the incipits have been identified as belonging to Philodemus and there are good reasons to think that all of them belonged to that author. If so, we have an incipit list organized to produce a selected edition of epigrams of Philodemus. It should be noted that these incipits are occasionally reversed, some crossed out, with occasional ticks in the margin, all of which suggests a process of reorganizing. The second is an unpublished Vienna papyrus (P. Vindob, G 40611) found with documents datable to the last third of the third century BC. This evidence suggests activities of selection and rearrangement, not just dissemination of standard formats. The thought that we might have not just Catullus' book or the editor's final cut but just one, or three or four, out of many competitive books of Catullus, each with some smart points in arrangement but none definitive, is frustrating, yet more realistic perhaps than idealizations of 1–116 as the perfect book of Roman lyric, complete with symmetries and definitive architecture. Yet we should also think in the opposite direction: those makers of non-authorial collections must have co-operated in spreading the culture of the poetry book, and even invented or perfected arrangements that were influential and meaningful, to some readers at least. In the past, critics have been insatiable about the amount of intentionality that is needed to authorize a 'perfect book'. Before the 1980s people would even deny that the *Odes* were a legitimate book because Horace presumably did not write his poems *after* designing the book. But this is to exorcize the amount of bricolage, improvisation, and workmanship that goes into literary practice. In epigram collections, plasticity and instability of the overall design does not mean bad quality: our Posidippus papyrus, for example, may have been ephemeral, but is beautifully structured.[43] If there were many texts around at this level of organization, this means that a reading public was being customized.

Intertextuality, as we all agree, does not require book format, nor even writing for that matter, but we also agree that between the third century BC and the first century AD a different poetics of reading, not only of writing and composing, was being popularized. We should reorient the model and accept that readers, editors, and transmission are just as important as authors, and sometimes do similar things:[44] if

---

[43] It is hardly a coincidence that the current rise of interest in the history of epigram collections takes place in the age of the electronic text and books on demand, with individual readers getting used to fashioning and refashioning the textual material.

[44] M. Beard, 'Ciceronian Correspondences', 123–4: 'the fact that we are not dealing with the design of the author himself does not mean that we are dealing with no design at all. The editors

we can reconstruct the emergence of a shared convention of reading, it is only by taking on board non-authorial collections of texts. For example, when we talk about the songs/texts of the canonical lyric authors, we tend to emphasize the difference between archaic poetics and the epoch-making invention of the scholarly *liber*, and so we normally think in terms of a loss of original meaning; but if we are interested in the Roman reception of that tradition, the change from song to book is also a production of new meanings. In the Roman (and Hellenistic) perspective, it is relevant to focus on ways in which the text of the lyric poets is assembled into book form[45] during the Alexandrian age and in turn, in that format, influences new practices of textual ordering. Alexandrian scholars who did new things with poems by Pindar, Sappho, Alcaeus, Archilochus, etc. must have been conditioned by some idea, and even ideal, of the poetry book; in turn, their choices influenced the genesis of new, and indeed authorial, poetry books, and of course of anthologies of more recent poetry, some authorial, some not. We should not separate the composition of new books of poetry from the reception of older texts simply because we know for a fact that those older books were not designed by the author of the text. Callimachus begins book 3 of his *Aitia* with a Nemean victory, and soon alludes to Pindar's *Nemean* 1; do we know for a fact that the choice has no relationship with the positioning of the poem as poem 1 in the learned Alexandrian edition? If this is an age when poems begin to signify 'by position' as well as 'by nature', it is hard to set limits to the osmosis between editorial practice and poetic intertextuality.

To mention one obvious example, there is much controversy about the origins and the ratio of book divisions of the *Iliad* and *Odyssey*, and general agreement that book divisions were not part of the original text (whatever this means), but nobody can deny that the influence of that surely non-authorial book structure was quick and active, and became inseparable from the authority of Homer. We can try to observe a few regularities in this editorial work, and one is the use of time-markers, especially descriptions of dawn, as a caesura between books. If we turn to what Roman epic poets do with their own book divisions, it seems likely that they perceived this device as a textual convention and did a lot of interesting manipulations

of these collections were assembling and arranging the letters in a literary world in which book organisation was taken seriously.'

[45] A few conjectures on this aspect in Barchiesi, 'Rituals in Ink'; id., 'Horace and Iambos', 156.

with it. Ovid, *Metamorphoses* 1 ends with the very word for a dawn, *ortus*, and 2 begins with the solemn words *Regia Solis erat*. This epic poet, it turns out, has decided to give us the real thing, a new day that trumps all previous epic dawns: an ecphrasis not of a regular part of day, but of the place where dawn actually is produced for the whole universe: the palace of the Sun in the Far Orient. Later on in the poem, book 8 starts with a very traditional-sounding sunrise, but after five lines the story is over and the characters have changed— a spoof of the convention of dawns as segmentations of long continuous actions, as their function was in Homer's corpus. Valerius Flaccus, who wants to be a more conservative epicist, expresses his participation to the tradition by starting, of all books, his book 3 with *Tertia . . . Tithonia,* and by marking the incipit of book 5, possibly a central point of his epic project, with *Altera lux.* Lucan, who is of course less traditional, starts the book of Pharsalus, his book VII, by saying that *day should have dawned* but the Sun did not want to rise the natural way, because of the curse on Pharsalus (Silius also starts his book VI with the topos, possibly as a homage to Lucan). Statius, who in the *Thebaid* is in a sense a malicious combination of all of the above, has his book 4 (not 3 like Valerius) begin *Tertius . . . Phoebus,* thus creating a *suggestio falsi* for the well-read audience: it looks like a typical dawn but this time the poet actually means 'the third year', an unusual time-lag in heroic epic. When we reach the end of his book 10 night falls—but hastened, preternatural, clearly a wink at the tradition of Lucan 7; when the final book, 12, starts, we learn that it was dawn—*but not quite,* it was a dark night still. All those games show that the Roman poets had been inspired by the technology of book-division, not just by the text of the Homeric poems: it would make little sense to separate authentic text from later manipulation in their own Homeric model. Similar thoughts are prompted by the tradition of Theocritus' *Idylls;*[46] here most people assume that Vergil's recreation of Theocritus in Rome is indebted to the new, larger, and more varied collection assembled by Artemidorus, and so there is agreement that the transformation of the text beyond authorial control can be seen as influential on the Romans. In fact, it is striking that none of the extant papyri, before the breakthrough of Artemidorus, preserves traces of pastoral and non-pastoral poems together. If the tendency was to circulate pastoral and non-pastoral Theocritus in separate bookrolls, this may have affected the Theocritean tradition in Roman times. In particular, the existence of a collection of pas-

[46] Examined in Gutzwiller, 'The Evidence for Theocritean Poetry Books', 119–48.

toral Theocritean idylls will have interfered with the evolution of late second-century Greek bucolics; by the times of Bion and Moschus it would be perverse to deny the recognizability of a 'bucolic' genre or mode, and this situation may have been influenced by, as well as influencing, the textual presentation of Theocritus. It could be significant, additionally, that Vergil, who derives from Theocritus a rigorous matrix of pastoral poetry, regularly based on recognizable pastoral models, has also opened his *Eclogues* to intertextuality with the non-pastoral 'Encomium to Ptolemy':[47] it could have been his own way to celebrate the reunification of the Theocritean flocks, and to show awareness of the entire poetic spectrum of his model.

The other question that we need to reopen is of course the issue of canonization and authenticity. We need more than a chain of important and transmitted authors, and more attention is necessary for adespota literature and pseudo-authors, as Richard Hunter has emphasized,[48] that is, real poems and often good poems by people mistaken for or posing as Theocritus, Ovid, Vergil, etc. They are often very good indications of how the search for the perfect book progresses between Alexandria and Imperial Rome.

So the impressive work on the Roman poetry book done during the 1970s and 1980s is more convincing when it takes into account the material constraints of the bookroll, less so when it enshrines individual Roman poets as inventors of the perfect art of book-planning. In recent years, work on Hellenistic books (for example by Gutzwiller on Hellenistic epigram collections, and on the transformation of the Theocritean corpus) has been suggesting a more gradual and less teleological image of the process, and the new Posidippus is now adding some brushstrokes. My paper has tried to comment on the present situation of research on Roman poetry books, and on the way research on Hellenistic antecedents can make a difference. I argue in favour of a fuzzy, messy, 'dirty' model of the development of poetry books, one in which the idea of the controlling author as editor and architect is complicated by the activity of readers, imitators, scribes, and scholars. I do not argue against the prominence of individual authors: Callimachus, for example, has often been idealized as the central influence on the genesis of the Roman poetry book, and my discussion of Catullus above has actually supported the importance of Callimachus in this respect. Yet I claim that there are at least

[47] As shown by Hunter, 'Virgil and Theocritus'. I will comment in detail on this aspect elsewhere.
[48] Hunter, 'The Sense of an Author'.

two areas where we need more connections, and in those areas the concept of the controlling author is not central at all—except that of course authors do imitate the practice of scholarly editing, as Nita Krevans argued long ago. The first is the expanding evidence on poetic anthologies, especially epigrams and short poems, and also, in prose, about collections of letters and other short pieces. This evidence suggests changes in reading habits and in cultural needs, not just innovations by individual geniuses of the poetic avant-garde. The second area is the messy history of texts by masters who did not think or care about writing for the perfect book. The story of the texts by Homer, Archilochus, Alcaeus, Sappho, and even Theocritus, even if we can only grasp some critical moments, is highly instructive because it shows that the transformation of a text, out of reach of authorial control, can become the matrix of successive imitations and traditions. This approach to the poetics of the book blurs the distinction between the ideal world where authors design, control, and transmit the formal structure of their opus, and the complex real world where editors and customers contribute to book design and mess it up, in a slow-moving collective reform of reading conventions.

Bibliography

ACCORINTI, DOMENICO, and CHUVIN, PIERRE (eds.), *Des géants à Dionysos: mélanges de mythologie et de poésie grecque offerts à Francis Vian* (Alessandria: Edizioni dell'Orso, 2003).

ACOSTA-HUGHES, BENJAMIN, and KOSMETATOU, ELIZABETH, 'New Poems Attributed to Posidippus', http://www.chs.harvard.edu/classicsat/issue_1/z_classat_pdf/posid_4-04_rev_4.doc.pdf.

——KOSMETATOU, ELIZABETH, and BAUMBACH, MANUEL (eds.), *Labored in Papyrus Leaves: Perspectives on an Epigram Collection Attributed to Posidippus* (Cambridge, MA: Harvard University Press, 2004).

————'Introduction', in eid. (eds.), *Labored in Papyrus Leaves*, 1–7.

——and STEPHENS, SUSAN, 'Rereading Callimachus' *Aetia* Fragment 1', *CPh* 97 (2002), 238–55.

AHRENS, H. L., *De Graecae linguae dialectis* (Göttingen, 1839–43).

ALBINO, D., 'La divisione in capitoli nelle opere degli antichi', *AFLN* 10 (1962/3), 219–34.

ALBRECHT, MARTIN, 'The Epigrams of Posidippus of Pella', MA thesis (Trinity College, Dublin, 1996).

ALCOCK, SUSAN, 'The Heroic Past in a Hellenistic Present', in Paul Cartledge et al. (eds.), *Hellenistic Constructs: Essays in Culture, History, and Historiography* (Berkeley, Los Angeles, and London: University of California Press, 1997), 20–34.

ANDERSON, R. D., PARSONS, P. J., and NISBET, R. G. M., 'Elegiacs by Gallus from Qaṣr Ibrîm', *JRS* 69 (1979), 125–55.

ANDREAE, BERNARD, *Schönheit des Realismus: Auftraggeber, Schöpfer, Betrachter hellenistischer Plastik* (Mainz: Philipp von Zabern, 1998).

ANGIÒ, FRANCESCA, 'Filita di Cos in bronzo (Ermesianatte, fr. 7, 75–78 Powell–P. Mil. Vogl. VIII 309, col. X, ll. 16–25)', *APF* 48 (2002), 17–24.

——'La statua in bronzo di Idomeneo, opera di Cresila (Posidippo di Pella, P. Mil. Vogl. VIII 309, col. X, ll. 26–29)', *MH* 59 (2002), 137–41.

ANGOUR, ARMAND D', 'Ad unguem', *AJPh* 120 (1999), 411–27.

ARGENTIERI, LORENZO, 'Epigramma e libro: morfologia delle raccolte epigrammatiche premeleagree', *ZPE* 121 (1998), 1–20.

ARNOLD, DOROTHEA, et al., *Ancient Art from the Shumei Family Collection, Metropolitan Museum of Art, June 20–Sept. 1, 1996* (New York: Metropolitan Museum of Art, 1996).

ARNOTT, W. G., 'Notes on *gavia* and *mergus* in Latin Authors', *CQ*, NS 14 (1964), 249–62.

ATHERTON, CATHERINE (ed.), *Form and Content in Didactic Poetry* (Bari: Levante, 1998).

Bibliography

Atti del XXII congresso internazionale di papirologia, Firenze 1998, ed. Isabella Andorlini, Guido Bastianini, Manfredo Manfredi, and Giovanna Menci, 2 vols. (Florence: Istituto papirologico 'G. Vitelli', 2001).

AUSTIN, COLIN, 'De nouveaux fragments de l'*Erechthée* d'Euripide', *Recherches de Papyrologie* IV, Presses Universitaires de France, Paris 1967, 11–67 (Planches I–II).

——'From Cratinus to Menander', *QUCC* 63/3 (1999), 37–48.

——'Paralipomena Posidippea', *ZPE* 136 (2001), 22, reprinted in expanded form in *Un poeta ritrovato*, 19–23.

——and BASTIANINI, GUIDO (eds.), *Posidippi Pellaei quae supersunt omnia* (Milan: LED, 2002).

————(eds.), 'Addenda et corrigenda ad editionem minorem', in Bastianini and Casanova, *Il papiro di Posidippo*, 161.

BAGNALL, ROGER S., *The Administration of the Ptolemaic Possessions outside Egypt* (Columbia Studies in the Classical Tradition, 4; Leiden: Brill, 1976).

——'Archaeological Work on Hellenistic and Roman Egypt, 1995–2000', *AJA* 105 (2001), 227–43.

BAILEY, D. M., 'The Canephore of Arsinoe Philadelphos: What Did She Look Like?', *CE* 74 (1999), 156–60.

BARBANTANI, SILVIA, 'I poeti lirici del canone alessandrino nell'epigrammatistica', *Aevum Antiquum* 6 (1993), 5–97.

——'Un epigramma encomiastico "alessandrino" per Augusto [*SH* 982]', *Aevum Antiquum* 11 (1998), 255–344.

——'Epinici in distici di età ellenistica: una composizione sul pugilato? Nota su *P. Schubart* 13 (*O. Berol.* 9303)', in Mario Capasso and Sergio Pernigotti (eds.), *Studium atque urbanitas: Miscellanea in onore di Sergio Daris* (Lecce: Congedo, 2001), 65–73.

——'Osservazioni sull'inno ad Afrodite-Arsinoe dell'antologia P. Goodspeed 101', in *La cultura ellenistica: il libro, l'opera letteraria e l'esegesi antica, Università di Roma, Tor Vergata, 22-24 settembre 2003* (Rome: Quasar, forthcoming).

BARCHIESI, ALESSANDRO, 'Discordant Muses', *PCPhS*, NS 37 (1991), 1–21.

——'Rituals in Ink: Horace on the Greek Lyric Tradition', in Mary Depew and Dirk Obbink (eds.), *Matrices of Genre* (Cambridge, MA: Harvard University Press, 2000), 167–82, 290–4.

——'Horace and Iambos: The Poet as Literary Historian', in Alberto Cavarzere, Antonio Aloni, and Alessandro Barchiesi (eds.), *Iambic Ideas* (Lanham, MD: Rowman & Littlefield, 2001), 141–64.

BARIGAZZI, ADELMO, 'Il testamento di Posidippo di Pella', *Hermes* 96 (1968), 190–216.

BARRY, MARGARET, 'Late Classical to Hellenistic', in Tony Hackens and Rolf Winkes (eds.), *Gold Jewelry: Craft, Style and Meaning from Mycenae to Constantinople* (*Aurifex*, 5 = Publications d'histoire de l'art et d'archéologie de l'Université catholique de Louvain, 36; Louvain-la-

Bibliography

Neuve: Institut supérieur d'archéologie et d'histoire de l'art — Collège Érasme, 1983), 63–8.

BARTHES, ROLAND, *The Rustle of Language*, trans. Richard Howard (New York: Hill and Wang, 1986); first publ. as *Le Bruissement de la langue* (Paris: Éditions du Seuil, 1984).

BASLEZ, MARIE-FRANÇOISE, 'Le sanctuaire de Délos dans le dernier tiers du IVe siècle: étude historique des premiers inventaires de l'indépendance', *REA* 99 (1997), 345–56.

BASTIANINI, GUIDO, 'Tipologie dei rotoli e problemi di ricostruzione', *PapLup* 4 (1995), 21–42.

——'Il rotolo degli epigrammi di Posidippo', in *Atti del XXII congresso*, 111–19.

——'Il papiro di Posidippo un anno dopo: presentazione', in Bastianini and Casanova, *Il papiro di Posidippo*, 1–5.

——and CASANOVA, ANGELO (eds.), *Il papiro di Posidippo un anno dopo* (Studi e Testi di Papirologia, NS 4; Florence: Istituto Papirologico 'G. Vitelli', 2002).

——and GALLAZZI, CLAUDIO, 'Il poeta ritrovato: scoperti gli epigrammi di Posidippo in un pettorale di mummia', in *Ca' de Sass*, 121 (March 1993), 28–39.

————(eds.), *Posidippo: Epigrammi* (Milan: Edizioni Il Polifilo, 1993).

————with AUSTIN, COLIN (eds.), *Posidippo di Pella: Epigrammi (P. Mil. Vogl. VIII 309)* (Papiri dell'Università degli Studi di Milano, VIII; Milan: LED, 2001).

BAUMBACH, MANUEL, '"Wanderer, kommst du nach Sparta...": Zur Rezeption eines Simonides-Epigramms', *Poetica* 32 (2000), 1–22.

——and TRAMPEDACH, KAI, '"Winged Words": Poetry and Divination in Posidippus' *Oionoskopika*', in Acosta-Hughes, Kosmetatou, and Baumbach (eds.), *Labored in Papyrus Leaves*, 123–60.

BAYNHAM, ELIZABETH, 'A Baleful Birth in Babylon: The Significance of the Prodigy in the *Liber de Morte*', in Bosworth and Baynham (eds.), *Alexander the Great in Fact and Fiction*, 242–62.

BEARD, MARY, 'Ciceronian Correspondences: Making a Book out of Letters', in T. P. Wiseman (ed.), *Classics in Progress* (Oxford: Oxford University Press, 2002), 130–44.

BEARZOT, CINZIA, 'Πτολεμαῖος Μακεδών: sentimento nazionale macedone e contrapposizioni etniche all'inizio del regno tolemaico', in Marta Sordi (ed.), *Autocoscienza e rappresentazione dei popoli nell'antichità* (Milan: Vita e Pensiero, 1992), 39–53.

BECHTEL, FRIEDRICH, *Lexilogus zu Homer* (Halle: M. Niemeyer, 1914).

BENNETT, C., 'The Children of Ptolemy III and the Date of the Exedra of Thermos', *ZPE* 138 (2002), 141–5.

BENVENISTE, ÉMILE, *Indo-European Language and Society*, trans. Elizabeth Palmer (London: Faber & Faber, 1973; orig. publ. as *Le Vocabulaire des institutions indo-européennes*, Paris: Éditions de Minuit, 1969).

BERG, LOUISE, and ALEXANDER, KAREN, 'Ancient Gold Work and Jewelry from Chicago Collections', *The Ancient World* 11/1–2 (1985), 3–32.

BERGMANN, BETTINA, 'Greek Masterpieces and Roman Recreative Fictions', *HSCPh* 97 (1995), 79–120.

——and KONDOLEON, CHRISTINE (eds.), *The Art of Ancient Spectacle* (Studies in the History of Art, 56; Washington, DC: National Gallery of Art, 1999).

BERGQUIST, BIRGITTA, 'Sympotic Space: A Functional Aspect of Greek Dining Rooms', in Oswyn Murray (ed.), *Sympotica: A Symposium on the Symposion* (Oxford: Clarendon Press; New York: Oxford University Press, 1990), 37–65.

BERNAND, ÉTIENNE, *Inscriptions métriques de l'Égypte gréco-romaine: recherches sur la poésie épigrammatique des grecs en Égypte* (Annales littéraires de l'Université de Besançon, 98; Paris: Les Belles Lettres, 1969).

BERNARDINI, PAOLA, and BRAVI, LUIGI, 'Note di lettura al nuovo Posidippo', *QUCC* 70 (2002), 147–63.

BERNSDORFF, HANS, 'Anmerkungen zum neuen Poseidipp (P. Mil. Vogl. VIII 309)', *GFA* 5 (2002), 11–44.

BERVE, HELMUT, *König Hieron II* (Abhandlungen der Bayerischen Akademie der Wissenschaften, 47; Munich: C. H. Beck, 1959).

BETTARINI, LUCA, 'Posidippo 37 A.-B. (= PMilVogl. VIII 309, col. VI, rr. 18-25)', *SemRom* 6/1 (2003), 43–64.

BILLOWS, RICHARD, *Kings and Colonists: Aspects of Macedonian Imperialism* (Leiden: E. J. Brill, 1995).

BING, PETER, 'A Note on the New "Musenanruf" in Callimachus' *Aetia*', *ZPE* 74 (1988), 273–5.

—— *The Well-Read Muse: Present and Past in Callimachus and the Hellenistic Poets* (Hypomnemata, 90; Göttingen: Vandenhoeck and Ruprecht, 1988).

—— 'The *Bios* and Poets' Lives as a Theme of Hellenistic Poetry', in Ralph M. Rosen and Joseph Farrell (eds.), *Nomodeiktes: Festschrift M. Ostwald* (Ann Arbor: University of Michigan Press, 1993), 619–31.

—— 'Between Literature and the Monuments', in Harder, Regtuit, and Wakker (eds.), *Genre in Hellenistic Poetry*, 21–43.

—— 'Posidippus on Stones. The First Section of the New Posidippus Papyrus (P. Mil Vogl. VIII 309, Col I–IV.6' (www.apaclassics.org/Publications/Posidippus/ posidippus.html, January 2002).

—— 'Medeios of Olynthos, Son of Lampon, and the *Iamatika* of Posidippus', *ZPE* 140 (2002), 297–300.

—— 'Posidippus and the Admiral: Kallikrates of Samos in the Milan Epigrams', *GRBS* 43 (2002/3), 243–66.

—— 'The Unruly Tongue: Philitas of Cos as Scholar and Poet', *CPh* 98 (2003), 330–48.

—— 'Posidippus' *Iamatika*', in Acosta-Hughes, Kosmetatou, and Baumbach (eds.), *Labored in Papyrus Leaves*, 276–91.

BINGEN, JEAN, '*I. Philae* I 4, un moment d'un règne, d'un temple et d'un culte', in *Akten des 21. Internationalen Papyrologenkongresses = Archiv für Papyrusforschung, Beiheft* 3/1 (1997), 88–97.

—— 'Posidippe: le poète et les princes', in *Un poeta ritrovato*, 47–59.

—— 'La victoire pythique de Callicratès de Samos (Posidippe, P. Mil. Vogl. VIII 309, XI. 33–XII. 7)', *CE* 77 (2002), 185–90.

BLANCHARD, ALAIN, 'Les papyrus littéraires grecs extraits de cartonnage: études de bibliologie', in Marilena Maniaci and Paola F. Munafò (eds.), *Ancient and Medieval Book Materials and Techniques: Erice, 18–25 September 1992*, 2 vols. (Studi e Testi, 357–8; Vatican City: Biblioteca Apostolica Vaticana, 1993), i. 15–40.

BLUM, RUDOLF, *Kallimachos: The Alexandrian Library and the Origins of Bibliography*, trans. H. H. Wellisch (Madison: University of Wisconsin Press, 1991); first publ. as *Kallimachos und die Literaturverzeichnung bei den Griechen: Untersuchungen zur Geschichte der Biobibliographie = Archiv für Geschichte des Buchwesens*, 18/1–20 (Frankfurt am Main: Buchhandler-Vereinigung, 1977).

BOARDMAN, JOHN, *Greek Gems and Finger Rings: Early Bronze Age to Late Classical* (New York: Abrams, 1970).

—— *Persia and the West: An Archaeological Investigation of the Genesis of Achaemenid Art* (London: Thames & Hudson, 2000).

BODEL, JOHN, *The Publication of Pliny's Letters* (Ann Arbor: Michigan University Press, forthcoming).

BOESSNECK, JOACHIM, *Die Tierwelt des alten Ägypten untersucht anhand kulturgeschichtlicher und zoologischer Quellen* (Munich: C. H. Beck, 1988).

BOHRINGER, FRANÇOIS, 'Cultes d'athlètes en Grèce classique', *REA* 81 (1979), 5–18.

BÖKER, ROBERT, 'Wetterzeichen', *RE* Supplb. ix (1962), 1609–92.

BOSWORTH, BRIAN, and BAYNHAM, ELIZABETH (eds.), *Alexander the Great in Fact and Fiction* (Oxford: Oxford University Press, 1999).

BOWERSOCK, GLEN W., *Roman Arabia* (Cambridge, MA: Harvard University Press, 1983).

BOWIE, E. L., 'Theocritus' Seventh Idyll, Philetas, and Longus', *CQ*, NS 35 (1985), 67–91.

BRACCHI, L. C., 'Orologi solari di Aquileia', *Aquileia Nostra* 30 (1960), 50–69.

BRETON, JEAN FRANÇOIS, *Arabia Felix from the Time of the Queen of Sheba, Eighth Century B.C. to First Century A.D.*, trans. Albert LaFarge (Notre Dame: Notre Dame University Press, 1999); first publ. as *L'Arabie heureuse au temps de la reine de Saba: VIIIᵉ–Iᵉʳ siècle av. J.-C.* (Paris: Hachette, 1998).

BRUN, PATRICE, 'Les Lagides à Lesbos: essai de chronologie', *ZPE* 85 (1991), 99–113.

BUCHHOLZ, H. G., *Methymna: Archäologische Beiträge zur Topographie und Geschichte von Nordlesbos* (Mainz: Philipp von Zabern, 1975).

BÜHLER, HANS-PETER, *Antike Gefäße aus Edelsteinen* (Mainz: Philipp von Zabern, 1973).

BULLOCH, ANTHONY, GRUEN, E. S., LONG, A. A., and STEWART, ANDREW (eds.), *Images and Ideologies: Self-Definition in the Hellenistic World* (Berkeley and Los Angeles: University of California Press, 1993).

BUNDY, ELROY L., 'The Eleventh Olympian Ode', in *Studia Pindarica* (Berkeley and Los Angeles: University of California Press, 1986), 1–33.

BURKERT, WALTER, *Homo Necans: The Anthropology of Ancient Greek Sacrificial Ritual and Myth*, trans. Peter Bing (Berkeley: University of California Press, 1983); first publ. as *Homo Necans: Interpretationen altgriechischer Opferriten und Mythen* (Berlin: Walter de Gruyter, 1972).

BURTON, JOAN B., *Theocritus's Urban Mimes* (Berkeley, Los Angeles, and London: University of California Press, 1995).

CAMERON, ALAN, *The Greek Anthology from Meleager to Planudes* (Oxford: Clarendon Press, 1993).

——*Callimachus and his Critics* (Princeton: Princeton University Press, 1995).

CARNEY, ELIZABETH, 'The Career of Adea-Eurydike', *Historia* 36 (1987), 496–502.

——*Women and Monarchy in Macedonia* (Norman: University of Oklahoma Press, 2000).

CARTLEDGE, PAUL, *Agesilaos and the Crisis of Sparta* (London: Duckworth, 1987).

CASSON, LIONEL, *Ancient Trade and Society* (Detroit: Wayne State University Press, 1984).

——(ed.), *The Periplus Maris Erythraei* (Princeton: Princeton University Press, 1989).

CATENACCI, CARMINE, 'Il tiranno alle Colonne di Eracle: l'agonistica e le tirannidi arcaiche', *Nikephoros* 5 (1992), 11–36.

CHAMOUX, FRANÇOIS, 'Le roi Magas', *Revue historique* 216 (1956), 18–34.

CHANTRAINE, PIERRE, *Dictionnaire étymologique de la langue grecque*, 4 vols. (Paris: Klincksieck, 1968–77; 2nd edn. with Supplement, 1999).

CHARPIN, DOMINIQUE, et JOANNÈS, FRANCIS (eds.), *La Circulation des biens, des personnes et des idées dans le Proche-Orient ancien: actes de la XXXVIIIᵉ rencontre assyriologique internationale (Paris, 8–10 juillet 1991)* (Paris: Éditions recherche sur les civilisations, 1992).

CITRONI, MARIO, 'Marziale e la letteratura per i Saturnali', *ICS* 14 (1989), 201–26.

CLARKE, JOHN R., *Looking at Lovemaking: Constructions of Sexuality in Roman Art, 100 B.C.–A.D. 250* (Berkeley and Los Angeles: University of California Press, 1998).

CLARYSSE, WILLY, 'Ethnic Diversity and Dialect among the Greeks of Hellenistic Egypt', in A. M. F. W. Verhoogt and S. P. Vleeming (eds.), *The Two Faces of Graeco-Roman Egypt* (Papyrologica Lugduno-Batava, 30; Leiden: E. J. Brill, 1998), 1–13.

——'The Ptolemies Visiting the Egyptian Chora', in Mooren (ed.), *Politics*, 29–53.

——*The Leuven Database of Ancient Books* (http://ldab.arts.kuleuven. ac.be/, November 2002).

——and VEKEN, G. DER VAN, *The Eponymous Priests of Ptolemaic Egypt* (Papyrologica Lugduno-Batava, 24; Leiden: E. J. Brill, 1983).

COCKLE, W. E. H., *Euripides: Hypsipyle* (Rome: Edizioni dell'Ateneo, 1987).

COLLINS, DEREK, 'Reading the Birds: *Oiônomanteia* in Early Epic', *Colby Quarterly* 38 (2002), 17–41.

CONNOLLY, JOY, 'Picture Arcadia: The Politics of Representation in Vergil's *Eclogues*', *Vergilius* 47 (2001), 89–116.

CRAMP, STANLEY, et al., *Handbook of the Birds of Europe, the Middle East and North Africa: The Birds of the Western Palearctic*, ii: *Hawks to Bustards* (Oxford and New York: Oxford University Press, 1998).

CRANE, GREGORY, 'Tithonus and the Prologue to Callimachus' *Aetia*', *ZPE* 66 (1986), 269–78.

——(ed.), *The Perseus Digital Library* (http://www.perseus.tufts.edu/: Dept. of the Classics, Tufts University).

CRIBIORE, RAFFAELLA, *Writing, Teachers, and Students in Graeco-Roman Egypt* (Atlanta: Scholars Press, 1996).

——'Literary School Exercises', *ZPE* 116 (1997), 53–60, with corrigenda in *ZPE* 117 (1997), 162.

——*Gymnastics of the Mind: Greek Education in Hellenistic and Roman Egypt* (Princeton: Princeton University Press, 2001).

CRISCUOLO, LUCIA, 'Agoni e politica alla corte di Alessandria: riflessioni su alcuni epigrammi di Posidippo', *Chiron* 33 (2003), 311–32.

CRUSIUS, OTTO, 'Dionysios (94)', *RE* v/1 (1903), 915–24.

DASZEWSKI, W. A., *Corpus of Mosaics from Egypt I: Hellenistic and Early Roman Period* (Mainz am Rhein: Philipp von Zabern, 1985).

DAVIES, J. K., *Wealth and the Power of Wealth in Classical Athens* (Salem, NH: Ayer, 1981).

DAVIS, NATALIE ZEMON, *The Gift in Sixteenth Century France* (Madison: University of Wisconsin Press, 2000).

DECKER, WOLFGANG, *Sport und Spiel im alten Ägypten* (Munich: Beck, 1987).

DE JULIIS, ETTORE M., ALESSIO, ARCANGELO, et al., *Gli ori di Taranto in età ellenistica* (Milan: Arnoldo Mondadori Editore Arte, 1989).

DEL CORNO, DARIO, 'Posidippo e il mestiere di poeta', in *Un poeta ritrovato*, 61–6.

DERRIDA, JACQUES, *The Truth in Painting*, trans. Geoff Bennington and Ian McLeod (Chicago: University of Chicago Press, 1987); first publ. as *La Vérité en peinture* (Paris: Flammarion, 1987).

DESANGES, JEHAN, 'Bérénice "comblée d'or": la ville ou la princesse?', *CRAI* 2001/2, 1187–95.

DE STEFANI, CLAUDIO, 'Una nota al "nuovo Posidippo" (P. Mil. Vogl. VIII 309, col. II 17–19)', *Eikasmos* 12 (2001), 139–40.

——'Integrazioni e congetture al nuovo Posidippo', *Eikasmos* 13 (2002), 165–8.

DETIENNE, MARCEL, *The Masters of Truth in Archaic Greece*, trans. Janet

Lloyd (New York and Cambridge, MA: Zone Books, 1996); first publ. as *Les Maîtres de vérité dans la Grèce archaïque* (Paris: F. Maspéro, 1967).

DETTMER, HELENA, *Horace: A Study in Structure* (Hildesheim: Olms-Weidmann, 1983).

DICKIE, MATTHEW, 'Which Posidippus?', *GRBS* 35 (1994), 373–83.

—— 'The Dionysiac Mysteries in Pella', *ZPE* 109 (1995), 81–6.

—— 'What was a *Kolossos* and How were *Kolossoi* Made in the Hellenistic Period?', *GRBS* 37 (1996), 237–57.

DIGNAS, BEATE, *Economy of the Sacred in Hellenistic and Roman Asia Minor* (Oxford: Oxford University Press, 2002).

—— '"Inventories" or "Offering Lists"? Assessing the Wealth of Apollo Didymaeus', *ZPE* 138 (2002), 235–44.

—— 'Posidippus and the Mysteries: *Epitymbia* Read by the Ancient Historian', in Acosta-Hughes, Kosmetatou, and Baumbach (eds.), *Labored in Papyrus Leaves*, 177–86.

DODDS, E. R., *Euripides: Bacchae*, 2nd edn. (Oxford: Clarendon Press, 1960).

DUCKWORTH, GEORGE, *Structural Patterns and Proportions in the 'Aeneid': A Study in Mathematical Composition* (Ann Arbor: University of Michigan Press, 1962).

EASTERLING, P. E., *Sophocles: Trachiniae* (Cambridge: Cambridge University Press, 1982).

EBERT, JOACHIM, *Griechische Epigramme auf Sieger an gymnischen und hippischen Agonen* (Berlin: Akademie, 1972).

EFFE, BERND, *Dichtung und Lehre: Untersuchungen zur Typologie des antiken Lehrgedichts* (Munich: C. H. Beck, 1977).

—— 'Die Destruktion der Tradition: Theokrits mythologische Gedichte', *RhM*, NF 121 (1978), 48–77.

EICHHOLZ, D. E. (ed.), *Theophrastus: De lapidibus* (Oxford: Clarendon Press, 1965).

ELSNER, JOHN, and CARDINAL, ROGER (eds.), *The Cultures of Collecting* (Cambridge, MA: Harvard University Press, 1994).

ERSKINE, ANDREW, 'Culture and Power in Ptolemaic Egypt: The Museum and Library of Alexandria', *G&R* 42 (1995), 38–48.

FAIRCLOUGH, H. RUSHTON, rev. GOOLD, G. P., *Virgil*, 2 vols. (Loeb Classical Library, 63–4; Cambridge, MA, and London: Harvard University Press, 1999–2000).

FAKAS, CHRISTOS, *Der hellenistische Hesiod: Arats Phainomena und die Tradition der antiken Lehrepik* (Beiträge zur Erforschung griechischer Texte, 11; Wiesbaden: Reichert, 2001).

FANTUZZI, MARCO, 'La tecnica versificatoria del P. Mil. Vogl. VIII 309', in Bastianini and Casanova, *Il papiro di Posidippo*, 79–97.

—— 'The Structure of the *Hippika* in P. Mil. Vogl. VIII 309', in Acosta-Hughes, Kosmetatou, and Baumbach (eds.), *Labored in Papyrus Leaves*, 212–24.

—— 'Sugli epp. 37 e 74 Austin-Bastianini del P. Mil. Vogl. VIII 309', *ZPE* 146 (2004) 31–5.

——and HUNTER, RICHARD, *Muse e modelli: la poesia ellenistica da Alessandro Magno ad Augusto* (Rome and Bari: Editori Laterza, 2002); revised and expanded English version *Tradition and Innovation in Hellenistic Poetry* (Cambridge: Cambridge University Press, 2004).

FERGUSON, JOHN, *Catullus* (Lawrence, KS: Coronado Press, 1985).

FERNÁNDEZ-GALIANO, Emilio, *Posidipo de Pela* (Madrid: Instituto de Filología, 1987).

FERRARI, FRANCO, 'Posidippus, the Milan Papyrus, and some Hellenistic Anthologies', www.chs.harvard.edu/classicsat/issue_1/2_classat_pdf/ferrari.pdf (as of December 2004).

FIRATLI, NEZIH, *Les Stèles funéraires de Byzance gréco-romaine* (Bibliothèque archéologique et historique de l'Institut français d'archéologie d'Istanbul, 15; Paris: Maisonneuve, 1964).

FITTSCHEN, KLAUS, 'Zur Rekonstruktion griechischer Dichterstatuen, 2 Teil: Die Statuen des Poseidippos und des pseudo-Menander', *AM* 107 (1992), 229–71.

FORRESTER, JOHN, '"Mille e tre": Freud and Collecting', in Elsner and Cardinal (eds.), *The Cultures of Collecting*, 224–51.

FOWLER, D. P., 'Martial and the Book', in A. J. Boyle (ed.), *Roman Literature and Ideology: Ramus Essays for J. P. Sullivan* (Bendigo: Aureal Publications, 1995), 199–226.

FRAENKEL, EDUARD, 'Eine Anfangsformal attischer Reden', *Glotta* 39 (1960), 1–5 = *Kleine Beiträge*, 2 vols. (Rome: Edizioni di Storia e Letteratura, 1964), i. 505–10.

FRÄNKEL, HERMANN, *Early Greek Poetry and Philosophy: A History of Greek Epic, Lyric, and Prose to the Middle of the Fifth Century*, trans. Moses Hadas and James Willis (New York: Harcourt Brace Jovanovich, 1973; Oxford: Blackwell, 1975), first publ. as *Dichtung und Philosophie des frühen Griechentums: Eine Geschichte der griechischen Literatur von Homer bis Pindar* (Philological Monographs, 13; New York: American Philological Association, 1951), 2nd edn. resubtitled *Eine Geschichte der griechischen Epik, Lyrik und Prosa bis zur Mitte des fünften Jahrhunderts* (Munich: C. H. Beck, 1962, rev. edn. 1969).

FRASER, P. M., *Ptolemaic Alexandria*, 3 vols. (Oxford: Clarendon Press, 1972).

FREDOUILLE, J.-C., et al. (eds.), *Titres et articulations du texte dans les œuvres antiques* (Paris: Institut d'études augustiniennes, 1997).

FUHRER, THERESE, *Die Auseinandersetzung mit den Chorlyrikern in den Epinikien des Kallimachos* (Basel and Kassel: Reinhardt, 1992).

FUMERTON, PATRICIA, *Cultural Aesthetics: Renaissance Literature and the Practice of Social Ornament* (Chicago: University of Chicago Press, 1991).

GALLAZZI, CLAUDIO, and KRAMER, BÄRBEL, 'Artemidor im Zeichensaal: Eine Papyrusrolle mit Text, Landkarte und Skizzenbüchern aus späthellenistischer Zeit', *APF* 44 (1998), 189–208.

GALLI CALDERINI, I. G., 'Su alcuni epigrammi dell'*Antologia Palatina* corredati di lemmi alternativi', *AAP* 39 (1982), 239–80.

GARZYA, ANTONIO, 'Sull'autore e il titolo del perduto poema "Sull'aucupio" attribuito ad Oppiano', *GIF* 10 (1957), 156–60.

GASPARRI, CARLO (ed.), *Le gemme Farnese* (Naples: Electa Napoli, 1994).

GAZDA, ELAINE, 'Roman Sculpture and the Ethos of Emulation: Reconsidering Repetition', *HSCPh* 97 (1995), 121–56.

——(ed.), *The Ancient Art of Emulation* (Ann Arbor: University of Michigan Press, 2002).

GEHRKE, H. J., 'Der siegreiche König: Überlegungen zur hellenistischen Monarchie', *Archiv für Kulturgeschichte* 64 (1982), 247–77.

GENTILI, BRUNO, 'Studi su Simonide I', *RCCM* 2 (1960), 113–23.

——ANGELI BERNARDINI, PAOLA, CINGANO, ETTORE, and GIANNINI, PIETRO (eds.), *Pindaro: Le Pitiche* (Milan: Fondazione Lorenzo Valla-Mondadori, 1995).

GEUS, KLAUS, *Eratosthenes von Kyrene* (Munich: C. H. Beck, 2002).

GIANNINI, ALESSANDRO, *Paradoxographorum Graecorum reliquiae* (Milan: Istituto Editoriale Italiano, 1966).

GIBBS, SHARON L., *Greek and Roman Sundials* (New Haven: Yale University Press, 1976).

La Gloire d'Alexandrie: Musée du Petit Palais, 7 mai–26 juillet 1998 (Paris: Paris-musées, 1998).

GOLDEN, MARK, *Sport and Society in Ancient Greece* (Cambridge: Cambridge University Press, 1998).

GOLDHILL, SIMON, 'The Naïve and Knowing Eye: Ecphrasis and the Culture of Viewing in the Hellenistic World', in Simon Goldhill and Robin Osborne (eds.), *Art and Text in Ancient Greece* (Cambridge: Cambridge University Press, 1994), 197–223.

GOMBRICH, E. H., *Norm and Form: Studies in the Art of the Renaissance*, i (London and New York: Phaidon Press, 1966).

GOW, A. S. F. (ed.), *Theocritus*, 2nd edn., 2 vols. (Cambridge: Cambridge University Press, 1952).

——and PAGE, D. L. (eds.), *The Greek Anthology: Hellenistic Epigrams*, 2 vols. (Cambridge: Cambridge University Press, 1965).

————(eds.), *The Greek Anthology: The Garland of Philip*, 2 vols. (Cambridge: Cambridge University Press, 1968).

GRAF, FRITZ, *Magic in the Ancient World*, trans. Franklin Philip (Cambridge, MA: Harvard University Press, 1997); first. publ. as *La Magie dans l'anti-quité gréco-romaine: idéologie et pratique* (Paris, Les Belles Lettres, 1994).

GRIFFITHS, F. T., *Theocritus at Court* (Leiden: Brill, 1979).

GRONEWALD, MICHAEL, 'Bemerkungen zum neuen Poseidippos', *ZPE* 137 (2001), 1–5.

——'Bemerkungen zu Poseidippos', *ZPE* 144 (2003), 63–6.

GRZYBEK, ERHARD, *Du calendrier macédonien au calendrier ptolémaïque* (Basel: F. Reinhardt, 1990).

GUÉRAUD, OCTAVE, and JOUGUET, PIERRE, *Un livre d'écolier du IIIᵉ siècle avant J.-C.* (Publications de la société royale égyptienne de papyrologie, Textes et documents, 2; Cairo: IFAO, 1938).

GUTZWILLER, KATHRYN, *Studies in the Hellenistic Epyllion* (Beiträge zur klassischen Philologie, 114; Meisenheim am Glan: Anton Hain, 1981).

—— *Theocritus' Pastoral Analogies: The Formation of a Genre* (Madison: University of Wisconsin Press, 1991).

—— 'The Nautilus, the Halcyon, and Selenaia: Callimachus Epigram 5 Pf. = 14 G–P', *CA* 11 (1992), 194–209.

—— 'Cleopatra's Ring', *GRBS* 36 (1995), 383–98.

—— 'Vergil and the Date of the Theocritean Epigram Book', *Philologus* 140 (1996), 92–9.

—— 'The Evidence for Theocritean Poetry Books', in M. A. Harder, R. F. Regtuit, and G. C. Wakker (eds.), *Theocritus* (Hellenistica Groningana, 2; Groningen: Egbert Forsten, 1996), 119–48.

—— 'The Poetics of Editing in Meleager's *Garland*', *TAPhA* 127 (1997), 169–200.

—— *Poetic Garlands: Hellenistic Epigrams in Context* (Berkeley: University of California Press, 1998).

—— 'Posidippus on Statuary', in Bastianini and Casanova, *Il papiro di Posidippo*, 41–60.

—— 'A New Hellenistic Poetry Book: P. Mil. Vogl. VIII 309', in Acosta-Hughes, Kosmetatou, and Baumbach (eds.), *Labored in Papyrus Leaves*, 84–93, expanded and revised version of 'A New Hellenistic Poetry Book. P. Mil. Vogl. VIII 309' (www.apaclassics.org/Publications/Posidippus/posidippus.html, January 2002).

—— 'Nikonoe's Rainbow (Posidippus 6 Austin–Bastianini)', *ZPE* 145 (2003), 44–6.

HABICHT, CHRISTIAN, *Gottmenschentum und die griechischen Städte* (Munich: Beck, 1970).

HALL, J. M., 'Contested Ethnicities: Perceptions of Macedonia within Evolving Definitions of Greek Identity', in Irad Malkin (ed.), *Ancient Perceptions of Greek Ethnicity* (Cambridge, MA: Harvard University Press, 2001), 159–86.

HALLETT, C. H. H., 'The Origins of the Classical Style in Sculpture', *JHS* 106 (1986), 71–84.

HALLEUX, ROBERT, and SCHAMP, JACQUES (eds.), *Les Lapidaires grecs* (Paris: Les Belles Lettres, 1985).

HALLIWELL, STEPHEN, *The Aesthetics of Mimesis: Ancient Texts and Modern Problems* (Princeton and Oxford: Princeton University Press, 2002).

HAMILTON, RICHARD, *Treasure Map: A Guide to the Delian Inventories* (Ann Arbor: University of Michigan Press, 2000).

—— review of Diane Harris, *The Treasures of the Parthenon and Erechtheion* (Oxford: Clarendon Press, 1995), *BMCR* 96.9.27.

HAMMA, KENNETH, and TRUE, MARION (eds.), *Alexandria and Alexandrianism: Papers Delivered at a Symposium Organized by the J. Paul Getty Museum and the Getty Center for the History of Art and the Humanities and Held at the Museum April 22–25, 1993* (Malibu: The J. Paul Getty Museum, 1996).

Bibliography

HANSEN, P. A. (ed.), *Carmina epigraphica Graeca*, 2 vols. (Berlin and New York: Walter de Gruyter, 1983–9).

HARDER, M. A., REGTUIT, R. F., and WAKKER, G. C. (eds.), *Genre in Hellenistic Poetry* (Hellenistica Groningana, 3; Groningen: Egbert Forsten, 1998).

———— (eds.), *Hellenistic Epigrams* (Hellenistica Groningana, 6; Leuven: Peeters, 2002).

HARDIE, ALEX, 'Philitas and the Plane Tree', *ZPE* 119 (1997), 21–36.

—— 'The Statue(s) of Philitas (P. Mil. Vogl. VIII 309 Col. X.16–25 and Hermesianax fr. 7.75–78P)', *ZPE* 143 (2003), 27–36.

HARRAUER, HERMANN, 'Epigrammincipit auf einem Papyrus aus dem 3. Jh. v. Chr., P. Vindob. G 40611: Ein Vorbericht', in *Proceedings of the XVI International Congress of Papyrology* (Chico, CA: Scholars Press, 1981), 49–53.

HARRELL, S. E., 'King or Private Citizen: Fifth-Century Sicilian Tyrants at Olympia and Delphi', *Mnemosyne*, 4th ser. 55 (2002), 439–64.

HAUBEN, HANS, *Callicrates of Samos: A Contribution to the Study of the Ptolemaic Admiralty* (Studia Hellenistica, 18; Leuven: Leuvense Universitaire Uitgaven, 1970).

—— 'Le transport fluvial en Égypte ptolémaïque: les bateaux du roi et de la reine', *Actes du XVᵉ Congrès international de papyrologie*, 4 (Brussels: FERE, 1979), 68–77.

—— 'La chronologie macédonienne et ptolémaïque mise à l'épreuve', *CE* 67 (1992), 143–71.

HAZZARD, R. A., 'The Regnal Years of Ptolemy II Philadelphos', *Phoenix* 41 (1987), 140–58.

—— *Imagination of a Monarchy: Studies in Ptolemaic Propaganda* (Toronto: University of Toronto Press, 2000).

HEADLAM, WALTER, and KNOX, A. D., *Herodas: The Mimes and Fragments* (Cambridge: Cambridge University Press, 1922).

HEEGER, MAXIMILIAN, *De Theophrasti qui fertur Περὶ ϲημείων libro* (Ph.D. diss., Leipzig, 1889).

HEITSCH, ERNST, *Die griechischen Dichterfragmente der römischen Kaiserzeit*, 2 vols., 2nd edn. (Göttingen: Vandenhoeck & Ruprecht, 1963–4).

HELLY, BRUNO, *L'État thessalien: Aleuas le roux, les tétrades et les tagoi* (Lyon: Maison de l'Orient méditerranéen, 1995).

HENGEL, MARTIN, *Die Evangelienüberschriften* (SB Heidelberg, phil.-hist. Kl., 1984/3).

HENIG, MARTIN, *The Content Family Collection of Ancient Cameos* (The Ashmolean Museum, Oxford: W. S. Maney and Sons Ltd., Leeds, 1990).

HENRICHS, ALBERT, 'Response to Part Two', in Bulloch et al., *Images and Ideologies*, 171–95.

—— 'Zur Meropis: Herakles' Löwenfell und Athenas zweite Haut', *ZPE* 27 (1977), 69–75.

HENRIKSSON, K.-E., *Griechische Büchertitel in der römischen Literatur*

(Suomalaisen Tiedeakatemian Toimituksia, Sarja B, 102; Helsinki: Akateeminen Kirjakauppa, 1956).

HESBERG, HENNER VON, 'The King on Stage', in Bergmann and Kondoleon, *The Art of Ancient Spectacle*, 65–73.

HEUBECK, ALFRED, and HOEKSTRA, ARIE, *A Commentary on Homer's Odyssey*, ii (Oxford: Clarendon Press, 1989).

HODKINSON, STEPHEN, 'An Agonistic Culture?', in id. and A. Powell (eds.), *Sparta: New Perspectives* (London: Duckworth, 1999), 147–87.

——*Property and Wealth in Classical Sparta* (London: Duckworth, 2000).

HÖCKMANN, URSULA, and KREIKENBOM, DETLEV (eds.), *Naukratis: Die Beziehungen zu Ostgriechenland, Ägypten und Zypern in archaischer Zeit* (Möhnesee: Bibliopolis, 2001).

HÖLBL, GÜNTHER, *A History of the Ptolemaic Empire* (London and New York: Routledge, 2001).

HOLFORD-STREVENS, LEOFRANC, *Aulus Gellius: An Antonine Scholar and his Achievement* (Oxford: Oxford University Press, 2003).

HOLLIS, A. S., 'Heroic Honours for Philitas?', *ZPE* 110 (1996), 56–62.

HOLZBERG, NIKLAS, *Catull: Der Dichter und sein erotisches Werk* (Munich: C. H. Beck, 2002).

HOPKINSON, NEIL, *Callimachus: Hymn to Demeter* (Cambridge: Cambridge University Press, 1984).

——*A Hellenistic Anthology* (Cambridge: Cambridge University Press, 1988).

HORSTMANN, AXEL E.-A., *Ironie und Humor bei Theokrit* (Meisenheim am Glan: Anton Hain, 1976).

HUNTER, RICHARD, 'Callimachean Echoes in Catullus 65', *ZPE* 96 (1993), 179–82.

——'Written in the Stars: Poetry and Philosophy in the *Phaenomena* of Aratus', *Arachnion* 2 (1995) 1–34 at http://www.cisi.unito.it/arachne/num2/hunter.html.

——*Theocritus and the Archaeology of Greek Poetry* (Cambridge: Cambridge University Press, 1996).

——*Theocritus: A Selection* (Cambridge: Cambridge University Press, 1999).

——'Virgil and Theocritus: A Note on the Reception of the *Encomium to Ptolemy Philadelphus*', *SemRom* 4 (2001), 159–63.

——'The Sense of an Author: Theocritus and [Theocritus]', in Roy Gibson and Christina Kraus (eds.), *The Classical Commentary* (Leiden: E. J. Brill, 2002), 89–108.

——'Osservazioni sui *Lithika* di Posidippo', in Bastianini and Casanova, *Il papiro di Posidippo*, 109–19; reprinted in revised and translated form as 'Notes on the *Lithika* of Posidippus', in Acosta-Hughes, Kosmetatou, and Baumbach (eds.), *Labored in Papyrus Leaves*, 94–104.

——'Reflecting on Writing and Culture: Theocritus and the Style of Cultural Change', in Harvey Yunis (ed.), *Written Texts and the Rise of Literate Culture in Ancient Greece* (Cambridge: Cambridge University Press, 2003), 213–34.

HUNTER, RICHARD, *Theocritus: Encomium of Ptolemy Philadelphus* (Berkeley, Los Angeles, and London: University of California Press, 2003).

HUSS, WERNER, *Der makedonische König und die ägyptischen Priester: Studien zur Geschichte des ptolemaischen Ägypten* (Stuttgart: F. Steiner, 1994).

——*Ägypten in hellenistischer Zeit 332–30 v. Chr.* (Munich: C. H. Beck, 2001).

HUTCHINSON, G. O., 'The New Posidippus and Latin Poetry', *ZPE* 138 (2002), 1–10.

——'The Catullan Corpus, Greek Epigram, and the Poetry of Objects', *CQ*, NS 53 (2003), 206–21.

INVERNIZZI, ANTONIO, and SALLES, JEAN-FRANÇOIS (eds.), *Arabia Antiqua: Hellenistic Centres around Arabia* (Rome: Istituto italiano per il Medio ed Estremo Oriente, 1993).

JANKO, RICHARD (ed.), *Philodemus On Poems, Book One* (Oxford: Oxford University Press, 2000).

JARDINE, LISA, *Worldly Goods: A New History of the Renaissance* (London: Macmillan, 1996).

JEBB, R. C., *The Plays and Fragments of Sophocles*, ii: *The Oedipus Coloneus* (Cambridge: Cambridge University Press, 1883).

JOHNSON, WILLIAM A., 'Pliny the Elder and Standardized Roll Heights in the Manufacture of Papyrus', *CPh* 88 (1993), 46–50.

——'Toward a Sociology of Reading in Classical Antiquity', *AJPh* 121 (2000), 593–627.

——*Bookrolls and Scribes in Oxyrhynchus* (Toronto: Toronto University Press, 2004).

——'Scholars' Texts and Reading Communities in Hellenic Egypt', in Alexander Jones (ed.), *Reconstructing Ancient Texts* (Toronto: Toronto University Press, forthcoming).

KAIBEL, GEORG, 'Zu den Epigrammen des Kallimachos', *Hermes* 31 (1896), 264–70.

KAMPEN, NATALIE B. (ed.), *Sexuality in Ancient Art: Near East, Egypt, Greece, and Italy* (Cambridge: Cambridge University Press, 1996).

KANNICHT, RICHARD, *Euripides: Helena* (Heidelberg: C. Winter, 1969).

KAROUZOS, CHRESTOS, "Τί τὸ κάλλιστον;", *Hellenika* 15 (1957), 286–92; repr. in B. C. Petrakos (ed.), Χρήστου Ι. Καρούζου Μικρὰ Κείμενα (Βιβλιοθήκη τῆς ἐν Ἀθήναις Ἀρχαιολογικῆς Ἑταιρείας, ἀρ. 149; Athens: Ἡ ἐν Ἀθήναις Ἀρχαιολογικὴ Ἑταιρεία, 1995), 375–81.

KASSER, RODOLPHE, with AUSTIN, COLIN, *Ménandre: Le Bouclier* (Papyrus Bodmer, 26; Cologny-Geneva: Bibliothèque Bodmer, 1969).

——*Ménandre: La Samienne* (Papyrus Bodmer, 25; Cologny-Geneva: Bibliothèque Bodmer, 1969).

KIDD, DOUGLAS (ed.), *Aratus: Phaenomena* (Cambridge: Cambridge University Press, 1997).

KIRK, G. S., *The Iliad: A Commentary*, i (Cambridge: Cambridge University Press, 1985).

Bibliography

KOENEN, LUDWIG, 'Die Adaptation ägyptischer Königsideologie am Ptolemäerhof', in Van 't Dack, Van Dessel, and Van Gucht, *Egypt and the Hellenistic World*, 143–90.

—— 'The Ptolemaic King as a Religious Figure', in Bulloch et al., *Images and Ideologies*, 25–115.

KONSTAN, DAVID, 'The Dynamics of Imitation: Callimachus' First Iambic', in Harder, Regtuit, and Wakker (eds.), *Genre in Hellenistic Poetry*, 133–42.

KOSMETATOU, ELIZABETH, 'Poseidippos, *Epigr.* 8 AB and Early Ptolemaic Cameos', *ZPE* 142 (2003), 35–42.

—— 'Vision and Visibility: Art Historical Theory Paints a Portrait of New Leadership in Posidippus' *Andriantopoiika*', in Acosta-Hughes, Kosmetatou, and Baumbach (eds.), *Labored in Papyrus Leaves*, 187–211.

—— and Papalexandrou, Nassos, 'Size Matters: Poseidippos and the Colossi', *ZPE* 143 (2003), 53–8.

KOZLOFF, ARIELLE, 'Is There an Alexandrian Style—What is Egyptian about It?', in Hamma and True (eds.), *Alexandria and Alexandrianism*, 247–60.

KRAMER, BÄRBEL, 'The Earliest Known Map of Spain (?) and the Geography of Artemidorus of Ephesus on Papyrus', *Imago Mundi* 53 (2001), 115–20.

—— 'Il rotolo di Milano e l'epigramma ellenistica', in *Un poeta ritrovato*, 33–45.

KREVANS, NITA, 'The Poet as Editor: Callimachus, Virgil, Horace, Propertius and the Development of the Poetic Book' (Ph.D. diss., Princeton, 1984).

—— 'Fighting Against Antimachus: The *Lyde* and the *Aetia* Reconsidered', in M. A. Harder, R. F. Regtuit, and G. C. Wakker (eds.), *Callimachus* (Hellenistica Groningana, 1; Groningen: Egbert Forsten, 1993), 149–60.

—— 'Callimachus and the Pedestrian Muse', in M. A. Harder, R. F. Regtuit, and G. C. Wakker (eds.), *Callimachus II* (Hellenistica Groningana, 7; Leuven: Peeters, 2004), 173–83.

KULLMANN, WOLFGANG, ALTHOFF, JOCHEN, and ASPER, MARKUS (eds.), *Gattungen wissenschaftlicher Literatur in der Antike* (Tübingen: G. Narr, 1998).

KURKE, LESLIE, *The Traffic in Praise: Pindar and the Poetics of Social Economy* (Ithaca, NY, and London: Cornell University Press, 1991).

—— 'The Economy of *Kudos*', in Carol Dougherty and Leslie Kurke (eds.), *Cultural Poetics in Archaic Greece* (Cambridge: Cambridge University Press, 1993), 131–63.

KUTTNER, ANN, *Dynasty and Empire in the Age of Augustus: The Case of the Boscoreale Cups* (Berkeley: University of California Press, 1995).

—— 'Republican Rome Looks at Pergamon', *HSCPh* 97 (1995), 158–78.

—— 'Hellenistic Images of Spectacle from Alexander to Augustus', in Bergmann and Kondoleon, *The Art of Ancient Spectacle*, 97–123.

KYRIELEIS, HELMUT, *Bildnisse der Ptolemäer* (Archäologische Forschungen, 2; Berlin: Gebr. Mann, 1975).

LABARRE, GUY, *Les Cités de Lesbos aux époques hellénistique et impériale* (Paris: Diffusion de Boccard, 1996).

357

Bibliography

LA'DA, CSABA A., *Foreign Ethnics in Hellenistic Egypt* (Studia Hellenistica, 38; Leuven: Peeters, 2002).

LAMBERT, S. D., 'Parerga II: The Date of the Nemean Games', *ZPE* 139 (2002), 72–4.

LAPINI, WALTER, 'Osservazioni sul nuovo Posidippo (P.Mil.Vogl. VIII 309)', *Lexis* 20 (2002), 35–60.

—— 'Posidippo, Epigr. 27 Austin–Bastianini', *ZPE* 142 (2003), 43.

—— 'Note posidippee', *ZPE* 143 (2003), 39–52.

LARONDE, ANDRÉ, *Cyrène et la Libye hellénistique: Libykai Historiai de l'époque républicaine au principat d'Auguste* (Paris: CNRS, 1987).

LAURENS, PIERRE, *L'Abeille dans l'ambre: célébration de l'épigramme de l'époque alexandrine à la fin de la Renaissance* (Paris: Les Belles Lettres, 1989).

LAUSBERG, HEINRICH, *Handbuch der literarischen Rhetorik: eine Grundlegung der Literaturwissenschaft*, 3rd edn. (Stuttgart: Steiner, 1990).

LAVIGNE, DONALD, and ROMANO, ALLEN, 'Reading the Signs: The Arrangement of the New Posidippus Roll (P. Mil. Vogl. VIII 309, IV.7–VI.8)', *ZPE* 146 (2004), 13–24.

LEACH, ELEANOR, 'Plautus' *Rudens*: Venus Born from a Shell', *Texas Studies in Literature and Language* 15 (1974), 915–31.

LEARY, T. J., *Martial Book XIV: The Apophoreta* (London: Duckworth, 1996).

—— *Martial Book XIII: The Xenia* (London: Duckworth, 2001).

LEFKOWITZ, MARY, *The Lives of the Greek Poets* (Baltimore: The Johns Hopkins University Press, 1981).

LEHNUS, LUIGI, 'Posidippean and Callimachean Queries', *ZPE* 138 (2002), 11–13.

LEWIS, SIAN, *The Athenian Woman: An Iconographic Handbook* (London and New York: Routledge, 2002).

LIDOV, JOEL B., 'Sappho, Herodotus, and the *Hetaira*', *CPh* 97 (2002), 203–37.

LINDSAY, JACK, *Leisure and Pleasure in Roman Egypt* (London: Frederick Muller, 1965; New York: Barnes and Noble, 1966).

LION, BRIGITTE, 'La circulation des animaux exotiques au Proche-Orient', in Charpin and Joannès (eds.), *Circulation*, 357–65.

LIVREA, ENRICO, 'Critica testuale ed esegesi del nuovo Posidippo', in Bastianini and Casanova, *Il papiro di Posidippo*, 61–77.

LLOYD, G. E. R., *Magic, Reason, and Experience: Studies in the Origins and Development of Greek Science* (Cambridge and New York: Cambridge University Press, 1979).

LLOYD-JONES, HUGH, 'The Seal of Poseidippus', *JHS* 83 (1963), 75–99, 84 (1964), 20; reprinted in *Greek Comedy, Hellenistic Literature, Greek Religion, and Miscellanea: The Academic Papers of Sir Hugh Lloyd-Jones* (Oxford: Clarendon Press; New York: Oxford University Press, 1990), 158–95.

—— 'Notes on P. Mil. Vogl. VIII 309', *ZPE* 137 (2001), 6.

—— 'Posidippus fr. 31 Austin–Bastianini (P. Mil. Vogl. 309, col. V 20–5)', *ZPE* 144 (2003), 62.

—— 'All by Posidippus?', in Accorinti and Chuvin (eds.), *Des géants à Dionysos*, 277–80.

—— review of Bastianini and Gallazzi (2001), *IJCT* 9 (2003), 612–16.

—— and PARSONS, P. J. (eds.), *Supplementum Hellenisticum* (Berlin: Walter de Gruyter, 1983).

LOMBARDO, STANLEY, and RAYOR, DIANE, *Callimachus: Hymns, Epigrams, Select Fragments* (Baltimore: The Johns Hopkins University Press, 1988).

LONG, A. A., 'Stoic Readings of Homer', in Robert Lamberton and John J. Keaney (eds.), *Homer's Ancient Readers: The Hermeneutics of Greek Epic's Earliest Exegetes* (Princeton: Princeton University Press, 1992), 41–66.

LOWRIE, MICHÈLE, *Horace's Narrative Odes* (Oxford: Clarendon Press; New York: Oxford University Press, 1997).

LUPPE, WOLFGANG, 'Rückseitentitel auf Papyrusrollen', *ZPE* 27 (1977), 89–99.

—— 'Weitere Überlegungen zu Poseidipps Λιθικά-Epigramm Kol. III 14ff', *APF* 47 (2001), 250–1.

—— 'Ein gastlicher Stein: Poseidipp, Epigramm Kol. III 20–27 (P. Mil. Vogl. VIII 309)', *MH* 59 (2002), 142–4.

—— 'Ein unbekannter Vogelname in Poseidipps Οἰωνοσκοπικά? (Kol. IV 24–29)', *APF* 48 (2002), 207–9.

—— 'Ein Leipziger Epigramm-Papyrus (P.Lips. inv. 1445 verso)', *APF* 48 (2002) 197–206.

—— 'Ein Weih-Epigramm Poseidipps auf Arsinoe', *APF* 49 (2003), 21–4.

—— 'Ein Habicht verheisst glückliche Seefahrt: Poseidipp Kol. IV 8–13/ NR. 21', *ZPE* 146 (2004), 39–40.

LURAGHI, NINO, *Tirannidi arcaiche in Sicilia e Magna Grecia da Panezio di Leontini alla caduta dei Dinomenidi* (Florence: Olschki, 1994).

MACLEOD, COLIN, 'Catullus 116', *CQ*, NS 23 (1973), 304–9 = *Collected Essays* (Oxford: Clarendon Press, 1983), 181–6.

MCNAMEE, KATHLEEN, 'Greek Literary Papyri Revised by Two or More Hands', in *Proceedings of the XVI International Congress of Papyrologists* (Chico, CA: Scholars Press 1981), 79–91.

MADDOLI, GIANFRANCO, NAFISSI, MASSIMO, and SALADINO, VINCENZO, *Pausania: guida della Grecia, Libro VI: l'Elide e Olimpia* (Fondazione Lorenzo Valla; Milan: Mondadori, 1999).

MAEHLER, HERWIG, *Die Lieder des Bakchylides* (Leiden: E. J. Brill, 1982).

MAGNELLI, ENRICO, 'Quelle bestie dei Telchini (sul v. 2 del prologo degli *Aitia*)', *ZPE* 127 (1999), 52–8.

—— (ed.), *Alexandri Aetoli testimonia et fragmenta* (Florence: Università degli Studi di Firenze, 1999).

MANETTI, GIOVANNI, *Theories of the Sign in Classical Antiquity*, trans. Christine Richardson (Bloomington: Indiana University Press, 1993); first publ. as *Le teorie del segno nell'antichità classica* (Milan: Bompiani,

1987).

MANN, MICHAEL, *The Sources of Social Power*, i: *A History of Power from the Beginning to A.D. 1760* (Cambridge: Cambridge University Press, 1986).

MANNING, JOSEPH, 'Twilight of the Gods: Economic Power and the Land Tenure Regime in Ptolemaic Egypt', in *Atti del XXII congresso*, ii. 861–78.

MANTEUFFEL, GEORGIUS [= JERZY], *De opusculis Graecis Aegypti e papyris, ostracis lapidibusque collectis* (Prace Towarzystwa Naukowego Warszawskiego, wydział 1, no. 12; Warsaw, 1930).

MARCHESI, ILARIA, 'A Complex Prose: The Poetics of Allusion in the Epistles of Pliny the Younger' (Ph.D. diss., Rutgers, 2002).

MARINONE, NINO, *Berenice da Callimaco a Catullo: testo critico, traduzione e commento. Nuova edizione ristrutturata, ampliata e aggiornata* (Bologna: Pàtron editore, 1997).

MARTIN, R. P., *The Language of Heroes* (Ithaca, NY, and London: Cornell University Press, 1989).

MASSIMILLA, GIULIO (ed.), *Callimacho: Aitia, libri primo e secondo* (Pisa: Giardini, 1996).

MASTRONARDE, D. J. (ed.), *Euripides: Phoenissae* (Leipzig: Teubner, 1988).

MATTHEWS, VICTOR, 'Sex and the Single Racehorse', *Eranos* 98 (2000), 32–8.

MATTUSCH, C. C., *Greek Bronze Statuary* (Ithaca, NY: Cornell University Press, 1988).

MEINCKE, WERNER, *Untersuchungen zu den enkomiastischen Gedichten Theokrits* (Ph.D. diss., Kiel, 1965).

MEISSNER, BURKHARD, *Die technologische Fachliteratur der Antike: Struktur, Überlieferung und Wirkung technischen Wissens in der Antike (ca. 400 v. Chr.-ca. 500 n. Chr.)* (Berlin: Akademie, 1999).

MICHEL, SIMONE, *Bunte Steine — dunkle Bilder: 'Magische Gemmen'* (Munich: Biering & Brinkmann, 2001).

—— 'Steinschneidekunst', *Der Neue Pauly*, xi (2001), 944–50.

MINEUR, W. H., *Callimachus: Hymn to Delos* (Mnemosyne Supplement, 83; Leiden: E. J. Brill, 1984).

MINNEN, PETER VAN, 'The Century of Papyrology (1892–1992)', *Bulletin of the American Society of Papyrologists* 30 (1993), 5–18.

MITCHELL, W. J. T., *Picture Theory* (Chicago and London: University of Chicago Press, 1994).

MÖLLER, ASTRID, *Naukratis: Trade in Archaic Greece* (Oxford: Oxford University Press, 2000).

MOLYNEUX, J. H., *Simonides: A Historical Study* (Wauconda, IL: Bolchazy-Carducci, 1992).

MONRO, D. B., *A Grammar of the Homeric Dialect*, 2nd edn. (Oxford: Clarendon Press, 1891).

MONTANARI, FRANCO, and LEHNUS, LUIGI (eds.), *Callimaque: sept exposés suivis de discussions* (Entretiens sur l'antiquité classique, 48; Vandœuvres-Geneva: Fondation Hardt, 2002).

Bibliography

MOOREN, LEON (ed.), *Politics, Administration and Society in the Hellenistic and Roman World: Proceedings of the International Colloquium, Bertinoro 19–24 July 1997* (Studia Hellenistica, 36; Leuven: Peeters, 2000).

MORELLI, A. M., *L'epigramma latino prima di Catullo* (Cassino: Edizioni dell'Università degli Studi di Cassino, 2000).

MORENO, PAOLO, *Testimonianze per la teoria artistica di Lisippo* (Treviso: Libreria Editrice Canova, 1973).

——*Lisippo*, i (Storia e civiltà, 11; Bari: Dedalo Libri, 1974).

——*Vita e arte di Lisippo* (La cultura, 47; Milan: Il Saggiatore, Arnoldo Mondadori, 1987).

——*Lisippo: l'arte e la fortuna* ([Milan]: Fabbri Editori, 1995).

——*Apelles: The Alexander Mosaic*, trans. David Stanton (Milan: Skira, 2001); first publ. as *Apelle: la battaglia d'Alessandro* (Milan: Skira, 2000).

MORGAN, TERESA, *Literate Education in the Hellenistic and Roman World* (Cambridge: Cambridge University Press, 1998).

MØRKHOLM, OTTO, *Early Hellenistic Coinage* (Cambridge and New York: Cambridge University Press, 1991).

MORTON, JAMIE, *The Role of the Physical Environment in Ancient Greek Seafaring* (Mnemosyne Supplementum, 213; Leiden: E. J. Brill, 2001).

MÜLLER, C. W., *Gleiches zu Gleichem: Ein Prinzip frühgriechischen Denkens* (Wiesbaden: Harrassowitz, 1965).

MURRAY, OSWYN, 'Aristeas and Ptolemaic Kingship', *JThS*, NS 18 (1967), 337–71.

——'Hellenistic Royal Symposia', in Per Bilde, Troels Engberg-Pedersen, Lise Hannestad, and Jan Zahle (eds.), *Aspects of Hellenistic Kingship* (Oakville, CT: Aarhus University Press), 15–27.

NACHMANSON, ERNST, *Der griechische Buchtitel* (Göteborgs Högskolas Årsskrift, 47. 19; Göteborg: Elanders boktryckeri aktiebolag, 1941).

NAGY, GREGORY, 'The Library of Pergamon as a Classical Model', in Helmut Koester (ed.), *Pergamon Citadel of the Gods: Archaeological Record, Literary Description, and Religious Development* (Harvard Theological Studies, 46; Harrisburg: Trinity Press International, 1998), 185–232.

——'Homeric Echoes in Posidippus', in Acosta-Hughes, Kosmetatou, and Baumbach (eds.), *Labored in Papyrus Leaves*, 57–64.

NARDELLI, M. L. 'P. Herc. 1676: contenuti di un libro dell'opera filodemea "sulla poetica"', in Roger Bagnall et al. (eds.), *Proceedings of the XVI International Congress of Papyrology* (Chico, CA: Scholars Press, 1981), 163–71.

NEER, R. T., *Style and Politics in Athenian Vasepainting: The Craft of Democracy, ca. 530–460 B.C.E.* (Cambridge: Cambridge University Press, 2002).

NENNA, M.-D., 'Gemmes et pierres dans le mobilier alexandrin', in *La Gloire d'Alexandrie* (1998), 156–61.

NISBET, GIDEON, *Greek Epigram in the Roman Empire: Martial's Forgotten Rivals* (Oxford: Oxford University Press, 2003).

——'Is There a Book in this Text? "Doing Genre" with the New Nikarkhos', in Mary Depew and Dirk Obbink, *Genre in Antiquity* (Cambridge: Cambridge University Press, forthcoming).

OATES, J. F., BAGNALL, R. S., CLACKSON, S. J., O'BRIEN, A. A., SOSIN, J. D., WILFONG, T. G., and WORP, D. A., *Checklist of Editions of Greek, Latin, Demotic and Coptic Papyri, Ostraca and Tablets*, 5th edn. (Bulletin of the American Society of Papyrologists, Supplement 9; Oakville, CT, and Oxford: American Society of Papyrologists, 2001).

OBBINK, DIRK, 'The Addressees of Empedocles', in Schiesaro, Mitsis, and Clay (eds.), *Mega nepios*, 51–98.

——*Philodemus, On Piety, Part 1* (Oxford: Clarendon Press, 1996).

——*Anubio: Carmen astrologicum elegiacum* (Munich: K. G. Saur, forthcoming).

—— 'Posidippus on Papyri Then and Now', in Acosta-Hughes, Kosmetatou, and Baumbach (eds.), *Labored in Papyrus Leaves*, 16–28.

——'*Tropoi* (Posidippus AB 102–103)', in Acosta-Hughes, Kosmetatou, and Baumbach (eds.), *Labored in Papyrus Leaves*, 292–301.

O'HARA, JAMES, *True Names: Vergil and the Alexandrian Tradition of Etymological Wordplay* (Ann Arbor: University of Michigan Press, 1996).

OHLY, KURT, *Stichometrische Untersuchungen* (Leipzig: Harrassowitz, 1928).

OLIVER, R. P., 'The First Medicean MS of Tacitus and the Titulature of Ancient Books', *TAPhA* 82 (1951), 232–61.

OLSON, S. DOUGLAS, and SENS, ALEXANDER (eds.), *Archestratos of Gela: Greek Culture and Cuisine in the Fourth Century BCE* (Oxford: Oxford University Press, 2000).

OSBORNE, CATHERINE, 'Was Verse the Default Form for Presocratic Philosophy?', in Atherton (ed.), *Form and Content*, 23–35.

OVERBECK, JOHANNES, Die antiken Schriftquellen zur Geschichte der bildenden Küste bei den Greichen (Leipzig: Engelmann, 1868).

PAGE, DENYS, *Greek Literary Papyri*, i (Cambridge, MA, and London: Harvard University Press, 1942).

——*Sappho and Alcaeus* (Oxford: Clarendon Press, 1955).

——(ed.), *Epigrammata Graeca* (Oxford: Clarendon Press, 1975).

PALAGIA, OLGA, 'Hephaestion's Pyre and the Royal Hunt of Alexander', in Bosworth and Baynham (eds.), *Alexander the Great in Fact and Fiction*, 167–206.

PAPALEXANDROU, NASSOS, 'Reading as Seeing: P. Mil. Vogl. VIII 309 and Greek Art', in Acosta-Hughes, Kosmetatou, and Baumbach (eds.), *Labored in Papyrus Leaves*, 247–58.

PARCA, MARYLINE G. (ed.), *Ptocheia, or Odysseus in Disguise at Troy (P. Köln VI 245)* (American Studies in Papyrology, 31; Atlanta, GA: Scholars Press, 1991).

PARSONS, P. J., 'Callimachus: Victoria Berenices', *ZPE* 25 (1977), 1–50.

—— 'Identities in Diversity', in Bulloch et al. (eds.), *Images and Ideologies*, 151–70.

—— 'Callimachus and the Hellenistic Epigram', in Montanari and Lehnus, *Callimaque*, 99–141.

PEARSON, LIONEL, *The Lost Histories of Alexander the Great* (American Philological Association Monographs, 20; London: William Clowes and Sons, 1960).

PERADOTTO, J. J., 'Cledonomancy in the *Oresteia*', *AJPh* 90 (1969), 1–21.

PERLMAN, PAULA, 'The Calendrical Position of the Nemean Games', *Athenaeum* 67 (1989), 57–90.

PETRAIN, DAVID, '*Πρέςβυς*: A Note on the New Posidippus (V 6–11)', *ZPE* 140 (2002), 9–12.

——'Homer, Theocritus, and the Milan Posidippus (P. Mil. Vogl. VIII 309)', *CJ* 98 (2003), 359–88.

PFEIFFER, RUDOLF (ed.), *Callimachus*, 2 vols. (Oxford: Clarendon Press, 1949–51).

——*History of Classical Scholarship from the Beginnings to the End of the Hellenistic Age*, i (Oxford: Clarendon Press, 1968).

PFISTER, FRIEDRICH, 'Das Alexander-Archiv und die hellenistisch-römische Wissenschaft', *Historia* 10 (1961), 30–67.

PFROMMER, MICHAEL, *Untersuchungen zu Chronologie früh- und hochhellenistischen Goldschmucks = Istanbuler Forschungen*, 37 (Tübingen: Wasmuth, 1990).

——*Metalwork from the Hellenized East: Catalogue of the Collections* (Malibu: The J. Paul Getty Museum, 1993).

——'Roots and Contacts: Aspects of Alexandrian Craftsmanship', in Hamma and True (eds.), *Alexandria and Alexandrianism*, 171–89.

——*Greek Gold from Hellenistic Egypt* (Los Angeles: Getty Publications, 2001).

PICARD, OLIVIER, 'Monnaies de fouille d'Alexandrie', *RA* 1998, 203–6.

——'Un monnayage alexandrin énigmatique: le trésor d'Alexandrie 1996', in Michel Amandry and Silvia Hurter (eds.), *Travaux de numismatique grecque offerts à Georges Le Rider* (London: Spink, 1999), 313–21.

PLANTZOS, DIMITRIS, *Hellenistic Engraved Gems* (Oxford: Clarendon Press; New York: Oxford University Press, 1999).

PLEKET, H. W., 'Games, Prizes, Athletes, and Ideology', *Stadion* 1 (1975), 49–89.

POLLARD, JOHN, *Birds in Greek Life and Myth* (London: Thames and Hudson, 1977).

POLLITT, J. J., *Art and Experience in Classical Greece* (Cambridge: Cambridge University Press, 1972).

——*The Ancient View of Greek Art: Criticism, History, and Terminology* (New Haven: Yale University Press, 1974).

POMEROY, SARAH B., *Women in Hellenistic Egypt from Alexander to Cleopatra* (New York: Schocken Books, 1984).

——*Families in Classical and Hellenistic Greece: Representations and Realities* (Oxford: Clarendon Press, 1997).

PONTANI, FILIPPOMARIA, 'The First Word of Callimachus' *Aitia*', *ZPE* 12 (1999), 57–9.

POWELL, J. U. (ed.), *Collectanea Alexandrina* (Oxford: Clarendon Press, 1925).

PUELMA, MARIO, 'Die Dichterbegegnung in Theokrits "Thalysien"', *MH* 17 (1960), 144–64.

QUAEGEBEUR, JAN, 'Cleopatra VII and the Cults of the Ptolemaic Queens', in *Cleopatra's Egypt: Age of the Ptolemies. Catalog of an Exhibition Held at the Brooklyn Museum Oct. 7, 1988–Jan. 2, 1989* (Mainz am Rhein: Philipp von Zabern, 1988), 41–54.

RADL, ALBERT, *Der Magnetstein in der Antike: Quellen und Zusammenhänge* (Boethius, 19; Stuttgart: F. Steiner, 1988).

REED, JOSEPH, 'Arsinoe's Adonis and the Poetics of Ptolemaic Imperialism', *TAPhA* 130 (2000), 319–51.

REGENBOGEN, OTTO, "Πίναξ", *RE* 20 (1950), 1409–82.

REINSCH-WERNER, HANNELORE, *Callimachus Hesiodicus: Die Rezeption der hesiodischen Dichtung durch Kallimachos von Kyrene* (Berlin: Mielke, 1976).

REITZENSTEIN, RICHARD, *Epigramm und Skolion: Ein Beitrag zur Geschichte der alexandrinischen Dichtung* (Giessen: J. Ricker, 1893).

REWALD, JOHN, *Cézanne: correspondance* (Paris: Bernard Grasset, 1995).

RICE, E. E., *The Grand Procession of Ptolemy Philadelphus* (New York: Oxford University Press, 1983).

RICHMOND, O. L. (ed.), *Sexti Properti quae supersunt omnia* (Cambridge: Cambridge University Press, 1928).

RICHTER, G. M. A., *The Portraits of the Greeks*, 3 vols. (London: Phaidon Press, 1967).

——*Engraved Gems of the Greeks and Etruscans* (London: Phaidon Press, 1968).

RIDGWAY, B. S., *Fourth-Century Styles in Greek Sculpture* (Madison: University of Wisconsin Press, 1997).

RIEU, E. V. (trans.), *The Voyage of Argo: The Argonautica* (Penguin Classics, L85; Harmondsworth: Penguin Books, 1959).

RISCH, ERNST, *Wortbildung der homerischen Sprache*, 2nd edn. (Berlin and New York: Walter de Gruyter, 1974).

ROBERT, CARL, 'Die Ordnung der olympischen Spiele und die Sieger der 75.–83. Olympiade', *Hermes* 35 (1900), 141–95.

ROBERT, LOUIS, 'Sur un décret des Korésiens au musée de Smyrne', *Hellenica* 11–12 (1960), 132–76.

——'Sur un décret d'Ilion et sur un papyrus concernant des cultes royaux', in A. E. Samuel (ed.), *Essays in Honor of C. Bradford Welles* (American Studies in Papyrology, 1; New Haven: Vernon Hunt Press, 1966), 175–211.

ROBERTSON, NOEL, 'The Thessalian Expedition of 480 BC', *JHS* 96 (1976), 100–20.

ROHR, RENÉ, 'Le cadran solaire romain de Bettwiller', *Cahiers alsaciens d'archéologie d'art et d'histoire* (1966), 47–58.

——*Sundials: History, Theory, and Practice*, trans. Gabriel Godin

(Toronto: University of Toronto Press, 1970); first publ. as *Les Cadrans solaires: traité de gnomonique théorique et appliquée* (Paris: Gauthier-Vilars, 1975), rev. edn. *Les Cadrans solaires: histoire, théorie, pratique* (Strasbourg: Oberlin, 1986).

ROLLEY, CLAUDE, *La Sculpture grecque*, ii (Paris: A. and J. Picard, 1999).

ROMAN, LUKE, 'The Representation of Literary Materiality in Martial's Epigrams', *JRS* 91 (2001), 113–45.

ROMMEL, HANS, 'Magnet', *RE* xiv/1 (1928), 474–86.

ROSENBERGER, VEIT, 'Der Ring des Polykrates im Licht der Zauberpapyri', *ZPE* 108 (1995), 69–71.

ROSENMEYER, P. A., 'Her Master's Voice: Sappho's Dialogue with Homer', in Stephen Hinds and D. P. Fowler (eds.), *Memory, Allusion, Intertextuality* = *MD* 39 (1997), 123–49.

—— 'Epistolary Epigrams in the *Greek Anthology*', in Harder, Regtuit, and Wakker (eds.), *Hellenistic Epigrams*, 137–49.

ROSSI, LAURA, 'Il testamento di Posidippo e le laminette auree di Pella', *ZPE* 112 (1996), 59–65.

—— *The Epigrams Ascribed to Theocritus: A Method of Approach* (Hellenistica Groningana, 5; Leuven: Peeters, 2001).

ROSSUM-STEENBEEK, M. VAN, *Greek Readers' Digests? Studies on a Selection of Subliterary Papyri* (Leiden: Brill, 1997).

ROTROFF, SUSAN I., review of Pfrommer, *Greek Gold from Hellenistic Egypt*, in *BMCR* 2002.05.14.

ROUVERET, AGNÈS, *Histoire et imaginaire de la peinture ancienne (Ve siècle av. J.-C. –I^e après J.-C.)* (Bibliothèque des écoles françaises d' Athènes et de Rome, fasc. 274; Rome: École française de Rome, 1989).

ROWLANDSON, JANE (ed.), *Women and Society in Greek and Roman Egypt: A Sourcebook* (Cambridge: Cambridge University Press, 1998).

RUDOLPH, WOLF, *A Golden Legacy: Ancient Jewelry from the Burton Y. Berry Collection at the Indiana University Art Museum* (Bloomington: Indiana University Art Museum, 1995).

RUSTEN, JEFFREY, *Theophrastus: Characters* (Cambridge, MA: Harvard University Press, 2002).

SAMUEL, A. E., 'The Ptolemies and the Ideology of Kingship', in Peter Green (ed.), *Hellenistic History and Culture* (Berkeley and Oxford: University of California Press, 1993), 168–92.

SANTIROCCO, MATTHEW, *Unity and Design in Horace's Odes* (Chapel Hill: University of North Carolina Press, 1986).

SBARDELLA, LIVIO (ed.), *Filita: testimonianze e frammenti poetici* (Rome: Quasar, 2000).

SBORDONE, FRANCESCO (ed.), *Ricerche sui papiri ercolanesi* (Naples: Giannini, 1976).

SCHIESARO, ALESSANDRO, MITSIS, PHILLIP, and CLAY, JENNY STRAUSS (eds.), *Mega nepios: il destinatario nell'epos didascalico, The Addressee in Didactic Epic* = *MD* 31 ([1993]; Pisa: Giardini, 1994).

SCHMALZRIEDT, EGIDIUS, Περὶ φύϲεωϲ: *Zur Frühgeschichte der Buchtitel* (Munich: Wilhelm Fink, 1970).

SCHMIDT, ERICH, *Persepolis II: Contents of the Treasuries and Other Discoveries* (Oriental Institute Publications, 69; Chicago: University of Chicago Press, 1958).

SCHMIDT, FRIEDRICH, *Die Pinakes des Kallimachos* (Klass.-philol. Studien, 1; Berlin: E. Ebering, 1922).

SCHOTT, PAUL, *Posidippi epigrammata* (Ph.D. diss. Berlin: E. Ebering, 1905).

SCHRÖDER, B.-J., *Titel und Text: Zur Entwicklung lateinischer Gedichtüberschriften* (Berlin: Walter de Gruyter, 1999).

SCHRÖDER, STEPHAN, 'Überlegungen zu zwei Epigrammen des neuen Mailänder Papyrus', *ZPE* 139 (2002), 27–9.

——'Skeptische Überlegungen zum Mailänder Epigrammpapyrus', *ZPE* 148 (2004), 29–73.

SCHULTZ, PETER, and HOFF, RALF VON DEN (eds.), *Early Hellenistic Portraiture: Image, Style, Context* (Cambridge: Cambridge University Press, forthcoming).

SCHUR, DAVID, 'A Garland of Stones: Hellenistic *Lithika* as Reflections on Poetic Transformations', in Acosta-Hughes, Kosmetatou, and Baumbach (eds.), *Labored in Papyrus Leaves*, 118–22.

SCHWEITZER, BERNHARD, 'Xenokrates von Athen', *Schriften der Königsberger Gelehrten Gesellschaft, Geisteswissenschaftliche Klasse*, 9 (1932), 1–52, reprinted in id., *Zur Kunst der Antike: Ausgewählte Schriften* (Tübingen: Wasmuth, 1963), 105–64.

SCODEL, RUTH, 'A Note on Posidippus 63 AB (P. Mil. Vogl. VIII 309 X 16–25)', *ZPE* 142 (2003), 44.

The Search for Alexander: An Exhibition (Boston: New York Graphic Society, 1980).

SEGAL, CHARLES, 'Simichidas' Modesty: Theocritus, *Idyll* 7. 44', *AJPh* 95 (1974), 128–36 = *Poetry and Myth in Ancient Pastoral* (Princeton: Princeton University Press, 1981), 161–75.

SELDEN, DANIEL, 'Alibis', *CA* 17 (1998), 289–412.

SENS, ALEX(ANDER), 'The New Posidippus, Asclepiades, and Hecataeus' Philitas-Statue', (www.apaclassics.org/Publications/Posidippus/posidippus.html, January 2002).

——'An Ecphrastic Pair: Asclepiades *AP* 12.75 and Asclepiades or Posidippus *APl* 68', *CJ* 97 (2002), 249–62.

——'Asclepiades, Erinna, and the Poetics of Labour', in Philip Thibodeau and Harry Haskell (eds.), *Being There Together: Essays in Honor of Michael C. J. Putnam* (Afton, MN: Afton Historical Society Press, 2003), 78–87.

——'Doricisms in the New and Old Posidippus', in Acosta-Hughes, Kosmetatou, and Baumbach (eds.), *Labored in Papyrus Leaves*, 65–83.

SERRAO, GREGORIO, *Problemi di poesia alessandrina*, i: *Studi su Teocrito* (Rome: Edizioni dell'Ateneo, 1971).

SETHE, KURT, *Hieroglyphische Urkunden der griechisch-römischen Zeit*, ii:

Bibliography

Historisch-biographische Urkunden aus der Zeit der makedonischen Könige (Leipzig: Hinrichs'sche Buchhandlung, 1904).

SHAW, IAN, BUNBURY, JUDITH, and JAMESON, ROBERT, 'Emerald Mining in Roman and Byzantine Egypt', *JRA* 12 (1999), 203–15.

SIDEBOTHAM, RICHARD, 'Ports of the Red Sea and the Arabia-India Trade', in Vimala Begley and Richard De Puma (eds.), *Rome and India: The Ancient Sea Trade* (Madison: University of Wisconsin Press, 1991), 12–38.

SIDER, DAVID (ed.), *The Epigrams of Philodemos* (New York: Oxford University Press, 1997).

——'Demokritos on the Weather', in André Laks and Claire Louguet (eds.), *Qu'est-ce que la philosophie présocratique?* (Villeneuve d'Ascq: Presses Universitaires du Septentrion, 2002), 287–302.

——'Posidippus Old and New', in Acosta-Hughes, Kosmetatou, and Baumbach (eds.), *Labored in Papyrus Leaves*, 29–41.

——'Pindar *Olympian* 11 and Greek Weather Lore', in Accorinti and Chuvin (eds.), *Des géants à Dionysos*, 167–72.

——'How to Commit Philosophy Obliquely: Philodemos' Epigrams in the Light of his *Frankness of Speech*', in John T. Fitzgerald, Dirk Obbink, and Glenn S. Holland (eds.), *Philodemus and the New Testament World* (Leiden: E. J. Brill, 2004), 85–101.

SISSA, GIULIA, *Greek Virginity*, trans. Arthur Goldhammer (Cambridge, MA, and London: Harvard University Press, 1990); first publ. as *Le Corps virginal: la virginité féminine en Grèce ancienne* (Paris: J. Vrin, 1987).

SKUTSCH, OTTO, 'The Structure of the Propertian *Monobiblos*', *CPh* 58 (1963), 238–9.

SMITH, E. MARION, *Naukratis: A Chapter in the History of the Hellenization of Egypt* (Vienna, 1926).

SMITH, MARTYN, 'Elusive Stones: Reading Posidippus' *Lithika* Through Technical Writing on Stones', in Acosta-Hughes, Kosmetatou, and Baumbach (eds.), *Labored in Papyrus Leaves*, 105–17.

SMITH, R. R. R., 'Spear-Won Land at Boscoreale: On the Royal Paintings of a Roman Villa', *JRA* 7 (1994), 100–28.

——'Ptolemaic Portraits: Alexandrian Types, Egyptian Versions', in Hamma and True (eds.), *Alexandria and Alexandrianism*, 203–13.

——'Theory and Criticism', in Martin Kemp (ed.), *The Oxford History of Western Art* (Oxford: Oxford University Press, 2000), 60–3.

SMITH, W. D., 'Analytical and Catalogue Structure in the *Corpus Hippocraticum*', in F. Lasserre and P. Mudry (eds.), *Formes de pensée dans la collection hippocratique*, Actes du IVe colloque international hippocratique, Lausenne, 21–26 septembre 1981 (Geneva: Droz, 1983), 277–84.

SPANOUDAKIS, KONSTANTINOS, *Philitas of Cos* (Leiden: Brill, 2002).

SPIER, JEFFREY, *Ancient Gems and Finger Rings: Catalogue of the Collections* (Malibu: The J. Paul Getty Museum, 1992).

SPRIGATH, GABRIELE, 'Der Fall Xenokrates von Athen: Zu den Methoden der Antike-Rezeption in der Quellenforschung', in Manuel Baumbach (ed.), *Tradita et Inventa: Beiträge zur Rezeption in der Antike* (Heidelberg: C. Winter, 2000), 407–28.

STADEN, HEINRICH VON, 'Gattung und Gedächtnis: Galen über Wahrheit und Lehrdichtung', in Kullmann, Althoff, and Asper (eds.), *Gattungen wissenschaftlicher Literatur*, 65–94.

STEINER, DEBORAH TARN, 'Eyeless in Argos: A Reading of *Agamemnon* 416–19', *JHS* 115 (1995), 175–82.

——*Images in Mind: Statues in Archaic and Classical Greek Literature and Thought* (Princeton and Oxford: Princeton University Press, 2001).

STEPHENS, SUSAN A., 'Egyptian Callimachus', in Montanari and Lehnus, *Callimaque*, 235–70.

——*Seeing Double: Intercultural Poetics in Ptolemaic Alexandria* (Berkeley: University of California Press, 2003).

——'For You, Arsinoe', in Acosta-Hughes, Kosmetatou, and Baumbach (eds.), *Labored in Papyrus Leaves*, 161–76.

——'Posidippus' Poetry Book: Where Macedon Meets Egypt', in W. V. Harris (ed.), *Ancient Alexandria: Between Greece and Egypt* (Leiden: Brill, 2004), 63–86.

——and OBBINK, DIRK, 'The Manuscript', in Acosta-Hughes, Kosmetatou, and Baumbach (eds.), *Labored in Papyrus Leaves*, 9–15.

STEVENS, SUSAN T., 'Image and Insight: Ecphrastic Epigrams in the *Latin Anthology*' (Ph.D. diss., University of Wisconsin-Madison, 1983).

STEWART, ANDREW, *Greek Sculpture: An Exploration*, 2 vols. (New Haven: Yale University Press, 1990).

——*Faces of Power: Alexander's Image and Hellenistic Politics* (Berkeley and Los Angeles: University of California Press, 1993).

——'The Alexandrian Style: A Mirage?', in Hamma and True (eds.), *Alexandria and Alexandrianism*, 231–46.

——'Two More Citations of Polykleitos's Canon', in 'Nuggets: Mining the Texts Again', *AJA* 108 (1998), 271–82.

——*One Hundred Greek Sculptors* (Perseus Web Project 1996) as of 15 January 2004: http://www.perseus.tufts.edu/cgi-bin/ptext?doc=Perseus%3Atext%3A1999.04.0008&query=head%3D%2314.

——'Alexander, Philitas, and the Skeletos: Poseidippos and Truth in Early Hellenistic Portraiture', in Schultz and von den Hoff (eds.), *Early Hellenistic Portraiture* (forthcoming).

STEWART, SUSAN, *On Longing: Narratives of the Miniature, the Gigantic, the Souvenir, the Collection* (Durham, NC: Duke University Press, 1993).

STROUP, SARAH, 'Invaluable Collections: The Illusion of Poetic Presence in Martial's *Xenia* and *Apophoreta*', in Ruurd Nauta et al. (eds.), *Flavian Poetry* (Leiden, forthcoming).

——*A Society of Patrons: Cicero, Catullus, and the Textual Body Politic* (forthcoming).

SUSEMIHL, FRANZ, *Geschichte der griechischen Literatur in der Alexanderzeit*, i (Leipzig: B. G. Teubner, 1891).

Bibliography

SVORONOS, J. N., *Die Münzen der Ptolemäer* = vol. iv of *Τὰ νομίσματα τοῦ κράτους τῶν Πτολεμαίων*, 4 vols. (Athens, 1904–8), German translation of vol. i, *Εἰσαγωγὴ ἀπονομὴ καὶ κατάταξις*.

TANCKE, KARIN, 'Wagenrennen: Ein Friesthema der aristokratischen Repräsentationskunst spätklassisch-frühhellenistischer Zeit', *JDAI* 105 (1990), 95–127.

TARDITI, GIOVANNI, 'Per una lettura degli epigrammatisti greci', *Aevum Antiquum* 1 (1988), 5–75.

THOMPSON, D'ARCY W., *A Glossary of Greek Birds*, 2nd edn. (London: Oxford University Press, 1936).

THOMPSON, DOROTHY B., *Ptolemaic Oinochoai and Portraits in Faience: Aspects of the Ruler-Cult* (Oxford: Clarendon Press, 1973).

THOMPSON, DOROTHY J., 'Ptolemaios and "The Lighthouse": Greek Culture in the Memphite Serapeum', *PCPhS* 213 = NS 33 (1987), 105–21.

——*Memphis under the Ptolemies* (Princeton: Princeton University Press, 1988).

——'Philadelphus' Procession: Dynastic Power in a Mediterranean Context', in Mooren (ed.), *Politics*, 365–88.

THREATTE, LESLIE, *The Grammar of Attic Inscriptions*, 2 vols. (Berlin and New York: Walter de Gruyter, 1980–96).

TOD, M. N., 'Greek Record-Keeping and Record-Breaking', *CQ* 43 (1949), 105–12.

TOOHEY, PETER, *Epic Lessons: An Introduction to Ancient Didactic Poetry* (London and New York: Routledge, 1996).

Treasures of Ancient Bactria (Shigaraki: The Miho Museum, 2002).

TRÜMPY, CATHERINE, *Untersuchungen zu den altgriechischen Monatsnamen und Monatsfolgen* (Heidelberg: C. Winter, 1997).

TURNER, E. G., *Catalogue of Greek and Latin Papyri and Ostraca in the Possession of the Unversity of Aberdeen* (Aberdeen: The University Press, 1939).

——*Greek Papyri*, 2nd edn. (Oxford: Clarendon Press, 1980).

——and P. J. PARSONS, *Greek Manuscripts of the Ancient World*, 2nd edn. (Bulletin of the Institute of Classical Studies, Supplement, 46; London: Institute of Classical Studies, 1987).

Un poeta ritrovato: Posidippo di Pella. Giornata di studio, Milano, 23 nov. 2001 (Milan: LED, 2002).

VAN SICKLE, JOHN, 'The Book-Roll and Some Conventions of the Poetry Book', *Arethusa* 13 (1980), 3–42.

VAN 'T DACK, EDMOND, VAN DESSEL, P., and VAN GUCHT, W. (eds.), *Egypt and the Hellenistic World: Proceedings of the International Colloquium, Leuven, 24–26 May 1982* (Studia Hellenistica, 27; Leuven: [Orientaliste], 1983).

VIRGILIO, BIAGIO, *Lancia, diadema e porpora: il re e la regalità ellenistica* (Studi ellenistici, 14; Pisa: Giardini, 2003).

VOLK, KATHARINA, *The Poetics of Latin Didactic: Lucretius, Vergil, Ovid, Manilius* (Oxford and New York: Oxford University Press, 2002).

WALBANK, F. W., *A Historical Commentary on Polybius*, 3 vols. (Oxford: Clarendon Press, 1957–79).

—— 'Monarchies and Monarchic Ideas', in *The Cambridge Ancient History*, 2nd edn., vii/1 (Cambridge: Cambridge University Press, 1984), 62–100.

WALKER, SUSAN, and HIGGS, PETER (eds.), *Cleopatra regina d'Egitto. Roma, Fondazione Memmo 12 ottobre 2000–25 febbraio 2001* (Milan: Electa, 2000).

—— *Cleopatra of Egypt* (London: The British Museum Press, 2001).

WALKINSHAW, LAWRENCE, *Cranes of the World* (New York: Winchester Press, 1973).

WEBER, GREGOR, *Dichtung und höfische Gesellschaft* (Stuttgart: Steiner, 1993).

WEST, M. L., '"Eumelos": A Corinthian Epic Cycle?', *JHS* 122 (2002), 109–33.

WESTENHOLZ, JOAN, 'Metaphorical Language in the Poetry of Love in the Ancient Near East', in Charpin and Joannès (eds.), *Circulation*, 381–7.

WILAMOWITZ-MOELLENDORF, ULRICH VON, *Antigonos von Karystos* (Philologische Untersuchungen, 4; Berlin: Weidmannsche Buchhandlung, 1881).

—— 'Heilige Gesetze: Eine Urkunde aus Kyrene', *SBBerl* 169 (1927), 155–76.

WILLIAMS, DYFRI, and OGDEN, JACK, *Greek Gold: Jewelry of the Classical World* (New York: The Metropolitan Museum of Art, 1994).

WINNICKI, J. K., 'Carrying Off and Bringing Home the Statues of the Gods', *JJP* 24 (1994), 149–90.

WISEMAN, T. P., *Catullan Questions* (Leicester: Leicester University Press, 1969).

WISSMANN, JESSICA, 'Hellenistic Epigrams as School-Texts in Classical Antiquity', in Harder, Regtuit, and Wakker (eds.), *Hellenistic Epigrams*, 215–30.

WÖHRLE, GEORG, 'Bemerkungen zur lehrhaften Dichtung zwischen Empedokles und Arat', in Kullmann, Althoff, and Asper (eds.), *Gattungen wissenschaftlicher Literatur*, 279–86.

WRAY, DAVID, 'Apollonius' Masterplot: Narrative Strategy in *Argonautica* 1', in M. A. Harder, R. F. Regtuit, and G. C. Wakker (eds.), *Apollonius Rhodius* (Hellenistica Groningana, 4; Leuven: Peeters, 2000), 239–65.

WRIGHT, M. R., 'Philosopher Poets: Parmenides and Empedocles', in Atherton (ed.), *Form and Content*, 1–22.

WROTH, WARWICK, *Catalogue of the Greek Coins in the British Museum*, xvii: *Troas, Aeolis, and Lesbos* (London: The Trustees of the British Museum, 1894).

ZANETTO, GIUSEPPE, 'Posidippo e i miracoli di Asclepio', in *Un poeta ritrovato*, 73–8.

ZANKER, GRAHAM, 'New Light on the Literary Category of "Ekphrastic Epigram" in Antiquity: The New Posidippus (col. X 7–XI 19 P. Mil. Vogl. VIII 309)', *ZPE* 143 (2003), 59–62.

Bibliography

ZANKER, PAUL, *The Mask of Socrates: The Image of the Intellectual in Antiquity*, trans. Alan Shapiro (Berkeley and Los Angeles: University of California Press, 1994); *Die Maske des Sokrates: das Bild des Intellektuellen in der antiken Kunst* (Munich: C. H. Beck, 1995).

ZETZEL, J. E. G., 'On the Opening of Callimachus, *Aetia* II', *ZPE* 42 (1981), 31–3.

—— 'Catullus, Ennius, and the Poetics of Allusion', *ICS* 8 (1983), 251–66.

ZIEGLER, KONRAT, 'Paradoxographoi', *RE* xviiiB (1949), 1137–66.

Index Locorum

Index Locorum

Dionysius of Halicarnassus *Dem.*
26   319

Diodorus Siculus
3. 12–15   159
3. 36. 3–37   157
19. 11   240

Diogenes Laertius *AP*
7. 744   88

Dionysius *de Aucup.*
2. 2   175
2. 9   167

Epicurus
fr. 183   220 n. 46

Euthydemus
SH 455   179

FGE
Adespota 134   210

Fouilles de Delphes
III 3, no. 192, *see* Posidippus AB T 2

GESA
33   253
64   254
68   254
69   254
71   254
72   254
73   254

Hedylus
AP
11. 61   5
11. 112–22   5
11. 123   5
11. 124–6   5
GP
4   148, 246 n. 68
7–9   289–90

Hermesianax
fr. 7. 75–8 Powell   197

Herodotus
1. 24   129
1. 30   295
1. 51   154–5, 314
2. 16   124
2. 22. 4   172–3
3. 41–3   155–6
3. 41   121, 154–5, 314
3. 121   121
4. 36–41   124

Hesiod
Op.
448–51   172
579–81   173
Th. 22–34   211

Homer
Il.
3. 3–6   230
3. 3–4   173
4. 82–4   165
7. 161   137
13. 62   306, 312
13. 70   306
13. 137–43   125–7
15. 237–8   306
17. 548–50   165 n. 5
Od.
15. 525–6   306
20. 101   170

[Homer] *AP*
7. 153 (or
[Cleobulus
of Lindus])   297–8

Homeric Hymn to Hermes
418–37   178–9

Horace
Epist. 2. 1. 269–70 328
Odes 1. 38   322–3, 325

Hyginus *Astr.*
2. 24   241–2, 264 n. 54, 274

IAG
16   254
45   254

General Index

Note: Greeks words are ordered as if transliterated in the Roman alphabet.

383

Heros (as artist) 145
Hesiod:
  as didactic poet 176, 179
  'mode' of composition in 113–14
  as source for Posidippus 180–1
  and truth 211–12
  and weather signs 172
hetairas 152, 162
Hieron II of Syracuse 250, 255
Hippolochus of Macedon 137
Homer:
  book division of 339–40, 342
  editions of 80, 342
  rivals of 211
  signs in 165, 169
  see also Milan Papyrus, allusions to;
    Posidippus, allusions to
Horace:
  and Catullus 328
  and Meleager 322–3, 325
  poetry books of 320–1, 338
Horus 281, 307
Hunter, Richard 290–1, 341
Hutchinson, G. O. 146, 161, 320, 337
Hydaspes River 122, 146, 282, 302

Ibycus 52, 314
idealism (categorical or phenomenal)
  192, 195
Idomeneus 57, 184, 216–20, 222
illusionism 193, 203
incipits 108, 333, 337–8
initiates, *see* mysteries
intaglios 142 n. 2, 153, 155, 163
iris/Iris 151, 303
ἱρος (ἱερός) 168–9, 306–7

jasper 157
jewellery, *see* gems; Milan Papyrus,
  λιθικά
Johnson, William 288, 311–12

καθαροπτέρυξ 167–8, 170
Keats, John 192
Kramer, Bärbel 68
Kres of Saqqara 101–2, 103
Krevans, Nita 288, 321, 325, 342
κῦδος 249, 253, 262–4, 268
Kuttner, Ann 242, 329

Lapini, Walter 168
lapis lazuli 151, 300–1, 302
λεπτός/λεπτότης 85, 120, 161, *see also*
  Philitas
Lloyd-Jones, Hugh 2
Lowrie, Michèle 321
Lucian 186
Luppe, Wolfgang 175
Lutatius Catulus 323
Lysippus of Sicyon 56
  Alexander(s) of 184, 189, 194–5,
    213–15, 220–2, 222, 300
  and Alexander 194–5, 313
  in ἀνδριαντοποιικά section 95–6, 168,
    183–4, 188, 208, 220–2, 291, 315
  Kairos of 7, 85, 109
  and mimesis 195, 313, 315
  in Pliny 187, 190–1, 194
  in 'old' Posidippus 109, 184–5, 190
  in Propertius 109
  in Xenocrates 188
Lysistratus, sculptor 188 n. 18, 191

Macedonia (personified) 239, 242
Macedonian queens 240–1, 272; *see
  also* Eurydice; Olympias
Maclead, Colin 334
Magas, king of Cyrene 242, 263, 276–7
magnets 92, 133–4, 158
Mago the Carthaginian 176
Mandene, Persian queen 152, 300, 302
Martial:
  arrangement in 324–30
  and Catullus 328
  gems in 145
  and Meleager 325
Matro, parodic poet 177
Mausoleion 250
Medeus of Olynthus 139 n. 53, 279,
  316
Meleager:
  epigrams of, in *Anthology* 115
  Garland 3, 5, 10, 81, 109–10, 322
  garlands in 325
  organization in 83, 94, 322
  prooemium of 312
  and Roman poetry 322–3, 325
  selection in 181–2, 311
  whether source of Lysippus epigram
    110